MAKIN[illegible] *[illegible]e* NEWS

An Anthology of the Newsbooks of Revolutionary England 1641-1660

THE EDITOR Joad Raymond was educated at Howardian High School, Cardiff and the University of East Anglia. He is currently a D. Phil student at Magdalen College, Oxford. *Making the News* is his first book.

MAKING
the
NEWS

An Anthology of the Newsbooks of Revolutionary England 1641-1660

edited by
Joad Raymond

foreword by
Christopher Hill

THE WINDRUSH PRESS · GLOUCESTERSHIRE

First published in Great Britain by
The Windrush Press
Little Window
High Street, Moreton-in-Marsh
Gloucestershire GL56 0LL

Telephone: 0608 652012
Fax: 0608 652125

British Library Cataloguing in Publication Data
A catalogue record for this book is available from
the British Library

Hardback: ISBN 0 900075 72 4
Paperback: ISBN 0 900075 53 8

Typeset by Archetype, Stow-on-the-Wold
Printed and bound in Slovenia

Printed and bound in Slovenia by printing house
DELO – Tiskarna by arrangement with Korotan
Italiana

for Lauren

Contents

Foreword		ix
Preface		xii
A Note on the Texts		xv
List of Illustrations		xvii
Introduction		1
ONE	To your Tents, O Israel: *The Long Parliament and the outbreak of hostilities*	26
TWO	The Voice is Jacob's voice, but the hands are the hands of Esau: *Linguistic aspects of war*	83
THREE	Sleeping with the Devil: *Women in newsbooks*	122
FOUR	The Hanged Woman Miraculously Revived: *Birth, life, sickness, death, providence and the inexplicable*	169
FIVE	That the people be not bound but free: *The trial and execution of Charles I*	203
SIX	A Prospect of the New Jerusalem: *Letters from abroad*	253
SEVEN	The head not quite cut off from the body: *Crime and punishment*	294
EIGHT	With a Pen like a Weaver's Beam: *Marchamont Nedham*	332
NINE	Men indued with new lights: *The inspiration and persecution of the people*	381
TEN	To Amuse and Abuse the People: *The Restoration*	423
Chronology of Events		475
Index of Newsbooks		479
Index		483

Foreword

The period between 1640 and 1660 is unique in English history. Before 1640 all publications were subject to a censorship which was religious, moral and political. There were no independent newspapers. Yet there was a thirst for news and views in the growing political crisis marked by Charles I's decision to rule without Parliaments after 1629, and his collection of taxes which many regarded as illegal because not voted by Parliament. On the continent the Thirty Years War (1618–1648) between Catholics and Protestants seemed likely to lead to victory for the former; and if protestantism were suppressed on the continent England's turn would come next. This concerned not only sincere protestants: the victories of Catholicism in Germany had been followed by resumption of church lands confiscated at the Reformation. This alarmed the many English gentlemen who had inherited monastic lands grabbed by their forebears.

Charles I's government, for good financial reasons, gave no support to our protestant brethren on the continent. Worse: Charles himself resumed church lands in Scotland, as well as imposing a prayer-book regarded as 'popish'. The combined result of these events was a revolt which led to a war in which England's army was defeated. This forced Charles to call a Parliament, since English tax-payers had gone on strike.

So there was much to discuss. Censorship collapsed with Charles's government, and there was an explosion of printing to meet this demand. Uncensored newsbooks were one aspect of this response. In 1640 there were none; by 1645 there were 722. Caroline Hibbard's *Charles I and the Popish Plot* (1983) has demonstrated the widespread suspicions among protestant Englishmen that the King was half-hearted in his protestantism. As Prince of Wales he had made a romantic dash to Spain to woo the Infanta, daughter of the most powerful Catholic ruler. When he returned unmarried popular delight was expressed by a spontaneous ringing of church bells such as London had never known.

But Charles ultimately married a French Catholic princess, to whom he was devoted and who was an ardent and successful proselytizer. A papal nuncio appeared at the English court in 1637, for the first time since the reign of Bloody Mary, whose burnings of protestants were still remembered. The Pope offered a cardinal's hat to the Archbishop of Canterbury. This was not publicly known, and Laud refused the offer; but the all-powerful Archbishop's ecclesiastical innovations, in England as in Scotland, laid him open to the charge of crypto-popery. When the Long Parliament met in November 1640 Laud was arrested, and ultimately tried, condemned and executed as a traitor. Many royalists in the civil war expressed alarm at the Queen's influence and intrigues, and at the number of papist officers in the royal army.

The newsbooks which responded to these concerns during the civil war were militantly propagandist: there was no pretence of impartiality on either side. Nobody was on oath. But, as Joad Raymond shows, we get far more out of newsbooks than reports of political and military events. His imaginative and wide-ranging selection from all the available newsbooks gives us an excellent impression of what life in England during those exciting years was like. It covers political ideas, social customs, crime and punishment, literary styles, strange happenings which were regarded as 'providences', foreign missions and the wilder political and religious groupings which surfaced during the revolutionary decades. Chapter 4 gives us insights into the lives, sicknesses and deaths of ordinary people.

That unique period of freedom to assemble and discuss matters previously forbidden to ordinary English men and women was celebrated proudly by Milton in *Areopagitica* (1644). Censorship, he declared, had been 'an undervaluing and vilifying of the whole nation', a reproach to the common people. 'Now the time has come, wherein... all the Lord's people are become prophets'. 'Give me the liberty to know, to utter, and to argue freely according to conscience, above all liberties'. Some political ideas were censored in the 1650s, but in the forties and early fifties we get more information about people below the level of the gentry, people with no university education, than we have again for a couple of centuries. For once women can be recognized as people of whom the historian should take cognizance (chapter 3). It is the world that simultaneously shocked and educated the country yokel John Bunyan (born 1628) and which he reproduces for us in *The Pilgrim's Progress* and *The Life and Death of Mr Badman*.

So this book gives us something valuable which we were perhaps unaware of lacking. All students of 17th-century English history know about the existence and importance of the innumerable newsbooks published between 1641 and 1660, but they are not easily accessible to the average reader. A complete reprint of the royalist *Mercurius Aulicus*, together with three other royalist Mercuries, *Rusticus, Anti-Britanicus* and *Academicus*, was published in four volumes by Cornmarket Press in 1971, edited by P.W. Thomas. He also edited *Mercurius Politicus* for the same publisher, in 19 volumes, in 1971–2. These were described respectively as *Newsbooks I* and *Newsbooks V*: but no others appear to have been published.

In this book, Joad Raymond makes an important contribution to social history, opening up for the general reader a new source which casts light on the ways of thinking and behaving of our ancestors of three-and-a-half centuries ago. 1640–60 is a period in which publication was freer and more open to ordinary people than it had ever been before 1640 and was to be for a long time after the censorship closed down again after 1660. He is much to be congratulated.

Christopher Hill

Preface

I owe many thanks. Their recipients include David Norbrook and Nigel Smith, who have commented on sections of the text, and guided me through the last year and a half at Oxford; Christopher Hill for reading the manuscript and venturing a foreword; then Victoria Huxley, my editor, for her pencil; and David Blake for his invaluable technical assistance. Secondly, I would like to thank the many librarians who have frequently offered their services beyond the call of duty: the bulk of my work was done in the Bodleian Library, Oxford; but I would also like to thank the staff of the New York Public Library; the Folger Shakespeare Library, Washington; the Library Company of Philadelphia; the Library of the University of Pennsylvania; the library of Worcester College, Oxford; and the McGill Library at Haverford College, Philadelphia. Penultimately I would like to thank Max, Peter, Carol, Hefin, Casey and Gwenny; and Neal and Nancy for their wonderful daughter. Most difficult to express is the burden of debt to Lauren Kassell, my wife, for bearing with me through it all, and lots more.

None of these people are responsible for any of the mistakes, which remain due to my own, persistent errors of judgement. This is the first anthology to offer a wide range of seventeenth-century newsbooks to a broad reading public. As such I have tried to steer a perilous course between appealing to many non-specialists, general readers and those interested in the history of journalism, and to an academic audience, the women and men with whom I work. While endeavouring to set straight a historical lacuna, I wanted my grandfather to gain pleasure from it. To some my comments and introductions may seem cursory and gratuitous, while others may find them insufficient, and will grope for signposts in order to understand the extracts here set before them. To these people I offer two consolations: some of the original readers of newsbooks may well have found difficulty in mastering the particular reading techniques necessary fully to appreciate this innovative form. Today, at least, we think we know what newspapers are for.

Secondly, this work is intended to stimulate interest in newsbooks. It contains a minute fraction of the many thousands of serials published between 1641 and 1660, each between eight and sixteen pages in length. Only a demented academic would try to read them all. Reviewers conventionally criticise omissions from anthologies: I look forward to hearing any complaints about missing favourites. If a few readers are persuaded to read the handful of texts herein contained in a fresh light, stimulating interest in them as literary forms as well as historical documents, then the project will have succeeded.

As those who read my introduction will find, newsbooks have suffered from a very bad press. This is something I want people to rethink. And although I suggest that we should be very careful about drawing comparisons between newsbooks and modern newspapers, it is inevitable, and not necessarily misguiding, that we should be pressed into rethinking our own journalistic machinery at the same time that we cast a fresh and estranged eye on the 'bad craziness' of November 1641. A few incidents forced this upon my attention in the last few weeks of writing this anthology. Firstly, I watched an election, and was made most conscious of the vicious instrumentalism of the fourth estate in the 1990s. *Instrumentalism* because all ideals of the improved distribution of information succumbed to simple aims. It seemed the newspaper war of the 1640s was fought within much broader horizons of ideals and objectives. Secondly, the Bodleian Library misplaced their volume 'Hope 8° 636', which contained the only copy of *Mercvrivs Pragmaticus* Numb.43 {5.16} listed in Caroline Nelson and Mathew Seccombe's Catalogue of British Newspapers and Periodicals. These are *very* rare texts. It is a privilege to be able to read them today, and without great care their print will fade and whole volumes will be devoured by time. Thirdly, Lauren made a thin blue line appear in a home pregnancy test kit. Suddenly the financial perils involved in living as a student, teacher and writer loomed very large. Patronage and politics and ideas all got messed up even more. It's the beginning of a great adventure.

Joad Raymond
Holywell Ford
1 May 1992.

A Note on the Texts

I have tried to make the entries as uncluttered by my apparatus as possible. A mass of editorial notes neither facilitate the re-evaluation of a text nor heighten its literary and formal qualities. Nevertheless some of the texts are accompanied by short introductions which provide some information or a context to guide non-specialist readers. Each passage is also accompanied by the title of the serial in which it appeared; the issue number, if printed on the original; the dates which the newsbook purported to cover; the Nelson and Seccombe STC number, which will aid the location of a copy of the newsbook concerned; and an entry number to which I refer in my own text thus {1.01}.

I have endeavoured to reproduce the basic typography of the texts. The use of italics and capitals was an integral part of the rhetoric of mid-seventeenth-century pamphlets. Where I feel that the compositor has simply made a mistake — for instance in inverting a letter and occasional transpositions — I have corrected it. Where this is uncertain I have tended to leave it as in the original. The typography of newsbooks is notoriously bad, but that is no reason to make it conform to modern practices. Where absolutely necessary I have, at the risk of cluttering the text, included interpolations. These are within brackets; {…}. Any text between other kinds of brackets; (…) and […]; is part of the original. Underlining — which — indicates an expanded abbreviation. These were sometimes used to cram extra text into a line, or to overcome lack of type.

Dates have been left as they were in the original texts. 'S.N.' or 'stilo novo' denotes the new style, Gregorian calender used on the continent, which was ten days ahead of the old style, Julian calender used in Britain. This may cause uncertainty over dates given by letters from overseas, but the context generally makes it clear where exactness is necessary.

My decisions over the selection of extracts have not been easy, and may sometimes seem entirely arbitrary. In chapters one, five and ten I have constructed a narrative of events. They cannot provide a complete picture, but they do suggest the kinds of impressions a seventeenth-century reader might have had of the pressing developments around him or her. The remaining chapters are thematically organised. They are a combination of material furnishing historical insight, texts rich in significance waiting to be unpacked and analysed, and purely entertaining pieces. Within each chapter the material is organised on a strictly chronological basis. The exception to this is chapter three, which concerns the representation of women in newsbooks. This is because it seemed that this section would benefit from juxtapositions which did not conform to temporal sequence, and therefore its organisation is intended to be purely suggestive.

It would have been futile to try accurately to represent in a single volume the whole spectrum of newsbook articles between 1641 and 1660. Reading newsbooks every day has continually forced upon my attention the fact that there is no such thing as objective editing — though there certainly can be effective editing. Thus the following anthology constitutes to some extent a conscious, polemical intervention; an attempt to put newsbooks back on the map and to stimulate a reconsideration of what they were and how they worked. Any objections to its selectivity, and suggestions of other texts which should have been included will therefore suggest that the debate has begun.

Abbreviations

N&S – Carolyn Nelson and Mathew Seccombe, *British Newspapers and Periodicals 1641–1700: A Short Title Catalogue*. New York: Modern Languages Association of America, 1987.

STC – A.W. Pollard and G.R. Redgrave, *A Short-Title Catalogue of Books Printed in England, Scotland and Ireland: And of English Books Printed Abroad 1475–1640*. London: Bibliographical Society, 1926; rev. edn. 1976–1991. 3 volumes.

Wing – Donald Wing, *Short-Title Catalogue of Books Printed in England, Scotland, Ireland, Wales, and British America and of English Books Printed in Other Countries 1641–1700*. New York: Modern Languages Association of America, 1972–1988. 3 volumes.

List of Illustrations

All reproduced by permission of the Bodleian Library, Oxford

1. *Mercurius Anti-Mercvrivs*. April 1648; Wing M1752; Hope Essays 634 (19)
2. *The Diurnall Occvrrances in Parliament*. 3–10 January 1642; N&S 99.01; Fairfax serial 99
3. *Speciall Passages And certain Informations*. 20–27 September 1642 ; N&S 605.07A; Fairfax newsbooks 2, numb. 7
4. *Mercurius Britanicus*, Numb.1. 23–29 August 1643; N&S 286.001; Fairfax serial 286
5. *Mercurius Civicus*, Numb.40. 22–29 February 1643{4}; N&S 298.040; Hope Adds 1133 Numb.40 (1643)
6. *Mercurius Civicus*, Numb.149. 2–9 April 1646; N&S 298.149; Hope Adds 1133 numb.149 (1646)
7. *Mercurius Medicus*, Numb.2. 15–22 October 1647; N&S 340.2; Hope Essays 634 (4)
8. *Mercurius Britanicus Alive Again*, Numb.1. 16 May 1648; N&S 282.01; [MS] Ashmole 720 (VII) numb.1 (1648)
9. *The Moderate*, Numb.39. 3–9 April 1649; N&S 413.2039; Hope 8o 666 number 39 (1649)
10. *A Perfect Diurnall*, Numb.84. 3–10 March 1644; N&S 504.084; Hope Adds 1128 (40) page 663
11. *Mercvrivs Pragmaticus*, Num.5. 12–20 October 1647; N&S 369.105; Fairfax newsbooks 14 numb.5
12. *Mercurius Honestus*, Numb 1. 19 May? 1648; N&S 331.1; [MS] Ashmole 720 (VIII) numb.1 (1648)

13. & 14. *Occurrences From Forraign Parts*, Numb.42. 22–29 November 1659; N&S 491.042; Fairfax serial 491 numb.42: recto and verso

15. *A Perfect Diurnall of the Passages in Parliament*, Numb.44. 10–17 April 1643; N&S 513.44A; Fairfax newsbooks 1 numb.44

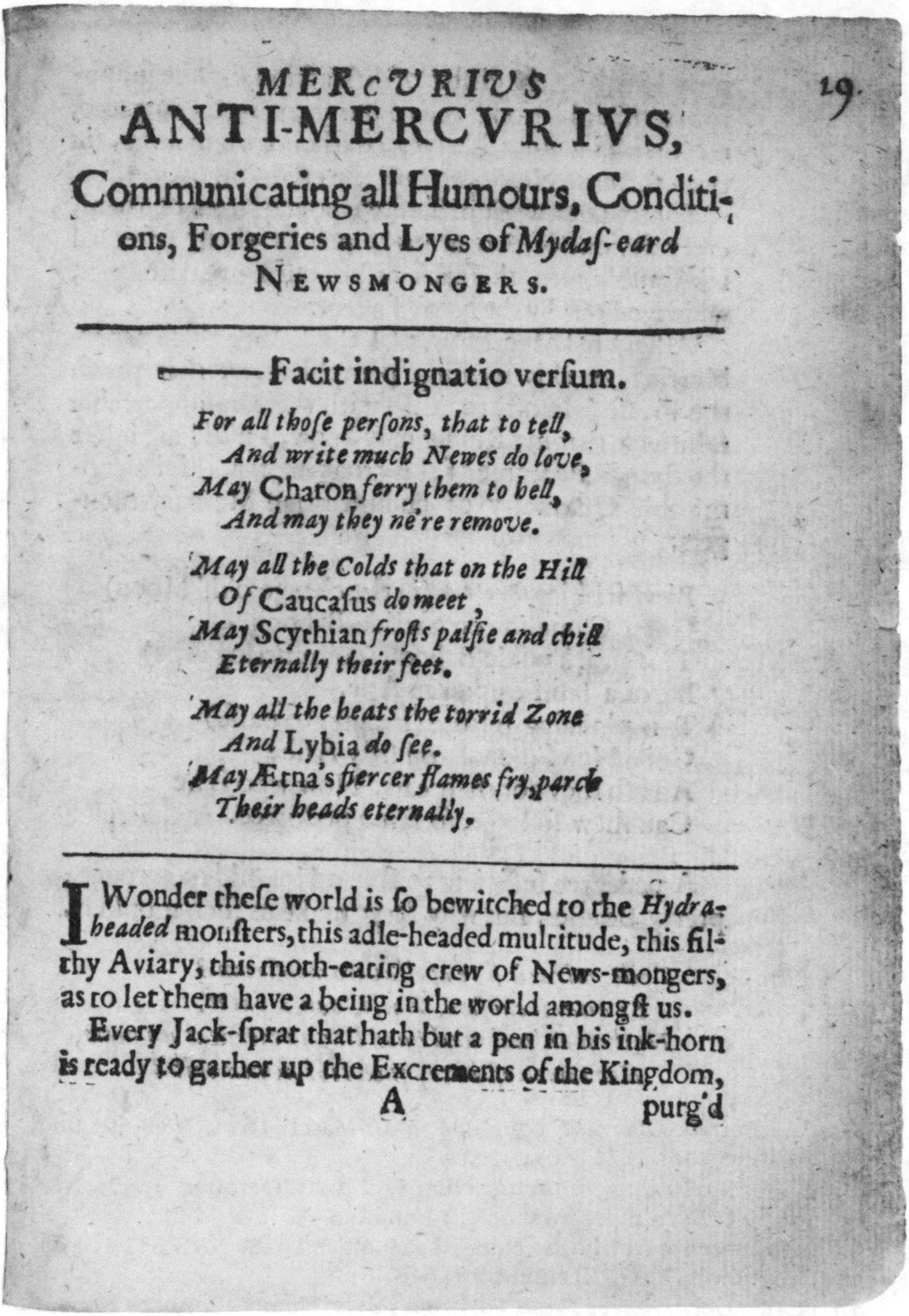

MERCVRIVS
ANTI-MERCVRIVS,
Communicating all Humours, Conditions, Forgeries and Lyes of *Mydaſ-eard* NEWSMONGERS.

19

——Facit indignatio verſum.

For all thoſe perſons, that to tell,
And write much Newes do love,
May Charon *ferry them to hell,*
And may they ne're remove.

May all the Colds that on the Hill
Of Caucaſus *do meet,*
May Scythian *froſts palſie and chill*
Eternally their feet.

May all the heats the torrid Zone
And Lybia *do ſee.*
May Ætna's *fiercer flames fry, parch*
Their heads eternally.

I Wonder theſe world is ſo bewitched to the *Hydra-headed* monſters, this adle-headed multitude, this filthy Aviary, this moth-eating crew of News-mongers, as to let them have a being in the world amongſt us.

Every Jack-ſprat that hath but a pen in his ink-horn is ready to gather up the Excrements of the Kingdom,

A purg'd

1. Mercurius Anti-Mercurius

Introduction

The invention of the newsbook

In the spring and summer of 1642 the three kingdoms of England and Wales, Ireland and Scotland, under the strain of a political rebellion, broke out into a great civil war which ravaged the kingdoms for four years. The discord between Charles and his parliament resulted in two decades of dramatic political and social changes, which were only terminated with the Restoration of Charles II in 1660. (Even then a lasting religious and political settlement was not achieved until the Rebellion of 1688.) Simultaneous with the outbreak of profound civil division and the consequent war, was the development of a new professional occupation, a breed of men, and perhaps one or two women, who, according to contemporaries, sowed sedition and spread great untruths. The products of these men and women, some said, were a contagion that flew into all quarters of the land to infect public opinion, ravage social hierarchies and lay the country waste. These people, a 'generation of Vipers', wreaked their damage by writing diurnals or mercuries. In modern language, they were journalists.

Hamlet, according to Shakespeare, said that actors were 'the abstracts and brief chronicles of the time. After your death you were better have a bad epitaph than their ill report while you live.' (II, ii) In the seventeenth century this role passed into other hands. In 1642 a parliamentary ordinance closed the theatres, and once and for all another medium supplanted the public stage, which was more influential than, perhaps even preceded the distribution of news and construction of public reputation by playwrights and poets. In the 1640s, journalism, and the *newsbook*, became a dominant literary form.[1]

The term 'journalism' can be misleading. The apparent (and to some extent genuine) continuity between the early newsbook and the modern daily newspaper makes it easy for us to assume that they meant similar kinds of things to their original readers as they do to us. To understand what the newsbook was, and how it came into being, it is necessary initially to dispense with modern categories and place the historical artefact in its own culture, in the context of the material, everyday life, the particular relationships, the means of production, and the modes of communication of the times. Historians need to be wary of attributing to newsbook writers such accolades as 'the first journalists', and their writings 'the first newspapers', because these phrases tend to reflect more upon the present age than the remote and only indirectly accessible period known as the English Revolution (or Civil War and Interregnum.)

For this reason I shall emphasise the term 'newsbook'. These early publications were not folio sheets, like modern newspapers, but small, weekly pamphlets. Contemporaries called them 'weekly pamphlets of news', 'newsbooks', 'diurnalls', 'mercuries', 'currants', 'corantos' or, occasionally, 'gazettes' in the Italian fashion.[2] The term newsbook is preferable not only because it most conveniently describes the object, but because it enables the historian to differentiate the publications between 1641 and 1660 from what came before and after.

The first newsbook appeared on the streets of London, probably in the vicinity of Holborn and Faringdon, on 29 November 1641. The title page announced the innovative nature of the contents in two ways. It was called 'THE HEADS OF SEVERALL PROCEEDINGS IN THIS PRESENT PARLIAMENT, from the 22 of *November*, to the 29. 1641. Wherein is contained the substance of severall Letters sent from *Ireland*, shewing what

1 D.F. McKenzie has argued that this transition began in the 1620s: see 'The London Book Trade in the Later Seventeenth Century', unpublished Sandars Lectures, 1976; and '*The Staple of News* and the Late Plays', in *A Celebration of Ben Jonson*, eds. W. Blissett, J. Patrick and R.W. Van Fossen (Toronto: University of Toronto Press, 1973).

2 There are two probable origins of this term: either it derives from 'gazetta', the small Venetian coin with which they were purchased, or from 'gaza', meaning 'treasury'. For a discussion of the etymology and its interpretation, see J.B. Williams, *A History of English Journalism to the Foundation of the Gazette* (London: Longmans, 1908), pp.6–7. 'Coranto' came from Latin, meaning 'running'. As with the term 'mercury', there is the implication of physical movement.

distresse and misery they are in With divers other passages of moment touching the Affaires of these Kingdomes.' The keywords in the context of the history of censorship here are 'this *Present* Parliament' and '*these* Kingdomes'.[3] The keywords in the history of the genre are 'from the 22 of November, to the 29.' The plain title page disguised something quite revolutionary.

Since 1594, *Mercurius Gallobelgicus*, a continental, twice-yearly news periodical in Latin, had been published in Cologne.[4] English periodical news publications began in 1620. Imitating a French newspaper printed in Amsterdam that year, a Dutch printer released an untitled sheet of news, '*Imprinted at Amsterdam by George Veseler, A°. 1620. The 2. of Decemember.* [sic] And are to be soulde by Petrus Keerius, dwelling in the Calver-streete, in the uncertaine time.' Later the same month another sheet, headed *Corrant out of Italy, Germany, &c*, was released with the same imprint.[5] These English language news sheets, as their titles suggest, contained news only of continental Europe. The phrase 'in the uncertaine time' implies that their appearance was an indirect consequence of the Thirty Years War. There is an element of truth in the commonplace association between news publications and warfare.[6] Some of the foreign language corantos had news of Britain, but at this point there were no English periodicals containing news of Britain and Ireland. In the 1620s Nathaniel Butter, Nicholas Bourne and other collaborators printed English language corantos in London, but these also limited themselves to foreign affairs.

The reason for these restrictions is fairly simple. It was illegal to print domestic news in England. There was a sense among the governors that too much information, a 'liberty of discourse', threatened to demystify and therefore undermine the nature of

3 'These Kingdomes' refers to Scotland, Ireland and England and Wales, three independent monarchies, all represented by the same monarch, Charles I. Wales was a dominion of England and was generally subsumed under the name of England, except when the Welsh flocked in great numbers to the aid of the Royalist cause. It is interesting that this invisibility of an important political body continues in the work of historians to the present day.

4 See Matthias A. Shaaber, *Some Forerunners of the Press In England, 1476–1622* (Philadelphia: University of Pennsylvania Press, 1929), pp.310ff.

5 For these early corantos, see Folke Dahl, *A Bibliography of English Corantos and Periodical Newsbooks 1620–1642* (London: The Bibliographical Society, 1952); Laurence Hanson, 'English Newsbooks, 1620–1641', *The Library*, 4th series, XVIII (1938); George F. Barwick, 'Corantos' *The Library*, 3rd series, IV (1913).

6 Stanley Morison, *Origins of the Newspaper* (London: The Times, 1954), p.5; Mrs. Herbert Richardson, *The Old English Newspaper* (London: The English Association, 1929), p.6; Barwick, 'Corantos', p.117.

proper government. Even foreign news was regarded with some suspicion: Thomas Archer was imprisoned in 1621 for publishing an unlicensed news sheet.[7] It was possible to make a living printing news, however, and throughout the 1620s Butter and Bourne, together with Archer, Downes and Sheffard steered a fine course in relation to the censors, issuing many periodicals of an indefinite periodicity. This publishing syndicate co-operated not only with each other but with a group of printers and correspondents to produce quickly and in large print runs.[8] The corantos were initially single sheets and then small volumes, anywhere between four and upwards of forty pages in length, but usually either sixteen or twenty-four pages, published whenever there was sufficient news to justify printing. In practice this was two to five times a month. By 1632 they had, however, annoyed the authorities enough to become the object of a Star Chamber decree:

> Upon Considerac[i]on had at the Board of the greate abuse in the printing & publishing of the ordenary Gazetts and Pamphletts of newes from forraign p[ar]t[e]s, And upon significa[ti]on of his ma[jes]t[ie]s expresse pleasure and Com[m]aund for the p[re]sent suppressing of the same, It was thought fitt and hereby ordered that all printing and publishing of the same be accordingly supprest and inhibited. And that as well Nathaniell Butter & Nicholas Bourne Booke Sellers, under whose names the said Gazetts have beene usually published, as all other Stationers, Printers and Booke Sellers, p[re]sume not from henceforth to print publish or sell any of the said Pamphletts, &c, as they will answer the Contrary at theire p[e]rills. And Mr Secr[etary]e Windebanke is lykewise prayed to send for the said Butter and Bourne, and to lay a strict Com[m]aund upon them on that behalfe.[9]

Until 1638, when they were granted a Royal Patent, Butter and Bourne published an occasional serial which did not contravene the wishes of the authorities. Thereafter they released a four-page periodical, once again at almost regular intervals, with some success. These continued to be exclusively concerned with foreign news. This contrasted with France, where the national, weekly newsbook was flourishing under the hand of Théophraste

7 Fredrick S. Siebert, *Freedom of the Press in England 1476–1776: The Rise and Decline of Government Controls* (Urbana: University of Illinois Press, 1952), pp.150–1.

8 See Williams, *A History of English Journalism*; McKenzie, 'The London Book Trade'.

9 Folke Dahl, 'Amsterdam – Cradle of English Newspapers', *The Library*, 5th series, IV (1949), 173–4.

Renaudot, with the patronage of Cardinal Richelieu.[10] It was only when the Scottish and Irish rebelled, and the three kingdoms erupted into substantial political conflict, and, as an adjunct to this internal disintegration, the mechanisms of censorship broke down, that the first English language periodical publications with domestic news could be printed.

Caroline censorship relied on three entities in addition to the king and the Archbishop of Canterbury: the Court of High Commission, Star Chamber and the Stationers' Company. In December 1640 Archbishop William Laud was impeached and imprisoned, and in July 1641 Star Chamber and the High Commission were abolished by the Long Parliament. Star Chamber had also been responsible for enforcing the unpopular church policy of Laud: the humble artisan Nehemiah Wallington had been brought before it, and the irrepressible and prolix pamphleteer William Prynne lost his ears as a consequence of its severe penalties. The unassisted Stationers' Company was equally unable to control printing: even before 1641 it had been subject to internal divisions. With the challenge to the king's prerogative and differences between the two Houses of Parliament there was no longer any single authority controlling the press.[11] The contradictory external forces operating on the Stationers' Company, and the continuing conflicts within it, ensured that any unified policy on printing rights was dissolved. Over a century after the event the *Boston Gazette* asserted that 'the original, true and real Cause' of the Civil War was press censorship, and that 'had not *Prynn* lost his *Ears*, K. *Charles* would never have lost his Head.'[12]

London witnessed an apparent increase in unlicensed printed books from 1640 onwards, and particularly during the summer of 1641. This is sometimes represented as an explosion in print, but it remains to be proved that the amount of paper coming off the presses rapidly increased. It is clear, however, that there was a significant change in the *kind* of books being published. Small, quickly composed and cheaply printed pamphlets had an impact out of proportion to their physical stature, simply because they were more easily available to greater numbers of readers. The newsbook began to cut into the market for more costly newsletters. (Newsbooks did not only display a physical continuity with

10 See Howard M. Solomon, *Public Welfare, Science and Propaganda in Seventeenth-Century France*, (New Jersey: Princeton University Press, 1972).

11 Siebert, *Freedom of the Press*, ch.8.

12 Quoted in Jeffery A. Smith, *Printers and Press Freedom: The Ideology of Early American Journalism* (New York & Oxford: Oxford University Press, 1988), p.21.

manuscript newsletters,[13] they overlapped in news content.) What was previously a more restricted, private experience was becoming widespread and available to less prestigious social groups. The cheap publications were generally unlicensed, and this meant that they could focus on new and contentious issues, and could bring a greater range of perspectives to bear upon those issues. Until the Parliamentary Printing Ordinance of 1643 they occasioned a continuous stream of complaints by individual members about unauthorised, scandalous and seditious pamphlets. To some contemporaries, these publications, including newsbooks, were dangerous not specifically because they were fictitious and prone to damage communication between the hostile factions; rather, the availability of news itself was represented as a destabilising force which exposed the workings of government, stripping it bare of its opaque privileges, and thereby led to unruly behaviour by the rude and undiscerning multitude.

One implication of this plague of pamphlets is that there was a dramatic transformation in both political consciousness and the distribution of information in early-modern society. Prior to this period such socially diverse individuals as John Rushworth (lawyer and later Secretary to the army,) George Thomason (member of the Stationers' Company,) Brilliana Lady Harley (correspondent and wife to Sir Robert, a member of the House of Lords,) and Nehemiah Wallington (devout Presbyterian and wood turner) had shown an interest in current affairs. Suddenly they started to collect its ephemera. Wallington spent so much on publications that he wrote in one of his notebooks; 'these little pamphlets of weekly news about my house ... were so many thieves that had stolen away my money before I was aware of them.'[14] Thomason amassed an enormous collection over the ensuing twenty years, not even allowing a spell in prison to interrupt his devoted purchasing.[15] Rushworth added to his manuscript accounts of councils and court meetings in the 1630s a considerable number of printed tracts, over which he scribbled notes in preparation for his voluminous history of the period.[16]

13 Stanley Morison, *Origins of the Newspaper*, p.9ff.

14 Paul S. Seaver, *Wallington's World: A Puritan Artisan in Seventeenth-Century London* (London: Methuen, 1985), p.156.

15 Lois Spencer, 'The Politics of George Thomason', The Library, 5th series, XIV (1969), p.20. For Thomason and Rushworth see also DNB. For Lady Harley, see Jacqueline Eales, *Puritans and Roundheads: The Harleys of Brampton Bryan and the Outbreak of the English Civil War* (Cambridge: Cambridge University Press, 1990), p.7ff.

16 See my forthcoming article, 'This Rushworthian inarticulate rubbish-continent: Newsbooks, politics and history'.

In some ways cheap and unlicensed publications helped to drive a wedge between king and parliament. By distributing information about the conflict they encouraged their readers to take a position on certain issues. They also spread anxieties about the central issues over which the opposing parties could not agree; for instance the response to the Irish Rebellion. In the prefatory address to his *Liberty of Conscience*, published in 1644, the same year as Milton's *Areopagitica*, Henry Robinson showed how the '*London* Pamphlets' and *Mercurius Aulicus*, the king's Oxford newsbook, were positioned in an argument which occluded the possibility of defining a middle ground. Private judgement, he argued, should lead to the discovery of truth, but in this case fear, mistrust and jealousy prevented any reconciliation or allowance of a liberty of conscience and so led inexorably to 'the firing of whole Townes, deflowring of Virgins, committing rapes, rapines, and a thousand other villanies'.[17] In the same year a victim of criticisms in newsbooks lashed back at their authors:

> who pretending to maintaine the cause of *Religion*, scandalize both it and all goodnesse, with malitious *Lyes*: whose anonymous *Reporters* have even sold themselves to the *Presse*, to abuse the Peace of this poore distracted Church and Kingdome, whose audacious *Pens* bedabbled in the Gall of bitternesse, set forth presumptuous things, maligning *Princes*, and speaking evill of *Dignities*, who aiming at the confusion of the *Church* strike at her very Pillars, casting their venomous *Froth* upon their Names, whose able and Religious Quils have vindicated the true Protestant Religion, from the dirty calumnies of learned Hereticks.[18]

The conflicts between newsbooks fed the political conflict. No contemporary reader of the mercuries would have believed that their country was unified, that their society was not in a state of tumultuous revolution, that they were not in some sense responsible for articulating their own position. The many petitions in the period, used by groups with various interests, appealed to a sphere of divided public opinion upon precisely the same conditions which newsbooks addressed their readers. Newsbooks were, as Robinson feared, implicated in the consolidation of these opposed positions.

17 Robinson, *Liberty of Conscience* in ed. William Haller, *Tracts on Liberty in the Puritan Revolution, 1638–1647*, 3 vols (New York: Columbia University Press, 1934), III, 109.

18 Daniel Featley, *The Gentle Lash, Or the Vindication of Dr. Featley* (Oxford, 1644), sig.A2. Wing F583. This passage appears not to have been written by Featley himself.

This was clear in the exchanges between king and parliament in late 1641 and early 1642. Representations of the proceedings in parliament tended to improve its reputation: these representations declined in number in periods of conflict within the Houses, when the news might be detrimental to their status.[19] The king showed some reluctance to employ the full potential of printed propaganda in his own interest, perhaps because he was distrustful of appeals to the public when he thought his own rights rested on the higher authority of divine jurisdiction. Later he realised the full importance of propaganda and oversaw the foundation of the highly successful Oxford court newsbook *Mercurius Aulicus*.[20]

In these ways, the pamphlets on politics, on Scotland (some of them printed in Edinburgh and distributed in England as propaganda) and on the rebellion in Ireland were inclined to side, actively or passively, with the parliament. Their effect was to shine a harsh light on the foundations of kingship, the person of the king and the nature of the church under Archbishop Laud. They stopped short of outright hostility, however; in these early days, it could be dangerous explicitly to attack the king's personal integrity, and as late as 1646 Marchamont Nedham, a tenacious, scurrilous and vituperative writer of newsbooks, was imprisoned and debarred from writing *Mercurius Britanicus* for too sharply satirising Charles {8.04}.[21]

Somewhere between the initial proliferation of pamphlets and the outbreak of war the first issue of *Heads of Severall Proceedings* appeared (see p.2 above.) The young publisher, John Thomas, who was later to gain a minor notoriety for disreputable publishing practices, was no doubt aware of the dangers he was potentially encroaching upon: he used only his initials on the title page, which made possible the transparent excuse that he was not responsible for the item, should he be brought before parliament.

But most remarkable of all was the conjunction of these facts with the dates on the title page of *The Heads of Severall Proceedings*: 'from the 22 of *November*, to the 29. 1641.' The

19 A.D.T. Cromartie, 'The Printing of Parliamentary Speeches in November 1640–July 1642', *The Historical Journal*, 33, 1 (1990), pp.23–44. Cromartie does not account for newsbooks in his article.

20 See P.W. Thomas, *Sir John Berkenhead 1617–1679: A Royalist Career in Politics and Polemics* (Oxford: Clarendon Press, 1969).

21 For more on Nedham see ch.8

newsbook purported to cover exactly one week. And though a novice purchaser would not necessarily have inferred this in November, the dates represented an intention to publish a second issue on the same day the next week. And perhaps the week after. With the coverage of domestic events and a weekly periodicity of publication the newsbook was invented.

Before and after November 1641

Newsbooks were a consequence of the English Revolution. Their existence depended on both the social and political changes which constituted that revolution: and the competitive market of weekly, serial news publications is one of the long-term inheritances of the 1640s. Their initial existence was closely bound with the Long Parliament, the group of men who came together at Westminster in 1640 with a view to bartering modest political and religious reforms in exchange for a supply to the king of money for military purposes, and who succeeded in creating the initial political revolution. The early existence of newsbooks reflects the relationship of some of these men with the press, notably their impression of the importance of publishing speeches, and of the exchange of publicity and propaganda with the king. Their existence through the revolutionary period was conditioned by their participation in the conflict between king, parliament and army. They are a consequence of the English Revolution, and evidence that there was a revolution in England between 1641 and 1660.

The English Revolution was actually a series of revolutions. These were not all defined by discrete events, and each participated in long and short term causes, but they can be differentiated for the convenience of a narrative. Some of the major developments are outlined in chapters one, five and ten, which chart newsbook representations of three of the transformations in government.

One aspect of the transformation in society which was both a cause and an effect of the newsbook was the expansion of a public sphere of political debate. A precondition of this was an increased political consciousness (not necessarily equivalent with literacy) among a broader section of the population, notably in urban centres, above all in London. The period following parliament's Grand Remonstrance, a petition of grievances and accusations addressed to the king, but framed in an appeal to the people,[22] saw mass demonstrations by the London apprentices. This was one of the moments in the mid-seventeenth century when the young, with their own subculture and experience of street politics, exerted a popular influence on the course of events in government.[23] The newsbook accounts are evocative of the excitement and fear on the streets of London in December 1641 and January 1642, when the king and parliament disputed the control of the militia and the apprentices mobbed the Lords and Commons crying for 'no Bishops' and the weeding-out of episcopacy, root and branch {1.2&5}. A generation of apprentices in 1640 had no experience of a parliament, having lived for eleven years under the 'Personal Rule' of Charles I: not remembering the dissolution of the 1628 Parliament, for them this revived government institution seemed to promise representation, a dissonant voice in the polity, and real political and religious change. Members of an impressively literate community,[24] their understanding and interpretation of political events and of history came in part from the expanding and mutating print culture in London. Those who could not read could be read to: and the practice of passing a pamphlet on to another reader, perhaps sending it by the Tuesday post to the provinces, and of reading aloud to a gathering, ensured a very high circulation for each printed text. Print runs were probably in the order of two hundred and fifty to perhaps a few thousand, in most cases closer to the smaller figure. The actual number of readers for a pamphlet with an average print run of 500 copies can only be conjectural. One individual about whom we do know quite a lot, however, confirms our impression about Puritan literacy, interest in current events and political intervention: Nehemiah Wallington exchanged ideas with a geographically widespread circle of friends, he bought and collected newsbooks, and he cried aloud for justice against the Earl of Strafford on the streets of London in May 1641.[25]

To some extent the readership was there before 1641, and our inference of a sudden historical rupture with the appearance of

22 This very public element of the Remonstrance was the aspect which caused most consternation. See Conrad Russell, *The Fall of the British Monarchies 1637–1642* (Oxford: Clarendon Press, 1991), p.427.

23 See Steven R. Smith, 'The London Apprentices as Seventeenth-Century Adolescents', *Past and Present*, 61 (1973), pp.155–7.

24 David Cressy, *Literacy and the Social Order: Reading and writing in Tudor and Stuart England* (Cambridge: Cambridge University Press, 1980), esp. chs. 6 & 7.

25 Paul Seaver, *Wallington's World*, pp.34, 48, 151, 174, 191.

the newsbook is deceptive. There is far too little evidence conclusively to determine to what extent the desire for news predated the first newsbook, and was only satisfied with the breakdown in censorship, and to what extent the events of the 1640s generated an interest in recent news. One source of evidence is the numerous accusations against news publications, their writers, printers, publishers and readers. These showed important relative modifications through the seventeenth century, but also revealed a persistence of a basic vocabulary of criticism which predated the civil wars and continued long after the Restoration.

In his masque, *Newes From the New World Discover'd in the Moone*, performed in 1620 although not published until 1640, Ben Jonson illustrated some enduring stereotypes. For instance the cynical avarice of the 'Printer':

> Indeed I am all for sale, Gentlemen, you say true, I am a Printer, and a Printer of Newes; and I doe hearken after 'hem, where ever they be, at any rates: I'le give anything for a good Copie now, be't true or false, so't be newes.

The 'Factor', author of manuscript newsletters, emphasises the irrelevance of accuracy to his credibility and creditablity when he observes:

> it is the Printing I am offended at, I would have no newes printed; for when they are printed they leave to bee newes; while they are written though they be false, they remaine newes still.

To which the Printer responds:

> It is the Printing of 'hem makes 'hem newes to a great many, who will indeed believe nothing but what's in Print. For those I doe keep my Presses, and so many Pens going to bring forth wholesome relations, which once in halfe a score yeares (as the age growes forgetfull) I Print over againe with a new date.[26]

Six years later, in *The Staple of Newes*, Jonson drew attention to the credulousness of the reader, to whom news was only a means to social exchange. The 'Register' of the staple of news describes his office:

> 'Tis the house of *Fame*, Sir,
> Where both the curious, and the negligent;
> The scrupulous, and carelesse; wilde, and stay'd;
> The idle, and laborious; all doe meet,

26 *Ben Jonson*, ed. C.H. Herford and Percy and Evelyn Simpson, 10 vols. (Oxford: Clarendon Press, 1925–50), VII, 514–5.

> To tast the *Cornu copiæ* of her rumors,
> Which she, the mother of sport, pleaseth to scatter
> Among the vulgar: Baites, Sir, for the people!
> And they will bite like fishes.[27]

His customers confirm his prejudices: a countrywoman asks for:

> A *groatsworth* of any *Newes*, I care not what,
> To carry downe this *Saturday*, to our *Vicar*.

The Register makes it clear whom the play is accusing:

> You are a Butterwoman, aske *Nathaniel*
> The *Clerke*, there.[28]

In 1631 in his character sketch of 'A Corranto-coiner', Richard Brathwait also designated Nathaniel Butter for personal satire, while contributing to these stereotypes.[29] He emphasised the provincial naivety of the audience of corantos, and the cynical manipulation of his readers by the coranto writer, whose 'owne *Genius* is his intelligencer', and whose news was pure fiction composed to coin a profit:

> He is all *ayre*; his eare alwayes open to all *reports*; which how incredible soever, must passe for *currant*, and find vent, purposely to get him *currant money*, and delude the vulgar. Yet our best comfort is, his *Chymera's* live not long; a weeke is the longest in the Citie, and after their arrivall, little longer in the Countrey.[30]

In 1632 Donald Lupton wrote that their untrustworthiness was proverbial: 'now every one can say, it's as true even as a Currantoe, meaning that it's all false.'[31]

These denunciations of early news publications were similar, often identical to complaints about newsbooks after 1641, a few, brief examples of which will illustrate the critical heritage within which newsbooks have been transmitted. These criticisms were mostly unimaginative and focused on a limited range of topics: firstly, the physical appearance of newsbooks; secondly, their untrustworthy content; thirdly, the motivation of their authors; fourthly, the credulousness and poor social standing of their

27 *Ben Jonson*, VI, 331–2.

28 *Ben Jonson*, VI, 293.

29 Richard Brathwait, *Whimzies: Or, A New Cast of Characters* (1631), p.22. STC 3591.

30 Brathwait, *Whimzies*, pp.15, 21–2.

31 Donald Lupton, *London and the Covntrey Carbanadoed and Quartered into seuerall Characters* (London, 1632), p.142. STC 16944.

readers; fifthly, the effect they had on society; and sixthly, their low esteem in a hierarchy of literary forms.

The title of one pamphlet explicitly associated poor typography with irresponsible text; the author of *A Presse full of Pamphlets: wherein, Are set Diversity of Prints, containing deformed and misfigured Letters: Composed into Books fraught with Libellous and Scandallous Sentences* underscored the danger to which the political process was subjected by the untruths told by newsbooks:

> My intentions in this Paper, is no otherwise but to describe the abuse of Printing, in publishing every Pamphlet that comes to their presse; abusing therin not only the persons of many Honourable, learned, and worthy Members of State, but even the Proceeding of the High Court of Parliament, and the worthy Members thereof, are by the same exposed to the view of all men, And were the same truly and really published, it would gain great Admiration & Renown. But in the description, it is so interlaced & intermixed with fictitious devisings of idle and rash wits, that the same are not credulous, and by that means lose that due and awfull respect, which otherwise ought to bee ascribed unto the same.[32]

Newsbooks were cheap, and looked cheap, being 'weekly Fragments' and mere 'penny-worths of History', 'peny-worths of paper,' 'penniworths of impiety'.[33] Their news was either invented or so utterly distorted that they were 'so many impostumated Fancies, so many Bladders of their own Blowing', full of 'parboyl'd Non-sense'.[34] Accordingly the authors were 'a company of impudent snakes', a 'Generation of *Vipers*', who were solely interested in their own profit. They 'gull'd' their readers 'out of their money'.[35] Marchamont Nedham, a newsbook writer who gained an enduring notoriety as a time-server, was particularly reputed for his avarice. Greed was no doubt associated with falsehood, and both led the perfidious newsbook writer to aim at the uneducated, 'poore deluded People', the 'credulous Vulgar',

32 *A Presse full of Pamphlets* (London, 1642), sig.A[2]v. Wing P3293.

33 J[ohn] C[leveland], *A Character of a Diurnal-Maker* (London, 1645) pp.2, 5. Wing C4657. *Mercurius Vrbanvs*, Numb.2, 9 November 1643. N&S 29.2. Featley, *The Gentle Lash*, sig.A2.

34 John Cleveland, *The Character of a London Diurnal* (London, 1644), p.8. Wing C4659. [Sam Sheppard], *Mercurius Mastix: Faithfully Lashing All Scouts, Mercuries, Posts, Spyes, and others; who cheat the Common-wealth under the name of Intelligence*, Numb.1, 20–27 August. 1652. N&S 339.1.

35 *Mercurius Mastix*; Featley, *The Gentle Lash*, sig.A2.

'unconsidering persons'.[36] Newsbooks were 'Calculated exactly to the low and sordid Capacities of the Vulgar'.[37]

Newsbooks were also said to cause real damage. The clergyman and church historian Thomas Fuller wrote that 'such scurrilous papers do more then conceivable mischief'; one anonymous pamphleteer, criticising Henry Walker, author of *Perfect Occurrences*, wrote that 'I do think that his, and many other scurillous Pamphlets, have done more mischief in this Kingdome then ever all my Lord of *Essex's* or Sir *Thomas Fairfaxes* whole train of Artillery ever did.'[38] The final theme of criticisms focused on the poor literary qualities of newsbooks. Their writers were not like a serious historian, 'a sage and solemn Author, one that curles his brow with sullen Gravity', but 'squealing Scribes'.[39] The author of *Mercurius Anti-Britanicus* wrote that the author of *Mercurius Britanicus* would not be able 'out of his *Writings* of Two whole yeares, to produce one Thing well, or sharply ill said, whereby the *People* might in pitty say, He was *hanged* for being *Witty*.'[40]

From these examples, it should be clear that the specific characteristics which contemporaries identified for censure reveal some continuity from Jonson in 1620 through to the 1640s. They suggest that while newsbooks were themselves new, some things about them were not absolutely unfamiliar. These repetitions can, however, also mask the remarkable innovations of the newsbooks of the 1640s: the continuities between criticisms are to be understood not as evidence of simple continuity in the news publications themselves. Instead the topics of these attacks represent elements of a genre, not a set of concrete rules, but a group of accumulated conventions and commonplaces from which a writer could choose or choose not to borrow. The tirades against newsbooks formed a tradition from which subsequent writers continued to draw. This is most important when we consider the way these hostile observations have formed the basis of the modern historians' understanding of what a newsbook was and how it worked, even infecting the diction used to describe

36 Featley, *The Gentle Lash*, sig.A2; John Nalson, *An Impartiall Collection of the Great Affairs of State*, vol.2 (London, 1683), p.807, Wing N107; [Roger L'Estrange], *A Rope for Pol, or, a hue and cry after Marchamont Nedham* (1660), 'Advertisement to the Reader', p.iv. Wing L1299A.

37 Nalson, *Impartiall Collection*, p.806.

38 Thomas Fuller, *The Holy State* (Cambridge, 1642), p.201. Wing F2443. *A Fresh Whip For all scandalous Lyers. or, A true description of the two eminent Pamphleteers, or Squibtellers of this Kingdome* (London, 1647), p.6. Wing F2199.

39 Cleveland, *A Character of a Diurnal-Maker*, p.5.

40 *Mercurius Anti-Britanicus* [Numb.1] (Oxford, August 1645), p.5. N&S 267.1.

them. Three hundred and fifty years of subsequent history has buried November 1641 deep in familiar contempt: this anthology is intended to encourage a re-reading and reassessment of some of these texts.

How to read newsbooks

In the nineteenth century James Grant remarked that the 'external appearances of the newspapers' of the mid-seventeenth century 'was in keeping with their low moral and intellectual character.'[41] If, for a modern reappraisal of the newsbook, it is necessary to dispel the unenlightening moral connotations which accompany such observations then it is perhaps necessary to describe what newsbooks looked like, why, and to suggest what inferences can be drawn from their external appearance. I hope this, with the illustrations, will serve as a framework for the reader to appreciate more fully the texts which constitute this anthology.

Early newsbooks certainly displayed some of the characteristics which they were critically accorded. This should not oblige us to concur with the moral disapproval. Newsbooks were, by 1643 at least, prone to printing stories which were basically untrue. The association between dishonest printing practices and newsbooks was probably encouraged, for instance, by John Thomas, the publisher of the first newsbook. In 1641 he may have had some semi-official connections inside parliament, but in 1642 he repeatedly offended against printing ordinances, published under other people's names, and was committed to Newgate prison.[42] He may have thereby fostered the reputation of publishers of the newsbooks for cynical malpractice.

The typography of newsbooks was often poor: the last pages were set very quickly, and type of uniform size was not always possible if there was a sudden influx or dearth of news. Fast and therefore relatively cheap typesetting would have made small print runs more economically feasible. Newsbooks were not conceived like large folio volumes. The royalist newsbook *Mercurius Aulicus*, the typography of which was exceptionally neat, with wide margins and accurate headings and pagination,

41 James Grant, *The Newspaper Press: Its Origin – Progress – and Present Position*, 2 vols. (London: Tinsley Brothers, 1871), p.38.

42 Sheila Lambert, 'The Beginning of Printing for the House of Commons, 1640–42', *The Library*, 6th series, III (1981), p.53. Cromartie, 'Printing of Parliamentary Speeches', p.38.

was established in opposition to London, parliamentary newsbooks. It was meant to look different. Awareness of presentation was by no means the preserve of self-consciously elitist publications, however: when *Mercurius Britanicus* was established to serve as counter-propaganda to *Aulicus*, it too was neatly organised, with an elegant commentary in smaller type in the margins, reminiscent of the marginalia of scholarly texts. The Leveller newsbook *The Moderate* was also well presented, with a plain, simple organisation, relatively accurate typesetting, and clear and evenly-sized type. Newsbooks were, at a penny each for the smaller ones, among the cheapest publications available, and they could appeal to the less literate and less educated as much as to the reader of luxuriant folios. Some newsbooks, for instance *The Scotish Dove*, written in a pious, intentionally 'populist' style, were intended for a less socially prestigious readership than others, for instance Pecke's *Perfect Diurnall*. Conclusions should not be inferred from insubstantial, internal evidence of style. Nonetheless, a newsbook would have been more accessible to a poor audience than a large, expensive volume, and it is reasonable to suggest that their audience included the middling and poorer sort (the 'vulgar'), whom some of the middling and better sort of people then and subsequently regarded as naïve, gullible and credulous.

As these divisions in the market suggests, newsbooks as a corpus of texts have no internal logic.[43] The newsbooks available during a given week differed in size, format, style and news content (and presumably price). There is no single, simple characteristic which makes an ordinary quarto news pamphlet a newsbook. Certain items which can be classified as serials are not really newsbooks: and some newsbooks never reached a second issue, even if they were ever intended to.[44] These differentiations reflect the variety of readers of different social statuses which read newsbooks. Each text shows indications of the historical circumstances in which it was produced, and of the hands of the individuals who wrote, published, sold and read it. Nevertheless it remains possible to make general observations about them.

There were physical continuities between all newsbooks. These are the kinds of things most apparent to someone looking

43 Individual newsbooks and serials do possess such a logic.

44 An example of the former is *The Wandering Whore*; the latter includes George Wither's *Mercurius Rusticus* {2.16}. N&S 668.1–3; Wing W3171 respectively.

through George Thomason's unparalleled collection of pamphlets purchased between 1640 and 1661.[45] Newsbooks were usually eight pages long, though the more confident and prestigious (and economically secure) could be twelve or sixteen. They had dates on their title pages, usually covering the week preceding their publication: for example, 'Friday 30 August to Friday 6 September, 1644'. The news of the end date could not actually be included, as the text would be printed on the preceding day and night, to be sold on that day. The date was generally positioned below the title, often with the publisher's and the bookseller's names. Some early newsbooks had a full title page, often with a blank verso, like most seventeenth-century publications, but their producers soon opted for a title covering only half a page or less, as this allocated more space to content.

After the first few months of their existence as a form, newsbooks tended to be numbered. This was co-ordinated with consecutive pagination and signatures (the mark at the bottom of the page which assists the identification, folding and binding of the separate sheets of a large book). The numbering of issues not only emphasised the fact that they were serials and aspired to comprehensive chronological coverage, but also encouraged the reader to purchase the same serial the next week. This was something of an innovation in the seventeenth century, when the habit of collecting was not as ingrained as it is today. When pirate publications appeared, as was the case with *Mercurius Pragmaticus* in 1649, they would imitate the original very closely, including the appropriate issue number.

Newsbooks also tended to divide their content into daily sections: thus the name 'diurnal'. Each day's news could be placed under a separate heading, and news brought by letters was often subdivided with a title, sometimes like a modern headline in appearance, noting the date and place of origin, and perhaps the day it was received. This partitioned the text as well as providing the news with some authentification and a mark of seriousness. While the physical appearance of the newsbook derived from older forms, such as letters and printed plays, it was also constrained by these formal innovations. No doubt such elements made newsbooks easier to read. For most in the seventeenth

45 For an account of the experience of reading the tracts, particularly in relation to newsbooks, see H.N. Brailsford, *The Levellers and the English Revolution*, ed. Christopher Hill (Nottingham: Spokesman, 1983 edn.), pp.401ff. The Thomason collection has a few newsbooks dating up to 1663.

century, reading would have been a struggle, a pained attempt to elicit meaning from obscure marks on the page. These problems would have been heightened when dealing with what was, after all, a new form. Pointers, such as headlines, could offer a momentary relief, as could a gap in an otherwise cramped page. Newsbooks were designed to be understood. Accordingly they summoned up old costumes and borrowed speech from other books, as well as devising new means to present unfamiliar material in an orderly fashion.

Regularity in periodicity, size and format were part of the basic identity of any newsbook. When Nedham was obliged to miss an issue or several issues of the *Mercurius Pragmaticus*, owing to a period spent evading the censors and prison, he would dutifully add their numbers to that of the next issue he succeeded in producing. He apologised when he had to diminish *Pragmaticus* to a 'single sheet ... because the *Curs* hunt so hot', that is, because he was being chased by parliamentary agents.[46] Some newsbooks ventured forth with novel and individual elements: *Certain Informations* grouped pithy headlines in the top left hand corner; *The Scotish Dove* introduced headlines in rhymed couplets in the top right hand corner; *Certaine Speciall and Remarkable Passages* had numbered headlines covering the front page, which more or less corresponded to the contents. *Mercurius Britanicus* used marginal annotations; in 1643 *Mercurius Civicus* illustrated its title page, usually with portraits of the protagonists in the war. These differentiations were nonetheless maintained within certain horizons of similarity, such as the positioning of the dates and issue numbers.

Although it seems to have been the custom for a new diurnal to be launched on a day of the week when there was less competition, the tendency in titles was towards similarity. There were numerous *A Perfect Diurnall of the Passages in Parliament* by different publishers through 1642. The familiar title was seen as a potential sales advantage, and each new editor intended to credit from the existing reputation of another. Other titles flaunted resemblance without being identical: *Some Speciall and Considerable Passages*, *Perfect Occurrences of Parliament*, *Diurnall Occurrences*, *Perfect Passages*, *Perfect Occurrences of Every Daies iournall in Parliament*, *The Kingdomes Weekly Post*, *The Kingdomes Weekly Intelligencer*, *The Moderate Intel-*

46 *Mercurius Pragmaticus*, Numb.32&33, 7–14 November 1648, sig.Zz(v). N&S 369.233.

ligencer, *The Moderate Messenger*, *The Moderate*. Newsbooks continued the seventeenth-century practice of not differentiating between title and subtitle or even the description of contents so some titles were particularly long and cumbersome. There were also many briefer and less pedestrian titles: *Hermes Stratjcus*, *Mercurius Rusticus*, *Mercurius Melancholicus*, *Mercurius Dogmaticus*, *Mercurius Poeticus*, *The Man in the Moon*. The popular use of 'Mercurius' led to the familiar appellation 'mercuries'. Mercury was the messenger of the Gods, winged and sandalled, and hence he was also an emblem of eloquence. The fantastical Elizabethan coiner of outlandish phrases, Thomas Nashe, employed this sense: 'The Mercurian heavenly charme of hys Rhetorique'. But the mercurial influence of the planet Mercury included being subject to whims and vagaries.[47] John Donne epigrammatically addressed *Mercurius Gallo-Belgicus*: 'Change thy name: thou art like/ *Mercury* in stealing, but lyest like a *Greek*.'[48] The mercuries as bearers of news were articulate, lively, mutable, transient and fair of speech.

The more incisive titles of the mercuries tended to belong to more polemical newsbooks, and this brings us to the most significant division among the group of publications collectively known as newsbooks. This is the opposition (which will become manifest in the following selections) between bland, plain-style texts, which describe the news in a dry, factual narrative, though sometimes with a more informal editorial; and the racy, rhetorical newsbooks, filled with spleen and invective, which relegated news to a secondary place. The aggressive, overtly propagandistic newsbook tends to be associated with the Royalist cause and with greater mendacity, though also with higher quality entertainment. This distinction has been exaggerated. Nedham's royalist *Mercurius Pragmaticus* was gloriously vitriolic about the parliamentary independents and the grandees in the Army Juncto, but also had mysteriously accurate sources of information, even inside parliament. There was also much excellent, self-consciously literary prose written by radical pro-parliamentarians and republicans: for instance in the 1648 *Mercurius Britanicus* by the prodigious John Hall (1627–1656). Hall, in pursuit of patronage from parliament, was an eloquent pamphleteer, with a talent for articulating the ideas of others as much as for producing his own. In his *Britanicus*

47 See the *Oxford English Dictionary*.

48 Donne, *The Satires, Epigrams and Verse Letters*, ed. W. Milgate (Oxford: Clarendon Press, 1967), p.53.

he appropriated the royalist practice, as found in *Pragmaticus*, *Melancholicus* and *Elencticus*, the supreme cavalier trinity of 1647–8, of opening his text with a four quatrain satiric poem. He also produced amusing and incisive readings of events, inverting the political stance of *Pragmaticus*. The editorials of *The Moderate* were both forceful and elegant in their support of a radical, leveller position. The single issue of *Hermes Stratjcus* in August 1648 also employed exciting rhetoric for the anti-royalist cause.

The authors of polemical newsbooks did not behave as if factual news was incompatible with concentrated invective. Newsbooks, like modern newspapers, participated in constructing the world around them, not only by means of polemical invention and political propaganda, but by arranging recent, unrecorded events in a narrative.[49] Although the resulting narrative might include elements of pure or partial fiction (as in the accounts in *Mercurius Aulicus* of numerous royalist military victories in 1645)[50] this did not make it any the less 'news'. An extreme and instructive example of mixing fact and fiction occurs in the anti-republican *Mercurius Fumigosus*. This was John Crouch's successor to *The Man in the Moon*; less overtly political, more frivolous and pornographic, and almost entirely devoid of news. Its contentiousness was as manifest and explicit as its anti-feminism. Yet *Fumigosus* number 37, like many newsbooks of the day, carried a medical advert (for which the advertiser paid a fee.)[51] The non-credibility of the context clearly did not imply that the advertiser was a mountebank, even in an age when a high number of medical men struggled for a share in a dubious market by advertising in newsbooks. A modern reader would probably be reluctant to buy a used car from Crouch: someone with a sincere profit motive was convinced that this was not so in February 1655.

Hall's 1648 *Britanicus* drew attention to a final and most important characteristic of newsbooks. In spite of their social prominence, most newsbooks did not acknowledge their authors. Lupton suggested that their authors were 'ashamed to put their

49 This apparent relationship between newsbooks and history was the reason why John Cleveland, in the texts I have cited above, was so eager to distinguish between sincere history and irreverent newsbooks.

50 P.W. Thomas argues that a new standard of accurate intelligence and reporting was set by *Aulicus*: yet he allows that inaccuracies were substantial by 1645. *Sir John Berkenhead*, pp.43–7, 67–72.

51 *The Man in the Moon*, Numb.37, 2–9 January 1650. N&S 322.37.

names to their Books.'[52] Yet Hall's mercury had an identity of its own, derived from its eponymous predecessor: when he wrote his *Mercurius Britanicus Alive Again*, Hall chose to keep the single 'n' in 'Britanicus'.[53] This conspicuous solecism had been committed by Captain Thomas Audley, or more likely his printer and compositor, in their first *Mercurius Britanicus* of 1643: *Aulicus* had duly mocked them, and consequently Audley and then Nedham had resolutely stuck to their patent, glaring error as a matter of pride. The title outlasted the demise of the scornful *Aulicus*. Thus *Mercurius Britanicus*, like several other titles, had a social existence not entirely dependent on Hall, and which Hall borrowed in order to make a public appearance. Historians who have (often successfully)[54] pursued the identity of authors have tended to overlook the significance of this anonymity. The author's name was not advertised because it was less important than the larger-than-life figure of the mercury itself. The mercury had a collective, social identity, and would only have been brought down to earth if too solidly attached to an author. To counterbalance this tendency I underplay questions of authorship in this anthology. The figure of the mercury was a larger, more public figure than the man or men behind it. It was an independent entity. The mercury had a forceful existence, wreaking damage through aggressive lies and misrepresentations: the author was merely an ugly man with a drink problem and a preternaturally vivid imagination.[55]

Writing the future

Probably the fiercest and craziest modern journalist has defined his style, known as 'Gonzo journalism', as 'essentially the "art" (or compulsion) of imposing a novelistic form on journalistic content'. He continues:

> on the high end there is only one real difference between the two forms – and that is the rigidly vested interest in the maintenance of a

52 *London and the Covntry*, p.143.

53 The imprint 'for Mercurius Britannicus' had been used for the corantos of Butter and Bourne in 1625. For another interesting use of the title see Martin Butler, 'A Case Study in Caroline Political Theatre: Braithwaite's "Mercurius Britannicus" (1641)' in *The Historical Journal*, 27, 4 (1984).

54 Williams, *A History of English Journalism*; Siebert, *Freedom of the Press in England*; Frank, *Beginnings of the English Newspaper*.

55 This alludes to a description of Nedham in [Francis Cheynell], *Aulicus, his Hue and Cry sent forth after Britanicus* (1645). Wing C3808.

> polar (or strictly polarized) separation of 'fiction' and 'journalism' by at least two generations of New York-anchored writers who spent most of their working lives learning, practicing, and finally insisting on the esthetic validity of that separation.[56]

Hunter S. Thompson is insisting on an important point: the distinction between fiction and journalism is one of practice, not of any inherent difference between the two forms. Both rely on the use of narrative to articulate their truths, and their segregation is maintained by the customs and fashions of the society in which they participate. But Thompson understates the longevity of the separation and the extent to which it is embedded in our culture and its notion of truth and representation. His observation is relatively applicable to seventeenth-century Britain (for 'New York' read 'London'). Furthermore, if the challenge to the barrier fabricated between fiction and journalism is the essence of Gonzo, then the title of Prince of Gonzo has a claimant prior to Doctor Thompson, in the form of Marchamont Nedham, sometime editor of *Mercurius Britanicus, Mercurius Pragmaticus* and *Mercurius Politicus*.

The distinction which Thompson is unpacking was established in British culture in the seventeenth century. It is predictable that a period which witnessed the invention of journalism and of the novel as linguistic forms would also beget explorations of the interchange between the two. Nedham did precisely this in his quasi-fictional editorials from Utopia {8.18ff}. He even pretended to have received letters from people who had been deceived by his fabrication, and looked for Utopia on the map. Perhaps he really did: it is conceivable that this was not a wildly gullible response. Many readers (though possibly not the ones who purchased maps) may have had no conception of where 'Cracovia' was, or what its global significance might have been. Nedham's last publication of the Interregnum period, a pamphlet titled *Newes from Brussels*, was an entirely fictitious letter from the continent in the voice of a cavalier, eagerly awaiting his king's restoration and revenge on the rebels. *Newes from Brussels* was an eleventh hour intervention, seeking to discredit the overtures of clemency which Charles was obliged to make in order to ensure his speedy return. Nedham's use of a certain inventiveness here

56 Dr. Hunter S. Thompson, *Songs of the Doomed: More Notes on the Death of the American Dream* (New York: Summit Books, 1990), p.184. The piece quoted here was written in 1977. See also *The Great Shark Hunt: Strange Tales from a Strange Time* (London: Picador, 1980 edn.), p.114.

did not make him an enemy to journalism, or a deceitful cynic. It is an amusing intervention and a shrewd political commentary, with which Nedham literally risked his neck.[57]

But there is a deeper significance to this parallel between journalism old and modern. In November 1641 the newsbook, despite its old costumes and borrowed speech, was a new form. Its existence was determined by many social, historical and culture forces, but these forces were realised by individual men and women who chose to venture into the literary marketplace with a weekly serial of domestic news. Print was not only reaching a new audience: its forms and horizons, its 'culture', were radically altering. Genres always change: like the restrictions of polite behaviour (whether it's polite to blow one's nose in one's hands at the dinner table) they are a series of customs, established by previous usages, which any writer can choose to adhere to or depart from. But in the 1640s, genres became a focus of ideological concern, and writers selected the forms they observed and alluded to with careful, political deliberation.[58] The political implications of genre were deployed in a more conscious fashion. Newsbooks were a form in which writers could act out their beliefs.

In a recently published 1974 statement on realpolitic, Hunter S. Thompson quotes Thomas Jefferson's timely parting-shot, written ten days before he died:

> All eyes are opened, or opening, to the rights of man. The general spread of the light of science has already laid open to every view the palpable truth, that the mass of mankind has not been born with saddles on their backs, nor a favoured few booted and spurred, ready to ride them legitimately, by the grace of God....[59]

By a curious conjunction Professor David Underdown, of Yale University, used this same inspired passage to conclude the 1992 Ford Lectures on Stuart History at Oxford University. As Underdown noted, Jefferson was quoting this carnivalesque image turned the right way up, of the master riding the servant. It is part of the common imagistic currency of the period 1641–1660. The Leveller Richard Rumbold said it at his execution in 1685. Jefferson was possibly aware of this; and it was also borrowed by,

57 *Newes from Brussels, In a Letter From a Neer Attendant on His Maiesties Person. To a Person of Honour here*. (London, 1660). Wing N398A.

58 On these points I am indebted to Nigel Smith's work on literary transformation and the English Revolution, forthcoming from Yale University Press.

59 Thompson, *Songs of the Doomed*, p.155.

among others, the journalist Daniel Defoe in 1705. Three years later the almanac writer John Partridge echoed it.[60] One of the shared interpretations, where Underdown concurs with Thompson, is the persistence of a radical discourse, with powerful imagery and egalitarian sentiments, the meaning of which, particularly of words like 'liberty' and 'freedom,' is subject to profound alterations and reversals. Jefferson was, of course, essentially an advocate of a free press, except where this infringed upon personal injuries. Yet he also stated in his 'Notes for a Constitution': 'Printing presses shall be free except as to false facts published maliciously ...'[61] He was deeply suspicious of the press, and thought that journalists manufactured lies. For him there was no straightforward link between Leveller discourse and the newspaper. Yet, as I hope to have suggested, newsbooks were intimately associated with the society which gave birth to Leveller arguments for political emancipation.

Newsbooks were by no means uniformly part of a radical political discourse. The writings of John Crouch, for example, were firmly in the tradition of conservative misrepresentation of sectarianism. Radical politics, religious dissent, female emancipation and plebeian activity were for Crouch all part of the same inversion of the way society, by the laws of nature and those of God, should be.[62] Nevertheless, even those reactionary newsbooks which did not overtly challenge the status quo are evidence of social as well as literary transformations. Making the news involved the reconstruction of the boundaries of truth, fiction and history, and was a most active activity.

According to Edward Hyde, Earl of Clarendon, on the first day to be covered by the first newsbook, a member of the Commons leaving the chamber, when the Grand Remonstrance had been passed after a long debate, said:

> 'that if the Remonstrance had been rejected he would have sold all he had the next morning, and never have seen England any more; and he knew there were many other honest men of the same resolution.'[63]

60 See Christopher Hill, 'From Lollards to Levellers' in *Religion and Politics in 17th Century England* (Brghton: Harvester, 1986); Bernard Capp, *Astrology and the Popular Press: English Almanacs 1500–1800* (London: Faber & Faber, 1979), p.249. I am indebted to Christopher Hill for this point.

61 Quoted in Smith, *Printers and Press Freedom*, p.89.

62 See the introduction to chapter 3.

63 Clarendon, *History of the Rebellion and Civil Wars In England*, ed. W. Dunn Macray, 6 vols. (Oxford: Clarendon Press, 1888), I, book 4, §53.

His name was Oliver Cromwell. His words were not recorded in a newsbook, but the kind of vision offered by the men who put forward the Remonstrance was paralleled in the creation of another new world. The fourth estate in its nascent form conjured a new space for new ways of speaking about (and in) society.

Newsbooks not only shaped events as they were happening, in their role as propaganda, but shaped events as they were to be recorded as history. In these days, when we are saturated by the media, we paradoxically believe that literary texts are necessarily passive documents. Newsbooks are a reminder that the world where some men and women were treated as if they were born for others to ride isn't so remote, and that in that world, writing was a way of inventing the future.

CHAPTER ONE
To your Tents, O Israel: The Long Parliament and the outbreak of hostilities

In the early seventeenth century news was not a freely available commodity, though if we believe *The Staple of Newes*, Ben Jonson's play of 1626, there was a market for it. The Staple of News, a place where news was sold for private profit, was for Jonson a mirror:

> wherein the age may see her owne folly, or hunger or thirst after publish'd pamphlets of *Newes*, set out every Saturday, but made all at home, & no syllable of truth in them: then which there cannot be a greater disease in nature, or a fouler scorne put vpon the times.[1]

In 1641 Autolycus was unbound. An expanding awareness of and interest in political news coincided with circumstances enabling publishers to supply it.[2] The first English newsbooks, in English and with domestic news, appeared in November 1641. Soon the features of the genre were established, and in any week several different newsbooks could be bought on the streets of London, and perhaps received in the provinces by the Tuesday post.

Some basic knowledge of the surrounding events is necessary to understand the context of the following extracts from the newsbooks themselves.[3] In May 1640 the Short Parliament had

1 This text is from the 1631 publication of the play, and was not part of the 1626 performance. *The Staple of Newes* in *The Workes of Benjamin Jonson* [the second volume] (1631), p.36. STC 14753.5. *Ben Jonson*, ed. C.H. Herford and Percy and Evelyn Simpson, VI, 325 (Oxford: Clarendon Press, 1938).

2 On censorship see F.S. Siebert, *Freedom of the Press in England 1476–1776: The Rise and Decline of Government Controls* (Urbana: University of Illinois Press, 1952); for a detailed analysis of these circumstances see my forthcoming *The Crisis of Eloquence: Reading and Writing English Newsbooks 1641–1649*.

3 The simplified summary of events which follows is drawn from the following

been dissolved without agreeing to provide King Charles with the financial supply he had requested, which was necessary to fund the war against Scotland. In October the English were defeated by the Scots in the Second Bishops' War, and the next month, in the face of imminent economic crisis, the Long Parliament was formed.

A parliament could not expect a continuous existence in the seventeenth century. They were called by the king only when he was in need of a subsidy, in return for which the gentry in the lower house expected to demand some legislatory concessions. When a bargain had been struck, the parliament was prorogued by the king until he had need of further resources. King Charles, lacking the skills in compromise of James and Elizabeth, was sceptical of the rights of others to impinge upon his God-given authority. Since the Parliament of 1628–9 and the furore over the forced loan, he had ruled through his Privy Council, without a parliament. In response to this and with an increasing county consciousness, often generated in response to the court,[4] members of parliament felt protective of their continued sitting. Accordingly, one of the earliest and more lasting pieces of legislation of the Long Parliament, to which Charles gave his reluctant assent, was to decree that the king had no right to prorogue parliament without the consent of its members.

The Commons proceeded to pursue a number of reforms relatively autonomous of the king's approval. In this they challenged the exclusive legislative authority of the monarchy, and sought to reverse the political and religious innovations of the previous eleven years of Charles' reign.

Firstly they attacked Arminianism, part of the broad spectrum of the Church of England which rejected the Calvinist doctrine of

works, which should be consulted for more satisfactory narratives: S.R. Gardiner, *History of England From the Accession of James I to the Outbreak of the Civil War 1603–1642*, vols. IX & X (London: Longmans, Green & Co., 1884); C.V. Wedgwood, *The King's Peace 1637–1641* (London: Collins, 1955); Anthony Fletcher, *The Outbreak of the English Civil War* (London: Edward Arnold, 1981, 1985); and Conrad Russell, *The Fall of the British Monarchies 1637–1642* (Oxford: Clarendon Press, 1991).

4 See Perez Zagorin, *The Court and the Country: The Beginning of the English Revolution* (London: Routledge and Kegan Paul, 1969); Alan Everitt, *The Local Community and the Great Rebellion* (London: The Historical Association, 1969); Robert Ashton, *The English Civil War: Conservatism and Revolution 1603–1649* (London: Weidenfeld and Nicolson, 1978, 1989); Clive Holmes, 'The County Community in Stuart Historiography', *Journal of British Studies*, XIX (1980); Victor Morgan, *Country, Court and Cambridge University, 1558–1640: A Study in the Evolution of a Political Culture* (UEA Phd. Thesis, 1983), pp.52ff.

predestination and emphasized the significance of religious forms and symbols as part of the means to salvation. It was this dominant strain in the English Church, as embodied by Archbishop Laud, which had encouraged Charles to impose the Book of Common Prayer on the Presbyterian Scots, an insensitive action which had precipitated the rebellion in Scotland. Arminianism was seen by many as a diluted form of Catholicism, and popular suspicion of it was allied to broader fears of Romish plots to overthrow the English government.[5] These fears were aggravated by the possibility of a Catholic rebellion in Ireland. One of the first moves of the Long Parliament was to overturn the Arminian Cannons of 1640, and to declare that the decrees of Convocation were only binding with the consent of parliament. By doing so they challenged the religious as well as the secular authority of bishops. In December parliament was supported in this by a petition presented by London Citizens which called for the abolition of episcopacy 'Root and Branch' {1.02&5}. Some progress towards this was made in February 1642 when bishops were excluded from the House of Lords {1.12}, although episcopacy was not abolished until October 1646. Popular intervention was also in evidence in the crowds of citizens and apprentices then daily forming around Westminster, and in the form of the taxpayers' strike which aggravated the financial problems of central government and disabled local government from functioning effectively. Parliament had already impeached Archbishop Laud and Thomas Wentworth, Earl of Strafford, both of whom had been particularly favoured by Charles. Wentworth was to be carried to the scaffold in May 1641; Laud lived in prison until his execution in 1645 {7.02}. More than censorship was breaking down in these last few months of 1640.

Up to October 1641 the legislation of the Long Parliament was to be relatively enduring. Then, soon after parliament reconvened following a six week recess, the news of the rebellion in Ireland reached England, bringing inflated stories of the massacre of English Protestants. The news served as a focus for emerging religious division, which was to be the single most important impediment to political stability for the next twenty years. On 22 November, having been delayed by the news from Ireland, the members of the Commons led by John Pym who formed an opposition to the king's supporters, passed a document known

5 See Caroline Hibbard, *Charles I and the Popish Plot* (Chapel Hill, NC: University of North Carolina Press, 1983).

as the Grand Remonstrance. The news from Ireland had led to urgent desires for action which ultimately favoured Pym and his colleagues. The Remonstrance was a document addressed to the nation in response to the king's declaration in support of present, episcopalian church policy. It blamed Charles for his susceptibility to the malign influence of bishops, papists and evil counsellors who sought to undermine the true Protestant faith of England. It implicitly attacked Charles' wife, the Catholic Henrietta Maria, who exerted significant influence over her husband. Charles' rule, it was claimed, had opened the gates to Jesuits and Catholics through his Arminian policy, while oppressing Puritans, using means, including innovatory forms of taxation, which had depressed and divided the people. The Remonstrance was a history of Charles' wrongs. The same week the first newsbook, *The Heads of Severall Proceedings*, reported the Remonstrance at some length {1.01}. One kind of history gave way to another.

The significance of the Remonstrance, like the 19 Propositions passed by the Commons on 1 June, 1642, was that in the guise of a document proffering reconciliation, new extents of legitimate parliamentary authority were being delineated. Both were focuses for the increasing polarization of the political nation into a Protestant or Puritan,[6] pro-parliament party, and an episcopalian royalist party, which accepted the aid of the small number of English Catholics. Both were frequently broached in newsbooks as possible sources of compromise and settlement between the two parties.

In January 1642, Charles impeached five members of the Commons, including John Pym, the leader of the radicals, for their own rumoured accusations against the queen. In spite of his dramatic entrance into the House of Commons {1.06,7}, the first time an English monarch had ever done this, he could not secure the necessary cooperation of parliament and other London authorities. In frustration he left the city. This served as a further catalyst for the polarization between those who supported the crown and those who believed that the parliamentary opposition offered the best basis for the restabilization of the kingdom and the settlement of the debts of the country. With the king's departure, angry at his failure to secure the imprisonment of the Five Members and at the uncompromising stance of parliament over its Grand Remonstrance, the newsbooks began to express

6 This term is much disputed, and historians continue to use it for convenience, in spite of its highly pejorative seventeenth-century meaning.

concern that even those at the top of the social hierarchy were irresponsibly contributing to the breakdown in the social fabric.

In spite of their reputation for sedition, most newsbooks of 1641 and 1642 assumed a sober, serious tone. They were primarily concerned with parliamentary news, that is, the debates and resolutions of, and the letters read before both Houses. Perhaps as a consequence of this they frequently suggest a weight of sympathy for parliament. This did not, of course, imply hostility towards the king. Rather such a position blamed malignants, Cavaliers, the hostile, crypto-Catholic advisers who were influencing the king and thereby forcing the split with his parliament. To fight for the parliament was to fight for king and kingdom. The newsbooks shared in anxieties over the seduction of the king and over a conjectured Catholic plot, which were particularly acute in the spring and summer of 1642 {1.13}.

Through the summer, communications between parliament and the king became less open to reconciliation, and instead both sides were more concerned with a propaganda effort which involved publicizing a sympathetic case in the summer Assizes, and in achieving control of the county militias. Parliament did this through its newly-established lieutenancy which devolved recruiting power to officials in the counties; the king through Commissions of Array by which he mustered troops in anticipation of conflict. Newsbooks increasingly participated in this publicity exercise.

Seven years later, a month before the king was executed, a satirical printed letter, addressed to the king from the Earl of Pembroke, interpreted his departure from London as the root of the miseries of the kingdom, and as a repeated motif in the history of the Civil War:

> I am now to take my leave of you; yet I intend not to leave you quite, and not see you againe, and yet by God I may too: Damme this Leaving has been the undoing of the Kingdom, for had not your Majestie left *White-hall*, the Parliament had not left you; nor had the Army seiz'd on you ...[7]

Explanations for the origins of the Civil War were never hard to find in this period, and in 1643 one newsbook blamed the City of London itself:

7 *The Earl of Pembroke's farewell to the King At his departure from the Treaty at the Isle of Wight*, Dec. 14, 1648, p.1. Wing P1118.

> If therefore *Posterity* shall aske, who broke downe the bounds, to those streams of blood, that have stained this earth, if they aske, who made Liberty captive, Truth Criminall, Rapine just, Tyranny, and Oppression Lawfull, who blanched Rebellion, with the specious pretence of defence of Lawes, and Liberties: Warre with the desire of an established Peace, Sacraledge and Prophanation, with the shew of Zeale, and Reformation: Lastly, if they aske who would have pulled the Crowne from the *Kings* head, taken the government of the Iudges, dissolved *Monarchy*, inslaved the *Lawes*, and ruined their *Country*, say, 'Twas the *proud, unthankefull, schismaticall, Rebellious, Bloody City of London*, so that they wanted of devouring this *Kingdome* by *cheating* and *couzening*, they mean to finish by the Sword.[8]

In *Behemoth*, his history of the war, Thomas Hobbes concurred with this perspective, arguing that the city had capitulated too easily to the stubborn and spiteful demands of the House of Commons. He wrote: 'London, you know, has a great belly, but no palate nor taste of right and wrong.'[9] It is true that London, and its crowds, were of focal importance for the outbreak of war, just as the capital was the nexus for the rapid economic development of the country as a whole.

All newsbooks looked at the prospect of an increasingly inevitable civil war, an *unnatural* war, with apprehension. The numerous reports of petitions from the counties, ceremoniously delivered to the House, praising the work of parliament and favouring the apposite punishment of his Majesty's evil advisers, expressed a hope for a settlement. This was also true of the many actions against 'scandalous Ministers' in the provinces, who were frequently brought before parliament and gaoled, though these actions must also be seen in the context of regional backlashes against their erstwhile domination by Laudian religion. As spring turned to summer hopes of peace became less prominent in newsbooks. Both sides argued for the good of the people. The newsbooks now focused on the king's Commissions of Array and on the Ordinance of Parliament for the bringing in of plate to fund their military exercises. Troops were enlisted, forces organized and moved, and the weekly reports described the injustices committed upon locals whose wealth was taken, often with violence, to support the military effort. During the early call to arms, newsbook writers frequently criticised the royalist party in

8 *A Letter from Mercurius Civicus to Mercurius Rusticus: or London's Confession but not Repentance*, August 25 1643, p.32. Wing B6323.

9 Thomas Hobbes, *Behemoth: or the Long Parliament*, ed. Ferdinand Tönnies (Chicago: University of Chicago Press, 1990), p.104.

socially elitist terms, picturing their troops as poorly fed and ill-clad vagabonds and Welshmen. But the soldiers on both sides were described as rowdy and potentially disruptive. Just as a few months earlier, the streets of London had witnessed the presence of threatening crowds, when the war commenced there were numerous accounts of drunkenness, swearing, pillage, assault, murder and rape in the north.

The initial hostilities broke out around Hull, which Sir John Hotham had occupied on behalf of parliament. Hull was a major port, and also contained the weapons of the army which had been disbanded in 1641 after the war against the Scots. It was therefore a centre of power in the north, which both sides sought to master while the provincial authorities attempted to maintain neutrality. When parliament ordered that the magazine at Hull be sent to London {1.18}, it became imperative to Charles that he make some kind of attempt on it. This he did on 23 April when he drew up to Hull, to find its gates closed to him. A nervous Sir John Hotham had decided, without the authorization of parliament, to deny his king admission. In this critical period parliamentary ordinances had established effective press control, and so this news was not reported in newsbooks.

The Commons, which declared on 20 May that the king was preparing for war {1.19}, formally approved of Hotham's actions. While Hotham shipped the magazine off to London, Charles raised an army. Fighting was ultimately precipitated when Queen Henrietta Maria brought on 3 July a ship with a cargo of munitions. Despite her interception by a parliament warship, the siege guns reached Charles, and were advanced on Hull. Accordingly Hotham opened the sluices and flooded the area around the town {1.23}. Canon fire was exchange from 10 July onwards. The king laid siege, but in spite of attempts to burn the city, his men spent much of their time jousting at windmills {1.26}.

On the 15 July the Earl of Essex was appointed as Captain General of the parliament's forces {1.24}. On 22 August, the king raised his Standard at Nottingham {1.34–9}. Soon parliamentary news shared space with reports of the horrors of war.

This, the opening passage from the first newsbook, covers the news from Ireland and the debate over the Grand Remonstrance and its publication.

The Heads of Severall Proceedings in this Present Parliament

22–29 November, 1641. 181.101 {1.01}

Monday in the House of Commons they received letters from *Ireland*, intimating that theire troubles are so great, that they have scarce time eyther day or night to write. That the Rebells doe much increase and presse hard towards *Dublin*, which putteth the Kingdom into great feare being scarce able to resist them. That they want mony to pay their Souldiers already entertained.

That the Rebels doe expect Armes and supply from forraine parts, both from *England, France* and *Spaine*.

That sending to the Rebels to demande the cause of theire taking up Armes, they returne a remonstrance that it is to maintaine the Kinges prerogative and the freedome of Conscience, in the exercising of religion, which if they may have confermed by Acte of Parliament they will lay downe theire Armes, and make restitution for the harmes done by them.

That the Governours returned answere to theire Remonstrance, that if they would lay down theire Armes and repaire to theire owne dwellings, they should have pardon and that they would bee a meanes to the Parliament for the satisfaction of theire demandes.

Vpon this letter there was a conference with the Lords for the leavying of 50000. pound more to that which is sent according as it is directed in the letter.

Also the examination of Sergeant Majour Shelley taken in Ireland against Sir *Henery Beddingfield* was then read. That he being at his house in Norfolke about Aprill last, the said Sir Henery asking how the Army stood in Ireland: and if there were good hawking and hunting there, he intended to goe over: but now hee would stay, for that before the next Christmas there would come the greatest troubls upon England and Ireland that have hapned these 100. Yeares.

After this, in the house of Commons they read the declaration of the State of the Kingdom; and how farre the grievances had beene reduced by this Parliament.

there was a great debate about divers clauses in it, and it was first put to the question that those clauses wherein the Bishops are tearmed malignant persons to the well-farre, and peace of this Kingdome in the particulars named should be altered, and the house being divided it was carried by the Majors part that it should so stand.

Afterwards the house was twice divided upon the question for the passing of the said Remonstrance without any alteration, and for the publishing thereof, and the greater part carried it, in both there being great oppositions, and debate about it.

Then *Master Peard* moved to have the remonstrance printed.

Master Palmer, presently standing up, offered eight times to make a certificate in the behalfe of himselfe, and the rest of that part; against the vote of the house, as was conceived for the publishing of the same, Presently thereupon the house rose having sate in debate about it, till three of the clocke in the morning, the trayned Band attending the House all that time. {...}

Wednesday morning, the house sate in debate about *Master Palmers* offence against the remonstrance, and there was a great conference, whither he spake against the vote of the house for publishing, or against the printing thereof; it being generally concluded that he spake against the vote of the house, and it was moved for his punishment.

First, that he should be called to the barre.

Secondly, committed to the Tower.

Thirdly, that hee should be expelled the house.

Fourthly, that he should be disabled for ever being a Parliament man, or to sit in any place of judicature; in this the house could not agree, but it was put to the question, and carried so, that he should be called to the bar to answere for himselfe, whereupon coming to the barre he said, that he was sensible of his misfortune to speake at that time: yet it was farre from his intentions to raise a muteny, or that he spake or intended any thing against the vote of the house, but onely aginst the printing of the same.

This debate held the house all that day, being great oppositions and debate about it.

Also there were Irish men lately come over and brought to the gate-house till further leisure to examine them.

Thursday, morning they againe fell into debate about *Master Palmer*, and it was put to the question and agreed upon that he should be sent to the Tower.

The Heads of Severall Proceedings in both Houses of Parliament

29 November – 6 December, 1641. 181.102 {1.02}

Mvnday *November* the 29. {…}

The Lords this evening ordered, they would receive no new Petitions, nor heare any private causes, till the first day of *Hillary* Terme, being the 23 of *February* next, that in the meane time, the great affaires of the Church and State might be settled: The howse of Commons this day fell upon divers complaints about Pole-mony, some for nonpayment, some for being over, and some under rated by the Assessors, and finding the want of that money to bee very prejuditiall to the affaires of State, they drew up a Certificate and an Order thereupon, & commanded it presently to be printed, for the generall taking notice of it, whereby power is given not onely for the speedy collection thereof, but the names of the defaulters to be returned, to receive punishment acording to their demerits according to the tenure of the Act of Parliament in that case provided. {…}

Tuesday, {…} This day againe many hundred of Cittizens flocking to the houses of Parliament, called earnestly vpon the members as they passed by from their houses, to suppresse Bishops, crying aloud noe Bishops, no Bishops, calling them the limbes of Antichrist, which caused a great dispute what Antichrist was, and whether Bishops could be accounted Antichristian, and other things pertaining to that purpose, and a conference for suppressing these tumults, this day Captaine Beale was released, putting in baile for his appearance.

This report (8 December) emphasises the importance of controlling the city and the presses.

The Diurnall: Or, The Heads of All the Proceedings in Parliament

6–13 December, 1641 109.1 {1.03}

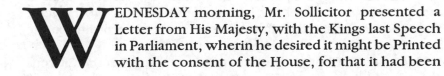

WEDNESDAY morning, Mr. Sollicitor presented a Letter from His Majesty, with the Kings last Speech in Parliament, wherin he desired it might be Printed with the consent of the House, for that it had been formerly Printed by a false Coppy: But the House would not condiscend unto it that it should be Printed by Vote of the House, but referred it to the Kings pleasure.

Then Master *Pymme* made Report from the Committee for the Irish affaires, of certaine Letters lately come from thence. Intimating, that the Revolt in *Ireland* was so generall, that whole Counties have joyned themselves to the Rebells. That they are come within 4. miles of *Dublin*, driving away their Cattle, and stopping the bringing in of Provisions to the City.

That they have made Protestation or Oath to maintain the Romish *Religion*, with their lives and fortunes.

That they acknowledge the King to be their lawfull Soveraigne, and that this their Rising is to relieve the oppressed in *Ireland*.

That they have writ a Letter to the Lord *Dillon*, to intreat him to goe for *England*, and acquainted his Majesty with their grievances, and desire tolleration for their Religion.

Presently thereupon the Lords sent a Message, informing the Commons that they had intelligence the Lord *Dillon* is come over, without giving any notice to the Privy Councell there.

Upon which, after some debate, it was Voted that the Parliament will not admit of any Tolleration of Religion in *Ireland*. And they referred the further consideration thereof to a Committee. {...}

FRIDAY Morning, they fell into debate of the Bill for the pressing of Men, which was sent back by the Lords for alteration of those words in the Preamble: That there might not bee any presse granted but by Act of *Parliament*.

Sergeant *Wylde* making a Report from the Committee upon the same, and maintaining it by Law, that the words could not be altered.

Wherfore it was againe sent up to the Lords; Then there was a Report made in the House of Commons, That there was 3. or 400. watchmen set about the *Parliament*: whereupon they sent for three or foure Constables before them, and demanded the cause of their comming with so many men, who made Answere, it was by vertue of a Warrant from the Justices of *midlesex*.

Whereupon further inquiry being made, it appeared the ground of their comming was upon a Warrant from the Lord Keeper to the Sheriffes of London, and from them to the Justices, That in case they should heare of any Tumults or Ryots at the *Parliament*, They speedily command aid to suppresse them according to the Statute.

Upon this Warrant, the Justices understanding that the Citizens of London had intended to come a great company of them with a Petition to the *Parliament*, caused the Constables to come with men to suppresse them.

Then the House falling into debate upon the matter, voted it; That to set a guard upon the *Parliament* without consent, is a breach of priviledge, and an offence of high nature.

Stories from Ireland tended to work in the favour of the radicals in parliament.

The Diurnall: Or, The Heads of All the Proceedings in Parliament

13–20 December, 1641 109.2 {1.04}

TUESDAY, The *Speaker* presents severall Letters to the House, one from the Justices in *Ireland*, another from the High-Sheriffe of *Leicester*, and another from the Attourney generall in *Ireland*, concerning some Ministers in *Ireland*, as hath been lately massacred by the Papists, as namely Mr. *German*, Minister of *Brides*, his body mangled, and his members cut off; and one *Fullerton* Minister of *Langhall;* and one *Hastings* his eares cut off; and one Blandry, his flesh pulled off from his bones in the presence of his wife: Which businesse did much trouble the Members of both *Houses*, and more at large reported by one *Portington*.

Repeated tumults on the streets of London were also a driving force for political change. This report is dated Monday 27 December.

Diurnall Occurrences in Parliament

27 December – 2 January, 1641{2} 97.1 {1.05}

This day a great company of Citizens attending about the Parliament, for answer to their Petition against Colonell *Lunsford*, as also to desire answer of their Petition against Bishops, crying out, *No Bishops, No Bishops:* the Bishop of Lincoln (now Bishop of York) comming along with the Earle of Dover towards the Lords house, observing a young youth in the company to cry out against Bishops, all the rest of the Citizens being silent, stept from the Earl of Dover, and laid hands on him, Which the Citizens observing, with-held the youth from him, and about an hundred of them comming about the Bishop, hem'd him in that he could not stirre; and then all of them with a loud voice cryed out, *No Bishops, No Bishops*; and presently after let him go. There were also three or four Gentlemen walking among the Citizens, and hearing them crying out against the Bishops, one of them in a desperate humour drew his sword, desiring the other Gentlemen to assist him, and he would cut the throats of them that cryed out against the Bishops; but they refusing, he in two severall places drew upon the Citizens; upon which he was apprehended by them, and brought before the House of Commons, and committed to prison.

The king made a rash and ineffectual appearance in the House of Commons on 4 January, accompanied by armed followers, hoping to secure the Five Members whom he had impeached of high treason.

The Diurnal Occvrrances, Touching the dayly proceedings in Parliament

3–10 January, 1642 106.3 {1.06}

The House of Commons upon their meeting, entred upon the scanning of the liberty of the Subject, and priviledges of Parliament, and having some time debated thereupon, notice was given of the Kings Majesties coming thither, which was about two of the clock in the after noone: His Majesty upon his entrance, demanded his Prisoners, *Mr. Pym*, &c, But they being not there present, hee made a short Speech wherein hee gave some reasons of their said accusation, desiring they might bee delivered to him: otherise hee would take them where he could finde them; further narrating his desire of his peoples welfare, and his concordancy with the Houses of Parliament in all things tending thereunto.

Diurnall Occurrences in Parliament

2–10 January, 1641{2} 97.2 {1.07}

Then Master *Pym* brought into the House the seven Articles exhibited by his Maiestie against him and the rest, which were read in the House: they all of them making severall replyes in answer thereunto. Master *Pym* moving that they might have a conference with the Lords, to cleere their innocencie therein, and

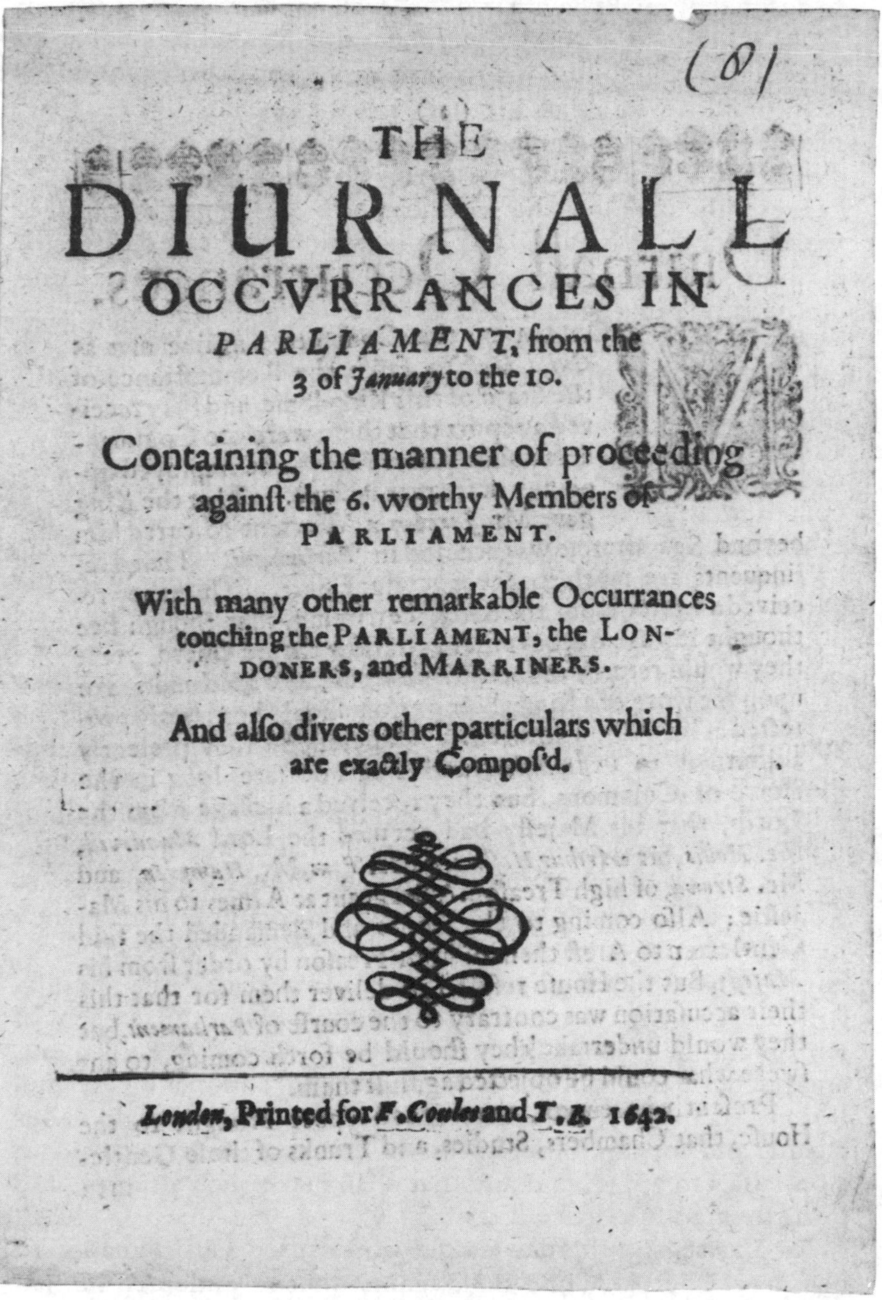

(8)

THE
DIURNALL
OCCVRRANCES IN
PARLIAMENT, from the
3 of January to the 10.

Containing the manner of proceeding
against the 6. worthy Members of
PARLIAMENT.

With many other remarkable Occurrances
touching the PARLIAMENT, the LONDONERS, and MARRINERS.

And also divers other particulars which
are exactly Compos'd.

London, Printed for F. Coules and T. B. 1642.

2. An early newsbook with a full title page

to desire they might have a sudden tryall upon it; which was done accordingly. And at that conference, they agreed to send some Members of the Commons to discharge the Guard of Souldiers that attend at White Hall, for that there ought not to be any Guard placed so neere the Parliament, without consent of Parliament, which was done accordingly.

Presently after this the King came to Westminster, guarded with two or three hundred Cavaleirs, which were that day feasted at Court, his Guard of yeomandry, Gent. Pencioners, his Serieants at Armes, and divers others.

All of them placing a Court of Guard along Westminster Hall to the House of Commons doore, whilst his Maiestie went into the House.

At which the House being much amazed to see his Maiesty, who had never before been at their House, and having no notice of his comming.

His Maiesty placing himselfe in the Speakers Chayr, Told them he came to demand those men of them which he had sent for the day before; but none of them being there, hee told them he expected they should send them to him so soone as they returned thither; and so left the House and went back to White-Hall guarded as before; and so soone as the King was gone, the House all adiourn'd till the next day one of the clock, to consult of the Kings demands. {...}

T*Hursday* morning the Committee met at Guild Hall, as was appointed, and they spent that day in drawing up a Declaration of the severall breaches of priviledge of Parliament his Majesty hath made concerning those men he hath accused; further declaring, that if any person shall arrest any of those Gentlemen, or any other member of Parliament, by a pretence of any warrant from the King, without the consent of Parliament, he is guilty of the breach of privilege of Parliament, and publicke enimy of the Common-wealth, and that it is lawfull for any such party, upon any such attempt; to stand upon his Guard, and for any other to assist him, and to require aid of Constables to apprehend any that shall make such attempt, and bring them to the House. {...}

His Majesty also this day {Friday 6th} caused a Proclamation to bee proclaimed at White Hall, against those Gentlemen he had accused, commanding all his Officers and Subjects, upon sight of any of them, to apprehend and carry them presently to the Tower; which Proclamation being sent to the Sheriffs of London, they refused to proclaime it.

Then {Saturday} the Kings Proclamation against the Gentlemen of the House was brought and read before the Committee, Mr. *Pym*, and the rest of the Gentlemen being then all present at the Committee, they all of them making severall replies in answer thereunto.

Vpon which it was voted by the Committee, after some debate, to be a forme like a Proclamation, but is nothing but a scandalous Paper and libell; and that there should be a Declaration published against it.

Parliament, protective of their existence, reacted violently to the Duke of Richmond's suggestion, on 26 January, that they adjourn in order to ameliorate deteriorating relations with the king.

Divrnall Occvrrences: Or, The last Weekes Proceedings in both Houses of Parliament ... Concerning the great Affayres of these Kingdomes

24–31 January, 1641{2} 181.204 {1.08}

But the *Duke* of *Richmond* in some discontent stood up, and sayd it was his motion that they might adjourne the whole Sessions of Parliament for Six Moneths. At which the Lords taking great distaste, that they should have spent so much time to settle the great distractions in *England* and *Ireland*, and so little as yet effected, both Kingdomes being as it were almost in a desperate condition, and that it should now be thought seasonable to adjourne the Sessions of Parliament for Six Moneths, desired the said Lord *Duke* might be called to the Barre which being agreed upon accordingly, and the said Lord Duke being brought on his knees to the Barre, made a short Speech in his owne defence, desiring their Lordships to make a faire construction of him and his actions and to excuse his errour for that motion.

But they being not fully satisfied herewith it was put to the Question, whether the sayd Lord Dukes submission at the Barre was satisfactory for his offence, and it was resolved upon that it was not, But that there should be a Commitee of Lords appoynted further to consider of the said words, and what reparation may be against him for it. {...}

THursday morning they againe met, and there was a Declaration or Remonstrance read in the House made by the Rebells in *Ireland*, and brought over by Mr. *Geo. Wentworth* who received it from the Rebells, when he was a prisoner with them.

Wherein they cast many aspersions vpon the Parliament, that they have in a malignant manner endeavored to subvert them and their Religion, and to oppose the effluence of his Maiesties gracious love vnto them in the exercise of their Religion, which they pretend to be the maine cause of their taking up Armes to maintaine his Majesties Royall Authority and Prerogative, and have to that end possessed themselves of many of the strong Forts of that Kingdome to enable them to serve his Majesty, and to defend themselves against the Tyrannous resolution of their Enemies, &c. {...}

Then the Lords having referred the businesse against the Duke of *Richmond* to the consideration of the House of Commons, which businesse, being fully laid open in their House, after some debate, they Voted him to be one of the malignant party to the good of the Common wealth, and not fit to be imployed in matters of trust, and that they should accordingly draw vp a Charge against him.

A Perfect Diurnall of The Passages in Parliament

24–31 January, 1641{2} 507.01 {1.09}

Thursday the 27. {...}

Then there was a paper brought to our House, and taken out of the Iournall of the Lords House, concerning a great offence made by the Duke of Richmond the night before, in the Lords House, for that the Lords being in earnest debate of the great affaires of England and Ireland; he moved the Lords it might be put to the question, to adiourne the whole Sessions of Parliament for six months.

For which he was called to the Barre upon his knees, where with great submission he acknowledged his errour, and desired to be excused for his fault. Vpon which the House being divided, it was carried by the maior part, that that submission for his fault was satisfactory for his offence.

Whereupon our House took the same into consideration, and it was generally conceived meet and fitting further to question him concerning it; whereupon wee fell into debate of the matter, and after great controversie and debate concerning him, he was voted to be an evill Counsellour to his Majesty, and one of the malignant party, and not fit to beare office in places of trust and eminency; and that we should take into consideration the drawing up of a charge against him. {...}

Then we had a third message from the Lords, that they had received a very gracious message from the Queene, in answer to the Request of the Parliament, that she would inform us by whom she received intelligence that the House of Commons were drawing up Articles against her.

To which she answered, that she was told so, but hath forgot by whom; but she gave no credit to it, for that her actions have bin all so clear both towards King and Parliament, that she hath ever desired and laboured with his Majesty, that he would unite himselfe to the Parliament in the satisfying of all their desires, that so there might be a right understanding between them.

With the exception of the queen, representations of women in the earliest newsbooks, before the outbreak of war, were generally positive.

Divrnall Occvrrences, Or, The Heads of the Proceedings in both Houses of Parliament
Numb. 5th.

31 January – 7 February, 1641{2} 181.205 {1.10}

The same day {31st} in the Lords House they sate again upon the *Irish* affaires, and there was also a *Petition* delivered to the Lords by a Company of women, containing their wants and necessities, by reason of the great decay of Trading occasioned by the present distempers and distractions of the State, and composing of differences between the two Houses of *Parliament*, That the Commons House they conceive have done what in them lay to relieve them, and redresse their grievances, but that such opposition being made in the Lords House, which is a great hinderance to their Reall intentions in their proceedings to perfect the same, that Religion may be established, and present ayd and assistance transported into *Ireland*, for the reliefe of the distressed *Protestants*, {...}

The True Diurnall Occvrrances: Or, The heads of the Proceednigs of both Hovses in Parliament

31 January – 7 February, 1642 621.2 {1.11}

On Tuesday the first of February, in the Lords House they sate upon the businesse concerning the Duke of *Lenox*, and after great debate thereupon the said Duke was voted still to sit in the House of Lords, and to continue his office at Court.

This day also was another Petition delivered to the Lords by a company of Women, about the number of 400. desiring an answer of their petition delivered the day before, and attending there for the delivery thereof, the Duke of *Lenox* coming to the House, they presented him their petition, who answered: Away with these women, wee were best to have a parliament of Women; Whereupon some of the Women interrupting his passage, catched hold of his staffe, humbly desiring him to receive their petition, upon which the Duke being moved, offered to draw back his staffe, but they holding it so fast between them, it was broken, whereupon the said Duke was enforced to send for another staffe; after which they delivered their petition to the Lord *Sawage*, who presented it to the Lords, and upon reading, and some debate thereof, they gave order that twelve of the petitioners should be called into the House, to declare their grievances, which was done accordingly.

Having made themselves 'an excrescence on political life' (Gardiner) the bishops were removed from the House of Lords. Twelve were then impeached and proceeded against.

The Continuation of the Divrnall Occurrences. Or. The Heads of all the Proceedings in both Houses of Parliament
Numb. 7

14–21 February, 1641{2} 181.207 {1.12}

SATVRDAY, the 19. of February.

THe 12. Bishops were brought from the Tower into the House of Peeres, to answer to the charge of high Treason lately preferred by the House of Commons against them upon their Petition or Remonstrance to his Majesty, the House of Commons upon the notice thereof came up likewise into the Peeres house, Mr. *Glyn* and Mr, *Maynard* (both Members of the Commons house) being appointed by their House to mannage their Charge against them; And then the Articles against the twelve Bishops were read, and the Bishops generally were demanded whether they were guilty or not, to which they answered, not guilty; then Mr. *Glyn* and Mr. *Maynard* began to expresse the haughtinesse and ambition of those Bishops, and their exorbitant power, but especially the Archbishop of *Yorke*, as an introducer of all the rest, and upon every particular Article expressed and explained the heynousnesse of their Treasons, in assuming to themselves the Regall power and Soveraigne authority unto his Majesty, and also their endeavouring to annihilate and suppresse the priviledges of Parliament, with divers other capitall crimes, which tended to no lesse then Treason.

To which the Bishops in generall answered, but more especially the Archbishop of *Yorke* (as his manner ever was) very boldly. That neither he nor any of the other Bishops in their Petition or otherwise did or intended to detract or deminish the least title of his Majesties Prerogative, nor the priviledges of Parliament, of which they were ever tender of, as the chiefe Pillars of this Kingdome; whereunto Mr. *Glyn* replyed, and vrged very stiffely strong Arguments, and cited some Presidents that some clauses in the Bishops Petition or Remonstrance were no lesse than high Treason, though very cunningly contriv'd and coucht in a Petitionary way; whereupon, after many Arguments on both sides (the Lords taking speciall notice of all the Passages) deferred the further hearing thereof, till Thursday next, whereupon the Bishops desired that their Councell at Law formerly assigned (namely Mr. *Fountaine*, Mr. *Chute*, and another Barrester at Law, might be admitted on Thursday next, to Pleade on their behalfe, which was condiscended vnto, and then the Bishops were againe remanded to the Tower.

This report, dated Monday 21 February, typifies the anxieties concomitant with the deterioration of relations between king and parliament.

A Perfect Diurnall of the Passages in Parliament

21–8 February, 1641{2} 507.05 {1.13}

Monday the 21. *of February*. {...}

There was a letter brought to the House from Lancashire, in discovery of certain dangerous plots of the Papists in that County, upon the examination of one that was drawn to that Religion by a Romish Priest: And afterwards being much troubled in his mind concerning the same, although he had sworn secrecie, made discovery of their intendments. The effect whereof was, That he was told by a Romish Priest of ten Barrels of powder in one Gentlemans House, and more in other places; which powder was to make Balls of wildfire, wherewith to set on fire divers chief Towns in this Kingdome: And that he replying to the Priest, It was a great pity to do such harm: the Priest told him, They were Hereticks, and it were no sin to destroy them: further adding, that when those Towns should be set on fire, all the Papists in England would rise. Whereupon there was an Order granted, to bring that Priest and hee that disclosed this to the Parliament.

William Prynne was a fierce anti-episcopalian and a prolific pamphleteer, much punished for his beliefs. In this report, dated 7 March, we see his qualities as a lawyer engaged in a dispute over printing rights.

A true Diurnall of the Passages in Parliament

March 7–14, 1642 625.1 {1.14}

MUNDAY-Morning the *Committee* concerning the Company of *Stationers* met, and Councell argued on both sides concerning the Point of Seisure and Patent; they of Councell for the Company pleaded First, that *Printing* is a *Prerogative* belonging to the *Crowne*. 2.That the King did grant these Letters *Patents* to *Bill* and *Barker* and to their Assignes to print the *Bible*, and to no other. 3.That it was effected at the sole charge of the Company of *Stationers*, which were at 4000.l. costs in the translating. 4.That there were a necessity it should be so restrained for the true *Printing* thereof, as being a matter of such high concernment as the Divine *Truth*. 5.That *Printing* is as inherent a *Prerogative* to the *Crowne* as *Coining* of *Money*. 6.That they were *Barkers* goods, and hee might lawfully ceize them. 7.That other *Printers* beyond the Seas have the sole disposing of the *Presse*; and that it might destroy this Manifacture, Mr. PRIN being of the adverse Counsell answered. First, That this *Prerogative* is not confirmed by *Parliament*. 2. That it was a *Monopoly*, and to countenance this is to confirme *Monopoly* for Law; and that it might be proved so by the signes, in that they have raised these *Bibles* to double the valew, and printed them upon worse Paper, and granted to the University of *Cambridge* 200.l. *per Ann.* to have it wholly in their hands; and that they are worse corrected then the old, and upon abusing of a *Patent* it is voyd, as in the Abbot of St. *Albons* case, &c. 3. That the Company have got for 4000.l. 60000.l. 4. Being refuted, *ut supra*, &c that as he is *Pater Patriæ* so he is *Defensor fidei*, and hath a care of the soules of his Subjects as well as their bodies; he answered it were not materiall for the *Printing*, so the matter printed were the truth, and so hath relation not to a particular Company, but to the Common-wealth in generall, and produced Presidents that divers have printed the *Bible,* and for these in grosse and unbound the Statute against importation of Bookes was out it selfe in one Volume, and the new in another and the *Psalmes* by themselves and Common-prayer booke by severall men they now ingrossed it into their owne hands. 5. That if it were as inherent to the *Crowne* as *Coining Money*, they might make a quick dispatch with their goods and lives, it would bee treason, and for the name it were no more then if an other man should marke his owne Cattell with another mans, that it were inconsistent and of dangerous consequence to admit of Presidents of other *Princes* in our State; and lastly it being a blessing to all in generall from God, it ought not to be restrained to particular Companies.

The unofficial leader of the Commons, John Pym, was frequently and unjustly attacked for usurping the king's prerogative. Parliament relied on provincial authorities to report those who spoke in malignant terms against it.

A True Diurnall of the Passages in Parliament
Numb. 10.

14–21 March, 1641{2} 626.10 {1.15}

On Tuesday, March 15.

TWo servants of the Inn-Keeper at the Spread-Eagle in Bread-street, upon examination testified, that Dr. *Showberry* of Queens College Cambridge, said, that if hee could meet with King *Pym*, hee would tell him that hee was a Rascall, and he would cut his throat and sinnewes. He was sent for as a Delinquent, and came to the Bar, and being examined, faintly denyed the words, but said, That if he uttered them, hee was in drink. Vpon the witnesse they were taken for grant to be said by him, and hee was fined an hundred pounds, and committed to the Gates house till it should be paid, and his Degree which he is about to take this yeare is stopped. Dr. *Eden* was appointed to send a letter to Cambridge for that purpose.

The following four entries show the consolidation of the positions of the two sides. King and parliament wrestled for control of the Militia as war approached, and sought to define the parameters of their own proper jurisdiction, notably over such essential issues as Ireland and the obedience of the subject.

A Perfect Diurnall of the Passages in Parliament Numb. 10

14–21 March 1641{2} 507.10B {1.16}

Wendsday the sixteenth. {...}

There was also a conference with the Lords, at which the Lord Keeper read a Message which he received from his Majesty, directed to both Houses, which was read tending to this effect: That his Majesty being now upon his journey to *York*, where he intends to make his residence for some time, thought fit to put his Parliament in minde that they use all possible industry for the speedy expediting of the forces for Ireland; in which his Majesty hath an especiall care, that no inconvenience may happen (on his part) to that service by his absence.

And concerning the *Militia*; as his Majesty hath himself been ever tender of the priviledges of Parliament, so he expecteth an equall tendernesse in them, of his unquestioned priviledges, amongst which he is assured this is a fundamentall one; and therefore he declareth, that by the Lawes his Subjects cannot be obliged to obey any Act; Order, or Injunction, to which his Majesty hath not given his consent; in which he expecteth and requireth obedience from all his Subjects, and that they presume not upon any pretence of Order or Ordinance (to which his Majesty is no party) concerning the *Militia*, or any other thing, to do or execute what is not warranted by those Laws, his Majesty being resolved to keep the Laws himself, and to require obedience to them from all his Subjects. After the reading of this message, the Lords declared how well they had approved of the Votes of the Commons the day before concerning the *Militia*; and that therefore they would referre the consideration of this message to the Commons. Whereupon there was a great debate concerning it in the House of Commons, a question being raised in the House, and much debated, whether this message was not sent in contradiction of the Votes of both Houses the day before, and how his Majesty should so suddenly have knowledge thereof, as to send an answer concerning them; and after some time spent in consultation about it, they digested his Majesties message into severall branches, and agreed upon certain Votes concerning it, *viz.*

1 That they would go on with their former Votes concerning the *Militia*.

2 That the Kings absence so farre remote from his Parliament is not only an obstruction, but may be a destruction to the affairs of *Ireland*.

3 That when the Lords and Commons in Parliament shall declare what the Lawes of the Land be, to have this not only questioned and controverted, but contradicted, and a command that it should not be obeyed, is a high breach of the priviledges of Parliament.

4 That a Committee of both Houses be appointed to enquire where this message was framed.

5 That those that did advise his Majesty to absent himself from the Parliament, and those that advised him to this message, are enimies to the peace of this Kingdom, and justly to be suspected to be favourers of the Rebellion in *Ireland*. All which Votes being sent up to the Lords, they also agreed with the Commons in them.

On Saturday 26 March a conference between both Houses read the King's Declaration, in which he attempted to justify the rationale of his position.

A Continuation of the true Diurnall

21–28 March, 1641{2} 68.11B {1.17}

Both Houses being met, his Majesties Declaration in answer to what had been late recommended unto him by both Houses, was presented and read before them, wherein he excused himselfe from those things wherein he thought himselfe to bee charged touching the breach of Parliament, the escape of Mr. *Jermyn* and the Lord *Digby*, and other advertisements from Rome, Venice, Paris, &c. and concluded how farre he had discended to comply with the Parliament, and to gaine the love of his subjects, intimating in the Bill, for the trieniall Parliament, relinquishing his title of imposition upon merchandizes, power of pressing of Souldiers, taking away the Starre-chamber and high Commission Courts, regulating the Councell Table, the limit of Forrests, Stanary Courts, &c. the votes of Bishops out of the Lords House, by which hee conceived the nature of Parliaments were not altered, and the constitution of this kingdome, whereby any diffidence might be raised betwixt him, his Parliament & Subjects. And touching his returne to London, hee would overtake their desires, and bee as soone with them as they could wish. In the meane time, neither the businesse of Ireland, nor any other advantage for the Kingdomes good should suffer through his default or absence, being so farre from repenting those Acts of Iustice and Grace which he had already performed to his people, that he shall with the same alacrity be ever ready to ad such new ones as may best advance the honour and prosperity of the Nation. The Lords after reading this, immediately rose, only appointed a Committee for the Irish affaires to meet in the afternoone.

A Perfect Diurnall of the Passages in Parliament
Numb. 12

28 March – 4 April, 1642 507.12 {1.18}

Friday, Aprill 1. {...}

Upon the meeting of both Houses, those members, of theirs, which went to his Majesty with their *Declaration*, being returned with his Majesties answer, upon a message sent, there was a conference, where the said Answer was read; which seemed somewhat to tax the Houses, touching their expression in the *Declaration*, as reflecting somwhat upon his Majesties Honor and Justice, as the doubt of his reall intention to joyn with his *Parliament* in all Acts for the security and good of his subjects; much complaining against scandalous Pamphlets, and the like, whereby he conceived himself much introduced, and the good affections of his; protesting his own integrity for the common good; denying any knowledge of his touching plots against the *Parliament*, either at home, or by calling in any forreign Force for his own protection (as not being to be credited) who only referred himself to God, and the love of his subjects; desiring some satisfaction, touching some things wherin he highly conceived himself wronged; utterly denying the consent to the Government of the *Militia* by Ordinance of *Parliament*, though ever willing (as never having denyed it) so it might passe by Bill, &c. which said Answer much troubled the Houses, and took each up severally some time in discussion thereof. {...}

Saturday, Aprill 2.

The House of Commons then entred again upon the consideration of his Majesties Message, and having some while consulted therupon, they sent a Message to the Lords, to desire a Conference, wherat it was moved, that the magazine at *Hull* might be removed (for the more security) to London, or some other place of strength; which the Lords having some time considered of, sent a message to the House, that they thought it fitting his Majesties consent might be gained therin: which said message caused another Conference, but they did not fully conclude thereupon.

Some Speciall Passages From London, Westminster, Yorke, Hull, Ireland. and other Parts Number 2.

17–24 May, 1642 606.02 {1.19}

The *House* tooke to consideration his *Majesties* summons of the 14. of *May* commanding the Gentry to appeare before him in their equipage; and they Voted, &c.

1. That it appeareth that his *Majestie* seduced by wicked *Councell,* intends to make Warre against the PARLIAMENT; who in all their Consultations and Actions have proposed no other end unto themselves, but the care of his Kingdome, and the performance of all dutie and Loyalty to his Person.

2. That whensoever the King maketh Warre upon the *Parliament,* it is a breach of the trust reposed in him, contrary to his Oath, and tending to the dissolution of this Government.

3. That whoever shall serve or assist him in such Warres, are Traytors to the Fundamentall Lawes of the Kingdome, and have beene so adjudged in two *Acts* of *Parliament*; II.*R*.2. & I.*H*.4. and ought to suffer as Traitors.

And both *Houses* inclosed their *Votes* in an humble *Petition* to his *Maiestie*; beseeching him to hearken to his great *Councell*; declaring, that as they are intrusted, they must endeavour to suppresse all Force that shall be raised to the disturbance of the Peace of the *Kingdome*; which was this day sent to the *Committees* at YORKE by an expresse.

This is an early account (8 June) of what was later to become a familiar story, except that in this case a member of parliament was involved. See also {1.32}.

Diurnall Occurrences in Parliament

6–13 June, 1642 100.2 {1.20}

WEDNESDAY, {...} Then the Commons received a *Petition* from the Lady *Sidney* a Widdow complaining against one Mr. *Griffith* a Member of the House of Commons, who had formerly beene a Suiter to her, who upon pretence of selling the said Lady a Iewell, invited her to his Lodging; whereupon the said Lady going according to the said Mr. *Griffith*, in a violent manner forc'd her to great incivility, for which shee desired Iustice against him. Whereupon the House being informed that hee is since fled, sent a *Warrant* to the Earle of *Warwick* to set strict watch at all Ports to prevent his escape by Sea, and that further search should bee made after him.

The king used some pointless delaying tactics with the commissioners from parliament, further hindering any personal reconciliation. This report is dated Thursday 16 June.

A Perfect Diurnall of The Passages in Parliament Numb. 1.

13–20 June, 1642 509.1 {1.21}

Then the Commons received Letters from the Committee at *Yorke:* Informing, that they had wayted these twelve dayes upon His Majesty, for answer to the nineteene Propositions, but could not obtaine any. And that they found so little respect from his Majesty, and such restraints laid upon him, that they desired they might have order to return back, and the rather for that they found the publicke resolution of the whole county, were so stedfast to the Parliament, there would be no changing of them.

The king's response to the 19 Propositions, and his treatment of the parliamentary committee tending them to him at York, further alienated the Commons. Many members of the Lords, however, felt sympathy with his declaration that he had not intended to instigate a war. The apparent discrepancy between the king's statements and his actions made reconciliation less probable: on 16 June, while still making overtures of peace, he put into effect his Commissions of Array.

Some Speciall Passages from Westminster, London, Yorke, and other parts. Number 5.

20–28 June, 1642 606.05 {1.22}

Tuesday the 21. *of June*. {...}

The Lords sent to the House of Commons a Letter from his Majesty, and an answer to the 19. Propositions containing seven sheets of paper close written on both sides, the Preamble of which did in effect expresse, *That the Parliament indeavoured to set up an upstart Authority (arbitrary power) That they had bestird Sir* John Hothams *boldface Treason, that their profession of establishing his Majesties honour and safety, was but a mockery and scorne, that they would widen the division between the King and Parliament, that their 19. Propositions were of that nature, that to grant them were in effect at once to depose the King and His posterity*, with such like expressions of asperity and bitternesse.

But the House being much moved at these vncharitable expressions (wounding the high Court of Parliament so much in Honour) they would have presently fallen upon the same to vindicate themselves from those aspersions; but in regard it was of that length, and that they might take some time to consider of it; they ordered on Tuesday next to take the same into a sad & serious consideration by a Committee of the whole House; that every Member might have liberty to speake as oft as they would, and what they would (bounding themselves within the rules of Modesty) declaring that never any thing yet came to this Parliament, which so much concerned the King and Kingdome, and preservation of both, as this did.

Later the Commons were to be less scrupulous about reading the king's letters {1.31}.

Some Speciall Passages from Westminster, London, Yorke, and other parts Number 7.

5–12 July, 1642 606.07B {1.23}

Tuesday the 5. of *Iune*. 1642

LEtters came from Sr. *Iohn Hotham*, Informing the House of the Ship *Providence*, laden with Ordinance, Armes, and Ammunition, and driven on the Sands neare *Hull* by Captaine *Pigotte*; that in the night time they (in the Shippe) got out foure Pieces of Ordinance, and planted them on the Bancke to guard the Shippe, so that when two little Barks, with 100. Musquetiers, sent from *Hull*, came to take the Ship, the Ordinance so planted, kept them off: But they took the Packet Boat, going with Letters to the Queen, wherein was Colonell *Ashburnham*, Sr. *Edward Stradling*, and others, who were brought into *Hull*, and are there in safe custodie. Sir *Iohn Hotham* sent the Pacquet to the Parliament, wherein was one Letter sealed with the Kings own Seal, which the Parliament (conceiving was for the Queen) would not open, though sent at such a time, when the Armes are landed to annoy the Parliament, and just cause of jealousie that the said Letter might nearely concern them in their safety. However, they returned the same in the name of both Houses, with all humility to His Majesty. But those Letters under the Signet Seale were read, some whereof required severall of the Commanders in our Fleet forthwith to repaire with their Ships from the *Downes* to *Humber* (neare *Hull)* and to *Newcastle*. {...}

Wednesday.

THe House received a more particular relation touching *Hull*, that on *Munday* last, the King came from *Yorke* with 3000 Foot, and 1000. Horse to *Beverly,* within 4 miles of HULL: there proclaimed that no Person whatsoever upon pain of death, should convey any manner of provision for the reliefe of *Hull* 200 Men were forthwith set worke in cutting of Trenches to divert the fresh water that runnes to *Hull,* likewise the 6 great Pieces of Batterie (that came with the rest of the Ordnance and Ammunition from *Holland,* in the ship called the Providence) were put into a condition for present service, and at the same time about 200 Horse were sent into *Lincoln-shire*: under the command of the Lord *Willoughby,* (sonne to the Lord of *Linsey*) and Sir *Thomas Glemham* stops all manner of provisions from *Barton* upon *Humber*, and other parts in *Lincoln-shire,* foregoing to *Hull.* The Cavaliers then with his Majestie often declared their admiration that Sir *Iohn Pennington* was not come with the Kings Ships from the Downes to stoppe all passage by Sea: being confident, that upon the discharge of the Earle of *Northumberland* from being Admirall, all the Captaines of the Ships would desert the commands of the Parliament: The Earle of *Warwick* and Sir *Iohn Hotham* being informed of all these passages, and the King being within an houre and a halfes march, hee sent 3 Messengers with a humble Petition to his Majestie, one after another, but none of them returned again: Sir *Iohn Pennington* called a Councell of Warre being satisfied, that his Maiesty had laid the Messenger fast (who at first inclined if his Maiestie appeared not there in person) to permit the Cavaliers to March neere the Towne with their Ordnance, and to hold them play off from the Walls, and out workes, till the Tyde came to it's height, and then to draw up the Sluice, and so force them to swim for their lives. But the Councell resolved rather (to invent losse of blood) presently to draw up the Sluice (having the advantage of a spring Tide, and damn'd the Countrey about *Hull,* which was done accordingly on *Munday* last in the Evening. But before it was done Sir *Iohn* gave the Inhabitants thereabouts, convenient notice to remove, their cattle and goods, and assured them what dammage soever they received thereby, the Parliament would make satisfaction to the full: (he hoped out of the estate of those Persons, most active to put the King upon such a designe.) And on *Tuesday* after, his Majestie returned from *Beverley* toward *Yorke*. {...}

The Houses (seeming to be satisfied that the Warre is begun already by his Maiestie) Ordered a *Declaration* to set forth the preparations for war that have beene making by some about his Maiestie, both in *England* and in *Holland*, and how long since: so the Kingdome may see, how they have beene deluded by those Lords that certified under their hands at *Yorke*: that there was no signe or intention of a preparation for Warre. {...}

MVnday the 10. of *Iuly*, {...} Letters of the 8. of *Iuly* were read, which came from Sir *Iohn Hotham,* which declared he expected every houre to be assaulted, that endeavour was used to blocke up *Humber* for any ships to passe, that as he had enemies without, so it was not unlikely but some were within, that if hee had (so it were speedily) but 500. men, money and victualls, neither respect of fortune, wife or children, shall make him desert the *Parliament,* but in this service for the good of *King* and *Parliament,* will sacrifice his life, rather then yeeld the Towne.

Oxford sided with the king from the beginning; in August Cambridge would also try to send Plate to the king, only to have it intercepted by the local Member of Parliament, Oliver Cromwell. The Earl of Essex, the hesitant and uncertain leader of the Parliament's forces until the creation of the New Model Army, was proclaimed with some sincere yet improbable sentiments. He was the son of the Elizabethan Earl who was executed for an abortive uprising.

Some Speciall Passages Number 8.

12–19 July, 1642 606.08 {1.24}

Tuesday the 12. of *Iuly*. 1642.

UPon Information given to both Houses of Parliament, That most of the Doctors and Heads of Colledges in the Vniversitie of *Oxford* had consultation there, about sending to His Majesty the Plate belonging to the severall Colledges (which by Law they could not doe) and that a Vote had passed in their Convocation House, that the same should be presently sent to *Yorke*, or a summe of Money, proportionable to their Plate: Thereupon both Houses passed a *Declaration*, setting forth the illegality of the Act: the injury done to those who had given Plate to remain to posterity; and not for the Fellowes of the Colledge to give away, or to convert to any other use; requiring the Schollers of the Vniversitie, and others, not to suffer the same to goe: And all the Counties adjoyning, to keep strict watch to hinder the passage thereof; and Doctor *Potter*, and others, therein most active, were sent for as Delinquents, for this their high contempt. {...}

The Committee appointed to consider of the defence of the Kingdome, presented their resolutions to the House, of having a Lord Generall, and raising an Armie: whereupon it was Resolved, *That an Armie should be raised for the safety of the Kings person, the defence of both Houses of Parliament, and of those who have obeyed their Orders and Commands, and preserving of the true Religion, Law, Liberty, and peace of the Kingdome*. They

Resolved, *That the Earle of* Essex *should be Generall of this Armie:* And both Houses, with much affection and cheerfullnesse, by Vote upon the Question, Declared, *They would Live and Dye with the Earle of* Essex *in this cause*.

A Diurnall out of the North: Or, The daily Occurrences of This Weeke

unto this present 16. of Iuly. 1642. 110.1 {1.25}

As the King was Bowling, there was scatter'd a paper with Verses, very scandalous against Mr. Pym, and shewed the King, who having read them, tore them in pieces, and with a sad looke said, *such libellous Rascals hath broke the peace of the Kingdom, and if Iustice did but lay hold of them, peoples minds would be quickly calm'd,* he that showed them very likely looked for better thankes.

Hotham's defence of the City of Hull and its munitions made it a locus for the early skirmishes. The terms 'Roundhead' and 'Cavalier' had been in existence roughly as long as newsbooks. The following letters were read in the House of Commons on Monday 18 July.

A Perfect Divrnall of the Passages in Parliament

18–25 July, 1642 509.6C {1.26}

Also, there was letters read from Sir *Iohn Hotham*, informing that the Cavaleers have made divers attempts by night against *Hull*, tending to burne the same in severall places, and that whilst the Souldiers should be busie in quenching the fire, they would scale the Walls and seize upon the Town; but this enterprise was prevented by Sir *Iohn Hothams* vigilancy, who so played upon them with his Cannon shot, that they soone left the enterprize, only they burned two Wind-Mills, which belonged to *Hull*: The Earle of *Newport* being also in this design, was by the waft of a Cannon shot dismounted from his horse, and cast into a deep ditch of water, where had he not been catcht hold of by the haire of the head, after once or twice sinking, he had lost his life; which passage being afterwards told to his Maiesty, the Archbishop of *York* being present, made answer it was well his Lordship was not a Round-head, if hee had, he might have been drowned, for that then he would have had little haire on his head to have been holden by.

This newsbook arranged an exchange between the king and parliament in clear and systematic typography. The report is dated Saturday 23 July.

A Perfect Diurnall, Or the proceedings in Parliament

18–25 July, 1642 517.2 {1.27}

This day, the Earle of *HOLLOND* brought a Message from his Majesty, in Answer to the late Petition of both Houses; consisting of fower points, *Viz.*

I.

That the Towne of Hull *should be surrendred vnto Him.*

II.

That the sole claime and interest in the Militia, *by the* Parliament; *should be vtterly disclaimed.*

III.

That all the Shipps now at Sea, should be Delivered up, into His Maiesties Hands.

IIII.

That the Parliament *should be adiourned to some other place, where His Maiesty should thinke fit.*

And after mature deliberation hereof, both Houses Voted.

I.

That it was not for the Kingdomes safety, to deliver up the Towne of *Hull*, untill such time as his Majesties Forces were disbanded.

II.

That for the *Militia*, they held it most fitting (according to his Majesties former desires) to settle it by Bill.

III.

For the Shipping, they thought it could not be put into more surer hands then now it is both for the defence of his Majesty and Kingdome.

IIII.

Fourthly that the Parliament was in the most Eminent place of the Kingdome, and where his Maiestie might abide in most peace and safetie, and there upon both Houses ordered that the Earle of *Essex* should forth with raise forces for the defence of his Maiestie and Kingdome.

Parliament was always careful to incriminate those around the king rather than the man himself. This was a longstanding political tradition. This report is dated 25 July.

Some Speciall Passages From Westminster, Hull, Yorke, and other parts. Number 9.

19–26 July, 1642 606.09 {1.28}

MVNDAY

The House fell seriously into debate of the Kings Answer brought by the Earl of *Holland*, and discended to this Resolution, *That they cannot yeeld to his Majesties Demands with the discharge of that trust which the Kingdom hath reposed in them for the security thereof*, and ordered a Declaration to be drawn (in as briefe a manner as may be) setting forth to the Kingdome; the particulars that is necessarie for them to insist upon, both for Religion, Liberty, and safety of the kingdome, the causes of these unpleasing Messages from his Majesty; that they may be removed from about him; and that so long as these Cavaliers are about his Majesty, and Delinquents of so high a Nature, (in removall of whom they will sacrifice their lives) the kingdome must not expect peace nor prosperity; and having laid this open, they have then discharged that trust reposed in them; and if the kingdome will not assist them, they are cleared to all the world of being guilty of the slavery (both for body and soule) which the Subjects and their posterity are like to fall into, by having authority by the sword imposed upon them.

Both the following accounts of the meeting between both Houses are dated Saturday 30 July. In the first, reference is made to the king's appearance in Parliament on 4 January, which was already being deployed as an historically significant event. See also {5.06}.

A Perfect Diurnall of the Passages in Parliament Numb. 7.

25 July – 1 August, 1642 510.07 {1.29}

Then the Lords desired a free Conference with the Commons, at which Conference the grand Declaration, shewing the emergent reasons the Parliament have, to take up Arms for a defensive war, was read: But before the reading thereof, Master *Hollis* made an excellent Speech, shewing the great danger wherein the Kingdom now standeth; and that the Malignant party about His Majesty, did aim at the overthrow and destruction of the whole Parliament; and so declared the just cause the Parliament had to make the best defence they can to prevent their wicked designes; for by destroying the Parliament they destroyed the King, and so consequently would bring ruine and destruction upon the whole Kingdom: He also gave some instances, wherein it plainly appeared, that if *Hull* should be delivered into His Majesties hands, and the Ordinance of the *Militia* laid down, &c. yet would not a peace thereby be setled, nor the Arms His Majesty hath raised be laid down, for that their malice is chiefly against the Parliament, and their endeavour is the utter extirpation thereof, which appears, because that before *Hull* was ever detained from His Majesty, or the Ordinance concerning the *Militia* ever so much as thought upon, there were strange and unheard of attempts against the Parliament; as namely, His Majesties coming to the House of Commons with a great number of Cavaliers, &c.

After this, the said Declaration was read, and being approved of by the Lords, was Ordered to be Printed.

A Perfect Diurnall of the Passages in Parliament
Numb. 7

25 July – 1 August, 1642 509.7A {1.30}

Saturday the 30. {...}

At that conference also, the Earle of *Essex* read a letter. which hee received from the Earle of *Warwick:* intimating, that he had intercepted a packet of letters at Sea, which were going to the Queene from his Majesty and some others, in a Tobacco ship, bound for *Holland*.

That the party, with whom the letters were intrusted, to prevent the delivery of one of them, which he conceived to bee of the chiefest concernment, gave it to another man in the ship, advising him, that he would forthwith put the same into a little box with a peece of lead in it, to make it sinke, and tie it with a string to some part of the outside of the ship; but the party being prevented of his purpose therein, by reason of the suddaine searching of the ship, (in hopes of a great reward,) conveyed himselfe into a Tobacco barrell, where hee continued for two or three dayes; the ship being for all that time kept at Sea, untill almost being starved for want of victuals; hee discovered himselfe, and the said letter was found about him, and also (with other letters) delivered to the Earle of *Warwick*, who sent them to the Parliament, which letters, the Lords delivered to the Commons, to consider, whether they should be opened or no; whereupon after some debate in the House of Commons, it was resolved upon the question, that they should be all opened by the House and referred to a Committee, to read and consider of, which was done accordingly.

Some Speciall Passages from Hull, Anlaby, and Yorke Number 10.

Truly informed Munday *the first of* August 1642. 606.10 {1.31}

Sir,

NOW others Intentions are discovered by their actions, what we have much and long feared is come upon Us: Here is no other found but Warre, and (notwithstanding pretences) that the intention thereof was before our feares: Drums beate up in diverse parts of this, and severall adjacent Counties, for Voluntiers for His Majesties seruice, albeit in this County very few come in. I heare the Parliament have replyed to His Majesty; they cannot agree to His Propositions (sent in Answere to their last Petition) and performe the trust reposed in them by the Kingdome: whereat our wretched Cavaliers are overjoyed, expecting from our Distractions, their Desires, from our Misery, their making. {...}

ON *Wedensday* night late about one of the Clock, there sallied out of *Hull* 40. Horse, and about 150. Foote, and fell upon the Cavaliers Trenches at *Anlaby*, where all the Souldiers deserted then, save two who stood Centinell, and (by their willfull refusall of friendly usage, attempting also to kill some of Sir *Iohns* party) were slaine. The Ensigne out ran his Colours, which Sir *Iohn* seized, also 70. Musquets, and took diverse Prisoners, like wise burnt the Barne, wherein the Granadoes, and other contrivements of the Cavaliers were preparing, intended for the burning of *Hull*, which to prevent occasioned this attempt; The fire for the time was very terrible to the Inhabitants, in regard of the noyse made by the Powder and Grenadoes. The night following 140. Souldiers more left their

Trenches, who resolved to dye, rather then to continue longer in that service, of whose mind are all the Trained Band generally, declaring publiquely they wil not exercise Armes against their friends, Neighbours and Countreymen, so as you will speedily heare of the Siege raised at *Hull,* if not already.

The allegiance of the counties was essential because they were the basis of military power.

A Perfect Diurnall of the Passages in Parliament Numb. 9

8–15 August, 1642 509.9A {1.32}

Munday 8. *of August*, 1642.

There was also Letters of Information from *Yorke*, That His Majestie hath had another meeting with the County, on *Thursday* last at *Yorke*, and that He made a Speech to them, much complayning against the late proceedings of the Parliament, and inciting the County to comply with Him, and lend him all ayde towards the raising of his Forces, especially a quantity of Armes out of the Store of the County, But that request would not be granted, the greatest part of the Countrey dayly more and more falling off from His Majesty to the Parliament, by reason of the late carriages of the Cavaliers. {...}

There was a Petition presented to both Houses from divers Gentlemen, of the Malignant party, in *Yorkeshire*, but drawne up by some Members of both Houses, now with his Majestie, It being a most invective Petition, full of rough, uncouth, and insolent Language, exclaiming against Sir *Iohn Hotham*, and the proceedings of Parliament. {...}

Wednesday the 10.

THere was a report made to the house, of the depositions of divers witnesses against Master *Griffith*, concerning his ravishing of the Lady *Sidny*; whereupon it was ordered, that there should be a charge drawne up against him, for the same, and it was then voted, that he should be disabled for being a member of the Commons house during this Parliament.

CHAPTER ONE

Some Speciall and Considerable Passages from London, Westminster, Portsmouth, Warwicke, Coventry, and other places. Numb. 1.

9–16 August, 1642 605.01 {1.33}

Thursday the 11. *of August.*

TO the great amazement (but nothing to the terror) of both Houses of Parliament, came a Letter from his Majesty to both Houses, and a Proclamation inclosed, which his Majesty commanded should be read in the House of Peeres, and afterwards in the House of Commons; the Lords discerning it to be of such a transcendent nature, fitter to be disposed of in another manner than to be read, were inclined not to reade it, yet at last read the same; It reciting that whereas both Houses have appointed the Earle of *Essex* Captaine Generall, doth proclaime the Earle of *Essex* Traytor, & all those Members of both Houses that are listed under him, and all persons that adhere unto him, expressing a resolution to set up his Standard: The Lords upon this declared (not one gainsaying it) (there being present the Earle of *Northumberland*, the Earle of *Pembrooke*, the Earle of *Clare*, the Earle of *Rutland*, the Earle of *Holland*, and eighteene Peeres besides) that this Proclamation would make the Earle of *Essex* as Captaine Generall, and in him the Parliament, (that so appointed him) Trators, and all that adhere to the Parliament to be Traytors, and in them the honest and well-affected partie of the Kingdome: That notwithstanding the great and big words of terror in this Proclamation, they are with one consent resolved to goe on with more united vigour than before, they having well considered their grounds before they entred into this action for the maintenance of Religion, Laws, & Liberty.

The Lords had no sooner declared this, but the Earle of *Essex* stood up and said, that this printed paper should not deterre him from discharging his duty to God, his King, & his Countrey, and that he would be as ready to sacrifice his life for the maintenance of the Lawes, as their new Generall should be to break the Lawes. {...}

Saterday the 13. *of August.*

THe Declaration passed both Houses against the printed paper proclaiming the Earl of *Essex* and those of both Houses that adhere unto him Traitors, which expresses that that scandalous paper is the venome of those traiterous Counsellors about his Majestie who endeavour to introduce Poperie, &c. which had been setled in this Kingdom ere now, had not the coming in of the *Scots* prevented it: And endeavouring to make the people subdue the Parliament; imploying outlawed persons to maintain the Law, Fugitives, Traitors and Delinquents to maintain the priviledges of Parliament, and Papists to maintain the Protestant Religion, declaring them Traitors that shall abet, publish or countenance that Proclamation; offering in the close of all, that if his Majestie will yet at last abandon those wicked Counsellors, and leave them to condigne punishment, and hearken to his great Counsell, they will make him as potent a Prince as ever bore Scepter in this Kingdom. {...}

Monday the 15. *of August*

THe honest men of Ware apprehended the zealous servant to the Cavaliers, who forebore to go to Church that he might the better fix this Proclamation (that the Parliament are Traitors) on the posts, which being espied by some few of the Town, they got heaps of stones which flew about his eares, and but that company came in he had felt the smart of it: So they seised on a cloak-bagge of his full of Proclamations and Commissions of Array; he at last confessing he received them as they passed the great Seal, and that he had left some of them at Lincolne, Cambridge, and other places by the way.

They brought him this day to the House of *Commons*, to the Barre, where he was committed to the Sergeant to be kept in safe custodie, and to be made exemplary for presuming (being a Commoner) to countenance any thing, endeavouring to make the Commoners of England traitors; It being advised that everie Member should write to some in each County to certifie the names of all such that dare take the boldnesse upon them to presume to read and publish those Proclamations, that they may be made examples to posterity.

Despite the casualties incurred before 22 August, the day on which the king set up his Standard has been interpreted by historians as the precipitatory moment of the Great Civil War. Its significance lies in the irreversible nature of this announcement of the conflict. In 1642 there were many ways of telling the story, even amongst those not explicitly siding with the king. The report is dated Wednesday 17 August.

A Perfect Diurnall of the Passages in Parliament *Num.* 10

15–22 August, 1642 511.10 {1.34}

Then the Lords sent a message to the Commons, declaring that they had received a letter out of *Yorkshire*, with a new *Proclamation* set out by his Majesty, declaring his Royall Intention to set up his *Standard* on *Monday* next at some convenient place which his Majesty should make choice of; thereby commanding all his dutifull Subjects that will aid and assist him to Repair thither, And proclaiming all those which shall refuse to obey the *Commission of Array*, and serve or adhere to the Earl of *Essex*, and submit to the *Ordinance of the Militia*, Traytors; and thereby appointing the Earl of *Cumberland* Generall for the raising of Forces in the Northern parts, which *Letter and Proclamation* was sent to the house of Commons, and after some debate therof, they desired a *Conference*, with the Lords, at which *Conference* the said *Proclamation* and *Letter* was read, which letter was to this effect, That the Cavaleers had violently taken many Arms from the Trayned Bands of that County, and plundered many Gentlemens houses, opening their Trunks and Chests, and taking away all they could find with many more Out-rages, which they daily committed, and that his Majesty intended to go from *Yorke* to *Nottingham* on the 16. of this instant *August*, and it was conceived he intended to set up his *Standard* there: And therfore the Gentlemen of the County of *York* desired that some considerable Forces might be sent into that County, and that power and authority might be given to such Gentlemen, whose names they presented to the house, being men of trust, to Raise Forces, and command them, for the defence and safety of that County, which was Referred to a Committee to consider of, and make Report to the house.

And a Committee was also appointed to draw up a Declaration to be published to the Kingdom, to declare to the Subject the legall proceedings of the Parliament, and the illegality of the said proclamation, and the violent procsecution in executing the Commmission of Array.

Certaine Speciall and Remarkable Passages from both Houses of Parliament

16–23 August, 1642 638.02 {1.35}

Monday the 22 of *August*, Both Houses received Letters of very ill newes from *Coventry*, that His Majesty in a warlike manner with 1500 Horse came thither on Satturday morning last, and demanded the Town, which they very willingly condiscended unto, with all dutifull obedience to His Majesty, but desired His Majestie would be pleased to discharge his extraordinary Guard of Cavaleers, for that they would be a very great affrightment to the Inhabitants; which His Majesty refusing, the Inhabitants taking into consideration the great outrage & spoyl that have been committed by the Cavaleers in other places where they have been; and fearing they would exercise the like cruelty against them, as their bold carriage and threatning language at first appearance with His Majesty did much foretell: For their own security, and to preserve the peace of the Citie, they shut the Gates against His Majesty and his Company, vntill such time as their feeres should be secured by his Majesties discharging the Cavaleers.

But his Majesty being impatient of delay, and much incensed thereunto by the rash counsell of the Cavaleers, layd strong siege against the Town and fell to Battery, and so still continues, and had battered down divers houses and had slain many men before the messenger that brought the newes to the Parliament came from thence, which was on Satturday in the afternoone.

A Perfect Diurnall of the Passages in Parliament
Numb. 11.

22–29 August, 1642 512.11 {1.36}

Munday the 22th. *of August*.

MUnday information was brought to the House by one of the Parishonors of St. *Andrews* Holborne, that one *Edw. Archer* living in Shooe Lane, in his table discourse speaketh very vile and outragious words against some particular Lords of the Parliament, viz. for the Earl of

Warwick he wished his heart in his Bootes, the Lord of Essex his guts upon a Dunghill, and such like desperate words vowing to be the death of the said Earl of Essex wheresome-ever he should meet him, & that he hath often endeavoured to put the said wicked enterprize in agitation, but never could have fit opportunity for so desperate a designe; upon which information present command was given to the Constable of the said Parish for the apprehending of the said *Archer*, and bring him to the Parliament, which was done accordingly, and committed to the Fleet. {...}

{Tuesday:} There was likewise report made to the House that divers Captaines cannot raise a sufficient number of Volunteers in London and Suburbs for this present expedition, except the Parliament pleased to grant the Officers warrants to raise them in some of his Majesties Counties; a Member of the House said, that he conceived the Parliament might grant Warrants to Constables to Presse his Majesties Subjects being in the King and Parliaments defence, for although this insurrection amongst our selves be termed Civill Warres, yet it was hatcht and set abroach in forraigne parts by the Jesuiticall Seckt, and seconded by those who are Delinquents to the Parliament, therefore it was held fitting that a Presse might be granted for some particular persons, as idle treacherous Marshalls men, and other loose persons of that profession, as their doggs they terme setters, many loose and deboyst Tapsters, and such like persons, which was referred to the consideration of a Committee.

Speciall Passages and certain Informations from severall places Numb. 3.

23–30 August, 1642 605.03 {1.37}

Nottingham, Munday, August 22. *Nine at night.*

THat this day about 6. at night, His Majesty came weary out of *Warwickshire* to *Nottingham*, and after halfe an houres repose, commanded the Standard to be brought forth, which was carryed by a Lord, His Majesty, the Prince, the Duke of *Yorke*, and divers Lords and Gentlemen accompanying the same, as soon as it was set up, His Majesty called for the printed Proclamation, mended with pen and inke some words misprinted, or not approved of, and caused the Herauld to reade the Proclamation three times, and so departed: The Cavaliers having disarmed all the Townesmen that had Armes sent them from the Parliament, three housholders refusing to deliver their Arms which they bought with their own mony, were committed close prisoners to *Nottingham* Castle: They plunder all mens houses whom they please to call *Roundheads*, and bring in Cart-loads of houshold stuffe, and sell them before the Court gate.

Certaine Speciall and Remarkable Passages from both Houses of Parliament

22–26 August, 1642 638.03 {1.38}

There was also credible information by Letters from *Nottingham*, that His Majesty hath set up His Standard there, and hath about three hundred Souldiers to Guard the same, and hath been under it himselfe three severall days, and made Proclamations for all his Subjects to come in unto him there, to ayde and assist him to suppresse the Earle of *Essex* Rebellion.

But the Countries are so well satisfied of the just and legall proceedings of the Parliament, in granting Commission to the Earle of *Essex* to raise forces That that there hath not beene as yet a 100 persons come in to His Majesty since the sitting up of the Standard.

The appeal to political and legal precedent was most important to both sides. The theatres were perceived as potential breeding grounds of civil unrest, and were closed for fear they might spread sedition. The attempt was not entirely successful.

A Perfect Diurnall of the Passages in Parliament *Num.* 12.

29 August – 5 September, 1642 511.12A {1.39}

Monday, the 29. *of August*.

MUnday the 29. of *August*, the Answer of the Lords and Commons in Parliament to the Message from his Majestie sent by the Earles of *Southampton* and *Dorset*, and Sir *Iohn Culpepper*, was returned to His Majestie, which was to this effect: That *Both Houses* do with much grief recent the dangerous and distracted State of this Kingdome, which they have by all means endeavoured to prevent, both by their severall advices and Petitions to his Majesty, which have not onely been without successe, but there hath followed that which no ill Counsell in former times hath produced, or any age hath seen: Namely, that severall Proclamations and Declarations against *Both Houses of Parliament*, whereby their Actions are declared treasonable, and their persons Traytors; and thereupon his Majestie hath set up his Standard against them, whereby he hath put the two houses of Parliament, and in them the whole Kingdom, out of his protection. So that untill his Majestie shall recall the said Proclamations and Declarations, whereby the said Earl of *Essex* and *Both Houses of Parliament*, and their adherents and assistants, and such as have obeyed and executed their commands and directions, according to their duties, are declared Traitors, or otherwise Delinquents; and untill the Standard set up in pursuance of the said Proclamations be taken down, his Majestie hath put them in such a condition, that whilst they remain so, they cannot by the fundamentall priviledge of Parliament, the publike trust reposed in them, or with the generall good and safetie of the Kingdome, give his Majestie any other answer to his Message. {...}

Friday the 2. *of September*. {...}

It was also Voted that there shall be no common Play-houses for the exercising of Stage Playes, and no common Interludes within this Kingdome. {...}

It is likewise reported that many of the Cavaleers being about two hundred in Number are come to *OXFORD*, and are made very welcome by the malignant Party there, and having a great part of the City and of the Vniversity of their Friends, they think to share their Plate before they goe, and when they have gorged themselves with Colledge Beere, they are of opinion that they are in very safe Trenches, and make some of the Schollers beleeve that they are able to defend the Town against forty thousand men.

It is said that since the skirmish at *SOVTHAM* in *WARWICKSHIRE*, many of the Cavaleers have beene found dead in the Corn-fields, being thrown there by those that fled away, and that they did much hurt to the Corn, by trampling and treading it down.

Episcopacy was not actually abolished until 1646. The common proverb cited in this report (dated Thursday 1 September) bodes ill for the newsbook.

A Continvation of certain Speciall and Remarkable passages Number 5.

30 August - 6 September, 1642 638.05 {1.40}

The Commons again falling into Debate of the *Scotch* Declaration for the uniformity in Church Government in the three Kingdoms; and taking into consideration the wicked practises of the Bishops and Prelaticall party, as having been the chiefe causers of the present distractions, and only Incendiaries between the King and Parliament: After long Debate, agreed in a Vote; That all Bishops, Deanes and Chapters, Prebends; all their adherents Root and Branch, shall be for ever eradicated, and others to be appointed in their places to order Ecclesiasticall affairs, according as the wisedome of Parliament shall further appoint.

This businesse cause so much joy in the City of *London*, that there was above 500 Bon-fires, and ringing of Bells in all Churches in the City that night; but indeed a great part of the vulgar people were in a mistake, it being rumor'd amongst them that the King was that night come to Towne, which occasioned a great part of their rejoycing; but that, as the common Proverbe is, was too good news to be true.

Quotidian Occurrences In and about London, And in other places of this Kingdome of England

5–12 September, 1642 579.01 {1.41}

MUNDAY *the fifth of* SEPTEMB.

AT a Conference of both the Houses of Parliament, there was read a message or Reply from the King, which came on Saturday last, purporting, that he did never declare, nor intended to declare his Houses of Parliament traytors, nor did hee set up his Standard against them, nor put them and the Kingdome out of his protection; but withall required, that if they would appoint a day to revoke their Declarations against those that assisted him, that upon the same day, he would recall his Proclamations and Declarations, and take downe his Standard.

The Houses upon consultation & consideration of these premises, presently set forth a Declaration to this effect: that the Armes which they have been forced, and shall be forced to take up, &c. shall not be laid downe, untill the King shall disprotect all that are, or shall be voted Delinquents, and remit them to punishment sutable to their deserts, that this and future ages may take precaution of involving themselves in the like offences. And that whatsoever detriment the Republique hath suffered since the Kings receding from the Parliament, shall be charged upon Delinquents Malignants and disaffected persons. And that well affected people, who have lent monies, or assisted, or shall assist the commonwealth in urgent pressures shall be repayed out of the estates of all offenders. {...}

A Paerfect Diurnall of the Proceedigns in Parliament

5–12 September, 1642. 515.1 {1.42}

Tuesday the sixth of September.

This day came letters from Oxford, intimating that the Schollars have joyned themselves to the Cavaliers, and have carried many great stones to the top of *Magdalens* Colledge, to the intent to cast them downe upon the heads of those that shall offer to oppose them, that they doe daily much hurt in the Citie; and have for their Captaine the Tapster of the Roe-buck, and Chamberlaine of the red Lion. Vpon which it was ordered the L. *Sey* with his Regiment should on Thursday next advance towards Oxford, for appeasing the disturbances raised in that County.

The charge of apostacy was repeatedly levelled at the parliament's army: Brownism, anabaptism and atheism were effectively homogenous terms, used to identify and condemn any form of religious unorthodoxy. In turn, parliament accused the king of enlisting the support of Papists.

England's Memorable Accidents

26 September – 3 October, 1642 579.04 {1.43}

Vpon the 19. of this instant, the King published Orders of Discipline to his Army, which being read, by word of mouth, he required them exactly to observe them, expressing that hee

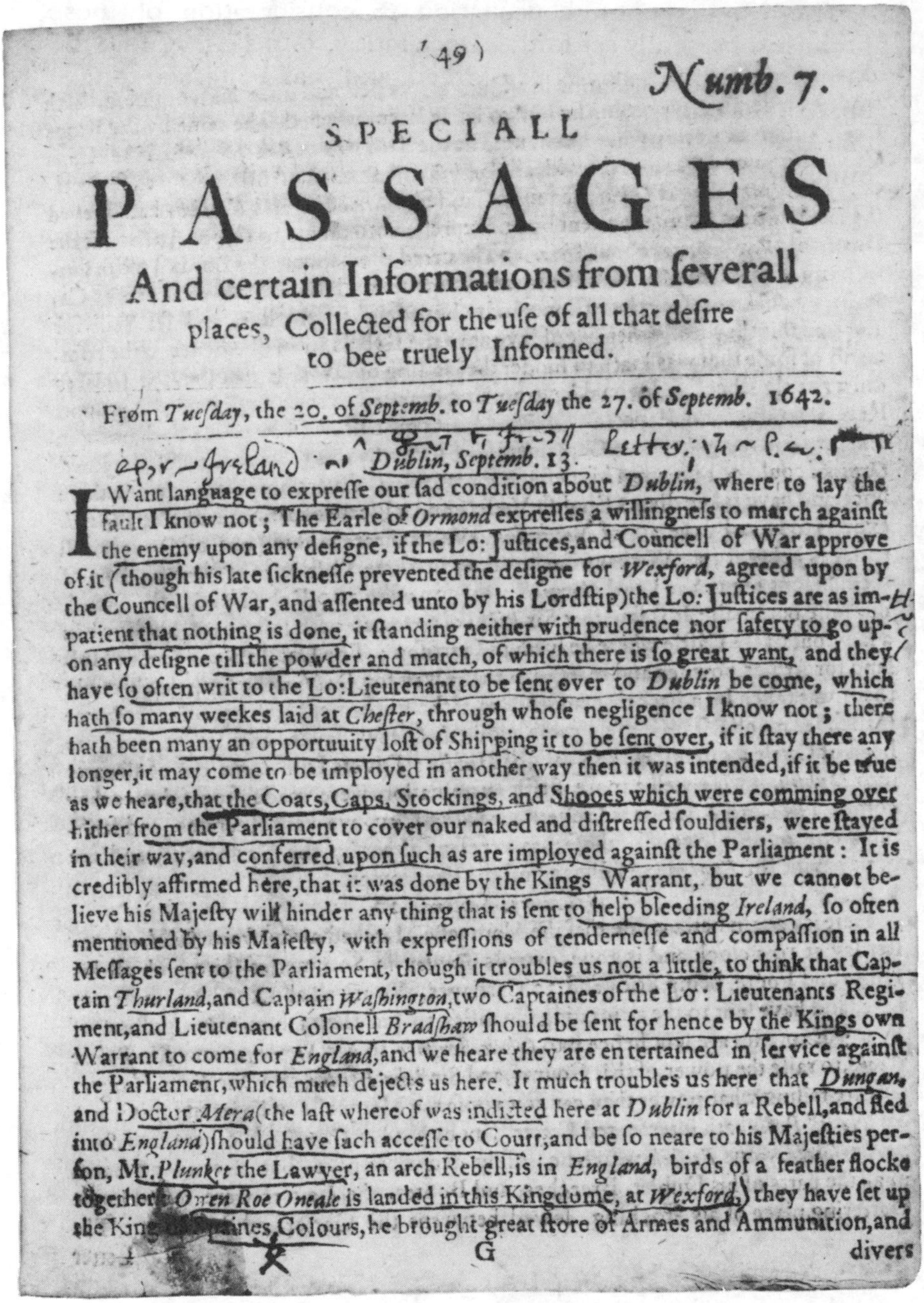

(49)

Numb. 7.

SPECIALL

PASSAGES

And certain Informations from severall places, Collected for the use of all that desire to bee truely Informed.

From Tuesday, the 20. of Septemb. to Tuesday the 27. of Septemb. 1642.

Dublin, Septemb. 13.

I Want language to expresse our sad condition about *Dublin*, where to lay the fault I know not; The Earle of *Ormond* expresses a willingnesse to march against the enemy upon any designe, if the Lo: Justices, and Councell of War approve of it (though his late sicknesse prevented the designe for *Wexford*, agreed upon by the Councell of War, and assented unto by his Lordship) the Lo: Justices are as impatient that nothing is done, it standing neither with prudence nor safety to go upon any designe till the powder and match, of which there is so great want, and they have so often writ to the Lo: Lieutenant to be sent over to *Dublin* be come, which hath so many weekes laid at *Chester*, through whose negligence I know not; there hath been many an opportunity lost of Shipping it to be sent over, if it stay there any longer, it may come to be imployed in another way then it was intended, if it be true as we heare, that the Coats, Caps, Stockings, and Shooes which were comming over hither from the Parliament to cover our naked and distressed souldiers, were stayed in their way, and conferred upon such as are imployed against the Parliament: It is credibly affirmed here, that it was done by the Kings Warrant, but we cannot beleive his Majesty will hinder any thing that is sent to help bleeding *Ireland*, so often mentioned by his Majesty, with expressions of tendernesse and compassion in all Messages sent to the Parliament, though it troubles us not a little, to think that Captain *Thurland*, and Captain *Washington*, two Captaines of the Lo: Lieutenants Regiment, and Lieutenant Colonell *Bradshaw* should be sent for hence by the Kings own Warrant to come for *England*, and we heare they are entertained in service against the Parliament, which much dejects us here. It much troubles us here that *Dungan*, and Doctor *Mera* (the last whereof was indicted here at *Dublin* for a Rebell, and fled into *England*) should have such accesse to Court, and be so neare to his Majesties person, Mr. *Plunket* the Lawyer, an arch Rebell, is in *England*, birds of a feather flocke together. *Owen Roe Oneale* is landed in this Kingdome, at *Wexford*, they have set up the Kings [illegible] Colours, he brought great store of Armes and Ammunition, and

G divers

3. *Speciall Passages* with John Rushworth's marginalia

would be very severe in punishing all the transgressors thereof, that they ought to be the more carefull of the performance of them, because the time approached to Action, that he could not suspect their courages, in regard that their Loyalties and consciences brought them to fight for their Religion, King and Lawes, against trayterous *Brownists, Anabaptists* and *Atheists*, who endeavour the destruction of Church and State, and have sentenced them to ruine for their Loyaltie to him: And that they might beleeve they could not fight in a better quarrell, they should heare his Protestation, which he made to this effect, he promised before God, and as he hoped for his blessing and protection to maintaine the true reformed Protestant Religion established in the Church of *England*, and to live and die in it. He desired to govern by the knowne Lawes of the Land, and to preserve the Liberty and propertie of the Subject, and if God should preserve him from this Rebellion by his blessing upon this Army, then he did promise before God, to maintaine the just Priviledges and freedome of *Parliament*, to governe by the known laws of the Land, and inviolably to observe the Lawes he had assented unto this Parliament, unlesse his great necessities and straites in this Warre, should drive him to violate them all, which he hoped God and Man would impute to the authors of this warre, and not to him who had laboured for the Peace of this Kingdome &c.

The Prince Elector of the Palatinate, Charles Louis, had been deprived of his kingdom by the Thirty Years War. Though neglected by his uncle he was always a favourite among parliamentary supporters of the Protestant cause: it was even suggested, some years later, that he should replace Charles on the throne.

A Perfect Divrnall of the Passages in Parliament *Number* 17.

26 September – 3 October, 1642 511.16C {1.44}

Tuesday the 27.

This day the House of Commons received Letters from the Prince *Elector* now in *Holland* with the Queen *Bohemia* his Mother, declaring in the same, his loyall affection to the Parliament, protesting that he hath no hand in his Brothers indeavours against the Parliament, but when he was in *England*, he indeavored to perswade the King his uncle to a unity with the

Parliament, but perceaving the same would not be hearkned unto, he departed for *Holland*, that he might have no hand in the Warre against the Parliament; and therefore desired the Pention allowed his Mother and him by the King, might be confirmed by the Parliament. And after some debate touching the same referred his request to the consideration of a Committee to make report thereof to the House on Thursday following.

On 30 September, parliament responded to the king's declaration which had implied that the army was constituted solely of Brownists, anabaptists and atheists.

A Contivation Of certain Speciall and Remarkable passages *Number* 11.

29 September – 1 October, 1642 638.11 {1.45}

There was also at a conference of both Houses a great debate concerning his Maiesties Speech and protestation which hee made in the head of his Army wherein hee termes the Parliament to bee no other but a company of Brownists Anabaptists and Shismatiques, and that they goe about to set up an Arbitrary Government in the state, and Innovation in the Church &c.

At which the Houses tooke great distast there being so many uniust aspersions cast upon them, and therefore Ordered that there should bee a Declaration forthwith drawne up to cleare the Parliament of those accusations, and to satisfie the Kingdome concerning their proceedings, and enforme them that although they have voted against the Government of Bishops for that it produced so many evills, it could not longer be borne withall, yet they never intended wholely to exterpate the Litturgy and Common prayer (as is pretended by his Majesty) but according to his Majesties owne proffer, to purge the same of such Corruptions as are inconsistant with the word of God, and offensive to tender and weake consciences; which Declaration they Ordered should be forthwith published to the Kingdome.

Moll Cutpurse was a legendary Jacobean heroine, based on a woman called Mary Frith, featured in pamphlets and in Middleton and Dekker's play *The Roaring Girl*. Here she seems to stand for the independence of London. The second report is from Worcester: it is a paraphrase of a letter from Nehemiah Wharton, a volunteer parliamentary soldier, to George Willingham, a London merchant. (See *Calendar of State Papers Domestic: 1641–3*.)

Weekly Intelligence From Severall parts of this Kingdome

10–18 October, 1642 686.2 {1.46}

The Commons understanding that there are divers that weare upon their hats a tauny colour'd Ribin, which is the colour his Majesties Souldiers weare, and that there are divers Officers in Towne that may take on these men to the great disturbance of the City of *London*, and the South parts of the Realme, have commanded the restraint of their meeting in *Pauls*, and given Order for the apprehending of them; and as a beginning, there was on saturday Justice *Longs* man taken following his Master with such colours (like man, like master,) the man being examined was found in severall Tales, but at last he refered the Committee that examined him to *Moll Cut-purse*, who being sent for, went to the Committee with Tauney and Orange colored Ribins saying she would were both, for she was for the King and Parliament. {...}

Worcester, Octob. the 9.

{...} on Sunday about the time of Morning Prayer, we went to the Minster, where we heard the Organs play, and the Queristers sing so sweetely that some of our Souldiers could not forbeare dancing in the holy Quire; the Anthome being ended they fell to praying devoutly for the King and Bishops, and one of our Souldiers said with a loud voyce, what never a fit for the Parliament, which offended them greatly.

A Continvation of certain Speciall and Remarkable passages *Number* 14.

8–12 October, 1642 638.14 {1.47}

Saterday the 12. *of* October.

It is also informed by letters from Rome that the Pope and Conclave have held an inquisition concerning the affaires of

England, and that they declare themselves with bitter invectives against the Parliament and upon consultation how they may best assist his Majestie against the Parliament, for the cutting off the Puritan faction in England, as they terme it.

In their propaganda parliament and the king disputed over who was promoting innovation: that is, whether Laudian Arminianism or Puritanism represented the true heritage of the English church.

A Collection of Speciall Passages and Certaine Informations

17 October – 1 November, 1642 Wing C5194 {1.48}

THere was a Declaration published by Order of both Houses of Parliament, setting forth the present condition of this kingdom, That his Majesty by advice and assistance of the evill and wicked counsell about him hath raised an Army, which are maintained with the spoyls of the Kings subjects; giving them leave to exact monies by force, plunder & spoyle all sorts of people. That this evil counsel doth not only hinder his Majesty from exercising the Iustice of a King towards his people, but even that honour which is observed betwixt enemies; {...}

As also in that Declaration the Houses make severall excellent Queries concerning the grounds of this warre, the result whereof in short is, That it is not feare of some Innovation or alteration in Religion or Church Goverment that hath occasioned this warre; for that the Parliament have fully declared that they intend to take away nothing but the Government of Bishops, which have been so evidently mischievous and dangerous to the Church and State; Nor is it to uphold the authority, Prerogative and honour of the King, as is so vainely alledged by them; But the true cause and matter of the quarrell is, That Priests and Iesuites may domineere and govern in the Kings councell as formerly, That the Bishops may suppresse powerfull preaching, and introduce the Popish Religion under colour of the Protestant profession, That the Earle of *Bristoll*, Lord *Digby*, Master *Iermyn*, and other Traytors may govern the affaires of State, and be distributers of Preferments; That Delinquents may escape the Iustice of Parliament, and triumph in the spoyles of honest men, That through our troubles the Rebels in *Ireland* may prevaile, That We may cease to be a free Nation, and become the object of cruelty and oppression at home, and of scorne and infamy abroad, &c. With this Declaration, there were certaine Votes published, resolved upon the Question by both Houses of Parliament, *viz*. That such persons as shall not contribute to the charge of the Common-wealth in this time of imminent necessity, shall bee disarmed and their persons secured.

The M.P. Sir John Evelyn was a committed member of the war party in 1642, and was one of the commissioners for peace against whom the king took exception. This report of his speech is dated 9 November. The passage continues with a contrasting and deatailed account of a battle.

Speciall Passages and Certain Informations
Numb. 14

8–15 November, 1642 605.14 {1.49}

SIR *JOHNEVELIN* this day made a Speech in the House of Commons to this purpose: That the troubles of his heart were such, that he could not protract the time any longer, but speak his mind, that his misfortune was great to be the man marked out (by the evill Counsellours about his Majestie) in such a way as to necessitate the breach of a Treaty of peace, so much sought for by the Parliament, and so much desired by the people, that if the laying down of his life and fortune would be a meanes of a happy reconciliation betweene the King and Parliament, hee would most cheerefully sacrifice both. That he cannot but account it a great honour both houses have done unto him (as a member of Parliament) to declare they cannot admit of the exception his Majestie hath taken to his person, and in him to the Parliament it selfe: but hee should account it a great honour, happinesse, and content to his own minde, that they would be pleased to waive him, and give way the rest designed for this service might goe with the Petition, that it may not be said that for a punctillo of honour, though the honour of the Kingdome must be upheld, thousands of persons of honour and wealth will perhaps be found wallowing in their owne blood, whereas upon the Treaty, if the King condiscend not to the just demands of Parliament to settle both matters concerning Religion and liberty, and the security and safety of the Parliament and Kingdome, and the priviledges of the Parliament so much violated by the King in this exception he hath taken, then are you cleare before God and man, of having sought all possible wayes and meanes to obtaine your rights: and then let us every man enter into a strict Oath of Association with life and fortune, not to lay downe Armes till we bring the King to his greatest honour, to sit in Parliament, and bring to justice those Traytors that have thus seduced his Majestie: and least the City (whose assistance to the Parliament in this imminent time of danger, is ever to be had in memory) should thinke that this Treaty will hinder our preparations, or marching towards the adverse party; let both Houses joyne in an Order, to desire the Lord Generall to draw out his Army to morrow, and the Drumme to beate this afternoone on paine of death, every man to be at his Coulours to morrow morning at eight of the clocke, and that at the same time the Parliament give some testimony to the Souldiers of their sensiblenesse of their faithfull service done by them in the late Battell, and to give each of the foote 2.s. 6.d. and 5.s. to every Horseman, and to encourage them for the future service they shall doe, they shall not need to doubt of the Parliaments care of them for a reward. And lastly, that the City be sent unto with all speed, to hasten the additional forces, under the Command of the Earle of *Warwicke* that they may march also. {...}

Upon Saturday the Kings answer was communicated to both Houses by the Earle of Northumberland, wherein his Majesty calls God to witnesse of his great desire of a peace, and to avoid the destruction and effusion of the blood of his Subjects, offering to treate at Windsor, or any where else where he shall reside, &c. This answer was received by both Houses, with a great deale of ioy, thinking his Maiesties heart had gone alongst with his expression, but it seemes it was the least of his thoughts, for that very morning (being Saturday, and a very great misty morning, fit to attempt and execute any bloody and treacherous designe) he sends from Colebrooke to Sion 8. Regiments of his foote, sixe pieces of Ordnance, and 20. Troopes of Horse, and suddenly they fell upon Colonell *Hollis* his Regiment that were quartered at Brainford (being the red Regiment, those honest religious souldiers, that to their great honour and fame, had fought so couragiously, and valiantly in the late Battle at Keneton, and cut off divers of them, who fought with all that force of the Kings from 12. a clock, untill halfe an houre past 3. in the afternoone, then my Lo, *Brookes* his Regiment came in to their reliefe, and at last the green Coats, Colonell *Hampdens* Regiment came and charged them five times over, whereupon they retreated, and the Lo: *Brookes*, with Colonell *Hampden*, and the remainder of Colonell *Hollis* his Regiment retreated to the Lord Generall: Newes of the cutting off the red Coats (the only terror of the Cavaliers) was carryed to the King at Hunsloe, who came with great ioy on Sunday morning to his souldiers at Brainford, encouraging them to goe on, and they should have brave and plentifull pillage in London; glorying at the sight of the dead bodies of our men as he went along, commending his souldiers for their valour in slaying of them; But God who is iust, and is the only searcher of hearts can vindicate his honour, and iustly punish in due time any that shall dissemblingly take his name in vaine, and call God to witnesse one thing, but intend another.

The King was so terrified with the sight of the Earle of Essex his Army, who faced him and his *Dammee* Regiments on Sunday morning till two of the clocke in the afternoone, and then the Kings Army not daring to stirre out of the Towne and their Trenches, they were forced and scattered with the Cannon onely, insomuch that the King was glad to make all hast away, and no doubt with a troubled conscience, for that he had consented to such a treacherous, Jesuiticall, unchristianly, and unkinglike accommodation, in being a cause of the shedding of so much blood, under the signed expression of calling God to witnesse, &c. This horrible and unnaturall accommodation of the Kings, so operated with the Parliament, that they voted that there should be no cessation of Armes, nor any accommodation but that the Lord Generall should revenge this bloody act of the Kings upon his Cavaliers: and on Sunday, when the Parliaments forces were disposed into a Battalia, the King sent one *White* a Courtier (commonly called *Dorset White*) with a Trumpeter to the Lord Generall to desire a parley, but the Parliament clapt him and the Trumpeter up in the Gatehouse, and would not hearken to a parley for that the King had dealt so unfaithfully with them, that when they had agreed to accommodation, and had his assent confirmed by his invocation of God to witnesse, &c. and that all the world may see the counsells and plots of Iesuits are prevalent with the King in causing him to violate his words, and the knowne law of Armes, even during the very time that *White* and the Trumpeter was comming with their message, and on their way almost at *Hammersmith*, and before he had delivered his message to the Lord Generall, the King himselfe in person (as divers in *Brainford* can witnesse) commanded them to give fire against a Pinnace imployed by the Parliament on Thames neare *Syon*, and plaid upon her with his Ordnance and Musqueteers for two houres, till the Saylers in her (having spent their shot) were forced to betake themselves to their long Boate, and having laid a traine of powder, they blew up the Pinnace, and so sunke her, that the King might make no advantage of her Guns, and the men got safe away with their Boate: This unkinglike accommodation, so to destroy his Subiects when the Accommodation was agreed unto, hath lost his Maiesty the hearts of many of the blinded Malignants that stood for him before, both in the City, and parts adiacent, for now they well perceive whereto the faire speeches of his Protestations, and Invocations tend: And for the carriage of the Kings Army, poore Brainford is made a miserable spectacle, for they have taken from them all the linnen, bedding, furniture for beds, pewter, brasse, pots, pans, bread, meale, in a word, all that ever they have, insomuch that when the Parliaments Army came into the Towne on Sunday in the evening, the Innekeepers and others begged of the souldiers a piece of bread, So that it may be truly said, a great part of the Kings Army consists of Rogues and Thieves, and in these their barbarous outrages they are cherished; it is feared by the King himselfe.

This report is dated 21 November.

A Continvation Of certain Speciall and Remarkable passages informed to both Houses of Parliament Number 20.

20–24 November, 1642 638.20 {1.50}

UPon Monday last as was appointed, the House of Commons entred into debate of the Kings Message which they received the Satterday before, wherein his Majesty againe urgeth the Parliament, that they would proceed in drawing up such propositions as may tend to peace and reconcile the differences betweene him and his Parliament; and that if the Parliament would speedily hasten the sending of the same to his Majesty, he was resolved to withdraw himselfe to Oxford, and would leave his Army at some distant whereby a Committee of the Houses might with more safty repaire to him to treat concerning the same.

But if the Houses refused to accept of his Maiesties Proffer to treat with him for a peace, his Majesty was willing to put an end to the pressures this Kingdome hath long groaned under by giving them a speedy battell.

The consideration of this businesse occasioned a very long debate in the House of Commons, many speeches being made about the same, some moving that to satisfie his Majesty and the whole Kingdome in the further expression of their willingnesse to imbrace a peace if it might bee obtained upon any honorable termes, and to send some propositions to his Majesty for a Treaty according to his desire.

Others alleadging what little effect their severall motions and Petitions to his Majestie concerning a Treaty hath wrought, his Majesty being so farre engaged to the Traitors and Malignants about him, who have hitherto frustrated all opportunities or appearances of peace: That there is little hopes of peace can bee procured so long as such evill and wicked Councellors are prevalent with his Maiestie, whose onely ayme in seeking of a Treaty is but to make delay and spin out time to tyre the Kingdome and wast their stocke, whereby at length they may procure their owne ends upon them.

The controversie was very great on both sides, there being a very full House that day in the Commons at least 200. of their members that debated the businesse, and at length it was resolved upon the Question that the House should bee turned into a Grand Committee to consider what answer should be returned to his Maiesty concerning his Propositions, which was done accordingly; and the Commons sate all day on Munday from nine of the clocke in the Morning till eight at night, and never refreshed themselves in all that tyme to consult thereof. And in the conclusion they agreed upon this vote: That his Maiestie should be desired himselfe in person to returne to his Parliament and treate with them in a Parliamentary way of such propositions as may reconcile the differences betweene them, the Parliament being the most properest place for a Treaty to settle the great distractions of the Kingdome.

And after the passing of that vote, it was put to the Question by the Commons whether there should be any additions made to that vote, or that it should passe as it was, and the House was devided upon the Question, but it was carried by the maior part, that there should be something further added to that vote by way of Proposition to his Maiesty, the debate of which businesse was referred till the next day.

On Tuesday last the Commons againe fell in debate of the busines for accomodation, and they agreed to some additions to the former vote for his Majesty returning to his Parliament.

That his Majesty would be pleased to give his consent to all those bills and Acts of grace which have been agreed upon by both Houses of Parliament and made ready for his Majesty to passe viz. the bill of Tonnage and Poundage, the bill for the assembly of the Clergy, the bill for the taking away of all innovations in the Church and the bill for the Militia (as I take it) is one, and some other Bills.

And it was further voted to be desired of his Majesty that he would give way and free liberty to the Parliament to settle Religion, the Lawes, and liberties of the subiect.

And also another vote was then agreed upon that his Majesty would deliver up delinquents to be proseeded against in a legall way according to Law and the course of parliament. And that in perticuler for the present his Majesty would forthwith deliver vp the Lord Digby and Comissary Wilmott to the Iustice of the Parliament being two notorious Traytors and chiefe agents in this Warr.

All which votes passing with consent in the House of Commons they were delivered to the Lords at a conference for their assent.

And the Commons also desired the Lords to ioyne with them in an addition to the foresaid votes, to acquaint his Majesty with the deep sence the Houses have of that strange and un-Kinglike expression of his Majesties in Challenging his Subjects to fight with him, and how contrary the same is to his Majesties late Propostitions, and often invocation to God to wittnes his tendernes, and unwillingnes to shedd the bloud of his Subiects.

The Commons likewise desiring the Lords to Ioyne with them in giveing order to the Lord Generall to advance with his Army in pursuit of the Kings forces and that he should omitt no opportunity of falling upon them not withstanding the foresaid propositions to be sent to his Majesty, untill such time as they should reseive his Majesties answer and consent to the same.

CHAPTER TWO

The Voice is Jacob's voice, but the hands are the hands of Esau: Linguistic aspects of war

> Pray now dear child, for sacred *Zions* sake,
> Oh pity me, in this sad perturbation,
> My plundered Townes, my houses devastation,
> My ravisht virgins, and my young men slain,
> My wealthy trading faln, my dearth of grain,
> The seed time's come, but Ploughman hath no hope,
> Because he knows not, who shall inn his crop:
> The poore they want their pay, their children bread,
> Their wofull mother's tears unpitied.
>
> (Anne Bradstreet)[1]

The Civil War brought with it the social consequences of civil war: riven families, atrocities, daily bloodshed. The newsbooks were fairly clear about that.

But there was political capital in stories which brought to the reader's attention the face of battle. Nehemiah Wallington, artisan and reader of newsbooks, referred to Prince Rupert, the royalist captain, as 'Prince Robber'. The reputation of the Cavaliers for cursing, drinking, whoring and committing execrable and merciless outrages was particularly conceived in the early years of the first civil war. Historians have tended to concur that Prince Rupert's cavalry were disorderly and ill-behaved, at least when away from the battlefield.

It was not only the royalist forces that were reported to transgress the boundaries of decency. *Mercurius Aulicus*, the first

1 From 'A Dialogue between Old *England* and New, concerning their present troubles. Anno 1642.' in *The Tenth Muse* (London, 1650), p.187. There is a modern facsimile edition, ed. Josephine K. Piercy (Gainesville, FL: Scholars' Facsimiles & Reprints, 1965).

issue of which appeared on Sunday, 7 January 1643 (probably to annoy the Puritans who thought that the Lord's day should be devoted to spiritual exercises), was the king's response to the London newsbooks. The reports in the latter legitimated the parliament's actions and largely blamed the war on the king's malignant and evil advisers: *Aulicus* sought to redress the balance by 'communicating the intelligence, and affaires of Court, to the rest of the Kingdome.' In its propaganda exercises it represented the parliamentarian troops as heretical rebels, led by men of low birth and only a selfish morality. Another Oxford newsbook, *Mercurius Rusticus*, written by Bruno Ryves, proclaimed itself 'The Covntries Complaint of the Murthers, Robberies, Plundrings, and *other Outrages*, Committed by the Rebells, on His Majesties faithful Subjects'. With the eighteenth issue this changed to concern itself with violences perpetrated 'On the Cathedrall Churches of this Kingdome', emphasising the apostacy of the rebels. More of a periodical than a newsbook, *Rusticus* documented at tedious length the parliamentarians' crimes, always stating in detail the financial losses of the victims, which Ryves juxtaposed against the economic and moral poverty of the criminals.

The apparent success of *Aulicus* concerned the supporters of parliament, and led them to commission Captain Thomas Audley to produce an alternative to the propaganda of the royalist editors Peter Heylin and John Berkenhead.[2] Audley employed Marchamont Nedham who soon entirely took over their newsbook, *Mercurius Britanicus*. Under Nedham, this witnessed the demise of *Aulicus* followed by successive crushing defeats of the king's forces. The more aggressive propaganda of the parliamentarians did not differ greatly in terms of technique from that of their enemy. They described in detail the war crimes committed by the king's soldiers, mocked their inept conduct, they overlooked or ignored their own side's failings: they sought to dispirit the enemy forces, implying that the soldiers of both sides read the other's propaganda. The parliamentarians could even mock the social station of the Welsh troops which assisted the royalists: and, unfortunately, their attitudes to women were roughly as unenlightened.

What these verbal encounters made clear was that the war was fought on paper as well as on the battlefield, and that both sides

2 On Berkenhead see P.W. Thomas, *Sir John Berkenhead 1617–1679: A Royalist Career in Politics and Polemics* (Oxford: Clarendon Press, 1969).

were quite prepared to sacrifice certain kinds of truth in return for the appearance of moral and military superiority. This is not to say that the newsbook writers consistently lied about the outcome of battles, though they certainly did that as well; but that linguistic strategies determined what was said as much as the records of events. In 1661 Lewis Griffin wrote:

> *Printing* and *Guns* are two modern inventions, & the one as well as the other hath made the *leaden Mine* as destructive to mankind as the golden; Men may be said to shoot from the *Press* as well as from the *Artillery*, some (like *Jehu*) to wound, others (like *Jonathan*) to warn; that is either by writing of *railing invectives*, or *sober exhortations*; *Polemicall discourses* are like shooting at a mark, which mark ought to be truth, *Schismatical Pamphlets* are *Granado's*, *Playes*, and *Romances* are squibs & crackers which though they wound not with their bullets, yet they blind with their powder.[3]

It was not that the pen, or moveable type, was mightier than the sword, but that they could do similar kinds of things. Certainly neither tended to increase the probability of political reconciliation. At a later date Andrew Marvell apostrophized: '*O Printing!* how hast thou disturb'd the Peace of Mankind! that Lead, when moulded into Bullets, is not so mortal as when founded into Letters!'[4]

The conflicts between truth and rhetoric as they appeared in exchanges between rival newsbooks no doubt gave ammunition to those who thought that all newsbook writers were scurrilous incendiaries. The following extracts outline some of the linguistic aspects of war, and evoke the confusion or uncertainty created amongst their contemporary readers, who by them could have been brought to confront the influence the distribution of information has upon human realities.

3 L[ewis]. G[riffin]. *Essayes and Characters* (London, 1661), sig.A5v-A6. Wing G1982A.

4 *The Rehearsal Transpros'd and The Rehearsal Transpros'd The Second Part*, ed. D.I.B. Smith (Oxford: Clarendon Press, 1971), p.5.

These first three entries describe individual encounters, acts of heroism and unusual military strategy. They represent early newsbook descriptions of battle at their most entertaining. The first was written 'by Master Godwin'.

A perfect Diurnall of All the proceedings of the English and Scotch Armies in Ireland
July 18. 1642

From the 14 of June to this present. {2.01}

June the 16. our men having made a breach in the Castle, assaulted it, but found the Enemie desperately resolute, reviling and calling them English doggs, Parliament Rebells, Puritan rogues, and holding up some of their best apparell and linnen at their sword points, and topps of Pikes, and setting fire unto them burnt them in our sight, saying, look here you pillaging Rascals there is pillage for you, and when our Gunners shot, they cryed shoot home you rogues, Captaine *Stutuile* having thrown in at the breach some hand grenadoes, part of the house took fire, which some of them seeing, resolutely burnt their armes, goods, and lastly themselves therein, others cryed for quarter, but none being granted but to the women and children, they resolutely defended themselves, and kept our men almost two houres at the breach at push of pike, throwing stones, slates, and hot liquor, in great abundance on them, spoyling many, yet our men encouraged by the example of Captain *Stutuile,* seconded him, and valiantly forced an entrance, killing many in the Castle, and found many that had bin killed by our shot, drawn into severall corners, the rest crying out, and begging for quarter, were brought out and stripped by our men and immediatly slain, being guessed in the totall at 140 persons, besides the women and children who had their liberty; we lost about 30 men, and many wounded, {...}

A letter from Scotland addressed to both houses, informing them of proposals for peace, also contained the following news story. The report is dated 15 August, the day the letter was read.

A Trve Relation of Certaine Speciall and Remarkable Passages from both Houses of Parliament

15–19 August, 1642 638.01 {2.02}

It was also by the said Letter informed that the Scottish Army in *Ireland* by a politick exployt have seized upon an eminent and chiefe Castle in the province of *Munster*, and killed a great number of the Rebells, the manner of the attempt was thus; The *Scotts* appeared upon a Hill neere the said Castle in two severall companies, one Company thereof had their owne Colours, with great store of Kyne and other booty; and the other had contrary colours, as if they were of the Rebells part, the two companies did skirmish with each other for some time upon the said Hill, with Pouder, shot, but no Bulletts; the greatest part of them with the Scottish Colours in a fained manner fell to the gound like dead men in the said skirmish: whereupon the Garison in the Castle having viewed the Battel, and the great overthrow given to the *Scotts*, the Rebells Colours having put the other to flight, and seized upon their booty with small joy ranne all out of the Castle unarmed with loud acclamations for the victory, expecting to take part of the spoyle, but the presupposed Rebels fell upon them, cut all their throats, and presently possessed themselves of the castle, where they found great booty.

Speciall Passages and certain Informations from severall places Numb. 4.

30 August – 6 September, 1642 605.04 {2.03}

Norhampton, Septemb. 1.

There was one passage this week in Warwickshire, I cannot but give you notice of it: Prince *Robert* with 300. Foot, and 600. Horse, beset Mr. *Purefeyes* house (who defends Warwick Castle against the Cavaliers) and demanded entrance, his Son in Law which kept the house, refused it, and said it was his Castle, yet if any

Gentleman desired singly to come in, he would give them entertainment, which was slighted, and the word past to give fire, which the Welch being his foot performed, and were presently answered with Musquet shot from the house, killing two of them dead, which made the rest to run, but a Colonell, a very proper man, calling them together, brought them on again, but with ill sucesse, for from the house they levelled so right, that they shot the Colonel, and Lieutenant Colonel dead in the place, and made the other to keep without shot, Then Prince *Robert* commands a Serjeant Major to Gallop up the Horse to the Gates of the house, to alight, and storm the house, upon their advance they made good marke, shot the Serjeant Major, and three more dead, wounding divers others, the rest glad to retreate, then they fired and burnt the out-houses to the ground: At last prince *Robert* beat for parley, those of the house advised upon it, being but 8. men, a Gentlewoman of 80. yeares age, and 2. maids, the old Gentlewoman advised them not to yeeld, but to fight it out to the last, and shee would make bullets for them, as fast as they could use them (most of their bullets being spent) and during the parley she made bullets accordingly, and caused the 12. men that staid within to appeare with Hats, sometimes with white Caps, other times with Hats and feathers in severall places of the house conspicuous to their adversaries, which made their number to be apprehended farre greater then it was: At last told Master *Abbot*, Mr. *Purefeyes* Son in Law, that he was a stout man, & had defended his house bravely, but that it might not be said that *Prince Robert* was compelled to retreate, not gaining of his ends, perswaded that he would yeeld himselfe, and the rest with him as his prisoners, and upon his honor he would see them safely conducted towards *Coventry*, and that a Lock should be hanged upon the doore, and no damage done to the house, which conditions for many respects Mr. *Abbot* accepted of, and prince *Robert* accordingly performed his word.

A Perfect Diurnall Of the Passages in Parliament *Numb.* 13.

5–12 September, 1642 512.13A {2.04}

Thursday. {8th ...}

There was also a petition presented to the House, with the names of divers poore Gentlemen Souldiers, who have spent long time and great estates in *Germany* and other places of War-like imployments, humbly beseeching the House that they may be intrusted in some Office of credit in this present Expedition, which for want of habit, money, and friends cannot get preferment so soone as many rawe giddy youth handicrafts-men, as Taylors, Barbers, players, nay Butchers now are imployed through the meanes of their money, or the loane of players garments, before such as have served an apprentiship in forraigne Nations, wee have observed in other parts, as *Germany, Swethland, Poland, Denmarke*, and *Holland*, the Schooles of Martiall Discipline, that no Officers or Commanders are made choice of to beare Office, but such as shall be knowne to be expert and skilfull in Martiall affaires, though perchance a younger brother may buy a Colours, yet seldome seene but of late, and in those parts it hath beene knowne that a Gentleman hath served seven, ten, yea fifteen yeeres before they could attaine to carry the Colours, but now we daily see a young Gentleman that hath spent three months study at the Universities, and from thence as much time in the Innes of Court or Chancery, he shall be exalted to a Captaines place, if not a Colonell, to command others, though not able to command himselfe, your Petitioner will maintaine and justifie these things with their lives: Referred to the consideration of a Councell of Warre.

The following three London newsbooks represent the irreligious and uncontrolled behaviour of royalist soldiers.

A Perfect Diurnall of the Passages in Paliament *Num.* 14

12–19 September, 1642 511.14D {2.05}

Tuesday. {13th}

LEtters of intelligence came to the House, that the Doctors of *Christ-Church-Colledge, Queens Colledge, Maudlins College,* S. *Iohns Colledge, New Colledge*, and *Corpus Christi Colledge*, have beene great agents and peace-breakers in assisting of the Cavaliers, whereof it is supposed Doctor *Pinckey* of S. *Iohns* Colledge is taken 15. miles beyond *Oxford*, riding to *Yorke*, and he with many others are comming to the Parliament, and that the Scholars and Inhabitants of the said City have left it a desolate wildernesse, so that what with the

Cavaliers and Scholars, that famous University, the flower of the world, is more like a barne, then a City of education and learning.

England's Memorable Accidents

19–26 September, 1642 579.03 {2.06}

MUNDAY, 19. *of Septemb.*

THe Cavaliers have made lately great havock in *Derbishire*, they draw Ordnance along with them to force men houses; they rifle all to a thread, they seize upon Pots, Ketles, Pannes and Pewter; they cut and breake in pieces Tables, Chaires, Stooles, Chests, Truncks and Bedsteads; they teare and cut in sunder pillowes, boulsters, and feather beds, strowe the feathers about the Chambers, and carry away the Tikes; they draine the Wine and Beere in sellers out of the vessells, and overturne the Milke-bowles in the dayries, they drive away all the cattell they can find of all sorts, they leave not a Pike, Musquet, Sword or Halbert in any mans house, and demeane themselves more barbarously and execrably, then the Immane Crabats did in desolate *Germany*.

Speciall Passages and certain Informations from severall places Numb. 9.

4–11 October, 1642 605.09A {2.07}

Out of Shropshire,

It is certainly informed by a godly Minister not far from *Shrewsbury*, that in one great house which the Cavaleers have plundered and pillaged, they did plainly and openly professe they had little to live on, but what they took from others; and that when they went to bed (being about 60. of them) divers of them had Crucifixes hanging about their necks. In another great house where they were, they dranke a health to the good successe of Sir *Philem O Neale* in *Ireland*, of the Gentlemans own Beere, and in presence of himselfe, and divers of his servants.

These relations are certaine, and will bee proved by divers faithfull eye and eare witnesses: by which we may see how likely these men are to maintain the true Protestant Religion, the Lawes of the Land, the lawfull liberties of the Subjects, whatsoever they pretend. And though they pretend they search only for Armour, yet they break up, and take away whatsoever is of worth, or can well be carried away, and spoil many other things, cutting them in pieces; and many of them (especially in out-townes and villages) where they are billetted, pay nothing for what they have, and take away many horses from the people.

Also the Cavaleers did ravish the wife of a very discreete, moderate, able and godly Minister in *Shropshire*, whose name is thought fit to conceale, out of respect to the person, who is a very sober and vertuous woman; and such was their impudence, that this was done whilest the Kings Majesty himselfe was in the Towne (or not far off) as is affirmed by divers persons of know credit in these parts.

A year after the London apprentices demonstrated for the uprooting of episcopacy, the atmosphere in London could be very different.

Speciall Passages And certain Informations Numb. 18

6–13 December, 1642 605.18 {2.08}

On Thursday last at Haberdashers Hall, there met divers people, many of them consisting of Proctors, Apparators, and persons of inferior quallity, to subscribe a Petition for Peace (as they termed it) and would have it presented to the Committee at Guild Hall, whether they came, who adviced them (if it were expressed in fitting language) to present it to the House: they all cryed *Peace, Peace* on any tearmes; others that were not privy to the Petition, said *Peace and truth together*; they replied, hand Truth, pox a God take Truth, let us have peace on any tearmes: and we resolve to die together if it bee not granted: The Lord Major seised on one of their Petitions with hands subscribed unto it, which advised the Parliament to follow the steps of the Petitioners predecessors, and to take a speedy course against Papists and Sectaries, and that so long as their proceedings were for peace, they would assist them, whereas hitherto scarce one man of all those that appeared, hath contributed one penny to the Parliament in all their great extremities. But this disorderly carriage of these men (of purpose to raise a combustion) pretending (though falsely) that a Petition was delivered against Peace in gennerall, whereas it was against peace that was not safe and honourable, did not divert the thoughts of the graver and wiser sort from subscribing to a Petition for Peace, in a modest, humble and respective manner (against which no man can speake) with reference to the wisdome of the Parliament in acquiring of it, whose indefatigable labours have sufficiently testified, it is the publique, and not their private ends, that have made them for above 2 yeares incessantly to serve the Common-wealth, even to the ruine of divers of their fortunes.

The following is the opening passage from the first dedicated Royalist newsbook, published at Oxford under the authority of the king, and initially edited by Peter Heylin. It may therefore be read as an attempt to define royalist journalism, with a set of values and style of authentication in opposition to the more common pro-parliament newsbook. In *Areopagitica* (1644) Milton described it as 'that continu'd Court-libell against the Parlament and City'.

Mercvrivs Avlicvs, Communicating the intelligence, and affaires of the Court, to the rest of the Kingdome. The first Weeke.

{1–7 January, 1643} 275.101B {2.09}

THe world hath long enough beene abused with falshoods: And there's a weekly cheat put out to nourish the abuse amongst the people, and make them pay for their seducement. And that the world may see that the Court is neither so barren of intelligence, as it is conceived; nor the affaires thereof in so unprosperous a condition, as these Pamphlets make them: it is thought fit to let them truly understand the estate of things that so they may no longer pretend ignorance, or be deceived with untruthes: which being premised once for all, we now go on unto the businesse; wherein we shall proceed with all truth and candor.

SUNDAY. *Jan.* 1.

New-yeares-day shall give entrance to this new designe. And that which was the greatest businesse and discourse thereof, was the report which came from *Burford* in the morning of Sir *John Byrons* carriage and behaviour there. At first reported variously (as in such actions commonly it doth use to be) according as men feared or hoped: but afterwards before night, a more exact and punctuall relation of it was brought from thence, which in briefe was thus. On Friday being the 30. day of *December*, Sir *John* had order to march with his whole Regiment to *Burford* (a towne about twelve miles from *Oxford*) to convey thither two cart loads of ammunition for the Lord Marquesse of *Hartford*, who was expected the next day at *Stow*, with all his forces. Being arrived at his quarter, his first enquiry was what forces the Rebels had at *Cyrencester*, or any other placce adjoyning. In which when as he could receive no satisfaction from the Townesmen there, hee sent a party of horse that night towards *Cyrencester*, who went within a mile & an halfe of the towne, and brought word, that there were not aboue 500 dragoons there quartered, the horse which had bin there being marched to *Tedbury*. The next day being Saturday there was little newes, more then the day before had yeelded. But about seaven of the clocke at night, a party that had beene sent forth towards the enemies, brought word, that about two miles from the towne in the way to *Cyrencester* they had discovered foure Dragoons with light matches, who so soone as they made towards them, rid backe so fast that they could by no means overtake them. Sir *John* imagining by this discovery that there might be some designe that night upon his Quarter, commanded Captaine St *John* to ride towards *Cyrencester* with forty horse; and that the whole Regiment should be in a readinesse at the first sound of the Trumpet, and went himselfe unto the top of the hill, where diverse wayes meets, where he placed a guard of 25. horse, and saw the Sentinell set forth upon the severall Avenues. At his returne, contrary unto his command and expectation, he found that one halfe of the men who were appointed to goe with Captaine St. *Iohn*, were not yet on horsebacke, but before farther Order could be given concerning them, a musket or two went off, and thererupon the Alarme was given, that the Rebels were entred into the towne already. On this Sir *Iohn* taking the next horse that came to hand, armed with his sword onely went towards the market place: where meeting his Lieutenant Colonell, hee commanded him to take a competent number of horse, and make good the bridge, lest if the enemy had tooke it the way might have beene stopped betwixt him and the Marquesse; the Ammunition being sent meane time, with a guard of 30 horse towards *Stow*, where the Marquesse was that day expected, as before was said. By this time it was known for certain both by the fire and by the report of the Muskets that the Rebels were about the white Hart, being an Inne in the utmost part of the Towne, from whence a lane leadeth to the Market Crosse. And therfore making thither with all the speed he could, he found the lane full of Musketeers, who were ready to enter the high street, & the guard of horse which had been left there, retreating as well as they could out of the danger of the shot. Sir *Iohn* considering hereupon, that should the enemy possesse the Crosse, and the houses on either side the streete, it was not possible for him to continue there, nor do any service with his horse against them beeing sheltred and defended: commanded those who were next to follow him, and rushed in upon them, laying about him with his sword, for other weapons hee had none, as was said before. No sooner was he got amongst them, but some of those which were furthest gave fire upon him; which doing no hurt, they presently betooke themselves to flight in a great confusion, some crying that they were for the King, and some for Prince *Rupert*. In this confusion hee drave them before him to the further end of the lane where the Inne standeth, into which they ran: & into which he entring pell mell with them, received a blow on the face with a Pole-axe or Holbard, wherewith hee was in danger to have fallen from his horse. But quickly recovering himselfe againe, hee saw the Inne-doore full of Musketeeres, and himselfe alone unarmed and naked of defence in the open street, and thereupon returned backe to the market crosse, where he found his men, who had mistaken his command conceiving that they were to have tarried there to make good that place. Upon his comming backe, Captaine *Apsley* rid up to the Inne-doore, which hee entred with much danger, but no hurt; a Trooper of Sir *Iohns* beeing kill'd in following him, and a few more wounded. But whilst he entred in at the fore-doore, the enemies despairing of successe, stole out at the backe-doore: and taking the benefit of a darke night, escaped the present danger, and recovered their horses: but fled not with such secrecie, but that their flight was quickly knowne, and themselves pursued; the chase being followed at the least sixe miles. But being the night was wondrous darke and the Moone not risen, few of them could be overtaken: so that the businesse ended with the losse of one man onely of Sir *Iohn Byrons*, and the hurting of fower onely besides himselfe; there being killed some twenty of the Enemies, or thereabouts. The whole number of them was conceived to be 200. whereof *Buck* was thought to be the Leader; but this uncertaine. The soldiers being returned from the chase, and the moone now up, Sir *Iohn* gave order to his Regiment to march away to *Stow* with the Ammunition, which he had caused to be conveyed beyond the bridge at the first alarme, himselfe with some few followers going to a friend, where he might both refresh his body, and apply fit things unto his wound. One passage must not be omitted, which in briefe is this. A Trooper of Sir *Iohns* had tooke a Prisoner, (who by his apparell seemed to be an officer) and asked him being sore wounded, who hee was for, he answered, for the devill I thinke; his conscience as it seemes, representing to him, the damnable and desperate cause hee was like to die in. And so much for the businesse of *Burford*, which I have here related with the more particulars, to satisfie all those who have beene otherwise informed of the carriage of it.

Newsbooks, both royalist and parliamentarian, scrutinized the words and actions of military men very closely, in search of divine interpretation. Compare with {2.25}.

Mercvrivs Avlicvs The eleventh Weeke

{12–18 March, 1643} 275.111 {2.10}

TUESDAY. *March* 14. {...}

This day also by letters out of *Stafford-shire* there came advertisement of some remarkeable pasages, preceding the Lord Brookes death, which were not signified before, *viz.* that at his going out of *Coventry* when he went towards *Lichfeild* he gave order to his Chaplaine, that he should preach upon this text, *if I perish I perish*, being the words of *Hester* in a different, but farre better cause, *Hest.*c.4.v.16: that in a prayer of two houres long which he conceived before his setting on the towne, he was heard to wish, that *if the cause he was in were not right and just, he might be presently cut off*; using the like expressions to his soldiers also. Which being compared with the event, may serve sufficiently to convince the *conscience* of those, who have beene hitherto seduced unto a good opinion of so fowle a cause, that it is neither *justifiable* in it selfe, nor *acceptable* unto God. And it was furthermore obsevred (besides his being killed on S. *Chads* day, by whose name, as being the first Bishop of the *Mercians* that Church which he assaulted, is, and hath anciently beene called) that he who had so often vaunted that he hoped to live to *see the day* when one stone of S. *Pauls* in *London* should not be left upon another, should be killed in the eye, and the lid not touched: that he who did dislike the *Letany* for no one thing more then for the prayer therein *against suddaine death* should be killed stone dead, (the bullet passing through the *eye* unto the *throat*) and not speake one word. Which passages and observations I wish were heartily considered of by his *Accomplices*; who being as deepe as he in this *Rebellion* against God and the King, have little reason to expect any better ends, if they have not worse.

Mercvrivs Avlicvs The foureteenth Weeke

2–9 April, 1643 275.114 {2.11}

In the *London* Diurnall for the last week, ending on Munday *April* 3. it is given out, that in the Earle of *Northampton's* pockets were found three *Crucifixes*, one *Agnus Dei*, and a protection from the *Pope*: a very fine impudent slander, and of no more truth then that Sir *Will. Waller* hath taken *Cyrencester*, which is reported confidently in one of their *Newes-bookes*, and that the Earle of *Essex* came on Sunday seavennight with all his forces unto the very walls of *Oxford*, and stroke up an *Alarme* in our very eares, and that no body durst come out, or shew themselves before his Excellencie: all which are as true as that Prince *Rupert* was buried at *Oxford*: or that Sir *Thomas Lunsford* feedeth upon children. They have likewise printed a Sermon pretended to be Preached before His Majesty at *Oxford* by Doctor *H.K.* which is an errant forgery, the supposed author having not beene at *Oxford* since His Majesties last comming thither, having beene detained by the Rebels forces. Neither is it usuall with His Majesty to cause those Sermons to be printed here, which are preached before His Majesty, it being a late custome of the House of Commons to Order their Sermons to be printed, whereof some Worthy Members have beene both auditours and composers, not onely giving them their Texts, but most of their Sermons, as we are able to prove. Also in their Diurnall they printed that one *Ed. Colser* Esq. (one of His Majesties Justices of Peace for *Norfolke*) was slaine by some of their Souldiers as he was comming last weeke out from *Norfolke*, the gentleman desires them to correct that passage, for he saies himselfe, he is very well, and being now listed in the Kings Troop, intends to stay with His Majesty till he may returne in peace to his own Country. And the reason (no question) why they printed him dead was, that they might be his Executours, and gather his rents for him, according to the ordinance of the two Houses.

The destruction of Cheapside Cross on 2 May was repeated in accounts of stereotypical Puritanical behaviour.

Mercvrivs Avlicvs The eighteenth Weeke

{30 April – 6 May, 1643} 275.118 {2.12}

It was advertised from *London*, that upon Tuesday last, according to the Order of the *Common-Councell* of that Citie before remembred, (the House of *Commons* choosing rather to act the businesse by their hands, then appeare in it themselves) the *Crosse* in *Cheapside* (an ancient and glorious Monument of *Christianity*) was pulled downe to the very ground; and that in so triumphant and brave a manner, with sound of Trumpet, and the noise of severall instruments, as if they had obtained some remarkable victory upon the greatest enemies of the *Christian* faith. As also, that according to the Order of the House of *Commons* spoken of before, all the glasse-windowes in the *Cathedrall Church* of *Westminster*, wherein was any *Imagery* or shew of painting, were defaced and broken, the Crosse upon the top thereof tooke downe, with many other horrible outrages; which as they were not fit for a *Christians* hand, so are they most unpleasing to a *Christian* eare. It is said also, that they have begun to deface the Tombes and Monuments of the *Kings, Queenes, Princes*, and other noble Personages, which are there interred: and to say truth 'tis wisely done. For if they should intend (as some thinke they doe) a change of Government, no better was then to remove all tokens and remembrances, by which the people at the present might be put in mind, (or in time to come be brought to know it) that ever there was such a thing as a King in *England*.

Mercurius Aulicus *The foure and thirtieth Weeke*

{20–26 August, 1643} 275.134A {2.13}

THURSDAY *August*. 24.

This day in the morning it was advertised, that on Tuesday night the distressed Rebells in *Gloucester* had made two sallies, the one upon the Lord Generals quarters, the other on Sir *Iacob Astley's*; but were soone beaten backe againe (as who could expect otherwise) with the losse of many of their men. And (which is worth your notice) those Rebels, which were taken prisoners at both these sallies, were most purely drunke, the faction in the City having (for the *Cause* as they call it) filled the poor Souldiers full of strong drinke, as the onely means to make them stand, that is, to poure out their owne bloud in the act of Rebellion. And I would faine know what kind of villany these profane Hypocrites have left unattempted to make this Rebellion the worst that ever was; who not content to rob all the Kingdome (by a spirituall clayme to the creatures of the earth) doe now like Atheists abuse those blessings by enticeing silly wretches to drinke away their senses, the more compleatly to damne soule and body, by leaving the world with all their sinnes about them.

The following two excerpts recount an exchange between *Aulicus* and *Britanicus*. The first is an attempt to demoralise London parliamentarians, the second an attempt to discredit the reporter of the first. Note the interesting use of typographical space in the latter, which was, strangely, published the day before the Earl of Caernarvon was killed in battle. The war between *Aulicus* and *Britanicus* was the longest and most spectacularly bitter of the newsbook wars.

Mercvrivs Avlicvs The sixe and thirtieth Weeke

{3–9 September, 1643} 275.136A {2.14}

SATURDAY, *Septemb.* 9.

Many letters were this weeke intercepted from *London*, most of which are perswasory Epistles from the Trainband wives, labouring to recall their militant husbands who (like true Londoners) are following their Leader the Earle of *Essex*; Take one for all, superscribed *To her deare husband Master* John Owen *under Leiutenant Colonell* West *in the Blue Regiment*; the Contents to a syllable as followeth;

Most tender and deare heart, my kind affection remembred unto you, I am like never to see thee more I feare, and if you aske the reason why, the reason is this, either I am afraid the Cavaleers will kill thee, or death will deprive thee of me, being full of greif for you, which I feare will cost me my life. I doe much greive that you be so hard hearted to me, why could you not come home with your Master Murfey *on Saturday? could you not venture as well as he? but you did it on purpose to shew your hatred to me; there is none of our Neighbours with you that hath a wife but Master* Fletcher *and Master* Norwood *and your selfe, every body can come but you. I have sent one to Oxford to get a passe for you to come home, but when you come you must use your wits; I am afraid if you do not come home, I shall much dishonour God more then you can honour him, therefore if I doe miscary, you shall answer for it, pitty me for Gods sake and come home. Will nothing prevaile with you My cosen* Jane *is now with me and prayes for your speedy returne, for Gods sake come home, so with my prayer for you I rest your loving wife*

London Sept. 5. SUSAN OWEN

What a horrid odious Rebellion is this that forceth good women to such piteous *miscarriages*! Here's poore Mistresse *Susanna* in danger to perish, through this unnaturall Rebellion. But the serious Reader may take notice, that divers of these intercepted London Letters come from factious Tradesmen to Officers in the Rebells Army, wherein these Londoners seeme to offer to the Souldiers more Apprentices if the former be cut off (whereby their Masters may have more mony with new) so that if any man have a desire that his sonne or kinsman should be knockt in the head for the good of his Master, let him send them now to London, and they will see them dispatched to the Army.

Mercurius Britanicus Numb. 4.

12–19 Sept, 1643 286.004 {2.15}

He jeers us with an intercepted Letter of Mistresse *Susans* the Citizens wife, complaining for her husbands company, which she utterly disavowes; we will show you one of your Cavaliers Epistles intercepted about the same time, to a friend in *London*, onely you must excuse me, I printed not the oathes, but left spaces.

Jack,

WE have not left one Woman Lady Gentlewoman Waytingmaid or other honest we have now some Irish and Frenchwomen come to us we intend not to leave till we have sinned with all Nations as well as our owne,

thine

Carnavan.

(1)

Numb. 1.

Mercurius Britanicus:

Communicating the affaires of great

BRITAINE:

For the better Information of the People.

From Tuesday the 23. of Aug. to Tuesday the 29. of Aug. 1643.

TO begin with the unconquered part of Britaine (where many of the inhabitants) even at this day are as ignorant as heathens, in exercise of piety and true godlinesse; and therefore no marvell the Papists work on such ignorant soules (under pretence to fight for *her King*) to engage themselves, Religion and Liberty: It is certified out of *Wales*, That the *Irish Rebels* daily *land* in small vessels, in those parts, and go for *Oxford*, and *pray* for the *Queene* (openly) for that *she* hath (as they say) *upheld the Catholiques in Ireland*. And those that land there, *informe* that the *Earle of Ormond* (craving leave to digresse a little, and touch on the neighbour Nation) is returned to his quarters at *Dublin*, with his five thousand men, without attempting any honourable action, and that it is most certaine, through the slownesse of his march, or the power of the *Oxford Adjuncto* at *Dublin* over his Councels, many protestants, men, women and children were all put to the sword in a castle, which his Lordship was going to relieve: And it is certified further, the better to bring to passe the Popish designes, the Irish at *Oxford* have prevailed, not onely *to put by his Lordship* from being any more a *Commissioner* to treat with the Rebels, by the *Kings authority*, but have put those in his stead that will (if it be not done already) conclude the *Cessation of Armes* with the Rebels and that it may be the better effected, By *Authority from Oxford*, a warrant is come thither for the *committing to the Castle of Dublin three privy Councellours* (deadly enemies to the Rebels) besides Sir *William Parsons*, namly, Sir *John Temple*, Sir *Adam Loftus*, and Sir *Robert Meredith*: If they would have connived at that bloudy Rebellion, & not *protested* against a Cessation of Armes with those infamous Rebells, the *Queene* would never have prevailed to have had them put out, and clapt up in prison, as now they are, and the greatest Irish Traitors there in the Castle at *Dublin* set at liberty on their words: And who are the *Accusers* of these Privy Councellours but *Brian Geneale*, a Jesuiticall Papist, Lord *Dillon* that writes usually to the Irish Rebels in his Majesties name, and *agitates* for them at Oxford, and the last is that treacherous faithlesse *Fortescue*; if these men are fit to be so

Wales.

Ireland.

A

far

4. Parliament's paper bullet: *Mercurius Britanicus*

This is part of George Wither's assay into writing newsbooks, in which he satirizes the values of the King and the royalist party. Wither did not produce a second issue.

Mercurius Rusticus: Or, A Countrey Messenger

{October 26 1643} Wing W3171 {2.16}

We are incredibly informed from *Oxford*, that the King had no considerable losse at the skirmish by *Alborne*, or at the battell neere *Newberie*, as we have been made beleeve. It is true indeed, that he lost many *Men* and *Subjects*; but they are but trifles, and it is almost generally supposed (though hoped otherwise by me) things which he regards not. He lost also many good horses, as his own partie doth confesse; but he had them onely for taking up, and hath takers enough to recrute them: He lost Lords, and a great Officer, &c. but that is a losse the least worth notice of all the rest, for they are toyes, which if he please he can make of the veryest rascals in his Army; they did wel therefore to give God thanks that their losses were no greater: But had they been so great on our side, we should rather have addressed our selves unto him by way of humiliation, then have mocked him with a counterfet Thanks-giving, as they have often done, and may now doe againe for their late overthrows in *Lincoln-shire* and at *Hull*. {...}

It is, there, thought also by some of His Majesties servants (as our *Mercurie* verily beleeveth) that the Queen will not have so many Masks at Christmas and Shrovetide this yeare as she was wont to have other yeares heretofore; because *Inigo Iones* cannot conveniently make such Heavens and Paradises at *Oxford* as he did at *White-hall*; & because the Poets are dead, beggered, or run away, who were wont in their Masks to make Gods and Goddesses of them, and shamefully to flatter them with Attributes neither fitting to be ascribed or accepted of; and some are of opinion, that this is one of the innumerable vanities which hath made them and us become so miserable at this day. We heare not yet any particulars of the late Ambassadours entertainment at *Oxford*, but wagers may be laid that he shall heare there many lying vaunts of their valorous atchievements, and untrue allegations against the Parl. for what will not they aver in private discourses, who are not ashamed to belie them in publique, and to their face?

The opening passage from a stylistically odd newsbook, revealing an equally odd piece of Welsh mythology. This transcription of a Welsh accent is not unique. It is curious that this did not seem to make the newsbook entirely unreliable, even though the Welsh were famed for their stupidity and deceptiveness as well as their bizarre pronunciation. Calling Mercuries 'Mr' (satirically) attributed to them a gentlemanly status which they were denied.

The Welch Mercury, Communicating remarkable Intelligences and true Newes to awle the whole Kingdome *Numb.* 1

21–28 October, 1643 708.1 {2.17}

HEr have read that in *Affrick*, wilde beasts of severall kinds doe meet at certain watering places, where they couple together, and doe beget monsters, and her have lately observed, that many writers, with their confederate Intelligencers, doe concur at the Wine-spring of Taverns, to invent mis-begotten Pamphlets, or indeed, monstrous Lies, but her will upon her credit give no Informations, but such as shall be true and currant, which her will carry on in a fayre and even manner, and with her swords and daggers maintain all her Reports to be certaine verities and truths, whereupon her will with bold Confidence come forth among the other crowdes of *Mercuries*, whom her doe far exceed in ingenuity, and generous educations, and therefore her will be called, *The new Welch Mr. Mercury*. {...}

Her doe hear for certain, that the Scots are in a cheerfull reddinesse to advance forward for England, which her Countreymen doe like very well, and will joyne with her in footing of a Northerne Gigge, while harmonious money doth lead the Morrice-dance, which is better musick then all her Welch-Harpes,

When pay day comes the Souldier drinks and sings,
There is no musick without silver strings.

But her shall have much to doe with Mr. *Blew-Cap*, when her come into *England* with her creat thousands of men, but her have a plot beyond her Northerne wit, for her have a Project to presse awle her Countrey-men that are under-ground, and doe live in her Mountains, which are a people called the *Ecchoes*, her ask her tother day, if her stood for the King, and her answered, the King; then her ask't if her stood for the Parlament, and her replied for the Parliament, so that her be no Delinquent, that doth stand for the King and Parliament; and therefore her will come with an Army of *Ecchoes* and voices, that shall cry *Vivez le Roy, & le Parliament.*

There is a *Diogenes* ghost that appears in two sheets, some call him Mr. *Aulicus*, but it was no Gentlemans qualitie to raile, Ile warrant you, and there are verie great enemies to *Aulicus*; but the *Welch Mercurie* could knock *Aulicus* into better manners with blowes and bobs for his railing, but her have better imployments. {...}

It is reported that Prince *Rupert* was make awle her Townes in *England* as poore as a Welch Village; and that her shall go bare-foot and bare-legg'd, as her doe in Wales; and was have an hungrie pelly, and live upon toasted sheese in London: her hope to see Prince *Rupert* taken prisoner by her Countrie men, and then her shall pay her good ransome for her selfe, and awle her Malignant tricks. {...}

Was heare that the Bishop of Canterburie should come to Triall, and was peached of treason in creat teale of matters, and her doe ferily believe, that her Grace was deserve to have her Lawn sleeves pull'd from over her Elbows, for he did plot to bring in her old religion: Let her goe when her head is off, and complain to the Earle of *Strafford* and her Pope.

This Rusticus, distinct from the *Mercuries* written by Wither and Ryves, may have been written by the prolific journalist Henry Walker, sometime editor, amongst others, of *Perfect Occurrences* and *Perfect Passages*.

Informator Rusticus: Or, The Countrey Intelligencer *Numb.* 1

27 October – 3 November, 1643 198.1 {2.18}

The Ordnance set forth by the Parliament for the releefe of maimed Souldiers, is a great incouragement to Souldiers, and the onely cause to maintaine and uphold an Army: It is one of the principallest means used by the Spaniard for the preserving and keeping his Souldiers together. For I have observed in Flanders, throughout all those Provinces, that Hospitalls and Guest houses are appointed for maimed Souldiers only, nay the Virgines themselves are their Physitians. But this charity only is extended to Papists: For when I was there I had a great sicknesse, and during my sicknesse professed my selfe to be a Papist, and was well provided for, and being recovered, a bald pated Fryar tooke me to taske, and told me I must confesse my sinnes to him; at which I laughed at this secondary God, whereupon I had present absolution, for I was presently thrust out of the house: and had it not pleased God of his mercy to preserve me, I had perished in the way. By this you may perceive how farre and to whom this papisticall piety is extended, not to Protestants, but themselves. I wish there may never in England be cause to make use of such mens charity; yet thankes be to God it is otherwise.

In November, *Aulicus* reported that 'by his exceeding temperance and strict diet (which made him languish and still looke thin)' John Pym had 'contracted the Dropsie, and Iaundyes, and Pthyriasis'. In December the man who was more concerned with body politic than the body natural died, leaving the moderate reform party in the Commons without a leader. *Aulicus* jeered at the justness of his death, *Britanicus* printed a dignified, sober elegy.

Mercvrivs Avlicvs *The fortie ninth Weeke*

{3–9 December, 1643} 275.149 {2.19}

SATURDAY. *Decemb*. 9. {...}

We are constrained to be larger in the relation of this dayes intelligence then we expected, in regard of the remarkable newes of *John Pym's* death, the most eminent of those Five *Members*, so justly on the 4th of *January* A° 1641. accused by His Majestie of that Treason, the fruits whereof have beene and are yet so visible to this distressed Kingdome: this I cannot say famous, but notorious man, loaded with other diseases, died this very day, chiefly of the *Herodian* visitation, so as he was certainly a most loathsome and foule carkasse. However the Preacher at *Warwicke* was sensible this might open the eyes of some well-meaning, but seduced persons, when he prayed that Master *Pym* might not die of this disease, least the Cavaliers should cry it up as Gods judgement. I will denounce no more of it, but that it is remarkable how this man died, observable how Master *Hampden* (approaching the Kings residence) received his death wound in *Chalgrave* field, where he first appeared in Armes to exercise that unjust and mischievous Ordinance of the *Militia*) and my Lord *Brooke*, who loved not our Church, was slaine from one. Besides, neither living nor dead, have the prime Authors of these miseries cause to rejoyce: for those that remember what seeds of the present mischiefes Sir *John Hotham* and his sonne were, and how active and fruitfull to this Faction Master *Nathaniel Fynes* was, would thinke it strange, if not wonderfull, that at their own Barre they should all Three be now attending the sentence upon their lives. But there are a sort of men apply nothing to themselves that befalls others; they may smart soone enough themselves, and then they will have more sence of the condition this Kingdome is brought into. I will let this man and the other rest in peace, though they first disturbed the peace of our then-flourishing Kingdome, and pray to God that he will remove his judgements from us.

Mercurius Britanicus *Numb.* 16.

7–14 December, 1643 286.016 {2.20}

An Elegie on Master *Pym*.

No immature nor sullen Fate
Did his immortall soul translate,
He passed *gravely* hence, even
Kept his old pace, from *earth* to *heaven*;
He had a *soule* did alwayes stand
Open for *businesse*, like his *hand*,
He took in so much, I could call
Him more then individuall,
And so much *businesse* waited by,
Would scarcely give *him* leave to *die*;
He knew the *bounds*, and every thing
Betwixt the people and the *King*;
He could the iust *Proportions* draw
Betwixt *Prerogative* and *Law*;
He liv'd a *Patriot* here so late,
He knew each syllable of *State*,
That had our *Charters* all beene gone,
In *him* we had them every one;
He durst be *good*, and at that time
When *innocence* was halfe a *crime*;
He had seen *death* before he went,
Once had it as a *token* sent:
He surfeted on *State-affaires*,
Di'd on a *Plurisie* of *caires*,
Nor doth he now his *mourners* lacke,
We have few *soules* but go in black,
And for his sake, have now put on
A *solemne* Meditation.
Teares are too narrow *drops* for him,

And *private* sighes, too *strait* for *Pym*;
None can compleatly *Pym* lament,
But *something* like a *Parliament*,
The *publicke sorrow* of a State,
Is but a griefe *commensurate*,
We must *enacted passions* have,
And *Laws* for weeping at his grave.

The following exchange between *Aulicus* and *Britanicus* illustrates the use of the moral upper hand in wartime propaganda exercises. Whoever won the moral debate, a later issue of *Aulicus* reports that the prisoner was executed.

Mercvrivs Avlicvs *The fifty first Weeke*

{17–23 December, 1643} 275.151 {2.21}

SUNDAY. *Decemb.* 17.

YOu may remember this day three weekes, how the Rebels railed on us for telling the world what they doe on *Sundayes*. Their reason is (for some allow Them to be reasonable creatures) this day revealed by an Expresse from *Shrewsbury*; wherein it was certified among other particulars, that on *Sunday* last *Decemb.* 9. while His Majesties Forces were at Church, one of their Prisoners was missed by his Keeper, who searching for him, and looking through a cranny into the Stable, he saw a ladder erected, and the holy Rebell (busie at a Conventicle) committing Buggery on the Keepers owne Mare. The Keeper seizing on him, brought him instantly before Sir *Richard Leveson*, where being examined, he openly and plainly confessed the whole fact, for which they will speedily proceed against him, though the poore Keeper is like to loose his Mare, which (according to the Statute) must be burned to death.

This Truth hath too mush horrour in it to admit of any descant, onely be pleased to subjoyne one passage which the SCOTTISH DOVE tells you in the last Paragraph of his Pamphlet this weeke; *We are credibly informed* (saith he) *from* Rothwell *in* Northamptonshire, *of a woman (well knowne to people of credit in this Citie) that hath brought forth a childe marvellous to behold; the lower part like a Wench, the breast as blacke as a Crow, the mouth contrary, no eyes, the one eare like unto a Hound, the other eare like unto the wattell of a Hog: the head* (round) *like a Coney, and the backe like a Fish.* Thus saith the DOVE, to which I shall adde nothing, but onely repeat those words, that *the woman is well knowne to people of credit in London*; and leave the Reader to make his inference from both these Relations.

Mercurius Britanicus *Numb*. 19.

28 December – 4 January, 1643{4} 286.019 {2.22}

He tells us that one of our party, their *prisoner*, that he sayes committed buggery on a Mare, now the truth is, for ought I hear yet, he committed but onely burglary; that is, he got into the Stable, and bridled the Mare, and was endeavouring to get away; but you may see what a lewd generation they are, and how they interpret every thing into sin; and now they have bethought them of this kinde of impiety, you shall have them *sinning* with the very beasts of the field shortly, and keeping Mares for *breeding* Cavaliers on, and they may do it as lawfully as the Ladies of honour may keep Stallions and Monkies, and their Bishops Shee-goates and Ganimedes, for they make nothing of such *prodigious fornication*, they make nothing of Sodomy and Gomorrahisme, especially your Italianated Lords, and your hot privy Counsellors, that have seen fashions abroad, as *Dorset* the Earle, that hath travelled to Venice for his sins, and *Littleton*, that was once Keeper of the *seduced Seale*, and had his Concubines as common as his Law, though I am not able to give you an account of his latter trespasses; perhaps he commits now with unreasonable creatures, as *Aulicus* sayes, for I hear he hath a pretty dappled Mare, which he keeps for his own saddle: But of all sinners, your *Cathedrall men* are the worst, some of your Prebends make nothing of sinning with the little singing boyes after an Anthem; Oh! this is prodigious lust, which rages after *Organ pipes*, and *Surplisses*; I could tell you a strange story of a reverend *Prelate* that you all know, you would little imagine what doings he hath had in his Vestry, but I leave his transgression to be inserted in the next Century.

Burglary no Buggery

This describes a wartime atrocity, followed by *Aulicus'* repudiation of the justifications of that atrocity in the London newsbooks. They demonstrate the very soluble relation between language and action, which is at the heart of war propaganda.

Mercvrivs Avlicvs *The eighteenth Weeke*

{28 April – 4 May, 1644} 275.218A {2.23}

TUESDAY. *April* 30.

This day we were certified from a very good hand, that that barbarous Mariner Captaine *Swanley* lately took some small vessels comming from *Ireland*, which he brought into *Pembrooke*, *Swanley* tender'd the Covenant to all the prisoners upon paine of death; some few tooke it, but most refused. But this bloody fellow tooke the refusers, bound them backe to backe, and cast them into the Sea. Those few that tooke it to avoid present death were not all set at liberty, for the Officers were imprisoned, and threatned that if the common Souldiers who had taken the Covenant should afterwards revolt to His Majesty, he swore he would see them both hang'd and quartered. This Intelligence we had from a worthy Gentleman who at that time was prisoner in *Pembrooke*.

Mercvrivs Avlicvs *The twentieth Weeke*

{12–18 May, 1644} 275.220A {2.24}

Last weeke we gave you notice of *Swanly's* barbarous murthering those Gentlemen at *Milford Haven*, and we then beleived that so bloudy, groundlesse, and unparallel'd murther, would have put the Rebells to frame some excuses to conceale such a villany from the eye of the world: but so shamelesse and impudent are these Rebells now growne, that they triumph and applaud it as a meritorious action; all their weekely Authors from the SCOUT downe to the very SCOTTISH-DOVE, please themselves with variety of expressions in approbation of the fact; One sayes, That *Captaine* Swanley *tooke sixscore English Irish, and sent them a fishing to the bottome of the Sea*: Another sayes, That *Captaine* Swanley *made those Irish drinke their bellies full of salt-water*: Another, that *Captaine* Swanley *made those that would not take the Covenant take the water with their heads downward*.

Another, That *the Captaine made triall if an Irish Cavalier could swimm without hands*. And the WEEKLIE ACCOUNT speakes it home, That *Captaine* Swanley *tooke good store of such as came from Ireland, tyed them backe to backe, and cast them into the sea for refusing the Covenant*. If to murther men for that they are unwilling to be perjur'd, be for *Lawes* and *Liberties*, then they at *Westminster* may goe for a *Parliament*. But the blood of these innocent Gentlemen doth cry so loud for vengeance, that we are confident the Rebels will prosper accordingly: Let them remember they are now foretold of it.

This newsbook was written by Simeon Ashe, the nonconformist chaplain to the Earl of Manchester.

A Continuation Of true Intelligence From the Armies in the North Numb. 6.

10–27 July, 1644 492.6 {2.25}

A man of qualitie belonging to the enemy, whose name, for some reasons, I may not mention, professed, That his conscience told him, our Cause was Gods, yet his honour would not suffer him to take part with us. The Lord *Grandeson*, who is under the Surgeons hand in *York*, told a friend who visited him, That he received ten wounds in the battle, one wound for the breach of every commandment in the decalogue. I will not glosse upon this expression, but rather relate an observable providence, which his Lordship, at the same time reported. Before the fight, while the Canon was playing on both sides, a Trooper hearing the singing of Psalms in our severall Regiments, came three times to his Lordship with bloody oaths and fearfull execrations in his mouth, telling him, That the Round-heads were singing Psalms, and therefore, they should be routed that say, and that himself should be slain: His Lordship did reprove him, and cane him for swearing and cursing, but he proceeded in his wickednesse: and as these words, God-damn-me, God-sink-me, were in his mouth, a Drake bullet killed him. This relation makes way for another. After the victory some few Troops came out of the Wood, and espying a body of foot in the Moor, made towards them, but hearing them sing Psalms, they swore, that thereby they knew them to be their enemy: Let this evermore be our discriminating character, to difference us from our enemies, That it is our constant practise to sing forth the praises of our God, professing our universall dependance upon His Majestie, both for safety and successe.

The *Scotish Dove*, the weekly slogan of which was 'be Wise as Serpents, Innocent as Doves', was a populist newsbook, with a personal style and an unsophisticated, pious analysis. Here the editor George Smith reflects on his job and on the nature of parliament, while trying not to offend anyone in power. Nonetheless his analysis might well have been in alignment with a large number of readers.

The Scotish Dove Numb. 52.

11–18 October, 1644 594.052 {2.26}

I Am not ignorant, (though innocent) that my *Dove* hath been, and is envyed and aspersed: One sayes, she meddles with things too serious, things not befitting a Pamphlet of this nature: Another sayes, she relates things incongruous to the way of Intelligence: Others say, she flies too high, and toucheth upon persons and things above her place. Thus she is diversly accused, acording to the diversity of mens fancies: All which troubles not me: My ayme is not to please all; for that were impossible. My resolutions are impartiall: my desire is, to speak truths: neither to call good evill, nor evill good. And as I would satisfie the desires of men in communicating Intelligence; so I would informe their judgements of the grounds and cause of the vicissitude of things, the alteration and changes of times and men, from prosperous to calamitous; that so there may be a healing of such evils as break out from corrupt causes. I would not give any just cause of offence to any: nor doe I envy the name or person of any, but sinne in the generall, and that I desire to beat down, and therefore endeavour to make men sensible of it, that by generall reproofes each man might apply it, and by diligent search, prove whether hee bee the man complained of.

Sure I am, that all these evils, and the great calamity that hath at this day overspread these Kingdomes of Great *Britaine* and *Ireland*, is from sinne: They are not sprung out of the dust, not hapned to us by chance, but sent from Heaven by an angry God, for our sins and obstinate impenitency. Idolatry was brought even into the House of God; and oppression was crept into the Throne of Justice: Every mans heart was filled with wickednesse, and their hands with violence; and there was almost an overture of all things, as if the Kingdomes period were fully come, destruction having environed all, had not God in great mercy given us a Parliament, such as is transcendent to all Parliaments before, for Religion and Justice. This I do with soul thankfulnesse to God acknowledge, with due honour to those our Worthies and *Zerubabels*, for their religious care of re-building the Temple of God, and constant endeavour not only to restore, but to establish our ancient rights, and to take off our heavy burdens, which corrupt men for self-ends, through wicked councels, shrouding themselves under the name of the King, did oppresse us with: Who will, doubtlesse, not suffer any that shroud themselves under their authority, to doe unjustly, if complained of: but severely punish all such self-seekers, although he were as neare as a Member. Ambition and covetousnesse are vices that all men are subject unto by nature: Among twelve Apostles, (all chosen by Christ) there was one Devill: and among 400 men, chosen by men, there may be diabolicall spirits: Many have shewed themselves, by open and shamefull revolt: and I conceive, we cannot but feare some are still remaining, secretly to act treason against God and the Kingdome, by corrupting good councell, as *Hushai*, by his wisdome, did change the evill counsell of *Achitophel*. I doe not think but our Armies, our Committees, yea, our happy Parliament, are more or lesse troubled with such spirits, who by false suggestions blow up hot contentions, and often raise such stormes, as drives our ship upon the dangerous rocks and sands, almost to shipwrack: Nor is this the worst; for the worst of these spirits have by their secret insinuations wound themselves into the affections of just men: so that the worst of men have some good man to plead in his behalfe. This is a misery, (I would it were not true) But I hope our honourable Worthies will eye it, and cure it: The eyes of the People are too much upon it, which causeth some discouragements to arise. But I say no more: I will only pray to God to reforme all that is amisse, That sinne lye not still upon us; For surely, till we resolve to sinne no more, and use diligent endeavour to pay our vowes to God, in keeping our covenant with God and man; we shall not see Peace, nor be freed of our bleeding miseries: Although the sinne of the Enemy be at the full, our humiliation is too empty: If we were as low, as they are high, the work would be done sodainly; till when, all Armies can do doe nothing: We may destroy one Army, and another will spring up in the roome; It is God that giveth Peace, and that createth Warre: while we warre against God by our sinnes, God will warre against us with the sword of his indignation: While we seek our selves,

God will leave us to our selves: While we suffer Ambition to reigne, and punish not covetous Oppressors, Idolaters, Libertines, Sectaries, &c. we shall be under thraldome.

The Weekly Account THE XXV. WEEK.

18–24 June, 1645 671.225 {2.27}

SEverall reports have been spread abroad concerning the person of the King; One sayes blood was seen upon his Arm, another that it was onely a sprain; But a third (with more confidence then the rest) affirmes, that having his sword at St. *Georges* guard, one that was by seeing the blow comming, cryed out; *Its the King, touch him not*! Upon which he stayed his hand, getting two or three good slaps, and so lost his Majestie: who (according to the best intelligence) had no hurt at all.

Some newsbook writers tended to exaggerate their accounts of war crimes, which, upon other occasions, necessitated equally exaggerated affirmations of accuracy. These atrocities are the familiar ones, coupled with stereotypical cavalier blasphemy.

The Parliaments Post *Num*. 7.

17–24 June, 1645 487.07 {2.28}

THe last News of concernment which we received was the surrendring of the Towne of *Leicester*, And the first Newes which this Weeke we will declare shall be cruelty of the Enemy practised upon the Inhabitants of the Towne of *Leicester*; for although through the liberality of too much Language and affection something heretofore delivered concerning the injuries there committed did exceede the Truth, yet what *this* Pen hath to impart unto you, shall not onely be confirmed by many of our owne men, but even by the Enemies themselves, who on Saturday last were brought to London, unlesse peradventure some few of them will be so impudent to deny it, who in this height of their affliction do carry themselves rather like to Conqueours then captives.

The subject of this sad discourse is that Leicester, being possessed by the force of the Enemy, they summond many of the

Inhabitants into one place where accordingly having made their appearance, they were demanded, if they would henceforth fight on the Kings side or on the Parliaments. The miserable Inhabitants receiving councell from their feare, and the present danger wherein they were, and not daring to professe the contrary, did make answer that they would fight on the Kings side. But how shall we be assured of it would the Caviliers in a reprobate pride and joy reply? Swear unto us God damne you, swear unto us God ramme you, that you will fight with us who stand for the King, which oath when many of the honest Inhabitants, out of the tendernesse of their conscience, would refuse to sweare, immediately the man was stripped, and the sword was drawn, and the Enemies (as if they would plunder their souls as well as their bodies) would cut them on their shoulders and armes to force them to forswear themselves, whiles the bloud running down, and the divided flesh rising up, their wounds with wide mouthes did seeme to cry unto heaven for vengeance, which indeed was not long deferred. There are many living Martyrs in the town of Leicester, who with their wounds as well as with their words can attest this truth. Neither is this all, but (as if they had been abhomind into beasts) they offred open and unmanly violence unto many wives and maides, nay we are informed they humbled some unto their lusts even at the foot of the Crosse, which they do pretend to reverence. Divers children of divers Gentlemen, and well-affected persons were taken from their parents, who (as if they had to deal with Turkes and Infidels) found no other means for their deliverance but to redeem them with their money. And are these the men that fight for our Religion, and for the Honour of the King. Can any vertue be safe in such an Army. May not the King himself feare that some sudden blow might overtake him, may he not suspect the safety of his person amongst such desperate Assassinats? Surely as it is the obligation of every honest man to tender the happinesse and the safety of his Prince, so it is the obligation of the Prince to remove himselfe from destroying Counsellours, and to tender the happinesse and the safety of himselfe.

But these cruelties in the adverse Army (though intollerable in themselves and odious) may passe for mercies compared with the barbarous proceedings of these monsters of mankinde in Ireland, who have made themselves and their Religion the abomination of both heaven and earth. The poore Indian could not be perswaded to think well of Heaven because he heard that a dying Spaniard was going thither. And the Divell I beleeve (knowing to what place the Irish after death must be assigned) will either be weary or ashamed of his Hell. They have hanged in one Town no lesse then threescore persons in one morning, for no other reason but that they were honest men and Protestants, they have by dishonest wounds disfigured the faces of many, by cutting off their noses, and they have increased their cruelty by dismembring others, they have done over all their Tragedies againe, which heretofore they acted, and left nothing unperformed which elaborate malice could either practise or invent. I remember that above two years since I heard a Recusant affirme that there was never any thing which fastned a greater scandall on the Catholike Church, then the horrid outrages committed in Ireland by those of their Religion. He expected some swift and heavie judgement to fall down upon them, and in an angry wonder he seemed to expostulate what was the justice that permitted them to live, And yet we see that they live, and they live not to depose, but to increase their fury.

A poem addressed to the parliament; this and the following extract are particularly interesting in the way they combine poetry and prose, mixing genres and showing the populist side of Civil War poetry. The premature elegy is not uncommon in newsbooks of the period.

Mercurius Elencticus Numb. 21

12–19 April, 1648 312.21 {2.29}

So exquisitely hath the *Devill* showne his *Master peece* in you, that now you have no more to doe, but indeavour either to appease *Gods wrath*, or to attend the *fatall stroke* of his *Iustice*, which by this time I have now limitted you, you shall be sure to tast of. In the meane time, if you *persist* in your *wickednesse*, I shall *continue* this manner of writing, and *Trace* you to your very *Graves* and there leave you with this *Inscription*.

Here lyes the *Ruines* (who can but *Lament* ?)
Of *England's Mad* and *Bloody Parliament*.
Here lyes *Rebellion, Murder, Sacriledge*,
Here are the *Achans* stole the *Golden wedge*:
Here lye the *Grand Impostors* of our *Nation*,
Who surfetted with too much *Revelation*.
Here lyes *Ambition, Envy, Pride*, and *Lust*,
All *hudled* up in this *Rebellious Dust*,

Here is *Hell's Suburbs*, the most *Perjur'd Knaves*
Of *England Crowded* in their *Cursed Graves*.
Her lyes *ungratefull Warwick*; There lyes *Say*
Choak'd of a *Surplesse*, and a *Holy-day*.
Herc's *Kent*, that *wadling, fliggering Baboone*,
There's *Lisle, Nottingham, Stamford, Algernoone*
Wise *Pembrooke* smoothered up in *oaths*. God blesse us,
Fierce Wharton de la Sawpit Baronettus!
The *Earle* of *Manchester pro temp[o]re*,
All here in *Silence*, not a *word* to *say*
Here lyes *Will Lenthall* and his *Dirty Law*,
Without a *Cushion, Chaire*, or *wad* of *straw*,
Here's *Pheasant, St. Iohn, Wild*, and *Bloody Rowles*,
And all the *Conclave* of their *Brother-fooles*.
Parker and *Beck*, and *Prinne* (all but his *Eares*)
With *Hayles* the *Pick-lock* and that man of *yeares*.
Grave Mr. Seldon, who doth now *repent*,
Hee ever *sercht* th'*Antiquities* of *Kent*.
Here is *Myles Corbet*, that perfideous *Iew*
And *Crooked Pierpoint*, (Men of *gastly Hew*:)
Chast *Harry Martin*, and his *Pretty ones*,
Poisning the Poore *wormes* with their *Pocky bone's*
Here is *Nath. Fiennes*, that famous *coward* of *Yore*,
Here's *Haslerig*, and *Mildmay*, Hundreds more
Of *Saints* interr'd: *King Noll, Black Tom*, and all
Sculke here, attending of a *dismall call*.
   Reader behold these *Monsters*! Then relate
   The *fate*, the *ruine* of a *rotten State*.

Mercurius Bellicus Numb. 19

30 May - 6 June, 1648 279.19 {2.30}

And therefore you shall heare that *Nol. Cromwell*, will ere long bee sent for by his Masters at *Westminster* from following his game in *Wales* where *Poyer* hath had many Skirmishes with him to the losse of many of his Saints, there was a confident report that he was dead, but it is not so for he is ordained not {to} die by any mans hands save the *hangmans*; yet in regard that hee is not long lived and because I would not have Posteritie ignorant of him; I have taken the paines to frame his Epitatph.

CROMWEL'S *Epitaph*.

HEre lyes Murther, faction, ire,
Oppression, Sacrilegious fire,
Cruelty, the very, oppression;
Wild Furie, beyond all expression.
Madnesse mixt with Melancholy,
Prophanesse in a shape most holy.
Here lyes a limbe of Reformation,
The curst of God, and his whole Nation.
Who did no Hell-bred evill want,
Yet chiefest of Saints Militant.
Who led them on, God to oppose,
By the bright radiance of his Nose.
Here lyes, the Devils eldest Son,
Nurst by the Hag, Sedition.
A Machiavillian for his wit,
Yet fraile in the disposing it.
A perjur'd Patricide, what not
Yea more, then *Hoskins* pointeth at.
All in one, conjoyned bee,
For here lyes *Cromwels* Majestie.

His sonne and heyre Prince *Cromwell*, was not long since at an Horse-race in *Hide*-Parke, where hee flaunted it Bragadochio like, throwing his money about with much magnificence, it hapned that two were to runne for a wager, and many were bettors on both sides; young *Cromwell* said to the next that stood by, heres five pound on the *bay Nag*, the other answered done, who shall keep stakes replyed *Cromwell* (for you must know that this young Saint is of his Fathers humour right, *mistrusted by all men* and mistrustfull himself) this Genleman replied the other, who hee, saith *Cromwell*, (and looking upon him with disdaine) why me thinks the fellow if his out-side bespeak him truly, never saw five pound in his dayes, the Gent: much inraged at his scornfull language (being indeed a Gent: of knowne worth and credit) replyed, sirrah *Cromwell*, you shall know, that I am master of more Crownes then thy Father, and better discended then thee, and with that bestowed some paines about him, till his *Cane* was weary with exercise and flew into shivers, and after hee switcht him on the face with his rod, the other Gentlemen hurrying together and having heard what had passed, much applauded the Gent: and streight began to showt, crying *King Cromwell, K. Cromwell*; which so terrified the Yonker, that setting spurres to his horse hee rode away like a whirlwind, and was never heard of since.

Militaris was a particulary well composed newsbook, by John Harris. This report is an allegory of the second civil war, made strange in order rationally to convince readers that treating with the king was against their interests.

Mercurius Militaris Numb. 1

{10–16 October, 1648} 346.1 {2.31}

Friday, *Octob*. 13. {...}

Just now comes to my hand *strange news*, such as the world never heard; There was a *battel* in the *Island of Wool* between the *sheep* and a *herd of wolves*, the *sheep* after the loss of 100000. and much of their wool, hapned to gain the *field*, and killed and dispersed the *whole herd*, and took the Captain of the *Wolves* Prisoner: many of the *Sheep* cry for Iustice against him, but the *Sheeps grand Councel* enters into *Treaty* with him, bows down and kisses his forefoot, and propose to him, that in case he will consent that they shall keep their own swords and make their own Priests, and two or three trivial things beside, then he shall be Captain of the *Sheep*, and shall have 800000 l. of their wool *per annum*: they shall never have any laws nor great officers but according to his will, and he shall never be questionable for the discharge of his trust; the *Sheep* are at present in great fear, but the *Treaty* is not yet concluded.

The defeat of Prince Charles' forces at Worcester by Cromwell was the final blow to Royalist military hopes. This passage has previously been attributed to John Milton, because it was supposed to have been too well-written to be by its probable author, Marchamont Nedham.

Mercurius Politicus Numb. 66

4–11 September, 1651 361.066 {2.32}

An exact Relation of the late glorious Victory, obtained (through Gods mercy) by the Forces of this Commonwealth, over the Scotish *Army at* Worcester, 3. *Sept*. 1651. *being an* Extract *of the chiefest of that intelligence which is yet come to hand*.

THough no Tongue or Pen be able to express the greatness of this Action, suitable to that magnificent appearance of God, in the behalf of *England*; yet becaus it is a main part of our duty, in any measure, to become subservient to his glory, it is conceived nothing can more advance it, than by recounting before all the world, the many wondrous and mighty dispensations of his mercy. This *Third day of September* hath been a very glorious day of Decision; This day twelvmonth was glorious at *Dunbar*, but this day hath been very glorious before *Worcester*: The *Word* then was, *The Lord of Hosts*, and so it was now, the *Lord of Hosts* indeed having been wonderfully with us. The same *Signall* wee had now as then, which was to have *no white about us*; yet the Lord hath cloathed us with *white Garments*, though to the Enemy they have been *bloody*: Only here lyes the difference, that at *Dunbar* our work was at break of *Day*, and done ere the morning was over; but now it began towards the close of the Evening, and ended not till the night came upon us. That was the beginning of their Fall before the appearance of the *Lord Iesus*; This seems to be the setting of the *yong Kings* glory.

This Battell was fought with various Successes for some hours, but still hopefull on the behalf of the *Commonwealth*, and inauspicious to the Enemy; of whom the more were slain, becaus the dispute was long, and very near at hand, and often at *push of Pike*, wherein the *new raised Forces* did perform very singular good service, for which they deserve a very high estimation and acknowledgement, since they have added very much to the reputation of our Affairs, by their alacrity and courage in the work; And it pleased God so to order this Affair in the hands of his weak instruments, that in the end it became an absolute *Victory*, determined by an immediate possession of the Town, with a totall ruine and defeat of the *Scotish* Army: Concerning which, be pleased to take a short view of the whole action, in the following Particulars.

Upon *Wednesday* morning 3 *Septemb*. between 5 and 6 a clock, the Forces under Lieut. generall *Fleetwood* began their march from *Upton*; but by reason of som hindrances in their way, reached not to *Team* River till betwixt 2 or 3 in the Evening. As soon as our Boats came up (which was much about the same time) a Bridge was presently made over the *Severn*, on our main Armys side, and another over the River *Team* on the *Lieut. Generals* side, who made way as far as *Powick*, half a mile on this side the Bridg with his *Van*, before the Enemy took the Alarm: but the Alarm being taken, they immediatly drew both their Hors and Foot from their Leaguer at St. *Jones*, to oppose the *Lieut. Generals* passage over our Bridges of Boats.

Whereupon the Generall presently commanded over Col. *Inglesbies* and Col. *Fairfax* their Regiments, with part of his own Regiment, and the Life-guard, and Col. *Hacker's* of hors over the *River*; his *Excellency* himself leading them in person, and being the first man that set foot on the Enemies ground: After these, the *Lieut. General* commanded Col. *Goffs*, and Major-gen. *Deans* Regiments, all which advanced towards the Enemy, who had wel-lined the hedges with men to impede the approach of our Forces; but it pleased the Lord after some sharp dispute (wherein ours beat them from hedg to hedg) to give a good issue there to our mens courage and resolution.

Then Col. *Blague*, and Col. *Gibbons*, with Col. *Marshe's* Regiment were comanded over *Team* as Seconds to the former, and to attempt the Enemy in other Places, where they had drawn their men; so which service the Lord *Greys* Regiment was likewise order'd over; who all acquitted themselves so valiantly, that after half an hour, or an hours dispute, it pleased the Lord that the Enemy quitted their ground, and fled away: Onely about *Powick* bridge, which they had broken down, having the advantage of Hedges and Ditches, they maintained a very hot dispute with Col. *Haynes* his Regiment and Col. *Cobbets*, Col. *Mathews* being as a Reserve to Them both; by which meanes it pleased the Lord, that the Enemy quitted that ground likewise, and ran away. As Col. *Haynes* his Regiment were wading over the River, to advance upon them, about a mile from *Powick*, the Enemy had broken down another bridg, upon a Pass unto which place were sent some of our Dragoons, who with assistance of som horse, forced the Enemy from that Place, and gained a passage over for the *Lieut. Generals* Regiment, Col. *Twistletons*, and Col. *Kendricks* that were commanded to pursue the Enemy, who (as it was supposed) made towards *Hereford* or *Ludlow*; but at length they wheeled off, and all ran into *Worcester*, except some few that were taken. The Ground where this Controversie was acted, was so combred with Hedges, that our Horse had not much liberty to engage; but yet both Hors and Foot, where they had opportunity, did (through the *Lords* presence assisting) approve themselves very gallantly.

After the Enemy had run away into *Worcester*, they renewed their Courage with apprehensions of shame and fury, and drew out what Hors and Foot they could upon the *Generals* side, supposing that most of his Army had bin advanced over the River, whereupon they made a very bold Sally on that side the Town in great Bodies, giving our men a very hot salute, insomuch that it put some of them to a little Retreat with disorder; but in a short space the Lord gave us Victory on this side also, being re-inforct with Major-gen. *Desborough's* Regiment of Horse, and Col. *Cobbets* of Foot. On that side was engaged part of the *Generals* Regiment of Hors, Major Gen. *Lambert*, Commissary gen. *Whalies*, Major-gen. *Harisons* Brigade, and Col. *Tomlinsons* Regiment, with some of the *Surry* and *Essex* Troops. Those of Foot, were the *Major gen*. Col. *Pride*, Col. *Coopers*, the *Cheshire* Brigade, and the *Essex* Foot: All these (as the Lord gave them opportunity) discharged themselves with much bravery; disputing also not only the hedges with the Enemy, but following them boldly to the very mouths of their Cannon; so that in the end they gained their Works, with their Fort-Royal, beating them into the Town, and turning their own Cannon upon them; which so wrapt them up with a Spirit of terror and confusion, that afterwards, the night being come, we soon gained an Entry, and became Masters of the Town, whilst the Enemy disposed themselves for a flight, the same way that they came in hither, and many of their Horse got away. Their King (it is said) went out very meanly, with only 12 Horse; in all there escaped not above 3000 Hors, and these not 1000 together in a Body; of whom, Col. *Barton*, being commanded to *Bewdly* the day before, with some Hors and Dragoons, took many Prisoners as they fled, to the number of 1200. And the next morning, persuit was made by 1500 Horse and Dragoons under Col. *Blundel*, and a stronger party under Major gen. *Harison*. In the flight, Col. *Lilburn*, and the *Generals* Regiment of Foot that was with him, met with their Antagonist the E. of *Derby*, *Lauderdale*, and about 140 persons of quality. These Forces of *Col, Lilburns*, with those lying at *Bewdly*, and in *Shropshire* and *Staffordshire*, seem to have bin so happily disposed there by Providence, as if we had foreseen this fatal Rout, and accordingly provided to intercept the Enemy in their return.

In all the Ingagements that ever we had, never did a more immediate hand of God appear, than in this, nor more courage and resolution in an Army, though no flesh hath cause to boast, becaus it is the Lord only that hath don all these things. The number of Prisoners is near 10000. near 3000 were slain of the Enemy; but of all on our side, not above 200. which adds much unto the Mercy. Of *Officers* very few slain; onely Quartermaster gen. *Mosely* and Capt. *Jones* of Col. *Cobbets* Regiment: Maj. gen. *Lamberts* hors was shot under him: The number of Arms and Colours is so great, that as yet no certain accompt of them hath been given. My *Lord Generall* did exceedingly hazard himself, riding up and down in the midst of the shot, and riding himself in person to the *Enemies* foot offering them *Quarter*, whereto they returned no answer, but shot. The *Major-generals*, and all the rest of the *Officers*, in their places, gave many eminent Testimonies of a noble courage and behaviour. Let us conclude therefore in the words of our renowned *General*, The dimensions of this mercy are above all our thoughts; It is, for ought I know, a *Crowning mercy*. Surely, if it be not, such a one we shall have, if this provoke those that are concerned in it to Thankfulnesse, and the *Parliament* to do the will of him, who hath don his will for it, and for the Nation; whose good pleasure it is to establish the Nation, and the Change of government, by making the people so willing for the defence therof, & so signally to bless the endevors of his Servants in this late great work. Let all our thoughts tend to the promoting of his honor, who hath wrought so great Salvation: Let not the fatness of these continued mercys occasion pride and wantonness, as formerly the like hath done to a chosen Nation; but let the fear of the Lord even for his Mercies, keep an Authority and a People, so prospered and blessed, and witnessed unto, humble and faithfull, that Justice and Righteousness, Mercy and Truth, may flow forth as a thankful Return to our gracious God, for all his mercies.

The following commemorative poem combines the sentimental conventions of glorifying battle with an attempt to revive a Lucanic republican and heroic tradition.

The Weekly Post *Numb.* 187.

11–18 July, 1654 544.187 {2.33}

The English having obtained a glorious Victory against the French, these lines were thought requisite to be inserted thereupon.

TAke wing my Muse, & mount the aery sky,
View winged Bullets how they stranglyfly
See how their swimming Castles march, they sayl,
As if their Timber, ah! would never fail.
See! how the glorious Lamp doth gaze to see
Cerulian Waves made, ah! a purple Sea;
Hark! how the warlike Trumpets call to fight,
And view the Monsieurs ship about, as light
As fancy sees them, BEN: doth bravely stand,
Upon the Poop discreetly gives command:
Ben: Follows with the Pearl, Foster is
Adding to's Canvass, each brave ship do'nt miss,
To plow the liquid Ocean, which doth swel,
Looks big: yet English spirits ne're could sell
To entertain base fear; the other run
As if they would set with the supping sun.
Ah! ah! immortal French are fear'd by Death,
The winds now give their scanted Canvass breath.
Ply after English hearts, and fetch from home
The haughty French. Let trembling Christendom
Hear of your Valours, were I Lucaniz'd,
My Pen this Victory had highly priz'd,
And made as famous as the Roman wars,
But I cannot by inauspicious stars.
Though in the fight, we saw Gods mighty hand,
And find he's great, both on the Sea and Land{.}

CHAPTER THREE
Sleeping with the Devil: Women in newsbooks

Most of the women in this chapter are either witches, whores, heretics or the Queen of Sweden. There are also some purely passive victims. The representation of women in newsbooks is much as we might expect.

Newsbooks, being concerned with public actions, generally reported the doings and fates of men. When women entered this public arena, it was either because they had transgressed beyond their proper, private interests, or because they were being used to punish men. The latter case might involve an heroic woman, keeping an army at bay {3.8} or fighting off the soldiers attempting to confiscate her unlicensed newsbooks {3.11}: but more usually the women were prostitutes who bequeathed their diseases to libidinous parliamentarians, or shrewish adulteresses who beat down their husbands and sacrificed their fidelity to the greater god of lust.

This was not always so. The newsbooks of early 1642 were sober, mostly parliamentary narratives, which, facing possible reprisals and political uncertainty, did not stray into comic libel. The London Citizens' wives, who presented petitions to parliament in January and February, were commended for their devotion: the Duke of Lenox/Richmond, who scorned their right to involve themselves in politics, was reprimanded, while Lord Savage, who was courteous, was implicitly praised {1.10&11}. This early condition of representation may partly have reflected an initial movement of women into a political sphere which followed the challenge to the king's undivided authority.[1] The fact of visible political change made likely the questioning of consolidated patriarchal authority, which was often associated with absolute monarchy. A year and a half after these accounts, a similarly composed group of women who petitioned parliament came into conflict with the trained band and were generally attacked by the newsbooks {3.7}. The change was, in general, a permanent one. Particularly when war broke out, women were a symbol used by propagandists to attack each other. The more polemical the newsbook, the more likely this was to be so. Perhaps for this reason, the more aggressive royalist newsbooks were, on the whole, greater offenders than the parliamentarian.

It is hardly surprising that writers should have chosen to foreground the potential of women to transgress the boundaries of social, political and religious norms, in a period of social, political and religious upheaval; nor that political instability should have been transcoded onto women's bodies.[2] As the many parallels drawn between family and state in seventeenth-century domestic and political treatises imply, the family was imagined as the basic unit of the socio-political order.[3] William Whately wrote in 1617:

> But what shall it auaile to maintaine a familie, without gouernment; or how can it bee gouerned but by them? so that they must also bee good rulers at home, and ioyne in guiding the household: the man as Gods immediat officer, and the King in his family: the woman as the Deputie subordinate, and associate to him, but not altogether equall; and both in their order must gouerne.[4]

In one of the texts to *Patriarcha*, his defence of absolute monarchy, Robert Filmer noted under the title 'That the first kings

1 See, for instance, Lawrence Stone, *The Family, Sex and Marriage In England 1500–1800* (Harmondsworth: Penguin, 1979 abridged edn.), p.225–6. See also David Underdown, *Revel, Riot and Rebellion: Popular Politics and Culture in England 1603–1660* (Oxford: Oxford University Press, 1985, 1987), p.154 and *passim*. I am most grateful to David Underdown for reading and commenting on this chapter and for allowing me to refer to his unpublished Ford's Lectures, delivered at the University of Oxford, 1992.

2 See Peter Stallybrass, 'Patriarchal Territories: The Body Enclosed', in Margaret W. Ferguson, Maureen Quilligan and Nancy J. Vickers, eds. *Rewriting the Renaissance: The Discourses of Sexual Difference in Early Modern Europe* (Chicago: University of Chicago Press, 1986).

3 See Susan Amussen, 'Gender, Family and the Social Order, 1560–1725' in Anthony Fletcher and John Stevenson, eds. *Order and Disorder in Early-Modern England* (Cambridge: Cambridge University Press, 1985).

4 William Whately, *A Bride-Bvsh, Or A Wedding Sermon* (London, 1617), p.16. This was published by the early coranto publisher Nicholas Bourne. STC 25296.

were fathers of families.'[5] Both of these examples were written before the Civil War, and predicted the response that many men would have had to the challenge to the king's supremacy in the 1640s. There was no absolute distinction in the mid seventeenth century between public institutions and the private institution of the family,[6] so a threat to one might implicitly place the other in jeopardy.

So while women were often used with deliberation in stories which libelled men (for instance, Henry Marten[7] and Miles Corbet {3.21&28}), their presence in newsbooks was often evidence of anxieties over a decayed political and gender hierarchy. The former found its most rarefied manifestation in the newsbooks of John Crouch, *The Man in the Moon*, *Mercurius Democritus* and *Mercurius Fumigosus*, with their minimal news content and melange of titillating wonder stories, slanderous attacks on prominent members of the army and parliament and outright pornography. As David Underdown has argued, in *The Man in the Moon* Crouch used a language which focused on an inverted moral and social order in order to articulate the reaction of a conservative, popular culture to political transformations.[8] Crouch's concupiscent Ranter women {3.31} reflected back on Ireton and Cromwell's blasphemous innovations. While rebellious women were an object for fascination earlier in the seventeenth century, the 1650s saw something new in an eight-page weekly almost entirely dedicated to cataloguing their pursuit of perversion.

Witchcraft was another cultural fantasy prominent in newsbooks. Witches were predominantly old, poor women, possibly known locally as scolds, whose persecution can be interpreted as the consequence of a breakdown in traditional social relationships and of new notions of identity which required the close surveill-

5 Sir Robert Filmer, *Patriarcha and Other Writings*, ed. Johann P. Sommerville (Cambridge: Cambridge University Press, 1991), p.1. Filmer was the friend of the co-editor of the *Mercurius Aulicus*, Peter Heylin.

6 Cp. David Underdown, 'The Taming of the Scold' in Fletcher and Stevenson, eds. *Order and Disorder*. If there was no boundary between the public and the private, the entrance of women into a public political sphere would not have been perceived as abnormal: yet if the boundary was uncrossable, there would have been no potential threat.

7 See C.M. Williams, 'The Anatomy of a Radical Gentleman: Henry Marten' in eds. Donald Pennington and Keith Thomas, *Puritans and Revolutionaries: Essays in Seventeenth-Century History presented to Christopher Hill* (Oxford: Clarendon Press, 1970).

8 David Underdown, '*The Man in the Moon*: Levelling, Gender and Popular Politics 1640–1660', unpublished Ford's Lecture.

ance of subjects for hidden forms of disobedience.[9] This is, of course, an enormous oversimplification, particularly of the distinctions between English and European practices of witch persecution, and there were several reports in newsbooks which display scepticism towards Scottish witchcraft trials {3.25; 7.04&05}. Nevertheless newsbooks always reported witch trials with some glee, and there were interesting stories of Cavaliers supposedly turning the women amongst their enemies into witches (actually merely the excuse for an extended meditation upon the nature of the diabolic pact {3.24}) and of a doctor who encouraged a woman to use white magic to find out who had bewitched her.

Newsbook writers may have reflected existing cultural fantasies, or they may have created them, deliberately investing them with added meaning. Alternatively newsbooks may have been a gauge to real social changes: for instance the heightened position women were occupying in religious observances. While women by no means achieved parity with men, in theory let alone in practice, the 'puritan revolution' did ameliorate religious inequality. The rapid growth of religious independency in the early 1640s gave to women the opportunity to participate in worship, even preaching and prophesying. Lady Eleanor Davis, neither low born nor a sectarian, utilized this right. The enthusiasts, the gathered churches, the Baptists, Diggers, Ranters and Quakers, all claimed to improve the lot of women, defining them as the spiritual peers of men.[10] Even the authorities could countenance female religious intervention: on 29 December 1648, Elizabeth Pool presented an allegorical vision to the Council of Officers, recommending that the cure for the distressed (feminine) land lay in the (masculine) army. She was listened to, within limits: her

9 There is a broad literature on the subject. Some of the texts on English and Scottish witchcraft are: Alan Macfarlane, *Witchcraft in Tudor and Stuart England: A Regional and Comparative Study* (London: Routledge & Kegan Paul, 1970); Keith Thomas, *Religion and the Decline of Magic: Studies in Popular Beliefs in Sixteenth and Seventeenth Century England* (Harmondsworth: Penguin, 1973); Christina Larner, *Enemies of God: The Witch-hunt in Scotland* (London: Chatto and Windus, 1981) and *Witchcraft and Religion: The Politics of Popular Belief*, ed. A. Macfarlane (Oxford: Basil Blackwell, 1984); Stuart Clark, 'Inversion, Misrule, and the Meaning of Witchcraft' *Past and Present*, 87 (1980).

10 See Christopher Hill, *The World Turned Upside Down: Radical Ideas During the English Revolution* (Harmondsworth: Penguin, 1972, 1975), ch.15; and Keith Thomas, 'Women and the Civil War Sects', *Past and Present*, 13 (1958). Also J.F. McGregor, 'The Baptists: Fount of all Heresy', pp.46–7, and B. Reay, 'Quakerism and Society', pp.143–6, in McGregor and Reay, eds. *Radical Religion in the English Revolution* (Oxford: Oxford University Press, 1984, 1986).

message was, more or less, what some of the Army leaders wished to hear. Uncertain which path to take, on 5 January the Council again consulted her, to receive the reply that while they had the right to imprison the king, it was not God's will that they should put him to death.[11]

Not all newsbooks had a conservative reaction to female preachers and prophets, though writers like John Crouch thought female vocality represented the bane of all social order, and associated it with sexual proclivity {3.32}. Anna Trapnel, whom a modern historian of journalism called a 'madwoman',[12] was associated with the Fifth Monarchists {3.37} and prophesied before the Council of State in London and while on a tour of Cornwall {3.39}.[13] Like Sarah Wight she combined her prophecies with fasting and periods of silence, and in many ways resembled the medieval mystics Margery Kempe and Julian of Norwich.[14] Trapnel, however, was more overtly politicised than her predecessors: in *The Cry of a Stone*, actually transcribed, like Kempe's book, by a male amanuensis, she observed that Cromwell had been put aside by God as an agent of great historical change.[15] She became a very public figure before Cromwell sent her to Bridewell to be flogged, and *Mercurius Politicus*, which, in spite of Nedham's irascible tendencies, could sometimes sound like Cromwell's mouthpiece, dismissed Trapnel's inspired outpourings as nonsense. *Severall Proceedings of State Affaires*, however, publicised her cause at some length {3.38}. Perhaps the interest of the newsbook editors in prediction and prophecy (Lilly loomed large in newsbooks both Royalist and Parliamentarian {3.13}) encouraged them to pay attention even to women.

Women were disorderly, and made 'other' to men, they could certainly be used as an indicator of when men had transgressed, and, being blamed for radical sensuality, for being what made men transgress.[16] They held an inferior position in relation to the law,

11 Gardiner, *History of the Great Civil War*, iv, 296; C.V. Wedgwood, *The Trial of Charles I* (London: Collins, 1964), pp.81, 89.

12 J.G. Muddiman, *The King's Journalist 1659–1689: Studies in the Reign of Charles II* (London: The Bodley Head, 1923), p.29.

13 Cp. Nigel Smith, *Perfection Proclaimed: Language and Literature in English Radical Religion 1640–1660* (Oxford: Clarendon Press, 1989), pp.45–53.

14 Cp. Caroline Walker Bynum, 'Fast, Feast, and Flesh: The Religious Significance of Food to Medieval Women', *Representations*, 11 (1985).

15 Anna Trapnel, *The Cry of a Stone* (1653[4]), p.10. Cromwell is referred to as 'Gideon'. Wing T2031.

16 Natalie Zemon Davies, *Society and Culture in Early Modern France* (Stanford: Stanford University Press, 1975), ch.5. See also Peter Burke, *Popular Culture in Early Modern Europe* (Aldershot: Wildwood House, 1978, 1988), ch.7.

and received harsher punishment for similar crimes. The mid-seventeenth century witnessed great anxieties concerning infanticide {3.14; 4.11&12; 7.06}: a woman was responsible for proving her innocence when her child died. The bodies of women were invested with meaning which might seem not entirely foreign: it was believed that the female orgasm was necessary for conception, and so a woman who was raped and made pregnant was believed to have enjoyed it, and therefore to have consented.[17] Newsbooks, of course, did not simply reflect these attitudes and beliefs or the concurrent changes in them; and neither did they substantially challenge them. Different writers used these images in different ways, for different purposes, but rarely stretching the limits of conventional representations. Perhaps the most surprising aspect of the position of women in newsbooks is that, for all the changes in historical circumstances, the stories have remained pretty much the same.

A Perfect Account *Num*. 211

17–24 January, 1654{5} 496.211 {3.01}

Munday Ian. 22.

Many strange disasters have fallen out this week, *viz*. At *Cobham* in Kent, a woman jealous of her husband, sent for the suspected female, and having drunk freely with her, she at the last demanded of her, if she would have her nose cut off, or her bearing part; and immediatly she and her maid servant fell to work, and exercised that part of her body which they thought had most offended. Not long after her husband came home, and demanding what there was to eat, she replyed, that she had got the best bit which he loved in the world, and so presented him with that most ungrateful object.

Amazed at the horrour of it, he addressed himself to the constable, who carrying both Mistriss and Maid to the next Justice, they were both committed to Maidstone Goal: But the dismembered woman being not dead, they have put in great bayl to be answerable to justice.

17 K. Thomas, 'The Double Standard', *Journal of the History of Ideas*, 20 (1959); Patricia Crawford, 'From the Woman's View: Pre-Industrial England 1500–1750', in Patricia Crawford, ed. *Exploring Women's Past* (Sidney, London, Boston: Allen and Unwin, 1983); Patricia Crawford, 'Attitudes to Menstruation in Seventeenth-Century England', *Past and Present*, 91 (1981). Cp. Wendy Gibson, *Women in Seventeenth-Century France* (Basingstoke: Macmillan, 1989).

One of the insights into the real, rather than the linguistic, treatment of women we can find in newsbooks is in the depressing catalogues of rapes and sexual abuse offered to women by the soldiers after victory. Newsbooks seized on these incidents, and if they persisted in representing such assaults to their readers and emphasising the relation between sexual drive and military violence in seventeenth-century masculinity, this is in part because of its basis in historical fact. It seems rape was as much a part of everyday life then as it is today, and though discourse of it was replete with moral condemnation, there was no more effective recourse for women then than today: only a trust to providence that one day the rapists would meet with their deserved punishment.

The Scotish Dove *Numb*. 88.

20–27 June, 1645. 594.088 {3.02}

The prisoners taken in the fight at *Naesby* field, were brought to *London* on Saturday, they were in number 4500, or thereabouts; of them, there was about 500 Commanders: there was neere 60 Colours, that were also taken in the fight, carryed before them through the streets. There are divers Colours more which were taken at *Leicester*, that are still lodged in *Leicester*, and not brought to *London* at all. The common souldiers were put into the Artillerie Garden in *Tothill* fields, the Officers into the Lord *Peters* house in *Aldersgate* street. On the Lords day last, there was two Sermons preached to the souldiers in the Artillerie Garden, by two able & reverend Divines: such is the care of the Parliament, they seeke to save the soules of their enemies, but our enemies labour to destroy us both body and soule; we shew mercie, they studie crueltie and mischiefe. The souldiers themselves confesse, the Parliaments Armie shewed themselves gallant in fight, and mercifull in quarter; not as the enemie did in *Cornwall*, nor at *Leicester:* They starve us, if prisoners; we feed them, and suffer multitudes of Malignants to come to them, now prisoners, who give them largely in Money, and other things: they destroy us with crueltie, and we put our selves in some danger by our too much lenitie. At *Leicester* and other parts they stript all, and not onely so, but afterwards tooke Virgins into the Market place, and most beast-like they abused them in the sight of all men, to satisfie their base lusts, one after another; and those in the Towne, or in the Countrey, of best esteeme and worth, were worst dealt with by them; the wives or daughters of the godlyer and most vertuous

Parents, were chiefely ravished: and (as I am assured) Sir *Robert Pye* (then their prisoner) observing their inhumane carriage and bestialitie, made complaint to some Officers and Commanders under whose power he then was (I need not name any more then a *Beard*) who replyed, they should satisfie themselves that way, so they did not kill them, he would doe so himselfe, &c. nay it is said, that some were forced till they dyed. I protest, I am ashamed to speak of the villainie that they there acted, as I have beene informed by the eye-witnesses, lest (as *Plutarch* saith in another case) I might thereby teach unheard villanie. Base are their actions, and base are their ends; their reward will be according.

This account reveals the author's standards of objectivity in reporting, and also his preconceptions of the role of women in battle. Women should be treated with somewhat more respect than 'Nigers', and certainly better than the Governor of Reading.

Speciall Passages And certain Informations
Numb. 37.

18–25 April, 1643 605.37 {3.03}

THat which first offers it selfe this weeke, is the continuation of the siege of *Reading*, and because there are so many strange and various reports, especially by the Adversary, permit a larger Narration, then you are usually troubled with in the weekly Passages, the intent thereof being to give true but short information.

The Lord Generall (as before) came Saturday the fifteenth of *Aprill*, before *Reading*, a place strongly fortified, with a deep ditch round, and strong workes neere and remote, he marched a compasse of some seven miles extraordinary, as if he had intended *Oxford*, by which meanes he got to the West and weakest side of the Towne, and possest himselfe of a hedge and ditch at the first, which gave him opportunitie of beginning his intrenchments, without any considerable losse of men, which are usually cut off in great numbers at the first breaking of ground: after his Excellency had got a good safe quarter at a Knights house about a mile from the Towne, and to the South-west, he began to make use of his Ordnance, against a worke neere to a barne, and continued playing for a good time, but finding that the subtle Governour (famous for the holding out Townes) made up as fast as the Cannon beat downe, he desisted that, and fell to intrenching, thereby intending to get by degrees to the said worke, and with as little losse as might be of men. The valiant and honest Major Generall, having learned in *Holland*, not to be prodigall of the lives of good Souldiers, there being not in six dayes above thirtie men wounded, and not twentie slaine, some of which being hurt by powder of their own, and some slaine by over-forwardnesse where there was no need: untill thursday towards night the Town was not circumvalated, which either for want of force or for what other reason the Reader may conjecture as he please: which not being done, the enemy got oppurtunitie to passe in three loades of Ammunition, and 700. fresh men: which could not but be a great incouragement to the besieged, and make the Governour able to make good his workes, that he need not have taken the women of the Towne to put before his men, to save them from the shot, as some affirme they saw upon the worke upon which the Parliament forces played, which if true, is more barbarous and inhumane, then can be parallelled; its true, the Turkes use to put Nigers before to dull the edge of their enemies swords, but that women should be so used, its pittie that ever such a Governour was borne of a woman, but that he had been some monster; and were the times setled, and he survive the troubles, it were a good worke for women to cut him in pieces, and send a piece to every Commander, as far as his carcasse would reach: but if mens eyes were not deceived, why might it not be some geare, or men in womens apparell, or the like: a favourable construction would be made, if possible.

Certaine Informations Numb. 27

17–24 July, 1643 36.27 {3.04}

Monday, Iuly 17.

OUT of *Yorkeshire* it is Informed, that at the last bataile betweene the Lord *Fairefaxe* and the *Newcastellians*, both the armies were forced to give over fighting and retreated for want of Gunpowder, the Lord *Fairefaxe* having received none from *Hull* in 19. weekes, whereupon they had a Parley, and agreed upon a Cessation of armes for a time, and the Lord *Fairefax* retired to *Leedes*, and Sir *Thomas Fairefaxe* his sonne went into *Bradforth*, whither his Father sent him some Gunpowder, which being intercepted by the Earle of *Newcastle*, he presently broke his promise, and before the time of Cessation was expired, he set upon *Bradforth* and discharged his Ordnance against it, therewith beating downe all the Chymnies, so that there are scarce sixe left standing in it; which forced Sir *Thomas Fairefaxe* with about 1500. men to quit the Towne, and leave it to the violence of the Popish Army, where also he was forced to leave his Lady, shee being wounded with a shot in the shoulder: after his departure from thence the barbrous and mercilesse Popish Souldiers entred the Towne, and slew many of the Inhabitants with their wives and children, and most inhumanely they threw one child into the River, and they have not left one man in the Towne under the age of sixtie, but have either slaine them or driven them away, and further, that most shamlessly they stripped the women and maidens naked, and ravished and deflowred them, and amongst the rest, after three of those barbarous Souldiers, had severally abused a maid servant belonging to the lady *Fairefaxe*, they shot her and killed her, and so they served divers other women, in a most execrable manner, which is horrible to be related, and therefore should open the eyes and understandings, of such as doe not seriously take to heart, these and such like detestable outrages, and endeavour to prevent the like usages of their wives and daughters, by a timely resisting of the perpetrators of these nefarious and abominable actions.

The Moderate Intelligencer *Num*. 27.

28 August – 4 September, 1645 419.027 {3.05}

Tuesday, Septemb. 2. {...}

This day we had a sad relation out of *Bedforshire*, of his Majesties Forces deportment among them; when the Enemy is gone, the Country unamazed, you may know the truth, we will give but a few particulars, but they are of an excellent Dye, {...} Another was the peece of justice done in *Huntington*; four having broken into a poor womans house, and plundered her chest filled with aples, being convicted, were condemned, and the dice being cast, he that threw least was hanged, but after there came complaints for great faults, as ravishing, &c. To this the like answer was given that the Queen gave to the people about *Newarke*, who Petitioning for redresse of such wrongs, answered, *Poor men they have been long from their Wives, can you blame them*.

The royalist *Aulicus*, though not so outrageous as *The Man in the Moon* or *Mercurius Fumigosus*, nevertheless made explicit the fantasised connection between rebellion and sexual activity. 'Zealous' is synonymous with 'Puritan', which in turn implies hypocritical.

Mercvrivs Avlicvs *The Second Weeke*

{7–13 January, 1644} 275.202A {3.06}

MONDAY. *Jan*: 8.

You may remember in the 36 Weeke of the last yeare, we told you of certaine zealous young Maids in the Citie of *Norwich*, who covenanted together to raise Troope of Horse for the Rebels service; and then we said these forward Girles (when honest times came againe) would either live to be stale Virgins, or else make use of these dayes of Reformation. And for a truth we are certified, that no lesse then five of this Virgin Troope are now great with childe, but by whom it is not yet signified: only 'tis said these Sisters are very busie, plundering for husbands against the good houre. And let all Virgins looke to it, for people hereafter will scarce thinke them honest, who are so bold and shamelesse as to joyne in a Rebellion against their owne Soveraigne.

Eighteen months earlier a group of London women had been commended for petitioning parliament: this time, as the royalist newsbooks recorded, their appeals resulted in violence.

Mercurius Civicus *Numb.* 11

3–11 August, 1643 298.011 {3.07}

On Wednesday August 9. about two or three thousand Women, most of them of the inferiour sort, inhabiting about the City of London and the Suburbs thereof, gathered together at Westminster, under pretence of presenting a Petition to both Houses of Parliament for peace. The Petition for better satisfaction I have here inserted.

The humble Petiton of many civilly disposed Women inhabiting in the Cities of London, Westminster, the Suburbs and parts adjacent.

SHewing unto your Honours, that your poore Petitioners (though the weaker Sex) doe too sensibly perceive the ensuing desolation of this Kingdome, unlesse by some timely meanes your Honours provide for the speedy recovery thereof; Your Honours are the Phisitians that can by Gods speciall and miraculous blessing, (which we humbly implore) restore this languishing Nation, and that our bleeding sister the Kingdome of Ireland, which hath now almost breathed her latest gaspe; we need not dictate to your Eagle-eyed judgements the way: Our onely desire is, That Gods glory in the true reformed Protestant Religion may be preserved, the just Prerogatives and Priviledges of King and Parliament maintained, the true Liberties and Properties of the Subject according to the knowne Lawes of the Land restored, and all Honourable waies and meanes for a speedy peace endeavoured.

May it therefore please your Honours to conceive that some speedy course may be taken for the settlement of the true reformed Protestant Religion for the glory of God, and the renovation of Trade for the benefit of the Subject, they being the soule and body of the Kingdome.

And they with many Millions of afflicted soules
groaning under the burthen of these times of
distresse (as bound) shall pray, &c.

Which Petition in regard of the Contents of it, I should not have much misliked, the Title being, the Petition of many civilly disposed women, who, had they behaved themselves accordingly in a civill manner, their meeting had not been so distastefull; but the greatest part of them carrying themselves very uncivilly towards divers Members of the House, and others, using many horrid execrations, that they would have the blood of those (whom they in their furious zeal conceived to be averse to peace) so that at last from words they fell to blowes, insomuch that upon their insolent abusing of divers men of quality, the trained Band and two Troops of Horse were forced to fall amongst them for feare of further danger; but they continuing their outrageous courses in casting stones and brickbats, they occasioned the more violence to be used towards them, wherein divers of them were dangerously hurt, and two men and two women slain, and at last upon the riding of the Troopers with their Horses among them, they were totally scattered, and many of those Medeans sent to Bridewell and severall Prisons, whereof one amongst the rest, being a most deformed Medusa or Hecuba, with an old rusty blade

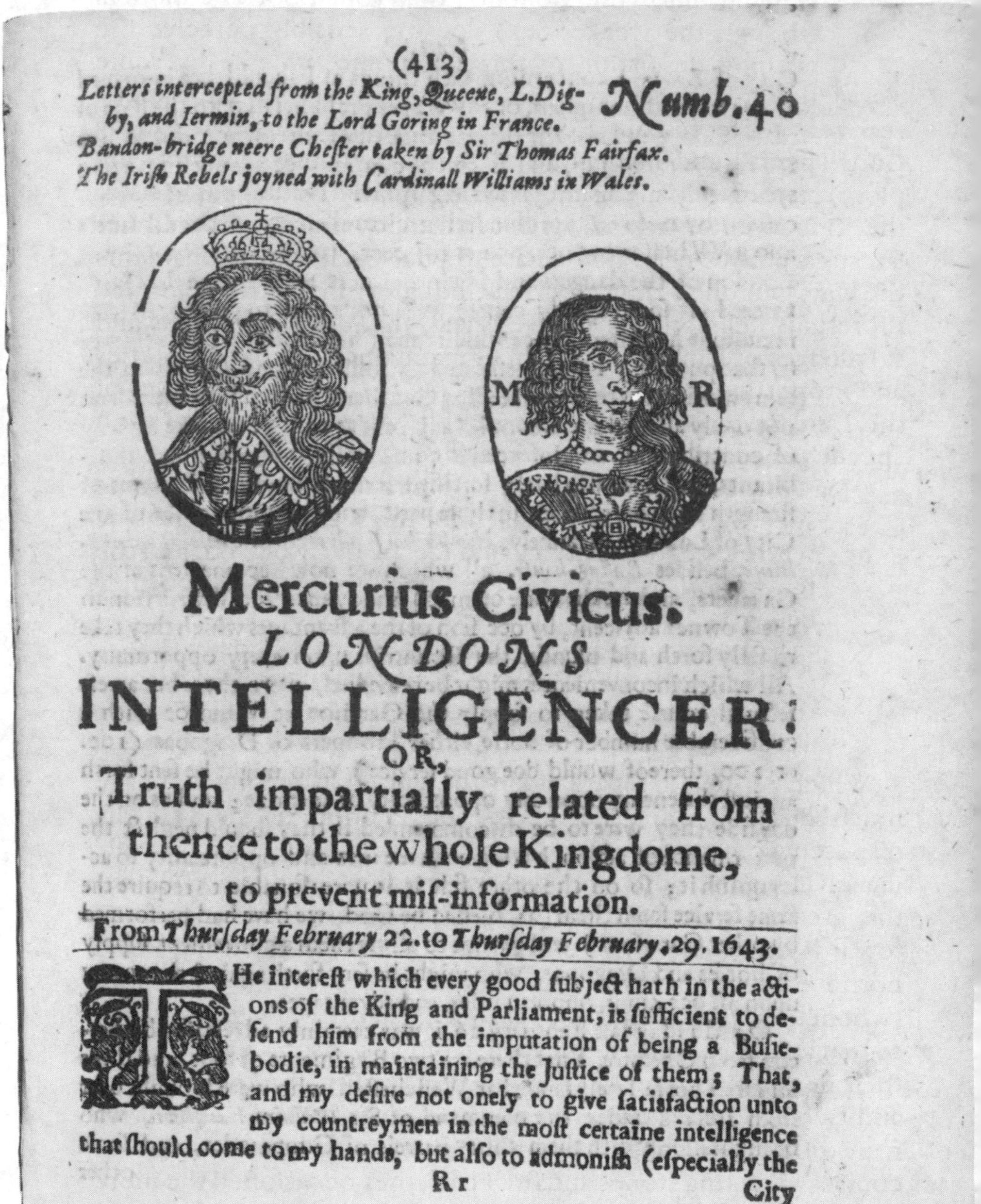

(413)

Letters intercepted from the King, Queene, L. Digby, and Iermin, to the Lord Goring in France. **Numb. 40**

Bandon-bridge neere Chester taken by Sir Thomas Fairfax.

The Irish Rebels joyned with Cardinall Williams in Wales.

M R

Mercurius Civicus.

LONDONS INTELLIGENCER:

OR,

Truth impartially related from thence to the whole Kingdome, to prevent mis-information.

From *Thursday February* 22. to *Thursday February*. 29. 1643.

THe interest which every good subject hath in the actions of the King and Parliament, is sufficient to defend him from the imputation of being a Busiebodie, in maintaining the Justice of them; That, and my desire not onely to give satisfaction unto my countreymen in the most certaine intelligence that should come to my hands, but also to admonish (especially the

Rr City

5. The Illustrated London newsbook, *Mercurius Civicus*

Numb. 149. (2095)

Mercurius Civicus.
LONDONS
INTELLIGENCER
OR,
Truth impartially related from thence to the whole Kingdome, to prevent mis-information.

From *Thursday, April* 2. to *Thursday April* 9. 1646.

ON Thursday *April* the second was the day for the Thanksgiving, for the victories obtained by Sir *Tho. Fairfax*, and his successefull armies in the West and by Sir *Will.Brereton* and Col. *Morgan* in the North-West. There preached before the house of Commons at Christ-church (where the Thanksgiving was solemnized by both houses of Parliament) M. *Peters*, and M. *Carrill*.

Cccccc This

6. *Mercurius Civicus*

by her side, had her hands tied behinde her with Match, and was guarded along by the trained Bands to prison, till further examination concerning the prime contrivers of this Designe.

The model woman, for royalist newsbooks, was the queen: some other high-born women were applauded for their political or military interventions. It was all the more humiliating for the enemy to be defeated by the efforts of the weaker sex. The report is from Portsmouth.

Mercvrivs Avlicvs

The three and thirtieth Weeke.

{13–19 August, 1643} 275.133 {3.08}

WEDNESDAY. *Aug*. 16. {...}

It was also signified from there that the Lady *Norton*, Mother to that most noble Colonell (who hath done such wonders of late daies) and Governesse for the present of the Towne of *Portsmouth*, (for the *Committee* dare doe nothing without her advice,) was very busily imployed in making some new works about *Portsey* bridge: and was not onely every day in person amongst the workemen (whom she encouraged much by her goodly presence) but brought also with her every day 30 or 40 maides and women in a Cart (they may perhaps live to be so coached hereafter) to digge and labour in the trenches. To the great honour of the Sex, of her person more, who in short time will grow as able to command in chiefe as the good Lady *Waller* to possesse the Pulpit. It was further signified from thence, that she, or the *Committee* by her direction, had caused a dungeon to be made there as darke as hell (that if the liberty of the Subject should be laied up there nobody should have hope to finde it) intended for such *Malefactors*, as it now appeares, who either doe refuse to take the new oath, or to pay their taxes, or otherwise shall shew any good affection to His sacred Majesty.

During the war, Mildmay had notoriously profited from selling the king's possessions; prior to the war he had been master of the king's jewel house. Here his wife is correspondingly castigated for parsimony.

Mercvrivs Avlicvs *The fortie fourth Weeke*

{29 October – 4 November, 1643} 275.144 {3.09}

SUNDAY. *Octob.* 29.

Hitherto we have acquainted you with the severall mischiefes of this Faction, but now I shall tell you what good I know of them; wherein I must be wondrous briefe, having onely one particular, and that one a woman, and that woman was guilty of one good thing, but the worst is, she knew not of it. For (as we were this day advertised) the Right Worshipfull the Lady *Mildmay*, whose husband we call Sir *Henry Mildmay* (one of His Majesties late good Servants.) This Lady being at Church on a *Fast* day, when there was a Collection for the poore Ministers of *Ireland*, saw people give money, and (like a true Christian Gentlewoman) threw into the Bason a peece of Gold of twenty shillings, but (good Lady) she had so wasted her eyes that day in beholding the face of the Preacher, that she tooke it for a shilling, and (as she sayes) meant it for no more, and therefore very ingenuously acknowledged her mistake, and sent to the Collectors for her peece of Gold; which they then denying, she peremptorily told them, *If they would not restore her Gold, she would never give the poore any thing as long as she lived*: The Collectors knowing this was the first time of her casting into the Bason, were unwilling to discourage a young beginner, and therefore returned her the very Gold she asked for, instead whereof she sent them a faire *Edward* shilling, whereat Sir *Henry* was very well pleased, telling her Ladiship, if he had kept His Majesties Jewels no better than she did her Gold, he had never gotten six pence by his place.

Mercurius Rusticus XV. Week.

*Octo.*7.1643 384.15 {3.10}

As the Rebells in their march towards *Glocester* passed through *Chiping Norton* in the County of *Oxford*: a woman of that Towne (whose zeal to the King and the Iustice of his cause could not containe it selfe though in the mid'st of his mortall Enimies) said in the hearing of some of the Rebells, *God blesse the Cavaliers*: (so are all good and faithfull Subjects called by the Rebells) This expression of the poore womans affection to the King and His loyall Subjects in so innocent a prayer, so highly insensed the Rebells, that to punish so hainous a Crime, presently they tyed her to the taile of one of their Carts, and stripping her to the Middle, for two miles march whipped her in so cruell a manner with their Cart-whips that her body in many places was cut so deep, as if she had been lanced with Knives, the torment being so great (as much as her straight bounds would give leave) she cast her selfe on the ground, so to shelter her selfe from their stripes, but in a most barbarous manner they dragged her along, in so much that her leggs and feet were so torne by the Stony rough wayes, that her flesh was worne off in many places to the very bones, at last having farre exceeded the number of stripes limited by God himselfe in the Law of *Moses* (though given by the hand of Iustice) *Forty stripes he may give him and not exceed, Deut*. 25. 3 they left her a Lamentable spectacle of their cruelty: in this miserable condition lay this poor soule for some few daies, and since died of those wounds which she received from them: The blood of this Innocent, mingled with the rest shed by their hands, crying loud with them under the Altar, *Revel*. 6.16. *How long, ô Lord, holy and true, doest thou not Judge and avenge our blood on them that dwell on earth?*

Mary-bones are knees, so named because of the Catholic predilection for kneeling.

The Man in the Moon (*Numb*. 12.)

27 June – 4 July, 1649 248.12 {3.11}

A hot combate lately happened at the *Salutation* Tavern in Holburn; where some of the Common-wealths vermin, called *souldiers* had seized on an Amazonian *Viraga* called Mrs *Strosse*, upon suspition of being a *Loyalist*, and selling *the Man in the Moons Book*; but she by applying beaten pepper to their *eyes*; disarmed them; and (with their own swords) forced them to aske her forgiveness; and down on their *mary-bones*, and pledge a health to the King; and confusion of their Masters the *Regicides*; and so honorably dismissed them. O for 20000 such gallant spirits to pepper the Roagues; you may see what valliant Puppies your *new Kings* be, when one woman can beat two or three of them.

There are several newsbook accounts of illicit or forced attempts to marry: this one involves the famous astrologer William Lilly. The editor of *Elencticus* was the royalist astrologer, George Wharton.

Mercurius Elencticus Numb. 3.

12–19 November, 1647 312.03 {3.12}

And because my taske is to reprove the Crimes of this mad age, it concernes me not to admit the fraile Practises of that Jugling Wizard *William Lilly*; the States Figure-Flinger Generall; a fellow made up of nothing but Mischiefe, Tautologies and Barbarisme; yet this Precious Youth hath beene lately the occasion of a great Blur in the ancient and Honourable Family of the *Scroopes*; namely, in the Marriage of the Lady *Annabella Scroope*, to one Mr. *John Howe* of *Lincoln-Inne* —— Thus. The Gentleman, (as who can blame him) scrues hopefully into the Acquaintance of this Lady (her fortune being no lesse then 2500 *l. per annum:*) and perceiving her Spirit a great deale to high for his Reach; applyes himselfe to this *Lilly* for advice, and (to say the Truth) for some unlawfull helpes for to gaine her Affection. The Jugler had large Promises made him of Reward, in Case he brought the businesse to perfection; and for the present, accepts of a good Round Fee; and thereupon resolves to Act by Policy, what he could not by Art: And to that end, advises the Gentleman to prepare some trusty friend to perswade the Innocent Lady to come to him upon a Horary Question, to know who should be her Husband: (For at this time she had Two Gallant Young Lords Sutors to her, which Mr. *Lilly* was fore-warn'd of) and to assure her that it was in his Power to resolve her truely. This was handsomely done, and the young Lady hastens with much Reverence and attention to this Lying Oracle: who tells her positively, That she should marry neither of the Lords that were then a Courting of her; but another Gentleman of such a Stature, Complexion, Haire, and Habite, as he then fully described to her in writing: and for her better satisfaction in the Poynt, wish'd her to goe into *Spring-Garden*, at such a time as he then appoynted her, and there (at the end of such a Walke) she should meet the very same Gentleman that the Heavens had ordained for her

Husband: And if she married him she should be the most fortunate Woman in the World; if not, the most unhappy under Heaven. Mr. *Howe* in the *Interim* is very Punctuall, and observ'd his directions to a haire; meets the betrayed Lady at the time appointed, and in the same habite which *Lilly* had cunningly, but most knavishly described unto her: The Appearance whereof, so amazed and bewitched the Good Lady, that she was never at quiet for them; but still with one device or other they so prosecuted the Plot, that she was (in a manner) forced through feare of the misfortune threatned her to marry him shortly after; to the utter undoing of a most Gallant Lady, and the extreame Griefe of her Noble Friends, who had provided more Honourably for her. This is a knowne Truth, which I thought fit to give the Kingdome notice thereof; that none be deluded with the abhominable Practices of this unworthy fellow *Lilly*: who deserves rather to be whipt about the Pig-market for this and other his Cheating Tricks upon Record, then to be countenanced and rewarded as he is by the Abettors of this Lying Age.

Certain Passages also recorded the results of these assizes, observing that not one man was to suffer. They represent some of the female crimes which caused the authorities most anxiety.

Perfect Proceedings of State-Affaires
Num. 306

2–9 August, 1655 599.306 {3.13}

Munday 6 *August*. {...}

This day was execution at *Kingstone* in *Surrey*, for the Gaol delivery of that County; where four women were put to death.

The first that was executed was a woman that had three Husbands, and the last of them was a Silck Throster, with whom shee had lived in good fashion, yet when hee was not well of a cold, and sent for some honey to take for it, she got poyson and mixed it with his honey, & so poysoned him, for which shee was this day burnt to death; And when shee came to the Stake, where was a Minister of the place, and Mr. *Bellers* of the Tower of *London*, a godly man well known, who called upon her to bee sensible of her condition, and seek for Peace with God, yet shee did not much regard it, calling it a trouble, which she desired she might not bee pressed with, only cryed out against pride, saying that that was the cause that brought her to this miserable end, and desired that all women would take warning by her example thereof.

The other three were hanged, they were all women, and al for murder also.

One of them was for killing her Child that was a Bastard.

The second was for killing one of her own Children, and being asked why she killed it, she said she did it because her Husband did not love it so well as he loved the rest of her Children.

And the third was a Woman that being in company with another woman they fell out, and she got a clout in her hand; and mastering the other woman, she stopped her mouth with the said clout, and choaked her to death.

Two Milk-women seeing a woman going very weakly in the fields neer Gileses, perceived that she had something in her lap, and when they came neer her they looked earnestly at her lap, and asking her what shee had in it that so wearied her, they received a crosse answer, but it so pleased God (as is said) that one of them espied the fingers of a child through an hole of her Apron, or Lap of her Coat, so that they would needs see what she had in her Lap, and there they found a new born Child alive, but the woman confessed that shee came to kill it, and throw it into some ditch or other place, and was two or three times about to do it, but still her heart misgave her, and shee could not find in her heart to do it; And had they gone away from her but an half quarter of an hour shee would have killed it; But by the means of these two women shee hath been prevented, and the Child is living.

Mercurius Politicus *Numb.* 362

14–21 May, 1657 361.362 {3.14}

At the Sessions in the Old Baily, 16 *May*, 1657.

There were five men and two women received Judgement to die; one of the women was for killing her Apprentice by immoderate correction, throwing him upon the ground, and stamping on the lower part of his belly; upon which violent and cruel usage he died.

The other woman was for stealing Five and twenty pound out of a Trunk; but she was reprieved by her belly. {...}

Women could be reprieved from death sentences (which were then not usually followed through) by 'their bellies', meaning pregnancy. This account contains an odd qualification.

Mercurius Politicus *Numb.* 275.

13–20 September, 1655 361.275 {3.15}

Cardigan, Sept. 8. 1655.

This place affords no matter of news, only it hath been a very wet Harvest; and we have suffered much by the floods, having taken away several bridges, and much Corn that lay on the low-lands. Last week there was a woman burnt to death in this Town, being sentenced to be so dealt with for stabbing of her own husband, she being drunk when she did it; she likewise pleaded that she was with child; on which a Jury of women was sworn, and they found her to be with child, but not quick. On which, the sentence pronounced was put in execution. {...}

An Advertisement.

WHereas Rebecca Bragg the Daughter of Rebecca Bragg, now the Wife of John Raymond of Bourley in the County of Essex, being under the age of fifteen year, is fraudulently carried away from her said Mother Mistress Raymond without her knowledge or consent, by Benjamin Dyster of Glensford in the County of Suffolk, and his Complices. These are to inform all Justices of the Peace to whom Marriages are committed by Law, that if the afore named Benjamin Dyster should appear before the said Justices or any of them, with the aforesaid Rebecca Brag, with intent to be married to her, that she the said Mistress Raymond her Mother, doth by these Presents forbid it, and desires the said Justices of the Peace not to marry them: In witness whereof she the said Mistress Raymond doth hereunto set her hand and seal in London, the 16 of September 1655.

This extended biography of Queen Christina of Sweden was probably published to distract attention from the trial of the English king, though certain elements were perhaps intended discreetly to suggest a comparison between the two monarchs. It serves as a treatise on proper female behaviour.

The Moderate Intelligencer Numb. 199

4–11 January, 1649 419.199 {3.16}

The Life and heroicall Imployments of Christina *the present Queen of* Swedland.

This Princesse, (th'onely Daughter & heire of the Great *Gustavus* King of the *Swedes, Gothes*, and *Vandales*,) was borne in *December*, 1626. Nature bestowed a new Sun upon the Northern Countries then, when th'old one was removed furthest from their Horizon. A yeare happy likewise in the glorious Defence of *Livonia*, and the Victory gotten by her Father of the *Lithuanians* in Fields of *Walovia*, and in that of the *Swedes* over the Polonians at *Riga*; *Dirschau*, and *Marienbourg*; the rest of the good Towns of *Prussia*, receiving Swedish Garrisons; and that of *Dantzic*, after an unprofitable tryall of her forces against them, being enforced to redeeme her selfe, and pay them a full price for her Liberty.

This great Kingdome *Swethland*, (so ancient as it reckons at this day, upon 52 Christian Kings, or Queens (making no difference of Sex in its Sovereignes vertue and worth being alike found in both) besides 102 that were Pagans, the last whereof was *Alaricus* the third) received, in the year 1597, a notable Change, by *Sigismond* the Third's Refusall to quit *Polonia* for the Kingdome of *Sweden*; whereby the Crowne thereof was transferred unto *Charles* the ninth of that Name; by whose deceass, happening the 29 of *Octob*. 1611, *Gustavus Adolphus* the Great, his Son, succeeded him, and was crowned in the yeare 1617 in the 21 yeare of his Age; and dying victorious, the 15 of *Novemb*. 1632, in the 21 yeare of his Reigne, in the famous Battell of *Lutzen*, this Princesse; then onely 6 yeares old, took in her hand the Scepter of this warlike Estate, supported, during her yonger yeares by a most generous Counsell.

Tis very much to have been borne of so great and redoubted a Prince, who in his life and death made tremble not onely all *Germanie*, but a great part of the Christian World by th'ever prosperous success of his victorious Armies. But because that true vertue, although it need exterior Ornaments yet it drawes no part of its unestimable worth from any thing but it selfe let's see by what meanes, and degrees the Princesse, whose life I describe; hath gotten the high esteeme, and full commendation which she hath, at this time, all the World over.

Having learnt of *Themistocles*, that Languages are like rich Hangings, the Beauty whereof no Report can so well, as th'Original, discover to th'eye, she would not rely on Interpreters in treating with the Neighbour Nations, but made 6 Tongues familiar unto her, *viz*; the German, the Swedish, the Latine, Greek, Frech, and Italian: she had, from her Infancy, learnt the German of her Mother, *Maria Eleonona* sister to the deceassed Elector of *Brandebourg*, as she had sucked in the Swedish, together with her milke, although they be more different one from th'other then the French is from the Spanish. The Latin she got from her School-Masters, & by Rules; and hath made it so easie unto her by conference with learned men, as she understandeth *Tacitus*, and all the Latine Poets; gives Audience, in that Language, to Ambassadours and Residents; and answers them at th'Instant, so elegantly, as they all depart from her ravished with admiration of such lively Eloquence in a Tongue that's dead. And as that Spirit, capable of all knowledge, meant lately to content her selfe with some sleight touch of the Greek, she got, in a few moneths, as great understanding therein as others are able to read it in that time.

The French she hath learnt so perfectly by Rules, and chiefly by her much conversing with the French Nobility in her Court, and th'Officers she hath of that Nation, that there is none in her Kingdome speaks it better; and the most neat Frenchmen would take her to be, by Birth, as she is in affection, really French: an affection which shee throughly expresses, not omitting any occasion of advancing the French; attiring herself after the Fashion of the Ladies of *France*: she likewise understands th'Italian so well, as she gives Audience to the Venetian Ambassadour, and to those that delight in that Tongue more than others. I leave them to judge that have tryed the hardnesse of making a forreigne Language familiar unto them, what difficulties shee may have met with in Learning so many different ones (whereof one commonly hinders th'other) and that so perfectly in so young an Age.

And because, me thinkes, you wish for the Portraiture of so perfect a Princesse, take as right a one as I can draw you, Her stature is neither too great nor too little; the constitution of her body of a middle size, neither leane, nor too fat: the forme thereof upright, and apt for all kinde of Exercises, especially Dancing, to which notwithstanding she is not further addicted then that she would be ignorant of nothing, The Lineaments of her face are very well proportioned, the tincture thereof mingled with white and red, as one may say with Lillies and Roses, the more agreeable because naturall, having never known what belongs unto Paint, not onely because she loves a naturalnesse in all things about her, but also for that such kinde of painting is hated and abominated all that Country over. In a word, her Grace, and Majesticall Carriage have formed in her such a connexion of sweetnesse, and gravity, that as she can winne by her looks and affability th'affection of all those that have th'honour to come neer her, so doe they imprint in them a modesty, and awfulnesse which Majestie brings ordinarily with it, and is by Nature stamped in the forehead of Sovereigne Power.

Likewise, notwithstanding her beauty and youth, her honour is not onely masculine, and vigorous, and such as is feigned to have been in those acceptable Pictures of *Pallas*, which lose no part of their lovelinesse because they are armed, but she, in her own disposition, prefers courageous before cowardly persons, not being able to perswade her selfe that any generous thing can proceed from a spirit that expresses any baseness in gesture or words; and believes that her Court, being a Theater of honour, there's nothing to be there hoped for by those that cannot boldly play their Parts therein.

She never bestows above an houre in dressing her selfe, and which is wonderfull, the skil by which the most part of Ladies endevour to make themselves the more acceptable, is found in her lesse prevalent then her neglect: and the grace of her Attire, chiefely, th'Ornament of her Haire, whereon others doe usually bestow so much time and tricking, seemes greatly increased by her neglecting of it.

Her ordinary employments in the Morning (which ever finde her up, not knowing how to turn day into night) are, after her Prayers and Studies, to goe unto the Manage, there to see her horses labour, and exercise themselves; by which care and others which she takes of War, and in the pleasure she hath in hearing men talke of it, *Ulysses* would have been deceived, doubting the truth of her sex, as he did that of *Achilles*: To goe a hunting, when the weather serves, and that on horsback, as her other Ladies, among whom she appears like an Amazon, managing her horse with such dexterity, as although she lets him run with full speed, yet shee shoots not off her Peece the lesse, nor hits her Game the worse, for all that.

At her return (for she never loseth dayes, no, not whole mornings, in that Royall exercise, she findes out another much more Royall then it) shee enters into her Councel-Chamber; where shee hath the patience to heare the opinions of all the Colledges, which are sometimes assembled all in one Body, though they be five in number, *viz.* 1 That of Justice, 2 That of War, 3 That of th' Admiralty, 4 Of State Affairs, and 5 Of the Treasury; composed each of foure Senators, and one President; besides, many Counsellours: and because the last of these Colledges disposes of the Sinews of War (her Element) she hath lately taken her selfe the most exact notice of the Revenues of her Kingdom: you would not believe how much all these exercises of the Body, and mind accompanied with sobriety, confirms her health, and th'vigour both of th'one and th'other, were it not that shee hath been but seldome, and that but a little, if at all, sick.

Th'Afternoon shee dedicates to Audiences, and honest Recreations of the mind, and such whereunto Invention, and Dexterity contribute more then hazard: That being a little refreshed, shee bestowes the rest of that time in the opening of Packets, and dictating Answers unto them; those which have instructed her to receive and return such Dispatches, remembering that it was by this industry, that one of our (French) Kings, to whom the Tutelage of *Charles* the Fifth was Committed, by his Father *Ferdinando*, made that Emperour so skilfull in affairs of State, especially in his own, as he cut out all his worke to *Francis* the First, which we read of in the History of the continual Wars they made th'one with th'other.

After her Ministers of State, she most esteems men of learning, in the study whereof, and to furnish her selfe with the knowledge of the best Sciences, by the reading of good Books, she spends not onely what part of the day remains after th'exercises and employment aforesaid, but oftentimes the greater halfe of the night, which often causes a feare among her Subjects (by whom she is no lesse beloved, then she is loving to them) that those her immoderate watchings, and over-earnest applications to reading, wil bring some prejudice to her health; the which objection she resolves by her experience to the contrary; and intreats them not to deny her this conference with the disinteressed Dead, which speak unto her and all Great ones more truely then those that are living dare doe, what Liberty soever is given them, or they pretend to take: and assures them, that she receives more satisfaction by them then all other her innocent and lawfull Recreations. And therefore one need not wonder that this her frequent conversation with the most skilfull and judicious spirits, hath made her one of the most prudent, sage, and vertuous Princesses of her Age, extraordinarily out-gone by her great Capacity, and th'experience of others; which she applyes unto herself: And her knowledge is in no sort Pedanticall but so applyed unto the Custome of her Court, that it is easie to judge how perfect an Owner she is of what she knows. And the care she hath of her Books is such, as fire having, by chance taken hold of a part of her Pallace, she never dreamt of saving her Cloth of gold and other rich Moveables wherewith it is most sumptuously furnished, but onely recommended her Books, and Papers unto her Officers care to see them preserved from that ravenous Element.

Her Majestie of *Sweden* is not onely content to give to the Publicke all these Testimonies of her Affections to Learning out of her knowledge that it is the support of Armes, and one of the most powerfull meanes of making States to flourish; but she goes two or three times a year to th'University of *Oupsal*, a days Journy from *Stockholme* (the chiefe Town where she usually resides, in the same Pallace with the Queen *Dowager* her Mother, holding both a most perfect correspondency together) to be present at the publick Exercises of the Students in that University; whereby you may judge what a vertuous Emulation is bred in all the Spirits both of the Masters & Schollers by the Royall presence of this learned Princesse, most able to judge of their Parts, and the fruits of their Studies.

But among all her goodliest, and most commendable Actions, we cannot forget without doing her much wrong, that although she expresses her constancy to war, when she findes she must follow it, yet she hath ever a greater disposition unto Peace. So that when she receiveth Intelligence of any Battel gotten, or Town taken, by her Commanders, or Allyes (as it often falls out, and whereof our Journalls are so full, as it were but, an abuse of time to repeat them unto you) her first word always is, *God be praised; this will certainely promote a Peace*; and to all th'Instructions which she hath given her Plenipotentiaries she always adjoyneth this, that they advance the Peace and hasten the Conclusion thereof, as soon as they can possibly to the glory of God, and the Good of her, and her Allyes Estates.

And this was the Condition of *Swethland*, and of its Queen towards th'end of this yeare; wherein the Senators of that Kingdome have resolved of a Generall Assembly (to be held the

13 of *January* next, at *Stockholme*) of all their foure States, (*viz.* the Nobility, Clergie, Townes, and Country-men,) to agree on a Day for the Coronation of this Princesse: of whom I have no more to say, but that I will admire the felicity of that Prince, who shall be so happy as to enjoy such a Treasure, and so may perfections: And perhaps it would be a lesse gracefull thing to describe her unto you after her Marriage then it is at this time, when her Condition of being a Virgin, which crownes all the rest of her vertues, makes her the more considerable, and th'admirable Object of all the Princes and Monarchs of the World.

One of a very large number of articles on the Queen of Sweden, who wandered across Europe, legend has it, dressed as a man. She was widely criticised first for refusing to marry and then for abdicating and converting to Catholicism.

Mercurius Politicus *Numb:* 217.

3–10 August, 1654 361.217 {3.17}

From Brussels the 9. *of August.*

Here is little news to write, by reason the Siege before *Arras* doth still continue in the same condition as was mentioned in my last. The fifth of this moneth at night *Christina* queen of *Sweden* arrived at *Antwerp*, in mans Apparel, coming there *incognito* with a small company, her Train arriving there the next day, at which time shee was drest in Womans cloaths, and was going abroad in the Coach of *Don Balthazar Mercader*, Governor of that City. The Queen hath fild all these parts with variety of discourse; and most extoll her above the rest of her Sexe for vertue and learning. From hence she goeth to the *Spaw*: She is lodged at one Seigneur *Garcia de Guiano*, a *Portuguese*; and so likewise at *Hamburgh* she lodged at a *Portuguese* Jews house. She hath the Earl of *Douau*, of *Steinbergern*, and the Baron of *Soop* in her company; travelling all *incognito*, as they did in the Country of *Denmark* and *Holstein*. {...}

From Hamburgh July 27.

There are but few passages here, to which I have only to add; That if *Charls Stuart* come hither, as the currant Report goes he will in a few dayes, then you may expect my next will tell you a story of it, and his entertainment here. The little Qu: of *Sweden* play'd Bo-peep with her Princes, whom she made believe she would goe to the *Spaw*; but its since certainly said she's gon to *Bruxels*, and that she will Winter there; he must be an *Oedipus* that Riddles her meaning in this Resignation, and manner of life she betakes herself unto; travailing from post to pillar without a Woman to wait on her.

The Weekly Intelligencer of the Common-Wealth Numb: 2

21–28 August, {1655} 688.306 {3.18}

Friday, August 24.

THere are many ships now under sail for VIRGINIA, in which are many Female Passengers, who during the aboad of the lusty Cavaliers in this City, and the Suburbs of it, are said to have been Ladies of Pleasure, but it is known that IRELAND or VIRGINIA, can make them honest again, and either by a pardoning silence, or by the indisputable necessity, and importunity of Nature, or by the candor of some nobler belief, they are able at any time to recover their crazy, or most debauched Reputation.

In John Crouch's version of commonwealth London, 'freedom' and 'liberty' become passwords for brothels, which maintain inverted social hierarchies in their purveyance of sin.

The Man in the Moon (*Numb*. 21.)

5–12 September, 1649 248.21 {3.19}

YEs, yes: Now it runs down by the *Rebels* heels, since the great mock-*Victory* of *Jones*, nothing but Joy, Feasting, Revelling, and another Recreation with the Saints called in plain English *Whoring*: Now their Bellies are full of all the good things belonging to *God*, the *King*, and *People*, they begin to say, *Soul take thy rest, eat, drink, and enjoy the pleasures of the Earth*; *as for* Heaven *and* Hell, *they are but meer Fables to scare Children with, &c*. which hath made some of the pamper'd rebellious *Iuncto* so lusty, that they have Erected about *Spring-Garden*, and Saint *Jameses*, no less then Three *Nurceries* of *Sodomy, Lust*, and *Uncleanness* to recreate their Spirits, and keep their Gifts and rebellious *members* in action.

The first is by my Lord *Gorings house*, or the *Mulbery-Garden*, called the *Whipping-School*, erected by the Worshipful Colonel *Martin* for the encrease of the Saints in the *Iuncto*: None is to enter here except a *Parliament man*, and not he neither without the *Word*, which is *Freedom*: At the Door (when he enters) he gives Five shillings the first time, and then he is after Free: So soon as he is come in, for his Ceremony, he is presented with a *naked wench* lying upon a Bed, to whom he approaches with bowing himself three times, and offers a Crown in Gold, and layes it upon her Chin, which she by a dexterious trick gives a toss and flings it into her *Tinder-box of Lust*; then afterwards he goes and chuseth which pleaseth him best, and so they go to their *Exercise*.

The Second is by Saint *Iamses*, and this is called the *Mopping School* (founded by one *Weaver*) and there so soon as a *Iuncto-man* comes to his Recreation, he gives the *Word* (which is *Liberty*) and but One shilling at the Door: So soon as he is entered, he is had up into a spacious Room, where the Wainscot of the Wall being but touch'd, falls down into an under Room, and along the Walk are several windows, through every of which are discovered their she *damnations*, one Singing, another playing on the Lute, another on Virginals, another reading a Lecture of Lust out of *Ovid*, and so they all employ themselves: to that which he likes best, he gives a Nod with his head, & presently she is ushered by the Matron or Bawd into a Room hung with all manner of Lacivious Pictures, with Perfumes burning, and musick unseen; and there they lie sometimes two, three, or four dayes together in a Close Committee of uncleanesse.

The Third is called *The Nunnery*, and thither their Inferior Clerks and other subordinate Officers, and Foot-men go, (not a man to enter there except the *word*, which is *Queen Mary*) they give no Money at entrance, but only Cross themselves on their Foreheads, in a mock to the sign in Baptisme, and to they enter, and for Three pence a Jigge, may use as many as they will; and all this under *Prides* very Nose, yet un-controul'd, so that *Pride* and *Lust* liveth together. Three Citizens Wives (pretending other business) were lately taken coming out of the *Mopping School* by their Husbands, who discovered this to me; but for their Names I have promised them to conceal.

Thus in base *Lust* and loathsome vile excess
They spend the Kingdoms wealth in wickednesse:
Whilst the poor *Commons* labour, but in vain
Vile *Luxury* and *Whoredome* to maintain.

The regicide Henry Marten was unjustly maligned as a notorious philanderer: unlike Restoration libertines his subsquent reputation has never been glamorised.

The Man in the Moon (*Numb.* 25.)

10–17 October, 1649 248.25 {3.20}

A *Bawd*, belonging to the *Mopping-School*, was likewise Sentenced to be *Carted*, that had Cozened *Harry Martyn* and some other Members of the *Juncto* in their *Venery*, and sold them *stale-flesh* for *Maids*: which was taken for a high *Contempt* against the Members of PARLIAMENT, because that *Harry Martyn* is disabled thereby (this fall of the leafe) to give any personal attendance in the *House*.

A Perfect Account Num. 110.

9–16 February, 1653 496.110 {3.21}

Beginning Wednesday, February 9.

FRom Edenburgh Feb. 5. The Judges have sate severall times this week upon criminal cases; upon triall they met with such as I think never came before any Judge on earth, viz. Margaret Rain (so called) of the age of eighteen years, who hath constantly been reputed a woman till of late, that she was accused of that detestable abomination of Buggery with a Mare, who upon ordinary search was thought to be an Hermophradite, but now by an inquest of Chyrurgians, is found to be a man of that sort the Phylosophers call Hypospadians, this creature by evidence of certain persons is convict of that beastly crime, and I believe will be burned together with thc beast, according to the Mosaical law.

Accounts of witches were used to represent an inverted political, social and gender order: during the civil wars and Interregnum period the political content often became very explicit. In practice, witchcraft cases were a nexus of accusation and counter accusation precipitated by local tensions.

Mercurius Politicus *Numb:* 181.

24 November – 2 December, 1653 361.181 {3.22}

From *Mylor* in *Cornwall*, Nov. 23.

We have a strange discovery of Witches about the *Lands-end*. One of them being taxed of witchcraft by a Neighbour, she instantly got a Warrant from Major *Ceely* to call the Party before him, who came, and by witnesses made it apparent. This wretch being discovered, she discovers others: Eight of them are sent to *Lanceton*, and seven more in durance.

One is a *black Witch*, who confesseth her cruelties in being the death of men, women, children, and cattel.

There is also a *white Witch*, who discovers many, and saith she never did harm, but healed many diseases, and unwitched many that had been bewitched by the *black Witches*. This skill of hers she imputes to Gods Spirit; only hath confessed, that she had an Appearance came to her once a year in the shape of a Dove, and upon its presence her skill was revived and renewed.

There was one who had her Milk bewitched, and could make neither Cream nor Butter, but in boiling the milk it would still crust, and at last kept boiling till the crust brake in the middle, and two Toads were seen therein, passing one by and over another.

Another confessed the Devil did suck her by the lip each moneth; and therein she felt such pain that to be rid of it she was forced to send the Devil on some destructive errand.

This philosophical statement on witchcraft discusses the way the Devil, with his limited powers, works to pervert existing human forms and ordinances. It is also an attempt to rationalise some theoretical statements on Daemonology.

The Parliaments Post *Num*. 13.

29 July – 5 August, 1645 487.13 {3.23}

THere is an infection in wickednesse; And the spirit of the Caviliers because it could not prevaile with our men, hath met with some of our women, and it hath turned them into Witches. Nothing doth more vexe my understanding, and disparage it into wonder, then to consider by what extent of spirituall power the devil can assume a body. Whither this body be reall or phantasticall I leave unto the *Casuists* to dispute. I am taught by the rule of Phylosophy to affirme that it is onely a phantasticall body: But by the delight which these Sorceresses doe receive from it, It should appeare to be a reall body. Howsoever the greatest delight in the act of lust consisting most in the imagination (as all Phylosophers do affirme) why may not the Divell abuse the imagination (the greatest faculty on which he workes) to apprehend those delights to be bodied and reall, which indeed are but imaginary. {...}

Howsoever it will be worth your meditation to observe how constantly the workes of darknesse do follow the workes of light, as the night doth follow the day. The institution of marriage was ordained in Heaven, and now forsooth the Divell must be married on earth. Nay, there must also be an obligation of words, such as are accustomed to be spoken by those who are united to one another in that honorable ordinance. The Devill hath an excellent memory, and it may be, that some such words were used at the first mariage in Paradise, howsoever the manner and method of it is descended to the Posterity of *Adam* all over the face of the earth. And now the Devill doth take the maide by the hand, and calling her by her name, doth say, I take thee *Rebecca* to be my wife, and doe promise to be thy loving husband untill death, defending thee from all harmes. And the mayde is taught to answer, I *Rebecca* doe take thee to be my husband, and doe promise to be an obedient wife till death, and faithfully to observe and performe all thy commands. Alas poore maide! How art thou betrayed? what a sad marriage is this, where the Divell is both the Husband and the *Officiate* too?

But *Why must the Divell be married to a maide*? The Divell indeed (though here in the shape of a young man) is an old sinner, and what a warme and soft restorative and cherishing comfort a young maide doth in the bed, bring to the decrepit coldnesse of decayed Age, the excellent *Fracanstorsius* can resolve you.

We finde that the Divell in the shape of a personable man hath had carnall copulation with these women. The pleasure which the Divell taketh by lust is not so much that it is lust, or that lust is a sinne, and a sin absolutely repugnant to the will of God, and indeed this is the worst condition that man or divell can be in, as to delight in sin, and to commit it onely, because that sinne is offensive unto God, I doe neither believe that the devil doth appeare in a reall body or (being a spirit) that he taketh any pleasure in the carnall acts of lust: but that the female being the weaker sexe, and the inclinations of the flesh being prone unto lust, the Divell maketh choyce by that way most to obliege his servants, which by nature most they are addicted to.

Severall Proceedings in Parliament *Num.* 15

4–11 January, 1649{50} 599.015 {3.24}

There is a great quarrell broken out in *Scotland*, between the Clergy and the Lawyers, each envying at the others ambition, but some talke that both of them have been to blame, in causing many hundreds of poore people to be burnt for Witches, in which some say there hath beene cruell tyranny, and many harmelesse people put to death, onely for their ignorance.

Mercurius Politicus *Numb.* 859. {589}

29 September – 6 October, 1659 361.589 {3.25}

From Rome, Septemb.3. {...}

This day here is to be an execution of seven women, who poysoned their husbands with the same subtile poyson, for which some others died about a quarter of a year ago.

Within these few days, a Lady of quality hath been apprehended and imprisoned for the same crime, which is now grown very common, notwithstanding the dreadful punishment of immuring them betwixt walls alive, that they may languish to death. It is hoped, that the severe Edicts published by the Pope, and the example of this execution, will prove a remedie for this evill in time to come.

The Moderate Intelligencer *Numb*. 7.

10–17 April, 1645 419.007 {3.26}

Sunday, April. 13.

GIve us leave to insert somewhat this day, and pardon the digression both to the day and also of the matter, it being not upon the subject of *Mars*, which is our busines, but of *Venus* and *Bacchus*, Its a strange custome in *Lincolnes Inne-fields*, not far from the *Portugall* Ambasadours house; the practise we conceive every way as bad, as any that were used when the book of Recreations commanded or permitted maygames, and revellings: but not to keep you from the matter any longer: There gathers many hundreds of men, women, maids, and boyes together, then comes *Negers*, and others of like rankes, these make sport with our English women and maids, offer in the *Venetian* manner, by way of introduction to that used in their *Stews*: why these black men should use our English maides and women upon the Lords day, or any other, in that manner, we know no reason for: but the truth is, the fault is wholly in those loose people that come there, and in the Officers of those Parishes where it is done.

In this rather offensive story, a woman functions as a cause for beating a parliamentarian. Note the mocking use of the term 'Gentlewoman', and the more direct 'Pusse'. A parson called Shepperd was sent for as a Delinquent by the Commons, for assaulting Corbet.

Mercurius Elencticus Numb. 45

27 September – 4 October, 1648 312.45 {3.27}

But that which most of all troubled them was an affront, (much like that of Sir *Henry Mildmays)* put upon *Myles Corbet*, the Iew, by some Cavaliers, against whom he made a most pitifull complaint to the House, having all the while his Arme [where his neck should be] *that is to say*, in a string; being sore wounded, and beaten [but not much blacker then before.] The story goes thus: On Wednesday last [being the *Fast Day*, by all good Tokens] Two Gentlemen going to take water, overtook *Corbet*, with a Whore at his Elbow, [her name I do not Remember, but the Drawers at the *Pye* without *Algate* perhaps may informe you, for there he meets the same *Gentlewoman* very often] and as it seemes took the Boldnesse to question what Interest *Myles Corbet* had in her, whose *Language* [proving as ugly as his Face] procured him a Kick or Two upon the Britch, which being hardened with so long *Sitting*, was perceived not to be much felt; and therefore one of the *Gentlemen* was pleased to supply that defect; and so *Caned* him over the Head and shoulders, very orderly into the *Boat*, and by that means Divors'd him from his Divine *Pusse*, who it seems knew the Gentleman, and hath since made Discovery of him to her *Sweeting*, who gave his Name to the Serjeant at Armes; And the House Voted it a high Breach of Priviledge for any Member to be *Robbd* of his Minion, or any way else to be Affronted, Assaulted, or Diverted from his Pleasure, whereupon the Persons of those Gentlemen were Ordered to be apprehended, which in my opinion have rather Merited their Thanks, then their Displeasure, who [for aught they know] have prevented the Issue of another Monster, that might have followed the Copulation with such a hiddeous Creature as *Myles Corbet*.

'Tom Lock', author of the short-lived *Jocosus*, produced a slightly less obscene pamphlet in the comical style of Crouch.

Mercurius Jocosus. Or The Merry Mercurie

28 July – 4 August, 1654 336.2 {3.28}

Female conscience.

A woman whose husband had been absent 7 yeers, and hee afterward coming home, and finding her married to another, yet demanded her as his wife, and her other husband refused to deliver her because legaly married unto her: The matter in difference was referred to a Iustice of peace, who placing her two husbands, the one at one end of the table, and the other opposite, bad her view them both wel, and told her insomuch as shee was lawfully married to them both, shee might have either of them, which shee would. the woman looking first upon one, and then on the other, said, May it please your worship sir, I hope I shal please them both.

The Kingdomes Weekly Intelligencer
Numb. 230.

12–19 October, 1647 214.230 {3.29}

There happened a passage or two this weeke which though not memorable, it is yet remarkeable, The one is of a Young Man, who being high in wine and reeling over the Bridge at *Stratford* upon *Avon*, it so fell out, that the neck of one of his spurs did fasten it selfe in the other, whereon he fell downe into the River and was drowned. The other was of a Yeoman not farre from *Warwick*, who for want of discretion or other discourse would sell his wife to his Companion. He asked what he would take for her, The Yeoman answered five pound. The other looking on her (for she was present) and conceiving with himselfe *that a good wife is worth gold*, he thought that she was worth five pound or worse then nothing; whereupon he presently layd downe the money, and tooke his purchase in his Armes and kissed her: Not a quarter of an houre after, The Yeoman repented of his bargaine, and offered to restore the money, and desired to have his wife returned. His Companion left it to her choyce, not without some intimation that he was loath to leave her; The good woman assured him that she was well content to live with him and had rather goe with the buyer then the seller, and accordingly expressing a courteous farewell to her Husband, she went along with his Companion. The poore Yeoman who (on better consideration) had rather lose his life then lose his wife, hath since made his complaint to all the Justices in that County, and because he cannot get her by love he is resolved to try if he can get her by law, and with extreame impatience attends the approach of the Tearme intending at the very first sitting, if he can, to have his cause heard in *Westminster* Hall before the Judges of the Common Pleas.

This passage employs the commonplace link between sexual and religious transgression, and anticipates Rochester's pornographic verse. 'Bedlam' was Crouch's name for Britain: 'Ranter' his general pejorative for unrestricted behaviour, usually female.

Mercurius Fumigosus, or the Smoaking Nocturnall [*Numb.* 10]

2–9 August, 1654 322.10 {3.30}

The last week the *Ranters* Exercised in a Parlour neer *Milk-street*, where they taught *liberty* to act *Evill*, and after the blessing of *increase* and *multiply*, they ended that daies Speaking of *Blasphemy* with this fine modest Sing-Song following.

You that can Revell Day and Night,
To enjoy the Fruits of Loves *Delight,*
With whomsoere you can acquire,
To quench the flames of Cupid's *fire,*
You must mark this, that when you meet
(In Garden, Orchard, Field or street)
With Feeble Brethren that scarce can
Perform the duty of a man,
Let them not sally from your lapp
Till you salute them with a Clap;
Dear Sisters, *you may freely doo't*
As easy as to stirr a foot,
But if you cannot, tell me now,
And I my self will teach you how.
When you meet lusty men of strength,
That will not bate a jot of length,
Oh hugg them hard, and suck them in,
Untill they even do burst your skin,
Spread forth the crannyes of those Rocks
That lie beneath your Holland smocks;
Stretch out your limbs, sigh, heave and straine,
Till you have opened every veine:
That so Loves *gentle juice that flowes*
Like Dewie Nectar, out of those
That press you down may run a tilt,
Into your wombs, and not be spilt
Do this (dear Sisters) *and hereby*
You shall increase and multiply,
And in some 20 *years you'l spread*
Further then Jacob's *Children did.*

> *But (like the* Saints*) I pray be sure*
> *Your speeches all be fine and pure;*
> *Let Gospel words, and sweet Expressions,*
> *Divine Narrations, and Confessions*
> *Be in your mouthes, though lusty T—ses,*
> *Are stoutly knocking at your A—ses.*

How like you this sport my bonny *Besses* of *Great Bedlam*? Is it not that *liberty* ye long look'd for; to lie with whom you list, live merrily, Eat, drink, sing, and enjoy the pleasures of the World.

Mercurius Fumigosus [Numb. 12.]

16–23 August, 1654 322.12 {3.31}

The *Celestiall Dogg-star* casts so Powerful an Influence this Week on Womens Cod-pieces, that it is impossible to carry a Virginity among them, which will not be seized on by these *Shee-Mastiffs*, that are so eager of their *Game*, that in *Sodom, Gomorah, Long-Acre, Drewry-lane, Ratliffe* High-way; and many other places, they run *open-mouth'd* at their Prey; As this last week, a Carter fetching *Grains* for his Horse, neer the Place last named, one of these *shee-Mastiffs*, set upon him; pulling him down into the Binn of *graines*, insomuch that the poor Carter had like to have been ravished by her, she biting so close by the *breech*, that she broak his *lusty Cod-piece Point*, making a second *Joseph* of the man, who fled from her with his Breeches about his heels; and when she could not have her *desire*, laid the blame on him, *that he would Ravish her*.

Another (being a *Coopers* maid at *Dowgate*) wanting a *Hoop* for her *Bucking-tubb*, had provided a *Coopers* man in *Lime-street* to do the *Jobb* for her, at 10 a Clock at *Night*, which they had done *undiscovered*, or *apprehended*, had not the Wenches Voice been heard by one of the Apprentices, saying; *It's in; It's in*; to which the *Cooper* replyd, *come buss me then.*

> 'Tis but the Text I have exprest,
> You may imagine all the rest.

Two of these *shee-Ranters*, walking lately a *clicketting* to *Rygate*, pick'd up two *Culls* or *Dicks* by the way, and ticing them to an *Ale-house*, kept them there all day till *Mid-Night*, about which time they all striped themselves *stark naked*, and fell to dancing about their *Roome*, which noise so disturbed the Master of the House, that he sent for Mr. *Constable*, who apprehending them, the *women* would not hide but the next day went *stark naked* about the *streets*; being demanded if they had Husbands? they replyed, *Their Husbands were within them, which was God*. Oh that Women (the shape of Angels) should prove worse then Devills!

The Kingdomes Weekly Intelligencer
Numb. 294.

9–16 January, 1648{9} 214.294 {3.32}

There is one thing worthy your observation, and it is most certaine. There was last yeer in *Scotland* a woman of threescore and ten yeers of age great with child, but what with the throng of people that daily came to see her, and crying out. It was a prodigy, and what with the fright of the Warre, for the Ingagement then broke forth, the poore woman miscarryed some five months before her time, but this yeer she is great with child againe, and is now threescore and eleven yeers of age, and hath a husband three yeers older then her selfe: This is a most certein truth, the woman lives in the South of *Scotland* adjacent to the Lands of my Lord *Lothian*, who (if I am not much mistaken) is now in *London*, and one of the Commissioners of the Kingdome of *Scotland*.

Mercurius Politicus *Numb*. 442.

11–18 November, 1658 361.442 {3.33}

Advertisements. {...}

WHereas *Penelope*, the Wife of *Erasmus Deligne* of *Harlaxton*, in the County of *Lincoln*, Esq; hath voluntarily deserted her said Husband, and accepted of a certain Annual allowance from him for Alimoney. He the said *Erasmus Deligne* doth therefore hereby publish and declare to all manner of persons, as well Tradesmen as others, residing within the Dominions and Territories of his Highness *Richard* Lord Protector, *&c.* not to Credit or Trust the said *Penelope Deligne* with any Wares, Merchandises, or other Commodities whatsoever. Forasmuch as the said *Erasmus Deligne* by the Laws of this Nation is not, so from henceforth he will not be liable to the payment or other satisfaction of any such person or persons, for any such Wares, Merchandises, or Commodities; nor for any other Debts which the said *Penelope Deligne*, or any other person or persons employed by her, shall contract on her behalf. Dated and published this Thirteenth day of *November*, 1658. *Erasmus Deligne.*

Milton published his first divorce tract in 1643. John Dillingham's *Parliament Scout* later expressed an interesting sympathy towards the plight of women in marriage.

The Parliament Scovt *Numb*. 77.

5–12 December, 1644 485.77 {3.34}

Friday the 6. *of* December.

The Commons took into consideration, that part of the Directory to marriage, which it seems is for matter, as before, and the party that is to marry, as before: we hope hereafter care will be taken for the relief of the husband and wife in case each denies cohabitation, &c. and also to punish the exorbitancies of the husband to the wife: if a Master strike a servant as is not fit, there is a remedy, but if a husband be never so cruell to the wife, unlesse to death, we know not where relief is to be had.

The civil wars increased the variety of roles with which women could participate in religion, notably in the sects. Here some challenge a group of self-confident students, who, threatened in the debate, protest that these inspired women have transgressed the boundaries of proper theological discourse, for which the women are punished. Sidney Sussex, once criticised by Laud for its puritan inclinations, was Cromwell's old college.

The Faithful Scout *Numb* 160

6–13 January, 1654 150.160A {3.35}

Beginning Friday, January 6.

IT is certified from *Cambridge*, that two *Petticoat-Preachers* came lately to *Sidney-Colledge*, and would needs enter into dispute with divers of the Collegians, who civilly and Scholastically answered all their positions; but those *weak Vessels* being not able to resist such able opposers, used very uncivil language, telling the Schollers *they were Antichrists, and their Colledge a cage of unclean Birds, with divers other invective speeches, &c.* Hereupon the Students made a complaint to the Mayor, who sent for them to appear before him; and demanded whence they came, and where they lay the last night; they said, *They were strangers and knew not the name of the place, but they payed for what they called for.* Then he asked them their names, they answered, *they were written in the Book of life.* Then desiring they would inform by what names their husbands were called, they answered, *they had no husband but Jesus Christ.* The honest Mayor seeing them so obstinate, that they not onely slighted the Ministery, but likewise all civil Government, caus'd them to be well lash'd for their obstinacy, and afterwards to be turn'd forth of the Town.

Anna Trapnel was a prophetess, gifted in producing spontaneous, rapturous verse. She was manipulated for political ends by the Fifth Monarchists; religious radicals and political dissidents who argued that the reign of Christ, as prophesied in the books of Daniel and of Revelation, would soon be settled on earth, bringing the downfall of priests, lawyers and landlords. Cromwell was also an obstacle to the rule of the saints. Trapnel was eventually ordered to be whipped. This story is followed by an account of the Welsh Fifth Monarchist Arise Evans presenting to Cromwell a prophecy which foretold the restoration of Charles before the end of 1653/4.

The Grand Politique Post Numb.127

10–17 January, 1653{4} 544.127A {3.36}

There is a Virgin Prophetess come to White-hall, who has declared great and wonderful touching this present Government, and saith that she comes from God, to declare a message to the Council; she has been sundry times in a Trance at M. *Roberts* his house, where many eminent persons frequented, and upon her awakening, she declared, That the eternal God was her refuge, and that he was leading her through the green Pastures, to his sacred Pavilion. Therefore, be encouraged in the Lord, ye children of the most High, and remember, that the Saints tryals shal end in tryumph, and the Night of Misery will have a most glorious Morning of Victory, for the exiled and banished wil be restored in the fifth Monarchy.

The *Bloody Vision* interpreted by *Arise Evans*, was presented to his Highness the Lord Protector by the said Author, who notwithstanding the high invectives therein contained, proving that the late Parliament was the mark of the Beast, mentioned in the Revelations, and that the fift Monarchy should suddenly be established under the power of *Charles Stuart*, &c. yet did the favourable clemency of his Highness extend so far, that he graciously remitted this imperious Representation, and permitted him his liberty. Nevertheless, when he departed, he went to White-hall, and there made Proclamation of what was published by him

Arise Evans:

Henry Walker's *Severall Proceedings* recorded Trapnel's beliefs and her trances in some detail. In the second story, on the advice of a doctor a woman practices white magic. *The Grand Politique Post* reported that the witch's name was Elizabeth Wenman, and that her victim's husband had pressed her own husband to go to sea.

Severall Proceedings of State Affaires
Num. 225

12–19 January, 1653{4} 599.225 {3.37}

A Breviate of Hannah *whom some call a Prophetesse in* White hall.

THere is one *Hannah* a Maid that lives at *Hackney* near the City of *London*, the same that was formerly at *Dunbar*, a Member of Mr. *John Simpsons* Church (as is said) who lives at one Mr. *Roberts* an Ordinary in White-Hall; to whom many hundreds do daily come to see and hear, who hath now been there about a fortnight: Those that look to her, and use to bee with her, sayes she neither eateth nor drinketh, save onely sometimes a Tost and drink, and that she is in a Trance, and some say that what she doth is by a mighty inspiration, others say they suppose her to be of a troubled mind, and people flocking to her so as they doe, causeth her to continue this way, and some say worse, so every one gives their opinions as they please. But this is visible to those that see and hear her.

1 That she is well in flesh in her hands and face, and seemingly lusty and strong; she hath Rings upon her fingers, and lyes in a bed continually in a Room where she is looked to.

2 She speaks to no body, but they that are about her, call it lying in a Trance; she lies as if she was continually asleep, save only when she prayes, sings, or drinks and eates the Tost, only she breaths, and sometimes she turns her selfe in her bed, and

sometimes covers herselfe, but most often others, some say, doth it.

3 In the afternoon (most commonly) every day she prayes and sings, begining about that usuall time that folk have dined, and continues sometimes two or three hours, sometimes foure or five hours never ceasing, but praying or singing until she hath finished for that time, and then seaceth, not speaking to any body, nor praying, nor singing until the next day again.

4 Her custom is to pray sometimes an houre, and sometimes two hours, and then sings two Hymnes in two several Tunes, and then prayes again, and sometimes sings again; sometimes oftener and sometimes fewer times; she is heard and understood very plainly by all when she prayes, but when shee sings, very little is to be understood what she saith.

5 Her prayers are in exceeding good method and order, good language, and such as indeed all that come doe much admire what they hear from her, excellent words, and well placed; such as are not ordinary.

6 Her matter is various, full of variety; for the Lord Protector, that God would keep him close to himselfe, as he hath hitherto, so stil to have his heart set upon the things of the Lord, not to be vain, nor regard earthly pomp and pleasure, and things below; but the things of God and his People, that he may be delivered from carnall Councels, and being seduced to please the men of the world, and those that seek unrighteousnesse, that he may not leave the councel of the Godly, to hearken to those who are worldly wise, and earthly Polititians, but wise in the Wisdom of God. That the Souldiery, whom God hath made Instrumental to overcome the enemy without, and in the world, may not be overcome of their inward spiritual enemies, to provoke God to lay them aside, and make use of others in the perfecting of that work, in which God hath so far employed them. That the Merchants of this Nation would not so far seek and minde their great profit by Trade at Sea, to fill their own Warehouses and Bags and be great in the world, as thereby to provoke an ungodly and wicked peace with the Dutch, to the dishonor of God, and hinderance of the carrying on of Gods work. That the people of God may not (as some of them have done) revile and scandalize the Lord Protector behinde his back, and speak reproachful words against him to others; (for, that she pleased before the Lord, was not the way of God;) but to deal faithfully and plainly with him, and go to him privately, to speak of those things to himself onely, according to the Rule of Gods Word, wherein they are offended

in any thing with him, or any thing that he doth; and that there may be love among the Saints and people of God. That the Lord would cause the people of this Nation, to leave their sins and profaneness, As Gentlewomens black Spots and Patches, Powderings of Hair, Gold and Silver-Lace, and other wickedness; and that she did believe God hath some of his Elect even among such, and prayed to God for their conversion. That the Lord will cause witches, and such as by false delusions seek to delude the people, to be discovered and suppressed; that troubled spirits may be comforted, and believe; and consider, that the Lord doth call such to come and reason with him; and that he will make their Scarlet and Crimson sins as Snow, and as Wool; and that the Saints and people of God would rejoyce in the Lords goodness to them. Consider, over what a Red-Sea and *Jordan*, he hath led them, and brought them into his Heavenly *Canaan*, where is no defilement, but all glorious, and peace. {...}

There are many for Robberies and Stealing, now, upon tryal at the Sessions. {...}

A Witch that upon malice bewicht a Woman and her Children, the Children blinde and lame by it; and the Mother pained in her side, and back, and bound in her body: She went to several Doctors, but could have no help, until at last one Doctor told her she was bewitched, but he would give her Physick, which if it did work, he would endeavor to help her: She took his Physick, it wrought, and she returned to him, who appointed her to make a Cake, and knead it with her own water, and eat it, using a form of words, which he gave her in writing, which she did; and when she had eaten it, was distracted, scarce knowing what she did, but went to the Witches house, and said she had her Picture; which making search in her house, she found, also of some of her Childrens, with divers Pictured more, which she carried home and burnt, and they did stink for two or three days like Sulphur, very strongly; she thrust an hot Iron into the breech of her own Picture, and presently went orderly to stool: And in those places of her body where she was pained, the Picture had had holes pierced in it; which she brought and shewed to the Bench.

But that which is most remarkable, is, That she would have received the Sacrament with a Gathered Church; where she was told, That she was not to be admitted, because she was reputed to be a Witch, which bewitched such a Woman and her Children: She denied it, appealing to her god. She was asked, who was her God? she said, the god of the world; and wished that she might never speak, if it was true; and that her god would shew her some eminent judgement upon her, if it was true. Whereupon she was presently struck lame and dumb, and ever since saith nothing, but I and No.

Mercurius Politicus *Numb:* 201.

13–20 April, 1654 361.201 {3.38}

From Truro in Cornwall, by the last.

Mrs. *Hannah Trapnel*, she that lately acted her part in a Trance so many dayes at Whitehal, hath for some time been in these parts. There seem to be two convincing Reasons against her Spirit; the one is, that it withdraws from Ordinances, and the other is, that it is Non-sensical. There are in her Company one Mr. *Langdon*, and Mr. *Bauden*, two Members of the late short-lived Parliament. The Justices of this County have taken notice of her wayes and practices; and Mr. *Lobb* giving the charge here this last Sessions, willed the Jury to enquire, 1 concerning Vagrants, 2 such as occasioned unlawful meetings, 3 Such as speak against the present Government. There were two Indictments drawn against her: *Langdon* and *Baudon*, her Compeers and Abettors, endeavored to make a learned Defence for her, but it was not suffered; only they entered into Bonds of three hundred pounds for her good behaviour and appearance at the next Assizes. If you had inquired better into her business, when she tranced it at White hall, it might have prevented the staggering of many a spirit in *Cornwal*. The design intended to be made use of by means of this woman, is (it seems) to compass *England*, and pass from one good Town to another to vent her Prophesies, and thereby disaffect the people to the present Authority. It calls to mind the old story of *Elizabeth Barton*, the holy maid of *Kent* (as she was called) in the dayes of *Henry* the 8. who was made use of by certain fanatick Popish Priests, by fained Miracles and Trances, to raise admiration in the multitude, and foment seditious humors against the Government; for which she and her accomplices had in the end their reward.

The Weekly Intelligencer of the Common-Wealth

17–24 July, 1655 688.301 {3.39}

Friday, July 20.

THis day we heard the story of a Female souldier that was brought to bed not far from the Tower, her love to her comerade was such, that in the habite of a young man she had followed him through all the dangers of the War, and had been a partaker of them with him as wel in *Ireland* as in *England*, a rare example of the powrful effects of love, which it seems on purpose did contrive she should prove now with Childe, that so rare an affection should not passe unobserved.

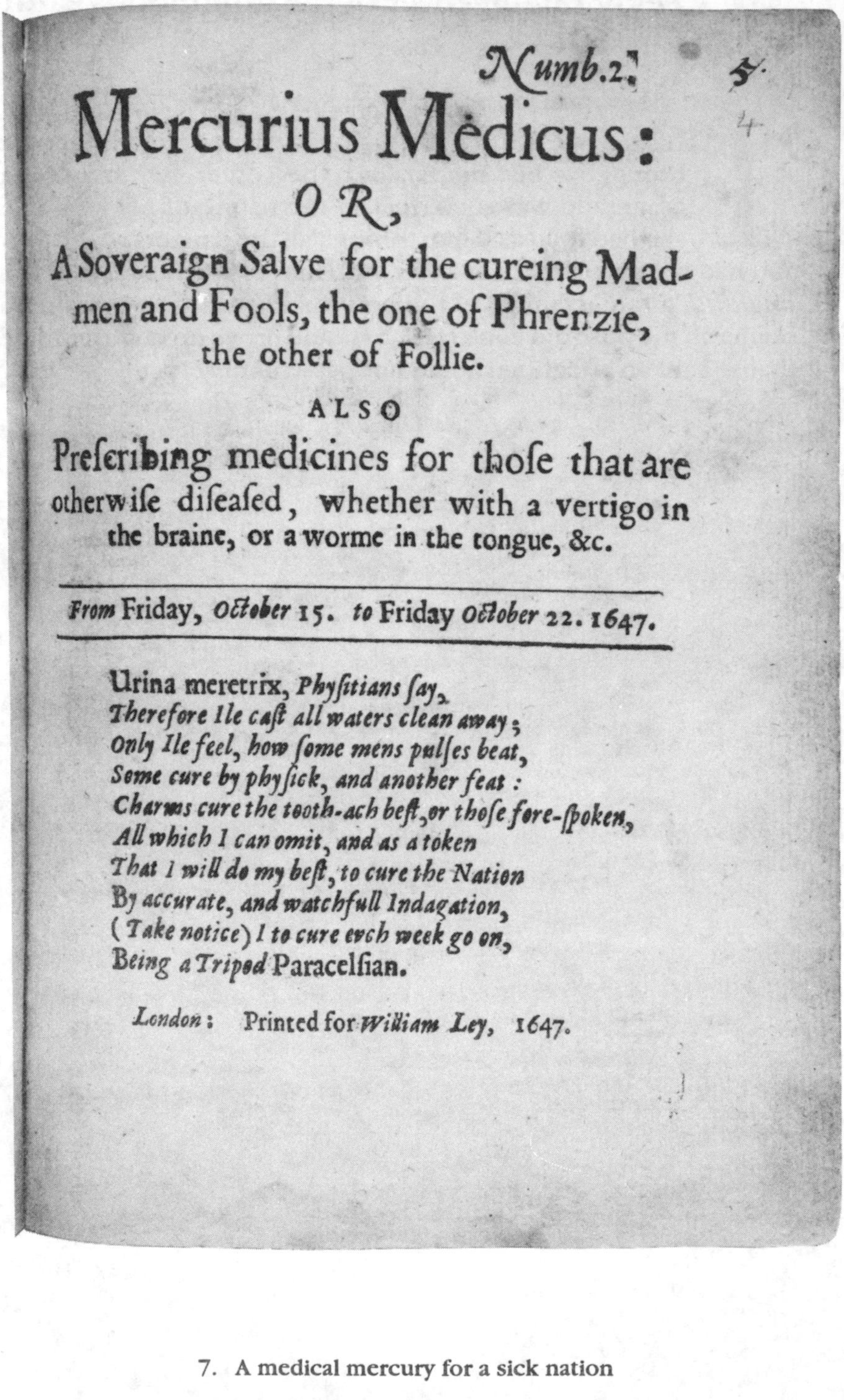

Numb.2. 5 4

Mercurius Medicus:

OR,

A Soveraign Salve for the cureing Mad-men and Fools, the one of Phrenzie, the other of Follie.

ALSO

Preſcribing medicines for thoſe that are otherwiſe diſeaſed, whether with a vertigo in the braine, or a worme in the tongue, &c.

From Friday, *October* 15. *to* Friday *October* 22. 1647.

Urina meretrix, *Phyſitians ſay,*
Therefore Ile caſt all waters clean away;
Only Ile feel, how ſome mens pulſes beat,
Some cure by phyſick, and another feat:
Charms cure the tooth-ach beſt, or thoſe fore-ſpoken,
All which I can omit, and as a token
That I will do my beſt, to cure the Nation
By accurate, and watchfull Indagation,
(Take notice) I to cure evch week go on,
Being a Tripod Paracelſian.

London: Printed for *William Ley*, 1647.

7. A medical mercury for a sick nation

CHAPTER FOUR
The Hanged Woman Miraculously Revived: Birth, life, sickness, death, providence and the inexplicable

Miracles are, from time to time, commonplace in newsbooks. A person living or dying by an act of God's will can subsist alongside another taken by a tertian ague, or being brought to health by the practice of medicine. The texts are unique only in their juxtaposition of stories freely available in other, separate sources. A modern reader is compelled to dismiss the wonder story either as a relic of a superstitious age or as evidence of a disingenuous author pandering to a foolish appetite in his readers. The same reader may attribute to the other, rational account the status of an historical fact. This dichotomous attitude would not necessarily reflect the response of a seventeenth-century reader.

Dismantling these boundaries and reconstructing early-modern reading practices is a most pressing and most difficult task. If it were the case that a person, a reader, either believed or did not believe, remained naïvely credulous or had learned a critical scepticism, then the historian's task would be relatively straightforward. She or he could study an individual and accordingly place him or her in one of the two categories. But even if, for example, a modern historian accepts that the belief in witches was a deluded one, it is nevertheless necessary for him or her to accept and analyse, even imaginatively to participate in, a 'mind-set' and its collective delusion which could instigate the massacre of thousands of more or less innocent, poor, old women.

Neither is the formulation 'mind-set' entirely satisfactory. The concept suggests a classless and ungendered, unified collection of shared beliefs, thereby limiting the debate. Rather, different structures of belief should be our focus, in an analysis in which the social effects of beliefs, conscious and unconscious, can be taken into consideration. Some beliefs lead to social action, others do not: the same authors who accused newsbook writers of shameless lies also accused them of having overthrown the king. The truth or absence of truth in these publications was only ever part of the story. How can we put this into practice in our modern reconstructions of seventeenth-century reading?

On 14 December 1650, a woman called Anne Green was executed for infanticide. She was hung for half-an-hour while merciful spectators swung on her legs to speed her death (a not uncommon practice,) and a soldier struck her with the butt of his musket. She was then cut down and her body carried in a coffin to a society of physicians who had begged the corpse for dissection, for the furtherance of medicine and the good of mankind. As the coffin was opened God intervened and brought her back to life. The physicians helped in this process, warming her body, feeding her elixirs and letting blood.

It transpired that she was innocent of infanticide, and the child had actually been miscarried, but the earthly means of justice had no way of accommodating this fact. Only God's great providence brought it to their attention.

There probably was a medical explanation behind this story, should we choose to reject the God principle. Alternatively the story may have been a complete fiction, devised by a proto-feminist concerned over infanticide prosecutions, and set at large by a number of sympathetic and influential collaborators.

On the other hand something similar happened near Rennes in 1588: but before turning to this incident, let us examine more closely the sources for the above historical event. Firstly there is the *Mercurius Politicus*, {4.10&11} published less than a week after the incident in December 1650, and reproduced in the following pages. Then there are *A Wonder of Wonders. Being a faithful Narrative and true Relation*...; secondly *A Declaration from Oxford, of Anne Green, A young woman that was lately, and unjustly hanged in the Castle-yard; but since recovered, her neck set straight, and her eyes fixed orderly and firmly in her head again*...; and, thirdly, *Newes from the Dead. or A True and Exact Narration of the miraculous deliverance of Anne Green*, all published in 1651, the former two probably in January, the latter in March.[1]

1 W. Burdet, *A Wonder of Wonders* (London, 1651), internally dated 13 January,

A Declaration from Oxford is an eight page pamphlet with a crude woodblock on the title page. Certain details corroborate with the *Politicus* account, but the narrative is rather different. As in *Politicus*, the infant is a span long, but there is no mention of it being discovered in sheets or a bed, only a dusty corner. It is a moralistic tract, with an overwhelmingly pious concern that thanks be given to God for the deliverance. The reader is pressed to show awe at Anne's vision of four angels. *A Wonder of Wonders* has the same woodblock, predominantly the same text, minus a couple of paragraphs, and is either the original of *A Declaration*, or stems from an identical source.[2] They are penny pamphlets, for the undiscerning audience of penny pamphlets.

Despite the sensationalistic title, *Newes from the Dead* is quite a different product. It opens with fourteen pages of poetry in Latin, English and French, expressing the authors' wonder at the affair. It is the report of a 'very rare and remarkeable accident' which has been 'variously and falsely reported amongst the vulgar', and elaborated upon by 'Ballad makers' until it has become a mere fiction.[3] Although one of the poems mentions a 'Belgian Headsman' who could slice off heads with his hand, this is meant to be a serious book, an analytic, rational text addressed to those of the same social stratum as the physicians who verify its authenticity. The authors consciously differentiate their publication from wonder pamphlets, repudiating stories of angels and eschewing an overt eschatological framework. Twenty-six pages in length, it contains the additional information that Anne Green was seduced by the son of the household in which she was working, and that the master, guilty by association, died three days after her recovery. Like the other pamphlets, it mentions the size of the infant as no more than a span in length: but does this in a discussion of the innocence of Anne. *Politicus, A Declaration* and *Wonder of Wonders* do not explicitly interpret this fact: *Newes from the Dead* uses it to demonstrate that the child must have been miscarried, going on to discuss Anne's menstruation. This kind of serious, scientific publication is discursively antithetical to the populist, cheaper pamphlets.

dated 10 January by Thomason (Wing B5620); *A Declaration from Oxford* (London, 1651; Wing D586); *Newes from the Dead,* attributed to Richard Watkins (London, 1651), dated 6 March 1650/1 by Thomason (Wing W1072).

2 The fact that *A Wonder of Wonders* names Burdet, the author of the letter from Oxford, suggests that it was probably the original.

3 *Newes from the Dead,* second pagination, pp.1, 10.

But what about *Politicus*? Do we ascribe this account to Marchamont Nedham's joco-serious style and his interest in keeping his readers entertained? And is this therefore evidence that our scepticism should restrict any reading of this story to the level of mere fantasy?

Nedham did not derive his account from any of these other publications, as his first letter on the subject was published before them. He published the news as it came into his hands. And this 'miracle' was subsequently read in two dominant fashions: as a scientific case and as a providential wonder story. Neither of these genres overcame and suppressed the other: each appealed to different responses from their audience. As with the nocturnal illuminations on 29 October 1643 {4.02&3}, there were 'many significations'. The same story was two stories, with quite different cultural resonances and different implications for understanding the world.

From this we can draw two conclusions. Firstly that the horizons of a story such as this extend beyond mere curiosity. The account is informative in two senses: it presents data, but it also furnishes the reader with a way of 'reading' the world, whether made by God or Descartes and Boyle. The story satisfies an appetite but also instructs, in several ways. And if the modern world chooses to prefer one of these interpretations as more conformable to our senses, then it is important to recognise that at this historical moment in 1651, one reading did not exist without the other. And secondly, that because the social function of a story is multiple and various, it cannot be dismissed as evidence of credulity. It is more important for the historian to reconstruct a repertoire of readings than for him or her to try to deduce (no doubt with the assistance of a modern medic) 'what really happened'.

Similar incidents were recounted earlier in seventeenth-century England. Moreover, Roger Chartier has analysed the mythology of a startlingly similar miracle near Rennes in 1588.[4] There a woman was condemned for infanticide who had been made pregnant by the son of the household in which she worked; at her execution the hangman kicked her in the ribs to speed her death, but she was saved by her faith, and thereby enabled to reveal her innocence. The French story was recounted in two

4 Roger Chartier, 'The Hanged Woman Miraculously Saved: An *occasionnel*' in *The Culture of Print: Power and the Uses of Print in Early Modern Europe*, ed. Chartier, trans. Lydia G. Cochrane (Cambridge: Polity Press, 1989).

pamphlets, with quite a different cultural orientation from the English: one of them affirming the dogmas of counter-Reformation propaganda. But the narrative was in all respects the same, and evolved out of medieval accounts of innocent men redeemed by miracles. Curiously, the woman's name was Anne de Grez.

We deduce from this not an instance of plagiarism, but a series of morphological similarities resulting from the oral transmission of stories. Such stories became folklore, and the narrative which resulted from a new event, a new hanged woman saved, was a synthesis of this time-served mythology and of new social conditions. This did not make it false.

The malformed infants and 'monstrous' births {4.13&31; 6.16} which constituted one of the more spectacular elements of newsbooks were not simply quirks of nature or outrageous appeals to sensation, though some of them may have been that as well. In a discourse thoroughly underwritten by parallels between political and natural bodies, a deformed progeny indicated that something was rotten in the state, and formed a text which could be interpreted. A headless body was a wonder, but it implied a kingless state. Medical authorities confirming the truth of such reports may have been displaced authorities diagnosing a sickness in the body politic: allegorical readings need not necessarily mean that the 'truth' of the natural phenomenon is undermined. As one Dutch correspondent wrote to the *Mercurius Politicus*, 'the Plague of the heart is greater than all.'[5]

This chapter contains reports of sickness and death, of strange births and unlikely cures, of indications that God shapes the way men and women live and that they are ultimately answerable to him. It should now be clear why these reports merit juxtaposition. The way a seventeenth-century man or woman experienced these mundane aspects of everyday life may well have been unfamiliar to us. When we read accounts of witchcraft persecution we automatically estrange ourselves from the beliefs of the persecutors, as we know that they are very distant from our own sensibilities. While there have been what we call political 'witch-hunts' in the twentieth century, the actions of those who burned their victims for making pacts with the devil seem remote. Some of the newsbook reports in this chapter suggest that even these most familiar aspects of our life which we seem to share with our past equally need to be estranged and carefully reworked before they can be understood.

5 *Mercurius Politicus*, Numb.118, 2–9 September 1652. N&S 361.118.

Strange lights and strange figures and fights in the sky are part of the staple material of newsbooks: for many of their contemporary readers they were deeply significant.

Speciall Passages And certain Informations
Numb. 24.

17–24 January, 1643 605.24 {4.01}

The Letters about *Banburie* say, that the Cavaliers in the Castle there are frighted at the sight of a great man that walkes in a Surplice, and that about *Edge-hill* and *Keinton*, there are men seene walking with one legge, and but one arme, and the like, passing to and fro in the night. This may be thought ridiculous, but those that have heard of the strange apparitions, and Rivers turned into bloud, and such like in *Germany*, and the frequentnesse of them, after great fights and ruine of Counties, will not onely credit this, but reckon it small in regard of those.

The Compleate Intelligencer and Resolver

The second of Novemb. 1643 52.1 {4.02}

Question.

Whether was the brightnesse of the last Sunday night extraordinary? and what could it signifie? &c.

Resolution.

1. It was extraordinary, because it exceeded all common Radiations and light, for the Moone was not in a capacity of shining, and the Starres could not doe it, their light was too faint and weake, though I beleeve God made use of a naturall cause in it too, as wee see it in the Elementary openings, and shuttings and coruscations.

2. It could not but signifie well, being a plaine and comfortable light without horrour, or other streaming Portent as Comets usually have.

3. It might signifie some new light of Reformation comming to us, for it was the night before the Assembly fell upon their great businesse of the Church.

4. It may have as many significations as light it selfe.

Certaine Informations From severall parts of the Kingdome *Numb.* 43.

6–13 November, 1643 36.43 {4.03}

Thursday, November 9.

Out of Suffolke they write, that *Sunday* night the 29. of *October* last, was very remarkable with them, for that evening after Sun set was extreame dark, till about eight of the clocke, then it began to grow light on the sudden, and was so light, that they could plainly see to read a great print, and could easily discerne written Letters and words, and yet there was no moon shine, for she rose not untill about five of the clocke the next morning. It was a quiet and calme light round about, and more then usually when the moone is at her full, and that the stars were rather dimmer then ordinarily they are: some clouds appeared in the North and East, and other where, with some streams of lightsomnesse in them, as if they had been illuminated from some place or other. And those that watched all night to see the event, affirmed, that it held so light even almost till morning.

At *Norwich* also they saw the very same light that night, onely this some persons of credit that sate up & watched have added, that about three a clock in the morning they saw a starre fall, longer then any starre that ever they saw, and it fell leasurely, a long time before it vanished, they had time to discourse together, from the time it began to fall, to the time it ceased. These things are not ordinary, what they portend God onely knoweth. In the Scripture light is alwayes taken in the good part, and signifies prosperity and joy.

And we have heard some affirme that are lately come out of Surrey, that at *Micham* in that County, they saw that *Sunday* night, strange apparitions in those white illuminated clouds towards the North, and amongst the rest a battell, as if it had been between two Armies, which no doubt threatneth a continuation of a Wars amongst us, but will end in a glorious and happy peace, as some Authours have written; but because this subject concerneth Astronomy, and it will aske some serious discourse, more then these short Informations will allow, we surcease untill a more fitting opportunity to decribe it to the full.

This editorial, followed by a fairly conservative wonder story, pursues the internal logic of the body-politic metaphor. The author, probably John Hackluyt, implies that the monstrous births represented in newsbooks are a product of the disorderly body politic of England. In one sense, though not necessarily the intended one, this was no doubt true. '*Lukes* note-book' refers derisively to Henry Walker's *Perfect Occurrences*, published under the anagrammatic pseudonym of Luke Harruney.

Mercurius Melancholicus: Or Newes from Westminster, and other Parts. Numb. 5.

25 September – 2 October, 1647 344.05 {4.04}

In the most palmed State, and flourishing age of Rome, a little before the mighty *Julius Cæsar* fell by the hands of the bloody Senators, (a preludium to the sack and ruine of the City, which shortly after did ensue) ther were strange and prodigious apparitions seen riding their Circuits in the Elements, as dreadfull Ecclipses, bushy Meteors, and staring Commets, wandring Ghosts, and Spirits shreeking, and gibbering in the streets of Rome, the Clouds instead of raine, droping bloud, and the like; these were but deaths harbingers, and as so many silent Prologues pointing to that fatall Tragedy which did ensue.

Not in Italies, but in Englands Rome more frightfull visions and amazing wonders dayly shew their gastly faces to the astonishment, not only of the present, but succeeding generations. To omit the marvelous countercourses of the heavens; yet fresh within our memories; let us reflect upon the earth, where wee may behold nature unnatured, Monsters reversed, heads where the feete, and the feete where the heads should be; Bodies divided, yea headlesse, and yet live, &c. These are nothing else but certaine presages of a sad Catastrophe, that as wee sowed in sorrow, so wee shall reape in teares, as wee began in blowes, so wee shall conclude in blood: For how doe calamities come rowling in like mighty waves, one upon the neck of another? And can it be otherwise? When he is accounted of best repute, that can with most dexterity undoe his brother. But let me whisper one word in his eare, his turne is next; all degrees, conditions, sexes, persons must dance fortunes jiggs, and have their rounds. But are these the errands wee are sent on into the World? What, to undoe each other? There is a life composed and constant, this at the best is but uncertaine; O why doe wee prize this span and neglect that which is so spacious? Ah my bowells! my bowells! I am pained at the heart: O that my head were a continuall spring of teares, that I might weepe day and night for the destruction of the Daughter of my people?

But no more of this I pray you, lest the Printer lose by the bargaine; for I must tell you one thing, and that's a true thing, and that's no new thing; one point of knavery will now a dayes finde more chap-men to buy it, then twelve points of honesty. Divinity Pamphlets are but standing-dishes in the Booke-sellers shops; whilst roguery in sippits is gobled up like Bells banquets by whole meales, and not so much as a scrap to be seene the next morning: And thus beginning with my selfe, let others beware their jackets, for *Melancholicus* meanes to sit upon some of their skirts, and yet be an honest man, though all the world say the contrary; for he hath learned that lesson long agoe; woe to him whom all men speake well of.

A strange apparition (or rather dilusion) neere Harrow of the Hill was seene the last weeke; (I wonder how it scaped *Lukes* note-booke) at a place called the Hermitage, the house of one Mr. *Rowse* (a Parliament man) about twelve of the clock at night (*Apollyons* chiefe tempting time) a horrible blacknesse arising as it were from the house, and passing on from it towards a caus-way close by, with a hideous noyse, as of many Coaches, the very fire (as by furious treading) sparkling out of the stones, and above the blacknesse a most melodious harmony of musick, much like to a consort of Cymballs; the relation is very true. This had been excellent newes this weeke for *Mercurius Diabolus*; surely that night the Devill was to be married to some one of the midnight sisters, and therefore had his Coach and horses made ready, with a noise of fidlers to fetch his faire Bride to the old Hermitage. I see the Divell makes bold with Parliament men sometimes; marry, I cannot tell whether upon free quarter or no; but 'tis like he is ever a good guest to his Landlord, and he knowes Parliament men want money.

A rationalistic repudiation of a wonder story reported in Nedham's *Pragmaticus*, in this case the kind of wonder story legitimated by a rapidly disintegrating philosophy of kingship. It also refers to the king's lechery, which was reputedly directed to lower-class women.

Mercurius Militaris
or The Armies Scout *Numb*. 2.

10–17 October, 1648 346.2 {4.05}

ITs my fortune to tell you of miracles, and *Pragmaticus* helps me to one in his news from *Newport, Octob*.16. he tells me, that his Majesty hath wrought a strange cure upon a child, whose left eye was closed up with the Evil, by prayer, and stroking it with fasting-spettle; how now *Prag*. Didst thou now intend to win the whetstone? Or art thou grown old in thy knavery, and they sight waxed dim, that thou couldst not see that this bait for the people did not cover the hooke? Every simple gull will know that this story intends only to foster an opinion amongst the people, that his Majesties person is sacred, or that he is Gods Vicegerent; but mark, the miracle the King (saith he) opened a blind eye; why *Prag*. are thy brains grown addle? Didst thou ever know a Tyrant or King, that was content the peoples eyes should be opened? It's against their interest; if the horse his eyes be not blinded, he will never grind in the mill, but let us mark the manner of the miracle, and that is as strange as the matter; it was cured (saith he) by the Kings prayer, and fasting-spettle; Why *Prag*. thou hast forgotten again, that a Lyar should always have a good memory; thou knowest it is against the Kings conscience to pray without the service book, and there is never a prayer in the book for the opening of an eye blinded by the Kings Evel; how then could the King pray, but the Kings spettle surely had the vertue to cure the swelling, it seems the King of late spits medicine; would not his Landress be questioned, whether the maids he desired her to prepare for him were wholsom, otherwise he may have taken some spitting pells for the French; but I beleeve *Prag*. had lately read of *Dionisius* flatteries, that licked up his spittle, and swore it was sweeter than *Nector* and *Ambrosia*, and he scorned to come behind them in his profession. I prethee, *Prag*. tell me next week whether thou didst beleeve this story when thou wrotest it, and tell me whence thou thinkest the virtue of his

Majesties touch proceeds? is't from the holiness of his Father *Jamees* his seed, or from the blood of the innocent that sticks to his hands? I do not much wonder that his slaver is wholsom, for I beleeve he dare not now spit out his poyson against the people.

The market for astrology no doubt led to some cynical fabrications.

The Kingdomes Faithfull And Impartiall Scout [*Numb*. 16.]

11–18 May, 1649 210.16 {4.06}

Saturday 14 {12} *May*. {...}

There was (this day) extant at the Exchange *London*, a Paper, called the Prophesie of *Paulus Grebnerus* (a German) concerning these Times; wherein he describeth the troubles of *Russia*, and the election of a Swedish King, *Sigismund* by name to be King of *Polonia*; by which he shall irrecoverably lose his own inheritance; That of the Swedish Race, there shall be one *Gustavus Adolphus* by name, that shall take heart from the distractions of *Germany*, to invade the Empire with a smal army, fight many battels prosperously, but should at last perish in a pitcht field. About that time a Northern King should reign, *Charles* by name, who shall take to wife *Mary* of the Popish Religion; whereupon, he shall be a most unfortunate Prince: then the people of his Dominions shall chuse to themselves another Commander or Governour, *viz*. an Earl, whose Government shall last three yeers, or thereabouts: and afterwards the same people shall chuse another commander or Governour, *viz*. a Knight, not of the same Family nor Dignity, &c. he shall endure somewhat longer time And after him shall appear one *Charles*, descended from *Charles* the I. who shall rule and govern all his Subjects in great peace and happinesse, &c. This is said to be found in the Library of Trinity Colledge in *Cambridge*, where it hath been published to the view of all persons resorting thither.

There was nothing particularly strange or miraculous about the Bills of Mortality, except occasionally the numbers of casualties. But their very existence and format is itself remarkable.

Severall Proceedings in Parliament *Num*. 13.

21–28 December, 1649 599.013 {4.07}

A General Bill of Mortallity for this year now past, according to the Report made to the Right Honorable the Lord Mayor of the City of London, By the Company of Parish Clerks of London, &c.
Buryed in the 97 Parishes within the Walls 2875. Plague 10.
Buryed in the 16 Parishes without the Wals 4750. Plague 36.
Buryed in the 10 out parishes in Middlesex and Surrey 2941. Plague 21.
The Totall of all the Burials this yeare 10566.
Whereof of the Plague 67. Bloody Flux, Scowring and Flux 802. Burnt and Scalded 10. Excessive drinking 2. Executed 29 Flox and Small Pox 1190. Dead in the streets &c, 9. French pox 15. Frighted 1. Hanged and made away themselves 13. Kild by severall accidents 39. Murthered 7. Overlaid and starved at Nurse 36. Smothered and Stifled 2. Starved 8. The rest of severall Diseases.
Christned 5825.
Increased in the Burials in the 123 Parishes and at the Pesthouse this yeare 672.
Decreased of the Plague in the 123 Parishes, and at the Pesthouse this yeare 544.
The Totall of all the Burials in the 7 out Parishes this year 1807. Whereof of the Plague 4.
The Totall of all the Christnings 1106.

The Bill of Mortality for London this week now past.

Buried within the 97 Parishes within the Walls,	33. Plague, 0.
Buried in the 16 Parishes without the Walls	77. Plague 0.
Buried in the tenne out Parishes	27. Plague 0.
The totall of all the Burials this week,	137.

Whereof of the Plague 0. Cut of the Stone. 1. Found dead two, one in the Glasse house at Olaves Southwarke, and one in the Common Sewer at Mary Whitechappell. French pox, 2. Kild by leaping out a Garret window at Ethelborow 1. Small pox, 5. Vomitting, 1.

Decreased in the Burialls this week 49,

The totall of the Burialls 7 out parishes 17. Plague 0

The Man in the Moon (*Numb.* 39)

16–23 January, 1650 248.39 {4.08}

The sad *Omens*, Apparitions, Thunders, and monstrous Births, lately seen in *England, Scotland*, and *Ireland*, are certainly as so many of Gods *Embassadours* to proclaime *open warres* against us; as on Christmas day, Thunder and the falling of strange Thunder-Bolts in divers Churches in *England*; the Child (or rather Angel) found in the Field; the strange *Comet* seene at *Dublin* in *Ireland*, and now lately in *Scotland*, the Powder-blast on *Tower-hill*, are questionlesse so many *Warning-pieces* to *Alarme* us out of our dull security, and to arme us against these monsters of Men that are now feeding upon our Carkasses, devouring Men, Women and Children.

Mercurius Politicus Numb. 14.

5–12 September, 1650 361.014 {4.09}

Certain Newes came from the Isle of *Wight*, of the death of the Lady *Elizabeth Stuart*, daughter to the late *King*; who being at *Bowls* (a sport wherein she much delighted) there fell a sudden Shower, which caused her to take cold, being of a sickly constitution; This hapned on *Monday* was fortnight, and the next day she complained of *head ach*, and a *feaverish distemper*; which by *fits* increased and remitted, till *Sunday* was sennight, at which time shee tooke to her Bed, and notwithstanding the care of that honest and faithfull Gentleman, *Anthony Mildmay*, Esquire, and all the Art of *Physicians*, her disease grew more upon her. Care was taken here by Sir *Theodore Mayern*, to send a *Physician* and remedies of his election to her; but being naturally of a weak body, and her Feaver growing sharp upon her, she departed this life on *Sunday* last the 8th of *September*, and care will be taken for her *Funerall*.

Mercurius Politicus *Numb*. 28.

12–19 December, 1650 361.028 {4.10}

Wednesday, Decemb. 18.

Came this notable one from *Oxford*.

SIR,

THere hath fallen out this week such a remarkable act of providence, that much amazeth the ordinary sort, and much affects the most discreet and reasonable men. One *Anne Green*, a servant in Sir *Thomas Reads* house at *Ounstu* in *Oxfordshire*, being gotten with child by Mr. *Ieffrey Read*, Grandchild to Sir *Thomas* (as the woman hath constantly affirmed when she maybe conceived to have no temptation to persist in a lye) near the fourth moneth of her time, with over-working her selfe about her ordinary employment of turning Mault, fell in Travell, and (neither her selfe nor her fellow servants well knowing what the matter might be) went to the house of Office, where with some straining, the child (not above a span long, and of whether sexe scarce distinguished) fell unawares, as she all along affirmeth, from her. Now there appearing something in the linnen where the wench lay, arguing suspition of some such thing: and she before confessing that she had bin guilty of that which might occasion her being with Child, although shee protested not to be certain thereof: the matter was further to be searched into, and an abortive Infant found in the top of the house of Office; whereupon, 3. dayes after her delivery, (in which time shee was carryed up and down to severall Justices of the Peace) shee was brought in an extream wet day, Prisoner to *Oxford*, and there condemned by one Mr. *Crook*, appointed to sit as a Judg in a Commission of *Oyer* and *Terminer*, death, and accordingly on *Saturday* morning the 14. of this present *Decemb.* was hang'd in the Castle yard. She hung near half an hour, in which time she was much pulled by the legs, and struck on the breast by divers other Friends, & other standers by; and above all, received severall violent stroaks on the stomack by a Soldier with the but-end of his Musquet. Being cut down, she was put into a Coffin, and brought to the house where the body was appointed to be dissected before the company of Physitians, and other ingenuous Gentlemen, who have a weekly meeting at Mr. *Clarks* the Apothecary, about naturall enquiries and experiments) by one Dr. *Petty*, lately come from *London* to the Anatomy Reader in this University. When they opened the Coffin to prepare the body for dissection, they perceived some small ratling in her throat: a lusty fellow standing by, thinking to do an act of charity, stamped upon her breast and belly: Dr. *Petty*, with Mr. *Clerk* of *Magdalen*-Colledg, and Mr. *Willis* of *Christ Church*, fell speedily to use means to bring her to life. They opened a vein, layed her in a warm bed, procured a woman to goe into bed to her, and continued the use of divers other remedies respecting her senslesnesse, head, throat, and breast, so that it pleased God within 14. hours she spake, and the next day talk'd and coughed very heartily, and is now in great hope of recovery. Upon this her Reprieve was granted, the Governour of this Garrison shewing much wisdome in obtaining thereof, and sense of this great providence. Thousands of people come from all parts to see her (notwithstanding the disswasion of those diligent Physitians) and all seeme to be satisfied of the wenches innocency to the murther, which she doth now, as on the Gallowes she did assert and stand in: so that 'tis apprehended to be such a contrary verdict from heaven that may strike terror to the consciences of those who have been any way faulty in this businesse.

Mercurius Politicus *Numb.* 32.

9–16 January, 1651 361.032 {4.11}

THVRSDAY, *January 9.*

Came this further Accompt from *Oxford*, concerning the Woman that was hang'd there, and now miraculously revived.

SIR,

THe Woman which so long hanged by the neck, and suffer'd so many strokes with the But-end of a Musquet, and stamping on the Breast, is now by the care of Doctor *Petty* our Anatomy-Reader (of whose reall worth I will inform you by the next) and other Physitians mentioned in my last, wholly recovered; the deadness of her Tongue, giddiness of her Head, and bruise made in her throat by the Rope wholly vanished. There is this farther remarkable, That when Doctor *Petty* heard she had spoken; and suspecting that the Women about her might suggest unto her to relate of strange Visions and apparitions to have been seen by her in that time wherein she seem'd Dead (which they had begun to doe) having caused all to depart the Room, but the other Gentlemen of the Faculty, enquired of her concerning her sense and apprehensions during that time, but found she spake somewhat impertinently, talking as if she had bin now to suffer; and when they spake unto her of her miraculous Deliverance from so great sufferings, she answered, *That she hoped that God would give her patience*, and the like. But the next morning being *Monday*, and the third day inclusively after her suffering, when she was better recovered, she then affirmed, and doth still, *That she neither remembreth how her Fetters were knocked off; how she went out of the Prison, when she was turned off the Ladder, whether any Psalm was sung, or not; nor was she sensible of any pain as she can remember*. And being told that she spake very well and pertinently on the Gallows such and such words; she confessed, *That she did not remember to have said them there, but that she resolved the day before to speak to that purpose*. Another thing observable is, That she came to her self, as if she had awakened out of a Sleep; not recovering the use of Speech by slow degrees, but in a manner altogether, beginning to speak just where she had left off on the Gallows, concerning Sir *Tho. Read's* house, and the leudness thereof, We hope there will come forth a more full and entire Relation of her Tryall, Sufferings, &c. to the end that this great work of God may be as fully and truly known, as becommeth so great a matter.

On *New-years day* the *Generall* was chosen our *Chancelor*.

Oxon, *6. Jan.*

1650.

The Faithful Scout [Numb. 44.]

14–21 November, 1651 150.044 {4.12}

Beginning, FRIDAY the 14 *of November*.{...}

This day Letters from *Brockeford* in *Sussex* intimate, That there hath been the body of a mighty *Giant* dig'd up neer *Ipswich*: the manner thus; At *Brockeford* Bridge, at the end of the street towards *Ipswich*, by the gravelly way, between the Lands-lace, one *John Vice* and another were digging gravel in the Road, and a little within the earth found the carcase of a *Giant* (for so I may rightly term him) for from the top of his scull to the bottome of the bones of his feet was ten foot; and overthwart his breast, from the ultimate of one shoulder to the other, as he lay interred, and before stirring, was four foot. His Scull was about the bignesse of a half bushel; the circumference of one of his thigh-bones of the bignesse of a middle sized womans waste; the nether Jaw-bone had in it firmly fixed 16 teeth of an extraordinary bignesse; the other none. Severall are the opinions of men in judging what time this man lived; some think him to be a Dane; others imagine he might belong to Prince *Arthur*; but for my part, I shall suspend my judgement: onely thus much I think I may say, That there hath not been seen such a man in *England* these hundred years.

This story was also recounted in a pamphlet titled *The Ranters Monster*, dated 30 March by Thomason, and advertised in the *French Intelligencer* on the same date.

The Faithful Scout [Numb. 60.]

5–12 March, 1652 150.060 {4.13}

Wednesday March 10.

This day came to my hands a paper, wherein is contained the most blasphemous actions, opinion and judgement, of one *Mary Adams*, living at *Tillingham* in *Essex*; who said, that she was the Virgin *Mary*, and that she was conceived with child by the Holy Ghost, and how all the Gospell that had been taught heretofore, was false; and that which was within her she said, was the true Messias: for which blasphemous words, and wicked opinion, she was committed to prison, there to remain untill the time came that she was to be deliver'd, to see what she would bring forth: But when the Midwife, and other good women came to her they did their best endeavors to bring her to a safe deliverance, but could not prevail; so that she lay in great misery and torment for the space of 8 dayes and nights, and at last brought forth the ugliest ill shapen Monster as ever eyes beheld; which being dead-born, they buried it with speed; for it was so loathsom to behold, that the womens hearts trembled to look upon it, having neither hands nor feet, but claws like a Toad in the place where the hands should have been, and every part of it was contrary to the shape of other Christians. And as for *Mary Adams*, she rotted and consumed as she lay, being from the head to the foot as full of botches, blains, boils, and stinking scabs, as ever one could stand by another. And miserable was her end; for being admonish'd to ask forgiveness for her sins; she answer'd, that her heart was so harden'd, that she could not repent but desired one of the women to lend her a knife to pair her nails, which when she had made use of, she laid the knife aside till the women were gone, and afterwards ript up her belly with it. The truth of this is affirmed by

M[r] *Hadley* Minister. *James Townsworth*, and *Andrew Farmer* Church-Wardens. *Richard Staff* Constable:
This was done *January* the 17. 1652.

Mercurius Politicus *Numb.* 108.

24 June – 1 July, 1652 361.108 {4.14}

By the late Thunder and Lightning there happened a very sad and lamentable Accident at a place called Church Lawton, within four miles of Congleton in the County of Chester, where divers, during Sermon, were stricken dead in the Congregation; the manner whereof being very strange, take the Relation thereof, as it was written by the Minister of the place to a Minister of a Neighbouring Congregation.

From Church-Lawton in Cheshire, June 25.

SIR, The Last Lords day, while we were waiting upon our great God in his own Ordinance in publick, there was a great deal of Thunder and frequent flashes of Lightning ushering in that Rain which we had so long implored and expected; and while the Thunder-claps were the loudest, we continued in prayer giving God the glory of his goodness and greatness. Prayer being ended, I read that portion of Scripture upon which I was then to speak unto the people, out of the third Chapter to the Philipians, the clause of the eight verse (and do count them but dung that I may win Christ) and had not spoken very many words in preferring of Christ above al other things, but a sudden noise was heard in the bell-house, like the discharge of many muskets at once, and a sudden flash of fire (as it seemed) dashed in my face, somewhat dazeled my eyes, and caused me a little to stoop, but presently looking up, I neither saw nor felt any thing, but presently a dog began to whelk much in the bell-house, and afterwards a boy cryed out for his brother, upon which followed a noise among the people, and a bussle as is usual when any thing is amiss in a Congregation: At first we had the report brought to the upper end of the Church that no harm was done, but a dog killed, the second report was that none were slain, but that two or three did bleed; the third relation was more sad, that three or four were slain, whereupon I spoke to the people and intreated them to be still, and they readily hearkened to my desire; some carried out their friends very silently, and the rest setled themselves to attend upon the business we had begun, wherein we continued the usuall time, and returned to God by prayer; after the publick work was done, we had a sad spectacle presented, eleven men and boys strucken immediately dead (for I cannot certainly hear that any of them either spoke, or groaned, or stir'd, but some sate and some lay as though they had been asleep, no wounds or bruises appeared on any of them, only one I saw to have his hair and ear burned a little, and they said another was somewhat scorched in the necke, on some of their cloaths there were some signes of fire, though very little; all of them died in the bell-house where they stood (by reason that the Congregation is usually very full, and the Church but little) except one boy sate in the lower end of the Church close to the bell-hous dore. Many were strucken down and many scorched, of which there is not one dead, but all like to recover, many of them being already perfectly well. The blow was admirable, and the providence wonderfull; for some had no harm at all while others were smitten dead that touched them; they who were smitten down and lay for dead, affirm they felt no sorrow at all, many were strucken quite lame for the present, and some continued so a day or two; others who were quickly well, felt their hands, arms and feet and legs, where the stroke was as though they had been on fire: The next morning I viewed the faces of the dead men; which were most of them black; one little boy who was my Schollar, a son of John Puersels I viewed all over, and from the top of his ear to the sole of his foot he was black on the left side. On Monday the deceased persons were decently interred in eleven several graves in our Churchyard at Lawton, where was a great throng of people, to whom I preached out of Luke 13.v.4,5. The names of those who fell by this mighty hand of God, were {...}

The Weekly Intelligencer of the Common-Wealth *Numb:* 131

2–9 August, 1653 688.131 {4.15}

Monday, August 8. {...}

We had this day from *Dundee* in *Scotland*, that there was lately in the River of *Dundee* in *Scotland* a most terrible and bloody fight between 80 Whales, who in their incounter made the River to rage like the Ocean in the height of a Tempest, and did discolour it all over with their blood. Two of the Whales being killed in the fight they were drawn to the shore, and in the body of one of them there was found the whole body of a man, and in his pocket 27 li: in silver, which my Lord *Doughee* being Lord of the place lays claim unto. Some who came in the last Catch from *Edenborough* have some part of the skin to shew to justifie the truth hereof.

The Perfect Diurnall *Num.* 214

9–15 January, 1653{4} 503.214 {4.16}

By Letters from *Madrid* of the 16th of December, 1653. {...} There is to be seen in this City a copy of a Letter in Print sent from the Jesuits in *Armenia* to those in this City, wherein they express a very strange thing happened in that Countrey, which is thus briefly; There being about five moneths since many Turkes and Moores met together at a Towne called *Medinatalvi*, (but commonly known by the name of *Mecha*) in the Mosquee, or Chappel where the body of their false Prophet hath layn many yeares; On a sudden, about ten of the clock in the forenoone, this Iron Chest (which for many years hath been suspended in the roof of that house, by vertue of the Load-stone fastned there) did fall down to the ground, which immediately opened, and swallowed up both the Chest, and what was therein; the ground remaining open about one quarter of an hour, and in that space came forth of that Abysse a great flame, and smoake, which rendred a great stench, and so the ground closed up as formerly; that thereupon all the Spectators fell on the ground, being struck with deadly feare at so dreadfull a spectacle, and some of them are since become Christians, leaving their superstitious service.

The Weekly Post *Numb.* 196

12–19 September, 1654 544.196 {4.17}

Strange News from the North.

Upon the third day of this moneth *September*, a day not onely remarkable for two notable and famous victories which the English had over the Scots; the one at Dunbar, the other at Worcester; but observable also as to be the day appointed for the sitting of this Parliament: Between 9 and 10 of the Clock at night, there was seen by *James Cook* Corporal, *Tho. Blossome*, and *Edward See*, all souldiers belonging to the Garison of *Hull*, this strange and unwonted Apparition.

These being (at the time before mentioned) on the top of the North-Block-house, having the Watch according to Order, on a sudden the skie seemed to be of a fiery colour, and to cast forth many streams. Whereupon *Tho. Blossome* observing the strangeness of the thing, began to tell the other two, how he had seen the very like appearance a little after the sitting of the first

Parliament; and after such fiery streams there appeared a great battel of horse and foot in the air. He had not ended his relation, but in the East appeared a huge Body of Pike-men, several parties marching before as a Forlorn Hope. Never saw they in their lives an Army (to their thinking) in better equipage. Suddenly they beheld in the North-west another Army, the which seemed unto them to march towards the Eastern Army with extraordinary speed.

And first, there was the representation of some skirmishes between parties of each Army, as the Forlorn Hope. Afterwards both Bodies did engage, and furiously charged each other with their pikes, breaking through one the other backwards and forwards, in such dreadfull sort, as the beholders were astonished thereat. Besides such was the order of the Battel, as the Wings of each Army came in to relieve their Bodies; and each had their Reserves, who accordingly came in: So that for an half quarter of an hour, there was a most terrible fight; but to their thinking the Army which came from the East had the worst. It is here to be noted, that both these Armies seemed to be of a Red colour.

Within a little while, there appeared another Army from the North-west, greater then the former, which marched directly to the place where the former Battel was fought. This Army was Black, and here they perceived horse as well as foot. And now begins another battel far exceeding the former for fierceness and cruelty. From the Black Army there went off Muskets and Cannons, insomuch that they clearly discerned the fire and smoak thereof. This battel was between the Black and the Eastern Red Army, being as they apprehended, the Reserve of the former Army which came forth from the North-west. These two Armies thus engaged, brake through one another, forward and backward; but the Black seemed still to have the best. But before both Bodies met, there were several skirmishes of parties between the Black and the Red, as in the former Battel. And when both Armies did encounter, they saw such fire and smoak, as if a dozen Cannons had been discharged together. A little beneath these Armies, not far from the earth, upon a black cloud, appeared Horsemen, and amongst them they could perceive nothing but rising of fire and smoak, and a multitude of spears as it were standing upright. This latter Battel continued a little longer then the former, the Black driving the Red before them, till all the Red vanished out of their sight. And the Black remained; who in a little time after, departed, and were not any more seen of them.

The Faithful Scout Numb. 198.

22–29 September, 1654 150.198 {4.18}

THere is a Gentleman, one *W. Elmy* now resident at *Lin* in *Norfolk*, that by the blessing of God undertakes the perfect cure of all men, women, & children, from the age of 7 years to 80 and upwards, of their Deafness in hearing, if any ways curable: he cures those that have bin so 20 or 30 years with much ease, & without any pain at all unto his Patient, within the space of one hour. He resolves them at sight whether they be curable or not; he takes not one penny of any except he makes a perfect Cure; and for the Poor he takes little. This wonderful mercy, many of the Gentry and others, have to their great comfort lately experienced; and at their earnest intreaty he hath thought good to let the Nation know so much. *You shall hear of him at the sign of the Bell at Kings Lyn in Norfolk*.

Oliver Cromwell's deliverance from danger when his coach-horses bolted was read as an act of providence, revealing how much one man's life could affect the destiny of a nation. Andrew Marvell, who recorded the incident in his poem 'The First Anniversary', may have read one or both of these accounts.

The Faithful Scout Numb. 199.

29 September – 6 October, 1654 150.199 {4.19}

Beginning, Friday Septem. *the* 29. {...}

This day his Highness the Lord Protector went in his Coach from White hall, to take the ayr in Hide-park; and the horses being exceedingly affrighted, set a running; insomuch that the Postilian fell, whereby his Highnesse was in some danger; but (blessed be GOD) there was little hurt.

This evening likewise (about ten of the clock) there appeared a blazing star over the River of Thames, neer the Tower of London, whose bright and glittering Rayes caused great admiration; What this great and wonderful Sign from Heaven portends, none can absolutely divine, or make evident, but the All seeing Creator of the glorious Sun, the Eye of the World.

The Faithful Scout *Numb*. 201.

13–20 October, 1654 150.201 {4.20}

A Rapture occasioned by the late miraculous Deliverance of his Highness the Lord Protector from a desperate Danger.

IF, what befell, must needs be understood
As Ominous; why, should it not of Good,
An Omen be? (as I believe it will,
Much rather, then prove Ominous for ill?
For, who can think, that He was saved from
A Mischief, that to Mischieves he might come?
Or, that we, by his safety, from the Curse
Of Anarchy, are saved for a worse?
Or, that when Mercies God is pleas'd to shew,
They do portend some Evils to ensue?
What inference more wicked, can be brought?
What, more prophanely! what, more vilely thought!
For 'twas not judged an Unprincely Game,
To drive a Chariot, when th'Olimpian Fame,
Was thirsted after; And when on that Hill,
Kings, with their Equals, therein shew'd their skill;
And wrapt in Clouds, rais'd by their horses heels,
And *thundrings*, from their furious *Chariot wheels*.
It was not want of skill to use the Rain,
That stout and chast *Hippolitus* was slain:
But an unlookt for dreadful Apparition,
(Of purpose rais'd, to hasten his perdition)
Frighted with horses; which, with head-strong fury,
Their Driver, from the beaten paths, did hurry
Among the Rocks: And, what thereon befell,
(The Story is so known) I need not tell.
And thus I hope) when we have sum'd up all
Which to his Highness hapned by his Fall,
His gains will be much greater then his *cost*,
And nothing but self-confidence be lost.

The following stories replaced the usual editorial, and thus were given a clear and morally didactic purpose.

The Faithful Scout Numb. 204

1–8 December, 1654 150.204E {4.21}

Beginning, Friday Decemb. *the* 1.

WHereas a certain Inn-keeper in the town of Rutlinguen, receiving a budget of money from a passenger to keep for him forswore the same before a Judge, giving himself to the Devil if he swore falsly, and was (by two that testified against him, which indeed were two Fiends of Hell) presently in presence of the Judge hoisted up into the air, where he vanished away with them, & was never found after.

One hearing perjury condemned by a godly Preacher, and how it never escaped unpunished, said in a bravery, *I have often forswore my self, and yet my right hand is no shorter then my left*; which words he had scarce uttered, when such an inflammation arose in the hand, that he was forced to go to the Chyrurgion, and cut it off, lest it should have infected his whole body, whereby it became shorter then the other.

A rich young maid in Saxony promised marriage to a young proper man, but poor: He fore-seeing that wealth and inconstancy might alter her mind, freely disclosed his thoughts to her: whereupon she made a thousand imprecations to the contrary, wishing, *That if ever she married another, the Devil might take her away on the Wedding day*: yet afterwards the fickle Wench was betrothed and married to another; and at Dinner two men on horseback came to the house, and was entertained at the feast: and after dinner one of them leading the Bride a dance, he took her by the hand, and led her a turn or two, and then in the presence of all her friends, he caught her, crying out for help, and went out at the Gate, where he hoisted her up in the air, and vanished away with his companion and horses, so that she was never seen more. *Most great and dreadful Judgements, yet Heavens just Revenging Power: May we not therefore fear the same Sword now impending over the heads of many in these our perilous times, who by breaking their Vows and Covenants, are guilty of the same provoking and Heaven outfacing sins.* Thus much touching Gods Judgements against perjury: in our next (by divine permission) we shall present you with an infallible Demonstration, by way of Example, of Gods judgments upon Swearers {…}

Mercurius Politicus *Numb:* 257.

10–17 May, 1655 361.257 {4.22}

That Excellent Cordial, called *The Countess of* KENT'S *Powder*, approved by long experience of the Nobility, Gentry, and best Physitians of this Nation, in any malign disease, *Plague, Small Pox, Burning Fevers, Wind-Collick, Women in Labor, Chiidren newly born, &c.* Is now made by one Mistress *Williamson*, living in *White-Friers*, near the late Countess's house, who was a Servant to her, and for many years compounded it by her Ladies direction. The whole stock of Powder, and of the Ingredients left by the Countess, was, after her death, given to the said Mistress *Williamson* by Mr. *Selden*, her Ladiships Executor.

This notice is published, because of the many counterfeit Powders uttered up and down by Apothecaries and others, under the same name, to the intent it may be known where the right Powder is to be had.

This graphic account of a medical prodigy followed an earlier, less detailed report.

The Faithful Scout *Numb.* 240

10–17 August, 1655 150.240 {4.23}

As touching the Truth of what is before specified, I am since given to understand by Mr. *Cook* the Chyrurgeon, that the aforesaid Mr. *Parrey* having a most intollerable pain in his head, sent (by the advice of his friends) immediately for him, and desired his counsel, for remedy (if possible) to his present condition, which the said Mr. *Cook* undertook, and after he had let him blood with Horse-Leaches, he then applyed him with 4 or 5 Pills, two nights together, which gave him 11 or 12 stooles, and wrought so excellently upon him, that the operation thereof proved so efficacious and effective, that it utterly destroyed this monstrous bed of Vermine, and caused them to come from him, at his going to stool, without any ordure at all, only abundance of slime and blood: This cause so much wonder and admiration, that Mr. *Cook* was forthwith sent for, who beholding the same, took them up, and laid them upon a Trencher, and turning them about, espyed the perfect figures of severall formes and shapes, as Serpents, Toads, Neuts, Sneaks, and the like, with strange and deformed faces, heads, and eys, and many of them had legs like frogs, as appears upon attestation, and withall some form and maturity of natural substance. For know, that after they were delivered by Mrs. *Parrey* to Mr. *Cook* he put them in a great Bason full of Water, where each of them disgorged almost a porenger full of blood. After which, he opened one of them with his instrument, and found some certain strings, like veins, but no bones; which things seeming strang, and not to be parallel'd in twice seven Ages, many Doctors and Physitians frequented his house in Cursisters Alley in Chancery Lane, where they declared and concluded, that the effects of this produced from some Natural Causes as well as Accidents, and that they chiefly subsisted meerly by blood, eating their passage through from one Member and Gut to another, which was the cause of all his distempers throughout head and body. In a word, 'tis said, that after he was dead, he purged many such like Creatures both upwards and downwards, but was soon after inwrapped in his Winding sheet, and nailed in his Coffin.

Mercurius Politicus *Numb.* 330.

2–9 October, 1656 361.330 {4.24}

London, October 3.

The River *Thames* Ebbed and Flowed twice in three hours space. At Seven a clock in the morning, it was high Water; it Ebbed for an hours time, and then it flowed again above an hour and a half, so that it made a very great Tide, and so ebbed again. Within the compasse of these dozen Years last past, the *Thames* has altered its Current thus, contrary to its usuall course, 3, or 4 times.

Mercurius Politicus *Numb.* 340.

11–18 December, 1656. 361.340 {4.25}

From Lisbon in Portugall, Novemb. 19.

Here hath happened a sudden alteration by reason of the Kings death, who departed this life on the 6. of this present month, about ten a clock in the morning. The disease that carryed him away was an obstruction of the kidneys, occasioned by the Stone and gravel; which was so sharp all the time of his sickness, that he seldom urined, and when he did, in so little quantity that he received no ease, and at length, after ten daies affliction, the disease made an end of him.

Politicus was the first newsbook to carry large numbers of adverts on a regular basis, from which Nedham probably made considerable amounts of money.

Mercurius Politicus *Numb*. 351

26 February – 5 March, 1657 361.351 {4.26}

An Advertisement.

SIr Edward Ford *Knight, hath accomplished his great Work, raised the* Thames *Water into all the highest Streets of* London, *Ninety three foot high in four eight inch Pipes. The like not known in any part of the World and so an honor to the Nation. All done at his own charge, and in one year: His Highnesses incouragement, and the Inhabitants intreaties, invited him to it: All publick spirits will honor him for it, and the whole Nation may finde benefit by it, in the draining of their Mines or Lands; which his Engine will do much better and cheaper, then ever yet hath been found out.*

Mercurius Politicus *Numb*. 358

16–23 April, 1657 361.358 {4.27}

From *Newcastle*, April 13.

AS touching that strange Accident concerning the Old man, so farr as is Truth I shall here relate.

They call his name Mr. *John Macklaine*, a Scotish man, Parson of *Lesbury* in *Northumberland*; about 20 or 25 miles from this Town, aged 116 yeares, who could not read without Spectacles for these 40 yeares last past, but hath his youth so renewed, that now he can read the smallest Print without Spectacles.

He had also lost most of his Teeth, but now he hath new Teeth come again. Moreover, he had lost his Haire, and now his Haire is coming again like a Childs Haire: And whereas hee was feeble and weake heretofore, he now begins to renew his strength likewise, and studieth much; and preacheth twice every Lords-day. This is All, and its Truth.

This is a follow-up to a story of an explosion and fire, which, if newsbooks are representative, was not an uncommon aspect of seventeenth-century life: though such events could nonetheless be read in a providential framework

Mercurius Politicus *Numb.* 370

2–9 July, 1657 361.370 {4.28}

Whitehal. July 4.

We had an account, That the late lamentable blow at *Ratcliff*, was occasioned by a Cooper, who going to hoop a Gun-powder Barrel, presumed to do it with an Iron Instrument, which lighting upon a Nail, struck fire, and the sparks occasioned that fatal mischief which ensued, to the ruine and destruction of many persons and families. Among the slain, was found a great-bellied woman, whose belly being immediately opened, the childe was taken out alive.

Superlatives were part of the formula for wonder stories: in this case they are prefaced to an account of an earthquake.

Mercurius Politicus *Numb.* 372

16–23 July, 1657 361.372 {4.29}

From *Barril* in the County of *Chester*: *Iuly* 11.

On Wednesday last being the eighth day of this instant *Iuly*, there hapned the strangest thing in our Neighborhood, which I believe this age hath produced in this Nation; which to prevent false reports, and in some measure to repay what I ow you for many kindnesses received, I shall briefly give you the sum of it, thus.

About three a clock the same day, I heard a very great noise like Thunder afar off, which indeed put me to gaze, and no little to admire at, in regard the Skies were clear, and no appearance of a cloud. Shortly after comes a Neighbor to me, and desired me to go along, and I should see the strangest sight, I ever saw: Where coming into a field called the *Leyfield*, lying in *Bickley*, in the County of *Chester*, we found a very great Bank of Earth, which had many tall Oak Trees growing on it, quite sunk under ground, Trees and all. Indeed at first we durst not go near it, in regard the Earth, for near twenty yards round about, is exceedingly much rent, and seems ready to fall in; but since then, namely this very instant, my self and some others, by Ropes or otherwise, have adventured to see the bottom, I mean to go to the brinck, so as to discern the visible bottom, which is Water, and conceived to be about thirty yards from us; under which is sunk all the Earth above it, for about sixteen yards round at least, three tall Oak Trees, a very tall Awber, and certain other small Trees, and not a Sprig of them to be seen above Water: Four or five Oaks more are expected to fall every moment, and a great quantity of Land is like to fall, indeed never ceasing, more or less; and when any considerable clod falls, we hear it much like the report of a Canon. Very great resort there is to see it, and many reports I know will be raised of it, which taking into consideration, not onely for your own satisfaction, but also for the common good, I have thus briefly given you a true Relation, as being an eye and ear-witness of all, as far as man can discern or judge.

We can discern the Ground hollow above the Water a very great depth; but how far hollow, or how deep, not to be found out by man.

Mercurius Politicus *Numb*. 391

19–26 November, 1657 361.391 {4.30}

From Amsterdam 18 Novemb. {...}

Last week, was found a Monster, yet alive, by Petten, at low water, called Zepia, which had 10 Horns: and Teeth, and a bill like that of a Parret, two Horns were like the Horns of a Goat; his body was like that of a Cat.

This account is accompanied by the testimony of medical experts, in order to increase its credibility.

Mercurius Politicus *Numb*. 398.

31 December – 7 January, 1657{8} 361.398 {4.31}

A Particular Relation sent from Sluys in the Low-Countries, touching a Monster there lately born; attested by persons of quality and learning.

WE whose Names are under written, Doctors of Physick, Surgeons, and Apothecaries, dwelling within the Town of *Sluys*, declare and certifie by these presents, upon request of *Louys* of *Bills*, Gentleman, Lord of *Coppensdam* and *Bonem*, Bailiff of the City and Jurisdiction of *Ardemburg*, That we being called by the foresaid Lord, to come to his House, he shewed unto us a Monstrous Birth of two late born Children, or one Monstrous Childe seeming to be two; of which, a Soldiers Wife was delivered at *Weerted*, on the *Elder-Sconce* near *Ardemburg*, which were of outward shape, as followeth.

To wit, That Birth had two Heads, and two Necks, and four Arms; two whereof were behinde, clipping about the Neck, the one Hand-rist lying on the other; the two other Arms hung across downward, on each side of the Body: The Hands which they said were closed one in another, were now unclosed, and were laid down on either side also of the Body. The Body upward was of double breadth, seeming to be of a double Brest, and all the other parts were double, yet with the skin covered, and lessening downward, appearing to unite at the Navel, which was but single; and from thence downward it was but small, as of one Body, and had but two Legs, and one Splay-foot; the shape of the one was Female; the Face was full and fair, but the other was altogether mishapen; the Eyes stood where the Mouth should be, both together opening without Ey lids, but above had Hairy Eye-brows: above the Eyes, just in the middle, stood a Masculine Member or Genital of an ordinary bigness, hanging down to the right Eye: It had no Nose, and seemed to have a Mouth under the Chin, like unto the Fundament; it had three Teats, two stood right as they are ordinary, but the other stood above. Betwixt the two united Shoulders there was a monstrous space of half an Ell long.

We have seen the Dissection, made by the said owner of the Monster, and it was performed without the issuing forth of any Blood; he shewing unto us, That the Arteries, Veins, and Sinews, had their meeting in the Skin, the same Arteries and Veins being yet full of Blood.

The Inner Constitution and Form of this Monstrous Chile or Children, shewed unto us, was as followeth, The Brain of the one, to wit, of the Female, had her due Constitution; but the other was of a Monstrous Constitution: For the *Dura Mater* had made a partition-cross from above to the lower part, from the one Ear to the other, and both sides had Brains, but very little: In the Brest were found two Concavities, on the right side of which there were Twelve Ribs, and there were Twelve Ribs also on the left side: Of the Male-Childe, the Back-bones spred downward at least four Fingers broad, and from thence running down, joyned all into one *Os sacrum*. There were found therein two Hearts, two Lungs, one great Liver, and one Gall; two Stomacks, the biggest whereof had joyned unto it a Milt and two Kidneys; that on the right, was bigger then that on the left: Of the Genital parts, is found onely that of the Female, the *Uterus*, with the Bladder and the Matrix, being fastned to it. In the Mouth of the Female Body were two firm Teeth; but the Male-body had a very little hole instead of a Mouth, but without a Chin. The Skin of this Monstrous Body, behinde as well as before, was found to be interlarded with Fat. We under written testifie this for a truth, confirming it with our Seals; *Actum* in *Sluys*, the Third of *December:* 1657.

John Moerman, Doctor of Medicin.
Francis de Raed, Doctor of Medicin:
Ippe Sixtus, Surgeon.
Joseph vander Heeden, Apothecary.
Cornelis de Coninck, Surgeon.

This Monster lived but few days, and presently after was Anatomised by an Ingenious Gentleman, named Mr *Louis de Bills*, Major of *Ardemberg*. who is very skilful in this very rare Method, particular to himself, of making Dissections and separation of the several parts of any man, or Beast, without Effusion of any drop of Blood, leaving the Brain, Eyes, Face, Veins, and all other, both inward parts and excrementitious, wholly within, and in embalming the same Bodies, so that they may be easily kept and known for many scores of years without deperdition of Substance.

Two Doctors of Physick, and two Chirurgeons, with an Apothecary, *viz. John Moerman, Francis de Raed, Ippe Sixtus, Cornelis de Coninck* and *Joseph vander Heeden*, all of the Town of *Sluys*, were present at the Dissection thereof, and do verifie the particulars of this Relation. There was an intent of having preserved the Monster, but some foolish women, who were kinred to the Mother, would by no means give way to the embalming, and so it was buried.

The said Mr *Louis de Bills*, who invented the aforesaid unusual way of Dissecting Bodies, is very well worthy the knowledge and imitation of the Physitians of *England*.

Reports of the near-deaths of foreign princes were repetitive and frequently founded on unreliable sources. This is a particularly confident relation.

Mercurius Politicus *Numb*. 424.

8–15 July, 1658 361.424 {4.32}

From Dunkirke, July 10. *S.N.*

The King of *France* is now very well recovered, and by the following means.

On the eighth instant his Physitians ordered his being let blood in the foot the second time, by which he was much refreshed about two a clock afternoon; and at that time the same day to take an Emetick or Vomitory Potion, which had so good an effect, that he passed that night with a great deal of rest and quietness and the next day being the nineth, he seemed in a manner free from his distemper. But the next after, it came on again with more trouble to him than before, for a little time, so that the Physitians judged there remained yet some vapors and humors which might occasion such Accessions and Accidents, as seemed to indicate a Maligne Fever; and therefore on the tenth instant in the morning, they gave him a Purgation, but very gentle, which wrought with so good success, that it rid away most of the remainders of the disease; by which means (through Gods blessing) we hope by the next to hear of his perfect state of recovery.

Mercurius Politicus Numb. 550

13–20 January, 1658{9} 361.550 {4.33}

An Advertisement

THere is lately a new Invention for a Bedstead, which is of a most admirable use for the ease and infinite convenience of all sick, lame, diseased, wounded or aged persons, so as they may be turned in bed without removing the bed-clothes, or touching the person; raising also the head and feet to what Proportion the Patient will require (though in their greatest sweat) to prevent taking cold; and in the greatest weakness to place a bed-pan without trouble, which before this Invention might not be done without much perturbation to sick and weak people. Divers have been made and sold with very high approbation by the Buyers. Also a most easie, plain and cheap Method for raising water, which takes little room, will last long, take up the greatest proportion of any way yet known, of most excellent use to clear Mines of any sort for Depth, for watering or draining of grounds, the supplying Cities, Towns, or Houses, and is fitted to be wrought by men or horses, by water or winde; to which also is adapted a Compendious Engine to go by all windes, without traversing the same; As also for all sorts of Mill-work, or all kindes of motions direct or circular, and to grinde Corn, Bark, Oad, Sugar; for the sawing of Timber, or any connatural to these before specified.

As also a new sort of Engines for extinguishing fire, plainer, stronger, cheaper, more traverseable, in less room, more portable then formerly used. *Thomas Oldfeild* Engineer, and workman for most of the particulars, who dwells next door to the sign of the Sun in the *Strand*, betwixt the *Savoy* and *Worcester-house*, who will direct unto Capt. *Benjamin Okeshott*, of the Regiment of the Right Honorable *Edward* Lord *Montague*, who will give him ample security to perform what is hereby proposed, upon equitable Considerations.

Mercurius Politicus *Numb*. 572.

16–23 June, 1659 361.572 {4.34}

Advertisements.

CHOCOLATE, an excellent *West-India* Drink, sold in Queens-head Alley in Bishopsgate-street by a French-man who did sell it formerly in Grace-Church-street, and in *Clements* Churchyard; being the first man who did sell it in *England*. There you may have it made ready to drink, and also unmade at easie Rates, and taught the use thereof; it being for its excellent properties so much esteemed in all places. It cures and preserves the Body of many diseases, as is to be seen by the Book, who hath it there to be sold also.

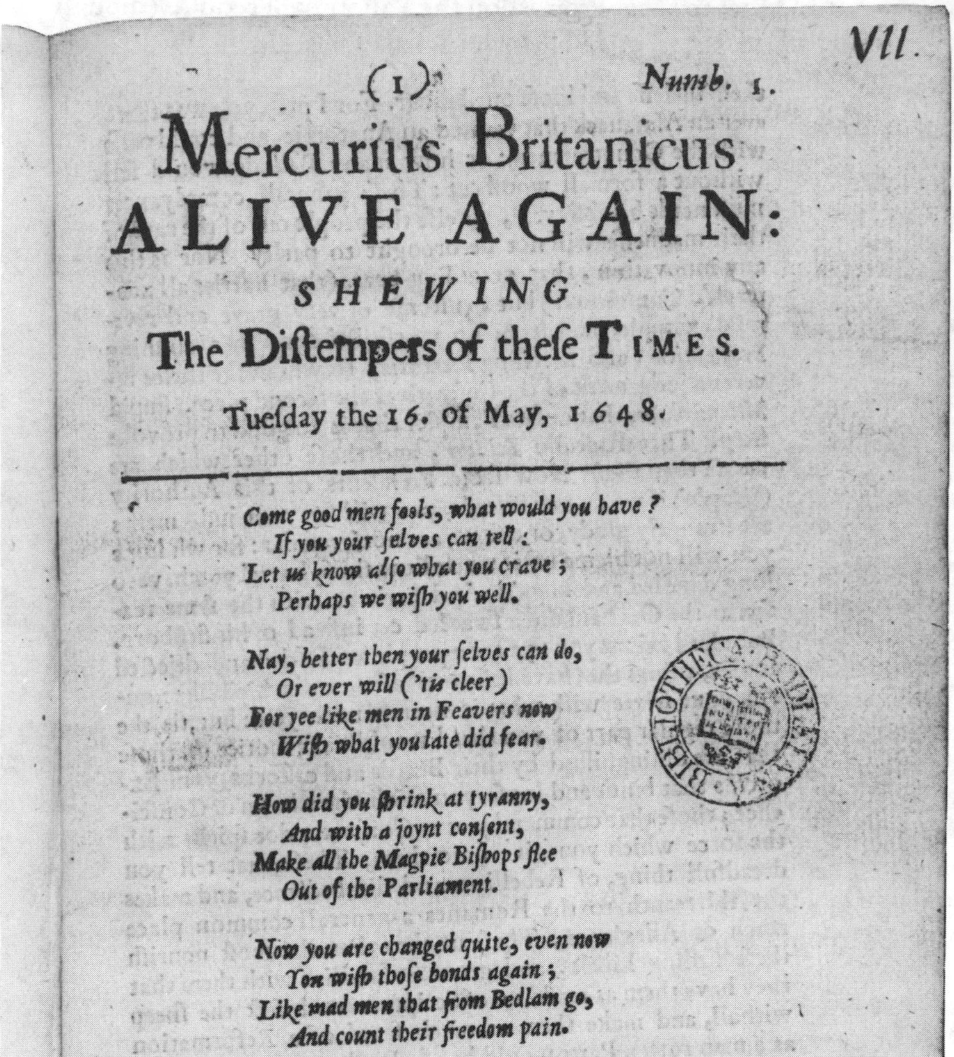

VII.

(1) Numb. 1.

Mercurius Britanicus ALIVE AGAIN:

SHEWING The Distempers of these TIMES.

Tuesday the 16. of May, 1648.

Come good men fools, what would you have?
If you your selves can tell:
Let us know also what you crave;
Perhaps we wish you well.

Nay, better then your selves can do,
Or ever will ('tis cleer)
For yee like men in Feavers now
Wish what you late did fear.

How did you shrink at tyranny,
And with a joynt consent,
Make all the Magpie Bishops flee
Out of the Parliament.

Now you are changed quite, even now
Yon wish those bonds again;
Like mad men that from Bedlam go,
And count their freedom pain.

THus do we according to the solemnity of a Pamplet begin with verses; for if we should not retain the accustomed ceremonies of abusing the people, we should render

B them

8. John Hall's revived *Britanicus*, complete with mis-spelling

CHAPTER FIVE
That the people be not bound but free: The trial and execution of Charles I

On 20 November 1648, the Army Council, in the knowledge that the king, then treating with parliament at Newport in the Isle of Wight, intended to leave the island, presented to parliament its Remonstrance, representing, amongst other things, that the king should be brought to a speedy trial for his responsibility in the late wars. Parliament thanked them but postponed a response to their demands until such time as the members had considered the latest peace propositions. Dissatisfied, some radical leaders of the army seized the king and moved him to more secure imprisonment, occupied London, purged parliament, forced the establishment of a Court of High Justice, tried the king for being a traitor, found him guilty, sentenced him to death, declared illegal the proclamation of a successor and then, on 30 January 1649, beheaded him in front of the Banqueting House in Whitehall.[1]

The king was actually sentenced for treason; but this charge was only secured by the introduction of an Ordinance on 1 January 1649, declaring it illegal for a king to wage war against the kingdom as represented by parliament. The trial was engineered by the Army Council, who distrusted the king and feared that parliament's peace negotiations of the summer and autumn of 1648 would either result in a civil war or in an unacceptable settlement; for instance, one in which Charles did not make the crucial concession of accepting the permanent establishment of

1 Narratives can be found in John Nalson, *The Trial of Charles the First, King of England* (Oxford, 1753); S.R. Gardiner, *History of the Great Civil War 1642–1649*, 4 vols. (London: Windrush Press, 1987) iv, 233–330; and C.V. Wedgwood, *The Trial of Charles I* (London: Collins, 1964).

Presbyterianism. The king had previously behaved with duplicity, and his negotiations were interpreted merely as a way of buying sufficient time to organise another royalist revolt. When parliament would not listen to their appeals, part of the Army Council, led by Cromwell's son in law Lieutenant-General Ireton, arranged the occupation of London and the ejection of the hostile members from the House of Commons. This latter action, known as Pride's Purge after the Colonel who stood at the top of the stairs in the House, checking each member as they entered and securing those on his list, and was the crux of the developments towards the abolition of monarchy in England.[2]

After Pride's Purge, which took place on the morning of 6 December {8.12}, those members of the lower house who were opposed to the trial of the king were quashed into obedience: many of those members not in captivity stayed away, and attendance at the House of Lords dramatically declined. The king, now deprived of newsbooks and pamphlets, was taken to Windsor, where he would be safe and ready for public action, and the House was obliged to vote against the treaty negotiations at Westminster. A committee was appointed by parliament to investigate how the king should be tried. Charles refused to consider the continuing overtures made to him by those who favoured reconciliation. At this point Cromwell, whose opinions remain partly veiled for this period, swung in favour of sacrificing the king in order to achieve a lasting political settlement. The execution of the king was ultimately motivated by a desire to secure peace. Cromwell's resolution resulted in the Ordinance for the king's trial, which appointed a committee of 150 who were to serve as jury and judges. This was transformed into an Act of Parliament on 6 January, in spite of opposition from the Lords. A new Great Seal was made, with the inscription, 'In the first year of freedom, by God's blessing restored, 1648.' The High Court of Justice met, after some obstacles in determining the number and identity of the individuals of which it was composed, and drew up a charge. Some Levellers were now pressing against the capital punishment of the king, but were unable to obstruct the will of the Army leaders including Ireton and Cromwell. On 19 January Charles was taken to St James's Palace, and the next day he appeared in Westminster before the Court {5.9}.

2 See David Underdown's seminal study, *Pride's Purge: Politics in the Puritan Revolution* (London: Allen and Unwin, 1971, 1985).

What happened next is represented in the texts which follow. The king was executed and monarchy abolished. The hitherto divine jurisdiction of the crown was scrutinised under secular analysis. Major White complained that the sword had become the authority under which the king was tried, and argued that 'it is not so much the person that can hurt as the power that is made up in the kingly office by the corrupt constitution; for if the person be taken away, presently another layeth claim to the kingly office...'[3] In once sense the Regicides obeyed White's logic and plucked monarchy up by the roots. Cromwell is reported to have said; 'We will cut off his head with the crown upon it.'[4]

Dispute between historians of the seventeenth century on the relative importance of short and long term causes of the revolution, has tended to focus on the outbreak of war rather than on the execution of the king, that quintessential image of social and political revolution. The internal logic of the economic and ideological circumstances which led to the former are often assumed to be sufficient to ensure progress to the latter. Thus in the narrative of the winter of 1648, the focus tends to fall on the actions and motivation of individuals. Sometimes this is further reduced to the 'characters' of the main protagonists; to the strength of Cromwell and the weakness of Charles; or to the single-mindedness of Cromwell, and the temperate indecisiveness of Charles.

So the movement from the 1648 Remonstrance through Pride's Purge to the execution of the king is generally understood to be the consequence of a fanatic and divided minority, in the Army Council and parliament, who manipulated their less dynamic peers into acquiescing to an action which was more or less shocking. Newsbooks, one of the staple sources for historical narratives of the trial of the king,[5] do not fundamentally challenge the basis of such an interpretation. The newsbooks represent the very public side of proceedings; the official documents and the licensed accounts of the exchanges within the High Court of Justice. The most detailed version of the latter was published in three parts as *A Perfect Narrative of the Proceedings of the High*

3 Gardiner, *History of the Great Civil War*, iv, 303.

4 Wedgwood, *Trial of Charles I*, p.99.

5 For instance, see Wedgwood, *Trial of Charles I*, pp.48–51, 123–7 and *passim*. Another detailed source, the records of the trials of the Regicides in 1660, are less reliable.

Court of Justice in the Tryal of the King, and its continuations, by Gilbert Mabbot.[6] To a greater or lesser extent the newsbook accounts conform to this official publication which, above all, was concerned to make the proceedings appear acceptable. But this public, dramatic mode of representation emphasized a dichotomy in the claims of the revolutionary minority: between constitutional innovations founded on notions of political and moral justice, and the language of ancient legal justice in which these innovations were expressed in order to legitimate them before a broader public.[7] The internal contradiction necessary for the appeal to the public was foregrounded as the arguments were represented in newsbooks, a public stage designed to inform and instruct popular opinion.

Other newsbooks, however, characterized the alternative face of mid-seventeenth-century press activity: the sustained invective against a caricature of another political position. The Royalist newsbooks, *Mercurius Pragmaticus, Mercurius Melancholicus*, and *Mercurius Elencticus*, continued through December and January to charge the Army Council and parliament as apostates, though they showed signs of disillusionment as the ineluctable approach of the regicide became increasingly apparent. Marchamont Nedham sporadically disappeared, chased by parliamentary agents in recognition of his polemical brilliance, and his publication was replaced by less incisive imitations. The insubstantial nature of the boundary between propaganda and news was apparent in *The Moderate* in this period. This pro-Leveller newsbook sustained detailed coverage of the trial while powerfully describing the political necessity of the action. The Earl of Leicester thought it would 'invite the people to overthrow all property as the original cause of sin, and by that to destroy all government, magistracy, honesty, civility and humanity'[8] which should also be read as a comment on its effectiveness. The editorials appealed to historical precedent, and the actions of Charles in the 1620s and 1630s as evidence of his untrustworthy character, in sophisticated arguments which betrayed a convic-

6 These have been omitted from this chapter, in favour of the more erratic reports in *Perfect Occurrences, Perfect Diurnall* and *The Moderate*, Mabbot's other organ.

7 Cp. Christopher Hill, *Puritanism and Revolution: Studies in Interpretation of the English Revolution of the 17th Century* (London: Martin Secker and Warburg, 1958), ch.3.

8 Quoted in Underdown, *Pride's Purge*, p.268.

tion that information and knowledge were powerful things, and not to be dissociated from a persuasive, rhetorical context.

But being a stage, where information and persuasion were involved with theatrical modes of presentation, the newsbook could claim to be an active part of the public arena. The Army did very little to suppress royalist publications in January 1649, apparently unafraid that Charles' words would triumph over their own in a public debate. Just as in 1642 the use of the press by parliament had participated in those historical forces which demystified the image of the king, thereby bringing his divine authority into dispute amongst a politicized reading public,[9] in 1648 newsbooks helped to shape the way Charles was perceived. Long before his death became a political inevitability, he was being prepared for martyrdom in the spring of 1648. The Army, which had been responsible for censorship since September 1647, was required to put down the provincial uprisings which constituted the second civil war, and the London presses once again experienced relative freedom. As the Royalist revolt was suppressed, fears for the king's safety were expressed in increasingly pessimistic tones, and he became figured as a Christian martyr, fated only to suffer while he remained on the earth. The king in turn emphasized the importance of the dictates of his own conscience, and with the newsbooks generated this cultural fantasy:

> His Majesty saith, if his two Houses will not receive in these {propositions} for a good peace, then hee can with Christ suffer any thing that can befall him, rather than deprive himselfe of any tranquility of mind (*in England though he did in Scotland*) and therefore adheres and hopes the Parliament will concur.[10]

The critical aside, noting that the king was content to allow Presbyterianism in Scotland, does not overcome the melancholy anticipation of Charles' martyrdom.

Brian Duppa, Bishop of Salisbury, had emphasised the theme when preaching to Charles at Newport, heavily underscoring the glamour of suffering:

> Consider I beseech you the value of the *Soule* that is thus *cast down*, that your Sighs are the breath of Heaven, your Teares are the Wine of Angels, your Groanes the Eechoes of the Holy Ghost, that therefore to

9 See Jürgen Habermas, *The Structural Transformation of the Public Sphere: An Inquiry into a Category of Bourgeois Society*, trans Thomas Burger and Frederick Lawrence (Cambridge: Polity Press, 1989).

10 *The Moderate Intelligencer*, Numb.193, 23–30 November 1648. N&S 419.193.

> imploy this sacred Treasure in prophane expences, to lay it out on the trifles of this world, is a Sin no lesse then Sacriledge; Bee therefore more thrifty of your sorrow, for the time may come, when you shall want those sighs, which now you so impertinently throw away; {...}
>
> The Angels are thy servants, they gather up thy tears; God is thy Treasurer, he lays them up in his bottle, the holy ghost is thy Comforter, he will not leave thee. Fear not then to be thus cast *down*, fear not to be thus *disquieted within thee*.[11]

The newsbooks participated in the making public of this very private advice to Charles. Its reproduction in newsbooks transformed it into a propaganda exercise, somewhere between history and fantasy. In this respect they prepared their readers for the mode in which the execution of the king was to be read. When Εικων Βασιλικη: *the Pourtraicture of His Sacred Maiestie in His Solitude and Sufferings* appeared on 9 February, the day after the King's funeral, its reception had already been constructed. This text, which implied that it had been written by the king himself, but was actually composed by John Gauden, possibly with the help of the king, used the king's prayers and meditations to define him as a protestant martyr. So powerful was the impact of this work that not even John Milton's exact repudiation of it, including the accusation that one of the prayers in a later edition was plagiarized from Sir Philip Sidney's *Arcadia*, could reverse its impact on the people.[12] A writer as ambivalent towards the king as Andrew Marvell could participate in this language:

> That thence the *Royall Actor* born
> The *Tragick Scaffold* might adorn: {...}
> *He* nothing common did or mean
> Upon that memorable Scene:[13]

In spite of what obviously was a feeling of powerlessness amongst writers of royalist newsbooks, they did contribute to an image of the king which received historical longevity. The

11 *Packets of Letters*, Numb.35, 7–14 November 1648. N&S 480.35.

12 *Eikonoklastes*, in *Complete Prose Works of John Milton*, ed. D.M. Wolfe, III, 362 (New Haven: Yale University Press, 1962). See also Christopher Hill, *Milton and the English Revolution* (London: Faber and Faber, 1977), ch.12.

13 'An *Horation* Ode upon *Cromwel's* Return from *Ireland*', *The Poems and Letters of Andrew Marvell*, ed. H.M. Margoliouth revised by Pierre Legouis and E.E. Duncan Jones (Oxford: Clarendon Press, 1971), I, 91–4. For strong readings of this poem, see David Norbrook, 'Marvell's "Horation Ode" and the politics of genre' in T. Healy and J. Sawday eds. *Literature and the English Civil War* (Cambridge: Cambridge University Press, 1990); and Blair Worden, 'Andrew Marvell, Oliver Cromwell, and the Horation Ode', in eds. Kevin Sharpe and Steven Zwicker, *Politics of Discourse: The Literature and History of Seventeenth-Century England* (Berkeley: University of California Press, 1987).

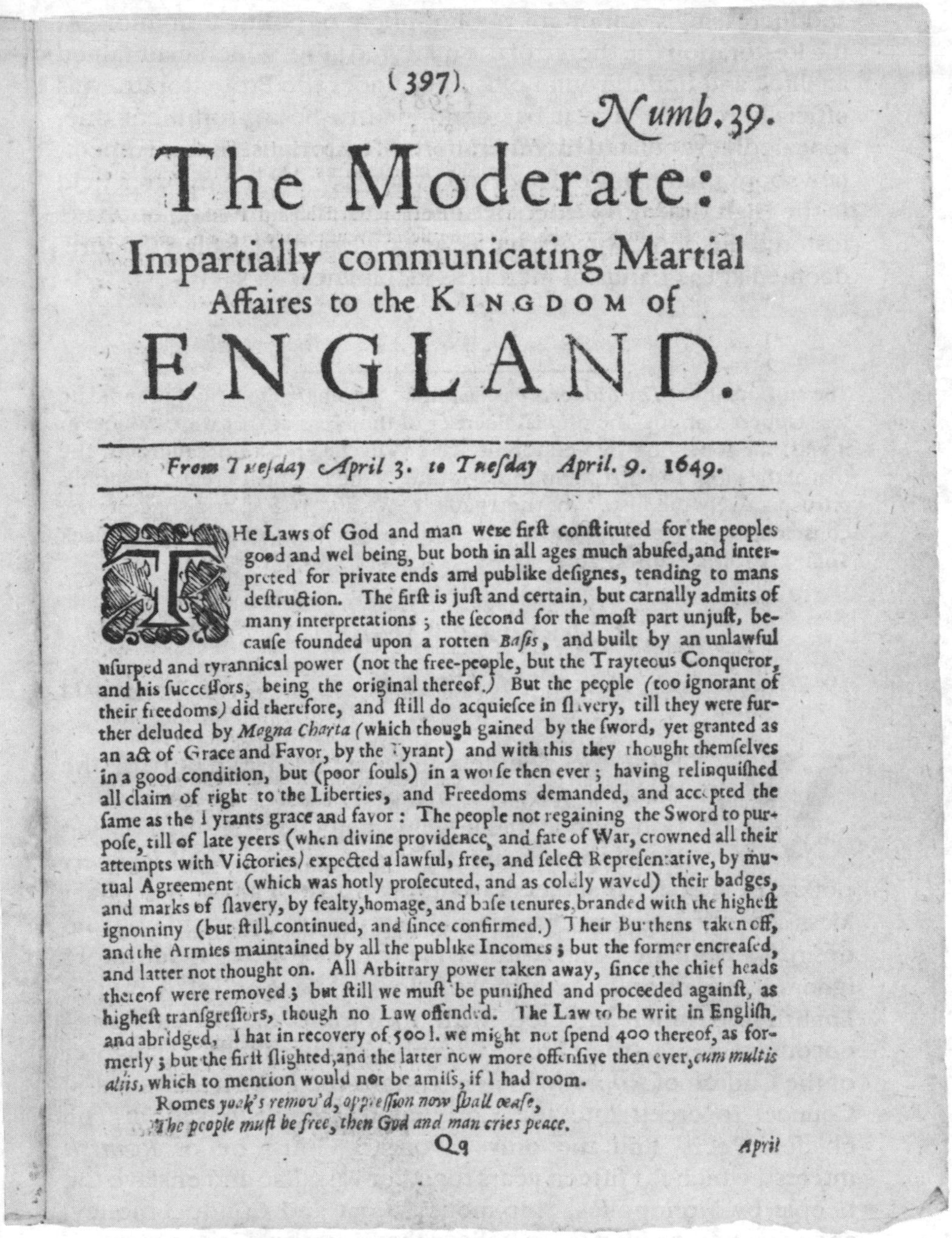

(397)

Numb. 39.

The Moderate:

Impartially communicating Martial Affaires to the KINGDOM of ENGLAND.

From Tuesday April 3. *to Tuesday April.* 9. 1649.

THe Laws of God and man were first constituted for the peoples good and wel being, but both in all ages much abused, and interpreted for private ends and publike designes, tending to mans destruction. The first is just and certain, but carnally admits of many interpretations; the second for the most part unjust, because founded upon a rotten *Basis*, and built by an unlawful usurped and tyrannical power (not the free-people, but the Trayteous Conqueror, and his successors, being the original thereof.) But the people (too ignorant of their freedoms) did therefore, and still do acquiesce in slavery, till they were further deluded by *Magna Charta* (which though gained by the sword, yet granted as an act of Grace and Favor, by the Tyrant) and with this they thought themselves in a good condition, but (poor souls) in a worse then ever; having relinquished all claim of right to the Liberties, and Freedoms demanded, and accepted the same as the Tyrants grace and favor: The people not regaining the Sword to purpose, till of late yeers (when divine providence, and fate of War, crowned all their attempts with Victories) expected a lawful, free, and select Representative, by mutual Agreement (which was hotly prosecuted, and as coldly waved) their badges, and marks of slavery, by fealty, homage, and base tenures, branded with the highest ignominy (but still continued, and since confirmed.) Their Burthens taken off, and the Armies maintained by all the publike Incomes; but the former encreased, and latter not thought on. All Arbitrary power taken away, since the chief heads thereof were removed; but still we must be punished and proceeded against, as highest transgressors, though no Law offended. The Law to be writ in English, and abridged, That in recovery of 500 l. we might not spend 400 thereof, as formerly; but the first slighted, and the latter now more offensive then ever, *cum multis aliis*, which to mention would not be amiss, if I had room.

Romes *yoak's remov'd, oppression now shall cease,*
The people must be free, then God and man cries peace.

Qq

April

9. A trenchant editorial in the Leveller *The Moderate*

newsbook was crucial in informing the attitude of a newly created and increasingly important public sphere of political opinion. At the Restoration the theme of the martyred king, which maintained an illicit and underground existence under the Protectorate, was officially revived, and it has continued to be a prominent one, repeatedly articulated by generations of historians. In this respect, newsbooks have not only served as sources for the debates held in the High Court of Justice between 20 and 27 January, but have fostered the depiction of Charles as a melancholy, isolated figure, doomed at the hands of merciless ideologues.

The authorship of *The Moderate* is disputed: the single most likely candidate was Gilbert Mabbot, the official licenser of the Press at that time. Whoever it was, the following two editorials state a Leveller position calling for the trial of the king. The first, written at the time of the Personal Treaty, describes retrospectively the history of the 1620s, 1630s and 1640s, and suggests the consciousness of a long history of grievances leading to the present. Black Tom was Fairfax's nickname.

The Moderate *Numb.* 11.

19–26 September, 1648 413.2011 {5.01}

WHere the people's judgements are rectified, the Traytors purposes are prevented; but when affections blinde the judgement, judgements by Treason bring speedy ruin. It is the greatest of all Princely policy, to keep their subjects in simplicity; the Papists must hear Mass, and say their Prayers in a Language they understand not, and desire of God they know not what, of their Laws made more ignorant, and consequently more fit for vassalage and slavery. The English too much affected with the Mode of *France*, gives encouragement to their Prince to espouse himself with a Daughter of the Church of *Rome*, which occasions the Popish Faction and Councel to creep into the Court of the *English* Nation: The chiefest Peers, and the only Favourites, must be of *Romish* interest, which for fifteen years together vassalize and enslave the people by Monopolies, Ship-money, Coat and Conduct-money, and what not; making them believe that Kings are Gods anointed, and Vicegerents, though Tirants; and that it is Damnation to oppose them in whatsoever they do, though it be to the ruine of the Nation; for the better effecting whereof, the people must be kept in greater ignorance by a Book of Common-Prayer; the Bishops must silence Preaching Ministers, and others of the Popish and Royal Faction must be preferred to great Benefices, to Preach down Puritans, and introduce Popery, by erecting of Altars, and bowing down with all reverence towards them, with Copes and Surplices, making the people believe that God was worshipped Complementally and Formally, more then Spiritually and Cordially; their Laws continued in French, that they may not understand their Liberty, or the bounded power of their Prince by them: The Bodies and Souls of the people thus enslaved *a la mode de France*, a Parliament is called, upon the peoples importunity; his gracious Majesty desires Subsidies may be levied before they proceed to redresse of grievances (to the end he might deceive them, as he had the Parliament of *Ireland*, in dissolving them before any private busines was heard) which denied, the King (by advice of the Popish Faction) Adjourns them: A second Parliament is soon after necessitated to be called, for raising money to see the *Scots* Army, to retreat out of this Kingdome: Justice is executed on one of his Maiesties dear Couzens, the Earl of *Strafford*, whose death his Maiesty had no way to revenge, but by Charging 5 of the Principall Members of both Houses, that managed the Tryal against him, of high Treason, (and consequently all the House, if he had pleased) his rashnesse in this unlawfull act (for which he afterwards cryed *Peccavi*) and his greedinesse of revenge invites him within few moneths after, to set up his Standard, and Proclaim warre against this Kingdome, which, with the assistance of all the Papists, Prelates, Monopolizers, Delinquents and all other the discontented persons, he maintaines for 5 years together against them, till Black *Tom* (the Conqueror) comes with his new dispised Model, with which he beats all his Armies, and takes away all his garrisons in 12 moneths time, and soon after secures his sacred person from danger, and most of his chiefe Coactors. By this time both Houses of Parliament draw up a Declaration against his sacred Maiesty, charging him with such high Crimes, as to make him the most Odious Prince in Christendome, (his Royall and deare consort having been charged of high Treason by the Parliament some yeares before.) Justice neglected, and the charge not prosecuted, his Sacred Fancy begins to work, how to raise another Army, to cut the throats of his Subjects, and yet to vassalize them if possible; the Scene is laid, and the Tragedie soon after acted by Sea and Land, Domestick and Forraign Enemies, and with fire and sword. All his Majesties Armies being routed, slain, and taken prisoners, and his Navy made unserviceable by the Armies great successes, and having no way left by the sword to recover his lost condition, and finding the people to gape after any Peace, prepares a gilded, poysoned Bait, on which he writes, *Peace, Peace*, which the people swallow with much greediness, the operation strong, the people swell, and rage with madness, which to qualifie, both Houses grant a Treaty with his sacred Maiesty, who desires no greater advantage against Parliament and Army, being the best Design that he ever yet had against them. {...}

The Moderate *Numb*. 19.

14–21 November, 1648. 413.2019 {5.02}

NO man lives happily if he want the freedom of liberty, because slavery's the greatest misery, which all the people under the sun (though free born) have been subjected unto by the sword: The King saith he is born a Monarch, and consequently the people slaves, and therefore some Authors say he is above Law by his absolute power {...} If so, how came *Hambdens* case to be condescended to by his Majesty and his privy Councell (in the case of ship-money) to be pleadable by Law, if his Majesties absolute power had been above Law? Why did not his said Romish Councell (who were select enemies to the people freedoms) advise him to insist on his said superlegall power? Or, how can a King be Arrested for debt *propria persona*, or dis-Throned, or executed by Law, and the representatives of the people, as many have been in this Nation, more in Scotland, and elsewhere, without number? And if Kings be subject to the Laws of the Land, and liable to Execution of death upon breach of Trust; and for Common safety, (which is above all Laws and powers whatsoever,) are not Parliaments likewise upon the same grounds? Did we elect Parliaments to redresse our grievances, take off our burthens, hold out our native freedoms and liberties against all pretended, Arbitrary, Tyrannicall, and destructive Kingly powers, and for our safety and well being? And do they instead thereof increase our grievances, by laying heavier, and as Arbitrary Taxes upon us, joyn with our enemies to destroy our freedoms and liberties (which our predecessors have bought dear with our blood,) and to maintain the Monarchicall, and Arbitrary power of the King, which was first gained, and since maintained by the sword, (though God hath freed us from it by two severall Conquests,) invited in a forraign enemy to destroy us, acted our enemies design in a Treaty, under a specious pretence of concluding a safe and well grounded Peace for the Nation, (though indeed for the destruction of all the honest and godly party of the Kingdom that ever engaged against the Common enemy.) Why do the people admire that the King (the great Delinquent of the Kingdom, and the Author of Englands ruine) should be secured, in order to a Tryall, (he having confest himself guilty of all the bloodshed in the three Nations, and of all the Rapine, Plunder, Taxes, and miseries therein by this war?) or that this Parliament shall be dissolved, and brought to an account for like breach of Trust, and for all the Treasure received by them, and most unjustly leavied upon us? Is it not the same course which the well-affected of the Kingdom of Scotland did take for the security of themselves, and that Kingdom? And was not the last Parliament there dissolved by advise of the Parliament of England, though but by the minor part of that Kingdom? And will not the same advise justifie the minor part of this Kingdom, in dissolving this Parliament of England upon the same grounds of *Salus Populi*, breach of Trust, and opposing and destroying the same Kingly, and Tyrannicall interest? Doth not all the Kingdom, and indeed all the world take notice that we are bought and sold as sheep for the slaughter by this Treaty (a design laid by the King, the eleven Members, and the Tower birds, and the rest of his Majesties new elected friends, ever since the Treaty at Uxbridge.)

Let the Enemies of God and his people perish, and let justice, and righteousnesse slow down like a mighty stream, let the Native rights and freedoms of the poor people be maintained, and they eased of their burthens, and let the power of Gods spirit break in upon them, and then, and not till then, can we expect peace in this Nation. {...}

The text of the Army's Remonstrance, of which parliament protracted its consideration until force was used, appeared to a greater or lesser extent in most newsbooks.

Perfect Occurrences. of Every Daie iournall
Numb. 99.

17–24 November, 1648 465.5099 {5.03}

Munday, Novem. 20. {...}

This day was presented to the Commons a REMONSTRANCE from the Army, inclosed in a Letter from the Lord Generall, which the Commons had read, and ordered to consider of it on Munday next.

Mr. Speaker THe Generall Councel of Officers, at their late meeting here, have unanimously agreed upon a Remonstrance, to be presented unto you, which is herewith sent by the hands of Col. *Ewers*, and other Officers; and in regard it concerns matters of highest, and present importance, to your self, to us, and the whole Kingdome, I doe, as the desire of the Officers, and in the behalf of them, and my self, most humbly and earnestly intreat, that it may have a present reading, and the things propounded therein, may be timely considered; And that no failing in circumstances or expressions may prejudice either the Reason or Justice of what is tendred, or their intention, of whose good affections, and constancy therein, you have had so long experience; I remain

Your most humble servant, T. FAIRFAX.

For the Honourable *William Lenthal* Esq; Speaker of the House of Commons.

Heads of the Remonstrance from the Army follow, (viz.)

FIrst we mind you of your Votes once passed concerning no more adresses to the King, &c. and our Engagement to adhere to you therein. What state you and the Kingdome were in then, and how it fared with you untill you began to recede. The House being called, you began to entertain motions tending to the unsettlement of what you had resolved. Multitudes Petition, and thence, under the pretence of freeing the Parliament from force, to raise Armes and leavy war against it (at best to inforce their Petitions, and under the notion of freeing the people from taxes to the Parliament, and quarter to the Army; to make them in our greater charges and burthens, for the King and His party, and (by withholding their taxes from the Parliament) to necessitate free quarter againe upon themselves, and ingage the people in another War on the Kings behalf, against the Parliament and their own Liberties, driving on a Personall Treaty to deceive you. {...} And against these matters of publicke interest this King hath (all along his raign) opposed, First, That there might be no Parliaments at all to restrain and check him. To support himslfe in height of Tyranny and make it absolute, Hee raised His first and second Armes against his people in both Kingdomes. At His will, would make you know, that, not you nor the Kingdom should have any Peace or quiet without him, that neither Parliament nor any Power on Earth (whatever ills He had done,) might for it attach or meddle with His Sacred Person.

Had He timely, freely and clearly confest, but so much as from conviction, or remorse, or from a sence of the hand of God against Him, or had left us but a ground of charity to believe so, we should have thought our selves bound to regard it with proportionable tendernes towards him; or at least, should have thought it not ingenious nor Christian to take advantage, from such confession, the more to prosecute Him for it; but having so long and so obstinatly, both in word and practise, till now, denied it; and never confessed it, untill all his other waies of force, policy, or fraud had failed him, and no other shift left, but by this forced acknowledgement to save Himselfe, and delude the People and confessing it but conditionally; does seeme to imply Hypocrisie, when at the same time, while thus in words he confesseth it, yet in practice he denies it still, by his continuing, and not recalling His Commissions to the Prince, and others, yea, to Ormond and his associated Irish Rebells. Besides the common voyce of them all in corners, that the King (good man) is meerly forced to what he grants, avowed by the Prince. The King in truth is in prison, and so it may serve in behalfe of the King, His Heirs, and whole party, as a protestation against any conclusion by the Treaty. For Divisions, He needs not come to make any amonst you, but to use them. 1 from the Jealousies which each party is apt to have of the tothers strengthening themselves, by Conjunction to Him and His. Secondly, What we declared was saving for the publicke Interest: We aimed not at the strengthning of our selves thereby to the ruine of any persons or party opposed did drive at any such end. {...}

Having thus endeavoured to Remonstrate, we proceed to offer; First, we conceive and hope, that you may finde abundant cause to forbear any further proceeding in this evill and most dangerous Treaty, and to return again to your former grounds in the Votes of Non-addresses, and thereupon proceed to the setling and securing of the Kingdom, without and against the King, upon such foundations as hereafter are tendered. We shall at least desire that you make sure to avoyd that main venome and mischief attending it, Viz. The Kings restitution with impunity, We propound, 1 That you would reject those demands of the King, sent to you on his and his Parties behalf, and that the Person of the King may, and shall be proceeded against in a way of justice, for the blood spilt. 2 That for other Delinquents you would lay aside that particular bargaining Proposition, that all Delinquents bee proceeded against according to justice, or with mercy, as cause shall appeare, and that none shall be exempted or protected therefrom, nor pardonable by any other power, then that of the Kingdome in parliament, by which they shall be judged. Thus Justice and Mercy being saved or reserved; we proceed to propound as:

1 That the capital and grand Author of our troubles, the person of the King may be speedily brought to justice, for the Treason, blood, and mischiefe hee is guilty of, 2 That a timely and peremptory day may bee set for the Prince of *Wales*, and the Duke of York to come in and render themselves, by which time (if they doe not) that then they may bee immediately declared incapable of any government; or trust, and to stand exiled for ever, as Enemies and Traytors, to dye without mercy. 3 That for further satisfaction to publique Justice, capitall punishment may bee speedily executed on a competent number of his chief Instruments also, both in the former and later Warre, as are really in your hands or reach. 4 That the rest of the Delinquents (English) in relation to the wars, may upon their submission and rendring themselves to Justice, have mercy extended to them for their lives, and that only Fines may be set upon them, and their persons further censured and declared to bee incapable of any Office or place of power, or of having any voyce in Elections thereto. 5 That the satisfaction of Arrears to the Souldiery, with other publique Debts, and the competent reparation of publique Dammages may be put into some orderly and equall, or proportionable way. After publique Justice, and therewith the present quieting of the Kingdome, we proceed in order.

1 That you would set some reasonable and certain period to your own power, by which time that great and supreame trust reposed in you, shall bee returned into the hands of the People. 2 That there may be a sound settlement of the peace and future Government of the Kingdom, upon grounds of common Right, Freedome, and safety to the effect here following: 1 That there be a certain succession of Parliaments (Annuall, or Bienniall). 2 That no King bee hereafter admitted, but upon the election of, and as upon trust from the people, by such their Representatives, nor without first disclaiming and disavowing all pretence to a negative voyce, against the determinations of the said Representatives, or Commons in Parliament. Servants may speak to their Masters, and ought to be heard and regarded, even when they speak for their own right only, and rather, when they speak for the good and safety of them they serve, but much more, when they speak of that wherein they have some joynt interest with them; and yet more when (those their immediate Masters being themselves also

servants, and Trustees for the benefit of others) they speak for the interest of those, for whom both are imployed.

By the appointment of his Excellency the Lord Generall, and his Generall Councell of Officers. *Signed,*
St. Albans Novemb. 18. 1648. *JOHN RUSHWORTH.*

When parliament overlooked the Remonstrance, the Army Council responded with a declaration which threatened future action against the Houses.

A Perfect Diurnall of Some Passages in Parliament *Numb.* 279

27 November – 4 December, 1648 504.279 {5.04}

Thursday Novemb. 30.

THe house had much debate this day whether the Remonstrance of the Army should be taken into speedy consideration, and it was resolved in the Negative neer by 90. Votes. {…}

From the Head-quarters was certified, That upon a very full Councell this day a Declaration was agreed upon in further prosecution of the ends of their late Remonstrance, and also to declare the Resolution of the Army to march up to *London*, The Declaration followes.

The Declaration of his Excellency the Lord Generall *Fairefax*, and His Generall Counsell of Officers, shewing the Grounds of the Armies advance towards the City of *London*.

BEing full of sad Apprehensions concerning the danger and evill of the Treaty with the King, and of any Accommodation with him, or Restitution of him thereupon, We did by our late Remonstrance, upon the reasons and grounds therein expressed, make our Application thereby unto the present House of Commons, that the dangerous evill of that way might be avoided, and the Peace of the Kingdome settled upon more righteous, safe and hopefull grounds, *viz* a more equall dispensing of Justice and Mercy in relation to things done or suffered in the late wars, and the establishing of the future Government of this Kingdome upon a safe succession and equall constitution of Parliaments, and that (for the ending of present, and avoiding of future Differences) to be ratified by an agreement and subscription of the people thereunto.

This course we took out of our tender care and earnest desire, That all wayes of extremity might be avoided, and that those matters of highest concernment to the publique interest of this Nation, might be pursued and provided for (if possible) by those whose proper Work and Trust it was. And herein we were willing to hope, That the persons so trusted, or the majority of them, might possibly have been either driven into that destructive way by forcible impulsions or lapsed thereinto through some inconsideration, or misapprehensions and conceived Jealousies: And therefore we did carefully decline the insisting upon any thing that might continue or renue any former Jealousies or Animosities, and kept onely to such things as were of necessity or advantage to the common Cause, and of common and equal concernment to those that have engaged in it; Which things we pressed in the way of Reason and Perswasion only, that they might be duly and timely considered. But to our griefe we finde, in stead of any satisfaction or a reasonable Answer thereto, they are wholly rejected, without any consideration of what ever Reason or Justice might be in the things set forth or propounded therein; for what lesse can be understood, when the things propounded were mainly for the avoidance of evils appearing in the Treaty with the King: And yet they put off the consideration of them, till there should be no place left for any consideration at all: First, laying it aside till *Munday* last, by which time the Treaty (as then supposed) would have been concluded; but that failing, and two dayes more being added to the Treaty, the consideration of our *Remonstrance*, on the day appointed, was waved and laid aside; the Treaty, the mean while, going on in the former way and termes, and like to be concluded the very next day.

Now, though we are far from that presumption, that the things should therefore be answered or considered, because propounded by us, save for the Reason, Justice, or publique concernment therein; yet, having no answer, or any thing shewed us to the contrary, we cannot but upon the grounds Remonstrated (and many more which might be added) remain confident in our former Apprehensions concerning them. And seeing the prevailing part of those, to whom we did apply, to have, as it were, their eyes wilfully shut, and ears stopt, against any thing of light or Reason offered to them, we find no place left for our former charitable or hopefull Apprehensions, concerning their error in such evill wayes; but remaining fully assured of the danger and destructivenesse thereof, as to all those publique ends for which they were intrusted, and also of the just advantage and necessity which lye in the things we have propounded and insist on, we now see nothing left, to which their engaging and persisting in such wayes, and rejection of those better things propounded, can rationally be attributed lesse then a treacherous or corrupt neglect of, and Apostacy from the publique Trust reposed in them; although we could wish from our souls, we might yet find the contrary. {...}

And therefore first, it should be our great rejoycing (if God saw it good) that the majority of the present house of Commons were become sensible of the evil and destructivenesse of their late way, and would resolvedly and vigorously apply themselves to the speedy execution of Justice, with the righting and easing of the oppressed people, and to a just and safe settlement of the Kingdom upon such foundations as have been propounded by us and others for that purpose, and would for the speedier and surer prosecution of these things exclude from communication in their Councels, all such corrupt and Apostatized Members as have appeared hitherto, but to obstruct and hinder such matter of Justice, Safety, and publique Interest, and to pervert their Councels a contrary way, and have therein so shamefully both falsified and forfaited their Trust.

But however (if God shall not see it good to vouchsafe that mercy to them and the Kingdom) we shall secondly desire, That so many of them as God hath kept upright, and shal touch with a just sence of those things, would by protestation or otherwise acquit themselves from such breach of Trust, and approve their faithfulnesse, by withdrawing from those that persist in the guilt thereof and would apply themselves to such a posture, whereby they may speedily and effectually prosecute those necessary and publique ends, without such Interruptions, Diversions or Depravations of their Councels from the rest, to their endlesse trouble, oppression, and hazzard of the Kingdome as formerly, and for so many of them whose hearts God shall stir up so to do, we shall therein, in this case of extremity, look upon them as persons having materially the chief trust of the Kingdom remaining in them; and though not a formal standing power to be continued in them, or drawn into ordinary Presidents; yet the best and most rightfull that can be had, as the present state and exigence of affairs now stand; And we shall accordingly own them, adhere to them and be guided by them in their faithfull prosecutions of that trust, in order unto, and untill the introducing of a more full and formall power in a just Representative to be speedily endeavoured.

Now yet further to take away all jealousies in relation to our selves, which might withold or discourse any honest Members from this courage, as we have the witnesse of God in our hearts, that in these proceedings we doe not seek, but even resolve we will not take advantages to our selves, either in point of profit or power; and that if God did open unto us a way, wherein with honesty and faithfulnesse to the publique Interest, and good people engaged for us, we might presently be discharged, so as we might not in our present Employments look on, and be accessory to, yea supporters of the Parliament, in the present corrupt, oppressive, & destructive proceedings, we should with rejoycing, and without more ado imbrace such a discharge, rather then interpose in these things to our own vast trouble and hazzard; so if we could but obtaine a rationall assurance for the effectuall prosecution of these things, we shall give any proportionable assurance on our parts, concerning our laying down of Arms, when, and as we should be required; But for the present, as the case stand, we apprehend our selves obliged in duty to god, this Kingdom, and good men therein, to improve our utmost abilities in all honest waies for the avoyding of these great evils we have remonstrated, and for prosecution of the good things we have propounded; and also that such persons who were the Inviters of the late Invasion from Scotland, the Instigators and the Incouragers of the late Insurrections within this Kingdom, and (those forcible waies failing) have still pursued the same wicked designes by treacherous and corrupt councels, may be brought to publique Justice, according to their severall demerits. For all these ends we are now drawing up with the Army to London, there to follow providence as God shall clear our way.

By the appointment of his Excellency the L. Fairfax, *Lord Generall, and his generall Councell of Officers held at Windsor*, Nov. 30. 1648.

Signed, J. Rushworth, Sce.

George Wharton's *Mercurius Elencticus* stated the royalist casc against the Army.

Mercurius Elencticus Numb. 57.

19–26 December, 1648 312.57 {5.05}

But we shall have *Law* and *Justice*, and every thing we want, if we will believe the Righteous *Buffle-heads* of the *City*, who call themselves *worthy persons of the Common Councell, and others of the City of London*. For

FRIDAY, Decemb. 22.

They published *severall Proposalls for Peace and Freedome, by an Agreement of the People, which* (as they say) *was offered unto Commissary General Ireton* (a Person indeed of incorrupt and un-biass'd judgement) *for the Concurrence of the Army* (the Sense whereof they presume virtually resides in his Breast.) It is Large and lubbardly, (like themselves) and therefore not here to be expected: But *ex ungue Leonem*, by the paw you may guesse at the nature and bulke of the Beast; and therefore I will give you a few of the prime heads of it. {...}

For the *KING*, they would have Him *guilty of all the Bloud, vast expence of Treasure and Ruine that hath been occasioned by these Warres, &c.* Yet, *if He will Assent to this Agreement of theirs*, they are content he shall *have mercy* (God a mercy Rebels!) *and that he may be crowned and Proclaimed KING againe* (till now they would never *(in Terminis)* acknowledge He was *Deposed) and may, in a Parliamentary way have as great a Revenue conferred upon Him, as (one yeare with another of His Reigne) was ever yet brought into the Exchequer:* (See how bountifull they are! But shall we believe them, that study nothing but the breach of Oaths and Promises?) well then! heres *meanes*, but where's the *power* he shall have? marry, not so much as the meanest Rebel in all His Dominions: For, (by this *Agreement)* if he shall but challenge his *Negative Voice*, or *refuse to consent and signe whatsoever the People shall present Him for Lawes, He shall be forthwith Deposed*. That's in the *second Branch* of their *Agreement*. Againe, though they allow Him the Title of *KING*, yet (hereby) He is to have no *Kingly Power*, nor any *power* at all that I can find: For, (1) that which they call the *Parliament*, is to be *summon'd* and *elected* by the *People*; not the *KING*. (2)

This *Parliament* is both to *make* and *repeale* Lawes without the *KING*. (3) A *Committee* of 32 consisting (for the greatest part) of the most factious, dissolute, and desperate of the whole Rabble, (whereof *Gibbs* and *Fouke, John Lilburne*, and *Harry Martin* are four) shall be enabled with *power* (till the next *Parliament*, after the *Dissolution* of this) *to regulate, place, dis-place, commissionate, or non-commissionate all the Judges, Justices of Peace, Sheriffs, and other Officers of the Kingdome whatsoever formerly granted by His Majesty*, &c. And all this (afterwards) *by succeeding Parliaments; and in Intervalls by a Committee of State, consisting of* 40 *of the Members thereof:* So that you see a *Jack a Lent*, or a *King of Clowts* would be full out as usefull to us, as *King CHARLES*, if they might but have their wills: Onely in this they desire His *help*, viz. *To degrade all such Persons on whom He hath heretofore conferred Honour for eminent and faithfull Services done him*; and to transferre them *to other unworthy Traytours of the Houses and Army, who have fought, and doe still indeavour His ruine:* And yet this neither, but *according to the judgement and wisdome of John Lilburne, Harry Martyn*, and the rest, or (as they say) of the *major part of that most excellent and honourable Committee*: Nor (after the Dissolution of that Committee) *shall it be lawfull for him to dignifie any with Titles of Honour, without Certificate* (forsooth) *of their Demerits or Services done the State, either from the Parliament or Committee of Estate* – But I will not trouble you any further with this trash; onely one thing I shall desire the Reader to observe in this their famous *modell of Government*, and that is, what *coherence* he finds betwixt the 7 and 14 of their *Proposalls*. In the first, they desire, *That all the Laws and Statutes now in force, and relating to the maintenance of Popery, Prelacy, Episcopacy, superstition, and all Ecclesiasticall Jurisdiction or Government, may be repealed*, &c. In the latter, *That Liberty of Conscience may be granted all these* (and many more) *by Courts and Offices for that purpose*. The words you had a little before, at large, but *Quære* the *meaning*.

> Thus have these *Common Coxcombs* thought it fit
> To *foole* themselves, to *exercise* their *wit*.
> Thus have these *Dolts* to gaine themselves *applause*,
> *Disgorg'd* this *filth* to *fortifie* their *Cause;*

The common Hackneys did nothing this day but abuse God according to *Order*, &c.

The day the Order for the king's trial was passed was a significant anniversary. See {1.06–7}.

Perfect Occurrences. of Every Daie iournall
Num. 105

29 December – 5 January, 1648{9} 465.5105 {5.06}

Thursday 4 *January*. {...}

The Commons finished the great Order for tryall of the King, And Ordered it to be forthwith ingrosse. And then the House proceeded to a Declaration concerning the *Legislative* power, and how it is originally not in the *King*, nor *Lords*, but in the *Commons. Jan*. 4. 1641. *The King came to seize the five Members*.

Perfect Occurrences of Every Daies iournall
Numb. 106

5–12 January, 1648{9} 465.5106 {5.07}

Begining Fryday Ian. the 5. {...}

A Message was ordered to be sent to the Lord Gen. to desire him to take care, that the *King* be strictly looked to, that he do not escape; and that none come to him, but such as are appointed. That care be taken for apprehending all Delinquents that stay neare the City, contrary to his Proclamation, for securing those under the Marshall Gen. And for suppressing scandalous Bookes and Pamphlets. And that the Chaines of the City of *London* be pulled down, which was done accordingly. {...}

Die Lunæ 8. *Ian*. 1648.

THe High Court of Justice for tryall of *Charles Stuart* King of *England*, met: And first called over the names. After which the Act of the House of Commons in Parliament assembled was read, giving power to the said Committee for present tryall of the said *Charles Stuart* King of *England*, And to adjudge him according to Law, and this to be finished within one months space. But as for the time and place, they are to adjourn from time to time as they shall see cause.

Perfect Occurrences. of Every Daie iournall
Num. 107

12–19 January, 1648{9} 465.5107 {5.08}

Beginning Friday January, 12.{...}

The High Court of Justice sat this afternoon, and Serjeant *Bradshaw* was extolled, and had the Mace carried before him as Lord President by Serjeant *Dendy* (not the old delinquent that was the great Courtier, but young Serjeant *Dendy* his son) Mr. *Broughton*, Mayor of *Maidstone*, was chosen Clerke instead of Mr. *Graves*; and Mr. *Litchmore* in place of *Radley* for one of the Messengers.

The Court had debates concerning the place for triall of the King, and severall places were argued, viz *Windsor*, St. *Jamses*, *Guild-hall London*, and *Westminster-hall*. 1 *Query*, Why not at *Windsor*? *Answ*, Because it will divide the Army. 2 *Query* Why not at St. *Jameses* ? *Answ*. Because it is one of the Kings houses, and thereupon envious people would say (if he should be put to death) that he was murdered, though the proceedings were never so just. 3 *Query*, Why not at *Guild-hall*? *Answ*. That may occasion a great disturbance. 4 *Query*, Why should it be in *Wesminster-hall*? *Answ*. 1 Because it is a place of publicke resort. 2 It is the place of the publicke Courts of Justice for the Kingdome.

A Committee was chosen, to determine the place, And another Committee to see the Scaffolds made, and power was given to the Lawyers for searching of all Records, and places; And bringing to the Court such writings as they shall see cause for.

Saturday Jan. 13.

THe Committee met this morning, and resolved, That *Westminster* hall shall be the place for Tryall of the King.

The Commons Voted that 1000*li*. should be advanced for the use of the Court for Tryall of the King. {...}

Munday Jan. 15.

The High Court of Justice sat againe this afternoon in the painted Chamber; they were called, and their Commissions and Instructions were read.

Instructions appointed by an Act of the House of Commons to the High Court for Tryall of Charles Stuart, *King of* England.

1. That they are appointed Commissioners and Judges for the hearing, trying and judging of the said *Charles Stuart*.

2. The said Commissioners, or any twenty or more of them shall be and hereby are Authorised and Constituted, An High Court

of Justice, to meet at such convenient time and place as the said Commissioners, or the major part of twenty, or more of them, under their hands and seals shall be appointed and notified by publicke Proclamation, in the great Hall or Pallace-yard of *Westminster*.

3. To adjourn from time to time, and from place to place, as the said High Court, or major part thereof meeting shall hold fit.

4. To take order for the charging of him, the said *Charles Stuart*, with the crimes mentioned in the said charge for the receiving of his Personall answer thereunto, and for the examination of witnesses upon oath (if need be) concerning the same.

5. Thereupon, or in default of such answer, to proceed to finall sentence, according to justice, and the merit of the cause, to be executed speedily, and impartially.

6. The said Court is hereby authorised and required to choose and appoint all such officers and attendants, as they, or the major part of them, shall in any sort judge necessary or usefull, for the orderly and good managing of the premises.

7. *Thomas* Lord *Fairfax* the Generall, with all officers of Justice, and other wel-affected persons, are hereby authorised, and required to be ayding and assisting unto the said Commissioners in the due execution of the trust hereby committed unto them.

8. Provided that this Ordinance, and the Authority hereby granted, to continue for the space of one moneth from the date of the making hereof, and no longer.

The Court (this day) had the charge brought in against the King, very large, and high, concerning *Rochel, Ireland, Scotland, England*; betraying, firing, murdering the people. A Committee was chosen to see the Scaffolds speedily set up for his Tryall in *Westminster-Hall*. And the charge was committed to a select number of them to be abreviated, to make the dispatch sooner. {...}

Wednesday, January 17.

THis morning the High Court of Justice sate, and reports were made from the Committee, about the manner of the Kings residence, and the Orders and Ceremonies of the Court, and upon the whole the Court passed severall Ordinances therein, (Viz.)

1 That the place to which the King shall be brought, shall be Sir *Robert Cottons* house, adjoyning to Westminster hall, and an house to be provided for the Lord President, neer to Westminster hall.

2 That a guard of Halberts be appoynted to guard the Kings person. Thirty whereof to attend in the Dining Roome, and two in the Kings Bed-chamber every night.

3 That there be also besides the Foot-guards, a Regiment of Horse appointed for a guard to the Court.

4 That the doore in the old Pallace be made up, to stop all passage that way, And a Court of Guard for 200 Souldiers to be made in Sir *Robert Cottons* Garden, towards the water side.

5 That the Members of the Court meet every day, first in the Chequer Chamber, and from thence goe together to the place appoynted in Westminster Hall, And a guard of Halberts be appointed to attend the Lord President, & a Sword, and a Mace, to be carryed before him.

Instructions also passed for the Order of bringing the King from Sir *Robert Cottons* house, through the Entry, at the South-end of Westminster hall; and Railes, and other conveniencies to bee made between the Kings lodgings and the Court.

And Instructions also for places for the Horse, and for the Foot that are to be upon the guard, during the sitting of the Court.

The Court chose Colonel *Humpheryes* to be the Sword Bearer.

A Perfect Diurnall of Some Passages in Parliament *Numb.* 288

15–22 January, 1648{9} 504.286 {5.09}

Saturday Ianuary 20. {...}

This day the high court of Justice for triall of the King sate in the Painted chamber, and from thence adjourned about two in the afternoon to the place built for that court in Westminster hall. The President had the Mace and Sword carried before him, and 20 Gentlemen attended as his Guard with Partizans, commanded by col. *Fox*. After an *O yes* made, and silence commanded, the Act of the Commons in Parliament for siting of the said court was read, and the court was called, there being above 60 Members of it present. Then the King (who lay the night before in S. *Iames*, and was brought this day to White hall, and thence by water guarded with Musketiers in Boats to sir *Rob. Cottons* house) was brought to the Barre, to which their attended him col. *Hacker* with about 30 Officers and Gentlemen, with Halberts. At his comming to the foot of the staires he was met with the Mace of the court, and conducted to a chaire within the Bar, where he sate down in the face of the court. The L. President in a short speech acquainted the King with the cause of his bringing thither, that it was in order to his Triall upon a charge against him by the Commons of England, which was then to be read, and the King to give his answer thereunto.

His Majesty made an offer to speake some thing before reading of the Charge, but upon some interruption was silent; And then his Charge was read. By which he was charged by the name of *Charles Stuart* King of *England*, as guilty of all the bloud that hath been shed in these warres at Kenton, Brainford, Newbery and such other places as he was present in Arms against the Parliament, and other perticulers very large, the King smiled at the reading of his Charge, And after reading of it, demanded of the Lord President by what lawfull authority he was brough thither? being answered in the name of the Commons of *England*, Hee replyed, He saw no Lords there (which should make a Parliament, including the King, and urged, That the Kingdome of *England* was Hereditary and not successive, and that he should betray His Trust, if he acknowledge or answer to them, for that he was not convinced, they were a lawfull authority, so that (after he had been often commanded to answer, and refused, he was remanded to Sir *Robert Cottens* house, and afterwards removed back to Saint *Iames*, where he lay that night, and the Court adjourned till Munday tenne a Clock in the forenoone, further to consider of this businesse.

Sunday, great recourse of people went out of London to Westminster but if to see the King they were disappointed; who was then at Saint *James* under strong guard. A solemne Fast was kept at White-Hall this day by the Commissioners for Tryall of the King.

The Moderate *Numb*. 28.

16–23 January, 1649 413.2028 {5.10}

At the High Court of Justice sitting in the great Hall of *Westminster*, Serjeant *Bradshaw* President, about 70 Members present. O yes made thrice, silence commanded. The President had the Sword and Mace carried before him, attended with Colonel *Fox*, and twenty other Officers and Gentlemen with Partizans. The Act of the Commons in Parliament for tryal of the King, read. After the Court was called, and each Member rising up, as he was called. The King came into the Court (with his Hat on) and the Commissioners with theirs on also; no congratulation or motion of hats at all. The Serjeant ushered Him in with the Mace, Colonel *Hacker* and about 30 Officers and Gentlemen more came as His guard; the President then spake in these words, *viz.*

Charls Stewart, King of *England*, the Commons of *England* assembled in Parliament being sensible of the great calamities that have been brought upon this Nation, of the innocent blood that hath been shed in this Nation, which is referred to You, as the Author of it; and according to that duty which they owe to God, to the Nation, and themselves, and according to that Fundamentall power and trust that is reposed in them by the people, Have constituted this High Court of Justice, before which You are now brought; and You are to hear the Charge; upon which the Court will proceed.

Mr. *Cook* Solicitor General. My Lord, in behalf of the Commons of *England*, and of all the people thereof: I do accuse *Charles Stuart*, here present, of High Treason, and High Misdemeanors; and I do in the name of the Commons of *England*, desire that the Charge may be read unto Him.

King. Hold a little, tapping the Solitcitor General twice on the shoulder with his Cane, which drawing towards Him again, the head thereon fell off, He stooping for it, put it presently into His pocket. This is conceived will be very ominous.

L. President. Sir, the Court commands the Charge to be read; if You have any thing to say after, You may be heard.

The Charge was read.

The King smiled often, during the time, especially at those words therein, *viz.* That *Charls Stewart* was a Tyrant, Traytor, Murtherer, and publike Enemy of the Commonwealth.

L. President. Sir, you have now heard Your Charge read, containing such Matter as appears in it: You finde that in the close of it, it is prayed to the Court in the behalf of all the Commons of *England*, that You Answer to Your Charge. The Court expects Your Answer.

King. I would know by what power I am called hither. I was not long ago in the Isle of *Wight*; how I came hither, is a larger story then I think is fit at this time for me to speak of: But there I entered into a Treaty with the two Houses of Parliament, with as much publike Faith as is possibly to be had of any people in the World. I treated there with a number of Honorable Lords and Gentlemen, and treated honestly and uprightly. I cannot say, but they did deal very nobly with Me: We were upon Conclusion of a Treaty. Now I would know by what Authority, I mean lawful;

there are many unlawful Authorities in the world, Theeves and Robbers by the High-ways: But I would know by what Authority I was brought from thence, and carried from place to place; and when I know by what lawful Authority, I shall Answer.

Remember, I am your King, your lawful King; and what sin you bring upon your heads, and the judgements of God upon this Land, think well upon it; I say think well upon it before you go further, from one sin, to a greater: Therefore let me know by what lawful Authority I am seated here, and I shall not be unwilling to Answer; in the mean time, I shall not betray my Trust. I have a Trust committed to me by God, by old and lawful discent. I will not betray it, to Answer to a new and unlawful Authority; therefore resolve Me that, and you shall hear more of Me.

L. President. If You had been pleased to have observed, what was hinted to You by the Court, at our first coming hither, You would have known by what Authority; which Authority requires You in the name of the people of *England*, of which You are elected King, to Answer them.

King. No sir, I deny that.

L. President. If You acknowledg not the Authority of the Court, they must proceed.

King. I do tell you so, *England* was never an Elective Kingdom, but an Hereditary Kingdom, for neer a 1000 yeers; therefore let Me know by what Authority I am called hither. I do stand more for the Liberty of My people, then any here that come to be My pretended Judges; and therefore let me know, by what lawful Authority I am seated here, and I will answer it, otherwise I will not answer it.

L. President told Him, He did interogate the Court, which be seemed not One in His condition; and it was known how He had managed His Trust.

King. Here is a Gentleman, Lieutenant Colonel *Cobbet*, ask him, if he did not bring Me from the Isle of *Wight* by force. I do not come here, as submitting to the Court, I will stand as much for the Priviledg of the House of Commons, rightly understood, as any man here whatsoever. I see no House of Lords here that may Constitute a Parliament, and (the King to) should have been. Is this the bringing of the King to His Parliament? Is this a bringing an end to the Treaty, in the Publike Faith of the World? Let Me see a legal Authority warranted, either by the Word of God, the Scripture, or warranted by the Constitution of the Kingdom, and I will Answer.

L. President. Sir, You have provided a Question, and have been Answered: Since You will not Answer, the Court will proceed; and those that brought You hither, take charge of Him. The Court desires to know, if this be all the Answer You will give.

King. I desire, that you would give Me, and all the world, satisfaction in this: For let Me tell you, it is not a slight thing you are about. I am sworn to keep the Peace, by the duty I owe to God, and my Country; and I will do it, to the last breath of My body: And therefore, you shall do well to satisfie, first God, and then the Country, by what Authority you do it; if by a reserved Authority, you cannot Answer it. There is a God in Heaven that will call you, and all that give you power, to an account. Satisfie Me me in that, and I will Answer; otherwise, I betray my Trust, and the Liberties of the People: And therefore think of that, and then I shall be willing. For I do vow, That it is as great a sin to withstand lawful Authority, as it is to submit to a tyrannical, or any otherways unlawful Authority: And therefore satisife Me that, and you shall receive My Answer.

L. *President*. The Court expects a final Answer, they are to adjourn till Munday. If You satisfie not Your Self, though we tell You our Authority; we are satisfied with our Authority, and it is upon Gods Authority, and the Kingdoms; and that Peace You speak of, will be kept in the doing of Justice; and that is our present work.

King. For Answer, let Me tell you, you have shewn no lawful Authority to satisfie any reasonable man.

L. *President*. This is in Your apprehension, we are satisfied that are the Judges.

King. It is not My apprehension, nor yours neither, that ought to decide it.

L. *President*. The Court hath heard You, and You are to be disposed of as they have commanded.

The Court adjourned till Munday ten of clock, to the Painted Chamber, and thence hither.

As the King went away, facing the Court, the King said, I fear not that, looking upon, and meaning the Sword.

Going down from the Court, the people cryed, *Justice, Justice, Justice*.

Jan. 21. The Commissioners kept a Fast this day in Whitehal, there preached before them, Mr. *Sprig*, whose Text was, *He that sheds blood, by man shall his blood be shed*. Mr. *Foxleys* was, *Judg not, lest you be judged*. And Mr. *Peters* was, *I will bind their*

Kings in chains, and their Nobles in fetters of iron. The last Sermon made amends for the two former.

A Perfect Diurnall *Numb.* 287

22–29 January 1648{9} 504.287 {5.11}

Beginning Munday, January 22.

THis day the Commissioners from the Kingdome of Scotland delivered into the House of Commons, some Papers, and a Declaration from the Parliament of Scotland, wherein they expresse a dislike of the present proceedings about tryall of the King, and declare, That the Kingdome of Scotland, have an undoubted Interest in the person of the King, who was not (they say) delivered to the English Commissioners as Newcastle for the Ruine of his Person, but for more speedy settlement of the peace of his Kingdomes. That they extreamly dissent and declare against the tryall of him, and that this present way of proceeding against him leaves a deep impression on them, and sits heavy on all their spirits, in regard of the great miseries that are like to insue upon the Kingdomes. {...}

This day the high court of Justice for tryall of the King, sat againe in *Westminster Hall*, for better satisfaction to the Kingdome, and for that severall imperfect Copies have been Printed, we will give you the proceedings of his Tryall exactly.

The Court being sat, O yes made and silence commanded, the King was sent for, whereupon Mr. *Soliciter Cooke* moved the Court, That whereas he had at the last Court in the behalf of the Commons of *England*, exhibited a charge of High Treason, and other high crimes against the Prisoner at the Barre, whereof he stands accused in the name of the People of *England*, and the charge was read unto him, and his Answer required, He was not then pleased to give an Answer, but instead of answering, did there dispute the Authority of this high court. His humble Motion was, That the Prisoner may be directed to make a positive Answer, either by way of Confession, or Negation; which if he shall refuse to do, That the matter of charge may be taken *pro confesso*, and the court may proceed according to Justice.

Lord President. Sir, You remember at the last court you were told the occasion of your being brought hither, and you heard a charge read against you containing a charge of high Treason and other high crimes against this Realme of *England*, and instead of answering, you interogued the courts authority and jurisdiction:

Sir, the authority is the Commons of *England* in Parliament assembled, who requires your answer to the charge either by confessing or denying.

The King. When I was here last, 'tis very true, I made that Question, and truly, if it were onely my own particular case, I would have satisfied my selfe with the Protestation I made the last time I was here against the legality of this court, and that a King cannot be tryed by any superiour jurisdiction on Earth; but it is not my case alone, it is the freedom and the liberty, of the People of *England*, and doe you pretend what you will, I stand more for their Liberties. For if power without Law may make Lawes, may alter the fundamentall Lawes of the Kingdome, I do not know what subject he is in *England*, that can be sure of his life or any thing that he calls his own; therefore when that I came here, I did expect particular reasons to know by what Law, what authority you did proceed against me here, and therefore I am a little to seek what to say to you in this particular, because the Affirmative is to be proved, the Negative often is very hard to doe: but since I cannot perswade you to do it, I shall tell you my Reasons as short as I can.

My Reasons why in Conscience and the duty I owe to God first, and my People next, for the preservation of their lives, Liberties and Estates; I conceive I cannot answer this, till I be satisfied of the legality of it. All proceedings against any man whatsoever ——

Lord. Sir, I must interrupt you, which I would not doe, but that what you doe is not agreeable to the proceedings of any court of Justice, you are about to enter into Argument, and dispute concerning the authority of this court, before whom you appeare as a prisoner, and are charged as an high Delinquent; if you take upon you to dispute the Authority of the court we may not do it, nor will any court give way unto it, you are to submit unto it, you are to give a punctuall and direct answer, whether you will answer your charge or no, and what your answer is.

The King. Sir, by your favour, I do not know the formes of Law, I do know Law and Reason, though I am no Lawyer profess'd, but I know as much Law as any Gentleman in *England*; and therefore (under favour) I do plead for the Liberties of the people of *England* more then you do, and therefore if I should impose a beliefe upon any man without reasons given for it, it were unreasonable, but I must tell you, that that reason that I have as thus informed I cannot yeeld unto it ——

Lord. Sir, I must interrupt you, you may not be permitted, you speak of Law and reason, it is fit there should be Law and reason, and there is both against you. Sir, the Vote of the Commons of *England* assembled in Parliament, it is the reason of the Kingdome, and they are these that have given to that Law, according to which you should have ruled and reigned: Sir, you are not to dispute our Authority; you are told it againe by the court. Sir, it will be taken notice of, that you stand in contempt of the court, and your contempt will be recorded accordingly.

The King. I do not know how the King can be a Delinquent; but, by any Law that ever I heard of, ill men (Delinquents or what you will) let me tell you they many in Demurs against any proceeding as legall, and I doe demand that, and demand to be heard with my Reasons, if you deny that, you deny reason.

Lord. Sir, you have offerd something to the Court, I will speak something unto you, the sense of the court. Sir, neither you nor any man are permitted to dispute that point; you are concluded, you must not demur the jurisdiction of the court; if you doe, I must let you know, that they over rule your Demurrer; they sit here by the authority of the Commons of England, and all your Predecessors, and you are responsible to them.

The King. I deny that; show me one president.

Lord. Sir, you ought not to interrupt while the Court is speaking to you, this point is not to be debated by you, neither will the court permit you to do it; if you offer it by way of Demurrer to the Jurisdiction of the court, they have considered of their Jurisdiction, they do affirm their own jurisdiction.

The King. I say sir, by your favour, that the commons of England was never a court of Judicature, I would know how they came to be so.

Lord. Sir, you are not permitted to go on in that speech and these discourses.

Then the clerk of the Court read as followeth: *Charles Stewart, King of England*, You have been accused on the behalf of the People of England of high Treason and other high crimes; the court have determined that you ought to answer the same.

The King. I will answer the same, so soon as I know by what authority you do this.

Lord. If this be all that you will say, then Gentlemen you that brought the Prisoner hither, take charge of him back again.

The King. I doe require that I may give in my reasons why I doe not answer, and give me time for that.

Lord. Sir, Tis not for Prisoners to require.

The King. Prisoners? sir, I am not an ordinary Prisoner.

Lord. The court hath considered of their jurisdiction, and they have already affirmd their jurisdiction; if you will not answer, we shall give order to record your default.

The King. You never heard my Reasons yet.

Lord. Sir, your Reasons are not to be heard against the highest jurisdiction.

The King. Shew me that Jurisdiction where Reason is not to be heard.

Lord. Sir, we shew it you here, the commons of England; and the next time you are brought you will know more of the pleasure of the court; and, it may be, their finall determination.

The King. Shew me where ever the House of commons was a court of Judicature of that kind.

Lord. Sergeant, take away the prisoner.

The King. Well sir, Remember that the King is not suffered to give in his Reasons for the Liberty and Freedom of all his subjects.

Lord. Sir, You are not to have liberty to use this language. How great a friend you have been to the Laws and Liberties of the People, let all England and the world judge.

The King. Sir, under favour, it was the Liberty, Freedom, and Laws of the subject that ever I took —— defended my selfe with Arms. I never took up Arms against the People, but for the Laws.

Lord. The command of the Court must be obeyed; no answer will be given to the charge.

The King. Well sir.

And so was guarded forth to sir *Robert Cottons* house: Then the court adjourned untill the next day.

Tuesday, Ianuary 23. {...}

This day the high court of Justice for tryall of the King sate againe in Westminster Hall, seventy three persons present.

The King comes in with his Guard, looks with an austere countenance upon the Court and sits downe.

Mr. *Cook* solicitor generall moved the court in effect, That whereas the prisoner at the Bar, instead of giving answer to the charge against him did still dispute the authority of the court, That as according to Law, if a prisoner shall stand as contumacious in contempt, and shall not put an issuable Plea, guilty or not guilty of the charge given against him, whereby he may come to a faire Tryall; That as by an implicite confession, it may be taken *pro confesso*, as it hath been done to those who have deserved more favour then the Prisoner at the Bar has done, and therefore that speedy Judgement be pronounced against him.

Lord President. Sir, You have heard what is moved by the councell on the behalfe of the Kingdom against you. Sir, You may well remember, and if you do not, the court cannot forget what dilatory dealings the court hath found at your hands, you were pleased to propound some questions, you have had your Resolution upon them. You were told over and over againe, That the court did affirm their own Jurisdiction, that it was not for you, nor any other man to dispute the Jurisdiction of the supream and highest authority of *England*, from which there is no appeal, and touching which there must be no dispute; yet you did persist in such carriage, as you gave no manner of obedience, nor did you acknowledge any authority in them, nor the high court, that constituted this court of Justice.

Sir, I must let you know from the court, That they are very sensible of these delayes of yours, and that they ought not, being thus authorized by the supream court of *England*, be thus trifled withall, and that they might in Justice, if they pleased, and according to the Rules of Justice, if they pleased, take advantage of these delayes, and proceed to pronounce judgement against you, yet neverthelesse they are pleased to give direction; and on their behalfs I do require you, That you make a positive Answer unto this charge that is against you sir, in plain termes, for justice knowes no respect of persons; you are to give your positive and finall Answer in plain English, whether you be guilty or not guilty of these Treasons laid to your charge.

The King after a little pause, said, When I was here yesterday I did desire to speake for the Liberties of the people of *England*; I was interrupted: I desire to know yet whether I may speak freely or not?

Lord President. Sir, You have had the Resolution of the court upon the like question the last day, and you were told, that having such charge of so high a nature against you, and your work was, that you ought to acknowledge the *Jurisdiction* of the *Court*, and to answer to your *Charge*. Sir, If you answer to your charge, which the court gives you leave now to do, though they might have taken the advantage of your contempt; yet if you be able to answer to your charge, when you have once answered, you shall be heard at large, make the best defence you can. But Sir I must let you know from the court, as their commands, that you are not to be permitted to issue out into any other discourses, till such time as you have given a positive answer concerning the matter that is charged upon you.

The King. For the Charge, I value it not a rush, it is the Liberty of the People of *England* that I stand for, for me to acknowledge a new Court I never heard of before, I that am your King, that should be an example to all the people of *England* for to uphold Justice, to maintaine the old Lawes; indeed I do not know how to doe it; you spoke very well the first day that I came here, (on Saturday) of the obligations that I had laid upon me by God, to the maintenance of the Liberties of my People: the same Obligation you spake of, I do acknowledge to God that I owe to him, and to my People, to defend as much as in me lies the ancient Lawes of the Kingdome, therefore untill that I may know that this is not against the fundamentall Lawes of the Kingdome, by your favour I can put in no particular Answer: If you will give me time, I will shew you my reasons why I cannot do it, and thus ———

Here being interrupted, he said, By your favour, you ought not to interrupt me; how I came here I know not, there's no Law for it to make your King your Prisoner; I was in a Treaty upon the publique Faith of the Kingdome, that was known —— two houses of Parliament that was the Representative of the Kingdome, and when that I had almost made an end of the Treaty, then I was hurried away and brought hither, and therefore ———

Here the Lord President said, Sir, you must know the pleasure of the Court.

The King. By your favour sir:

L. *President*. Nay sir, by your favour, you may not be permitted to fall into these discourses; you appeare as a Delinquent, you have not acknowledged the authority of the court, the court craves it not of you, but once more they command you to give your positive answer, — *Clark*. Do your Duty.

The King. Duty sir!

The Clark reads a Paper, requiring the King to give a positive and finall answer by way of confession or deniall of the charge.

The King. Sir, I say again to you, so that I might give satisfaction to the people of England of the cleernesse of my proceeding, not by way of answer, not in this way, but to satisfie them that I have done nothing against that trust that hath been committed to me, I would do it; but to acknowledge a new Court, against their priviledges, to alter the fundamentall Lawes of the kingdome, sir you must excuse me.

L. *Presid*. Sir, this is the third time that you have publiquely disownd this Court, and put an affront upon it; how far you have preservd the priviledges of the people your actions have spoke it; but truly sir, mens intentions ought to be known by their actions, you have written your meaning in bloody characters throughout the whole kingdom: But sir, you understand the pleasure of the Court — Clark, record the default, — and Gentlemen, you that took charge of the prisoner, take him back again.

The King. I will onely say this one word more unto you; if it were onely my one particular, I would not say an more, nor interrupt you.

L. *Presid*. Sir, you have heard the pleasure of the Court, and you are (notwithstanding you will not understand it) to finde that you are before a court of Justice.

Then the King went forth with the Guard to *Sir Robert Cottons* house, where he lay the last night and this. The Court adjourned till the next day.

Perfect Occurrences of Every Daies iournall

Numb. 108.

18–25 January, 1648{9} 465.5108 {5.12}

Wednesday Jan. 24. {...}

At the brazen Serpent in *Pauls* Church-yard, is to be sold a new book, of the beauty of Providence, very usefull to support the hart of Gods people these trying times.

The High Court sate this morning in the Painted Chamber, upon hearing of witnesses, against the King; And sent the Serjant with one of the Ushers, to the Hall with a Declaration which was read. *That the High Court then sitting in the Painted Chamber, were like to spend most part of this day there, upon the great affaires of the* Kindome. *And that therefore, those that were in the Hall, might depart thence.*

There were this day some 30. witnesses brought in against the *King*, giving Testimony of his setting up his Standard at *Nottingham*, himself in the head of the Army, and acting in severall other places, exprest in the Charge against him. A Committee was appointed to take all those Testimonies, and report them to the Court in the Painted Chamber on the morrow.

Thursday 24. *Ianuary*.

THe High Court took the Depositions of the witnesses against the King, in the Painted Chamber, of his raising his Standard, giving Commissions, Marching into the Field, fighting, killing; And the severall battels he was personally in; As also the Letters when he treated with the

Parliament, under his hand and Seal, for the Prince, the Marquis of *Hardford*, &c to goe on, and looke on what he did, as invalid; giving thanks to all his Friends that did adhere to him, assuring them, that he will not desert them.

The *King* is at St. *Jameses* untill the depositions be all taken. He saith that his Conscience tells him not to be guilty of any blood-shed, but the E. of *Strafford*, He desires when he comes again, to be heard of what he hath to offer, before the Court do any thing, or the Solicitor move: it is offered that he may send something before he comes in writing if he will. The Lord Gen. is so full of great affaires, that he could not yet come to sit when the King was there, but he sate in the Painted Chamber; And he being Gen. & by Malignants falsly accused to seek to be *King* himself, doth the rather refrain, leaving it the rest to judge.

This, *The Moderate* announced in Numb.29, was to be the official version of proceedings. The editorial began: 'Not death, but the cause, makes a Martyr'.

The Moderate *Numb*. 30.

30 January – 6 February, 1649 413.2030 {5.13}

The last Proceedings of the High Court of Iustice, sitting at Westminster Hall, Saturday, Ianuary 27. 1648.

VPon the Kings coming he desired to be heard. To which the Lord President answered, That it might be in time, but that he must hear the Court first.

The King prest it, for that he believed it would be in order to what the Court would say, and that an hasty Iudgement was not so soon recalled.

Then the Lord President spake as followeth. Gentlemen, It is well known to all, or most of you here present, that the Prisoner at the Bar hath been several times convented, and brought before this Court to make Answer to a Charge of Treason, and other high Crimes exhibited against him in the name of the people of England. To which Charge, being required to Answer, he hath been so far from obeying the commands of the Court, by submitting to their Iustice, as he began to take upon him reasoning and debate unto the Authority of the Court, and to the highest Court that appointed them, and to trie, and to judg him; but being over-ruled in that, and required to make his Answer, he was still pleased to continue Contumelious, and to refuse to submit to answer; hereupon the Court, that they may not be wanting to themselvs, nor the Trust reposed in them, nor that any mans wilfulnesse prevent Iustice, they have thought fit to take the matter into their consideration; they have considered of the Charge, they have considered of Contumacy, and of that confession, which in Law doth arise upon that Contumacy; they have likewise considered of the Notoriety of the Fact Charged upon this Prisoner, and upon the whole matter: They are resolved, and agreed upon a Sentence to be pronounced against this prisoner, but in respect he doth desire to be heard before the Sentence be read, and pronounced; the Court hath resolved that they will hear him. Yet Sir, Thus much I tell you before hand, which you have been minded of at other Courts, That if that which you have to say, be to offer any debate concerning the Iurisdiction, you are not to be heard in it, you have offered it formerly and you have struck at the root, that is, the Power, and the supream Authority of the Commons of England, which this Court will not admit a Debate of, and which indeed it is an irrational thing in them to do, being a Court that Acts upon Authority derived from them. But Sir, if you have any thing to say in defence of your self, concerning the matter Charged, the Court hath given me in command to let you know that will hear you.

Then the King answered, Since that I see you will not hear any thing of Debate, concerning that which I confesse I thought most material for the Peace of the Kingdom, and for the Liberty of the Subject, I shall wave it, I shall speak nothing to it; but only I must tell you, that this many a day all things have been taken away from me, but that I call dearer to me then my life, which is my Conscience and my Honour; and if I had a respect to my life more then the Peace of the Kingdom, and the Liberty of the Subject, certainly I should have made a particular defence for my self, for by that, at leastwise, I might have delaied an ugly Sentence, which I believe will passe upon me; therefore certainly, Sir, as a man that hath some understanding, some knowledge of the world; if that my true zeal to my countrey had not overborn the care that I have for my own preservation, I should have gone another way to work then that I have done: Now Sir, I conceive, that an hasty sentence once past, may sooner be repented of, then recalled; and truly the self same desire that I have for the Peace of the Kingdome, and the Liberty of the Subject more then my own particular ends, makes me now at last desire, that I having something to say that concerns both: I desire before sentence be given, that I may be heard in the Painted Chamber before the Lords and Commons:

This delay cannot be prejudicial unto you, whatsoever I say: if that I say no Reason, those that hear me must be Iudges, I cannot be Iudge of that that I have; if it be reason, and really for the welfare of the Kingdom, and the Liberty of the Subject, I am sure on't it is very well worth the hearing; therefore I do conjure you, as you love that that you pretend, (I hope its real,) the Liberty of the Subject, the Peace of the Kingdom, that you will grant me this hearing, before any Sentence be past; I only desire this, That you will take this into your consideration, it may be you have not heard of it before hand, if you will, I will retire, and you may think of it; but if I cannot get this Liberty, I do protest, That these fair shews of Liberty and Peace are pure shews, and that you will not hear your King.

The Lord President said, That what the King had said, was a declining of the Jurisdiction of the Court, which was the thing wherein he was limited before.

The King urged, That what he had to say was not a declining of the Court, but for the Peace of the Kingdom, and Liberty of the Subject.

Lord President. Sir, This is not altogether new that you have moved unto us, though it is the first time that in person you have offered it to the Court: And afterwards, that though what he had urged might seem to tend to delays, yet according to that which the King seemed to desire, the Court would withdraw for a time, and he should hear their pleasure.

Then the Court withdrawing into the Court of Wards, the Sergeant at Arms had command to withdraw the Prisoner, and to give Order for his return again.

The Court after half an hours Debate, returned from the Court of Wards Chamber, and the King being sent for, the Lord President spake to this effect;

Sir, You were pleased to make a motion here to the Court, touching the propounding of somewhat to the Lords and Commons in the Painted Chamber, for the Peace of the Kingdom; you did in effect receive an Answer, before their Adjourning, being *pro forma tantum*; for it did not seem to them that there was any difficulty in the thing; they have considered of what you have moved, and of their own Authority: The return from the Court is this, That they have been too much delayed by you already, and they are Judges appointed by the Highest Authority, and Judges are no more to delay, then they are to deny Iustice; they are good words in the great old Charter of England, *Nulli negabimus, nulli condemus, & nulli deferremus justitiam:* but every man observes you have delayed them in your Contempt and Default, for which they might long since have proceeded to Iudgement against you, and notwithstanding what you have offered, they are resolved to proceed to Sentence and to Iudgment, and thats their unanimous resolution.

King. Sir, I know it is in vain for me to dispute, I am no Septrick {i.e. sceptic}, for to deny the power that you have; I know that you have power enough: Sir I must confesse I think it would have been for the Kingdoms peace, if you would have taken the pains for to have shewn the lawfulnesse of your power: for this delay that I have desired, I confesse it is a delay, but it is a delay very important for the Peace of the Kingdom; for it is not my person that I look at alone, it is the Kingdoms welfare and the Kingdoms Peace: It is an old Sentence, *That we should think on long before we have resolved of great matters suddainly*, therefore Sir, I do say again, that I do put at your doors all the inconveniency of a hasty Sentence. I confesse I have been here now I think this week, this day eight dayes was the day I came here first, but a little delay of a day or two further may give Peace, whereas an hasty Iudgement may bring on that trouble and perpetual inconveniency to the Kingdom, that the childe that is unborn may repent it; and therefore again, out of the duty I owe to God, and to my countrey, I do desire that I may be heard by the Lords and Commons in the painted Chamber, or any other Chamber that you will appoint me.

The President replied, that what he desired, was no more then what he had moved before, and therefore the Court expected to hear what he would say before they proceeded to Sentence.

King. This I say, that if you will hear me, I do not doubt to give satisfaction to you, and to my people, and therefore I do require you, (as you will answer it at the dreadful Day of Judgement) that you will consider it once again.

President. The Court will proceed to Sentence if you have no more to say.

King. Sir, I have nothing more to say, but I shall desire that this may be entred what I have said.

The Lord President then proceeded to declare the grounds of the Sentence in a long speech, which you may see at large in what the High Court shall set forth.

The Lord President having cited many things in relation to the power of Kings, and their being called to account for breach of Trust, and expressed in what sence this present King had been guilty, according to his Charge, of being a Tyrant, Traytor,

Murtherer, and publike Enemy to the Common wealth. He further declared in the name of the Court, That they did heartily wish, that he would be so penitent for what he had done amisse, that God might have mercy, at leastwise upon his better part; for the other it was their duty to do it, and to do that which the Law prescribes, they were not there *jus dare*, but *jus dicere*; that they could not but remember what the Scripture said, *For to acquit the guilty, it is equal abomination, as to condemn the innocent*; we may not acquit the guilty, what sentence the Law affirms to a Traytor, a Tyrant, a Murtherer, and a publick Enemy to the Countrey, that sentence he was to hear read unto him.

Then the Clerk read the Sentence drawn up in Parchment.

That whereas the Commons of England *in Parliament, had appointed them an high Court of Justice, for the trying of* Charls Stuart, *King of* England; *before whom he had been three times convented, and at the first time a Charge of high Treason, and other crimes and misdemeanors was read in the behalf of the Kingdom of* England, *&c.*

Here the Clerk read the Charge.

Which Charge being read unto him, as aforesaid, he the said *Charls Stuart*, was required to give his Answer, but he refused so to do; and so exprest the several passages at his Tryal in refusing to answer.

For all which Treasons and Crimes, this Court doth adjudg, That He the said Charls Stuart, *as a Tyrant, Traytor, Murtherer, and a publike Enemy, shall be put to death, by the severing of his Head from his Body.*

After the Sentence was read, the Lord President said,

This Sentence now read and published, it is the Act, Sentence, Judgment, and Resolution of the whole Court: Here the Court stood up, as assenting to what the President said.

King. Will you hear me a word Sir?

Lord President. Sir, you are not to be heard after the Sentence.

King. No Sir?

Lord President. No Sir, by your favour Sir. Guard, withdraw your prisoner.

King. I may speak after the Sentence.

By your favour Sir, I may speak after the Sentence ever.

By your favour (hold) the Sentence Sir ——

I say Sir I do ——

I am not suffered for to speak, expect what Justice other people will have.

This counterfeit *Mercurius Pragmaticus*, which attempted to imitate Nedham's incisive rhetoric, appeared on the morning of the king's execution. Nedham himself did not publish during this week.

Mercvrivs Pragmaticvs Numb. 42

16–30 January, 1649 369.242 {5.14}

And now let me *knott* my Satyrick *Whip-coard*, and sting your cauterized Consciences a little with some more *rugged* and serious Reprehensions; ye obdurate Rebells at *Westminster*, that dare thus go on, and Act that, which Heaven hath but *Ordain'd*; Or rather with a Sacrilegious ACT, pull downe the Sacred *Ordinance* of GOD: But shall ye prosper thus in this Hellish Enterprize; and will not heaven controul you, and timely step in and avenge the Quarrell of his *Vicegerent*? Yes; expect a *Iulian* dart in the midst of your Carrier to ceaze you: look for a dismall day, when ye shall houl for a drop of that sacred *Oile* of Kingly Unction which ye now so much dispise, to poure into the Wounds of your festered *Consciences*: Youl wish for that one day to cure you, which now you take to be your greatest grievance. {...}

But what? then you mean to goe on my brave Blades of *Steel*, and gallant Gown men in your Deposing Designe, and the murderous machination of your KING: Yes, the feat is now done, and Law and Equity must both give way: the Trayterous Tragedians are upon their *Exit*, and poor King CHARLES at the Brinke of the *Pitt*; The *Prologue* is past, the *Proclamation made*, His Sentence is given, and we daily expect the sad *Catastrophie*; and then behold! The Sceane is *chang'd*;

> *England* but now a glorious *Monarchy*
> Degraded to a base *Democracy*.

The *Play* thus done, or rather the *WORKE Finish'd*; the Epilogue remains, to wit the Epitaph of a slaughter'd King; which I reserve to another Opportunity; hoping Heaven may prevent you, ere your Sceane be finish'd; (as you did those poor Players lately in the middle of their's; not onely depriving them of their present subsistance, but the meanes of future) but what doe we talke of such slight Injuries to them that are now undoing Kingdomes; Yes, not onely *England* and *Ireland* (the one by their

Care, the other by their neglect) but *France* too, as farre as lies in them; so great is their spight and mallice against their Soveraigne; that it reaches as farre as he dare claime a Title: to this purpose; *Iohn Lilburne* the Licentious Libertine was lately they say sent over to make Proselytes, and instill into those poor Peasants the pleasing Principles of Faction in the notion of *Freedome*: and certainly, they may soon be perswaded to shake off their Iron yoake of Slavery, that have seen us before them break the Golden *Band* of Subjection, and cast away the easie Coards of Loyalty.

They may well thow off their Cloggs of Oppression, that have seen us unloose the Latchet of Obedience. {...}

Accursed PRIDE, thou destroyer of *Man*-kinde, that dost miraculously creep into the *Hearts* of thy Dearly beloved Sisters, and workest strange *Effects* within them, and makest them *swell*, as if they had drunke New *Ale*, insomuch that they scorne to drinke the *water of Humillity*; 'Tis thou that hast stole (Oh may'st thou be hang'd for a Thief) into the hearts of *Fairfax, Crumwell, Ireton*, and the rest, and has incensed them against their KING; and made them build *Scaffolds* in Westminster, to Try him for his Life; 'Tis thought that thou art the *Father* of *Rebellion, Murder* and *Independency*, and the Confounder of all Civillity, which is as harmlesse as small *Beere*; thou wert once (by the Report of thy Neighbours) Moderately honest, and didst live at home by thy owne *Fatt*, but now canst live abroad by the *Fatt* of other *Lands*; Thou art that Evill thing, that hast advanced the *lowest*, and tumbled downe the Highest from before thy Presence; 'Twas thou that causedst *Fairfax* and his *Army* to come into *London*, that they might be admired at for their *Vertues*; 'Tis thou, *O Pride*, that art Famous in nothing but *Infamy*; 'Tis thou art Respected for nothing but for *Disrespecting* thy Superiours; 'Tis thou that canst agree in nothing but in *Disagreeing*; 'Tis thou that risest high, that thy *Fall* may be the greater: Oh never was *Pride* so *rich*, nor *Humility* so *Poore*; Now *Pride* I will leave thee, for thou wer't never good, nor will I ever meddle with thee more till thou art better; and so farewell and be hang'd, that's twice *Good bye*.

This account was adapted from the official source: Charles' death speech was probably completely inaudible to the noisy crowd, and was really addressed to those with him on the scaffold. This narrative does understate the king's hesitation in laying his head on the execution block; which was low in order to facilitate restraining him, in case he tried to resist.

A Perfect Diurnall of Some Passages in Parliament *Numb*. 288

29 January – 5 February, 1648{9} 504.288 {5.15}

Beginning Munday, Ianuary 29. {...}

This day the high Court for triall of the King met, and appointed the place for his execution to be over against the Banqueting house of Whitehall, in order whereunto a Scaffold was preparing: the time, betweene the houres of ten and three to morrow.

The King Saterday and Sunday at Whitehall, D[r] *Iuxton* sat up with him all Saturday night, Sunday he din'd and sup'd in his Bedchamber and seemd very cheerfull. This day means was made to deliver a Letter to him from the Prince, which the King no sooner received, but burnt it.

This day the King was removed to S. James, where his children from Syon house came to visit him, but stayed not long, he took the Princesse in his arms and kissed her, gave her his blessing, and two seales that he had wherein were two Diamonds, she wept bitterly. The P. Elector, D. of Richmond, and others, made suit to see him, which he refused. This night he lay at S. James. {...}

Tuesday, Ianuary 30.

THis day the King was beheaded, over against the Banquetting house by White-Hall, The manner of Execution, and what passed before his death take thus.

He was brought from Saint *James* about ten in the morning, walking on foot through the Park, with a Regiment of Foot for his guard, with Colours flying, Drums beating, his private Guard of Partizans, with some of his Gentlemen before, and some behind bareheaded, Doctor *Juxon* late Bishop of *London* next behinde him, and Col. *Thomlinson* (who had the charge of him) to the Gallery in Whitehall, and so into the Cabinet Chamber, where he used to lye, where he continued at his Devotion, refusing to dine (having before taken the Sacrament) onely about 12. at noone he drank a Glasse of Claret Wine, and eat a peece of bread. From thence he was accompanyed by Dr. *Juxon*, Col.

Thomlinson, Col. *Hacker*, and the Guards before mentioned through the Banqueting house adjoyning, to which the Scaffold was erected, between Whitehall Gate, and the Gate leading into the Gallery from Saint. *James*: The Scaffold was hung round with black, and the floor covered with black, and the Ax and Block laid in the middle of the Scaffold. There were divers companies of Foot and Horse, on every side the Scaffold, and the multitudes of people that came to be Spectators, very great. The King making a Passe upon the Scaffold, look'd very earnestly on the Block, and asked Col. *Hacker* if there were no higher; and then spake thus) directing his speech to the Gentlemen upon the Scaffold.

King. I Shall be very little heard of any body here, I shall therefore speak a word unto you here; indeed I could hold my peace very well, if I did not think that holding my peace, would make some men think that I did submit to the guilt, as well as to the punishment; but I think it is my duty to God first, and to my Countrey, for to clear my selfe both as an honest man, and a good king, and a good Christian. I shall begin first with my Innocency, In troth I thinke it not very needfull for me to insist long upon this, for all the world knowes that I never did beginne a Warre with the two houses of Parliament, and I call God to witnesse, to whom I must shortly make an account, that I never did intend for to incroach upon their Priviledges, they began upon me, it is the Militia, they began upon; they confest that the Militia was mine, but they thought it fit to have it from me; and to be short, if any body will look to the dates of Commissions, theirs and mine, and likewise to the Declarations, will see clearly that they began these unhappy troubles, not I; so that as the guilt of these Enormous crimes that are laid against me, I hope in God that God will cleare me of it, I will not, I am in charity; God forbid that I should lay it upon the two Houses of Parliament, there is no necessity of either, I hope they are free of this guilt; for I doe beleeve that ill instruments between them and me, has been the chiefe cause of all this bloodshed; so that by way of speaking, as I find my selfe cleare of this, I hope (and pray God) that they may too: yet for all this, God forbid that I should be so ill a Christian, as not to say that Gods Judgements are just upon me: Many times he does pay Justice by an unjust Sentence, that is ordinary; I only say this, That an unjust sentence (meaning Strafford) that I suffered for to take effect, is punished now, by an unjust sentence upon me; that is, so far I have said, to shew you that I am an innocent man. Now for to shew you that I am a good Christian: I hope there is (pointing to

Dr. *Iuxon*) a good man that will beare me witnesse, That I have forgiven all the world, and those in particular that have been the chiefe causers of my death; who they are, God knowes, I doe not desire to know, I pray God forgive them. But this is not all, my Charity must goe farther, I wish that they may repent, for indeed they have committed a great sin in that particular, I pray God with St. *Stephen*, That this be not laid to their charge; nay, not onely so, but that they may take the right way to the Peace of the Kingdom, for Charity commands me not onely to forgive perticular men, but to endeavor to the last gasp the Peace of the Kingdom: so (sirs) I doe wish with all my soul, and I do hope (there is some here will carry it further) that they may endeavor the Peace of the Kingdom. Now (sirs) I must shew you both how you are out of the way, and will put you in a way; first, you are out of the way, for certainly all the way you ever have had yet as I could find by any thing, is in the way of Conquest; certainly this is an ill way, for Conquest (sir) in my opinion is never just, except there be a good just cause, either for matter of wrong or just Title, and then if you goe beyond it, the first quarrell that you have to it, that makes it unjust at the end, that was just at first: But if it be only matter of Conquest, then it is a great Robbery; as a Pirat said to *Alexander*; that he was a great Robber, hee was but a petty Robber; and so, sir, I do thinke the way that you are in, is much out of the way. Now Sir, for to put you in the way, beleeve it you will never doe right, nor God will never prosper you; untill you give him his due, the King his due (that is, my Successors) and the People their due; I am as much for them as any of you: You must give God his due, by regulating rightly his Church (according to his Scripture) which is now out of order: For to set you in a way particulary now I cannot, but onely this, A Nationall Synod freely called, freely debating among themselves, must settle this; when that every Opinion is freely and clearly heard. For the King, indeed I will not, (then turning to a Gentleman that touched the Ax, said, Hurt not the Ax that may hurt me. For the King:) The Lawes of the Land will clearly instruct you for that; therefore, because it concerns My own particular, I onely give you a touch of it. For the people. And truly I desire their Liberty and Freedom, as much as any body whomsoever; but I must tell you, That their Liberty and their Freedome, consists in having of Government; those Lawes, by which their Life and their Goods, may be most their own. It is not for having share in Government (sir) that is nothing pertaining to them. A subject and a Soveraign, are clean different things; and therefore, untill they do that, I mean, That you doe put the people in that Liberty as I say, certainly they will never enjoy themselves. Sirs, It was for this that now I am come here: If I would have given way to an Arbitrary way, for to have all Laws changed according to the power of the Sword, I needed not to have come here; and therefore, I tell you (and I pray God it be not laid to your charge) That I Am the Martyr of the People. Introth sirs, I shall not hold you much longer; for I will onely say this to you, That in truth, I could have desired some little time longer, because that I would have put this that I have said, in a little more order, and a little better digested, then I have done; and therefore I hope you will excuse Me. I have delivered my Conscience, I pray God that you doe take those courses, that are best for the good of the Kingdome, and your own salvations.

Dr *Juxton*. Will Your Majesty (though it may be very well known Your Majesties affections to Religion, yet it may be expected that you should say somewhat for the worlds satisfaction.

King. I thanke you very heartily me Lord, for that I had almost forgotten it; Introth sirs, my conscience in Religion, I think is very well known to the world; and therefore I declare before you all, That I die a Christian, according to the profession of the Church of England, as I found it left me by my Father; and this honest man, I think will witnesse it. Then turning to the Officers said, sirs, excuse me for this same: I have a good cause, and I have a gracious God; I will say no more: Then turning to col. *Hacker*, he said, Take care that they do not put me to pain; and sir this, and it please you: But then a Gentleman comming neer the Ax, the King said, Take heed of the Ax, pray take heed of the Ax: Then the King speaking to the executioner said, I shall say but very short prayers, and then thrust out my hands: Then the King called to D. *Iuxton* for his Night-cap, and having put it on, he said to the Executioner, does my haire trouble you? Who desired him to put it all under his cap, which the King did accordingly, by the help of the Executioner and the Bishop. Then the King turning to D. *Juxton* said, I have a good cause, and a gracious God on my side.

Dr. *Iuxton*, There is but one stage more: This stage is turbulent and troublesome; it is a short one: But You may consider it will soon carry You a very great way, it will carry you from Earth to Heaven; and there You shall finde a great deale of cordiall joy and comfort.

King. I go from a corruptible to an incorruptible Crown, where no disturbance can be.

D. *Iuxton*. You are exchanged from a Temporall to an Eternall Crown, a good exchange.
Then the King took off his cloak, and his George, giving his George to D. *Iuxton*, saying Remember, (*it is thought for the Prince*,) and some other small ceremonies past: After which the king stooping down laid his necke upon the blocke, and after a very little pause stretching forth his hands, the Executioner at one blow severed his head from his Body. Then his Body was put in a coffin covered with black Velvet, and removed to his lodging chamber in White hall. {...}

Thursday February 1. {...}

The Kings head is sowed on, and his corps removed to *St James* and embalmed, a committee to consider of the time, manner and place of his Funerall, by his Ancestors, but not yet agreed upon.

This *Pragmaticus* also lacked Nedham's style.

Mercvrivs Pragmaticus Numb. 43

30 January – 6 February, 1649 369.243 {5.16}

NAy, you may ene goe to rest now, your *Great* and *Acceptable* WORKE is done; the *Fatall Blow* is given, the Kingdome is translated to the *Saints* — Oh Horror! Blood! Death! Had you none else to reak your cursed *mallice* on, but the sacred Person of the King? *cursed be your* rage *for it is fierce, and your* malice *for it is implacable*.

Good God, how every day adds fresh supplyes of *Miseries* to poor dying *England*; enough of *Care*, but little enough of *Cure*; though yeers and moneths end, yet your sorrows are still beginning, and out Calamities ceaze not; not long a goe we were comforted, and hop'd there would be a happy reconcilement of King, Parliament and People, (by a Treaty) but now we fear; then we laugh'd, but now we languish; one day we are comforted, the next confounded.

Beware the building, for the *Foundation* is taken away, the windes begin to blow, and the waves to beate, the Restlesse *Arke* is toss'd; none but uncleane Beasts are entred into her, the *Dove* will not returne, neither will the *Olive Branch* appear. The *Axe* is laid to the *Root*, even of the *Royal Cedar*, then what can the Inferior *Tree* expect but to be crush'd and bruis'd in His fall, and afterwards hewn down and cast into the fire. {...}

Tuesday, *Ian*. 30. a day more ominous and fatall to all true Protestants then *November* the Fift, for what was then but intended, is now Acted, and indeed never two such horrible *Acts* were committed in *England* as came forth this day, to the abundant joy of the *Saints*, The one ACT was for murdering the King, the other for the prohibiting the Proclaiming of his Highness the Prince of *Wales*, or any other Person to be King of *England*, or *Ireland*, or the Dominions thereof under the heavy penalty of being adjudged Traytors to the *Comon-wealth*, and to suffer the pains of Death, and such other Punishments as belong to the Crimes of *High Treason*, that is as much as to say, such *Punishments* as belong unto themselves, being the most notoriously known *Traytors* that ever the Sunne shin'd upon {...}

This day a Letter came to the King from the Prince of *Wales*, which the messenger delivered to the Captain of the Guard, who opening it, read the same to all the Tatterdemallions, and after, came smoaking with his Tobacco in the very face of the King, and offered him the Letter, which his Majesty refused to receive.

This day a Warrant came from the *High-Treason Court* for the Execution of the King, between the houres of 10. and 3. He came from St. *Iamses* to *Whitehall* on foot, accompanied by Dr. *Iuxon*, and mounting the *Scaffold*, with an undaunted Resolution He made a Speech to the People, which because it hath been published already, I shall onely give you the Heads thereof.

1. That His Majesty began not the Warre, but the Parliament began with Him.

2. That giving consent for the beheading of the *Earl* of *Strafford*, was that (His Majesty said) for which Gods judgement was just upon Him.

3. That they will never have Blessing, till God have his due, the succeeding King his due, and the *People* their due: God by his due, by a right regulating of the Church, the King his due, by investing him in his Rights, and the People their due, by enjoying those Laws, by which their Lives and goods may be most properly known to be their owne.

4. That He was His Peoples *Martyr*, and dyed for maintaining the Laws.

5. That he dyed a true Protestant according to the Profession of the Church of *England*, as he found it left him by his Royall Father.

And so with much constancy, he yeelded His body to the block: and here wee may see, That *Mutability* is but *Times* Ensigne; nothing visible is permanent, the most Glorious King, or palmed

State, is but the recorded *Monument* of *Vncertainty*. *England*, that but lately appear'd like the bright Moon amongst the Starrs, the most Beautifull of all other Nations, but now alas her light is put out, her beauty faded, and all her glory departed from her.

The king was buried on 8 February at Windsor, in the space which had once been intended for Katherine Parr, the sixth wife of Henry VIII, who had survived her husband to remarry.

Perfect Occurrences *Num.* 111

9–16 February 1648{9} 465.5111 {5.17}

The late King *Charles* is buryed at *Windsor*. The manner thus.

The first night he was brought into his bed-chamber, the next day the Deans Hall was prepared with mourning, then he was brought thither, the room being made dark, and lightened by Torches, where the body was, till the time of buriall, which was about two in the afternoon. The Duke of *Lenox* caused this Inscription to be cut in Letters, & put upon the Coffin [KING CHARLES 1648]. And he was buried in the Vault with King *Henry* the eight.

The manner of his carriage to the Grave, thus: The Kings Servants that waited all the time of the Kings imprisonment, went first before the body, the Governour, and Dr. *Juxon* went next to the Course; the four Lords, *Richmond, Hertford, Southampton*, and *Lindsay*, carryed the foure corners of the Velvet over the Corps, which was carryed by Souldiers. It was desired by the Duke of *Richmond*, that the Bishop might use the Ceremonies used at the Buriall of the dead; but it was the opinion of the Governour, and those Gentlemen imployed by the Parliament, that hee ought not to use the Book of Common Prayer, although the Parliament did permit to use such decency as the Duke should think fit; but if the Doctor had any exhortation to say without booke, hee should have leave, but he could say nothing without book.

Stories of the Regicides' haunted consciences abounded.

The Man in the Moon, Discovering a World of Knavery Vnder the Sunne (*Numb.* 2.)

16–23 April, 1649 248.02 {5.18}

Reports flie about, That *Fairfax* and *Cromwell* cannot sleep, they are so haunted with evill Spirits, that sometimes they start in their sleeps, rise from their beds, draw their *naked weapons*, and cry *charge, charge*; this may be true, for Ile assure you 'tis reported so by their owne household servants, and surely they cannot chuse but know that are about them; they are sonnes of *darknesse*, and the *Man in the Moon* loathes the sight of them; One thing is worthy of laughter, and I beleeve it for truth; in briefe, thus it was, His Excellency having businesse late in Whitehall, and comming out hastily to take Coach in the muckish of the Evening, it happened, that his Coach stood just on the place where the King was murdered, and Mr. *Miles Corbet* a Parliament man standing by the Boot of the Coach, to sollicite him about something concerning the *Navy*, who making towards *Fairfax*, his *Excellency* turned suddenly about, mistaking *Corbet* (being of a black Complexion,) for the Devill; left his Coach, and run home into Queen-street in a great agony, and was so frighted, that he would eate nothing in two or three dayes after; at last asking his Coach-man if he observ'd nobody stand at the Boot of the Coach, who inform'd him, That it was Mr. *Corbet*, that had some businesse with his Honor; presently after he had a very good stomach, and fell heartily to his meate.

A guilty Conscience is on earth a hell,
If that were all his punishment, 'twere well.

CHAPTER SIX
A Prospect of the New Jerusalem: Letters from abroad

A single report in *The Kingdomes Faithfull and Impartiall Scout* justifies modern attention to the representation of the geographic other in seventeenth-century newsbooks. It described two Amerindians being displayed in France by merchants, as objects of curiosity, as the animate testimony to the existence of another world where they do things differently. Through the presence of a translator, an interesting fact in itself, one of them was allowed to speak, and thereby moved from being an object to subject; from a curious artefact to a critical interpreter of early-modern Europe. Though in the third person, the newsbook account offered a glimpse onto a heavily accented speech act framed by an encounter between two discrete cultures. He said:

> That since his coming thither, He observed two things which he stood amazed at. First, that so many gallant men which seemed to have stout and generous Spirits, should all stand bare, and be subject to the will and pleasure of a Child. Secondly, that some in the City were clad in very rich and costly Apparel, and others so extream poor, that they were ready to famish for hunger; that he conceived them to be all equaliz'd in the ballance of Nature, and not one to be exalted above another. {6.08}

The 'Child' was Louis XIV. The speech and its values are surprisingly familiar, as the editor of the story noted in his aside that this was '*A worthy expression of two Heathen Levellers*.' This egalitarian discourse was not only available in England in 1649, it had a prominent status among the radical members of the Army who had pressed for a broader political franchise, better pay and a society in which it was acknowledged that some men weren't born with saddles on their backs, nor others booted and spurred to ride them. As a mirror reflecting the distorted reality of European culture, it is a device Jonathan Swift would have been pleased with.

On their first contact with Amerindian culture, Europeans were struck by their physical differences: this news report focused instead on social organisation,[1] and compared the aspirations of the more frightening political dissidents of England in 1649 to the savages which destroyed settlements and engendered so much fear. Europeans had also, of course, been killing through the transmission of diseases and, later, active genocide, since their arrival.[2] The political dissidents might look to the New World in a corresponding fashion, as a place where they might live freed from oppressive masters. New worlds and new cultures were powerful symbols in Revolutionary England. Whereas the New World tended to be described in the terms of the old, it was possible to reverse this process, and to turn the old world upside down, by pointing out, as Montaigne did, that some people ate their parents as a gesture of respect.[3]

In fact the use of the new world to interpret the old reaches an extreme in the news item concerning the Leveller Indians. Daniel Border, the editor of the paper, stole it from Montaigne's *Essayes*. Here is the passage in John Florio's 1603 translation:

> Three of that nation ignoring how deare the knowledge of our corruptions will one day cost their repose, securitie, and happinesse, and how their ruine shall proceede from this comerce, which I imagine is already well advanced, (miserable as they are to have suffered themselves to be so cosened by a desire of newfangled novelties, and to have quit the calmnesse of their climate, to come and see ours) were at *Roane* in the time of our late King *Charles* the ninth, who talked with them a great while. They were shewed our fashions, our pompe, and the forme of a faire Cittie; afterward some demanded their advise, and would needes knowe of them what things of note and admirable they had observed amongst-vs: they answered three things, the last of which I had forgotten, and am very sorie for-it, the other two I yet remember. They saide, *First, they found-it very strange, that so many tall men with long beardes, strong and well armed, as were about the Kings person (it is very likely they meant the swizzers of his guarde) would submit themselves to obey a beardlesse childe, and*

1 Cp. Richard Bonney, *The European Dynastic States, 1494–1660* (Oxford: Oxford University Press, 1991), p.362.

2 William H. McNeill, *Plagues and Peoples* (New York: Anchor Press/Doubleday, 1976).

3 Anthony Pagden, *The Fall of Natural Man: The American Indian and the origins of comparative ethnography* (Cambridge: Cambridge University Press, 1982).

> *that we did not rather chuse one amongst them to commaund the rest.* Secondly (they have a maner of phrase whereby they call men but moytie of men from others.) *They had perceived, there were many amongst vs full gorged with all sortes of commodities, and others which, hunger-starven, and bare with neede and povertie, begged at their gates: and found it strange, these moyties so needie could endure such as iniustice, and that they tooke not the others by the throte, or set fire on their houses.*[4]

In 1649, when *The Kingdomes Faithfull and Impartiall Scout* was published, the young Louis XIV was on the throne, France being under the regency of Anne of Austria: this enabled a comparison with Charles IX, also a minor when he inherited the crown, to whom Montaigne referred. An historical coincidence enabled Border to translate the passage. A writer more hostile to the Commonwealth than Border would not have omitted the suggestion that the strongest man should be elected ruler: this might have seemed an adequate parallel to the land where there was no power but the sword. From this reworking it is possible to deduce that Border, like Montaigne, was not being simply malicious. Instead he used the foreigner's observation to pick out exactly what was sympathetic in the Levellers' cause. In the light of Montaigne's imaginative sympathy with the Indians it is no coincidence that the Leveller propagandist William Walwyn expressed the 'deep impression' the essayist made upon him: 'I have been long accustomed to read *Montaigns Essaies*, an author perhaps youl startl at; nor do I approve of him in all things, but ile read you a peece or two, that will be worth your study...'[5]

While we should read European representations of America in the light of domestic politics, and not as some objective commentary, this does not mean that all observations on the new world are merely reflections of the old. Amerindian culture was experiencing drastic changes in its social stratification, some areas having their distinct hierarchies destroyed, as a consequence of contact with the Europeans.[6] The depiction of the colonial

4 Michel de Montaigne, *The Essayes Or Morall, Politike and Millitarie Discourses*, trans. John Florio (Menston: The Scolar Press, facsimile edition, 1969), p.106. STC 18041.

5 William Walwyn, *Walwyns Just Defence Against the Aspertions Cast Upon him* (London, 1649), pp.10–13. Wing W685. This has been reprinted in William Haller and Godfrey Davies, *The Leveller Tracts 1647–1653* (Gloucester, Mass.: Peter Smith, 1964), pp.350–398. On Walwyn and Montaigne see also Nigel Smith, 'The Charge of Atheism and the Language of Radical Speculation, 1640–1660' in eds. Michael Hunter and David Wootton, *Atheism from the Reformation to the Enlightenment* (Oxford: Clarendon Press, 1992).

6 Alfred W. Crosby, *Ecological Imperialism: The Biological Expansion of Europe,*

encounter depended on an exchange, however restricted.[7] So while the Leveller Indians may have been plagiarised from another text, translated across time until it became a mediated fiction, other letters from abroad provide insights into the influence of new sights, new smells, new spices and new meats on the travellers who recorded them. The colonists, at least those organising and funding the settlements, ventured over the Atlantic with the theories of Pliny and Machiavelli behind them, but soon left these influences behind in their daily experiences of the plantations.[8] Poy, a newsletter writer who had assisted Richard Hakluyt with the third volume of his *The principal navigations*, invested in the Virginia plantation, and eventually settled there as a colonial governor.

These letters from abroad stand somewhere between representations of political utopias, travel writing and exotic fiction. The new world was a crux of fantasies. It is the land to which Oliver Cromwell perhaps almost departed late in 1641 when he despaired of political reform in England. In these letters experiences were recounted with the wonder of a prospect of a world literally expanding. The Americas were at once a haven for the godly,[9] a place where the new Jerusalem might be built, and a land of Cockaigne, a natural paradise where the fruit fell into the hand and fish leapt onto the banks of the river, a land of cakes and ale where crops grew abundantly in the dark soil, where the air was clear and warm, where the golden fleece might be found. At the same time there was danger. The Indians were sometimes represented as innocents with an essentially noble nature, in the tradition of Montaigne and Rousseau. Upon other occasions they were portrayed as barely human savages, always preparing to massacre Christians with the most cowardly devices.

Foreign countries were different places and their ways could not always be understood. This was particularly evoked by letters from Europe. Although the world was being increasingly inte-

900–*1900* (Cambridge: Cambridge University Press, 1986), pp.209–15.

7 Crosby, *The Columbian Exchange: Biological and Cultural Consequences of 1492* (Westport, CT: Greenwood Publishing Co., 1972), ch.2.

8 David B. Quinn, 'Renaissance Influences in English Colonization', in his *Explorers and Colonies: America, 1500–1625* (London: Hambledon Press, 1990), pp.97–117. Crosby, *The Columbian Exchange*, ch.1.

9 See William Haller, *The Puritan Frontier: Town-Planting in New England Colonial Development, 1630–1660* (New York: Columbia University Press, 1951), ch.5; David Cressy, *Coming Over: Migration and Communication between England and New England in the Seventeenth Century* (Cambridge: Cambridge University Press, 1987), ch.3.

grated by trade and commerce and consequently news reports of overseas events, such as the Thirty Years War, were of importance to an expanding domestic audience, cultural barriers continued to impede translation {6.25}. Foreign correspondents had the opportunity to become anthropologists, devising detailed accounts of ceremonies, and trying to reconstruct their meaning in the form of a symbolic narrative. A description of the coronation of the Turkish king, consisting of a ceremonial circumcision followed by the presentation of a sword, gestured towards an interesting, neo-Freudian interpretation {6.06&09}.

We cannot know the extent to which such readings may intentionally have been implied, but the efforts directed towards accuracy and detail were evidence of a desire to understand the 'other' by unravelling its peculiar practices. Others emphasised the similarity between foreign practices and domestic ones. Encounters with narratives of other cultures also furnished the reader with a means of understanding the integrity of his or her own. Such an act of intellectual conceptualization, encouraged by the account of the Leveller Indians, questioned the values of society and asked what made them cohere. If England remained God's chosen land, it was not without the understanding that other ways of living, involving male polygamy or eating one's parents, could make sense.

The distribution of foreign news was both a consequence of, and a condition for foreign trade. The importance of information to trade and investment stimulated interest in newsbooks. Here economics is mixed with astrology.

Certaine Informations *Numb.* 46.

27 November – 4 December, 1643 36.46 {6.01}

Friday, December 1.

By Letters from Lisbon in Portugall it is informed, that the King of that Kingdome hath lately conquered the Kingdome of Algarve, which lyeth upon the South of Portugall, and hath alwayes belonged unto it, as a member thereof, and that he hath gotten the Country of Segovia, from whence cometh all the fine rich woolls that make the best Spanish Cloath, and finest Felt hats, which is of great importance, and will bring him in much treasure. And that his Army marched so far Southwards, that they came within a few miles of the great City of Sevill, in the Spanish

Province of Andaluzia, which put the Sevillians in such a fright, that they sent to St. Lucars their sea Port, for some hundreds of men to aide them against the Portugalls. And if it should so happen, that the King of Portugall should get possession of Sevill and St. Lucars, the Spaniards trade for gold and silver to the West Indies, would be absolutely intercepted, and quite lost, and then the Spaniard would become the poorest and most despicable Nation in Europe. Thus the Spaniard yearely looseth, and the Pope his ghostly Father daily looseth, the Italian Princes still getting some part or other of his territories from him. These are the two main supporters of Antichristian tyranny in the world, who if they fall, as the last great conjunction of Saturn and Jupiter presageth they must, according to the judgements of learned Mathematicians, Popish Idolatry will soone be driven out of the world.

This letter from Virginia offers an American perspective on the English Revolution, as well as on domestic politics.

Mercurius Civicus *Numb.* 104

15–22 May, 1645 298.104 {6.02}

I doe not usually acquaint you with any forraine intelligence, conceiving the affaires at home to be more lookt after, yet having this weeke received some matters of importance in reference to this Kingdome in divers letters from Virginy, I shall for once give you a relation of their contents, which are thus:

We are still troubled with the Indians upon the frontier part of the Country, and therefore wee are now providing three forts in the middle of the Country being in the Kings Territories, which is not far from us, that so we may have a power amongst them able to destroy them and to deprive them of their livelihood. They lately in a treacherous manner cut off 400 of our people, they have not courage to doe it otherwise: we take this course now that so wee may follow our businesse in the summer. How ever the crops we make now cannot be so great as they have bin, and I think we shall be at the charge of halfe our labours to maintaine these forts, and the Souldiers at the middle plantation which is a narrow passage the Indians have into the Forrest, this is our onely charge that dwell on the Northside of the *Iameses* River, the people on the other side are to deale with the Indians there: This way though chargeable is thought most convenient to extirpate and subdue this people that doe much annoy us: they are so cowardly that ten of ours will make an hundred of them run away. We are at peace among our selves and have beene so ever since the massacre; Sir *William Barclay* went for Bristoll and left Master *Kempe* his Deputy and is not yet returned: It is my opinion that the massacre (though a judgement) did divert a great mischiefe that was growing among us by Sir *William Barclay's* courses; for divers of the most religious and honest inhabitants, were mark't out to be plundered and imprisoned for the refusall of an Oath that was imposed upon the people, in referrence to the King of England. It was tendered at mens houses, the people murmured, and most refused to take it: Those few that tooke it did it more for feare then affection; so that it is the opinion of judicious men that if the Indians had but forborne for a month longer, they had found us in such a combustion among our selves that they might with ease have cut of every man if once we had spent that little powder and shot that we had among our selves. I must not omit to give you notice of the governour of Mary-lands commissions lately brought hither in the Bristoll ship, though it may be you have already notice of in *England*: The governour of Mary-land very tenderly discovered a commission that he had from His Majesty to take the *London* ships, to seize upon all debts due to *London* Merchants, to build custome-houses, and to receive the custome of Tobacco heere, and also to erect Castles and build Forts for the defence of the Country, and out of this revenue hee was to pay the governour of this Colony 2000l. The Assembly seemed to comply with him and pretended the accomplishment of all his desires, and when they had gotten as much out of him as they could they seemed to commend the ingenious contrivance of the businesse, hee replied that was the only agent in the businesse himselfe, which they tooke good notice of, withdrew themselves, dissolved the Assembly, but published a Proclamation that all ships from *London*, and elsewhere should have free Trade, and so departed leaving him and his commissions.

Since the massacre because men should not be disabled to defend themselves, and their Plantations, it was thought fit to make a Law that no mans servant, his corne, or Ammunition should be taken in execution, but when it shall please God we shall suppresse our enemy, this Act will be repealed.

Certaine newes is brought hither by a credible person, That *Ingle* hath taken and plundered all the Papists except the governour of Mary-land, and some few that are gone away among the Poluxant Indians for refuge, and that he hath sent 40 men by land, and 60 by water to fetch them by violence.

I should now leave the forraigne newes were it not that upon the day of execution of the massacre upon the Christains by the Indians there hapned a great wonder (which to many may seeme incredible, and the rather for that it is related at so great a distance from this Kingdome; and indeed there are some people so criticall that they will believe no more then they see of the affaires of this Kingdome, and much lesse further of: yet for the satisfaction of such as are desirous, I shall onely set down the words of the Letter comming from an honest and knowne hand in that Plantation, to a person of good repute in this City, Gods goodnesse hath beene lately very eminent in delivering me and my family from the Indian massacre. Upon the first day of April my wife was washing a bucket of clothes, and of a sudden her clothes were all besprinkled with blood from the first beginning to the rincing of them, at last in such abundance as if an hand should invisibly take handfuls of gore blood and throw it upon the linnen. When it lay all of an heape in the washing-tub, she sent for me in, and I tooke up one gobbet of blood as big as my fingers end, and stirring it in my hand it did not staine my fingers nor the linnen: Upon this miraculous premonition and warning from God having some kinde of intimation of some designe of the Indians (though nothing appeared till that day) I provided for defence, and though we were but five men and mistrusted not any villany towards us before: yet we secured our selves against 20 savages which were three houres that day about my house. Blessed be the name of God.

This newsbook offered eminently practical advice on settling in the West Indies.

A Continvation Of certain speciall an Remarkable passages *Numb.* 21.

6–13 February, 1645{6} 61.21 {6.03}

Beginning the 6. of February

THe tottering condition of the Kings Army is much noysed abroad beyond Seas, for amongst some Letters intercepted, wee finde one from the Spanish Islands, advising his friend in arms against the Parliament to leave the

Warres and goe over thither to make a new Plantation, and withal incloseth a note of what provisions are needfull for him to ship with him for that voyage, and would have him take shiping at *Dartmouth*.

A Note of the Provisions followeth.

Imprimis, one firkin of flower or more with a Lock and a Key to it, this is for Pancakes and Puddings, a bushell of Wheat beaten and Oat-meale, three dozen of Bread, buy it in the West Country as you come to spend in the forepart of your voyage, and save your allowance of biskets which else wilbe short if the voyage prove long, a firkin of butter, a firkin of Egges, three or foure hundred in Bran, bring a Coopefull of pullen and barley, and Gravell for their food, bring with you Cheeses, Rice, and a Hogge to kill by Sea, as for sheepe they will pine away if they bee not brought up at hard meat get two or three Sea Chists to put all these things in and a large Cellar to put your waters in, For your necessary use, get a small Frying pan, a little Kittle, two or three bottles to keepe your beere in and some other necessaries for your Table as you see cause for the ship will not afford them lay in at your owne cost a barrell of good beare, and another of water least you be scanted, a pot of Honey, Sugar, spice, Sack, burnt Clarret wine, Vinegar, hot waters, Ioyce of Lemon, Mustard seed, a pot of Greene Ginger, Meridate and some Cordialls, and for your cloathing in the ship get a warme Wascot, two paire of Linnen drawers to lye in, two or three paire of Hose for change, bands, shirts, &c. a furre Gowne, a fur Cap, scant not your selfe in any of these things least you repent it, for you may have use for all, and you pay nothing for the carriage of them, and if any thing be spared there will be no losse, and if with them you bring but 500.l. either in money or English Commodities, you may do well but however I would not have you faile to bring with you three or foure labouring men, by whose paines and your mannaging of their endeavours you may doe well.

The conservative editor of *The true Informer* used an American perspective to reflect back on developments in England, where the rattlesnakes were the Independents.

The true Informer *Numb*. 44.

21–28 February, 1646 498.44 {6.04}

And this came in a Letter from New England, being written by a Magistrate of the Towne called *Concord*, representing the danger of errours in Religion, and a greater danger by the tolleration. The Letter followeth in these words, as it was written to a Divine in London.

Reverend and dearly beloved in our Lord Jesus:

YOur Letter 21 Febr. last I received, and do unfainedly rejoyce to heare, that God hath mercifully hitherto preserved you and yours in these calamitous times. It is no marvell the war is not likely yet to end, when there are such divisions of those, which should joyne heart and hand as one man against the common Enemy. I have heard also, that there was never of late times such a generall inundation of hellish opinions spred amongst the Professours of the Gospell, as amongst you now; which, if it be not suppressed seasonably, will doubtlesse eat up the marrow of all true Religion amongst you; and then wo be to the Land, when the power of Godlinesse is rarely to be found amongst you. It is also reported, that pride in apparrell was never so excessively generall as now, such as being of meane qualitie going ordinarily in silk; and is it not a time rather to put on sack-cloth, and to meet the Lord in an humble abasement, to try if yet there may be hope to stay the over-flowing scourge, that it passe not over all the Land. The latest newes with us as yet, is the battell at Naesby, where wee heard God gave the Parliaments Forces a glorious victorie; the Lord give you and us in all his gracious dealings, to owne his hands, and to blesse his Name. But surely, Sir, it would be more joyous to mee, to heare that the people turne to Him that smites them, than to heare of many victories; for though there were but a few wounded men left in the Enemies Camp, they would serve as a rod of Gods anger, to work what desolations he hath appointed. Remember my love (I pray you) to each of our Derby-shire friends, amongst whom, if any have turned aside to these, and the like sinfull opinions, as Familisme, Anabaptisme, or Antinomianisme, that from all that I have heard or seene of such wicked opinions in these parts (except they speedily repent, and rise out of such errours, before they have too deeply drunk them in) the next thing, I feare, I shall heare of them, is that they are become Libertines, or worse. Wee were this yeare in great danger to have fallen into a war with the Indians, but the Lord in mercie prevented it. Wee have had a verie dry Summer, wee have our health verie well in these parts, through mercie; the winters here are much colder than in England, but when the skie is cleare, and the Sun of any height, it is verie warme under the shelter of the wind. I have enclosed the taile of a Rattle-Snake, when any creature comes neare them, I killed her in the way from the Bay to our Towne; they are the most venomous creatures in the Country; such as have been bitten with them, have within few houres been all over spotted like the Snaile, but having some Snaile-weed in season, have recovered: In some places they have many of them, I never heard of above three, as I remember, in all the bounds of our Towne. Thus my love to your selfe, and all the rest of our friends, I rest,

Concord, the ninth of the tenth month, 1645.

Yours ever in the Lord,
Thomas Flint.

The foreign news in John Dillingham's *Moderate Intelligencer* was generally good. The issue previous to this mentioned 'the sport of the combate of Bulls' and the political intrigues of Venice: this report describes the treating which ended the Thirty Years War. The large sum of money which the Palatine Elector was supposed to pay was erroneous: the next issue noted that the actual figure was 23612. This is another instance of the importance of news to the economy: the peace was to have a very bad effect on English trade, because the Hispano-Dutch peace treaty enabled the United Provinces to resume mercantile competition.

The Moderate Intelligencer *Numb*. 191

9–16 November, 1648 419.191 {6.05}

Muster 24 of Octob.

The Lord Deputies of the Empire, about eight this day, went to the *Swedish Plenipotentiaries*, and delivered their last conclusion about the military satisfaction for the *Heshish*, which as it seemed, was onely to delay the signing of the general Peace till old and new *Prague* might be taken: which conference held til 11 of the clock. This being done, there was nominated the houre for subscription, the House of *Count* of *Nassau* was appointed for the *French* Embassador, the House of *Count* of *Lamberg*, for the *Swedish Plenipotentiary*. At one in the afternoon the *Swedish* came first into *Count Lamberts* with five coaches six horses before each, in the last coach sate the Lord *Plenipotentiary*, and with the Resident *Berenslau*; one quarter of an houre after came *Monsieur Servient* with a great Train, of which first all the Pages and Lacques in Green; War is as Winter, Peace as the Spring; trimm'd with Orange Velvet and Silver, about 40 or 50 in number. Secondly, a gilded coach covered with red Velvet, in which sate the Lord *Servient* and Resident *de la Court*. *Servient* was very richly clothed, as ever was seen. After him followed the Captain *du Garde*, and the Gentlemen of the Horse, with a Guard of six and twenty horse and persons of quality: then followed five other coaches, with 6 horses before each; all which went to the house of *Count* of *Nassau*. In both which places they were busie in conferring the *Instrumentum Pacis*, after that the *Swedish* and *French* Embassadours subscribed, and then after complementing one with another, they went home to their severall Lodgings. Thereupon the Imperiall Lord *Count* of *Nassau*, and *Count* of *Volmar* went to *Monsieur Sevient: Count de Lamberg*, and Lord *Craane* went to the *Swedish Plenipotentiarie*, subscribed and sealed the *Instumentum Pacis* solemnly, which being brought by the Secretaries of the severall Embassadors to *Bishopshoff*, were ratified by the Deputies of the Electors and States of the Empire: About eight or nine of the clock it was happily finished; then went off 108 great shots. In the afternoon about three of the clock there was seen a Storke, never at that time in that place before (an Embleme of Love and Unity) which flying about the Lodgings of the *Imperiall* Lords rested; at last upon the Councel House.

The next day was so cleer a Sun-shine without any clouds, that it seemed, Heaven it self was wel pleased with this general Peace: in the Chuches thanks was given to God.

About ten of the clock the high Tower of *St. Lambert*, and the Councel house were hang'd with all manner of Ensignes, with the Eagle. The City Secretary accompanied with eight Trumpets, and two Kettle-drums, road through the whole City, and made publication of it: in the interim many Volleys of shots were made here and there. On the Market, about the Councel house stood 400 Musquetiers, and the City Train in all 1500, who stood in arms, shooting so many Volleys that hardly a house could be seen for the smoake of Gunpowder: these being marcht off, there were made 226 great shots, which shootings continued till 12 at night. In the interim the several Embassadors send by special Cavalliers their reciprocall congratulations one to another. The same evening the *Spanish* Embassador *Monsieur Brown* sent a Gentleman to the *French* Embassador, congratulating him for this Peace, telling further that His Master hopeth, that this *German* Peace wil be a way, that *Spain* and *France* may enjoy the like Peace, to the welfare of Christendom. {...}

Since the Treaty betwixt *Spain* and *France* are reassumed, in which to day a solemne conference shall be held; and on both parties they labour strongly, that the *Swedish* Embassadors would be pleased to mediate therein, and to see the differences reconciled, that an universall Peace in Christendome may be enjoyed, to which both parties seem to incline very much.

It is observable, That amongst other harsh conditions of this Peace to the Calvinists, The Prince Elector *Palatine*, and his Brothers are to renounce for themselves, & their heires their right to the Upper *Palatinate*. And though the Elector should if his Brothers refuse, he is not able to perform, and so not enjoy the benefit of the Treaty, it being not cleerly expressed. His Highnesse is also to pay within two moneths to satisfie the *Swedish Militia* for the first tearm, according to the ancient taxation for the Warre against the *Turk*, to the value of 236122 pound sterling, in ready money notwithstanding. The losse of the Upper *Palatinate,* and the *Bergstrass*, being a considerable part in the Lower *Palatinate*, besides the excessive miseries, which that poore Country hath endured, during these 30 yeers Wars.

There are also some lands (Fees) of the Lower *Palatinate*, bestowed by the Emperour and the Duke of *Bavaria* upon foure Noblemen, their Counsellors, who have beene always the greatest enemies to the House Palatine, and the Prince Elector is obleiged by this Treaty to confirme them, though it be not particularized, what these lands are: and for ought Hee knows, it may be the greatest part of his Dominions: Let all take notice of the different disposition and affection in (Profession) to the *Palatine* Family in *England* now, and 30 yeers, when Prayers, Fasts, Men and Money was offered in abundance.

See also {6.09}

The Moderate Intelligencer *Numb*. 196.

14–21 December, 1648 419.196 {6.06}

From Smyrna, *the* 11*th*. *of* October.

The 8*th*. of *August* last, was *Sultan Mahomet*, th'eldest Son of *Sultan Ibrahim*, placed in the Ottoman Throne, and was, the next day after, Circumcised with all the Ceremonies usuall thereunto, and the 16 day following, he took possession of the Sword, *Aivan Seray*; which denotes the full possession of the Empire; making that day his publick entrie in *Constantinople*, attended on by his principal *Visier*, called, *Kadgi Mahomet Pacha*, (70 yeers old, and of very great accompt among the Turks) the *Visiers, Cadis, Emiris, Capigis, Chiaoux, Spahis, Janizaries*, and a great number of other persons. The 18 *Sultan Ibrahim*, who was, the 9th. day, thrust into a Chamber of the *Serail*, and afterward into a darker place, accompanied only by two old women, upon information given that he intended to escape, there died, as tis reported, desperate. Howsoever hee was buried the same day, neer the *Sultan Mustapha*, his Uncle: We have understood since the death of the Grand *Visier*, that he purposed to have made a Peace with the Venetians; but now there is small appearance thereof; {...}

An entertaining letter, evocative of place and material culture and descriptive of trade. It suggests integration of States through mercantile encounters. The enormous time lag in its arrival may be a consequence of it having been held back until the preparations for the trial of the king made domestic news restricted and politically delicate.

The Moderate Intelligencer *Numb*. 198.

28 December – 4 January, 1649 419.198 {6.07}

From the East Indies *the* 3. *of* July 1648.

If any Island deserve the name of *Colchos*, from whence the *Argonauts* are said to have fetched the golden fleece, tis surely that of *Goa*; not onely in respect of the excessive riches found, and traded for, in that Haven, (a scantling whereof you may have in the fraught of three ships lately come thence to *Lisborne*, loaden partly with Ingots or wedges of Gold, Ambergris, Diamonds, and other precious Stones) wherein no Port in the World is able to compare with it, but because there is no place affords more hope of discoverie of Mines of Gold and Silver, the soyle thereof being neere of the colour of the better of those mettals: which hath perswaded many *Philosophers* that they shall find there stuffe enough for the Phylosophers Stone, their great work. And in truth, notwithstanding many inhibitions to the contrary made by the Portugall Viceroy, fearing that the reputation thereof will excite th'envie and appetite of other Princes and States to come and attempt the gaining of it, even at this present many Alchymists and men experienced in Mines, are very busie in that place.

This Island (whose principall Town beares the name of it, and is the Metropolis of all the Indies) is watered all about by a River three miles broad, and so farre distant from the maine land; the Houses of the Town are built *à la Portugais*, though not so high rooffed because of th'excessive heat of th'Ayre; yet very much tempered by the shadow of the Gardens belonging to every House, and replenished with Trees bearing most delicious fruits.

The Portingals are there in peace with all the world, and yet they keepe their Frontiers continually in a state of Defence whatsoever should happen; especially since the Moores endeavoured to get the Forteresse of *Chuell*, by surprizall (for otherwise they could not get it.) In the meane while we are told that the Hollanders being returned unto the *Philippines* to attempt againe the investing of *Manilla* (the principall Forteresse held by the Spaniards in that Countrey) have in that Enterprize lost many ships, and a great number of men. And that they are also driven from *Mangnazachi*, a Haven in *Japan*, because they were not punctuall enough in their payments, which otherwise, as tis said were not always found lawfull.

The best, and greatest part of *China* is yet in the power of the Tartarians, a Nation farre more, warlike then, but not so politick as these, *Chineses* whose King holds now, no more but the Province of *Cantan* in the confines whereof is the Town of *Macao* possessed by the Portingals, between whom and the Spaniards of *Manilla* Commerce being established, both th'one and th'other, carry their commodities to *Mocassar*, whose King being Newter, is become a surety for both Nations.

The English, on the contrary, have abandoned the businesse of *Coroari*, a Forteresse within the kingdome of *Canara* (neere to this Island of *Goa*) wherein there grow many Spices, because, they say they got but little by it.

The Trade of *Moca* in the Red Sea is also well nigh destroyed, by reason of too great a number of English, Portingale, and Holland Ships, which bring thither any their Marchandice, growen, by that meanes, almost out of request. The like is also become of the Traffick of *Ormus*, by which the English heretofore gained so much. On th'other side, that of the Forteresse of *Mascats* (which belongs to the Portingals, and stand over aginst *Ormus* within the Persian strait) increases, and becomes thereby more and more considerable.

The Portingales did the last yeere set out a Fleet of light and nimble Barks, which they call *Periches* to drive the *Malabar* Pirats, and Moores from the Coasts of th'Indies (continually ravaged and ransacked by them) and have succeeded so well therein, that they have already taken a good number of those Rovers, and thereby well-nigh rid those Seas of that mischievous generation.

The Kingdomes Faithfull and Impartiall Scout [*Numb.* 11]

6–13 April, 1649 210.11 {6.08}

☞ Two of the Savage Indians were brought into France by some Merchants; they were shewed at Court, and afterwards in the City of *Paris:* One that understood their language, asked one of them, how he liked the countrey, and the condition of Christians, the Indian replyed, That since his coming thither, He observed two things which he stood amazed at. First, that so many gallant men which seemed to have stout and generous Spirits, should all stand bare, and be subject to the will and pleasure of a Child. Secondly, that some in the City were clad in very rich and costly Apparel, and others so extream poor, that they were ready to famish for hunger; that he conceived them to be all equaliz'd in the ballance of Nature, and not one to be exalted above another. (*A worthy expression of two Heathen Levellers.*)

This describes a veritable land of Cockayne, where the fruit falls into the hand. Perhaps the advertisement was unsuccessful, because it was repeated in *A Perfect Diurnall* at the end of the month. It is followed by a later, more detailed report of the ceremonial circumcision in Constantinople {6.06}.

The Moderate Intelligencer *Numb.* 215.

26 April – 2 May, 1649 419.215 {6.09}

At the intreaty of a well-willer, the following lines are inserted.
There is a Gentleman going over Governour into Carolana *in* America, *and many Gentlemen of quality and their families with him.*

THis place is of a temperate Climate, not so hot as *Barbado's* nor so cold as *Virginia*; the Winter much like our *March* here in *England*. The Northern latitude begins where *Virginia* ends, at 37, neer Cape *Henry*, and takes in six degrees Southerly; no bounds to the East and West, but the Seas. At point *Comfort,* neer Cape *Henry*, you enter into a fair Navigable River, called *James* River, about two leagues over: on both sides that River, are the chiefe Plantations in *Virginia*, and their chief Town *James* Town. On the South side of this River, are two Rivers, *Elisabeth*, and *Nansamond*, which convey you into *Carolana*; so that this River is a Haven to both Colonies. This

Carolana, besides the temperature of the Climate, hath many Native Commodities to feed and cloath the body: Deer in abundance, bigger and better meat then ours in *England*, having two young ones at a time; their skins good cloathing, being better dressed by the *Indians* then ours: Elkes of a large size, admirable meat, having three young at a time; their Hides make good Buffe: besides Hares and Conies, and many other that are good meat: Beasts of prey, that are profitable for their Furres, as Bevers, Otters, Foxes, Martins, Minches, and Musk-Cats, their Cods better scented then those of *East-India*, and more lasting: Fowle of all sorts, Patridges and wild Turkies 100 in a stock, some of the Turkies weighing 40 pound. Fish there are in great abundance, of all sorts. In the Woods are sundry kinds of Fruits, as Strawberries, Raspices, Gooseberries, Plums, and Cherries; three several kinds of Grapes, large, and of a delicious taste. In these Woods are herbes and flowers of fragrant smels, many kinds of singing Birds, which have varieties of sweet Notes. Though this Countrey be for the most part woody, but where the *Indians* have cleared, for their Corne and Tobacco, or where the fresh marshes and medowes are, yet they are pleasant and profitable; pleasant, in respect of the stately growth and distance of the Trees one from the other, that you may travail and see a Deere at a great distance; profitable, being of divers kinds, both for Shipping, Pot-ashes, Mulberry trees for Silk-wormes, Walnut trees, and stately Cedars; so that when of necessity you must cut down for Building, and other uses, you are recompenced for your labour. You also have many pleasant Ascents, Hills and Valleys, Springs of wholsome waters, Rivers, and Rivolets. Now you see you are plentifully fed and cloathed with the naturall Commodities of the Country, which fall into your hands without labour or toyle, for in the obtaining of them you have a delightful recreation. Now fearing you should out of this abundance, in the excesse take a Surfet, you have many Physical herbs and Drugs, Allom, *Nitrum, Terra Sigillata*, Tarre, Rosin, Turpentine, Oyle of Olives, Oyle of Walnuts, and other Berries; Honey from wild Bees, Sugar-Canes, Mulberries, divers sorts of Gums and Dyes, which the *Indians* use for paint. Within the ground, Mines of Copper, Lead, Tinne, Pearle, and Emroydes. Having the profit and pleasure of the natural Commodities, you shall see what Art and Industry may produce. The Soyle is for the most part of a black mould about two feet deepe, you may trust it with any thing. The *Indian* Corne yeelds 200 for one, they have two Crops in six moneths; *English* Wheat, Barley, and Pease, yeeld 30 for one; Hempe, Flax, Rice, and Rape-seed have a large encrease: What *English* Fruits are planted there, improve in quantity and quality. Besides all this is said, we shall shake, hands with *Virginia*, a flourishing Plantation, which is not onely able to strengthen and assist us, but furnish us with all *English* Provision, Cowes and Oxen, Horses, and Mares, Sheepe and Hogs, which they abound in now, which they and other Plantations were enforced to bring out of other Countries with great difficulty and charge, these are ready to our hands.

If this that hath been said give incouragement to any, let them repaire to Mr. Edmond Thorowgood, *a* Virginia *Merchant, living in* White-Cross-street, *at the house that was Justice* Fosters. *He will informe you of the Governour, from whom you will understand when and how to prepare themselves (not exceed* August) *and what Conditions shall be given to Adventurers, Planters, and Servants; which shall be as good, if not better, then have been given to other Plantations.*

Plantations in *America* were first famous in King *James* his time, the arguments to draw people over were the bringing the Gospell to the Indians, inriching men that went and adventured, and extending Dominion, the fruit whereof is visible, in King *Charles* his time, the persecution of men diffring in opinion revived this undertaking, and thousands went to *New-England* whose condition is also known, now their seems to be great designes of this nature which arise out of the discontents at the present state of affairs, alterations, & the wants which the late War hath brought many unto, for which their seems no blame. For consent be advised to make no use of the Merchant farther then transportation, part with nothing, if an adventurer, but what you are willing to loose to accomodate your friend, lay no foundation of a Plantation for your perticular before you go, when you begin to disburst, resolve to go, leave more or lesse behind you in *England* that may supply the first necessities, which wil be greatest, and thus much be sure, if the Countrey be healthfull to English, its seated as well as any upon which the English are, if not better.

The Ceremonies used in Constantinople *at the Coronation of* Mehemet, *the new great Turke, and Successor to* Sultan Ibrahim *his Father.*

Sultan Mehemet having been proclaimed Emperour the 8 of *August* last past, he was, according to the custome of that Countrey, circumcised the next day following: And untill he had recovered his strength (much impaired, as well by the bloud he had lost, as the pain he suffered thereby) the wives of the last

Grand Signior were removed into the old *Seraglio*; no more of them remayning in the Pallace but the Mother, and Grandmother of the present Emperor. Whereupon he being wel again of the said wound, went, the 16 of the same moneth, to receive the Sword in performance of the Ceremony observed at the Coronation of the *Great Turk*, which was accomplished in the manner following.

Being arrived, by break of day, at the *Mosquee* of *Subvanceri*, scituate in th'end of the Town, and of the Port, he entred under a Tribunall, or Pavillion prepared, and set of purpose in the middle of a great Court, upon foure pillars of Marble; whereupon the *Mufti* comming thither, to put the Sword into his hand, as a speciall mark of th'Empire; He presented unto him an ordinary Sword, an Alcoran, and a loaf of Bread, covered over with a piece of Linnen (which Ceremony they observe, upon a belief they have, that on which so ever of these their Prince shall first lay his hand, rather by chance then any choice, it infallibly denoteth his Disposition, and Inclination; so that if it be upon the Sword, they judge he will be addicted unto War; if upon th'Alcoran, hee will be a man given to the Laws; and if upon the Bread, he wil be gentle and peaceable: According to which Superstition, this Prince having touched the Sword, they judg that he will be warlike: And this being done, he return'd on horsback, throughout the Town unto the *Seraglio*.

{Goes on to describe in ornate detail the procession...} His Highness, in the midst of so great Riches, had on a most goodly Vesture of the *Persian* fashion, and of a Rose colour, set off upon silver, and furred with Ermins; a Turbrnt on his head, with two Heron-plumes, tyed together by two Emeralds; each as big as a Wal-nut; and between his Ey-brows a Fly, painted with Inke, to hinder him, as they said, from being bewitched; but which, in truth, served to render him more ougly then he was of himself; having great goggle-eyes, a high-raised forehead, and a very stern aspect; his sadded countenance shewing that he disdained all this Pomp, which other men so admired, and delighted in, as being no better then a Consequence of the Disgrace done unto his Father.

He was followed by his Sword-bearer, Clokeback-bearer, & Stirrup-holder; who are commonly called *Celictar, Chaonnadar*; and *Requiptar*; wearing Caps of white felt, like the *Janizaries*, save that they wanter the silver hooks for Feathers: and after them went the Falkeners of the *Serrail*, with their Velvet Bonnets; which had better countenances, and better clothes then those that had gon before them; to the end they might not leave, being the last, any other then goodly representations in the memory of such as were present at this Ceremony; which continuing till night, received a new lustre by the Lamps that were alighted in many places, by reason of the solemnity kept by the *Turks* that Day, when they imagine that their Prophet mounts up to Heaven to confer with God.

A revival of *Hamlet* in Naples.

The Moderate *Numb.* 57.

7–14 August, 1649 413.2057 {6.10}

Naples, July 24.

The fourth instant our Vice-King had a Comedy acted before him, wherein was represented the miseries and calamities which are procured by a civill war, and the great benefit which is reaped by peace and tranquillity, and all under the shadow of Poeticall Fictions; to this was invited our Archbishop, the Popes Nuntio, with all the Princes, Nobility and Gentry of this Court, but it had a Tragicall end, for ere the week was expired, severall persons were executed, and among them Monsier *Fabroni* Secretary to the Duke of Guise, who being arrived in Spain, hath been carried prisoner into the Castle of Escicha, where he is used with all respect and civility, the King of Spain having sent 24000. Crowns for his maintenance.

The missionary John Eliot, 'Apostle to the Indians', displayed an exceptional sympathy for the heathen; his letter also provides an unusual insight into missionary psychology. His sense of isolation was typical among Puritans. The letter also mentions the terrible impact European diseases had on the indigenous inhabitants of America.

Severall Proceedings in Parliament *Num.* 105

25 September – 2 October, 1651 599.105 {6.11}

A Letter from New-England, *from Mr.* Eliot, *preacher of the Word there, of the glorious progresse of the Gospell among the Heathen there.*

Much honoured and beloved in Christ,

THe Providence of God giving this unexpected opportunity of sending. I thought it my duty not to omit it, that so the Saints and people of God with you (especially your selfe, with the rest of the worshipfull Corporation) might understand the progresse and present state of this work of the Lord among the *Indians*, for we meet with changes of providence, and tryalls in this our day of small things, it hath pleased the Lord to try them, so soon as they have but tasted of his holy wayes for our natures cannot live without Phisicke, nor grace without affliction, more or lesse, sooner or later.

The Winter before this last past, it pleased God to work wonderfully for the *Indians* who call upon God in preserving them from the Pox, when their prophane neighbours were cut off by it.

This Winter it hath pleased God to make lesse difference, for some of ours were also visited by that disease; yet this the Lord hath done for them, that fewer of them have dyed thereof, then of others who call not upon the Lord, only three dyed of it, but five more (young and old of other diseases,) now (through the Lords mercy) they are well, though not without ordinary infirmities which befall mankind.

In matters of Religion they go on, not only in attendance on such meanes as they have, nor only in knowledge, which beginneth to have some clearnes in the fundamental points of salvation, but also in the practice and power of grace, both in constant care in attendance on the worship of God, on Sabbath dayes and Lecture dayes, especially profitting in the gift of prayer, and also in the exercise of love to such as be in affliction, either by sicknesse or poverty.

I have seen lively actings of charity, out of reverence unto the command of the Lord, when such as had not that Principle, were far from such works of mercy. It pleased God to try them in the time of the Pox, for some of them did hazzard their own lives (for to them it is very mortall) in obedience unto the command of the Lord, to shew mercy to them that were sick, and some were infected thereby, and fell sicke; and lay with much chearfulnesse and patience under Gods hand, and through the Lords mercy are wel again, and others who did shew mercy in that case, escaped the sicknesse to the praise of God. {…}

Likewise God is pleased to try their charity by an old paralitick or palsie sick man, whose own children being prophane, and tyred with the burden of him (his retentive power of holding excrement being loosened) and having a loosenesse, sometimes he is very noysome and burdensome) they forsook him, and he had perished, but that the Lord stirred up (by the word of his grace) their hearts to shew mercy unto him: he was while he was sick at six shillings a week charge, for we offered one shilling a night to any to tend him, and for meer hire none would abide it, but out of mercy and charity some of the Families did take care of him, and gave freely some weeks, and for others were paid out of their publick monies, namely, such as hath been paid by such as have bin Transgressors, by Fine or mulct; and still he is at 4*s*. a week charge, being better in health; insomuch that all their publique mony is spent, and much more, and we have collections among them for the same use.

The old man who hath been and still is wise, doth wisely testifie that their love is sincere, and that they truly pray to God, and I hope so doth he, and shall be saved.

I could with a word speaking in our Churches, have this poor man releived, but I do not, because I think the Lord hath done it for the tryall of their grace, and exercise of their love, and to traine them up in workes of charity, and in the way of Christ to make collections for the poor.

I see how the Lord provideth to further the progresse of the Gospell by these tryalls and afflictions: Yea, there be more passages of this Winters work wherein the Lord hath taught us by the crosse. For one of our first and principall men is dead, which though it be a great blow and damping to our work in some respect, yet the Lord hath not left the rest to discouragement thereby, nay the work is greatly furthered. For he made so gracious an end of his life, and imbraced death with such holy submission to the Lord, and was so little terrified at it, as that it hath greatly strengthened the faith of the living, to be constant and not to fear death, greatly commending of the death of *Wampooas*, for that was his name. I think he did more good by hs death, then he could have done by his life.

One of his sayings was, *That God giveth three mercies in this world, The first is, strength and health. The second is food and clothes. The third is, sicknesse and death, and when we have had our share in the two first, why should not wee bee willing to take our part in the third, for his part he was,* I heard him speak thus, and at other times also; and at his last he so spake, and it so took with them, that I observe it in their prayers, that they so reckon up Gods dispensations to them. His last words which he spake in this world was these, *Jehovah aninnumah Jesus Christ*, that is, *Oh Lord give me Jesus Christ*. And when he could speak no more, he continued to lift up his hands to heaven according as his strength lasted unto his last breath, so that they say of him, he dyed praying.

When I visited him the last time that I saw him in this world, (not doubting but I shal see him again with Christ in glory) one of his saying was this; Foure years and a quarter since, I came to your house and brought some of our children to dwell with the English, now I dye, but I strongly intreat you (for that is their phrase) that you would strongly intreat Elder *Heath* (with whom his Son liveth) and the rest which have our children, that they may be taught to know God, so as that they may teach their Country men, because such an example would doe great good among them. His heart was much upon our intended work to gather a Church among them.

I told him I greatly desired he might live (if it were Gods wil) to be one in that work, but if he should now dye, he should goe to a better Church, where *Abraham, Isaack* and *Jacob*, *Moses* and all the dead Saints were with Jesus Christ in the presence of God in all happinesse, and Glory. He said he feared not death, he was willing to dye, and turning to the company which were present, hee spake unto them thus: I now shall dye, but Jesus Christ calleth you that live to go to *Natik*: that there the Lord might rule over you, that you might make a Church, and have the Ordinances of God among you; beleeve in his world, and doe as he commandeth you, with many such words exhorting them, which they could not hear without weeping.

A little before his death he spake many gracious words unto them, whereof one passage was this: Some delight to hear and speak idle and foolish words, but I desire to hear and speak only the Word of God, exhorting them to do likewise: His gracious words were so acceptable and affecting, that whereas they used to fly and avoyd with terror such as lye dying: now on the contrary they flocked together to hear his dying words: whose death and burial they beheld with may tears, nor am I able to write his story without weeping.

Another affliction and damping to our work was this, that it hath pleased God to take away that Indian who was most active in Carpentry, & who had framed me an house with a little direction of some English, whom I sometimes procured to goe with mee to guide him, and set out his work. Hee dyed of the Pox this Winter, so that our house lyeth, not yet raised, which maketh my abode among them more difficult, and my tarriance shorter then else I would, but the Lord helpeth me to remember that he hath said, endure thou hardness as a good Souldier of Jesus Christ, these are some of the gracious trials and corrections the Lord hath exercised us withall, yet hee hath mingled them with much love and favour in other respects. For it hath pleased God this Winter, much to inlarge the ability of him, whose help I use in translating the Scriptures, which I account a great furtherance of that which I most desire, namely, to communicate unto them as much of the Scriptures in their own language as I am able, besides it hath pleased God to stir up the hearts of many of them this winter, to learn to read and write, wherein they do very much profit with a very little help, especially some of them, for they are very ingenious. And whereas I had thoughts that wee must have an English man to bee their Schoolemaster, I now hope that the Lord will raise up some of themselves, and inable them unto that work, with my care to teach them well in the reason of the sounds of Letters and spellings. I trust in the Lord that we shal have sundry of them able to read and write, who shall write every man for himselfe, so much of the Bible as the Lord shal please to enable me to translate. Besides these workes which concerne Religion and learning we are also a doing (according to the measure of our day of small things) in the civil part of this worke we have set out some part of the Towne in severall streets, measuring out and dividing of lots, which I still set them to doe, and teach them how to do it, many have planted Apple Trees, and they have begun divers Orchards.

Its now planting time, and they are full of businesse, yet we are doing some publique work. The last week I appointed our lecture to be at a water which is a comon passage, and where the fish we call Ale-wives come, there we built a bridge and made a Wyre to catch fish, and being many of them, some appointed to one work, some to another, through the blessing of God wee brought both these workes to perfection. We also have begun a Pallizadoe Fort, in the midst whereof, we intend a Meeting-house, and School-house, but we are in great want of tooles and many necessaries. And when we cannot go we must be content to creep.

This present week I am going to *Pawtukes* the great fishing place upon *Merimacke*, where I hear sundry do expect my comming, with a purpose to submit themselves unto the Lord, but the successe is in the Lords hand, the ship is like to be gone before my returne. I hear nothing of your Family but health and welfare, but I have not heard any thing lately. I doubt not but you will hear from them.

Sir, I doe earnestly beg your prayers both for me, and for this worke of the Lord which he hath set me about, and being now in hast upon my journey, I can proceed no further, but commending you to the Lord, and to the Word of his God, I rest,

Roxbury this 28*th* of the second Moneth. 1651.

Yours in our deare Saviour Christ Jesus *JOHN ELLIOT*.

Sir I am in much want of Bibles for the Indians, as also paper, Ink hornes, Primers, &c.

Mercurius Politicus had the finest foreign news of any newsbook. Nedham's correspondent in Amsterdam repeatedly represented the insufferable arrogance of Claudius Salmasius, the Catholic intellectual whom Milton had challenged in his *Defence of the People of England*. Here another man of letters also receives a rare mention.

Mercurius Politicus *Numb*. 84.

8–15 January, 1652 361.084 {6.12}

{...} They write also from *Paris*, that M. *Hobbs* (he that wrote the Book of *Common-wealth*) sent one of his Books as a Present to the King of *Scots*, which he accepted, in regard he had formerly been his Tutor in the *Mathematicks*; but being afterward informed by some of his *Priests*, that that Book did not only contain many Principles of Atheism and grosse Impiety, (for so they call every thing that squares not with their corrupt *Clergy-Interest*) but also such as were prejudicial to the Church, and reflected dangerously upon the Majesty of *Soveraign Princes*, therefore when M. *Hobbs* came to make a tender of his service to him in person, he was rejected, and word brought him by the Marquiss of *Ormond*, that the King would not admit him, and withal told him the reason, by which means M. *Hobbs* declines in credit with his friends there of the *Royal stamp*, as men shall, that run not to the same height and excess of madnesse with themselves.

Our *Salmasius* bites his thumbs still in silence at *Leyden*, and gives out, that he scorns to give any Answer to *Milton*; but the truth is, I believe he knows not how to salve those wounds and scars that have been given him. He is now more haughty then ever; and takes himself (I think) for some great Emperor: There is no man so much a *Sot*, as he that is drunk with pride and ambition.

The Pope was notorious in England for his parsimony: this narrative plays on the insincerity and vanity of Catholics in general.

Severall Proceedings of State Affaires
Num. 256

17–24 August, 1654 599.256 {6.13}

Saturday 19 *July*. {...}

There is an Irish man formerly a Popish Priest in *Ireland*, newly come from *Rome* into *England*, being converted thus:

He had been with the Pope, to whom he made an Address, and had audience in behalf of the Irish Papists lately of that Country, and being come before the Pope, he made a pittifull Declaration of the miserable and distressed condition of the Romish Catholicks of *Ireland*, through the Wars, after which the Pope lift up his hand, and prayed in Latine, *The Lord help you*.

The Priest told him that he did thank his Highness for praying to God to help them, but withall desired help from him, they being in a miserable suffering condition, and like to perish if he did not something for them, to which the Pope replyed, That he had little enough for the supply of himself, and those that are under his charge, and had nothing that he could spare for them.

The Priest replied to the Pope, that the Hereticks (for so they call the Protestants) had driven them out of their Country, and they are undone, and have nothing to subsist, all being taken from them. To which the Pope replyed, Why did you let them drive you out of your Country, you should have staid there and fought it out, and rather have laid down your lives then suffered them to take your Country from you.

The Priest again replyed to the Pope, that they did fight whilst they had power, and many thousands slain of them, and that they had lost all for Religion, and suffered out of their affection to the Romish Catholick Religion, and therefore left their Country, and their Estates that they might enjoy their Religion.

The Pope told him, that they were the more fools for their labor, and that it had been better for them to have staid and kept what they had, and then (holding out his Foot to kiss his Toe) dismist him, who is now come into *England* and pretends to be a Convert.

Nedham's eager anticipation of the Pope's death reached comical proportions. After many false reports, however, the Pope did die.

Mercurius Politicus *Numb:* 243

1–8 February, 1654{5} 361.243 {6.14}

From Paris February 6. *stilo novo.*{...}

The lastest advice from *Rome*, of the 12 of the last month confirms the death of the Pope, which was somewhat dreadfull, he lying 4 days in an agony, not taking any sustenance, and making strange outcrys, lilling out his Tongue, which was very much sweld, and black and blue: He dyed the 7 of the last month about 8 in the morning; whereupon the Cardinall *Anthonio Barberini*, with the Clerks of the Chamber, made proclamation of his death, taking into his custody the Seal called *Annulus Piscatoris*, which he brake in presence of the colledg of Cardinals. About 3 a clock the next morning, the Popes body was carryed in funerall pomp from *Monte Cavallo* where he dyed, as farr as the *Vatican* in a Litter of red crimson Velvet, which is the usual mourning colour for the Popes. The next day, the Cannons and clergy of *St Peters* went to receive him, and carried him into their church. But it is very remarkable, that so great a stench issued from his body, that a man could not endure to come near it. And while they were carrying it, there fell out so great a tempest with Thunder and Lightning, that all the Inhabitants of the city were much terrified at it. Being placed in the church, he was there exposed to the open view of the people till Sunday, being cloathed in red, and his Pontificall habit upon a Bed of state, and that night he was interred.

Mercurius Politicus *Numb:* 245

15–22 February, 1654{5} 361.245 {6.15}

From *Rome*, January 25. {...}

The late Pope, a little before his death, took a Ring off his finger, of very great value, which he delivered to the Sieur *Scotty-Major*, to be by him presented to the succeeding Pope; which the Lady *Olympia* desiring to view, he refused her. The common people of this City, and others, are very much offended, that this Lady, and the Prince *Pamphilio* her son, and the rest of the Popes Kinred, shewed so little of charity, and honor, at his funeral, that they did not provide for him two Chests, one of Lead, and another of Cypress-wood, according to the usual manner of Popes, insomuch that for want thereof, his body was left in the lower Hall, in a nasty pickle, to the mercy of Rats and Mice, which gnawed part of his Nose and Face, through the negligence and drowsiness of those that watched it; which verifies the Prophesie delivered some time since by an Astrologer concerning this last Pope, *Carebit propriâ Sepulturâ, He shall want a convenient Burial.*

Notwithstanding all diligence hath been used, in enquiring after the Authors of those bitter Pasquils, which proclaim most horrid things touching the deceased Pope, and most severe punishments are threatned against them, yet they proceed in revilings every day; so the Father *Olivia*, a Jesuit, his Ghostly Father, to vindicate him, hath put forth a brief Relation of all that passed at the death of his Holiness, assuring the world, that before he died, he gave very eminent Testimonies of his Piety, and manifested an entire resignation to the Will of God, and a very great willingness to part with the world.

New England, a refuge for the godly, was not necessarily a refuge for *all* the godly, and soon became a seat of intolerance. Pamphlets describing the transgressions of New-England Puritans disillusioned those who had been inspired by the prospect of a New Jerusalem, and served to frighten others who were themselves hostile to sectaries.

The Weekly Post Numb.221

3–10 April, 1655 544.221 {6.16}

From New-England we have received intelligence, That many there are who hold sundry heretical Opinions; amongst the rest, one Mrs. Dyer, held a monstrous opinion, uttering several blasphemous expressions against the Nativity of Jesus Christ, and the Virgin Mary; and being big with child, was brought to bed of a Monster, which had no head, the face stood low upon the breast, the eares like an Apes grew upon the shoulders, the eyes stood far out, and so did the mouth, the Navel, belly, and distinction of the Sexe, were where the hips should have been, and those back parts were on the same side with the face, the armes, thighs, and legs, were as other childrens: but in stead of toes it had on each foot three claws, with Tallons like a Fowl: upon the back above the belly, it had two great holes like mouths, and in each of them stood out two pieces of flesh: it had no forehead, but in the place above the eys it had 4 horns, two of which above an inch long, hard and sharp, and the other two somewhat less: it was of the Female Sex; both the Father and Mother of it were great Familists, but now reported to be turn'd Quakers.

The conquest of the New World, over the efforts of other European States, had ultimately utilitarian ends which could overcome mere expressions of wonder.

Mercurius Politicus *Numb:* 256.

3–10 May, 1655 361.256 {6.17}

Another from *Barbado's* Island, March 16.

Through Mercy we arived safe here in five weeks time, a passage seldom known to be so comfortable, and more it would be, had we our stores from London, which we expect. Had they come along with us, and not been lockt up by these Easterly winds, in the River Thames, which carried us from Portsmouth, we had now been upon the execution of our design; whereas now we stay in expectation of their coming in every day; but by this delay we had the opportunity to deal the more favorably here with the Inhabitants, in compleating our Regiments to a competent number, and raising one whole one upon the place, whereby we hope our Land-Army will be doubled.

We are taken up with many businesses, and so much the more, by reason of our making prize of the Dutch ships, which we found here, and must help to transport our new Levies.

But what debts the Dutch Traders have due to them, we are feign to enquire after on shore, because they being stubborn will acknowledge nothing, nor will the Inhabitants, because they love to trade with the Dutch, though they can give no solid reason for it, and they are no great well-wishers to this expedition, fearing it may spoil this Island. Indeed, we found our *English* Merchants utterly discouraged here, and their factors wearied out here, because of the Dutch, who carry away the harvest of Barbadas. They had sold off most of their goods before we came, or else we had met with them to purpose; however, we have once more rooted them here, and sent force to the Lee-ward Islands to do the like: And we have settled a Court by Commission here, not onely to levy what shall appear to be theirs, or owing to them, but to make seizures from time to time of all such as shall attempt to trade here. The most we have gotten (beside vessels) is, that a Dutch Merchantman, since our Arival, coming in with 246 Negroes, we have sold them for about 5762 l. and another vessel which had in her about 23 Asses, is not yet sold.

The Gentlemen of the Island are very civil to us, and give us many costly Entertainments at their Plantations, though the Quartering of our Forces lies heavy upon them, who (for their parts) do very much honour our Expedition, and will give all possible Assistance to dipatch us away; wherein the honour of his Highness and our Nation engaged, our lives we shall not account dear unto us to preserve the same. We have laboured and wrastled with difficulties, and at length so far supplyed our selves one way or other, as we intend to set sail hence the 26 instant. We have raised 3000 men, and two Troops of horse, raised and armed by particular persons, who mount themselves as a Life-guard to our General. We are now 6000 Land, and 5000 seamen. The Lord in mercy go along with us.

The massacre of the Piedmont Protestants by Italian soldiers was, like the 1641 rebellion in Ireland, startling news in Britain. The butchering of the faithful, God's chosen people, surrounded by vast numbers of Catholics, bred anxious speculation at a distance from which intervention was impossible. Milton wrote a fierce sonnet on the subject: 'Avenge, O Lord, thy slaughtered saints ... Slain by the bloody Piemontese that rolled Mother with infant down the rocks.'

Mercurius Politicus *Numb:* 257.

10–17 May, 1655 361.257 {6.18}

From Lyons may 8.

We have received certain aviso, that the poor Protestants in the valleys of Angrogne, Lucerna, and St Martin within Piedmont, have of late bin sorely vexed and persecuted by the Duke of Savoy, whose Subjects they are: he being moved to it by that Devilish crew of Priests and Jesuites, who prevailed so far with the Duke, that first he affrighted them with great threatnings; next they proceeded to take away their goods and estates, putting them in prison, carrying away their children, and using all means that can be imagined, with all violence, to make them revolt and forsake their Religion; notwithstanding all which, and the many miseries and heavy pressures they still lye under, for the maintaining of the true and orthodox Religion, according to the purity of the Gospel, which they still constantly profess, their enemies perceiving that they could avail nothing their rage was so inflamed, that they have perswaded the said Duke of *Savoy*, to constrain them with violence; who thereupon sent an Army to destroy them, although they have been always true and faithful Subjects. The Army was of above eight thousand men, under the command of the Marquess *de Pianella*, and the Earl of *Quince*, who set upon these poor people living quietly at hom (therein shewing their great valour) who seeing themselves thus assaulted, and that they aimed at their lives, and of their wives and children, stood in their defence, and made what resistance they could against them, there were many of them slain, and some of the Enemy; many carried away prisoners, upon whom they have used all manner of cruelties that could be invented, before they put them to death; some residue that have escaped the slaughter, are got into the Mountains with their Wives and Children, while the Enemy set their Churches on fire, plunder their houses, and then fired them; a very small number with their families are got into the *Daufine* in the French Dominions, and some others in *Switzerland* : It may easily be gathered from the premises, what a sad and lamentable condition they are now in, after long and heavy sufferings; all the true Protestants being bound by charity to have a fellow feeling of their miseries: so much the more, by reason that it will appear by good proofs, that they have retained among them the purity of the Gospel ever since the Apostles time, notwithstanding many cruel persecutions raised against them, by the malice of the Devil & Antichrist, without any mixture of Idolatry or Superstition. These are those who were cruelly persecuted by the Papists, about five hundred years since, and then were called *Vaudois* and *Albigois*, by the next you will have more particulars about this business.

Mercurius Politicus *Numb*. 262.

13–20 June, 1655 361.262 {6.19}

***Take next part of a brief Account (as it was sent from beyond sea) of the inhumane Bucheries acted upon the poor Protestants under the Duke of* Savoy; *which is as followeth*;**

AMongst so many furious assaults, so many violent attempts, and so black deceits and treacheries, the ayr being all on fire by reason of the flames, or all duskish by the smoak of burnt Houses and Churches, did resound nothing else but the Crys, Lamentations and fearful Scrichings, made yet more pitiful by the multitude of those Eccho's which are in those Mountains and Rocks.

The Mother hath lost her suckling Child, the Husband his Wife, the Brother his Brother, some have been barbarously massacred, whilst they were busie in saving some of their goods, others having fled to escape to the tops of the Mountains, were forced to cast themselves into the hollows of Rocks, and amongst the snow, without fire, without nourishment, without covering, sick, old, wounded, women with child, of whom many miscarried, and lay dead near their children, after they had sustained themselves with a little Snow, which was put and melted in their mouthes instead of Sugar. Amongst many who were forced to run away bare foot and bare legg'd, several persons of great quality had their legs and feet so long frozen by snow and ice, that they have altogether lost them.

On the morrow after, being the 21. the boutefeus and murtherers were not idle. A Monk, of the Order of S. *Francis*, and a Priest, who were desirous to have the honor to be the chief incendiaries, with their fire works (which they easily could do) did not fail to set on fire the Church of S. *John*, and almost all the remaining houses, part in *Angrogne*, and part in *la Tour*. And where they found any corner free from the first fires, the Priest did but discharge his carbine to make an end of it; and the Souldiers being fleshed with blood, did run to the very tops of the Rocks and places, which seemed to be inaccessible, to cut the throats of all such as they should find there. It was not a difficult thing for them so to do, since they were not in a posture to make any other resistance, but by their tears, which might have caused the most barbarous Tartarians and Cannibals, to let fall their arms out of their hands. At *Taillareta*, a very small village scituated upon one of the highest hills of *la Tour*, they offered a thousand injuries to an hundred and fifty Women and little children, and then cut off their heads; whereof they did boil many, and eat their brains, but left off, saying, they were too unsavoury, and that it went against their stomach; they cut many others in pieces and bits, which they threw the one at the other. From a poor woman that escaped them, and is yet living, although she was cruelly treated by them, they took her little child in swadling Bands, and threw him from a precipice with many others. And there have been many others who have been torn and split in the middle by two Souldiers, who took those innocent creatures, one by one leg, and the other by the other, and after they had torn each one his half, they beat one another with it. They stripped naked many people, without either distinction of age or sex, and cut their bodies after such a manner, as would make one tremble to hear it recited, and then threw upon them Salt and Gunpowder, and then putting on them their shirts again, they set them on fire, making them burn upon these poor martyrized bodies. Other being naked, were tyed neck and heels together, and rouled down some precipices. They were so barbarous, as not to exempt one *Peter Symonde* of *Angrogne*, being a hundred years old, nor his wife, who was ninety five; they burnt a great many in their houses, refusing to kil them before, though they requested it: to others they opened their breasts; to others they pulled out their guts, and cut off their privy parts; after they had abused several women, they thrust many stones in their privy parts, and walked them in this posture till they dyed.

They hanged others upon Trees by the feet, and left them in that estate till they dyed. They gaunched many, both by the Fundament, after the Turkish manner, and across. They staked others through the Belly to the ground, and drove the stakes into the earth as far as they could. Of those whom they brought before the Marquis, & who would not abjure their Religion, they carryed away to *Turin*; and among others Mr *Cross*, and Mr *Aghit*, Ministers of *Villars* and *Boby*; and that after they had seen the admirable constancy of *John Paikas*, and Mr *Paul Clement*, that a poor peasant, this an Elder and Deacon of the Church of *la Tour*; the former having chosen the Gibbet rather then the Mass, the other was carryed near him to appale him; but as hee was on the top of the Ladder, & the Missionaries redoubling their exhortations, saying it was yet time enough if he would turn Catholique; he spake to the Executioner to do his duty, desiring him to dispatch, & pray'd God to pardon those Murderers, although (said he) he saw, as present, the vengeance that God would take for so much innocent blood spilt.

My pen falls from my hand in describing these things; yea, the very thoughts of them makes my whole body to tremble, my hair to stand up; a heart of Adamant, a hand of steel, and a pen of Iron, could not express, half the horrid prodigies of cruelty and lamentable spectacles which were seen, unheard of among the most barbarous in former ages; far from ever being exercised in Christendom. You might have seen here the leg of a Woman, there the head of a Child, sometimes the privie members of a man, the intrails of another, and sometimes the pieces of another, which the Beasts had not yet made an end of eating. Tears obscure my sight, and the violence of sobbing hinders me from proceeding further.

Having paused here a little and taken breath, I shall say farther, that a poor old man, being ninty five years old, called Mr *Thomas Margher*, having been taken among the rest, a French Officer, who was present at his Martyrdome, relates of him, that at the first time he refused to go to Mass, his Nose was cut off; then being asked again, Whether he would go to Mass, and having answered, he would rather choose to dye, one of his Eares was cut off, and then the other; and so every time he said he would not go to the mass, one or other of his Limbs was cut off; at length they hanged him as they did the other two abovenamed; and then this good old man with a smiling countenance would say to his Executioners, *Do ye tye and torment my Body as much as you please, yet you cannot touch my Soul, nor have ye any prisons or chains that can keep it from going to heaven; but on the contrary, according to the course of nature, having so little time yet to live in this world, ye doe but hasten my deliverance, and my happiness*. Then having given thanks to God for the honor hee did him to suffer for his name, he prayed the Hangman to perform his duty.

Of the spoil of Provisions, of Wine spilt in abundance by those who puld off the Iron hoops from the Vessels, or of the Cattell, or of their plunder, say we any thing; The very Women came from the farthest part of *Piedmont*, and carryed away all to the very Brooms.

There were military as well as commercial aspirations involved in the exploration of New Worlds. Jamaica was one of the permanent territorial gains of the Protectorate, acquired during an otherwise ruinous expedition. This story suggests that the soldiers' very wonder at the vegetation presented them with danger. It is an odd mixture of delight and violence.

Mercurius Politicus *Numb.* 269.

2–9 August, 1655 361.269 {6.20}

August 8 To speak more fully and exactly to our *West-Indian* affairs, know that upon Saturday last there arrived an Express from the Fleet and Army in the West-Indies, with Letters from the Generals and Commissioners there to his Highness, to the effect following.

We left *Barbadoes* the last of March, and came to St. *Christophers*, where we found a Regiment formed, which we received into our company, not staying to anchor. Thence passing forward, we came in sight of *Sancta Luz, Porto Rico*, and some other Ilands, and on the 13 of April arived before *Sancto Domingo*, part of our forces landing within six miles of the Town, without any opposition, but the main of the Army landed near 40 miles beyond it, contrary to what was intended; which fell out in respect of the absence of the Pilot, who being sent out to discover, returned not in time. This occasioned a very long march for the army through Woods and narrow Lanes, and all without any guide; which with the heat of the weather, and want of water, put the Army into some weakness and distemper, and made them very unfit for service. The Soldiers likewise stragled from their Colours to gather Oranges, Lemons, Pines, &c. the extraordinary eating whereof put many of them into the Flux, and Feavers. In this condition we advanced near the Town, where our forlorn, being surprised by an Ambush, and their Leader Adjutant-General *Jackson* running away, were put to a retreat by 300 men; and there Major-General *Heans* keeping his ground, was slain. This Ambuscado was afterwards routed by some of the Sea-men, who came up to relieve the Forlorn. *Jackson* was cashiered for cowardize, and he had his sword broken over his head.

After this, the Army retreating for some refreshment, it was thought most convenient by the Officers, and most for the service, to leave that Iland (the Army being weakened by their aforesaid long march) and to attempt the Iland of *Jamaica*: And having shipped the Army, we arived there upon the 10 of *May*, and took the Town of *St. Jago de la Vega*, having beat the Enemy from their Forts and Ordnance, who were got together in a body, consisting of about 3000 men. And from this place nothing did divert our first attempt, but that it had not a name in the world; for, we finde the Country equal, if not superior to *Hispaniola*, and in four miles march here, we saw more Cattle and Plantations then in 40 in *Hispaniola*, and a better air; and the scituation thereof much more advantageous to all purposes. We are now getting horses, whereof there are great abundance in the Iland to make Troopers and Dragoons, to pursue the Enemy, who are fled unto the Woods, and endeavour to get away into the Iland of *Cuba*, twenty Leagues from this; for prevention whereof we have laid some Frigots in the way. The Fleet got safe into the Harbor, which is indeed a very safe and gallant one for riding in all winds. We finde here *Ebonie* in great plenty, store of large Cattle, and Timber in abundance for shipping, and some ships on the stocks in building; the Ground very Fertile, and full of brave Plains and Rivers. There is likewise great store of Salt Peter, which some men among us, who are Powder-men of *London*, do affirm, may be had as good and as plentifully, as in any place in the world, and in three years time they will undertake to serve *England* with it, woods and rivers for carriage being easie here, with choice places to erect Mills. We want onely Workmen, some of our men are already beginning to Plant.

We lost in *Hispaniola* between two and three hundred men by sickness and Skirmishes with the enemy, and killed in the Woods by the Cow-killers, as they were stragling to gather fruit. The Town where our Army is, is a well built Town, of Stone and Brick, above two miles about, and is able to Quarter Twenty thousand men.

The English found it easier to treat 'Indians' as human beings when they were being murdered by the Spanish. This story followed soon after the news of the massacre in Piedmont.

Perfect Proceedings of State-Affaires *Num.* 309

23–30 August, 1655 599.309 {6.21}

From Generall *Penns* Fleet, and the Forces at *Jamaica* in the West India's, it is advertized that they have an army there in the Field, & have had some skirmishes with parties of the *Spaniards* that lye in the woods, and hope shortly to quit that Island of them, But there are very few Indians there, those they had were slaves, though when the *Spaniards* first came thither, there were in that Island of *Jamaica*, and the Island of St. *John*, six hundred thousand Inhabitants; but all destroyed by the Wars, except those few they reserved for slaves, and shared them amongst them; who are now almost extinct in this Island, and the rest of the adjacent Islands. Instead of teaching them the knowledge of God, they were cruell and covetous towards them. Some men have been spent in the Mines, some women consumed in Tillage; and many men and women by heavy burthens which they made them carry, by Famine, by scourges, and other miseries have been destroyed. They have ripped up women with childe, lay wagers who could be most exact in cutting off an Indians head, or cut him asunder in the midst; take Infants from their mothers breasts and dash out their brains, and drawn others with tearing; hang'd some, burnd others, cut some of their hands almost off, and hanging by a little, bad them to carry those Letters to their Country men. Broyled the Nobles and Commanders on Grid Irons, stopping their mouths till they dyed; worryed them with Dogges. And since they have been setled there, they have by wiles several times seduced English ships to come in and Trade with them (of which there is good testimony) and when they have gotten them safe to those Islands, they have basely murthered them and seized upon their ships and goods; For which facts of theirs certainly God hath a great controversy with them; The English are in a better condition, as to their own security and supply, then if they had been in *Hispaniola*, only that had been more honorable, but Gods own way is best.

The strange sartorial ways of the French were not without their complications.

Mercurius Politicus *Numb*. 294.

24–31 January, 1655{6} 361.294 {6.22}

From Paris, January 2. stilo novo

On Saturday last, the King being with his mother the Queen, in her Chamber, many Ladies there present took occasion to make Complaint of the Insolences offered by the officers of the Lieutenant Civill to all Ladies and Gentlewomen that pass the

Streets, taking from them their long Scarfs, which are now become a great fashion. These Scarfs being made of *Taffata*, reach to the Feet behinde and before, by which meanes many Thieves and Robbers disguising themselves with them, came into Citizens houses as Women, and so gained access and opportunity to use violence and plunder, and retire undiscovered; which was the reason the Lieutenant Civil put forth an Ordinance prohibiting the use of such kinde of Scarfs, and impowering his Officers to take them away in the Streets: Hereupon the Court Ladies not enduring the Affront, have prevailed so far, that the K: hath promised to take order about it.

Mercurius Politicus *Numb*. 330.

2–9 October, 1656. 361.330 {6.23}

From Cape St Antonio, the West-End of Cuba, in the Indies, July 10.

IN my other Letter I mentioned to you our expectation of a sudden departure from *Iamaica* to Cape *St Antonio*, which hath since succeeded, where wee met with these ships in their way home, they having made some stay at the *Caymanes* to get Turtles, where we also have been since our coming forth, and in one nights time got as many as Victualled our ships for a Fortnight. It is a Fish that eates much like Veale, and of light digestion, which is an excellent commendation in this Country. This is a singular Refreshment to our men, and puts them in heart and patience to expect the Spanish *Armada*, which we are in continuall hope of meeting; and doubt but not in the end we shall be able to return his Highness and the Commonwealth a good Account of our Services.

Mercurius Politicus *Numb*. 334.

29 October – 6 November, 1656 361.334 {6.24}

This following Letter having lain by me for some time, because the Contents seem to exceed all belief; yet seeing it is justified as writen by so judicious a person as *Sir Kenelm Digby*, take it as it came to hand,

And Extract of Sir Kenelm Digby's *Letter to a Friend, From Tholouse in France, Septemeber* 27, 1656.

Sir, I entertain'd you from *Paris* with Miracles of Grace, from hence receive one of Nature. The following are the words of Mr *Fitton's* Letter of July 2, from Florence. *Sir*, This is to present my humble service to you, and to let you know of a strange Metamorphosis hapned in *Barbary* not long since; which is, the turning of a whole City into Stone; that is, men, beasts, trees, houses, utensils, &c. every thing remaining in the same posture (as Children at their Mothers brests &c) when the petrifying Vapor fell upon this place. This City is under the King of *Tripoli*, some 4 days journy into the Land. One *Whiting* the Capt. of an English ship (who had bin a slave in these parts) coming to *Florence*, told the great Duke of this accident, and he himself had seen the City. The Duke desirous to know the truth, wrote to the Bassa of *Tripoli* about it, there having been a friendly correspondence between them these many years: The Bassa hath now answered the Dukes Letter, and assures him, that the thing is most true, and that he himself is an Ey-witness of it, going to the place purposely to see it, & that it hapned in the space of very few hours; and withall he hath sent to the great Duke divers of those things petrified; and among the rest, (Venetian Zecchines) turned into stone: Thus Mr *Fitton*.

It seems strangest to me, that an unactive body (as all dry and cold earthy ones are) should thus change Gold, the strongest Resistent in Nature: But it is true also, that little dense Atoms force their way most unresistably into all bodies, when some impellent drives them violently.

This story is a reminder of the danger which could ensue difficulties in translating codes of manners and politeness between cultures. The solution here was to circumvent such codes.

Mercurius Politicus *Numb*. 376

13–20 August, 1657 361.376 {6.25}

From the *Hague* Aug. 16.

On Sunday the 12 of this instant here fell out an odd kind of Accident, which because unusual, I shall relate.

About 7 a clock that day in the Evening, the French Ambassador came riding out of the Park in a Coach and six horses, and by chance met the *Spanish* Ambassador in a Coach with two horses in the walk before the Queen of *Bohemia's* house; which being separated with a Raile from the Coach-way or Walke which goeth about it, the next therefore to the Raile was supposed by the *French* to be the upper hand. Heretofore, when they met one another, they were wont to passe by each other on the right-hand, not takeing notice who was next to the Raile, which in *France* is taken for the upper-hand, but not here. This fell out just in the nick of time when news was brought of the taking of *Montmedi*, which perhaps put the French Coach-man into a fit of braveing, and perhaps made the Spanish Coach-man think himself the more concerned to put a confident countenance upon a bad business: however, so it was that both the Coaches met one another near the Raile, and neither would give way, but stood still with their Horses heads against each other, and the Attendants stood still on both sides.

After a while the People flockt to look upon them, it being Sunday a time of leisure. Divers Sword men came to the *French*, and others with Swords and Pistols, so that there was an appearance of a combat. This brought a great concourse of People about them, so that there was a great fear of a tumult. Hereupon the Lords of *Holland* sent a Company of the Guard, and a Troop of horse to attend by the Boots of each Coach, and another Troop to stand betwixt the coach-horses. The Commissioners of *Holland* in the mean time walked between the Ambassadors, tendring several Propositions. The readiest way to compose the matter, they thought was, to cause both horses and Coaches of both parties to retire back; and if any in the name of this state, whether Soldiers or others, should have caused either of them to retreat back, it would have been taken as an Act of Force: So that after many overtures, when nothing else would do, this expedient was found out; the Railes were sawed and broken down in two Places, and thereupon the *Spanish* Ambassador rod away with his Coach on the right-hand; and the *French* thought he had the upper hand, because he kept the way strait on, without turning to the right or left; the *Spaniard* being as much satisfied, that he had given the *French* so long a stand.

Mercurius Politicus *Numb*. 422.

24 June – 1 July, 1658 361.422 {6.26}

From Suratt in the East-Indies, Jan. 16. 1657{8}. {...}

Of all the treasures of these *Indias*, they have of late lost the most precious, in the death of so wise and fortunate a Prince, that his Subjects do despair, of ever seeing a Successor to his vertues. He had lived to fair Age of 73 years, and possibly you will say to a Doteage, when you hear, that at those years, a person so renowned for his prudence should become fondly enamourd of a young Lady, and grow so extravagant in the passion, as to attempt a reparation to the decays of nature by artificial provocations, which proved violent enough, to dispatch the young Lady as well as the old man. Such was the Exit of the Great Mogol.

CHAPTER SEVEN

The head not quite cut off from the body: Crime and punishment

Henry Burton and John Bastwick, Puritan preachers, both had their ears cut off. William Prynne had his ears clipped twice, was branded on the cheek and pilloried. James Naylor had his tongue bored through with a hot iron {9.21&23}. The body of Oliver Cromwell, sixteen months dead, was disinterred then publicly hung, and his head displayed in a progress around the city, impaled on a pole {10.36–7}.

There are a number of things the historian can do with these facts. The past is, no doubt, a different country where they do things differently; but this should compel the modern reader to observe caution when drawing the conclusion that life in the mid-seventeenth century was nasty, brutal and short. Thomas Babington Macaulay wrote that:

> It is pleasing to reflect that the public mind of England has softened while it has ripened, and that we have, in the course of ages, become, not only a wiser, but also a kinder people.[1]

More recently historians have contested these assertions concerning the quantity of violence in early modern England, and particularly the relation between the quantity of measured violence and the quality of life.[2]

1 T.B. Macaulay, *The History of England*, ed. C.H. Firth (London: Macmillan and Co. 1913), I, 417.

2 Lawrence Stone, 'Interpersonal Violence in English Society 1300–1980', in *Past and Present*, 101 (1983); J.A. Sharpe, 'The History of Violence in England: Some Observations' and Stone's rejoinder, in *Past and Present*, 108 (1985). On the relations between crime, violence and the law see as a background to this chapter; F.G. Emmison, *Elizabethan Life: Disorder* (Chelmsford: Essex Record Office, 1970); J.M. Beattie, 'The Pattern of Crime in England 1660–1800' in *Past and*

It is difficult to reconstruct the levels of violence in the period, and newsbooks cannot contribute anything to the issue of quantity. Nor can they provide a substantial insight into quality. In fact the newsbook accounts in this chapter chart a very limited horizon: their function is not to suggest a picture of the nature of life but to delineate a very public notion of death.

The following extracts are dominated by *Mercurius Politicus* and its Monday counterpart *Publick Intelligencer*. This is in part deliberate: *Politicus* had a detailed, fluent style which lent itself to seductive narration. It is also, in part, a contingency: *Politicus* was the main propaganda organ of the Protectorate, and had a privileged position from which to report the executions of traitors condemned for attempting to overthrow the government in the 1650s.

Executions of traitors also predominate in the following pages. These were the most public kind of execution: and though the individual means of death vary but little, they are also the most instructive. Writing the crime upon the body was not the only way to make a criminal's death meaningful {7.06&09; 9.23}. The narrative by which a death was represented, a familiar genre to the seventeenth-century reader, also took a didactic form.

Instruction was the emphasis both of public executions and of the pamphlets which accompanied them. These were often written to the rules of the genre and printed prior to the actual event, so they could be sold immediately afterwards. They invested the moment of death with significance, according to the means of killing employed and the lengthy death speech, usually with an extended account of the criminal's penitence. Often this repentance did not solely concern the crime which had brought on the punishment, but represented a much more general sense of guilt.[3] This characteristic, though undoubtedly partly attributable to the conventions of the genre, demonstrates the extent to which the death scene combined the action of internal as well as

Present, 62 (1974); J.S. Cockburn, 'The Nature and Incidence of Crime in England 1559–1625: A Preliminary survey' in Cockburn, ed. *Crime in England* (London: Methuen, 1977); J.A. Sharpe, 'Enforcing the Law in the Seventeenth-Century English Village', in V.A.C. Gattrell, Bruce Lenman and Geoffrey Parker, eds. *Crime and the Law: The Social History of Crime in Western Europe since 1500* (London: Europa Publications, 1980); and Alan Macfarlane, *The Justice and the Mare's Ale: Law and disorder in seventeenth-century England* (Oxford: Basil Blackwell, 1981). For a more general introduction, see J.A. Sharpe, *Crime in Early Modern England 1550–1750* (London: Longman, 1984).

3 J.A. Sharpe, '"Last Dying Speeches": Religion, Ideology and Public Executions in Seventeenth-Century England' in *Past and Present*, 107 (1985).

external restraints on behaviour. As Erasmus said, 'Men, I believe, are not born, but made',[4] and in early modern society internalised constraints were an increasing part of everyday life, replacing less reliable external sanctions.[5] The public execution was one way of communicating an idealised version of the emotional responses of the obedient subject as well as the fate accorded to the disobedient. The scaffold was indeed a stage, but like the (then closed) theatres, its role involved the deliberate transmission of information through mundanely literal, verbal means, as well as through the edifying spectacle of the body subjected to the instruments of death.[6] The scene of death was acted out as a drama, with established roles within which the participants usually performed.[7] The elements of the genre included confessions, not just to the given crime, but representing a much wider sense of guilt and misbehaviour, for instance, disobedience to one's parents {7.08}. Those, like Charles Stuart, who professed their innocence on the Scaffold could attribute their fate to a providential punishment for other sins {7.01,07&11; 5.15}. The texts of these dying speeches would be sold after the execution. Pamphlet accounts of executions placed the theatre of death before an even bigger audience, and served some of the same functions as the executions themselves: the dissemination of the state's idea of the law.

Executions, particularly those of traitors, were displays of the ultimate power of what was in reality a less than omnipotent state. For this reason some of the accounts which follow are brutal. But they are even more tedious than violent. The moment of death is frequently located in a curt sentence after pages of sanctimonious

4 Quoted in Wayne A. Rebhorn, *Courtly Performances: Masking and Festivity in Castiglione's Book of the Courtier* (Detroit: Wayne State University press, 1978), pp.27, 208n.8.

5 Mervyn James, *English Politics and the Concept of Honour, 1485–1642* (Oxford: Past and Present Supplement 3, 1978); and Norbert Elias, *The Civilizing Process*, two volumes, *The History Of Manners* and *State Formation and Civilization*, trans. E. Jephcott (New York: Pantheon Books, 1978).

6 On the latter see Michel Foucault, *Discipline and Punish: The Birth of the Prison*, trans. Alan Sheridan (London: Allen Lane, 1977), part 1. Both Foucault (pp.65–9) and Stephen Greenblatt emphasise the performative nature of the event and its concomitant texts to the exclusion of the informative aspects. Before newsbooks the theatre was for some was a primary secular source of news. See Greenblatt, *Shakespearean Negotiations: The Circulation of Social Energy in Renaissance England* (Oxford: Clarendon Press, 1988), ch.5.

7 Peter Burke, *Popular Culture in Early Modern Europe* (Aldershot: Wildwood House, 1988, orig. 1978), p.197.

sermon and detailed contrition. They therefore cut against the grain of what has been a tendency amongst recent cultural critics to fetishize corporeal punishments, to dwell on texts describing dismemberment and to translate the anatomizing action into an ambivalent symbolic language. Because of the prominent seventeenth-century conception of the body politic, all bodies as represented in texts have become trite analogies for social structures and institutions, for 'technologies of social power'. Too often accounts of physical punishment have turned them into semiotic celebrations of the hierarchies of power (the pinacle of which, in the hands of critics, is another body, that of the immortal Queen Elizabeth, the apotheosis of the hegemonic state.)[8]

It would be unsatisfactory to argue that these metaphoric readings overlook the *real* bodies which are being broken and penetrated and severed. The ostentatious and catholic rhetoric of a debt to the dead, multitudinous and unknown, would be somewhat out of place in the present context, because the newsbook accounts which follow are very remote from real bodies, they are texts, often texts representing a polity staging the basis of its own power by the ultimate public humiliation of its antagonists. As texts they offer themselves up to hermeneutic and metaphoric exercises.

The marrow of the following chapter is a single account from *The Publick Intelligencer*. It describes the execution of three men, and the reprieve of three others, who were condemned to death with the more celebrated Hewet and Sligsby, for conspiring to overthrow the Protectorate. The trial, like that of the king, required the establishing of a High Court of Justice to ensure satisfactory convictions. This passage is particularly interesting and useful because it consists of about half of the newsbook, and contains most of the characteristic elements of accounts of executions. As Edward Hyde, Earl of Clarendon noted, the punishment served a public function:

> besides the two before mentioned, to whom they granted the favour to be beheaded, {Hewet and Sligsby} there were three others, colonel Ashton, Stacy, and Betteley, condemned by the same court, who were treated with more severity, and were hanged, drawn, and quartered, with the utmost rigour, in several great streets in the city, to make the deeper impression upon the people, the last two being citizens. But all

8 Joel Fineman, 'The History of the Anecdote: Fiction and Fiction' in H. Aram Veeser, *The New Historicism* (London: Routledge, 1989); James Holstun, 'Ranting at the New Historicism' in *English Literary Renaissance*, 19 (1989); and David Norbrook, 'Life and Death of Renaissance Man' in *Raritan*, 8:4 (1989).

> men appeared so nauseated with blood, and so tired with those abominable spectacles, that Cromwell thought it best to pardon the rest who were condemned, or rather to [reprieve] them {...}[9]

Actually Stacy's sentence was remitted so he was only hanged. Yet in spite of his unmasked hostility to Cromwell, Clarendon was right to draw attention to the trial and punishments as a statement to the citizens of London. In the last summer of his life, with insuperable financial problems and dissatisfaction among broad sections of the people as well as the army, Cromwell was dying of a political illness.

Some of the following texts are concerned not with executions but with crimes. What they can add to Assize courts and other records, like the accounts of executions is a use of language. This is one of the primary sources for social history, the history of *mentalités*, of belief and scepticism. The study of these accounts and the generic rules they represent does have something to contribute to the sociology of seventeenth-century crime.

An image of a head not quite severed from a body is a dramatic, violent moment, which has both an incommunicable, personal dimension,[10] and a politically charged meaning; but it is also a very small component of a mundane and didactic exercise, often a very boring one.

9 For 'reprieve' manuscript reads 'reproove'. *History of the Rebellion and Civil Wars In England*, ed. W. Dunn Macray, 6 vols. (Oxford: Clarendon Press, 1888), VI, book 14, §102.

10 See Elaine Scarry, *The Body in Pain: The Making and Unmaking of the World* (New York & Oxford: Oxford University Press, 1985).

In April 1642 Sir John Hotham decided, on the behalf of Parliament, to deny the king entry into Hull. Charles proclaimed Hotham a traitor, and in July Hotham, accompanied by his son, was required to defend the port by force. In June 1643, he elected to hasten the conclusion of the war by attempting to surrender the city to the enemy's forces. He was prevented from doing so by his brother-in-law, and was once again declared a traitor, this time by Parliament, and was condemned to death along with his son, Captain John Hotham. The House of Lords attempted to force a reprieve, but the Commons harshly insisted on the superiority of their judgement. The following account from Pecke's *Perfect Diurnall* also mentions Roger l'Estrange, who was to secure a reprieve, and subsequently became the chief journalist of the restored Charles II.

A Perfect Diurnall of Some Passages in Parliament *Numb.* 75

30 December – 6 January, 1644{5} 504.075 {7.01}

Munday the 30. *of December.*

THe House of Peeres this day sent to the Commons for an answer to their message upon Sir *John Hothams* petition the last weeke, for pardon of his life, to which the Lords had agreed, and the businesse being further debated by the Commons, whether it should be put to the vote for concurrence with the Lords, it was voted Negative as before; and a message was sent to the Lords concerning the same, and to acquaint them that the house of Commons had made an order, that no private businesse should be taken into consideration by them for ten daies. {...}

Tuesday, Decemb. 31. {...}

There was great expectation this day of Sir *Iohn Hothams* execution, and great numbers of people went to Tower hill to behold the action, where the Scaffold, his Coffen the executioner, and all things were in a readinesse, but about eleven of the clocke in the forenoone, as he was comming from the Tower towards the hill, attended by the Lieutenant, the Provost martiall, the guard, and divers Gentleman and Ministers in company, a messenger came riding with a reprieve from the house of Peeres, directed to the Lieutenant of the Tower and Provost martiall, requiring them to defer his execution till Saturday next; upon which he was carried backe to the Tower.

The house of Commons having intelligence concerning this businesse that the Execution was deferred, they not assenting to any reprieve or had knowledge thereof, sent an order to the Lieutenant of the Tower, to know the cause why Execution was not done on Sir *Iohn Hotham*, according to the sentence of the Councell of War.

The Speaker falling very ill suddainly in the house, left the chaire, and the house adjorned till the next day. {...}

Wednesday, Ianuary 1. {...}

A report was made to the house of the examinations taken by the Court Martiall of the reprieve of Sir *Iohn Hotham*, which occasioned some debate, and an Order was then made, *That no Officers and ministers of Iustice, established by Ordinance of both houses of Parliament shall hereafter stay the execution of Iustice upon any perticular order, or repreive from either house of Parliament, without the concurrence of both houses, and this Order to be sent to the Commissioners for martiall Law, to the Lieutenant of the Tower and Provost Martiall.*

And it was also further Ordered, *That the Lieutenant of the Tower do proceed to the Execution of Sir* John Hotham *according to the sentence of the Court Martiall on Thursday next.*

Captaine *Hotham* was executed this Day, and this morning before his Execution (having notice by a quick Intelligence (as it appeares) that there would be no pardon granted to his Father) sent a petition to the house of Peeres, writ with his own hand, and another to the house of Commons, for his own pardon, but it would not be granted, the petitions for better satisfaction I shall insert verbatim, *viz.*

To the Right Honorable the house of Peeres in Parliament,

The humble petition of Captaine *Hotham*.

Humbly sheweth,

T*Hat hee acknowledgeth that hee hath justly merited, your heavy displeasure, and deserved the greatest punishment that can bee inflicted upon him, for that hee hath requited your abundant favours with ingratitude, arrogance, and folly, hee well knowes he deserves not any mercy, neither should hee have moved you in it, if your favours clemency, his desolate family, the teares and lamentations of a poore Wife, and helplesse Children, did not move him to sue for mercy, he hath forborne to trouble you, or interest your good intentions, while there was hope of mercy to his distressed Father: but hearing to his great griefe that sentence is un-*

revoked, he is bold to present his miserable condition to your mercifull consideration,

And humbly prayes, that whereas a sentence of death is passed upon him, by the councell of War, that you would mitigate his punishment, and change it, into Fine, or Banishment, or both; and your petitioner will dayly, and duly pray, &c.

Iohn Hotham

To the Honorable house of Commons in Parliament, the humble Petition of Captaine *John Hotham*.

Humble sheweth,

T*Hat he acknowledgeth his faults and his follies, committed by him against you are so many, that all the punishment you can inflict will be according to Iustice, your great abundant favours, he hath requited with arrogance and negligence, so that if his knowledge of your great mercy to offenders did not encourage him, the conscionablenesse of his own unworthinesse would have kept him from hoping for favour, but the cryes and feares of a poore Wife, helplesse children, desolated family, hath moved him a poore condemned Commoner to fly for mercy to the Commons of* England; *and he hath forborne thus long to petition you, because there was hopes, your mercy would have bin extended to his poore distressed Father, and he would not give interruption to his petition, although it had cost him his own life, but since to his great grief he heares that sentence is unrevoked,*

He humbly prayes that your great clemency, and mercy, will look upon him in the next place, and mitigate his heavy sentence of Death, into banishment and fine, or what other punishment you please, and your petitioner, his Wife, and poore Children will ever pray for prosperity to your affaires, and will remaine, *Your humble Petitioner*

John Hotham.

But these petitions not taking effect, though no doubt Captaine *Hotham* had great expectation thereof, he was about eleven of the Clock this forenoone brought from the Tower, to the place of Execution on Tower-Hill, At his first comming upon the Scaffold Mr. *Coleman* Minister of the Tower, and an other Minister, had some conference with him, admonishing him to cleere his conscience both towards God and man, after which Mr. *Coleman* made an excellent Prayer for the occasion, Captaine *Hotham* joyning with him, and after that the Captaine made a prayer himselfe, and at the ending thereof stood up, and turned to the people, made a short Speech, but said little by way of satisfaction touching the matters for which he was to die, but rather contrary in many particulars to the foregoing Petition; I am unwilling to censure the words of a dying man, but otherwayes it might well be conjectured, that he had some confident hopes of pardon for himselfe or his Father; His Speech to the people was much to this effect: *That in regard of the condition wherein he stood, he was lookt upon as an object of shame, and justice, That it had pleased God to bring him to that end for his sins, which he acknowledged to be just, That he had done the Parliament many services, in the preserving of Hull, their Forts, Magazines, Townes and Forces, and (as he said) never miscarried in any attempt*, with some other generall expressions to that effect, and added further, *That he knew no matter of Treason by his distressed Father, that stood in the same condition, as himself (as Treason might be interpreted) against the Parliament, and arrained the proceedings of Parliament in a great measure*.

Upon the conclusion of his speech, Mr. *Coleman* prayed againe, at the ending whereof Captaine *Hotham* prepared himselfe for the Block, whereon having laid his head, the Executioner severed the same from his body at one blow, which his Brother Master *Durant Hotham* standing by tooke up, wrapt in a Scarfe, and laid it in the Coffen.

Mr. *Roger-le-Strange* who as you heard was condemned by the Court Martiall on Saturday last, and the Execution appointed to be this next Thursday in Smith-field, petitioned the house of Peeres, that the businesse upon which he was condemned, might receive a further hearing before the Parliament, and in the meane time Execution to be deferred, to which the Lords agreed, And sent a Message to the Commons, that the councell of War might certifie the State of Mr. *Le-Strange* his case, and the Commons after some debate, concurred with their Lordships therein. {...}

Thursday, January 2. {...}

Sir *Iohn Hotham* (according to the last order) was this day brought to his execution upon Tower hill, it was about 12 of the clocke before he came from the Tower to the Scaffold, and it was neere two of the clocke before execution was done, his unwillingnesse to die appeared by his many delayes, and no doubt but he had thoughts of pardon to the last; to which purpose he had so far prevailed notwithstanding the former denials, that another motion was made to the house of Commons this day, for the pardoning of his life. But such was the resolution of the house to doe justice upon so eminent an offender, that it was again denied: At his first comming upon the Scaffold Mr. *Peters* the Minster told the people, that it was the desire of Sir *Iohn Hotham*, that since he had in his Chamber fully discovered his mind to him, and other Ministers, that many questions might not be put to him, but that he might have liberty to speak what he thought fit concerning himselfe. After which Sir *John* standing before the raile, and his head uncovered, made a Speech to the people, wherein he declared, *That for the businesse of Hull, the Ministers had been with him, and given him good counsell, and that he had declared his mind to them; that for other offences, as rash words, anger, and such things, no man had been more guilty then himselfe. That he had received many mercies from God, for which he had been ungratefull, but he hoped God Almighty had forgiven him, and desired the people to pray for him*. With many other generall expressions to that effect.

Upon the ending of his speech Mr. *Peters* spake againe, and told the people he had something further to commend unto them from Sir *Iohn Hotham*, which was, *That they would take notice in him the vanity of all things here below, as wit, parts, prowesse, strength, honour, or what else. That he had lived in abundance of plenty, his estate very large,* 3000 *li. per annum, and that he had gained much to it. That in the beginning of his daies he was a Souldier in the low Countries, and was at the battell at Prauge*. And one thing very observable Mr. *Peters* desired them to take notice, that he was told by Sir *John Hotham*, that at his first going out for a souldier, his father spake to him to this effect: *Sonne, when the Crown of England lies at stake you will have fighting enough*.

After these speeches Mr. *Peters* made a very pertinent Prayer for the occasion, and after him Sir *John* prayed himselfe; then they sung the 38 Psalme, which Mr. *Peters* read, with some pertinent verses out of other Psalmes, and then Sir *Iohn* prepared himselfe for the block, and after he had put off his doublet kneeled behind the block above a quarter of an houre, which he spent in private prayer, after which he laid himselfe down, and the executioner did his Office at one blow.

Later the same month Archbishop William Laud, who had been languishing in the Tower of London since 1640, was also dragged to the executioner's block. Pecke's account of the execution of Laud animadverted with the Archibishop's death speech, interpolating his own criticisms. There was still a lot of resentment of Laud, though some thought the punishment of an albeit vindictive old man of seventy was tardy and pointless.

A Perfect Diurnall of Some Passages in Parliament *Numb.* 76

6–13 January, 1644{5}   504.076   {7.02}

Friday, January 10.

I Shall begin this day with the execution of the Bishop of Canterbury, who according to the sentence of Parliament was beheaded on Tower-hill this day. At his first comming upon the Scaffold he made his last Sermon (as he tearmed it) or Speech to the people; but how far he dissembled his treasons therein may appeare to any that have had the least knowledge of his life, and carriage. He hath now past the hands of justice, and I have no more to say of him. But will give you the summe of his Sermon or Speech and some observations thereon, to this effect:

G*Ood people*, I am an old man, and my memory short, and therefore being come to this place, I must crave leave to make use of my papers, I dare not trust to my memory.

Good people, this is a very uncomfortable place to preach in, and yet I come to doe it, with this Text, *Heb*. 12. desiring to imitate those that runne with patience the race that was set before them, looking to *Iesus Christ, the author and finisher of our faith, who for the joy that was set before him, endured the crosse, despised the shame, and is set down at the right hand of God*. [*A good Text, but how consonant to this occasion, (judge Reader)* Jesus Christ the author and finisher of our faith, for the joy that was set before him endured the Crosse: *and the Bishop of Canterbury, after a very faire and legall triall for his treasons against the State, is condemned to the block*.

I have been long in my race, I have looked unto Jesus, the Author and finisher of my faith; his blessed and only will be done. I am come to the end of my race, and here I feare not death, the *King of terrours*, so I might be with Jesus, who is locally at the right hand of God: he despised the shame for me, and (God knowes) I despise the shame for Jesus Christ, I am to passe through the red Sea, and my feet are upon the very brink of it; an Argument (I hope) that God is bringing of me to the *Land of promise*: for, that was the way through which of old he led his people: for, before they came to the Sea, he instituted a Passeover for them, a Lamb: Now, if it be to be eaten with sowre herbs, I shall obey it, and labour to digest the sowre hearbs, as well as the Lamb; I shall not think much of the herbs, nor be angry with the hand that gathers them, but look to him who alone governes both the one and the other; for men can have no more power over me then they have given them from above. I am not afraid of this passage through the Red-Sea, for what I could not indure of my selfe, but Christ hath gone through before me, and I shall most willingly drink of this cup, though not as deep as he did: and entring into the Sea, I shall passe through it in the way that he shall please to lead me.

{...} concerning this great and populous City, where it hath been usuall of late, to gather hands, and goe to the great and high Court, to clamour the Parliament, as if they must be guided by them, a way that may endanger a Minister of States life, [*If such a Minister of State as his Grace hath been*.] and bring much judgement upon their own heads: and this hath lately been practised against my selfe, God forgive the abettors, and I forgive them with all my heart. I remember how it was in S. *Stephens* case, [*A good case, but very badly applyed*.] when nothing else would serve, they stirred up the people against him & *Herod* went the same way, for when he took S. *Iames* he would not put him to death, without the people: But take heed of having your hands full of bloud: This is a time, when God, above other things, makes inquisition for bloud, and when inquisition is on foot, *Iere*. 7. The Prophet tells them, what cause they had to take heed of this: It is a fearfull thing, at any time, to fall into the hands of the living God, but then, especially when he makes inquisition for blood, [*Sure the Archbishop forgot, that Israel could not prosper, till Iustice was executed upon* Achan, *and* Sauls *Sons, and we hope our Israel, will now prosper against the common enemy, having executed Iustice upon so great a persecutor of the Church of God.*]

England hath flourished, and been a shelter unto other Nations, when they have been in a storme, but alas now is in a storme it selfe, and God knowes when it shall get out, and is now become like an Oake broaken in shivers, and at every step prophanesse and irreligion entering on apace, (while a prosperous peace did establish it) [*His Grace might well have been put in remembrance here, who were the first disturbers of the peace of Church and State, both in England and Scotland.*] for now we have in a manner almost lost the Church, [*too much by your means*] and too much in this City, and that which all the Jesuits could not do, is brought into a great danger.

Lastly, for my selfe: I shall not be too tedious, I shall hasten to goe out of the world, and I beseech as many as are in hearing to observe; I was a member of the bosome of the *Church of England* as it stands established by Law; in that profession I have ever been brought up, and in that profession I now come to die. This is no time to dissemble with God, at least in matter of Religion; and therefore I have alwaies been estalished in the Protestant Religion, and in that I come to die. What clamour underwent I for labouring to establish an uniformity [*or rather conformity to the Church of Rome*] in the ceremonies and discipline of the Church.

I am accused of high Treason by the Parliament, a crime which my soule ever abhorred; this Treason was charged upon me to consist of two parts: *An endeavour to overthrow the fundamentall Lawes of the Kingdome*; *and, to alter the Religion established*. Besides the answer I gave to the severall Charges, I professed my innocency in both Houses, it was then at the Barre: and now I must come to my Protestation, not at the Barre, but to my Protestation at this houre and instant of my death; in which (I hope) all men will be such charitable Christians as not to thinke that I would hide or dissemble my religion; [*a right Iesuiticall plea*] I doe therefore here (with that caution I did before) submit with all due respect to the wisdome and judgement of my Judges who are to proceed *secundum allegata & probata*.

I have been accused, likewise, of being an Enemy to Parliaments, and to indeavour their destruction: I understood them, and the benefit that comes by them, too well to be so: [*No, then what meanes that counsell of yours to His Majesty, besides the dissolution of the former, before the last, if this Parliament prove peevish, break it off.*] But I misliked the misgovernment of some one or two Parliaments, [*Observe Reader, the Bishop disliked the government of one or two Parliaments, because they went about to regulate the abuses of the Bishop and the Lordly prelacy*; *And therfore the Bishop would breake the neck of all Parliaments hereafter*] and did conceive they might have done well with moderation: *Corruptio optimi est pessima*, there is no corruptions in the world, is so bad, as the corruption of that which is good it self.

Then he prayed God to direct the Parliament, and blesse them, that they may not fall under any misgovernment.

I will not now be long, I have done, I forgive all the world, all, and every one, bitter enemies, or others, whatsoever they have been, which have any way prosecuted me, in this case: And I humbly desire, to be forgiven, first of God, and then of Man, whether I have offended them, or they think I have: Lord forgive them, and now I desire you to joyn with me in prayer.

Upon the conclusion of this his last Sermon, he made a short prayer audibly, kneeling at the Raile, and after he had put off his Canonicall Gowne, another kneeling behind the block, upon the conclusion whereof, the Execution{er}, upon a word given him, cut off his head the first strok.

An example of the didactic nature of punishments.

Mercurius Politicus *Numb*. 8.

25 July – 1 August, 1650 361.008 {7.03}

Monday, July 29.

FRom *Genoa*, notice is given of the discovery of a Plot carried on by divers of their *Nobility*, for the destruction of that *Common-wealth*, and an alteration of the Government, by cutting the Throats of the *Senate*. The *Ring-leader* was convicted in prison, who afterwards laid violent hands on himselfe: Neverthelesse, his corps were exposed upon the *Gallows*, his estate confiscated, his Children degraded, and banish't for ever. A *Pillar* also will be erected, with an *Inscription* of the foul *Crime* thereupon, that it may, together with his Infamy, bee transmitted to posterity.

(663) Numb. 84.

A Perfect Diurnall OF SOME PASSGEAS IN PARLIAMENT, And from other parts of this Kingdome.

From Munday the 3. of *March*, till Mund. the 10. of *March* 1644.
Collected for the satisfaction of such as desire to be truly informed.

Printed for *Francis Coles*, and *Lawrence Blaikelook*, and are to be sold at their Shops in the *Old-Baily*, and at *Temple-Barr*.

Munday the 3. of *March*.

THe House of Commons this day past the List of the Officers under command of Sir *Thomas Fairfax*, and by a Message sent the same up to the Lords, desiring their speedy Concurrence.

An Order was made by the Commons that Mr. *Pryn* should print and publish all the proceedings of the tryall of the late Arch-bishop of *Canterbury*, and to send for all the Papers and Records in relation to that businesse, it were well it were printed in all languages and sent abroad, for the Sermon he made when he lost his head, is translated into severall languages, and published in all Christendome such is the diligence of the Enemy to get advantages.

The Committee appointed to draw up the Declaration and the proceedings of the Treaty, were ordered to hasten the same.

News came to the House of the taking of *Sherrington* Talbot, and Mr. *Dowdswell*, two great Commissioners of Array in *Worcestershire*, and it was Ordered they should be sent for up to the Parliament in safe custody.

The Commons received advertisement by letters from Sir *William Waller*, of the

Pppp

Letters from Sir William Waller to the Parliament of a late defeate given to the Winchester Cavaleers, Col. Phillips slayne Liftenant Colonell Gardiner, and divers others of the enemy taken Prisoners. Severall other late successes by the Parliaments forces at large imparted.

The late fight betwixt the L. Fairfax and Sir Marmaduke Langdaels forces in Yorkeshire at the releiving of Pomfreite Castle fully and truly related.

40

10. *A Perfect Diurnall,* with marginal headlines, reports the epitaph of Laud

---

County Assizes for England, Scotland and Wales were regularly reported in newsbooks. This Scottish example contains a critique of the Presbyterian system of church government and its role in social control. The tortures employed in pursuit of confessions of witchcraft are also criticised.

Mercurius Politicus *Numb.* 126

28 October – 4 November, 1652 361.126 {7.04}

From Lieth, October 23.

On Wednesday last the English Commissioners for Administration of Justice, sat upon Criminall matters at Edinburgh. The first day was spent in reading their Commission from the Commissioners at Dalkeith, calling the Sheriffs of these severall Counties on this side the *Firth*, viz. *Barwick, Selkerke, Peebles, Louthian, Linlithgewe, Haddington*, and *Roxborgh*, and those Sheriffs that appeared not were fined 200 *l.* Scots each, afterwards the Gent' of the severall Counties who were to doe their service, were called, and such as appeared {not} fined 100 *l.* Scotch, and then severall Delinquents were called, and set down for Tryall. Since that, these 3 days have bin spent in the Tryall and Fining of severall persons for Adultery, Incest, and Fornication, for which there were above 60 persons brought before the Judges in a day; and its observable, That such is the malice of these people, that most of them were accused for facts don divers yeares since, and the chief proof against them was their own confession before the Kirk, who are in this worse then those of the Roman Religion, who doe not make so ill an use of their Auricular Confession: som of the facts were committed 5, 6, 10, nay 20 years. There was one *Ephraim Bennet* a Gunner in *Lieth*, indicted, convicted and condemned for coyning Six pences, Shillings, and half Crowns. Also 2 Englishmen, *Wilkinson* & *Newcome* condemned for robbing 3 men, and for killing a Scotchman near *Haddington* in March last. But that which is most observable is, that some were brought before them for Witches, 2 wherof had bin brought before the Kirk about the time of the Armies coming in to *Scotland*, and having confessed it, were turn'd over to the Civil Magistrate; The Court demanding how they came to be proved Witches, they declared that they were forced to it, by the exceeding torture they were put to, which was by tying their Thumbs behind them, and then hanging them up by them, 2 Highlanders whipt them; after which they set lighted Candles to the Soles of their Feet, and between their Toes; then burnt them by putting lighted Candles into their Mouths, and then burning them in the head. There were 6 of them accused in all, 4 whereof dyed of the torture. The Judges are resolved to inquire into the business, and have appointed the Sheriff, Ministers, and tormentors to be found out, and to have an account of the ground of this Cruelty.

Another Woman that was suspected according to their thoughts to be a Witch, was 28 days and nights with Bread and Water, being stript stark naked and laid upon a cold stone, with only an hair Cloath over her; Others had Hair shirts dipp'd in Vinegar put on them to fetch off the skin. Its probable there will be more discoveries shortly of this kind of *Amboyna* usage; but here is enough for reasonable Men to lament upon.

Cromwell supported Mathew Hopkins, the witch hunter, and under Hopkins, the persecution of witches in England increasingly resembled the more vigorous practices in Scotland and on the Continent (though this had been a gradual development through the century). It was easier to adopt a sceptical position towards witchcraft trials in Scotland {3.24}.

Mercurius Politicus *Numb.* 127

4–11 November, 1652 361.127 {7.05}

From *Edenburgh*, November 2:{...}

There was a man condemned for a witch, a very simple Fellow, but he was reprieved. It is very observable in him, that upon a Commission from the Judges in *June* last, and afterwards before the Judges; he confessed himself to have had familiar Converse many times with the Devill. That he gave him a Piece of silver which was put into a Crevice of his Neighbours hous who had cross't him, and thereupon all his Cattel and horses died; and (after 2 years languishment) the woman her self. He said also that he had renounced his name, for which the Devill gave him a new one, which is *Alexander* or *Sandy*. That he sometimes lay with the Devill in the likenes of a woman, with many other stories of that nature; and yet most of them that have conversed with him say they cannot believe him to be indeed a witch. Before the Judges, at his Triall, he denied all that he confessed before, and said he was in a dream. Yea, the very day that he should have been executed, he was not at all afraid, but seemed indifferent, whether to live or die.

The Trueth is, he lived in so poor a condition, and was (through his simplicity) so unable to get a livelyhood, that he confessed, or rather said any thing that was put into his head by some that first accused him, upon the confession of some who have died for witches. By this you may guess upon what Grounds many hundreds have heretofore been burnt in this Country for *Witches*.

Another didactic piece of extreme violence, in which the punishment fitted the crime.

Mercurius Politicus *Numb:* 179.

10–17 November, 1653 361.179 {7.06}

From Paris Novemb. 15. S.N. {...}

There has been a remarkable piece of Justice done at *Mastricht* of late worth taking notice of; A woman having most lamentably murthered her husbands child he had by a former wife, was afterwards apprehended; who presently confessed the fact and was thereupon sentenced to be executed after the same manner. In the River of the *Mase* where she had flung in her child, was a scaffold built, upon which she was brought, and strangled at a stake, and presently her hands and legs were chopt off with the same chopping knife wherewith she had cut off those of her childe, and afterwards she was put into a bag and flung into the *Mase*.

The following two accounts describe the sentencing and punishment of the accused in one of the big treason trials of the Protectorate, which received much publicity in the newsbooks. John Gerard was a Royalist intriguer who recruited help from Peter Vowel, a relation of his, and Somerset Fox, an Islington schoolmaster. Cromwell's Council soon gathered intelligence of their plot, and caused a number of arrests, from whom these three were selected. As in the case of Charles and John Lilburne, a High Court of Justice was established in order to ensure the outcome of the trial. The execution of the three conspirators coincided with the punishment meted on Dom Pantaleon Sa, brother to the Portuguese Ambassador. In November 1653, Dom Pantaleon had been involved in a scuffle with Gerard at the New Exchange, and his attempt to exact revenge had resulted in the murder of a bystander. The first account begins 6 July.

Mercurius Politicus *Numb:* 213.

6–13 July, 1654 361.213 {7.07}

This afternoon also the high Court of Justice sat again in *Westminster hall*, and there was brought before them Mr. *Gerhard*, Mr. *Vowel*, and Mr. *Fox*; the Prisoners were demanded what they had more to say for themselves, and Mr. *Gerrard* and Mr. *Vowel* spake much to excuse themselves, notwithstanding what had been proved against them. After with the L. President *Lisle* made a learned speech, to convince them of the desperate wickedness of their design, and how fully the particulars of the Charge had bin proved, and what punishments the Law had provided in such cases, after which, the sentence of the Court was read severally against all three to this effect, *That upon mature consideration of the Treasons and Murthers plotted, and contrived by them against his Highness the Lord Protector and the Commonwealth, and raising a bloody war in the same, the Court did adjudge them to be hanged by the neck until they be dead*. Mr. *Gerrard* desired the Court that the Execution might be altered, and that he might either be beheaded, or shot to death like a souldier: A Petition to this purpose was also presented to the Lord *Protector*. {...}

Friday, Iuly 7 The high Court of Justice were pleased to send M. *Bond* master of the *Savoy*, to the three persons by them sentenced the day before, to advise and prepare them for another world; In which Christian work having offer'd his best assistance, he found master *Vowel*, the Schoolmaster of *Islington*, very stiff and conceited in his way, as he had appeared at the time of his

Tryall, and so utterly refused to entertaine any discourse at all about the concernment of his soulc.

Summerset Fox did now, as at his Triall, behave himself with much ingenuity and sorrow for his offence, so that mercy hath been shown him, and it pleased his Highness the *Lord Protector* to grant him a Reprieve.

As for Mr. *Iohn Gerrard*, he carried himself to the Minister, with handsomnes and Freedom, but appeared perfect *Cavalier*, alledging his affection to the late King, and that Interest. *Fox* being reprieved, it was determined the other 2 should be hanged together on Monday morning, *July* 10 upon a gallows to be erected at *Charing-Crosse*. {...}

Whitehall Iuly 10.

As concerning the Prisoners lately condemned at the *Upper Bench* about the *Portugall* Riot and Murther at the *New Exchange*, and those that were the same day also sentenced by the *high Court of Iustice* for Treason, they are thus disposed of. It pleased his Highness the Lord *Protector* to reprieve *Summerset Fox,* because of his ingenuous Confession, but this day the other 2 were executed for their Treasons against his Highnesss and the Common wealth, *Vowel*, a Schoolmaster that lived at *Islington*, was in the morning executed upon a Gallows erected at *Charing-Crosse*, and in the same place it was expected *Gerhard* should have suffered the same death, but that he had the favour granted him to loose his head. *Vowel* spake little of the crime for which he suffered but the main of his discourse was to proclaim how great a Zelot he was to the old way of Religion, and to the cause of the late King and his family; wherein he let fall divers expressions tending to sedition, and few of repentance for his fault, touching which he would not speak out, but willed the executioner to doe his office, and so after half an hours hanging he was cut down, and conveyed away in a Coach.

About 4 in the afternoon *Iohn Gerhard* was brought to the Scaffold on *Tower-hill*, his behaviour was sprightly, the substance of his discourse *Cavalier-like*, boasting himself to be of the profession of Religion which was established by *Q. Elizabeth, K. Iames* and *Charls*, to which family he declared his affection. He acknowledged himself guilty of former sins (but named them not) for which he had deserved death heretofore; but as touching the crime for which he was to die, he spent not many words, only he confessed that he knew of the plot. At length he submited his neck to the Executioner; who at once sever'd the Head from the Body.

But a little before he lay down, came the Portugal Ambassadors brother, Don *Pontaleon Sa*. A very observable hand of Providence, that these two persons, *Gerhard* and the *Don*, who began that quarrel, in the prosecution whereof the murther was committed at the New-Exchange, should meet thus to die at the same time and place, for different crimes. It is also to be noted, that God did even mark out this Portugal for justice: For when he escaped out of Newgate at first, he was immediately found out; and now having by order of the Court been remanded to the Keeper of New gate, he was very near an escape thence again, but the Lord prevented him: For yesternight, being the Lords day at night, a new plot was laid for his escaping by two women; the principal Contriver was one Mrs. *Gourdon*, who brought along with her to the prison another woman, who under her womans apparel had a Foot-boys suit on: The womans clothes being taken off, they drest up the Don in them, and so he came down with Mrs. *Gourdon* to the door, where the Keeper narrowly prying under the hood, discovered the fraud, and spoil'd the business, for which perhaps Mrs. Gourdon may receive her reward. This failing, and the hour of execution next day approaching, he was conveyed from Newgate to Tower-hill in a Coach and six horses in mourning, having divers of his Brothers Retinue with him, much lamenting his condition. Being upon the scaffold, he spake somwhat to those that understood him, in excuse of his offence, laying the blame of the quarrel and murther upon the English in that business. So after some few private words and passages of Popish devotion with his Confessor, he surrendred to him his Beads and Crucifix, and his Head to the Block, which was chopt off with somwhat more then a single blow. The rest condemned about that murther, were reprieved all, save an Irish man, who was executed also this day early in the morning at Tiborn.

Severall Proceedings of State Affaires *Num*. 250.

6–13 July, 1654 599.250 {7.08}

Monday 10 *July*.

THis morning the English youth that was in the Ryot, and joyned with the *Portugals* Brother at the New Exchange, was hanged at *Tyburn*, who confest his disobedience to his Parents, his running away from them, and prayed to

God to save his soul, but there was no great considerable thing that he spoke.

This morning also Mr. *Peter Vowel* Schoolmaster of *Islington*, was hanged near the Mews gate, by the place where Charing Cross stood, where were an abundance of people to see him executed.

He had a Roman carriage, a thing too many glory in; many were sorry to see him die so desperately, he being upon the Ladder, put off his Hat, and took his leave of the people several times, & did speak near half an hour; the cheif substance of his discourse was, that he was of the Religion of the Church of *England* as it was established in the late Kings daies, and reproached the present power, but chiefly the Court that condemned him; dyed in a confidence of the work to be carried on by somebody else, though he died in this Cause, to which he declared great affection and willingness to dye, as also his confidence of going to Heaven.

He pulled out two or three handfuls of money which he gave to the Minister that was the Ordinary with him, which he took out of his pockets, and delivered to him, and desired the prayers of the people.

But he declared no compunction at all for the murderous, bloody Design intended, for which he was condemned and suffered death: Praying to the Lord to receive his soul, he was turned off and hanged, and so soon as he was dead, was presently cut downe, and his friends with a Coach which they had brought for that purpose carried away his Corps. {...}

This afternoon *Don Pantaleon Sa*, Brother to the *Portugall* Ambassadour, and Mr. *John Gerhard* were both beheaded together on the Scaffold at Tower-hill, at which time a great arme of a tree, on which many were got up to see their heads cut off, brake, and severall of them are hurt. Where Providence had so brought it about, that those two persons who had begun the Fray at the Exchange (for *Gerhard* was the chief of the English, as the Portugall Ambassadors Brother was chief of the *Portugals*) were both beheaded on the same Scaffold at the same time successively, the one for that Fact, the other for another; for Mr. *Gerhard* was beheaded for the late Plot, as one of the chief of those who should have led on the party that should have murthred the Lord Protector.

Mr. *Gerhard* coming to the place of execution was much agast and his countenance fell, and his spirit much flagged, so that hee with much weaknesse went up to the Scaffold; and being got up had little strength to do any thing, being ready to sink down before the people, and hee spake very little.

The substance of what hee said was, That hee dyed a true Son of the Church of *England*, as it was established in the Reign of the late King *Charles*, whom hee loved with all his heart, and had fought for, and that hee was a faithfull loyall subject to *Charles Stuart* (whom hee called his King) and was willing to dye in his cause; and declared much affection to him, and to his Interest; Hee was so weak that hee said little more; Hee prayed, and being helped to prepare himself, laid himself down, and was even dead in the judgement of those that were upon the Scaffold so soon as hee lay down, before the blow was given, insomuch that hee was not able to give the Executioner the sign, by stretching out his hand, or voyce, or any thing.

The Executioner at one blow cut off his Head, and his body and head being taken up, were put into a Coffin, and carryed away in a Coach.

Don Pantaleon Sa being brought upon the Scaffold, had two Popish Priets with him, and some other Friends, the Ambassadour himself was not there, who had resolved before not to see him in any prison, nor under any restraint, holding it that that would bee a dis-honour to his King; And besides, the Ambasadour was now preparing to bee gone away from the City, and was gone as far as *Graves end*, having packed up his goods two or three days before, but owing many thousands of pounds, some followed him, and sought for satisfaction, and it is said that hee is putting in security by some Merchants, to pay them that followed after him.

The *Portugall* Ambassadors Brother spent a good part of the time in Devotion with those Priests upon the Scaffold, having his Crucifix, and Beads, and other Popish trumpery there with him.

His speech was in Latine, declaring that hee dyed a Son of the Romish Catholick Church, and that hee was willing to dye a Martyr, and such kind of Popish discourse.

When hee kneeled down to the Block, hee laid down his Crucifix at his mouth, esteeming that great Devotion, and in that posture had his head cut off, and was immediately dead upon the blow, but the head was not quite cut off from the body, but hung by some skin, and sinews, or some such like, which by a sliding of the Axe was presently also cut and so severed.

A Coach with six Horses which brought him, did also carry away the Corpse put into a Coffin, brought for that purpose.

Severall Proceedings of State Affaires
Num. 255.

10–17 August, 1655 599.255 {7.09}

Saturday 12 *August*. {...}

A Soldier was this day burnt in the Fore-head at Charing cross with a hot iron and cashiered, for stealing of cloaths in the house where he quartered.

There are two Youths; the one called *Holgate*, and the other *Harlow* brought up prisoners from the fleet, to be tryed at the Goal Delivery for most horrid Buggery with each other, who were first discovered to five young godly Youths of the ships, that had several consultations about it, and upon their discovery revealed it to the Officers, and two more were sent up for that filthy Crime a while before, that are to be tryed the next Sessions.

Severall Letters from other parts of *England* speak much of that horrible sin, being committed by many in *England*, which may endanger its destruction, if the Lords great mercy prevent not. But among others there was the last Assizes at *Lincoln* a Schoolmaster hanged for Buggering one of his Schollars; He was a man that did often preach, and held forth strange Notions; but when he was to die, confest that he was a Papist.

These reports of Scottish Assizes represent some of the crimes in which newsbook writers appear to have assumed that their readers were interested. Adultery was made a capital offence by a 1650 Act of Parliament. In general the impulses of central government in enforcing discipline through legal reform did not carry to the provinces: very few were actually executed for adultery. One interesting aspect of the following report is the case of 'Jock of Broad Scotland', who was punished under the Blasphemy Act, also of 1650, for a kind of irreverent materialistic pantheism. His case is an example of the kind of irreligious belief concerning which there is very little evidence.

Mercurius Politicus *Numb*. 316.

26 June – 3 July, 1656 361.316 {7.10}

From Dalkeith, Iune 21.

THe inclosed proceedings of the Judges in *Scotland* coming to my hands, and conceiving them of publique use, they contain many things remarkable, I thought fit to send them to you, that they may be published.

The names of the Judges that rode the Circuit were *Iudge Smith* and *Iudge Laurence*.

The names of those who were adjudg'd to die this Circuite, and the Causes of their sufferings.

Glasgowe, Aprill 30. 1656.

Iohn Read Accused for the Crime of Buggery with Mares, Kyne and sheep, and found guilty thereof, by an assise, conform to his own Confession, was adjudged to be taken upon *May* 3. to the ordinary place of execution at *Glasgow*, there to bee strangled till he be dead, and afterward his Body to bee burnt to ashes, and his goods to be Escheat for the use of the Commonwealth; and the Mares, Kyne and sheep with whom he polluted himself, to bee searched for, killed and burnt.

Christian Mathie, convict of severall Adulteries with marryed men, she herself being a marryed Woman; *viz*: for adulteries committed by her with *Robert Hill* a marryed man, to whom she bare 3 Children; with *Patrick Hodge*, to whom shee bare one Child; with *Alexander Brackanrege* a marryed man, to whom she bear two children; shee was ordered to be hanged on Wednesday *May* 7. {...}

Ayre, May 6, 1656.

David Old, and *Agnes Dick* his Wives brothers daughter for Incest with other, confest judicially, and found guilty thereof by an Assise, ordained on the first Wednesday of *June* next to the ordinary place of execution for the Burgh of *Air*, and there betwixt two and four hours in the afternoon, to be hanged till they be dead, and all their moveable Goods to be Escheat. The Commissioners at the earnest desire of severall Gentlemen of the Countrey, both English and Scots, delayd the execution of the same sentence pronounced against them, as it is said, untill the first Wednesday of *November* next, 1656.

Helene Wallace, accused for murther of her own child, convict thereof by an assise, and ordained therefore by the Commissioners upon Saturday the 17 of *May* 1656. to be taken to the ordinary place of Execution for the Burgh of *Aire*, and there betwixt 2, and 4 houres in the afternoon to be hanged while she be dead, and all her moveable goods to be Escheat.

Dumfrieze, May 13.

Jane Cranfaird accused for the murther of her own childe, gotten by her in adultery with *Alex: mac Culloch* in *Ringany*, a marryed man, and being put to an assise therefore, was found guilty both of the adultery and murther, and ordained by the

Commissioners therefore to be hanged at the Burgh of *Dumfrieze*, and all her moveables to be escheat.

William Maklehassie accused of bestiality with his own Mare, being put to an assise therefore, was convict of the said Crime, and ordained to be taken to the ordinary place of Execution for the Burgh of *Dumfrieze*, upon *May* 21, and there betwixt 2, and 4 houres in the afternoon to be strangled at a stake till he be dead, and thereafter his body to be burnt to ashes, and his goods to bee Escheat, and the Mare to be killed and burnt so soon as shee can be found.

Alexander Agnew, commonly called *Jock of broad Scotland*, being accused; Forasmuch as by the Divine Law of Almighty God, and Acts of Parliament of this Nation, the committers of the horrid crime of Blasphemy are punished by Death; nevertheless in plain contempt of the said Lawes and Acts of Parliament, the said *Alexander Agnew* uttered hainous and grievous blasphemies against the Omnipotent and Almighty God, and second and third persons of the Trinity, as the same is set down in divers Articles in manner following; to wit,

First, the said *Alexander* being desired to go to Church answered, hang God, God was hanged long since, what had he to do with God, he had nothing to do with God. Secondly, he answeared, he was nothing in Gods Comon, God gave him nothing, and he was no more obliged to God then to the Devill, and God was very greedy. Thirdly when he was desired to seek any thing in Gods name, he said he would never seek any thing for Gods sake, and that it was neither God nor the Devill that gave the fruits of the ground, the wives of the Country gave him his meate. Fourthly being asked, wherein he beleeved, answeared, he beleeved in white meale, water, and salt. Fifthly being asked how many persons were in the Godhead, answered there was onely one person in the Godhead who made all, but for Christ he was not God, because he was made, and came into the world after it was made, and died as other men, being nothing but a meere man.

Sixtly he declared that he knew not whether God or the Devill had the greater power, but he thought the Devill had the greatest, and when I dye (said he) let God and the Devill strive for my soul, and let him that is strongest take it. Seventhly, he denyed there was a holy Ghost, or knew there was a Spirit, and denied he was a sinner or needed mercy. Eightly he denyed he was a sinner and that he scorned to seeke Gods mercy. Ninthly he ordinarily mocked all exercise of Gods worship; and envocacion on his name, in derision saying, pray you to your God and I will pray to mine when I think time. And when he was desired by some to give thankes for his meate, he said, take a sackfull of prayers to the mill and shill them, and grind them and take your breakfast of them: to others he said, I will give you a twopence, and pray vntill a boll of meale and one stone of butter fall down from heaven through the house rigging to you: to others he said when bread and cheese was given him, and was laid on the ground by him, he said, If I leave this, I will long cry to God before he give it me again: to others he said, take a Banock and breake it in two, and lay downe the one half thereof, and ye will long pray to God before he put the other half to it againe.

Tenthly, being posed whether or not he knew God or Christ, he answered, he had never had any profession, nor never would; he never had any Religion, nor never would: also that there was no God nor Christ, and that he never received any thing from God but from nature, which he said ever raigned, and ever would, and that to speake of God and their persons was an idle thing, and that he would never name such names, for he had shaken his cap of these things long since, and he denied that a man has a soule, or that there is a heaven or a hell, or that the Scriptures are the word of God. Concerning Christ he said, that he heard of such a man, but for the second person of the Trinity, hee had been the second person of the Trinity, if the Ministers had not put him in prison, and that he was no more obliged to God nor the Devill. And these aforesaid blasphemies are not rarely or seldome vttered by him, but frequently and ordinarily in severall places where he resorted, to the entangling, deluding, and seduceing of the common people: through the committing of which blasphemies he hath contravened the tenour of the said Laws and acts of Parliament and incured the paine of death mentioned therein, which ought to bee inflicted upon him with all rigor, in manner specified in the Indictment.

Which indictment being put to the knowledge of an Assise, the said *Alexander Agnew*, called *Iock of broad Scotland*, was by the said Assise, all in one voice, by the mouth of *William Carlile*, late Baily of *Dumfrize* their Chancellor, found guilty of the Cryme of Blasphemy mentioned in his Indictment. For which the Commissioners ordeined him upon Wednesday 21 *May* 1656; betwixt 2 and 4 houres in the afternoone to be taken to the ordinary place of Execution for the Burgh of *Dumfrize*, and there to be hanged on a Gibbet while he bee dead, And all his movable goods to be escheate.

The following newsbook, the Monday companion to *Mercurius Politicus*, is dismally crammed with stories of death, six men condemned for the Treason of plotting to start a war against the Lord Protector and to replace him with Charles Stuart. This, the last royalist plot against Cromwell took place in his final summer. Though such plots failed significantly to threaten the Protectorate, the money required to support an adequate Militia contributed to the financial problems of the government. This report is included here because it typifies such accounts in its reliance on the commonplaces of representation, though it is atypical in its extensiveness. The mention of the French King's health seems ironic in context.

The Publick Intelligencer *Numb.* 133.

Monday 5–12 July 1658 575.133 {7.11}

IT was on the first of this moneth that his Majesty of *France* was surprised by a continuall Fever, accompanied with the pain of his head. He was let blood several times, by means whereof, with other remedies, he was presently well amended in health, through the care of his Physitians, to the great Joy of his Subjects, who are abundantly satisfied in observing the great care of the Queen, and of the Chief Minister the Cardinal, who by his presence gave assistance night and day. {...}

London, July 7.

This Morning between Nine and Ten of the Clock, Col. *Ashton*, who was by the Court of Justice sentenced to suffer death as this day, was accordingly conveyed in a Sled from Newgate, drawn with four horses (Dr. *Warmstry* sitting in the Sled with him) to *Towerstreet*, overagainst *Mark lane*-end; where a Gibbet was erected: being come to the place of Execution and taken off the Sled, at his going up the Ladder, he desired Dr. *Warmstry* to pray with him, which Prayer was to this effect.

Dr Warmstry's Prayer at the Ladder-foor in Towerstreet:

O Lord prepare our hearts; Enter not into Judgment with thy servant O Lord, for in thy sight shall no man living be justified. O most great, most glorious, most holy, most merciful, and gracious Lord God, we thy poor unworthy servants, humbly desire to lye low at this place, in this time of extremity, at the footstoole of thy Mercy-seate, beseeching thee for the Lord Jesus Christ his sake to have mercy upon this thy servant. Thou are the God of life, and thou art the God of comfort, thou art the God of all mercy and compassion; In thy hands are the soules of every living creature and the breath of all mankind, thou ownest us, thou healest us, thou killest us, thou makest alive, thou bringest us to the grave, and thou bringest us back again, and thou saiest come again ye Children of men; Thou dost whatever pleases thee in Heaven and in Earth, and in all things. And as for us, O Lord, we are all the work of thy hand and we are in thy hands as the clay in the hands of the Potter; Thou preservest us here, and then we turne again to our dust, and after death come to Judgment, to render an account to thee of the whole course of our lives and conversations, and to receive sentence from God for what we have done in the body, whether good or evill. Have mercy upon thy poor, weak, fraile and mortall creatures, give us not up to utter ruine and destruction, but grant us grace, that wee may glorifie thee both in life and death, that we may be eternally happy; Look in great mercy upon this thy servant here, he is before thee now ready to come to thee, and desirous to lay himself down at the footstoole of thy mercy, and there to beg for a pardon. Thou hast been pleased to bring him to shame here bring him to glory and eternall happiness of felicity by and by. Pardon his sins, O Lord, wash away all his iniquities with the precious blood of thy dear son; he hath mourned for it, thou hast seen his tears Lord, put them into thy bottle and let the water of his tears be turned into the wine of spiritual joy, and everlasting comfort. Grant he may be more and more humbled for his sins, that thou mayest more and more exalt him, and that there may be a holy purpose in his soul, and that unfeigned; that if his life were longer, to spend it wholly in thy service. Give him a stedfast faith in thy promises, and in thy great mercies in Christ Jesus: make him to know, that though he is miserable himself, and hath deserved damnation, yet the death and passion of Christ hath satisfied for his sins: {...} Remember us in mercy, and pardon the sins and transgressions of this City and Nation, that thou mayest be reconciled to us, and repair us, and restore us, and be a God of blessing again; remember thy mercies for thy Sons sake, in whose Name we commit thy servant, to thee, into thy bosom, and under the shadow of thy wings: Give him strength, patience, meekness and humility; give him a sure and stedfast faith in thy mercies, and give him a flaming love to thee, and a heavenly mind desirous to come to his Saviour; that he may say, *Come, Lord Jesus, come quickly*; we desire to give him up to thee; send thy holy Angels with a Commission of mercy from the throne of Mercy to convey his soul to eternal hapiness. Amen, Blessed Jesus. *Our Father which art in Heaven*, &c.

And just as he was going up the Ladder, the Doctor used these following words to him: [*Almighty God who is a strong Tower, be with thee, and make thee know and feel, that there is none other name given under Heaven, whereby to attain everlasting life, but by the Name of Jesus. The blessing of God the Father, the Son, and the Holy Ghost be with you henceforth and for ever.* Amen.]

When he was upon the Ladder, he spake thus.

Ashton. I hope I see my Lord and Saviour Jesus Christ.

Dr Warmestry. *I hope so (says the Doctor) passe on from the Cross to the Crown. Remember who went before you.*

Ashton. I am brought here to a shameful death. I am an English man born, and (as many know) a Gentleman born; I am brought here by occasion of two fellows that corrupted me, namely, *Topham* and *Langhorn*, who were the men that brought me acquainted with one *Manley*. And *Manley* and the rest told me they would raise a Regiment for me, and then I told them I would command it. I was drawn into the business. And now I am brought here for my former sins; God hath delivered me several times from several Judgements; he hath visited me at this time, because I slighted, and did not follow that Repentance that I promised. Therefore I desire all Protestants to leave off their sins for Christ his sake, and become new men, for it is that that brings all men to ruine; I beseech God of mercy, have mercy upon my Soul; Lord God, I come to thee; Lord the Father of Heaven have mercy upon me, O God the son Redeemer of the World have mercy upon me, O God the holy Ghost, proceeding from the Father and the Son, have mercy upon me. Remember not my offences, but spare me, good Lord God. I beseech thee spare thy servant whom thou hast redeemed, for thy dear Sons sake. I have no more to say, but desire the prayers of all good people.

Doctor. One word, remember that saying of the Psalmist, *Thou shalt answer for me O Lord*.

Ashton. The Executioner asking him, if he had any more to say, he answered, No. But concluded thus; *I commit my spirit into thy hands O God; the Lord have mercy upon my Soul*. Which being said, the Executioner turned him off the Ladder; and afterwards being cut down, he ripped up his Belly, took out the Bowels, and burnt them in a fire readie prepared upon the place. Then his head was cut off, and his Bodie divided into four Quarters.

Execution being done upon Colonel *Ashton*, and his Quarters convyed away in a Basket upon a Cart, to *Newgate*; The Sheriffs officers went to the Tower, to fetch *John Betteley* to his Execution, (who was likewise drawn upon the same sled) into Cheapside; (where formerly the Cross stood) where was likewise a Gibbet erected.

The Manner of the Execution of John Betteley *in Cheapside*.

Being come to the Gibbet on a Sled with a Minister, the Minister read, and the people sung with him a Psalm beginnning thus, *O Lord consider my distress*, &c. After which, the Traitor kneeling on the Sled the Minister prayed to this effect, *viz*.

O Lord prepare our hearts to pray. O most holy and most glorious Lord God, a God of infinite justice, and of infinite mercy in Christ Jesus, we thy humble servants intirely desire thy fatherly goodness mercifully to look upon this they servant, who is now (according to the Sentence which he hath received) to die: O Lord prepare him for that instant of death by all those means and wayes which thou knowest far more necessary, then we can ask; O Lord, give him a true sight of his sins so far, that he may be truly sorrowful for them, and having a true repentance may obtain mercy. Let not Satan have so great a power over him, as to bring him to the least degree of dispair, but shew him thy mercy in thy onely begotten Son, and open the Fountain that was set open for the House of *David*; open it, and shew him that there is no other name whereby he can be saved, but by the Name of Jesus. And when he doth look upon his Saviour (which was crucified) let him know and feel, and understand, that by true faith in him all his sins are forgiven; That howsoever he hath transgressed the Law in this life, yet all those transgressions are satisified for by the blood of Christ. Speak peace to his conscience, and give him rest and quietness, that he may patiently submit; he acknowledges, that these things are not out of the dust, or from chance; he is sensible of thy providence, and that his sins have brought him to this painfull and shameful death. O Lord, be merciful to his soule, and speak peace to his Conscience, be mercifull to that soule that seeks thee, and is ready to submit himself to thee; Infuse those things into him that thou requirest of him; give him a true remorse for his sins, and unfeigned faith and reliance, and confidence in Christ. Give him true charity and love to all men whatsoever, enemies or others, that bear the names of men; give him a heart to forgive them all, that he may receive forgivenes at thy hands. O Lord, do not proportion thy guifts according to our deserts; we are fraile and weak, and our prayers are such, but for thy Sons sake, give him all these things that are necessary; let not the narrownes of our hearts, or of our prayers, any way prejudice thy gifts. Thou that art the Fountain of all goodnes, shew thy goodnes to this thy servant, let the light of thy countenance shine upon him, and let him know and feel and see that his sins are forgiven. Grant this for thy only begotten sons sake, and heare the prayers of all thy people and heare his Petitions, and grant these Petitions we beseech thee, not for any thing that we can speak either for him or our selves, but for that blood of Christ that speaks better things then the blood of *Abel*, who died for our sins. Whatsoever, O Lord, thou hast commanded make good, that, for the doing of that which thou requirest, thou mayst give that which thou hast promised, even for thy Sons sake; To whom be ascribed all honor, glory, and praise, now and for ever *Amen*. *O Lord, be merciful to him*.

Betteley. *I trust in him that he will certainly save me.*

Then he went up the Ladder.

His Confession followeth.

LOrd receive my Soul, and be merciful to me: I commit my Soul into Almighty Gods hands; for he is my Protector and Redeemer. I am not ashamed to live, nor affraid to die; for, my conversation hath been such, in Christ Jesus I hope I shall finde mercy.

As concerning them that are my enemies, I pray God forgive them their sins, I freely forgive them all that have done me wrong.

As for the late Plot, I was never but once in company with them concerned therein: I did know of such a thing, but deny that I acted therein. Shall I damn my Soul at this instant? I will speak the truth.

I do acknowledge I offended God in it, and wronged this Nation in hearing it, and not discovering it.

One *Brandon* that was one of them, drew me into the business, and his man. I carrying work to him, could not refrain his house, and so he often inticed me thereto, and would not let me alone, till he had got me into a house where we drank together.

I have no more to say as to the Plot, but desire mercy from God.

Having thus done, the Executioner turned him off, and the rest of the Sentence was executed upon him, as before upon Col. *Ashton*, and his Head and Quarters were conveyed also to *Newgate*.

As for the third man, *Fryer*, who was to have been executed this day in *Smithfield*, he was drawn on a Sled also from the Tower in the afternoon to *Smithfield*, where after he had performed his Devotions, being upon the Ladder, and the Executioner ready to turn him off, a Reprieve came, and he was carried back again to the Tower by the Officers in a Coach. {...}

A Particular Relation of all the Passages concerning John Sumner, Edmond Stacy, *and* Oliver Allen, *being appointed to be executed this day, according to the Sentences given against them by the Court of Justice, with the Prayer and Discourses of Dr.* Warmstrey *at the place of Execution over against the* Old-Exchange, *and Speech at large spoken by* Edmond Stacy *upon the Ladder, &c. Friday, 9 July* 1658.

ABout Ten of the Clock the Sled went to Newgate, and brought from thence *John Sumner* and *Edmond Stacy* both together to Cornhil, where coming to the Gibbet erected for *Stacy, Sumner* was carried to the Victualling house, at the sign of the black Boy. And *Stacy* coming out of the Sled, and standing at the Ladder foot, Dr. *Warmstrey* spake to him as followeth.

Dr. Warmstrey, I would have you declare your Faith, that you dye a true Protestant of the Church of *England*, Do you not.

Stacy, For my Faith, so far as God shall give me Assistance, I will declare it. I do beleive that God is the Creator of all things, I do beleive that my Saviour Jesus Christ was his only begotten son from all Eternity, and the absolute Saviour of all the World: And I do believe (as really) he suffered upon a Tree for all the sins of the World (I hope for mine as well as others) And though it hath bin my sad fortune to fall into the hands of two men, whose names I am unwilling to declare, but forgive them, my hope is fixed upon God through his Death and Passion, and by his Righteousness, to be made Righteous.

Dr. You have received this day the Seal and Pledg of Gods mercy through Jesus Christ, he hath given you the Seale of your Interest in his sufferings; And he hath given you the Seale and Pledge of everlasting life; I hope your Faith hath laid hold upon this mercy.

Stacy, I have cast my self wholly upon Jesus Christ. I have no other hopes or refuge but only the Salvation of Jesus Christ.

Dr. Remember that expression, Lamentations. 3, *Wherefore doth a living man complain, a man for the punishment of his sins? Let us search and try our waies, and turne again to the Lord*. And so it concerns you to humble your self under the mighty hand of God and fall down at his mercy seate, and to justifie God, and to cry out with *Daniel, Righteousness belongeth to thee, but to us confusion of faces; but there is mercy with thee that thou mayest be feared, and with thee there is plenteous redemption. If that thou shouldest marke iniquities, who should stand before thee?* Remember that God hath received a satisfaction to his Justice by the sufferings of Christ Jesus, and he hath purchased a general pardon for penitent sinners and true beleivers. And let that great tenor of the Gospel, 24 Luke 47 be in your heart. Thus it is written saies our Saviour, when he was departing from his Disciples, and it is the sum of the Gospell; And thus it behoved Christ to suffer and to rise from the dead the third day, and that repentance and remission of sins should be preached. And the fruit of the Gospel is this, a general pardon in the blood of Christ to all penitent sinners, repentance and pardon; The Lord in the Gospel cals all to repentance, and proclaimes a general pardon. Now let us pray.

{...} *Our Father &c.*

After this, he went up the Ladder.

Dr. The God of Heaven take thee into his armes, and dispose of thee according to his great goodness.

Edmond Stacys *Speech upon the Ladder.*

GEntlemen, I am under the condemnation of men for High Treason, yet I bless God in my heart I ever from a child hated Treason, Treachery, Plots and Conspiracies. When I served the Parliament I served them faithfully, and truly I could have wished with all my soul that I had served God so faithfully. No man heretofore ever knew me a Traytor, or ever knew me have a hand in human blood, but what I did as I was a Soldier. And it is not unknown, that I was never taxed for a Theif, for, I ever hated it, but it is for my sins and transgressions that I have offended God, who hath suffered me to fall into the snares of the Devill. For I met with one *Sumner*, as I was talking with one in *Soperlaine*; this man came to me by accident and invited me to drink. I went with him, but nothing passed then as to this business for which I now suffer; I went homeward and this man (taking his leave of me) told me he would come again to mee in the afternoon, which he did, and so brought me acquainted with *Topham*. *Sumner*, he told me at first I should be promoted for *Swethland*; and *Topham* spake of another busines, of several Merchants; these men since have been found with their Cellars full of powder, &c. It was a thing I ever hated to plot or intercept any mans blood, and yet the Lord left me to my self, to the blindness of my heart. I knew not the time that was prefixed for this business at first; I did not know the ground of the matter, till such time as I was told; and so now I come to suffer, but Lord, of thy mercy grant that I may never be under thy condemnation. O good God, had I but served thee faithfully and truly, these things could never have been, but God in mercy forgive mine enemies; I beseech thee O God forgive them, and have mercy upon my soule for this offence. For, I must confess I deserve Damnation from thee, O God, but yet Lord have mercy upon me. I bear no malice at all to any man.

Executioner. Are you ready?

Stacy. I am going a great journey, and therefore desire you to stay a little. I tell you loving Friends, it is for my sins and transgressions whereby I offended God, that he hath brought me to this condemnation; but blessed be the Lord God that hath given me a true Faith and a Hope in Jesus Christ. These afflictions hath brought me to know my sins aright, I never knew what Grace was before; therefore, most gracious God have mercy upon me, and for the merits of my Saviour Jesus Christ, look down upon me. Let not this sin, for which I suffer, or any other be laid to my charge, but let me have a share in Christ, O my God. My loving Country-men, Oh! the thing that was propounded, I knew not any more of the proceedings, than onely what they told me through clouds.

For the firing of the City, I never knew of it, I am an Englishman born, and should I burn my own Country? I abhor the thoughts of it. There are them that meant to do strange things, who have had their Cellars full of Powder, and they hedged me in to my confusion. Therefore most gracious God look down upon us all. O my God, my God, have mercy upon me; give me I beseech thee, a true faith and confidence in thee, that I may go through stitch with all my afflictions. Thou knowest, O Lord, what supplications I have made to thee; therefore, good God, strengthen me, that I may not fail at the last minute, that I may have a true faith in thee, that the shadow of death may be nothing in comparison of the life to come.

Blessed be God, I forgive all, I have neither malice to old nor yong; the Lord bless me, the Lord deliver me, I hope he will: I have a true lively faith in Christ Jesus, Lord have mercy upon me, make my salvation sure. Good God hear me; gracious Father hear me, let my sinful cryes come up to Heaven; thou knowest how wicked I have been, I justly have deserved this for my sins. Jesus Christ died for all my sins, apply Jesus Christ to my soul, that his sufferings may be a comfort to me that suffer in this World: Grant that in the World to come, I may live with thee. O my God, how loth is mortal flesh to die! This is a shameful death, yet my Saviour Jesus Christ died as shameful a death; and therefore why should I be ashamed? I hope the Lord will have mercy upon my Soul.

I desire you all to have a special care of your selves and servants; for, the too many meetings in several corners have brought many yong men to confusion. O my God, help me O Lord to go out of this vale of misery, strenghthen me I beseech thee, that the sting of death may not go through me: Pluck it out O God, before I depart, that I may escape the second death, and have a glorious Resurrection.

O my God! I could speak a great deal more to you, I would fain deliver all my self to you, because I would discharge my conscience: As I told you before in the first place (God is my Witness and Record) I ever did hate Treason, Plots, and Thievery. For Murder, the Lord knows I am innocent. The Lord knows the secrets of all hearts, and knows who was the beginner of this Plot, and knows the latitude of it. But O Lord God, Creator of all the World, against whom I have more transgressed, then I am able to speak of, Have mercy upon me, and deal favorably with me, and grant that I may have a lively faith in the merits of Christ, that those sins that I have committed here in this, or any other business, may never be laid to my charge in the World to come.

O blessed Saviour Jesus Christ, direct my Prayers to God; O Holy Ghost strengthen me to the last minute. O good God, forsake me not, but not my will, but thy will be done. In mercy, O God, look down upon my poor wife, and be to her a strong Tower of defence; be to her a Husband and Friend. In mercy look down upon all those that are afflicted, that are engaged in this most horrid act: Good Lord deliver them out of all their troubles; look down in mercy upon them. O God the Father, Creator of the World. O God the Son, Redeemer of the World. O God the Holy Ghost proceeding from the Father and the Son, have mercy upon me. Let my sinful supplications come to thee; Lord remember the promise thou hast made, *That at what time soever a sinner doth repent of his sins, from the bottom of his heart, thou wilt blot out his transgressions*. O my blessed God, that suffered a shame for my sins, let me have a portion in thy grace, that I may have a reconciliation with thee after this life is ended. O my good God, how tedious death is to mortal men! Especially to such a sinner as I am! I beseech you to pray for me, lift up your Prayers to God for me a poor wretched sinner. O that I could have served my God so faithfully as I should! My neglect of duty to thee hath brought this evil upon me; for that which I ever hated, through thy over-ruling power, hath brought me to this shame. How loth is mortal flesh to die! Pray for me. Blessed God hearken to me, and give me a heart faithful to believe; give me a spirit to feel no pain in death, in comparison of the heavenly joyes that are with thee: Strengthen my faith, now I am to feel the pains; more and more strengthen me; I beseech you bear with my weakness. Many brave Gentlemen have been brought to this, and very lately; and therefore I beseech you all to have a special care, that by other mens harms you may learn to beware: For, if I had had the foresight of the thing, surely I should have escaped this. It was my unworthiness towards God that hath caused this sin, for which I now suffer, to fall upon me. God have mercy upon my Soul, and forgive all those that have done me wrong. How fearful is the sting of death to a sinner! But blessed be God, that thou hast sanctified this affliction to me, that since I have been afflicted for this most horrid act, I have known more of my sins then in all my life time, I could discern or see.

Blessed be thou, O Lord God, that I have a true and lively faith in Christ, that when this life shall pass away, I shall have true consolation with thee for evermore.

Stacy. Doctor may I sing a *Psalm?*

Doctor. Yes.

Then Stacy *having a Bible delivered him, read and sung the Five and twentieth* Psalm; *and after that*, The Lamentation of a Sinner. *and went on thus*:

You have heard what I have said, I have three or four words more. O Lord God, Creator of the World, Father of our Lord Jesus Christ. I humbly entreat thee to strengthen me to the very last minute. Remember thy promise to sinners, That at what time soever a sinner doth repent, thou wilt be gracious to him. O Lord let thy holy Spirit convey my spirit into happiness with thee for evermore. Lord, for thy mercy sake look down upon me; Gracious Christ have mercy upon me, O Holy Ghost have mercy upon me. How loth is this sinful flesh to leave this wicked World! O God strengthen me, O blessed Christ strengthen me. O Holy Ghost strengthen me, Lord for thy mercy sake, Christ for thy mercy sake, Holy Ghost for thy mercy sake. Lord have mercy upon me, and that for my Saviour Jesus Christ his sake. O blessed God have mercy upon me; for, into thy hands I commit my spirit; in whose name I further call to thee.

Our Father, &c.

After Execution done upon *Stacy* (whose Sentence was so far remitted that he onely was hanged, and not quartered) *Sumner* was again brought to the Sled, and from the Old Exchange drawn into Bishopsgate-street, where was likewise a Gibbet erected;

under which, *Sumner* being arived, his Highness having been graciously pleased to grant him a Reprieve, it was there produced: Then the Officers took him thence, and conveyed him to a private house, and afterwards they returned with him in a Coach back to *Newgate*. And it is observable, That when news was told him of a Reprieve, the said *Sumner* wept for Joy, and blessed God and his Highness for the mercy.

The Sheriffs Officers having disposed thus of *Sumner*, they next went with the Sled to the Tower to fetch *Oliver Allen* (a third person condemned for Treason) to his Execution, who was in a like manner drawn on the Sled to the Four Spouts at the upper-end of *Grace-Church-street*, where was likewise a Gibbet erected; whither being come, his Highness was likewise graciously pleased to grant him a Reprieve. And it is remarkable, that all the way he passed he wept and much lamented his crime; and when he had information of his Reprieve, he burst forth into a greater passion of weeping, expressing his unworthiness of so great a favor, as the saving of his life.

Being taken off the Sled, he was conveyed to his Masters-house in *Grace-Church-street*, and from thence transmitted back again to the Tower. {...}

From Dunkirk, July 16. *S.N.*

The King of France is now very well recovered; and by the next through Gods blessing we doubt not to give you an account of his perfect state of recovery.

CHAPTER EIGHT
With a Pen like a Weaver's Beam: Marchamont Nedham

Marchamont Nedham was one of the most widely read writers of the seventeenth century. Since the publication of his very first newsbook to the present day he has been a spectre haunting the margins of historical writing, sometimes grudgingly praised for the brilliance of his ebullient prose, and simultaneously condemned as a man without principles, a time-server guided only by financial self-interest, prepared to change sides at the glimpse of greater reward.

One contemporary called him 'the writing Attila' and 'the politick Shuttle-cock', and accused him of having a 'publique Brothel in his Mouth'.[1] Another contemporary, arguing the case for bringing Nedham to the scaffold after the Restoration, wrote a most vehement attack which can almost be read as an encomium:

> {...} what was by other singly attempted in several waies, has been in all practis'd by the late writer of *Politicus*, *Marchemont Nedham*, whose scurrilous Pamphlets flying every Week into all parts of the Nation, 'tis incredible what influence they had upon numbers of inconsidering persons, who have a strange presumption that all must needs be true that is in Print. This was the *Goliah* of the *Philistines*, the great Champion of the late Vsurper, whose Pen was in comparison of others like a Weavers beam: {...} had the Devil himself (the Father of Lies) and who has his name from Calumny been in this mans office, he could not have exceeded him.[2]

1 *The character of Mercurius Politicus* (1650). Wing C2021.

2 [Roger L'Estrange], *A Rope for Pol* (1660), 'Advertisement to the Reader'. Wing L1299A.

It is telling that that such scathing praise was incorporated without parentheses into the earliest biography of Nedham.[3] Even his relatively sympathetic modern biographer finds him 'venal and unprincipled'.[4]

The shadow hanging over Nedham's head, on several occasions dangerously close to being transformed into a rope, was his history of writing for paymasters, particularly those fated for a reversal of fortunes. In 1643, at the age of 23, he joined Thomas Audley to assist in the production of *Mercurius Britanicus*, for which he later assumed full responsibility. *Britanicus* was parliament's answer to an Oxford royalist newsbook, *Mercurius Aulicus*, which since the first of January, 1643, had become a significant propaganda force behind the king, with a large print run and a network of distributors prepared to risk their necks in carrying it to London and other parts of the kingdom. Other newsbooks, which were London based and generally pro-parliament, could not match Aulicus for popularity, nor could they succeed in duplicating its racy style. *Britanicus* did this and more, and survived to gloat over the demise of its rival.

The enforced conclusion to *Britanicus* came not at the hands of the Royalists, but as a consequence of offending parliament. Through the early 1640s Nedham had increasingly come to side with the Independent faction, and rejected solutions of political compromise. In *Britanicus* he began to propound views which rejected the language of conciliation which was being uneasily maintained by parliamentarians, and tested the water for radical positions which were later to become a more common currency. This has been overlooked by those historians who label him a liar and time-server. In 1645 he found himself in trouble for publishing a hue and cry after the king {8.03}. This time he escaped with a reprimand, while Thomas Audley, his erstwhile collaborator and now assistant to the censor, found himself in prison. Then in 1646 he attacked the king and called for the trial of those responsible for spilling the blood of the saints, hinting that this might include the king himself {8.04}. Nedham blamed not malicious advisers, but the man. He was discharged after about two weeks in the Fleet

3 Anthony A Wood, *Athenæ Oxoniensis*, third edition, ed. Philip Bliss, Vol.3 (London, Rivington et al. 1817)

4 Joseph Frank, *Cromwell's Press Agent: A Critical Biography of Marchamont Nedham, 1620–1678* (Lanham MD: University Press of America, 1980), p.vii. This, Wood's *Athenæ Oxoniensens* and *The Dictionary Of National Biography* are the main secondary sources for Nedham's life.

prison, upon a promise not to write any more pamphlets without the permission of the House of Lords.

Nedham had begun to practise medicine in 1645 and he now turned to it full time: his journalistic prose employed many medical metaphors, and he later wrote a treatise on the need for the adoption of new ideas in medical practice. He resorted to it again after the Restoration, and Bulstrode Whitelocke, the Interregnum parliamentarian and ambassador, recorded that he was attended by Nedham in 1665, being charged no fee for this service.[5]

Nedham eschewed the restrictions of parliament, however, and medicine did not attract his undivided attention for long. In 1647 he knelt before and begged forgiveness of the king. In return he was appointed editor of what was to replace the now defunct *Aulicus* as the archetypal Royalist newsbook, to the polemic and political insight of which his peers could only aspire. Much has been made of this *volte-face*, and it is no doubt true that Nedham was taking advantage of a considerable salary and a chance to exact personal revenge against those who had debarred him from writing. It may also be the case that sincere, pragmatic motives caused him to trim through fear of an Presbyterian ascendancy, and what that might bring {8.05}.

Nedham outlined the purpose of his joco-serious style, notably the blending of verse and prose, in the first issue of the *Mercurius Pragmaticus*:

> NOt that I am a whit opinionated of this way of *Riming* constantly, but only to tickle and charme the more *vulgar phant'sies*, who little regard *Truths* in a grave and serious *garb*, have I hitherto been thus light and *Phantastick*, both in *Verse* and *Prose*. And so I must still continue; but yet I would have you know, in the midst of *jest* I am much in *earnest*: And of all those *Nuts* which I give the *Members* to crack in *merriment*, I hope themselves and others, will be able to pick out the kernell.[6]

There was a change in rhetoric, however: the writer who had encouraged the readers of *Britanicus* to have faith in their sheer overwhelming numbers, which would force the Cavaliers to take notice of them, now called the people the 'dregs', the 'mob', 'rascals' and 'the prophane'.[7]

5 *Diary of Bulstrode Whitelock 1605–1675*, ed. Ruth Spalding (Oxford: Oxford University Press, 1990), 29 March, 1665.

6 *Mercurius Pragmaticus*, Num.1, 4 April 1648. N&S 369.101

7 To a contemporary this would not have indicated an anti-populism: in this context there is a clear cut distinction between 'the people' as victims who were being betrayed by their politcal leaders, and the 'many-headed multitude', the people as

Though the censors never relented in hounding Nedham, late in 1648 his editorials betrayed a certain hopelessness concerning the king's cause. He skipped a few issues in November and December 1648, and eventually resigned himself to defeat in January 1649. He reappeared with a *Mercurius Pragmaticus (For King Charles II)* in April that year, but two months later was taken and committed to Newgate. There he did not languish, but negotiated with Britain's new political leaders and was given a pension in return for appearing in his third major journalistic guise, as editor of *Mercurius Politicus*. This was to be the longest lived newsbook of the civil war and interregnum period, and for ten years was the dominant organ of propaganda for the Commonwealth and Protectorate.

In June 1650 a prospectus for *Politicus* was presented before the Privy Council, which echoed the first issue of *Pragmaticus*:

> The designe of this Pamphlett being to vndeceive the People, it must bee written in a Jocular way, or else it will never bee cryed vp: For those truths which the Multitude regard not in a serious dresse, being represented in pleasing popular Aires, make Musick to the Common sence, and charme the Phantsie; which ever swayes the Scepter in Vulgar Judgements; much more then Reason.
>
> I entitle it Politicus, because the present Gouernment is veram πολιτεία as it is opposed to the despotick forme. It shalbee my care to sayle in a middle way, between the Scylla and Charybdis of Scurrility and prophanes. {...} I desire suplyes of the best Intelligence of State; and that Tuesday may bee the weekly day, because most convenient for dispersing it through the Nation.[8]

This was not an entirely accurate description of *Politicus*, though it can probably be attributed to Nedham. Over ten years the newsbook underwent changes in style and content, but it remained a complicated beast. For editorials through 1650-1 {8.13-6}, Nedham reprinted extracts from his *The Case of the Commonwealth of England, Stated*, which he had published in 1650 as part of his new deal with the Cromwellian Government.[9]

an anarchic and destructive force. See Christopher Hill, 'The Many-Headed Monster' in *Change and Continuity in Seventeenth-Century England* (New Haven and London: Yale University Press, 1991 rev. edn.); and 'The Poor and the People in Seventeenth-Century England' in ed Frederick Krantz, *History From Below: Studies in Popular Protest and Popular Ideology* (Oxford: Basil Blackwell, 1988).

8 *The Life Records of John Milton*, ed. J. Milton French (New Brunswick: Rutgers University Press, 1950), II, 310-1. I have expanded the abbreviations.

9 There is a modern edition of this: Philip Knachel, ed. *The Case of the Commonwealth of England, Stated, by Marchamont Nedham* (Washington: Folger Shakespeare Library, 1969).

Then, when he had used up this text, he published passages from what was to become *The Excellencie of a Free State* (1656).[10] These editorials were sophisticated political analyses, much influenced by Hobbes and Machiavelli and showed Nedham adeptly handling Republican ideas, and attempting to convey them with confidence and persuasive force. The originality not only of his style but of his ideas suggest that his convictions genuinely lay with his paymasters at this point.

In October 1655, Cromwell ordered that the licensing laws should be more thoroughly applyed. From then until April 1659, The Thursday *Mercurius Politicus*, with its Monday counterpart *The Publick Intelligencer*, were almost alone in the marketplace. Nedham's coverage of foreign affairs remained superlatively good, though the style of his newsbooks flattened. The challenging editorials had disappeared, though in 1657 he wrote a series of spoof letters from Oceana (alluding to James Harrington's *The Common-Wealth of Oceana*, published in 1656) and Utopia {8.17–21}. In these his joco-serious style reached its apogee, and he most closely welded serious political criticism with a dry, comic style. His Utopian correspondent attributes the invention of this rhetorical technique to Sir Thomas More, author of *Utopia* (1516), who, the letter claims, was condemned to death for transgressions committed when he momentarily ceased to pitch his speech betwixt jest and earnest. This notion of Drollery was central to Nedham's political and literary style.[11]

When Cromwell died, Nedham's position was jeopardized as much as anybody's. He wrote a magnificent obituary for Oliver Cromwell, threw in his lot with the Protectorate under Richard, and with the collapse of the Protectorate, the reconvened Rump Parliament ejected him from the editorship of *Politicus* in May 1659. He proceeded to write a singularly inopportunistic pamphlet, *Interest will not Lie*, which rationally demonstrated that the restoration of Charles Stuart was in the interest of none but the Catholics. Nedham soon found himself reinstated as the editor of *Politicus* and the *Intelligencer* by the Army leaders. One contemporary attacked this action thus:

10 On these texts, see in addition to Frank, H.R. Fox Bourne, *English Newspapers: Chapters in the History of Journalism* (London: Chatto and Windus, 1887), pp.21ff.; H. Silvia Anthony, 'Mercurius Politicus Under Milton', *Journal of the History of Ideas*, XXVII (1966); and J. Milton French, 'Milton, Needham, and "Mercurius Politicus"', *Studies in Philology*, XXVI (1936).

11 It is the failure to recognise the structure of Nedham's satire that constitutes Frank's mis-reading of these editorials, *Cromwell's Press Agent*, p.101–2.

> *Nedham* the Pamphletter, who formerly writ *Pragmaticus* and told lies for the King, afterward writ Intelligence for the Parliament, and in that day told lies for the Protector, in the mean time endeavouring all he could (by scandalous, and lying reports which he sent of them about the Nation) to render them {honest persons} odious to the people, and as much in him lay, to cast dirt upon, and make null, and void their faithful testimony against the late Apostacy; who though he gives out in his Book that *Interest will not lye*, will for his own Interest (like the corrupt Lawyers) tell lyes and maintain a wicked Cause for any that will best reward him for so doing. Yet this fellow, though turned out for this since the Protector was laid aside, lately received again, to write Intelligence for the Parliament, contrary to their own Declaration and Resolves, which is so wretched an action, as it stinks in the Nostrils of God, and his faithful people, The good Old Cause of Christ needs no liars to be employed to help bear it up.[12]

As the City of London warmed to the idea of a settlement with the future king, Nedham produced his newsbooks in an increasingly subdued form until the Declaration of Breda, when the Restoration settlement was sketched in a broad outline. The Council of State once again removed him, and the last issues of *Politicus* were probably not his. He had just published his parting-shot *Newes from Brussels*, a sharp and uncompromising satire, and to a chorus of unforgiving pamphlet attacks, which have served historians so well in their accounts of him, he fled to Holland, his newsbook career over at the age of forty.

Though he was not exempted from the King's general pardon, he was later granted a personal royal pardon and therefore returned to England. Though he may have been many times bent, he was not bowed, and he did continue to write, including books on education, medicine and *A Short History of the English Rebellion*, which consisted of the poems on the title pages of *Mercurius Pragmaticus*. In the 1670s, he even became a propagandist for Charles II; but he never returned to newsbooks, now monopolised by Henry Muddiman, followed by Roger L'Estrange.

The attacks on him mainly focussed on two issues: his prose style and his greed. In a serial dedicated to attacking his *Britanicus*, one contemporary wrote:

> As for his writings, there is as much difference between them and finer Invectives, as there is between a man cut with a Rasor, and spew'd upon. For as such a one cannot be said to be wounded, but bemired,

12 *A True Catalogue, Or, Account of the several Places and most Eminent Persons in the three Nations, and elsewhere, where, and by whom Richard Cromwell was Proclaimed Lord Protector of the Commonwealth of England, Scotland, and Ireland* (28 September, 1659). Wing T2593.

> so we cannot say, that this Fellow writes, but vomits. His compositions have not that thing which we call Salt, but a kind of boysterous Gall, which makes them venemous, not sharpe. Have you ever at a Carting, seen People throw rotten Egges. Such is his stile. A friend of mine gives another Character of him; and saies, There is as much difference between his Invectives, and a true Satyre, as between the prick of a Needle, and the biting of Mad-Dogge, the one is all poynt, the other all Rage.[13]

Another contemporary compared his prose to that of the Elizabethan pamphleteer and writer of fiction, Thomas Nashe, whose prose has undergone something of a critical renascence in this century.[14] Unfortunately this is not true of Nedham.

His greed was legendary, and it is true that he made considerable sums of money by publishing and by his rationalization of the use of advertising. Other journalists, including Nathaniel Butter and Bruno Ryves, author of *Mercurius Rusticus*, experienced great poverty. But whether these accusations of greed are a consequence of his political shiftings, or whether his political timeserving was a consequence of unbound avarice, is a complex problem which has not yet been satisfactorily accounted for. The issue is buried deep in some highly prejudiced historiography and the time is long overdue that historians should question and revise the misleading categorisation of Nedham as 'Hell's barking cur'[15] a liar,[16] a political Vicar of Bray[17] and a literary Mountebank.[18]

13 *Mercurius Anti-Britanicus*, Numb.2. (Oxford, August 1645). N&S 267.2.

14 *Mercurius Anti-Pragmaticus*, Num.1, 12–19 October 1647, p.2. N&S 270.01.

15 Francis Wortley, *Mercurius Britanicus His Welcome to Hell* (London, 1647). Wing W3641.

16 J.H. Hexter, *The Reign of King Pym* (Cambridge: Harvard University Press, 1941).

17 J.G. Muddiman, *The King's Journalist 1659–1689: Studies in the Reign of Charles II* (London: The Bodley Head, 1923), p.14. Douglas Bush also uses this phrase in *English Literature in the Earlier Seventeenth Century 1600–1660* (Oxford: Clarendon Press, 1962), p.261.

18 *Mercurius Anti-Britanicus*, Numb.2.

CHAPTER EIGHT

When the king's private correspondence was captured by Fairfax at Naseby, many newsbooks commented on it, marking a new sensibility towards the mystical nature of kingship, but none with such blatant hostility (nor at such length) as Nedham. *Britanicus'* criticisms reproduced here are arduous, but are a landmark in the development of explicitly hostile attitudes towards the king. The first begins with Nedham's excuse for a week's absence.

Mercurius Britanicus *Numb*. 90.

14–21 July, 1645 286.090 {8.01}

A Man cannot rest himselfe a *week* in silence, but there is such a deale of *enquiring:* I must needs say, it had been a hard matter to find me out; for I was very private, and seriously imployed making a *Key* to open the Kings *Cabinet*: yet there are so many privy *Drawers* in it, strange *Conveyances*, so many deceitfull *Windings* and *Turnings*, that I mistook it for a *Juglers* Boxe, and so it required some time to fit it, and open all the *mysteries*. For *pence* apeece then (*Malignants*) I will shew you more *Tricks* here, than ever *Hocus-Pocus* did in *Smithfield* at *Bartholomew*-Faire: *Aulicus*, and *Canterbury's* Sermon were nothing to this, for it will yield us at least a *Moneths* sport; and I mean to *anatomize* every *Paper*, week after week, till I have gone quite through; keeping still to my old Motto, *For the better Information of the People*.

A Key for the Kings Cabinet.

Resolution of *Britanicus.*

What, no *Aulicus*, nor like to be? The *Pamphlet* yielded up its last in *two sheets and a halfe*, and rests in hope of Resurrection in the *West*, which may be at *Doomes-day*; for till then they will have little to do but *despaire* and *die:* Then Queen *Mary's* Cabinet will be opened too, and all the Cabinets, Tricks, Devices, and Labyrinths of *State-Policie*. But in the mean time, we having occasion to make use of the *Kings*, it hath pleased *God* (who brings the hidden things of darknesse to light) to give it unto our hands; and with admiration we entertaine it, as an *Omen*, that seeing the *secret intentions* of our enemies (by this happy *Providence*) are fully discovered unto the world, now (certainly) is the time, wherein *God* will set a *fatall period* to their mischievous *Practises*.

No *Aulicus.*

The takeing of the Kings cabinet, a great mercy.

Now let us rifle the *Cabinet*. In the first place a *Letter* from the *King* to the *Queene*, dated from *Oxford* January 9. 1644. Yes, from *Oxford*, thence comes all the mischiefe; It begins thus, *Deare Heart*; this is the *complementall compellation* all along, and she

The Kingdom should be dearest to the King.

hath so much of it, that none at all is left for *Great Britaine:* This is the *Deare Heart* which hath cost him almost three *Kingdoms*: Now to the *Letter* it self.

Dear Heart,

A Letter to the Queen.

S*Ince my last which was by* Talbot, *the* Scots *Commissioners have sent to desire me to send a Commission to the generall Assembly in* Edenburgh, *which I am resolved not to do; but to the end of making some use of this occasion, by sending an honest man to* London, *and that I may have the more time for the making a handsome Negative, I have demanded a Passeport for* Philip Warwicke, *by whom to returne my answer.* [This is the old *Court-humour*, they do not love to heare of *generall Assemblies* and *Parliaments*; and here you may see, whatsoever *good motion* comes from the *Subject*, there is a resolution ready to thwart it, and a policy to make use of it for *by-ends:* From whence I raise this observation for the future, that *the People* may have reason to be *jealous*, when the *King* shall delay an *Answer* to reasonable and necessary *Demands*.]

An Observ-ation.

I forgot in my former to tell thee, that Lentall *the Speaker brags that Cardinall* Mazarin *keeps a strict Intelligence with him: though I will not sweare that* Lentall *sayes true, I am sure it is fit for thee to know. As for* Sabrian, *I am confident that either he, or his Instructions are not right for him who is eternally thine*. [See how their heads work at *Oxford!* they know how odious the *Queens designes are to all true French-men*, and therefore dream of the *Cardinals* holding Intelligence with us. I could easily have believed this, but that the language of the *Letter* seems to detract from the *wisdome* of that noble faithfull Gentleman the *Speaker*, in whose breast all secrets of *State* have ever been so surely lockt up, that I ghesse this to be the issue of their own *jealousie*, rather then any *expression* of his.]

An *Oxford* conceit.

Then writing to the *Queen* concerning the *Treaty* at *Uxbridge*, he signifies his mind to her in the Postscript of this Letter, which is this:

A discovery of the Mock-Treaty at *Uxbridge*.

The setling of Religion, *and the* Militia, *are the first to be treated on: and be confident, that I will neither quit* Episcopacie, *nor that* Sword *which God hath given into my hands*. [I say no more then, but let the World judge what his intentions were for *Peace*, and what was the end of *Treating*.]

In a second Letter there is this passage: *I must again tell thee, that most assuredly* France *will be the best way for transportation of the Duke of* Lorain's *Army, there being divers fit and safe places of landing for them upon the Western Coasts, besides*

The second Letter to the Queen.

the Ports under my obedience, as Shelsey *neer* Chichester, *and others, of which I will advertise thee when the time comes*. [Did ever any Prince take such strange courses to ruine his own Kingdome, that rather than yield to his Subjects their just demands, he strives to introduce *Foraigners*, the most outragious *fuell* in *Civill Combustions*; and the worst of *Foraigners* too in respect of our *Religion*; for who knowes not that the Duke of *Lorain's* Army are the most absolute *Popish* of any now on foot in *Christendome*? But (God be thanked) the Duke of *Loraine* hath otherwhere to *fish* than in the *troubled waters* of *Great Britaine:* and for ought I can heare, there is no *State* abroad (whether *Protestant* or *Popish*) but either admires, or laughs at the *Kings* engagement in this his groundlesse *unnaturall War*.]

Endevour to bring in Forainers.

The Letter concludes thus: *By my next I think to tell thee when I shall march into the field, for which money is now his greatest want (I need say no more) who is eternally thine*. [Yes, *eternally thine*; this is the *burden* of the *song*, so that you must never look to see him his *own man* again; for himselfe, all, *Breeches* and all, are resigned up into her hands for all eternity. This word (*eternally*) is a wild word for a *Complement*, a little too arrogant an *Hyperbole* in a mortal mans mouth, upon so frivolous an occasion.] {...}

A most vain expression.

In a seventh *Letter* dated *Oxford* Febr. 25. 1645. He writes to the *Queen* thus: *I assure thee that thou needst not doubt the Issue of this Treaty; for my Commisioners are so well chosen (though I say it) that they will neither be threatned nor disputed from the grounds I have given them; which (upon my word) is according to the little note thou so well remembers. In short, there is little or no appearance, but that this Summer will be the hotest for war of any that hath been yet: and be confident, that in making peace, I shall ever shew my constancy in adhering to Bishops, and all our Friends, and not forget to put a short period to this perpetuall Parliament. But as thou loves me, let none perswade thee to slacken thine assistance for him who is eternally thine*. C.R.

Seventh Letter to the Queen

[Where note, that in telling Her She *need not doubt the issue of the Treaty*, it is plaine he meant to conclude nothing but what should please her: that his *Commissioners* were to do nothing, but according to such grounds, wherewith she had been acquainted; which no man will imagine, such as could have been accepted by the *Parliament*, she being so inveterate an enemy to our *Religion*, and the intended *Reformation* both in Church and State: That he professes his constant adhering to *Bishops*, and an

A full discovery of the *Uxbridge* Mock-Treaty.

absolute endeavour to overthrow this *Parliament:* In order whereunto he is very earnest with her for foraigne assistance, and all this during the time of *Treaty:* Now let the world judge, whether he ever intended any good end by Treating.

The eighth Letter to the Queen

In an eighth Letter dated *March* 5. 1645. He writes to the *Queen* ——— *It being presumption and no piety, so to trust to a good Cause, as not to use all lawfull means to maintain it; I have thought of one meanes more to furnish thee with for my assistance, than hitherto thou hast had: It is, that I give thee power to promise in my name (to whom thou thinkest most fit) that I will take away all the Penal Lawes against the* Romane Catholiques *in* England, *as soon as God shall inable me to do it; so as by their meanes, or in their favours, I may have so powerfull assistance as may deserve so great a favour, and enable me to do it*. [Where note, that he esteems the arming of *Papists* (professed Enemies to the *Protestant* Religion) a *lawfull meanes* to maintain his *Cause*; Sure then none will believe his *Cause* to have any relation to the *Protestant* Religion: That the *Penal Lawes* against *Papists* being once removed, who knowes not what dammages and miseries would befall *Protestants* ? and yet he professes the maintenance of this Religion. Lastly, that he intends to repeale those Lawes by the *Sword*; the *Atheisme* and *Cruelty* of which resolution will be detestable to all Posterity.]

All Lawes against Popery to be repealed.

Ninth Letter.

A ninth containes only matter of Complement to the *Queen*, with complaint of some about him, that they are a *vexation to his life*; *for some* (says he) *are too wise, other too foolish, some too busie, others too reserved, and many fantastick*.

Tenth.

In a tenth Letter nothing much materiall. In the eleventh he complains to the *Queen* of the *Prince* in these words: *Now I must make a complaint to thee of my Son* Charles, *which troubles me the more, that thou maist suspect I seek by equivocating to hide the breach of my word, which I hate above all things, especially to thee*, [but to the Parliament it hath been ordinary.] *It is this: He hath sent to desire me that Sir* John Greenfield *may be sworne Gentleman of his Bed-chamber, but already so publikely ingaged in it, that the refusing would be a great disgrace both to my Son and the young Gentleman, to whom it is not fit to give a just distaste, especially now, considering his Fathers merits, his own hopefulnes, besides the great power that Family hath in the West: Yet I have refused the admitting of him untill I shall hear from thee. Wherefore I desire thee first to chide my Sonne, for engaging himselfe without one of our consents; then, not to refuse thy own consent; and lastly, to believe, that directly or*

Eleventh.

Never man thus enslaved to a Woman.

indirectly I never knew of this till yesterday, at the delivery of my Sonnes Letter. So farewell, Sweet-heart, and God send me good newes from thee. [Could any man believe him guilty of so weak a Passage as this, had not his own *hand writing* testified it? It were ridiculous in a private man, much more a *King*, to submit to the will of his Wife upon every *trifle*. It seems he had promised her to prefer another to the place; which being otherwise disposed of, and fearing thereupon a *chiding*, the fault is laid upon the *Prince*: But to qualifie the matter to her, he promises the *Gentleman* shal not be admitted without her consent: to excuse himself, wishes her to chide the *Prince*, and concludes with a serious asseveration, that he never knew of the busines. Now let all men consider what a necessity lies upon this Nation, in defence of their own safety, and of their Religion, when no Affaires (of concernment, or frivolous) are transacted, but according to the will and pleasure of the *Queen*.]

A very childish passage.

My sole aim in medling with these Letters of the *Kings*, is to open the eyes of the *wilfully obstinate*, and such as are *seduced*, and for the confirmation of *well-affected* persons: and with the same intention I shall proceed next week upon as many more of them. In the mean time I appeale to the *Consciences* of all men, whether we have not evidence enough in these, to manifest those destructive courses he now walks in, to the breach of his most solemn *Vowes* and *Protestations*.

Britanicus his intent.

Mercurius Britanicus *Numb*. 91.

21–28 July, 1645. 286.091 {8.02}

NOw there is some hope, when *Malignants* begin to have *Qualmes* of *Conversion*; for they cry up my *Papers* for no lesse than *Prophesie*, and say that those in the King's *Cabinet* are a plaine *Revelation* of all those *mysterious Court-abominations* which I told them of long since: Now *Aulicus* (if ever he appeare again) must *officiate* in *Lady Cloaca's* Kitchin, and not be treasured up any more in *Malignant Chambers* and *Closets*; for they vow never to have faith again in any *single-sheeted Creature* but *Britanicus*; poor neglected *Britanicus*, that uses to tell them *Truth* of all from the *King* to the *Traitour:* And yet there are a *sort* of idle *paltry Fellowes* still, a *Non-sence Corporation* of *Humourists*, which maintaine the old *garbe* of *prating*; and seeing they cannot deny the *Letters* they wil undertake to justifie the *King* by them.

Some hope of Malignants

Refractory Cox-combes.

First, they say he writes *well and wisely:* But I dare say Himself is ashamed of it. They say farther, that what he wrote was *out of policy:* These men do him ill service to Proclaime him so notorious a *Iuggler*, as to dissemble with all *Parties*. Others there are, and those especially of the *tatling Sexe*, which extoll him for his *love* to his *Wife*: I pray you take notice of these *women*, it is ten to one but they have the *Breeches*; for (I beleeve) no discreet ones will expect, much lesse challenge so much from their *Husbands*, nor any *wise man* yield so much unto his *wife*. But what may we say, when a *King* (whose private affections ought not sway him in publique Affaires) shall forsake the *Great Councell* of his Kingdome, to be ruled wholly by his *Wife*? and in a matter too of so high concernment as *Religion*, by a Wife of a contrary Religion? and in affaires touching his Subjects *Liberties*, by a Wife of so imperious a nature, as himselfe hath had by experience, and often complained?

The *Kings* prepost-erous courses.

The *Queens* imperious-nes

The truth of this will also be confirmed out of the *Cabinet*; and therefore I think it very convenient, before I proceed to any more of the *Letters*, to shew you how the *King* himselfe complaines of his Wife's *disposition*, to the *French King* her Brother, not long after her comming hither; as will appear out of those *Instructions* given by him at *Wansteed* to his *Agent*, who was then to be imployed in *France*, which were signed the 24. of *July* 1626. and a Copy of them found in the *Cabinet*, as followeth:

CHARLES Rex.

She began betimes.

The endeavor of the *Queens* Priests.

"It is not unknown both to the *French King* and his *Mother*, what unkindnesses and distastes have fallen between my Wife and Me, which hitherto I have borne with great patience (as all the World knowes) ever expecting and hoping an amendment, knowing her to be but young, and perceiving it to be the ill crafty counsels of her Servants for advancing of their own ends, rather than her own inclination." [Here he is willing to excuse her in regard of her young yeares, and other occasions, pretending her to be of *another Inclination:* but you shall perceive by what followes, that this was but a *Complement* rather then *Truth*. We grant it might proceed from the *crafty counsels* of her *servants*, and it was evident enough; for the *Jesuits* and *Priests* about her had taken the *just length of her Foot* (as we say) and of the *King's* too; they had found out the dispositions of both, and plaid their *game* accordingly: They knew how to set her on work, and if she got the better of him at first, what *advantage* might be made of it ever after. And now the *Game* begins.]

"At my first meeting of her at *Dover*, I could not expect more testimonies of Respect and Love than she shewed; As to give one instance: Her first suit to me was, That she being young, and comming into a strange Country, both by her yeares, and ignorance of the Customes of the place, might commit many errors, therefore that I would not be angry with her for her faults of Ignorance, before I had with my instructions learned her to eschew them, and desired me in these cases to use no third person, but to tell her my selfe, when I found her to do any thing amisse: I both granted her request, and thanked her for it, but desired that she would use me as she had desired me to use her; which she willingly promised me, which promise she never kept; for a little after this, *Madam St. George* taking a distaste because I would not let her ride with us in the Coach, when there were women of better quality to fill her room, claiming it as her due, (which in *England* we think a very strange thing) set my Wife in such a humour of distaste against me, as from that very houre to this no man can say that ever she used me two dayes together with so much respect as I deserved of her: but by the contrary hath put so many dis-respects on me, as it were too long to set down all, some I will relate."

It was Hony-moon at *Dover* then

The first ill cariage upon a slight occasion.

[What *King* then (think you) but himselfe, could ever have endured this? This *Madam St. George* (as I take it) was her *Nurse*; from her she suckt the *peevishnesse:* It was fine, that the pride and pretended *priviledge* of a *French Pusse* should be valued before the pleasure of her *Husband* and *Soveraigne*; yet upon this she takes (as I believe she sought) occasion of discontent, whereby to enter upon the *Stage*, to act that *Part* of Impudence (now plotted) upon her *Husband*. But He (good man!) goes on still complaining to the *French King*, thus:]

A most high affront.

"As I take it, it was at her first comming to *Hampton Court*, I sent some of my Councel to her with those Orders that were kept in the Queen my mothers house, desiring she would command the Count of *Tilliers* that the same might be kept in hers: Her answer was, that she hoped I would give her leave to order her house as she list her selfe. (Now if she had said that she would speak with me, not doubting to give me satisfaction in it, I could have found no fault with her, whatsoever she would have said of this to my selfe, for I could only impute it to Ignorance; but I could not imagine that she affronted me so, as to refuse me in such a thing publikely.) After I heard this Answer, I took a time (when I thought we had both best leisure to dispute it) to tell her calmly both her fault in the publike deniall, as her mistaking of the

Another high affront.

An intolerable affront.

busines it selfe: She, in stead of acknowledging her fault and mistaking, gave me so ill an answer that I omit, not to be tedious, the relation of that discourse, having too much hereafter of that nature to relate."

[This is a new strain of a *feminine spirit*: that scorns to be bounded by *Precedent:* She thinks it an indignity to do as the *Queenes* of *England* before her. The *King* desires to have her *House* govern'd as his *Mothers* was; and for that purpose presents her with the *Orders* by persons of Honour, In whose presence she openly returns such an unworthy answer, as well expressed the pride of an absurd *imperious nature*. Notwithstanding this, all is well enough taken, only he tels her of it calmly and privately; in requitall whereof she returns him such an unfitting answer, that he is ashamed to mention it. Did ever man heare of such a *silken Thunder-bolt*? I suppose no *King* of *England* before him would have endured it. But more is behind.]

A Continuation of Affronts.

"Many little neglects I will not take the paines to set down, as Her eschewing to be in my company when I have any thing to speake to Her, I must make meanes to Her servants first, else I am sure to be denyed, Her neglect of the *English Tongue* & of the Nation in general, I will also omit the affront She did Me, before My going to this last unhappy Assembly of Parliament, because there has been talke enough of that already, &c. the Author of it is before you in *France*."

[What this *Affront* was I have not had opportunity to inquire, but the other seeme to exceed all credit in the *Relation*; that any woman should be so daring to act; that any *Monarch* should be so stupid (rather than patient) to beare them.]

A Quarrell about the Officers of her Revenue.

"To be short, omitting all other passages, comming only to that which is most recent in memory: I having made a Commission to make my wives Ioincture, &c. to assigne her those Lands She is to live upon, and it being brought to such a ripenes that it wanted but my consent to the particulars they had chosen: She taking notice that it was now time to name the Officers for Her Revenue, one night when I was a bed, put a paper in My hand, telling Me it was a list of those that she desired to be of Her Revenue; I took it, and said I would read it next morning, but withall told Her, that by agreement in *France*, I had the naming of them: She said there were both *English* & *French* in the note; I replyed, that those *English* I thought fit to serue Her I would confirme, but for the *French* it was impossible for them to serve Her in that nature: Then She said, all those in the paper had breviates from Her Mother and Her self, and that she could admit of no other."

The Queen Mother tampering here long before she came over

[Where note what an influence the *Queen Mother* had upon Her long before Her comming hither.]

"Then I said, it was neither in Her Mothers power, nor Hers, to admit any without My leave, and that if She stood upon that, whomsoever She recommended should not come in; then She bade me plainly take My Lands to My Self, for if She had no power to put in whom She would in those places, She would have neither Lands nor House of Me, but bade Me give her what I thought fit in pension; I bade Her then remember to whom She spake, and told Her that She ought not to use me so: Then She fell into a passionate discourse, how She is miserable in having no power to place Servants, and that businesses succeeded the worse for her recommendation; which when I offered to answer, She would not so much as heare me; Then She went on, saying, She was not of that base quality to be used so ill, then I made Her both heare me, and end that discourse."

Peevish passion.

[Had ever any *Agent* (thinke you) such a strange parcell of *Stuffe* as this to deliver in his *Negotiation* ? What, that the *nightly passages* between a man and his wife should be sent into *France*, in such a *Sheepish stile*, to be laugh't at? Me thinkes, his own *Authority* had been sufficient to correct and reforme an *obstinate woman*, without giving notice to any *Foraigne State*, of such ridiculous provocations. Now he concludes.]

"Thus having had so long patience, with the disturbance of that that should be one of My greatest contentments, I can no longer suffer those that I know to be the cause & fomenters of these humours, to be about my Wife any longer, which I must do if it were but for one action they made My Wife do, which is to make Her go to *Tiburn* in devotion to pray, which action can have no greater invective made against it, than the Relation. Therefore you shall tell my Brother the *French King*, as likewise His *Mother* that this being an action of so much necessity, I doubt not but he will be satisfyed with it, especially since He hath done the like Himself, not staying till he had so much reason: And being an action that some may interpret to be of Harshness to His Nation, I thought good to give him an Accompt of it, because that in all things I would preserve the good correspondency, and Brotherly affection that is between us."

A strange kind of Penance.

[You see here who those are which he accuses of fomenting *peevish humours* in the *Queen*, even those which caused Her to go on *Penance* to *Tyborne*, the *Iesuites* and *Priests* about Her: Why then did He so often afterwards condescend to Her *Humours*, and continue stil to do so upon all occasions? For even

Fomenters of discontent between the King & Queen,

now it plainly appeares (and none can denie) that all things whatsoever are transacted according to her will and pleasure. What is this, but to tell us, that though He knew these *humours* were caused by the *Priests*, and consequently could not but imagine them to have their designe therein, yet that He was so supine and carelesse, as to yield Her the better? which (it is evident) She holds to this day; nothing being done but by Her motion or consent, to the manifest prejudice and ruine of our *Religion* and *Nation*.]

Who weares the Breeches.

It was for this hue and cry, in which he was so insolent as to refer to the king's famous stammer, that Nedham arrived in his first serious trouble with the censors.

Mercurius Britanicus *Numb*. 92.

28 July – 4 August, 1645 286.092 {8.03}

Rumours concerning the King.

WHere is *King Charles*? What's become of him? The strange variety of opinions leaves nothing certain: for some say, when he saw the Storm comming after him as far as *Bridgwater*, he ran away to his *dearly beloved* in *Ireland*; yes, they say he *ran away* out of his own *Kingdome* very *Majestically:* Others will have him erecting a new *Monarchy* in the Isle of *Anglesey:* A third sort there are which say he hath hid himselfe. I will not now determine the matter, because there is such a deale of uncertainty; and therefore (for the satisfaction of my Countrymen) it were best to send *Hue and Cry* after him.

Hue and Cry after him.

*If any man can bring any tale or tiding of a wilfull King, which hath gone astray these foure yeares from his Parliament, with a guilty Conscience, bloody Hands, a Heart full of broken Vowes and Protestations: If these marks be not sufficient, there is another in the * mouth; for bid him speak, and you will soon know him: Then give notice to* Britanicus, *and you shall be well paid for your paines: So God save the Parliament.*

* *Bos in lingua.*

A Prince irrecoverably lost.

But now I think on't (Reader) I know not what to say to him; for I have been *telling him his owne* this good while, and yet no *amendment* at all: Nay, the dying *groanes* and *pangs* of this poor *bleeding Kingdom*, could never wring one *sigh* or *Teare* from him; but on the contrary, rejoyced in the *ruine* of his faithfull *Subjects*, falsly branding them for *Rebels* and *Enemies*, and cheerefully siding with the *known Enemies* and *Rebels* to his *Crown* and *Dignity:* What remedy then for such obstinacie? I have said nothing here, which I have not already made apparent out of his own *Letters*; but the rest behind speak more plainly and odiously, concerning *Ireland*; especially those to the Marquis of *Ormond*, which whosoever reades, will rather wonder he should proceed so irreligiously, than that *Britanicus* dares write so boldly.

No man of Con-science or Honesty but must condemne him,

Here Nedham tested the margins of political discourse in 1646, and fell out on the wrong side of what Parliament permitted. He was, it seems, too early: the next year the Army took over censorship, which created quite a different situation. The suffering of the Scots under tyrant kings was almost proverbial, and later became a repeated motif in Republican thought, for instance in John Hall's *The Grounds and Reasons of Monarchy* (1650).

Mercurius Britanicus *Numb*. 130.

11–18 May, 1646 286.130 {8.04}

WIll the *Scots* send the *King* to his *Parliament*, or not? Ye shall know more, when 'tis determined in the *upper House* what to do, how He shall be *demanded*, and how *received*. Have we been all this while in earnest, and now stand we upon *Ceremony*? Be resolved, O ye *Commons* of the *Kingdom*; you have paid deare for your *Liberties*, and whosoever he was that endeavoured to *rob* you of them, is *ipso facto* a * *Tyrant*, by consent of all that ever wrote *History* or *Politiques*; and no doubt the consideration of this is enough to *weane* our *Brethren*, for this poore *Island* hath groned under many *Tyrants*, all hatcht under the *Prerogative*; and the *Scots* have smarted so much heretofore by the power of that brood of *Vipers*, that they have little reason to make their *Camp* the *Court*. Should it settle long there, much *jealousie* must needs ensue; for when we know where the *Head* is, we may imagine the other *Members* are, or may be there: where a *King* comes for entertainment, sure his *Councellours* may follow; a *Prince* cannot be long without his *Secretary*, nor can *Charles* without his *Digby*.

No time to dally now.

* Read old *George Buchanan*.

The *Court* ever an enemy to the *Scots*.

But—sure all this is but a *dream*, and we more afraid then hurt: It cannot be but the *Scots* will send us the *King* suddenly, only you must conceive (for *Country's* sake) they must make much of him a little; beside, you know he came but bare * and ill provided

* So it is reported.

thither, so that a new *Suit* or two will do well before he come, only the *Scotch* Tailour may be a little too long in fitting him with the *English* fashion: perhaps when that's done, he may have a mind to come from *Newcastle* by water, and to land at the *Parliament-stairs* before we are aware. If not so, perhaps he may endeavour to settle himself there *level-coyle* between the *Nations*, stake one *Crown* against the other, have the two *Kingdoms* at each *elbow* both sides of the *Tables* before him, that he may be able to manage the after-game in either upon occasion. This is but a *guesse*, God forbid it should be *prophesie*.

Careat successibus opto.

In his Royalist guise Nedham continued to incorporate racy polemic and vernacular diction into political criticism, now adding verse. His repeated motifs were to mock individual Independents as religious fanatics of low birth, relying on stereotypes to attack presbyterianism as a form of tyranny (his distrust of presbyterianism is some thing in which he was consistent) and to play up his own role in prophesying the political future. The following passage refers to the Putney debates of 1647, where members of the New Model Army discussed political liberty. The Agitators were the elected representatives of each regiment.

Mercurius Pragmaticus *Num*. 9

9–16 November, 1648 369.109A {8.05}

Now, now wee see 'twas for the *Crowne*
The *Houses* both did *fight*:
For, since the *Cavaliers* are downe,
They put the *King* to flight.

The *Adjutators* sterne and proud.
Said he should have no QUA{R}TER,
Because he is a *King* and vow'd
To make the *Saint* a MARTYR.

Their *Officers* cri'd HAILE O KING;
The rest made *Mocks* and Scornes;
The *Houses* Vinegar did bring,
And all did *platt* the *Thornes*.

Thus CRUCIFI'D great *Charles* did live,
As *dead,* is gone away;
For RESURRECTION *God* will give
A new *Cor'onation-day*.
—— *Nemo me impunè lacessit.*

Come, come away *Gentlemen* of the *Houses*; winde your *Horns*, and let's to the old sport of *King-catching* once againe. The *Adjutators* can provide you good *Blood-hounds*: and you had best set them on foote some way or other, lest they leave *senting* after his *Majesty* and come to unkennell the *State-hackneyes* at *Westminster* (you know who I meane) that are grown Resty with *sitting*: nay, put *lying* in to boote, and *cogging* and *couzening*, and all the virtuous *tricks* that could possibly be invented, to contribute to the ruine of a *gracious Prince*, and a *glorious* People.

For, they have brought our new *Israel* now into the same frame with the *old*, when there was no *King*, and every man did what was *right in his own eyes*: and since his *Majesty* hath beene *weighed in the ballance* at *Putney*, his Kingdome must be *divided*, and given to the godly *Medes* and *Persians*; only 'tis supposed they will never agree how to part *stakes*: nor is it known yet whether we shall ever have a *King* again, or not, because the name *Subject* is a *heathenish* invection, and not fit to be put upon the *Kings, Priests* and *Prophets* that *Troope*, and *Trump* it about the *Kingdome*; So that wee are like to have a brave world, when the Saints *Rampant* have reduced our *wives*, our *daughters*, our *Estates* into a holy *community*: For, I have heard it disputed, That *marriage* was but an Ordinance *typicall* to the first *Adam*; and is now abolished in the *second*; whereby it appears, that *Matrimony* must be converted into a kinde of religious *Caterwaule*, when the *model* of this new *Common-wealth* hath cast all its *Kittens*.

And now I am thus farre in, I must tell you too that this *designe* against *Propriety* is the reason why they are such enemies against *Lawyers*, there being no further use of *meum* and *tuum*, nor of *Lawes*, to lay *Lime-twigs* upon *liberty of Conscience*, nor of a *King* to execute them, nor of *Lords* to assist him; insomuch that *John Lilburne* and I are all-to-peeces in this businesse, because hee hath studied the *Lawes* so long, that he findes that the only fault in them is, that they allowe any *Lords* at all, and saies he is resolved to lay the *House of Lords* flat upon their backs; not considering, that he may be sufficiently revenged upon these *Members* of it that have abused him, when the *Adjutators* prove good *mid-wives*, and the *Kingdome* shall bee *brought to bed* of that prodigious *Monster* which they call a *full and free Parliament*, wherein the *high-shoes*, the Reverend *Coblers*, and *Kettle-menders*, must all come a *gossiping*. And shall wee not have jolly doings then, think ye?

Yes, and the first businesse they pitch upon, will be to call his *Majesty* to an *Accompt*, when they can catch him; but because there is no likelyhood of that, the *Commissioners* of both *Houses* have taken his *Dog* (a poore *Curre* that his *Majesty* kept for pleasure) into safe Custody; for, he was not suffered to have any *Creature* else that was *loyall* to be familiar with; which being by great misfortune left behinde, it is supposed the supreme Councell of *Adjutators* are drawing up an *Impeachment* against him, for being privy to the escape of his *Master*.

But the *Question* is, whether they have not called him to an *Acompt* already in *private*, considering the madnesse of a former *Age* hath given them a *Precedent* for the practise of as damnable a *vilany*, when they carried that unfortunate Prince *Edward* the second from place to place (un-known and un-heard of by the People) for the space of two whole yeeres, till at length he was murdered in *Berkeley* Castle.

Avarice was one of the motives of which Nedham was consistently accused. Here he is at the other end of the charge, attacking the appointment of the Earl of Pembroke as the Chancellor of the University of Oxford, where Nedham had himself been a student.

Mercurius Pragmaticus *Numb*. 21

1–8 February, 1648 369.121 {8.06}

MONEY, *thou soul of Men and Wit,*
But yet no Saint *of mine* !
*While th'*Houses *vote, and* Synod *sit,*
Thou ne're shall want a Shrine.

REFORMING *is a dull device,*
Breeds nought but strife and rage;
Thou putt'st us into Paradice,
And bring'st the Golden-age.

Thou art Religion, God, *and all*
That we may call Divine;
Thy Temple *is* Westminster-hall,
And all our Priests *are thine*.

Tush, tell not us the way to Heaven
Thou iuggling Clergy-Elf,
That sett'st the world at six and seven;
MONEY *is* Heaven *it self.*
—— *Nemo me impunè lacessit.*

LEt none censure me of *Atheisme*, while I set down the *Religion* of the *Money-drivers* of the times. These are they that have blown away *Popery* and *Protestantisme* all in a breath, to make way for that grand *Idolatry* Covetousnes; the *roote* of al our *evils*, and the fruitfull mother of all our *new Opinions*. And now the work being done, it is high time they should make *Holy-day*, and enjoy the *Creatures* in ease, as we suppose they will suddenly: for, they sit and doe just nothing; in so much that their whole *weekes proceedings* will hardly amount to a penny-worth of *Newes*, though (perhaps) they may cost the kingdome many *thousand pounds*. They roll but one *stone*, and that is as precious as the *Philosopher's,* which they *gueld* out of the purses of the people. As for other matters, they are left to our *State-Committee*, or the new *States:* as to secure the King till the *Resurrection*; themselves from an *Insurrection*, and *Accompts*; the impeached *Lords* and *Commons* from a *Restauration*; the *Scots* and *Irish* from making an *Invasion*; and to take care that the *Mouse-traps* of the *State* be well baited with *tosted Cheese* to catch the rebellious *Welchmen* in the County of *Pembroke*.

All which is left for them; and yet my Lord of *Pembroke* himself is none of the *Committe*, being left out for a *Bawler*, and to stop his mouth, the Vniversity of *Oxford* must bee plagued with him as a second *Visitation*; for the *Members* (supposing any thing good enough for *Vniversities*) have voted him to be their *Chancellor*, because little money is to bee made of *Books* and *Schollars*; or else you may be sure their would have been no lesse then a *Committee*, to have had a feeling in the dignity: so that it is possible now, if our *Colledges* scape the desteny of *Monastries* and *Abbies*, that *Learning* may be voted no *Treason*, and our *Libraries* passe for *Christians*, seeing neither of them will yeeld any profit to the *Elders* of the last years, or the brethren of this years *Translation*.

Nedham explains the project of his jocular style: to attack hypocritical precisians (i.e. puritans) in spite of his printer's shortcomings.

Mercurius Pragmaticus *Num.* 25

29 February – 7 March, 1648 369.125 {8.07}

I Was once in good hope no *Faults* would be found, but what the *Printers* leave me, which I must needs say are too many every weeke: And the mischiefe is, that I know not how to mend them: for, they are a generation so lost in *Ale* and *Smoake*, that they will neither take, nor give due *Correction*. But I heare there is a curious *Tribe* of *Criticks* abroad, *Precisians* of the same *cut* and *garb*, with the *Synod*, that are offended, because I mingle *Scripture-phrase* with my *Relations*. But what I doe in this way, I would have them to know, is done in emulation of the more serious *Rabbies* of the Times, those *Linsie-wolsie Elders* of the People, that with their *Shuttle-heads,* weave their home-spun *Lectures*, with *Newes* and *Divinity*, and dresse all their *Politiques & Discourses* in a *Scripture-mode*, to make them passe the more current among their *Proselytes:* So that what I doe this way, is but in *derision* of them, who set both *Scripture* and *Conscience* upon the *wracke*, to bring about their owne ends. And I hope to represent them in their *hypocriticall* prophanations, shall be accounted no more *prophanenesse* in me, than in a true *Divine*, whose Office it is to strip the *Vices* of the Times, and expose them to the contempt and hatred of the *People*, in their proper *Colours*.

Here he reflects upon his broader historical project

Mercurius Pragmaticvs *Numb.* 20.

8–15 August, 1648 369.220A {8.08}

IT is now almost *Twelve-months*, since I first set pen to *Paper*; and having reflected seriously upon all that I have done, I find (after a strict *Survey*) that as it was my care ever to write nothing but *Truth*, in matter of *design* or *action*; so all hitherto have proved true to a *Tittle*. And this I dare boast, that he which is *Master* of these *Pamphlets*, needs no other *Comment* upon this last yeares *Proceedings*, of the *Houses* and the *Army*.

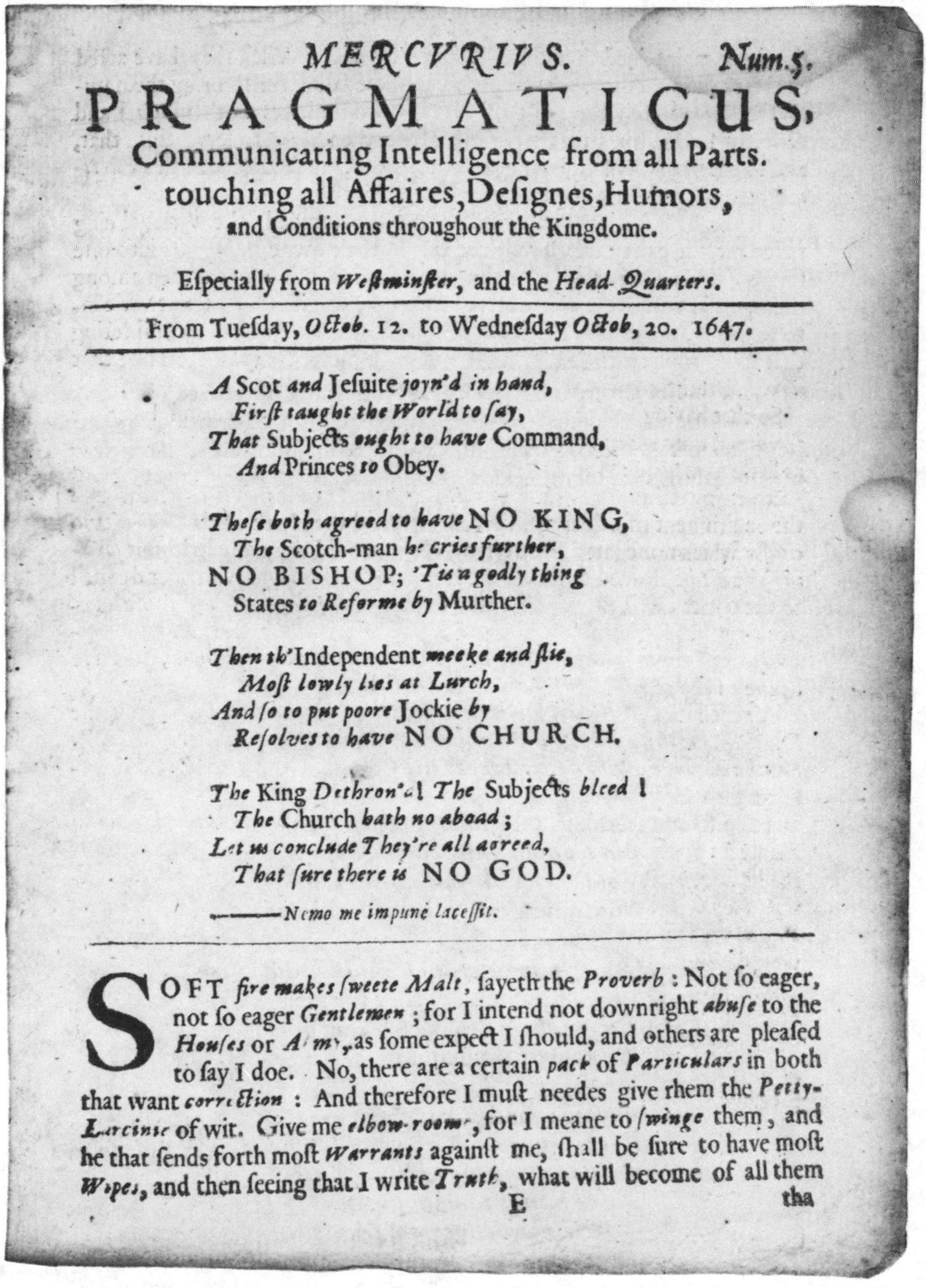

MERCURIUS. Num.5.

PRAGMATICUS,

Communicating Intelligence from all Parts.
touching all Affaires, Designes, Humors,
and Conditions throughout the Kingdome.

Especially from *Westminster*, and the *Head-Quarters.*

From Tuesday, *Octob.* 12. to Wednesday *Octob*, 20. 1647.

A Scot *and* Jesuite *joyn'd in hand,*
First taught the World to say,
That Subjects *ought to have* Command,
And Princes *to* Obey.

These both agreed to have NO KING,
The Scotch-man *he cries further,*
NO BISHOP; *'Tis a godly thing*
States *to Reforme by* Murther.

Then th' Independent *meeke and slie,*
Most lowly lies at Lurch,
And so to put poore Jockie *by*
Resolves to have NO CHURCH.

The King *Dethron'd! The* Subjects *bleed!*
The Church *hath no aboad;*
Let us conclude They're all agreed,
That sure there is NO GOD.

——*Nemo me impune lacessit.*

SOFT *fire makes sweete Malt*, sayeth the *Proverb* : Not so eager, not so eager *Gentlemen* ; for I intend not downright *abuse* to the *Houses* or *A m y*, as some expect I should, and others are pleased to say I doe. No, there are a certain *pack* of *Particulars* in both that want *correction* : And therefore I must needes give them the *Petty-Larcinie* of wit. Give me *elbow-roome*, for I meane to *swinge* them, and he that sends forth most *Warrants* against me, shall be sure to have most *Wipes*, and then seeing that I write *Truth*, what will become of all them

E tha

11. Nedham's Royalist *Pragmaticus*

The principall end whereof having been only to abuse the *Kingdom* (but especially the *City*.) And this course mannaged not so much by the *Houses*, as against them, by an inconsiderable *Faction* in them; who being back't with an over-awing *Army*, made it their busines to Impeach their *Fellow Members*, and turn the Houses *topsy-turvy*, that they might (at pleasure) bring us all to *slavery*. These things (I say) being visible, it was high time for all men to seeke *remedy*, and cast off that monstrous *yoke* of the Monster, *Independency*.

The size and hue of Cromwell's nose was something no satirist overlooked. Here Nedham is at his most anti-presbyterian, though he does make an argument against it on the basis of Cromwell's self-interest. This was to become one of his dominant modes of analysis.

Mercurius Pragmaticus *Numb*. 29.

10–17 October, 1648 369.229 {8.09}

Let me be Turke, *or any Thing*
But a Scot'ch *Calvinist*:
First he damn'd Bishops, *next his* King,
Now he cashieres his Christ.

Gude Faith Sir, *they the Pulpit bang;*
But let their Gospell *downe*:
For, the old Saviour *needs must* gang
Now a new one *is come to Towne*.

The Saints, *whom once their mouths did curse*,
Deare Brethren *are and* Friends;
Which proves their Zeale *a* Stalking horse
For knavish-godly *Ends*.

Then raile no more at Antichrist,
But learne ye to be civill;
And since ye have King Cromwell *Kiss't*,
Shake hands to with the Devil.
—— *Nemo me Impuné Lacessit*.

WHO would have imagined a *Twelvemonth* since, that *Nol. Cromwells Nose* could ever have entred *Edenburgh*, without putting it into a *Combustion*? But see what change of weather there is in the *Common-*

wealth: This *Oliver*, whom they proclaimed the very *Abaddon*, and all his *Traine* to be no lesse than the *Taile of Antichrist*, is now become the only Friend of *Reformation*; and for his better entertainment, the *Damosells* of the *Scotish-Kirke* have met him with their *Timbrels*, and the blue Brethren of the *generall Assembly* blow their *Bag-pipes* in the *Pulpit*, with an *Hosanna*, or a *Song of deliverance*. Yes, and to manifest their *Brotherly affection*, the old *Discipline* of good *Cheer* is so set on foot among them, after the *Scotish* Fashion; that is, not with *Capon*, and *Custard*, those rare Appertenances of the *London* Presbyterie, but in a new way every iot as savoury in a cold *Climat*, and that is with a glorious oyle of *Pottage*, commonly calles *Brewis* and *Bannocks*, which on the other side of *Tweed* exceeds *Chicken-broth*, and in a *Scotc'h* stomack, tends every jot as well to *edification*. {...}

Yet let them *Juggle* and do what they can, I warrant you *Oliver* is more wise, than to admit of a *Scotish* Presbyterie in *England*, since wheresoever it *settles*, it layes an intollerable *Burthen* upon all, from the *King* to the *Beggar*, without exception. Of this we have a very notable example, which should have been mentioned in the last, and hath been since in another: But that the *Current* of it may be the more universall, it is here againe inserted; and so much the rather, because it hath been confirmed since the first publication, by many considerable hands, The busines concernes the Lord *Loudoun*, Lord Chancellor of the Kingdom of *Scotland*; who was convented lately before the Commissioners of the *generall Assembly*, and accused of complying too farre with the *King*; when he was last with him at *Hampton*-Court. Now, though few that know his *Lordship's* Temper, will beleeve, that he ever complyed really with his *Maiesties Interest*; yet the *Iealousie* of the *Kirk* is sufficient to condemne the greatest men: And therefore having *delivered him over to the Devill* (their grand *Chapman*) no *Absolution* would be yeelded to, without *Penance* and *Satisfaction*; so that his *Lordship* was glad to exchange his *English Scarlet* for *Scotch Canvase*, and mortifie the *Body* for the saving of his *Soule*, upon the *Stoole of Repentance*: But it was done somewhat the more privately at present, in regard of the *Scandall* which might be given to the Brethren of *Independency* now among them; especially at this Instant, when the *holy Discipline* is to bee setled.

Here then, O ye *Nobles* and *Gentry* of *England* learn to be wise; behold in this *Glasse* the *Model* of your *holy Slavery*, if you yield to *Presbyterie*.

Nedham mocks the Commons and its agents who sought to track down *Pragmaticus* and stifle his press.

Mercurius Pragmaticus *Numb.* 34.

14–21 November, 1648 369.234 {8.10}

Satterday, Novem.18.{...}

A little before the *House rose*, there was a heavy *Complaint* made by the godly Crew of *Independents* against *Mercurius Pragmaticus*, for revealing the Knavery of that *Faction*, in all their *Debates, Councells*, and *Proceedings*, whereby they are made odious in the eyes of the world; and therefore they pressed he might be severely dealt with, above all other *Malignant* and scandalous Authors, boasting, that now they had him in their *Clutches*. Now you are to understand, that their *Beagles* have been hunting up and downe after me, and that they might seem to doe somewhat worthy of their *Pension*, they seized upon some honest man or other upon suspition, and brought him in to the *Lobby* at the doore of the House of *Commons*, where the *Members* of the *Faction* came in hope to triumph over poore *Prag*. and made report unto their *Fellowes*, what a prize they had gotten, and after they had declaimed a while, and rip't up all their *Transgressions* against the *Godly Party*, at length it was moved eagerly, that a Committee of themselves might be pack't, which was accordingly done; to bring poore *Prag*. into the *Inquisition*, when they know where to catch him.

CHAPTER EIGHT

This covers one of the critical weeks in the progress of events towards the execution of the king. Frustrated by the persistence of the Commons in dealing with the king, the Army imprisoned several of the members of the house, in an action which became known as Pride's Purge. This cleared the way for the trial of the king. Central to Nedham's editorial is the concept of 'interest', influenced by his reading of Machiavelli, which in his Republican guise he later used to argue for the stability of the Commonwealth.

Mercurius Pragmaticus Numb. 36, 37.

5–12 December, 1648 369.236 {8.11}

TO say, that *Government is mutable at the pleasure of the People*, is a bold *Assertion* destructive to the common weale of *Nations*; forasmuch as it leaves the *yoake* loose upon their necks, and gives them a liberty of resisting all *Authority* whatsoever; nor would any *Governours* be safe, longer than they flatter and sooth the *rascall Multitude*: so that the *Purple-robe*, which ought to be accounted venerable and sacred, shall be prostituted to the lust and pleasure of the *Prophane vulgar*, that are as mutable as the *Aire*, and never content with their present condition.

From whence these Inconveniencies will follow: *First*, The *Lawes* which are the *supporters* of a *Nation* will never be safe, nor certain, but alter according to the humor of every new Faction, which must needs introduce confusion of the *Commonwealth* in general, and of many thousand particular persons, whose livelyhood depended on the *Lawes established*.

Secondly, The *Commonwealth* will never be free from *Factions* and *divisions*, because every man will envie his *Neighbour* that is greater or richer than himself; especially, if he be in *authority*, and apply *themselves* and *friends* to any *Party*, that is most likely to suppresse him; by which means no man of wealth and power will be secure from the malice of his *Inferior*, who will endeavour to inrich themselves by his ruine.

Thirdly, There will be no end of *Rebellion*, as long as *Ambition* is in the world: For, every *aspiring person* considering by what means the last *Rebells* attained to dominion, will practise the same *principles* and *pretences*, to ingage the people perpetually against the new *Usurpers*. An example of this we have here in *England*. Upon the same *Termes* that the *Houses* quarrel'd with the *King*, doe the Army now with the Houses, in defyance of their *authority*: and if it should happen (which God forbid) that the

Grandees of the Army can establish themselves in the intended *Tyranny* (be it an *Oligarchy*, or a *Democracy*, or what you please) then admit the same *Principle* of changing *Government* at the pleasure of the *People*, and it will be made use of in a short time by persons of the same *aspiring humor*, to cashire them likewise: And so instead of a *peaceable Government* under *heriditary Kings*, the Land shall groan under the burden of *successive Tyrants*, and be tormented with *Usurpation* upon *Usurpation*, and Rebellion upon Rebellion *in Infinitum*.

Fourthly, If there be not a *supreme trust* and *power* (from whence there ought to be no *Appeale*) in the hands of a *single*, or *severall persons*, there can be no *Government*, for, in this *supreme Trust* or *non-Appeale*, lies the very essence of *Soveraignty*: And therefore to pronounce a liberty in the people of changing the *Government* (what ever it be) or to question the *Governor*, is to take away the Relation of *Governour* and *Governed, Soveraign* and *Subiect*. It is in effect, as much as to say, there ought to be a *Government*, but none to be *governed*; which is a rediculous absurd *Foppery*, destructive to the very nature of *Government*, and must introduce meer *Anarchy* and *Confusion*.

Last week I was routed by the *Mirmydons*, but now you shall see me rout them, if they doe not rout themselves with these *wild courses*, and save me a labour: And therefore (to set them out in their proper Colours) I must needs re-collect part of the last weeks proceedings in the Houses and Army, that passed on *Friday, Saturday*, and *Monday*, December 1. 2. 4. which being matters of an eminent nature, the carriage of them must by no meanes be buried in *Oblivion*. {...}

Saturday, Decem. 2. {...}

This day his *Excellency* took up his Quarters at *White-Hall*, as if he meant to *King* it, and brought along with him 4. Regiments of Foote; part of which became *Courtiers*, and the rest were dispersed into *Yorke* House, and other noble Houses. There came also 6. Regiments of Horse; part of which made bold with the King's *Stables*, and turned out the *Hourse guards* of the *Houses* to grasse.

Sunday. Decem. 3. the *Mirmydons* swagger'd above the Streets, and took a view of the *City*, as if they meant to divide the inheritance by *Lot*, among the Brethren: But his *Excellency* himself (God blesse us) took state at home, and would not admit so much as one *Member* to kisse his hand.

Monday, December. 4. produced *Newes* of his *Majestie's* being seized in his Bed-chamber, by Order from the *Generall*, and committed to *Hurst*-Castle, a place farr more barbarous than *Carisbrooke*, being seated in the *Sea*, and so noysom, that the *Guards* themselves are not able to indure it, but shift ever and anon into fresh Quarters; and therefore we must conceive, that this is done, in hope to stifle him up with *Fogs* and *Mists*, as a more plausible way of murther, than by *Pistoll* or *Poyson*. Lay this to heart, O ye people of *England*, and pitty [as I know you will] the miserable condition of the best of *Princes*.

Vpon this *Intelligence*, the *Houses* presently voted, that this removall of his *Maiesty* was *without their consent or previty*; and all that was said to it among the *Commons* was this, by a resolute *Gentleman* who reported it; That it was a most *insolent rebellious act*. Neverthelesse, they resolved to proceed upon his *Maiesties Concessions*, and resumed their *Saturday's* debate; and all the day it was argued to and fro, whether they were *Satisfactory*? It was maintained very bravely in the affirmative by the ancient men of the House, as Sir *Robert Harlow*, Sir *Ben. Radyer*, Sir *Simonds D'ewes*, Mr. *Edward Stephens*, Sir *Harbottle Grimston*, Mr. *Walker and many others*; who were opposed by the Skip Iacks, such as *Prideaux* and his Lacquey Sir *Thomas Wroth*, Sir *Peter Wentworth*, Sir *Whimzy Mildmay*, *Harvey, Ash Ven, Blakiston, Scot, Hoyle* of *Yorke*, the two Iews *Miles Corbet* and *Gourdon*, young and old *Harry Vane*, and divers others. It were endles to relate the severall *Speeches*; but for the concessions it was agreed, that his Majesty had condiscended farr enough for the securing all the maine ends of the Parliaments first engaging, and therefore had given sufficient satisfaction: Against which the *Faction had not a word of reason to reply*, but founded their *Arguments* wholly upon the *Resolutions* of the *Army*; that without complying with them, there could be no hope of a Settlement, and they must look some other way then toward the King for it, who as his Majesties good old Servant Sir *Whimzy Mildmay* said *was no more to be trusted then a Lyon that had been caged, and let loose again at liberty*. Well said Sir *Whimzy*; for, he led the way, and his *Brethren* followed with most impudent *Revilings* and *Reproaches* against his *Majesty*.

Night drawing on, and it being perceived by divers honest *gentlemen*, that they could hardly vote the Concessions *satisfactory*, they presently waved that, and Candles being brought in, they framed a new question, *Whether his Maiesties Concessions were a sufficient Ground to proceed upon to a setling of the*

Kingdom? The *wrangling* continued all night, and till 8 a clock the next morning, the *Levelling Conspirators* hoping by this meanes to tire out the rest, and then carry things at pleasure: But it would not be, and so it being put to the *Vote* was carried bravely in the *Affirmative*, 129. being for it, and but 84. on the contrary. Vpon this they adiourned till *Wednesday*, and appointed a Committee of six, to goe and maintain a Correspond in the mean time with the *Generall*, who (in state, God wot) made them coole their heeles, and nod after their *night watching* at least three houres before admission; and then having delivered their *Message*, they were dismissed with a surly kind of *ceremony*, and this answer, that the way to corrispond was to comply with the *Remonstrance*,

Wednesday, Decem. 6. The *Saints* being over heated with the former daies work of the *House*, and finding that all went crosse to their wild *Remonstrance*, They sent a paper this day to the Commons, requiring that the *Members Impeached* in the year 1647. and Maior Gen. *Brown*, who (they say invited in the *Scots*) may be secured, and brought to Iustice; and that the *ninety odd* Members, who refused to vote against the late *Scotish* Ingagement, and all those that voted the recalling the Votes of *non-Addresses*, and voted for the *Treaty*, and concurred in yesterdayes *votes*, declaring the Kings *Concessions to be a Ground for the house to proceed upon to the settlement of the Kingdom*, may be immediately suspended the *House*. This paper being delivered in, their *zeale* was so sharp set, that they scorned to stay for an *Answer*, but the *Grandees* immediately sent their *Janisaries*, with a List of those *Members* names which they aimed at; most of which were seized as they were going in, and some pulled out of the *House*, (as Col. *Birch* and Mr *Edw. Stephens*) and carried into the *Queens Court* Prisoners, to the number of 41. persons, by name Sir *Ro. Harley*, Col. *Harley*, Sir *William Waller*, Sir *Walter Earle*, Sir *Sam. Luke*, Sir *Rich. Onslow*, Sir *Io. Merrick*, Sir *Martin Lyster*, *Lo. Wenman*, Mr. *Knightly*, Sir *Gil. Gerard*, Mr. *Fra. Gerard*, Sir *Ben. Rudyer* {...} and Mr. *Nath. Fines*, who demanding *by what power he was committed*, it was answered, *By the power of the sword*; but he was soon set at liberty.

Hugh Peters (that knowes all) came to the rest, and avowed this to be the Act of the *Generall*, and *Lieut. Gen* O brave *Blades*! The House sent the *Sergeant at Armes* twice to the *Queenes Court* to demand their Members, but they refused to render them, and carried them to *Hell* in the *Palace yard*, where their only Torment all night was want of Beds and other Necessaries. All that the House did upon this, was only to appoint a Committee to conferre with the Generall, in the behalf of their Members apprehended; and when all was done, in came *Nol. Cromwell* to Towne at night, as if he (poore man) had no hand in the Busines.

Thursday, Decem. 7 divers other *Members* were kept back from entring the *House*, and those apprehended the day before were sent for to attend the *Generall*, where they were made to stay in a tedious cold season in an outer roome, at least 4. houres, without fire, or so much as a stoole to sit on, though there were many *Gentlemen* ancient and Feeble. At length they were told his *Excellency* was not at leisure (forsooth) to admit them now, but had ordered them, to be conveyed to severall Innes in the *Strand*. This was a pretty new kind of *petty-larciny*, for *Parliament men*, to be posted away Prisoners from *Ale-house* to *Ale-house*, and was done in a very strange manner; for, as they were conducted from *White hall* to the *Strand*, Soldiers were appointed to lead each of them by the Arme, as if they had been doom'd to present *Execution*, the rest of their Fellowes with Musquets and Pikes, making a Lane on both sides, and reviling them with opprobrious Speeches; as *how that they had cozened the Kingdom of its Treasure, and them of their Arrears*, but the Members replyed, that they *should make it appeare to the Soldiers ere long, that their Arrears were in the pockets of their* Commanders, *and the rest of their own Party*.

The House being thus clensed, in came that pure holy Goblin *Nol. Cromwell*, who brought in along with him his Fellow-Saint *Harry Marten*, who looks as thin, as if he had gotten a *Scotch* Clap, after the *Northern* Victory, and the case of the apprehended Members being reported, how that they had been kept up all night out of bed in the Cooks house called *Hell*, *Harry* would needs break a Iest; that *since* Tophet *was prepared for Kings, it was fit their friends should goe to Hell*: And therefore desired them to lay that busines aside, and consider the deserts of the Lievtenant Generall; which was done accordingly, and thankes given by Mr. *Speaker*; who likewise moved, that to morrow might be a day of *Humiliation* for the House; which some looked upon as a *Jeere* at first, till it was voted in good earnest to be on the morrow in the *House*, and that 3. Sermons should be preached by the three *Gunpowder Polititians*, viz. *Marshall, Caryll*, and *Peters*.

These things being considered by the *Lords*, they presently adiourned for feare of an Humiliation by the Soldiers, and (for ought I know) the next time they may adiourn for ever, and be scaetered about as Limbs of the *Prerogative*. Oh, my Lords, sure this tryall of patience will teach you how to be truly Noble, and fright your posterity for ever, from the plague of popular Ingagements.

Nedham announced his return in an exuberant style. Young Tarquin was his name for the prospective tyrant, Charles Stuart, 'King of Scots.' In this editorial he mocks Tarquin and his supporters for compromising themselves with the Scots.

Mercurius Politicus Numb. 5.

4–11 July, 1650. 361.005 {8.12}

HOw sweet the Air of a *Commonwealth* is beyond that of a *Monarchy!* Is it not much better then to breath freely, and be lively, upon a new score of *Allegiance*, than pine, and fret, and fume, in behalf of the old *Non-entity*, till wit, Soul, and all be drowned in *Ale* and *Melancholy*?

But oh ——! *Young Tarquin* is a coming with a world of *Majesty* and *Vermin*; and there's not a Royalist in *England* but dreams of an Office (Sir *Reverence*) to be at least *Groom of the Stool* (if the *Kirk* do not rob him) or *Lord Chamberlain* among the *Ladies*, if his nose be not put out of joynt by Some hot-metalled *Laird*, or *nine peny Scotchman*. This is the *blessed work*, for which the *Lay-Elders* of *London* lay out in contribution, that the honest men of the *City* may be turned out of Office, and themselves mounted on hors-back, with *golden Sausedges* about their *Necks*, for the entertainment of *their Majesty*. This is it, for which the *City Sir Johns*, and their *secluded Members*, do *feast* and *pray*, and plot to no purpose, unless it be to halter their *Flocks*, and their necks in the new *Noose* of *sequestration*. Now (they say) is the time of *Triall*; and oh, what a world of Comfort there is in a little *Tribulation* and *Faction*! The *pale Horse* of persecution begins to range about the streets; and (they say) Rabbi *Jenkins* had his *Conscience* coached away in Triumph, with no less than *six* all a row, to play the second part of the *Pharisee*, root up *heresie*, and sow *sedition* in the *Country*.

In the following four editorials Nedham uses Machiavellian and Hobbesian concepts to legitimate the Commonwealth in 1650 and 1651. He also employs the Humanist method of alluding to the Roman and Athenian republics in order to place the English body politic in a classical tradition: here we see Nedham's political discourse in its most serious, intellectual form. Ironically, his Machiavellian ambivalence to purely moralistic accounts of power and authority was to become the focus on many attacks on him for self-interest and greed, by critics who had read Machiavelli a lot less closely. These editorials, and the Oceana 'letters' which follow, demonstrate Nedham's importance in British Republican thought.

Mercurius Politicus *Numb*. 20.

17–24 October, 1650 361.020 {8.13}

THAT a *Call from the People is necessary and essentiall to make a lawfull Magistracy*, is an *Objection* worn out in the mouths of many. To which it's answer'd; That if only a *Call from the People* constitute a lawfull Magistracy, then it follows, there hath very rarely ever been any lawfull Magistracy in the world, nor among us long before, or since the *Conquest*; For, it is evident out of Histories, from the very beginning, that all the world over, *Princes* came into the Seate of Authority, not only without a *Call* or *Consent*, but absolutely against the wills of the People; and so they exercise their Soveraignty to this very day.

More particularly, here in *England*, most of our owne *Kings* reigned not only without any *Call*, but made way by their *Swords*; there being of those 25. Kings, that have King'd it among us since the *Conquest*, not above halfe a dozen that came to the Crown in an orderly Succession, either by *lineal* or *collaterall* Title: And not any one of those *halfe dozen* but laid Claim to it, by vertue of his Predecessors usurpation, without any *Call* from the People; only, in the Investiture They had their silent Consent; because out of a Love of publique peace none would, or out of Feare none durst, offer to question their Titles.

Now, if the former part of this *Objection* were true, that a *Call* were the only *Essential* constituting a lawfull Government, then it would follow, that, as all the world, so *Wee* and our *Ancestors* have lived and paid Obedience, in times past, under an unlawfull Magistracie; which, sure, no sober man wil affirm: But if any will be so loose as to say it, then in sober sadnesse I would fain know, why we may not now as lawfully submit to the present Magistracy, in case it were unlawfull, as our Ancestors did heretofore to theirs, for the publique Peace of the Nation.

But as in this Case, there is no need of the Peoples *expresse positive Consent*, to justifie a new Government, so a *Tacit* or *Implied Consent* is sufficient; which Consent is the very Dictate of Nature, or common Reason, because it is better to have some Justice than none at all; And there is a necessity of som coercive Power or Government, lest all be left to disorder, violence, and Confusion; which, after a *Civill Warre*, none (even of the *Conquered Party*) can be so unnaturall as to desire; And therefore they do *tacitly consent*, that be administred by the *Conquerers*, because it is a lesse evill to be governed by Them, than altogether to want *due Coaction*, and Direction.

Mercurius Politicus *Numb*. 31.

2–9 January, 1651 361.031 {8.14}

THe Cause in generall which moveth one man to become subject to another, is the fear of not otherwise preserving himself. And if a man may subject himself to him that invadeth; or if men may joyn among Themselves, to subject Themselves, to such as they shall agree upon, for fear of others; And seeing that when many men subject Themselves the former way, there ariseth thence a *Body politick*, as it were naturally; Then it is evident, that since there is no other possible way to preserve the wel-being of this Nation, but by a submission to the *present Powers*, we may, and must pay a subjection to them in order to our own security: Nor can any hold a Plea for *Non-submission*, upon pretence of having been invaded, or over-master'd by those whom he reckons here as *Invaders* or *Usurpers*: nor can the *prevailing Part* of this Nation be blamed in any wise, for joyning among Themselves, to subject Themselves to such as are now in Authority, for fear of domestick Conspirators and foreign Invaders; but having thus subjected Themselves, They are naturally, lawfully, and completely united in the Form of a *Body politick*, or *Common-wealth*, truly called *The Commonwealth of England*.

Mercurius Politicus *Numb*. 32.

9–16 January, 1651 361.032 {8.15}

IT may be further added, that the end for which one man giveth up and relinquisheth to another, or others, the right of protecting or defending himselfe by his own power, is the security which he expecteth thereby, of protection and defence from those to whom he doth so relinquish it: And a man may then account himselfe in the state of security, when he can foresee no violence to be done unto him, from which the doer may not be deterred by the power of that soveraigne or supream Authority that is set over them: how far therefore in the making of a Common-wealth, man subjecteth his will to the power of others, must appear from the end, namely, *Security*.

From whence may plainly be inferred, that since no security for *Life, Limbs,* and *Liberty* (which is the end of all Government) can now be had here in *England*, by relinquishing our right of Self-protection, and giving it up to any other Power beside the present; Therefore it is a very unreasonable Course in any man, to put himself out of the Protection of this Power, by opposing it, and reserving his Obedience to the K. of *Scots*, or any other Power whatsoever; it being clear, that neither he nor any other can now protect us, by affording present Security from Violence and Injury.

Mercurius Politicus *Numb*. 68.

18–25 September, 1651 361.068 {8.16}

IT is a noble saying, though *Machiavel's*; *Not he that placeth a vertuous government in his own Hands, or Family, but he that establisheth a free and lasting Form, for the peoples constant security, is most to be commended*. Whosoever hath this opportunity, may improve his actions to a greater height of Glory, than ever followed the fame of any ambitious Idol that hath graspt a Monarchy: For, as *Cato* saith in *Plutarch*, even the greatest Kings or Tyrants, are farre inferior to those that are eminent in *Free-States* and Commonwealths; nor were those mighty Monarchs of old worthy to be compared with *Epaminondas, Pericles, Themistocles, Marcus Curius, Amilcar, Fabius*, and *Scipio*, and other excellent Captains in *Free States*, which purchased themselves a Fame, in defence of their Liberties. And though the very name of Liberty were for a time grown odious, or ridiculous among us, it having been long a stranger in these, and other parts; yet in antient time, Nations were wont to reckon themselves so much the more noble, if they were free from the Regall Yoak; which was the cause why there were so many Free States in all parts of the world,

In our own Countrey here, before that *Cæsars* Tyranny took place, there was no such thing as Monarchy: For, the same *Cæsar* tels us how the *Britains* were divided into so many severall States; relates how *Cassevellanus* was by the *Common Councell* of the Nation, elected in that their publique danger, to have the principall Administration of State, with the business of War; And afterward; how the severall Cities sent their Hostages unto him; whereby we perceive, it was of old no Monarchy, but like to the *Gauls* (with whom it was then one also in Religion) divided into *Provinciall Regiments*, without any entire Rule or Combination; onely in case of common peril by Invasion, &c. they were wont to chuse a Commander in Chief, much like the Dictator chosen by the *Romans* upon the like occasion. And now we see all the *Western World* (lately discovered) to be, as generally all other Countries are *in puris naturalibus*, in their first and most innocent condition, setled in the same Form, before they came to be inslaved, either by some predominant Power from abroad, or some one among themselves, more potent and ambitious then his neighbours. Such also was the State heretofore, not onely of our Nation, but of *France, Spain, Germany*, and all the West parts of *Europe*, before the Romans did by strength and cunning unlock their Liberties: And such as were then termed Kings, were but as Generalls in War, without any other great Jurisdiction.

If we reflect likewise upon the antient State of *Italy*, we finde no other forms of Government but those of Free States and Commonweals, as the *Tuscans, Romans, Samnits*, and many others; nor is there any mention made of Kings in *Italy*, besides those of the *Romans*, and of *Tuscany*, which continued but a short time; for *Tuscany* soon became a free State, and as absolute enemies of Monarchy as the *Romans*; in the continuation of which enmity, they placed a kinde of an Heroick bravery.

Nor is it only a meer gallantry of Spirit that excites men to the love of Freedom; but experience assures it to be the most commodious and profitable way of Government, conducing every way to the inlargement of a People in wealth and Dominion. It is incredible to be spoken (saith *Salust*) how exceedingly the *Roman* Commonwealth increased in a short time, after they had obtained Liberty. And *Guicciardin* affirms, that Free States must needs be more pleasing to God than any other Form; because that in them more regard is had to the common good, more care for the impartiall distribution of Justice, and the minds of men are more inflamed thereby to the love of glory and vertue, and become much more zealous in the love of Religion than in any other Government whatsoever.

It is wonderfull to consider, how mightily the *Athenians* were augmented in a few years, both in wealth and power, after they had freed themselves from the Tyranny of *Pisistratus*; But the *Romans* arrived to such a height as was beyond all imagination, after the expulsion of their Kings. Nor do these things happen without special reason, for as much as it is usuall in Free-States to be more tender of the Publique in all their decrees, than of particular interests; whereas the case is otherwise in a Monarchy, because in this Form the Princes pleasure usually weighs down all considerations of the Common good. And hence it is, that a Nation hath no sooner lost its Liberty, and stoopt under the Yoak of a single Tyrant, but it immediately loseth its former Lusture: The bodie fills with ill humours, and may swell in Title, but cannot thrive either in Power or Riches, according to that proportion which it formerly enjoyed; because all new acquisitions are appropriated as the Princes peculiar, and in no wise conduce to the ease and benefit of the Publique.

These are the editorials from Utopia and Oceana. The first contains an early suggestion of the utility of corrective brainsurgery.

Mercurius Politicus *Numb*. 352

5–12 March, 1657 361.352 {8.17}

From *Utopia*, February 15.

SIR, Notwithstanding your many months silence, I am not out of charity with you, nor if I were would I tell you, because my Designe is only to give you a friendly provocation, to maintaine a correspondence with me in the future, for (me thinks) neither you and I, nor our Countries, should be so strange to each other, especially seeing we *Utopians* are of your extraction, the famous Sir *Thomas More* having been the Founder of this our Republick. Of him our Annalls say, that as an Eminent Statesman, he had the right Knack of living in the World, his *motto* being *Ioco-Serio, Betwixt Jest and Earnest*, which the most learned in the Languages of the Suburbs have translated *Drolling*; and he kept to it a long while, but at length leaving it off, and falling from his Principle, by being but once in his daies in earnest (and that was when he stood for his supremacie who is the greatest *Droll* in the world) you see what became of him them; he brought himself to the block by it, and there finding his error he fell to *Drolling* again when 'twas too late, and so (the Story saith) he took his leave of Mortality, as a sad example to such as shall venture to be in earnest, among the great *Politicoes* of the captious World.

Upon consideration of so lamentable a Fate befaling this our Founder, we *Utopians* and our Ancestors, in all succeeding times, have set it down for a sure Maxim of State, *To live in Jest, and never to be in Earnest, except it be in order to die*. And This being premised as the prime Point of Policie, you are thereupon to understand, throughout the whole Course of my Correspondence with you, that whatever I write is no further in earnest than you please to make it so. Indeed (Sir) 'tis but *Drolling*.

Now (Sir) for News, you are to know, that for these seven years last past, this renowned City and Commonwealth of *Utopia* hath been sorely afflicted with an infectious Itch of scribling political discourses, caused by a Salt humour first bottel'd in the Braine pan, and then breaking out at the fingers ends. The world hath run a madding here in disputes about Government, that is to say, about Notions, Forms, and Shadows, and the *grand Pols* of the Town being wisely convened and assisted by the vertue of a sixpenny Club, have so often (like Lucians philosophers) ended their Conventions in a Quarrel, that the Magistrate taking notice of these disorders, must himself determine the matter; and to that end he gave order to put the whole society of Pols into the Hospital of the *Incurabili*, to have their Sculls opened and searched with a long Sword, and so served up with green-sauce, as a fit punishment for presuming to break the Fundamentall Law of *Utopia*, by daring to be in earnest, and appear in print so profound and serious Projectors.

The day for Operation being come, viz the 13 of February wherein wee were to trie whether any good could be done for the recovery of these lost men, there was held in the *Hospital-hall* a celebrious meeting of Operators of all sorts and sizes, *Surgeons, Apothecaries, Methodical Doctors, Quacks Mountebanks, Leeches, Simplers, cunning Women, Midwives, Nurses, Chymists, Trepanners, Sowguelders, and Druggers*, with all other the Appendants of the profound Mysterie, that nothing might be wanting to restore the wits of the Commonwealth, that have so long run a wool-gathering after Government.

The Patients of our own Country being searcht, *secundum Artem*, at the Day appointed, the Artists found they had swallowed many a Gudgeon, which swimming in the Brain, were converted into Notions, and therefore pronounced them incurable, yet said, much might be done, if they could but take down Pompions instead of Mastick Pills; of which a Tryall is to be made.

Yesterday, the very next day after the Operation, it being a Cure that this Country is famous for, here landed a jolly Crew of the Inhabitants of the Island of *Oceana*, in company of the learned Author himself, they having been sent hither with him, by order of the most Renowned Prince *Archon*; *viz* Doctor *Ferne*, Mr *Hobbs*, Mr *White*, Mr *John Hall* of *Richmond*, together with the *High-Notionall-Knight*, and the Author of the *late Animadversions* upon the Welsh; and that wondrous wise Republican called *Mercurius Politicus* (who served up the Politicks in Sippets) Of all whose Concernments in the way of Cure, as also of all the other Occurrences and Affairs of State in this Countrey, you may expect an Account by the Post from time to time.

Mercurius Politicus *Numb*. 353

12–19 March, 1657 361.353 {8.18}

From *Utopia*, February 15.

SIR, Though my Correspondence with you be not liked by many, yet glad I am that you are pleased to accept it; And for your encouragement, you may rest assured, that you will not lose your labor, because whatever you write, our *Utopians* pretend readily to understand you; for, wee have no *Drols* here, except my self; most of the rest of my Countrimen are errant Statesmen, born so into the world, not bred; for, alas (Sir) they think learning is foolery, Education but time lost and Civility converts a man to a Crocodile upon these shores. Besides (Sir) Government is to coarse a thing, wee are many of us perfect, have long since thrown away the poor Crutches of Humane Reason and Policie, and leave them to those mean Spirits who are Creeples in their own Conceit, and have not the capering trick of disputing Government everlastingly, instead of obeying. O Sir, the *Grecians* were a dull People; They had but seven wise men; we have seven Thousand that understand All, except Themselves, and are so valiant that loking soure and grave they dare play at Push-pin with *Pompey*, or *Cæsar* himselfe for the whole Empire of *Utopia*.

Now (Sir) for News, I thought I might have been able to give you some Account concerning the Cures of those *Pols* that were put last week into the Hospital, but so many are landed here every day upon the same occasion, and the place is so crouded, that no orderly progress can be made; only the opinion of the learned, who have cast the water of the State, is This; That those of them who have their Phansies hung with fine Cobwebs of Notions be dismissed with a Feather in the Cap, and a Whiske in the Braine; That those who halt and are ill at ease with Scruples about Government, be sent to the Corn-cutters; And that the Mangie Scriblers of the Politicks may all have the Unguent for the Itch, except *Mercurius Politicus*, who gave over in time, and now for *Drolling* deserves to be condemned to the perpetuall drudgerie of a Pamphlet.

These Courses being appointed for those infected persons, there is no doubt but the rest of our *Utopians* will be ruled well enough, and keep sober, especially seeing it hath pleased the Lord *Basilides*, that most excellent Prince, to give order for the Assembling of the Senate this week, to consult about the waies and means of reducing this Commonwealth to a happy Establishment; So that now I can promise you somwhat will bear the Charges of the Post, seeing this Busines will occasion a through discussing of all the points of Prudence. But still all must be taken jovially, according to the Law of *Utopia*.

Mercurius Politicus *Numb*. 354

19–26 March, 1657 361.354 {8.19}

From *Utopia*, March 1.

SIR, Sorry I am that so many of your Countrimen have been searching the Map and cannot tell in what part of it to find out our *Utopia*. But the truth is, they are the more to be excused, because we our selves, with all the learned in Geographie, as yet know not in what Longitude or Latitude to describe it; though I may tell you, we had some heretofore that traveld for it at least a dozen years together, and like Sir *Francis Drake*, went round and round the world, and so went home again. Why then should any be angry, that in all the voyages made through the *Terra Incognita* of three Forms of Government, and the Four Monarchies of the world, no safe Footing should be found, nor any like to be, but by landing in a Fifth? Indeed (Sir) all that we have learnt by travelling is this, now to live at home and be quiet, having gained so much experience, as to know there is a necessity of a settlement, and that it matters not what the Form be, so we attain the ends of Government.

To this purpose, our Senate being Assembled this week, I shall now performe my promise by giving you some brief Account of their first daies Transactions.

And in the first place, because the Affairs of *Utopia* are no less urgent than arduous, it was thought requisite, for the more quick dispatch, to resolve, *That no man should make a speech above* 2 *hours long*; in regard our Ancestors thought a quarter, or half an houre long enough; and truly that was enough for them, because they were so dull as to pen all, and living in the Infancie of time, were content to learn to spell before they spake.

This being premised, our Senators presently fell upon their work, and it was resolved *nemine contradicente*, That wee *Utopians* had hitherto been mistaken touching the notion of *Liberty*, as of late years it hath been stated in this Country, Alas (Sir) the *High Shoon*, the *Leveller*, and the *Enthusiast*, thought it lay in having no land-Lord no *Law*, no *Religion*, save his own Phantsie; They thought we ought to have been as boundless as the Sea, as common as the Earth, as free as the Aire, and as wild as the Fire, that by combustion, like rare Chymists, we might extract somwhat more fine than ever was known to our Predecessors; Thus we might have been reduced to our primitive freedom: for, do you think fit, that Free-borne man should be pinion'd with Policie seeing of late the whole race of *Adam* became Politicians and Princes by the Law of Nature? Indeed, it ought not so to be; there was a readier way to rule the world by leaving every man to himself, it being then understood, that this only is perfect Liberty, where none obey all command, & every one doth what he list.

Yet give me leave to tell you (Sir) for all this, we had no Free State then, save that the People were free to feed themselves with Phantsies, and were told that they were the supreme Power, and should come to use it in a Revolution or Rotation of their Assemblies, the consideration whereof made their Worships giddy, in those days, with expectation, and the Senate so wise as to hold up the Humor.

Thus while they sate still, and the People ran out into endless Factions, still further and further from a Settlement, there was in conclusion no visible means left, to keep the old Race of Kings from over-running our Estates and Liberties, had not the most excellent *Basilides*, that Renowned Prince, resolved to encounter all the Monsters of Scandal, Prejudice, Ignorance and Faction at home, and the Common Enemy abroad.

You see then by this, it is not without Reason, that our present Senate have concluded, that the People were mistaken about the point of *Liberty* in former time.

After this Resolve, two more were immediatly passed, and because the Post cals on me to dispatch, I can but only name them.

The one is this, *That our Utopians have hitherto been extremely mistaken in the Ground of all their Arguments about Matter of Government*. They fetch their Arguments from principles of naturall Right and Freedom, whereas the truth is, Government is an Art or Artifice (call it which you will) found out by Mans Wisdom, and occasioned by necessity, he being (as I may say) necessitated in order to the more secure enjoying of his Freedom, to resign up his natural private Right for the publick convenience of himself, and the Community where he lives; and so the Reasons constituting Government are not to be derived from Mans naturall Right, for, that must be presumed a nullity before there can be a Government, and yet there is no possibility of preserving it but by Government.

The other is this, *That there is no everlasting Principle in Government, as to any one particular Form*. For, the Rules and Reasons of Government cannot be always the same, it depending upon future Contingents; and therefore must be alterable according to the variety of emergent Circumstances and Accidents; so that no certain Form can be prescribed at all times, seeing that which may be most commendable at one time, may be most condemnable at another, and that is ever best which best fits the present State and Temper of Affairs and is most conducible to the end of Government: and so a Free State may be no less, and many times much more, in that which Men call Monarchy, than in any other Form. 'Tis not the name of a Free State or Commonwealth that makes it to be so indeed, but that is a free State in every form, where Men are put into the way of a free enjoyment and security of their Rights and Properties. Which being so, it is a fundamentall Article of our State-Creed in *Utopia*, That he who cals his brother an Apostate for moving, according to Reason, with the great Wheel of Government, may himself, if he happen to suffer for his obstinacy, be justly esteemed his own Martyr, not the Publick.

But more another time; at present I fear I have been too serious, and exceeded the Bounds of an Epistle, therefore beg your pardon.

This editorial contains an argument against censorship, somewhat at odds with the ideology of Nedham's paymasters in the Spring of 1657.

Mercurius Politicus *Numb.* 355

26 March – 2 April, 1657 361.355 {8.20}

From *Utopia* March 8.

SIR, yours bearing date the last of *February*, came safe to hand. Glad I am, our Returnes are certain, and like to be, for the wind over all this Commonwealth, is generally so favourable and faire, that I see now there is hope you may come hereafter to know which way it blowes, without the help of a Weather-Cock; Therefore be sure you keep Touch with the Post, otherwise I shall hold on my Course, and perhaps leave you ignorant of the rare Mistery of *Drolling*. This is a secret that we have had great Experience and use of in our *Utopia*; for, truly Sir, too many of our Countrymens Crownes, were once even quite Addle betwixt Dreaming and Disputation; besides, their Combs were grown so big with high Conceit, that it was no easie matter to Cut them, being ready to Crow over all the Learned of all Ages and Orders, that ever durst enter the Pit, in point of Argument; neither University nor Academy, nor Common-sense, was able to come neer them, till at length, a certain *Droll* undertook them, who never plaid at the Pate, because he found it so well Lined, that no Reason, though never so Accute, was able to enter, but yet with short Girds under the Ribbs, and smart Touches on the Sides, he made a shift to Confute some, to Convert the rest, and in conclusion to carry away the Cudgels from all our wise men of *Utopia*. Since which time, it has been the Policy of this Country, to retain a *State Droll* in pension, as a most necessary Officer, to Correct all that presume to Print or Dispute about Models of Government.

Now the benefit which redounds to this State; by the instituting of such an Officer, is so considerable, that the little Wits of the City, being duly Lasht, are kept from Lashing out; so that the Actions of our Renowned Prince, and the Prudent Resolves of the Senate, may chance to walk the Town without Examination, and the Texts of Law both Divine and Humane, may scape the Torments they are put to by every smal Faction.

In the mean time, you are to know, that things are growing here to an indifferent good pass, by the diligence and wisdome of the

Senate, who proceed in their Resolutions with great Alacrity, of some of which you had a Taste, by the last Return of Post.

Since which, the first Resolve passed this Week, was to this effect, *That in the Electing of Members to serve for the respective Provinces and Boroughs in the Senate of Utopia, the People do, together with the Interests and Trusts reposed in those Members, resign up to them all their Wit, Wisdome, and Understanding; so that the Wisdome of the Senate, is the Wisdome of the whole people, and contrary Opinion, (whatever the pretence be) is adjudged Faction*. At first our *Utopians* looked very blew upon this Resolve, supposing it was unreasonable they should part with that Wit which they never had, because not a man of them but thought he could Conquer the World with a Bulrush, and turn it upon the Axletree of Government, with a little Finger. And truly it was a hard matter to weane them from this Princely Humour, till time taught them to understand, That where a Civill Power is to be setled, we cannot all be Princes.

Then they began to see plainly, that mankind must of necessity yeeld up their natural Faculties, as well as Rights, to their chosen Trustees, before there can be an acting in a politick capacity of any kind, for the benefit of all; Then they began to understand too, that though all men are equally born Princes, by deriving their Pedigree from the blood-royall of *Adam*, yet they cannot all live Princes; and there was never any Free State in the world wherein it was so, though it was fit men should be told so, there being no other way in that Form, to back the Beast of many Heads, and keep him from casting his Rider. Then they began to see, that in Government; 'Tis but to catch Butterflies to run a gadding after Forms, or like the Dogg in the Fable, by catching at the shadow, to venture the losse of the Mutton. And at length, they made a shift to see the Truth of all, That men are as Free, every jot under a Right Principality, as under a Popular Forme; seeing every Form of Government, is (as was said) an Act or Artifice, a Fiction or Figment of the brain, which is nothing in it self, further then as it is a necessary device, for putting men into a way convenient for the acting and exercising of their naturall Rights and Judgements, sometimes after one manner, sometimes after another, as occasion requires in prudence, for the common Good. So our *Utopians* having been satisfied in this Point, began to hate Faction grounded upon Forms and Notions, and became Fitter to live under a Prince in time to come.

Another Resolve was, *That our Utopians have bin extreamly mistaken in their suppositions, touching the ground of our*

Quarrel with that Forreign race of Kings, which lately ruled here; and most justly deserve to be for ever excluded. It was neither against their Name, Title, Dignity, nor Office, that Armes were taken up, but against their Enormities and Irregularities. So the Senate understood, so they Declared, and in their Declarations commended the Form of the *Three Estates*, as most excellent, most suiting with the *Genius* of our People, the Insular scituation of our Dominions, its Magnificence equall to the most glorious Nations, and that under which our Ancestors became happy and famous both at home and abroad. And in this Resolution the Senate continued till the latter end of the Year 1646. at which time they did put forth a Declaration to all the World, shewing how unwilling they were to part with that Form of Government. And doubtless it had never been parted with, but that He who was dignified with the supreme Title, made it altogether impossible to secure the Interest of Religion and Liberty, if respect were had any longer to himself or Family; then the Reason of State, Publick Necessity and Convenience altering, it made way (and that justly too) for the altering and changing the Old Form of Government, and introducing a New one, which was called a *Free-State*, and intended to be so for ever, but never was so in the exercise of that popular interest, which had been declared for. But growing into Exesses altogether intolerable they soon followed the Fate of the former: Other wayes and Forms being made use of afterwards as well as this, and all proving ineffectual; It was resolved thus much further by the Senate, *That every one of those Forms ought to be looked upon in their Times, but as* Ultima tabula post naufragium, *that is to say, the last Plank (as it were) after shipwrack, laid hold on out of necessity, to save a Commonwealth from sinking, and so no longer to be made use of, then till they could get a shore upon some sure and lasting settlement*. This our Utopians now generally understand, and begin to see, That all Forms of Government are but temporary Expedients, to be taken upon Tryal, as necessity and right Reason of State enjoyns in order to the publike safety; and that as 'tis a madness to contend for any Form, when the Reason of it is gone, so 'tis neither dishonour nor scandal, by following right Reason, to shift through every Form, and after all other Experiments made in vain, when the ends of Government cannot otherwise be conserved, to revert upon the old bottom and Foundation.–Till the next I rest,– *Joco-Serio,*

Your most humble Servant.

Mercurius Politicus *Numb*. 356

2–9 April, 1657 361.356 {8.21}

From Oceana, April 1.

SIR;

I Desire you would not foul your fingers any more with your foolish Correspondent of *Utopia*; for, the *Agrarian*-Wits of the five and fiftheth order, of the Commonwealth of *Oceana*, do humbly conceive, That no Government whatsoever is of any Weight but in their Balance; and that if you go to *Venice* to learn to Cog a Die with a Balloting Box, you'll soon get money enough to purchase a better Island then *Utopia*, and there you may erect a Commonwealth of your own. For, (SIR) you are to know, its no great Charge, when the accompt is cast up, as it is set down by the learned Author and founder of our most famous *Oceania*, because, as he orders the matter, very ordinary Tools will serve the Turn; Therefore, though he tells us of his *Nebulosa*, (or *Nebulones*, if you please) his *Phylarchs*, his *Tribes*, his *Censors*, his *Knights Errant*, and *Garbatissimi Signori*, whom he cals the most compleat Gentlemen of this Age, yet you are to know, that a High-Constable is a Prime officer of State amongst them if he Ken the Knack of Balloting, and can but tell Noses; by which means he may perchance amount to the Dignity of a *Non-sincer*, whose Office it is to provide Boxes of all Colours of the Rainbow. And as to the whole Charges of this famous institution, he has left the Account of it upon Record for the Instruction of Posterity that they may know, if they please to Repair, but to Bartholmew Fair, a small Matter will serve to buy knacks to Govern the world.

Imprimis, Urns, Balls and Balloting Boxes; for ten thousand Parishes the same being wodden ware.	20000*l*. 0 *s*.
Item, Provisions of like kind for a Thousand Hundreds	3000. 00.
Item, Urns and Balls of Mettall, with Balloting Boxes, for Fifty Tribes	2000. 00.
Item, for erecting of fifty Pavilions	60000. 00.
Item, wages for 4 *Surveyors General, at a* 1000*l. a man.*	4000. 00.
Item, Wages for the rest of the Surveyors, being 1000. *at* 250*l. a man*	250000. 00.
Sum totall	339000. 00.

This is his own Account to a tittle, and he tells us, tis no great matter of Charge for the building of a Commonwealth, in Regard it has Cost as much to Rigg a few ships; and now we talk of ships, they may serve to transport him to the Tribe of *Nubia*, where *Hermes de Caducea*, Lord Orator of that tribe, stands ready to bid him welcome for his rare Invention.

In the mean time you may take notice, That we have quitted the Island of *Utopia* for a time, and perhaps for ever, being now landed in *Oceana*, to carry on the Plantation of that Country, where the learned Discoverer, has promised to settle Doctor *Ferne* in a fat Bishoprick, if he please but to wright against him. For my part, I have done with him, and all the Builders of Castles in the aire, only it was fit he should be known, because he gave the occasion, and I desire the Wits to beware of him and his Antagonist; for those Worms in their Brains, which were at first but as *Mogats*, are improved to such a magnitude, by feeding upon Politick Notions, that their Sculls being opened with a Goose-quill of their own, the one was delivered of that Monster *Leviathan*, and the other lately voided at least a Conger.

Twice Nedham was removed from his editorship of the *Mercurius Politicus*, and after the second time, he didn't write a newsbook again. This made the front page.

The Parliamentary Intelligencer *Numb.* 14.

26 March – 2 April, 1660 486.114 {8.22}

WHereas *Marchemont Nedham*, the Author of the weekly News books, called *Mercurius Politicus*, and the *Publique Intelligencer*, is, by Order of the Council of State, discharged from Writing or Publishing any publique Intelligence: The Reader is desired to take notice, that by Order of the said Council, *Giles Dury*, and *Henry Muddiman*, are authorised henceforth to Write and Publish the said *Intelligence*, the one upon the *Thursday*, and the other upon the *Monday*; which they do intend to set out under the Titles of the *Parliamentary Intelligencer*, and of *Mercurius Publicus*.

VIII.

MERCURIUS Numb 1.

HONESTUS.

OR,

NEWES from WESTMINSTER;

Touching the unfolding of *Elencticus* and *Pragmaticus*, the distempering of the Members, the beating of the Pulses, the under-hand working of the franzie brains, and the sudden Visitation of a Welch Plurisie, with the danger of their Disease, and the opinion of their great Doctors,

Pragmaticus *what is't you meane,*
the States *to scandalize:*
Or why dost thou make publike seen
Conceits for Victories.
Will whimsies think'st thou strike us dumbe?
thy party thou dost cheat:
Else where's the Welch *Conquest become?*
or where's thy North Defeat?
Though that you speak, write what you list,
Is't you can pull States *down?*
O no! a thing Greg. *'gins to twist,*
you take it, 't is your own.
How now Elencticus, *where is*
March's *eight and twentieth day?*
Oh! Oh! that's gone, and turned 'tis
Into the Eighth of May.
This fatall day in Poyers *eares,*
such terrours deepe did smight,
That in his heart it left such feares,
he cannot sleepe all night.
Now Elencticus *thou'lt lye we see,*
then prethee turn thy tune;
For now wee'l neither credit thee,
nor yet thy end of June.

London, Printed for *R. G.* 1648.

12. An honest mercury?

CHAPTER NINE

Men indued with new lights: The inspiration and persecution of the people

One of the social consequences of the English Revolution was the increased possibility of popular participation in religious debate. This both broadened the appeal of dissenting doctrines and practices, and made these sectarian tendencies more sustainedly spectacular than ever they had been before. From a broad background of class hostility sprang the impulse to alter the precepts, language and gestures of religious worship, transforming it into something the respectable and orthodox saw as antichristian. The Diggers, whose political doctrine was also a religious one, and for whom secular actions necessarily were subject to eschatological reading, argued that Heaven and Hell were states of mind and that private property was a consequence of the fall of mankind, and a form of theft {9.08&09}. 'Freedom', their spokesman Gerard Winstanley wrote, 'is the man that will turn the world upside down, therefore no wonder he hath enemies.'[1] For many in England through the 1640s, the world of Winstanley and of others must have seemed, in truth, a world upside down, used as an inverted and distorted order to define a more sober faith, but nonetheless real for all that.[2]

While the political turmoil of 1641–1660 produced new varieties of religious experience and belief, this is not to imply that

1 Winstanley, *The Law of Freedom and Other Writings*, ed. Christopher Hill (Harmondsworth: Penguin, 1973), p.128.

2 On Winstanley and many other radical worshippers in the seventeenth century, see Christopher Hill, *The World Turned Upside Down: Radical Ideas During the English Revolution* (Harmondsworth: Penguin, 1972, 1975); on the textual culture of radicalism, and particularly the importance of gesture, see Nigel Smith, *Perfection Proclaimed: Language and Literature in English Radical Religion 1640–1660* (Oxford: Clarendon Press, 1989).

England before 1641 was free from heresy. In that year the authors of the Grand Remonstrance had written:

> The malignant party tell the people that our meddling with the power of Episcopacy hath caused sectaries and conventicles, when idolatry and Popish ceremonies introduced into the Church by command of the Bishops have not only debarred the people from thence, but expelled them from the kingdom. Thus, with Elijah, we are called by this malignant party the troublers of the State, and still, while we endeavour to reform their abuses, they make us the authors of those mischiefs we study to prevent.[3]

Mortalism (the belief that the soul died with the body), Lollardism and Familism continued to exist in some form or another through the early seventeenth century. This underground existence became more public with the reduction in press controls and the diminished effectiveness of religious censorship. Likewise some radical ideas appeared to have had a quasi-continuous, though insufficiently traced existence through the later seventeenth and eighteenth centuries until they influenced the work of, among others, William Blake; they became particularly visible after the French Revolution.

But the predominant cause of the energetic and exuberant displays of religious dissent in the 1640s and 1650s was not a continuing tradition of subversive theology, but the tumultuous times themselves. The Ranters {9.11–15; 4.13}, who were the most elusive and certainly the most extravagant of the religious radicals, flourished between 1649 and 1651, and were probably grounded in an itinerant culture. They swore oaths for the very pleasure of them, extemporized and literally ranted in order to attack the neo-scholasticism of respectable theological debate. They praised beer and tobacco, believing them to be an aid to worship. Some claimed to be God. Their behaviour was a rejection of theological tradition and it insisted upon the present as the moment for religious inspiration.[4]

The Quakers, another group which features strongly in the following excerpts, were similarly spectacular. Like the Ranters,

3 Cited in S.R. Gardiner, *History of England* (London: Longmans, 1884), X, 63.

4 On the Ranters, see A.L. Morton, *The World of the Ranters: Religious Radicalism in the English Revolution* (London: Lawrence & Wishart, 1970); Christopher Hill, *The World Turned Upside Down*, ch.9 and *passim*; Nigel Smith, *A Collection of Ranter Writings from the 17th Century* (London: Junction Books, 1983); J.F. McGregor, 'The Ranters: A Study in Free Spirit in English Sectarian Religion, 1648–1660' (Oxford B.Litt thesis, 1968); and 'Seekers and Ranters', in McGregor and Barry Reay eds. *Radical Religion in the English Revolution* (Oxford: Oxford University Press, 1984).

they rejected the dead text of scripture in favour of the inner spiritual light of the inspired individual. They literally quaked: their early meetings were characterised by ecstatic fits and other displays of exuberance. The aspect of their practices espoused by their best-known seventeenth-century proponent, George Fox (who led them into pacifism after the Restoration), had a very different face in James Naylor, who, in their early years, was considered the spokesman and leader of the Quakers. It was Naylor's style of worship represented the aspect of Quakerism which, it has been argued, developed out of Ranterism. Naylor's influence was curbed when he was punished for blasphemy. He had imitated Christ's entry into Jerusalem by riding into Bristol on the back of a donkey while palm leaves were strewn at his feet. The second Protectorate Parliament wasted precious time in devising a vicious sentence for Naylor, and secured Cromwell's reluctant consent {9.21}.[5]

Cromwell was basically in favour of toleration, but the Quakers caused great anxiety amongst many in government, not least because of their unparalleled popularity. They appealed to the middling sort, not the poorer sort or the elite, and spread, particularly in rural areas, at a rate that promised to convert all of England in a few years. They aimed at social change prior to, and as a means to political reform: they therefore addressed themselves to the people, and accordingly generated popular hatred as well as support. Like newsbooks, those other conveyers of sedition, Quakers were considered viprous; they communicated and multiplied by contamination. County officials were eager to place them in confinement: they were a threat to law and order and to social hierarchies maintained by quiet deference. They refused to remove their hats to social superiors, they addressed everyone by the same, egalitarian pronoun 'thou', and they encouraged their followers to challenge ungodly clergy in the middle of sermons.[6] It seemed to some of their contemporaries that these gestures touched the basis of the social fabric. They appear frequently in the following pages because they were a very strong presence both in society and in newsbooks through the 1650s.

5 See Ronald Hutton, *The Restoration: A Political and Religious History of England and Wales 1658–1667* (Oxford: Clarendon Press, 1985), pp.10–11.

6 See Barry Reay, 'Quakerism and Society' in McGregor and Reay, *Radical Religion in the English Revolution*; Christopher Hill, *World Turned Upside Down*, ch.10.

The sources for the history of religious radicalism generally have, to say the least, their limitations. Newsbooks are no exception. Sympathy for radicals can be found in the Leveller newsbook, *The Moderate*, but most newsbooks formed part of that conservative culture, constituted by a reaction against irreverent, egalitarian and populist eschatology and worship. Formal innovation was by no means inherently linked to political radicalism: conservative reaction could don carnivalesque forms, as the men who dressed as women in order to attack the Diggers demonstrated. As an organ of the state, newsbooks represent propaganda urging the populace in the provinces to police the extravagances of their neighbours: as a voice of their respectable readers, they are an instrument of pressure upon the Commonwealth and Protectorate governments, pushing against the Army's advocation of religious toleration.

The thoroughly biased nature of the sources (except for Quaker history, which offers an exceptionally large number of autobiographies and other inside material) has recently been used to argue that the Ranters did not exist. The Ranter craze, according to J.C. Davis, was a 'projection of deviance', and there was 'no Ranter movement, no Ranter sect, no Ranter theology'.[7] We are left with a group of individuals, all associated with radical puritanism, and with some similar ideas. Davis' argument shows that using limited, printed sources (and literalistic modes of reading) historians cannot conclusively demonstrate the existence of an organised relationship amongst persons who were almost universally reviled. This does not mean, of course, that the individuals concerned did not share in the fantasies of their contemporaries. The argument that the anxiety over social disorder could be focused on an antinomian position, and could follow through its internal logic without need of a 'real' object, is of course quite a distinct issue from whether the Ranters existed or not. To draw some parallels: because the communist-hunt under McCarthy was based upon crazed paranoia and mass delusion, does not mean that there were no real individuals who believed that communism offered a better way of life: and because the witch-craze of the sixteenth and seventeenth centuries was a violent, collective fantasy repugnant to the modern age, does not

7 J.C. Davis, 'Fear, Myth and Furore: Reappraising the "Ranters"' in *Past and Present*, 129 (1990), p.82; *Fear, Myth and History: The Ranters and the Historians* (Cambridge: Cambridge University Press, 1986), p.124.

mean that there were no individuals who believed that they were witches and were accordingly possessed of supernatural powers. Ranters were so far from the jurisdiction of orthodox Protestantism that their fellow radicals, including the Quakers and Levellers, sought to distance themselves from them. Cromwell, who generally encouraged toleration, detested them for their antinomianism {9.16},[8] the belief that God's elect could not be touched by sin, and that it was therefore a pretty good idea to explore sinful activities as a sign of one's blessed status. Consequently their position in radical puritan society is especially difficult to reconstruct. But we are left with a number of accounts of believers who, particularly under the Blasphemy act of 1650, were accused of Ranterism, and did not deny it. What are we to do with these people?

One of the games which can be played with newsbook accounts of the religiously irreligious is the truth game. This is the means by which historians unpack historical facts from accounts motivated by unashamed hostility. No one would deny that Thomas Edwards' heresiography *Gangraena* (1646) is an unpleasant, distorted attack which homogenises some of the varied and particular beliefs of individuals: but it remains an important source for approaching the doctrines of non-elite members of society.

The printed sources we have for religion are only a thin patina on what was a mass activity. To rationalise these sources, as Davis does, is clearly a methodological error. To apply an intellectual Occam's Razor to the evidence, and argue that we should believe no more than we can see, or hold in our hands, is hardly satisfactory. Perhaps as a corrective we should emphasise the reasonableness (rather than the irrationality and therefore the probable non-existence) of the Ranter's position: swearing, smoking, drinking and inspired ranting seems to me an attractive form of worship. This does not mean that therefore someone must necessarily have done it three hundred and fifty years ago, but that it may have made sense in a certain context.

So what should be done with the printed sources that follow is a creative reading, an interpretation that tries to relate these images to group activity. We certainly do not know enough about the distribution and readership of newsbooks, or any seventeenth-

8 See Gardiner, *History of the Commonwealth and Protectorate*, 4 vols. (Adlestrop: Windrush Press, 1988–9), II, 2–3.

century texts; but as mass-circulated representations they had a social influence that participated in the creation of Ranters both as a material reality and as the reality of a social fantasy. Who knows whether newsbooks didn't encourage someone to curse and rant and adopt a position of materialistic pantheism?

The Book of Common Prayer was central to the issues over which war had broken out. Charles had attempted to force it on Presbyterian Scotland in 1637 with disastrous consequences. This report is from a Royalist newsbook written by Bruno Ryves and published in Oxford.

Mercvrivs Rvsticvs IV. Week

June 10. 1643. 384.04. {9.01}

At *Pebmarsh* in the same County of *Essex*, on the Lords day, divers of the Parliament Voluntiers came into the Church, while the Parson M. *Wiborow* was in his prayer before Sermon, and placed themselves neere the Pulpit, and while he was in his prayer, one of them strook divers times with his staffe against the Pulpit to interrupt him, and while he was in his Sermon in contempt of the place where they were, and the sacred action in doing, they were almost as loud as the Preacher, to the great disturbace of the Congregation: no sooner was the Sermon ended and the Parson come out of the Pulpit as farre as the Reading-desk, but they lay violent hands upon him, rent his Clothes and threaten to pull him in peices in the Church: with much intreaty they spare him there, and permit him to goe into the Church-yard, he is no sooner come thither, but they assault him more violently then before: Master *Wiborow* seeing the Constable (who all this while stood a Spectator of his hard usage) calls unto him, and charges him in the Kings name to keep the Kings peace: at his Request they did a little forbeare him: but before he could get halfe wayes home, they assault him again, and demand his book of Common-Prayer which he used in the Church (That which was found by the Parish being torne in peeces before) which he refusing to deliver up unto them, they wrecke their fury on him: they Tugge and haile him and vow to kill him unlesse he deliver up the booke of Common Prayer to their pleasure: he stoutly refuseth, hereupon they fall upon him, strike up his heeles and take it from him by force, and so carry it away in Triumph.

M[r] *Blakerby* (a silenced Minister heretofore) preaching at *Halstead* in the same County, told them that to bow at the name of *Iesus* was to thrust a Speare into Christs side, and such Ministers as signed Children with the signe of the Crosse, did as much as in them lay to send such Children unto the Divell.

A puritanical suggestion that another irreligious institution be dispensed with.

The true Informer Numb. 42

7–14 February, 1646 498.42 {9.02}

MVNDAY, *Febr.* 9.

EPiscopacy being abolished, I see no reason why this day in which this book is extant, should be honoured in the commemoration of Bishop Valentine, or by what anomalous power of the Church of Rome, he should be made the Patron of copulation; there is no doubt but he was a Bishop, & I am afraid a very wanton one, for otherwise why should that lusty heat which in this pregnant season, make proud the blood, receive from him not only an allowance, but protection: Surely if his condition were correspondent to his title, everie piece of paper which the petulant youth weare this day in their hats, and every little scroule which the bashfull and conscious Virgins keep more concealed under their cuffe, are all but libells against his Gravity, whatsoever Epitome that custome heretofore have had I do believe the practice idle and unlawfull, yet peradventure as the Swedes will allow none to sell ale, or to keep such houses of hospitality, but unlesse such who serve their Ministers, because that by their neglect of sordid gaine, and the civility of their conversation they should give good examples unto others; so Antiquitie of Superstition, made this Bishop provident of this day, that in the remembrance of the excellence of his continence, and the severity of his life he might correct the fires and distempers of youth, which otherwise would be too unbridled and licentious; but of this enough {...}

Baptists practised adult baptism and regarded infant baptism as at best pointless, and at worst a serious abuse of a divine ordinance. In the 1640s they were one of the major focuses for anxiety over the social order. They were also known as 'Dippers' because of their practice of total submersion. The following account associates this ritual with promiscuity, one of the charges conventionally made against the 'Anabaptists', with whom Baptists were frequently associated by those hostile to them.

Mercurius Civicus *Numb*. 177.

8–15 October, 1646 298.177 {9.03}

We have been importuned to give you the relation of the rebaptizing of a woman at *Hempstead* in *Hartfordshire*, in a River called *Bourn End*, hard by *Bourn Mill*; which to shew the strangenes of the manner, and the madnesse of that Sect, we have here inserted, as from authenticke hands it was sent unto us.

A Relation of the Rebaptizing a Woman at Hempsted *in* Hartfordshire *in* September *last past*, 1646. *by one* James Brown *a Sawyer*.

In the parish of *Hempsted* in *Hartfordshire*, there liveth one *James Browne*, by trade, a Sawyer; by calling, a converter of holy Sisters; by person, of a very big and tall Stature; by Religion, formerly, a good Protestant, diligent in hearing of Sermons, and alwayes seeking to heare the best men: Now of late time, within these six or seven years, he hath quite left the Church: and instead of hearing Gods Ministers in publique, he is become a preacher and teacher of others, (especially of women) going about from house to house preaching and teaching, Instructing and Baptizing; (or Rebaptizing) doing good as they say, to so many as adhere to his kinde of Teaching: and he is either the second or third man of note for spirituall abilities (as the Brethren are pleased there to call them) in all that part of the Country.

About the middle of *September* now last past. 1646. This *James Browne*, having on a day Preached (or as they call it spoken) unto an assembly of Brethren, where he inveighed against Baptizing of Infants; affirming it to be a most damnable popishe sinne: and that all true Christians ought more to mourne and lament for that they were Baptized when they were Infants, then for all the sinnes that ever they committed in the whole course of thier lives; and further shewing, how necessary and needfull it was to salvation (having attayned unto a sufficient measure of Faith) to be rebaptized. One

Mary Halsey, wife of *William Halsey*, a holy woman of the company, desired to be Baptized a new: shewing her selfe to be very sorrowfull for the blindnesse of her Parents, that would have her Baptized in her Infancy, before she knew what it meant, and she (being then without Faith) unworthy of it. *Browne* having thoroughly examined this his new convert, and found her to have attayned to a competent knowledge, the examination ended, This woman with *Browne* went into a River, neere-hand to the house of that dayes exercise, called *Bourn End* River; and there neere unto *Bourne End* Mill, in a place of the River somewhat deeper then the ordinary Channell, where having joyned together they went down into the water: *Browne* went down in his leather Breeches, in which he used to go to Sawing: And the woman went into the water in a paire of Linnen Drawers onely to cover her shame; made of purpose for such like uses, the rest of her body being all quite naked.

In this water, *Browne* washed her body all over from top to toe, rubbing her with his hands, as men doe their sheep when they wash them; and so clensed her from all filthinesse, (as he saith both of body and spirit) and throwing water upon her, used the words of Baptisme, *I Baptize thee, in the name of the Father, and of the Sonne, and of the Holy Ghost*: thrusting her head three times into the water, because three persons in Trenity: and in this water I wash and purge away all thy sinnes; sending them down the stream, together with this water that runneth off thy body: so that now thou art made as cleane againe from all sinne and wickednesse, as ever thou wast in thy Infancy; nay, cleaner, for now thy originall sinne if thou hadst any, is quite taken away, and thou art now received into the number of Christs chosen Children; and made a member of his mysticall body, and mayest be fully assured of the Kingdome of Heaven.

This being done, they departed out of the water, and went to the place of that dayes exercise.

This was seene and heard by the Miller of *Bourn End*, and some others, who got behind a hedge to heare and see the action. As they were going out of the water, the Miller called to them, and wished *Brown* to rub her a little more; for there is (saith he) I doubt one spot that is not yet made white, and they departed making no answer, and a man with them, that the woman brought downe with her to looke to her apparell, which she put off neere the River side, when she went into the water: and had not that man kept her apparell, the Miller would have conveyed it out of the way, and made her go naked to the assembly, from whence she came.

Antinomianism, the doctrine that the godly could not sin, or in effect could sin as much as they wanted because it made no difference, caused particular anxiety in the interregnum. This was the central doctrine attributed to and stated by the Ranters.

Mercurius Pragmaticvs *Numb.* 22.

22–29 August, 1648 369.222A {9.04}

And whereas they {the Commons} boast, that the *bright* and *morning star* is risen upon them, they walk yet but by *Moon light*, being stark *lunatick*, and of a *reprobate sence*. For the truth whereof we have daily experience, but this day especially I received very memorable and sure *Intelligence*, concerning the *Examination* of one *Wiliam Harris*, taken before two *Iustices* of the *Peace* for the County of *Huntington*, upon the 29. of *July*. 1648. which being a *Rarity* I must needs publish. He avowes himself to bee *God*, and that there is no *God* besides him, with many other high *Blasphemies*. There is likewise with him in prison a good *Sister* of his, one *Lockington's* wife of *Godmanchester*, committed for the like damnable expressions, whereof that the whole *Kingdome* may take notice, and also what this *Reformation* is come to, give me leave to set forth a *Copie* of the mans examination, *verbatim*.

Being demanded why he did lately commit Adultery upon the Lords day, with Lockington's *wife of* Godmanchester, *he confesseth she did come to his Bed's side and kisse him, and then did lie down upon the Bed by him, and that he did then kisse her, and that she stay'd above an houre with him. He further saith, she came to him by the will of God, and could not keep away, and that when God extends himself to any man, he must doe whatsoever he would have him, though it be to the committing of Adultery (as some call it) or killing of a man. And being demanded in particular, whether then he had the carnall knowledge of the said* Lockington's *wife, he saith he will not answer, but referreth himself to the witnesses, And he further saith, that which we call Adultery, or any other sin, is no sin, but that it is the suggestion of the Devill, he saith is a mistake of those that are not* Called, *there being* no Devill: *But* God *being in him,*

***and he in* God, *all his Actions (how weak so ever seeming to us) are no sin, but his Commands*.** Unto which *Examination* he set his *hand*; and both he and his *Adultresse* lie now committed in *Huntington* Goale.

This *Lockington's* wife being asked by the *Iustices* why she would break the Bond of *Matrimony* betwixt her and her Husband, she answered, shee *had Idolized her husband too long already*. So that since *Superstition* is fled out of *painted windows*, and Surplices into *Sheets*, judge you whether the *Synod* and the rest of them had not best hasten the setling of *Church government*, lest the new *Planters* and *Waterers* make this *Doctrine* spread, and cause poore *Lockington's* Branch of *Reformation*, to sprout forth in time, upon the *Brow-antlers* of all the *Belweathers* of the *Faction*.

One of Cromwell's laudable and lasting innovations was the admission of the Jews, who had been banished in the reign of Richard II, into Britain. The conversion of the Jews to Christianity was one of the signs that the Kingdom of God on earth was soon approaching.

The Perfect Weekly Account

10–17 January, 1649 533.44 {9.05}

Thursday Ian. 14. {...}

After this the General Councel of the Army, ordered two petitions to be drawn up to be presented to the Parliament; the one for the taking away of tythes; the other for the repealing of the Statutes heretofore made for banishing the Iewes out of this Kingdom {...}

As to the repealing of the Statutes for banishing the Iewes out of this Kingdom, It is the rather desired because it is not thought fit to be mentioned in the *Agreement of the People*. And as for the further reasons thereof, I shall referre you to the Peti{ti}on of *Iohanna Cartenright* Widdow and her son *Ebeneezer Cartenright* freeborne of *England*, and now inhabitants of the City of *Amsterdam*.

Humbly sheweth,

THat your Petitioners being conversant in that City, with and amongst some of *Izraels* race called *Iewes*, and growing sencible of their heavy out-cries and clamours against the intolerable cruelty of this our English Nation, exercised against them by that (and other) inhumane exceeding great Massacry of them, in the raign of *Richard* the second King of this land, and their banishment ever since, with the penalty of death to be inflicted upon any of their return into this land, that by discourse with them, and serious perusall of the prophets, both they and we find, that the time of her call draweth nigh; whereby they together with us, shall come to know the *Emanuel* the Lord of life, light, and glory, even as we are now known of him, And that this Nation of *England* with the Inhabitants of the Netherlands, shall be the first and readiest to transport *Israels* Sons and daughters in their ships to the land promised to their forefathers, *Abraham Isaac* and *Iacob*, for an everlasting Inheritance.

For the glorious manifestation whereof, and pious means thereunto, your petitioners humbly pray that the inhumane cruell Statute of banishment made against them may be repealed, and they under the Christian banner of charity and brotherly love, may againe be received and permitted to trade and dwell among you in this land, as now they do in the Netherlands.

By which act of mercy, your Petitioners are assured the wrath of God, will be much appeased towards you, for their innocent blood shed, and they thereby dayly enlightened in the saving knowledge of him, for whom they look dayly and expect as their King of eternall glory, and both their and our Lord God of salvation Christ Jesus, for the glorious accomplishing whereof, your Petitioners do, and shall ever addresse themselves to the true Peace, and pray, &c.

The Diggers, or True Levellers, established their commune of common property for common good, in which the earth would be a treasury of wealth for all, on St. George's Hill on 1 April 1649. They were mobbed by locals, threatened by soldiers, their seeds dug up and their camp eventually demolished, though Fairfax did attempt to provide them with some protection. The following account relates the appearance of two of their spokesmen before him.

A Perfect Diurnall of Some Passages in Parliament Numb. 298

16–23 April, 1649 504.299 {9.06}

Friday April 20. {…}

This day *Everard* and *Winstanly*, two of the chief Actors in the late businesse we mentioned of Surrey, came to White-hall to give the Lord Generall an account of their digging up the grounds on S. Georges hill in Surrey; they made a large Declaration to justifie their proceedings, but it may be all briefly summed up thus: *Everard* sayd, *That he was of the race of the Jews and that all the Liberties of the People were lost by the comming in of William the Conqueror: and that, ever since the people of God have lived under Tyranny and Oppression, worse then that of our Forefathers under the Egyptians. But now the time of the deliverance was at hand, and God would bring his people out of this slavery and restore them to their Freedoms in enjoying the fruits and benefits of the Earth: And that there had lately appeared a Vision to him, which bad him, Arise, and dig and plow the Earth, and receive the fruits thereof: And that their intent is to restore the Creation to its former condition. And that as God had promised to make the barren Ground fruitfull: So now, what they did was to renew the ancient Community of the enjoying the fruits of the Earth and to distribute the benefit thereof to the Poore and needy, and to feed the Hungry, and to cloath the Naked. And that they intend not to meddle with any mans Propriety, nor to break down any Payls or inclosures, but onely to meddle with what was common and untilled, and to make it fruitfull for the use of man; but that the time will suddenly be that all men should willingly come in, and give up their Lands and Estates, and willingly to submit to this Community. And for those that will come in and worke, they shall have meat, drinke, and clothes, which is all that is necessary for the life of man; and that for money, there was not any need of it, nor of any clothes more then to cover their nakednesse. And that they will not defend themselves by Arms, but will submit unto Authority, and wait till the promised opportunity be offered which they conceive to be neer at hand. And that as their forefathers lived in Tents, so it would be suitable to their condition now to live in the same.* With many other things, to this purpose.

This one observation further may not be forgotten, That while *Everard* and *Winstanly* were before the Generall they stood with their Hats on, and being demanded the reason, sayd, he was but their fellow Creature. Being askt the meaning of that place, *Give honour to whom Honour is due*, they seemed to be offended, and said, That their mouths should be stopped who gave them that offence.

The Kingdomes Faithfull and Impartiall Scout
[*Numb.* 13.]

20–27 April, 1649 210.13 {9.07}

Beginning Friday the 20 *of Aprill.* {...}

The new fangled people that begin to dig on St. *Georges* Hill in Surrey, say, they are like Adam, they expect a generall restauration of the Earth to its first condition, that themselves were called to seek and begin this great work, which will shortly go on throughout the whole world: and therefore they begin to dig and dresse the Earth: (*One of them getting up a great burden of thorns and bryers; thrust them into the pulpit at the Church at* Walton, *to stop out the Parson.*) They professe a great deal of mildnesse, and would have the world believe, they have dreamt Dreams, seen Visions, heard strange voyces, and have dictates beyond mans teaching. They professe they will not fight, *knowing that not to be good for them*. They would have none to work for hire, or be servants to other men, and say that there is no need of money: yet they offer, that if any Gentleman, &c. that hath not bin brought up to labour, shall bring a stock, and put it into their hand, he shall have part with them; (*a pure contradiction of themselves.*) They alleadge, that the Prophesie in *Ezek.* is to be made good at this time, where is promised so great a change, that the travellers which passe by, shall take notice, and say, *This Land which was barren and wast is now become fruitfull and pleasant like the Garden of* Eden.

The Ring-leaders of these were brought up to *London*, and the rest dispiersed, but they said they would come again. {...}

Saturday 14 Aprill. {...}

The new Plantation in Surrey is re-levelled by the Country people, and many of the Levelling Seekers forced to fly (in the heat of their zeal) for refuge.

Munday Aprill 23. {...}

There be some which come from St Georges hill in Surrey: who say that a considerable party of the diggers, met againe in pursuance of what they had begun, a modest Gentleman came to them and for a time he expostulated the cause with some of them, and after a short discourse the Gentleman being moved strook one of them a box on the eare. The Leveller said it was again{st} their principles to return it againe, but rather to turn the other eare so the businesse was soon pacified, yet the digger shortly after

shewed much choller and in discontent said, that on all that he digged he would sow Hempseed.

In the following passage Nedham defends the Levellers and their prominent spokesman John Lilburne against the tyrannical Army Council who had attempted to make them appear ridiculous by associating them with the Diggers. Nedham had no deep sympathy with the Levellers, but briefly supported them in 1649 when their political objectives led to an apparent allegiance with the king.

Mercurius Pragmaticus, (For King Charles II.) {2 pars. Num.1.

17–24 April, 1649 370.01 {9.08}

No doubt they {the Army Councell} might {restore freedom}, if gallant *John* were once redeem'd from the *Lyons* and *Catamountains*, and men truly understood what they are which we call *Levellers*; not that they aim at the *Levelling* of mens *Estates*, but at the new *State-Tyranny*: And therefore it is, that the mercifull *Hoghen Mogens* of *Derby-House* having nigh starved the Kingdom, and a few poor people making bold with a little *wast-ground* in *Surrey*, to sow a few *Turnips* and *Carrets* to sustein their *Families*, they wrest this act to the disrepute of the *Levellers*, as if they mean't to make all *common*; and to make a huge businesse of it, their *Pamphleters* proclaim it about the Kingdom, and divers troops of *Janisaries* were sent prauncing into *Surrey* to make a *Conquest* over those *feeble souls* and *empty bellies*. But that you may not be scared with the *Levellers* hereafter, I tell you they are such as stand for an *equall Interest* in Freedom against the present *Tyranny*, and are so much the more tolerable in that a little experience will teach them, that a just *Monarch* is the best *Guardian* of *publique Liberty*; besides, the passage is very quick and easie, from a *popular Government* to a well-regulated *Monarchy*.

The following account relates the execution of the Levellers, army radicals who had recently refused to serve in Cromwell's campaign in Ireland, perceiving it as a means of crushing resistance to the tyrannical impulses of the State. They were shot down in the Church yard at Burford, which by a curious juxtaposition was the place of Nedham's birth; All Souls, where Fairfax and Cromwell rested the same night, before being awarded honorary degrees by the University, was Nedham's old college. It is difficult to prove that Nedham wrote this late issue of *Pragmaticus*, but the style is certainly close to his.

Mercurius Pragmaticus. (For King Charles II.)
{2 Pars Num. 6.

22–29 May, 1649 370.06A {9.09}

THe *Proverbe* saith, *A Dog hath his day*, and so hath the *Independent*; for *Brother-Leveller* hath had his *good-night* as well as Sir *Iohn Presbyter*, and must be forced, like him, to live upon the mercy of the *ruling-faction*. Indeed, this *Reformation* hath brought forth a pretty *litter*, and whosoever looks seriously upon them all, may soon see who, and what were their *Parents*: For; by their *Religion* and *Manners*, and their *Practises* upon each other, any one must conclude that the *Turke* and the *Canniball* were chief in their generation.

And this appears by the bringing in the *Levellers* like *minc't-meat*, for the *second-course*, after they had eaten up the *Presbyters*; wherein King *Nol* (as I told you) spared for no cost to catch the *Birds of Righteousness* in a *Net* at *Burford*; And so it concerned him, for that his *Spies* had given him notice of their brave Resolution to have stood to their *tackling*, and fought it out to the last man; as they had reason (sure) to bid high, when so glorious a *prize* was set before their eyes, as the *Prerogative* of *Saint-ship* over all the *Purses* in the Kingdom,

By vertue whereof it is, that *Oliver* hath all along carried the day against his *Enemies*, and now especially at *Burford*; whither he came having that day marched 40 miles, and prepared his way with many a Blessed Troop of *Angels*, which so converted the *Levelling-Captain* of the Guard, that made his *Old friends* secure, by assuring them that no *Enemy* was or would be at hand; and so having bid them *good-night*, he and the *Scouts* (being *Brethren in iniquity*) made a *match* to go and meet his *Highness* and his

Excellency, and so brought them on (by night) to spoyl all the *dreams* and *visions* of *victory* by a *surprisall* in their *quarters*.

The issue whereof was, that the *Free-born Champions* were brought into *Bondage*, and used by *Oliver's Israel* like *Egyptians*, being spoyled of their *horses* and *arms*, though most of the men made a shift to escape, not above 200 taken, who being all turn'd into the *Church*, and so the *Church* into a *Conventicle*, a *Councel of War* made short work with two *Cornets* and two *Corporals*, by an absolute *sentence* of death upon them; but the rest for being enemies against *tithes*, were sentenced to *tithe* their own destruction; and for being Adversaries to *Churches*, destined every *Tenth* man to hang like *Bel's* in the *Steeple*, and ring his *Highnesse* and his *Excellency* a sad *Peale* upon their departure.

But here lyes the *mystery*, that of the 4 sentenced absolutely Cornet *Denne* obtained a *Writ* of Relief (caled a *Pardon*) at the place of *Execution*; which is much to be wondred at, considering that the *Bowels* of the *Saints* are *just* and *tender* as their *consciences*, and may help to make *Fiddle-strings* like *Cats-guts*, or rather serve like *wire* to make *Harpsicle*, to make *musick* and *mischief*. But *Denne* was no sooner condemned, but he *wheeled* about immediatly, if he did not before, forasmuch as his *canting Recantation* hath given the world cause to beleeve (what many of his *old friends* say) that he was imployed among them all along, on purpose to heighten, and then betray the businesse; it being none of Oliver's least Arts (by Advice of his Son *Henry*) to hatch factions and then crush them in the *shell*, for the Advance of his Reputation.

As for the other 3 Comrades of *Denne*, whose names were *Thompson* (brother to *Thompson* the stout Leader) *Church* and *Perkins*, They were *shot*, carrying the businesse most gallantly, and looking death in the face with a world of Magnanimity; which *Saint-like dispatch* being over, King *Oliver* went into the *Church*, and sang a *Psalm of mercy* to their fellows, extolling the service of *Ireland* to no purpose, whilst his *Excellency* sent out *warrants* to catch *Rebels* at home, and directed them to all the *Bumkin-Justices* and *Club-men* that are crept into *Commission*.

In like manner, the *supreme things* here at *Westminster* are fallen a voting of severall *particulars*, to give the *free-born* humor a *thorough-purge* out of the *Army, City* and *Kingdom*. The first is an *Order* for a Commission of *Oyer* and *Terminer*, to be issued out under the great *Butter-print* of *England*, to bring all the *Saints* that are in prison in *Northampton* and *Oxford*, to pass the *fiery tryall*, and lay those new *Pillars* of *Reformation* in *dust* and *ashes*.

Secondly, That the *Counsell of State* is enjoyned to take care; that is, the *Councel of State* hath enjoyned the *supreme Voters* to fall a voting and ordering, that the *Lord Mayor Andrews*, squeaking *Skippon, Robert Tichburn* the rare *Rattoon*, and all the Ministers of *Injustice* in *London*, shall become the *State's Catch-poles*, to hunt out all the *Rebels* that were in the late *Rebellion* against *Nol*. That was well put in, or else if all *old Rebels* must have been *ferreted*, then this truth would have been verified to some purpose, that the *City* hath often been swept more clean by an Order of the *House*, then ever it was by the *plague*. Then judge you whether they are not a *supreme pestilent Generation*.

The third *Order* is, that *Mun Prideaux*, Atturney, or *Dul-man* Generall for the *State*; do prepare a *Proclamation* to be sent into all *Counties*, for the apprehending all new *Rebels*: And if he cannot do this of himselfe, I *Prag*, that am a notable *Rag* of the *Supreme Authority*, do *Order* and *Ordain*, or *inact*, that *Bolstrode Whitlock*; the prime *Squire*, be an assistant, the world having taken as much notice of his rare *faculty* in *drawing* up, & *declaring*, as they have of the *wild Baron* for *hanging* and *quartering*.

Now the *Question* is, whether this *Proclamation* would have put any metall into the men of *Northampton*, had it come down when gallant *Thompson* (with his 13 men) kept the *Town* in possession, with all *Arms* and *Ammunition*, and plundred the *holy treasure* of the *Excise*, and distributed it among the poor, out of whose *purses* it was wrack't by the device of an *Ordinance*. After this, having notice of his Brothers being shot at *Burford*, and that himself was pursued, he publickly declared, that yet it was not impossible but he might meet with *Cromwell* or *Fairfax*, and then he would charge his *Birding-peece* too in a *Councel of war*, and make no more then a *Cock-Sparrow* of his *Highnesse* or his *Excellency*.

Which being don, and *Intelligence* given that the *Persuers* were at hand, he fled out of *Town*, and being followed hard, his men were taken; but himself better mounted than the rest, escaped into a wood neer *Wellingborough*, where being hunted out, and resolved to take *no quarter*, he charged the party of Horse most bravely 3 several times, and sent some of them to be his *Harbingers* in the other world; whether himself followed immediately being at his *third charge* shot by a Carbine with seven Bullets into the belly. Thus fell the great *Achylles*, or that *Alexander* of the *Levellers*, who wanted nothing but a *Royal Cause*, and a better *Fortune*, to have built himself a *Monument* as large as either of those: however, let him live among his own party by the name of *Tompson the great*.

This *Tragedy* being over, & the *Lion* dead whom *Cromwel* feared living, & his *Highness* & his *Excelency* having their hearts now at ease, they set forward from *Burford* to *Oxford*, to have their *Triumphs* celebrated by the *spurious Brats* of the *University*; where they were lodged in *All-Souls* Colledg, heretofore a neat *nursery* of civility and learning.

This editorial appeals to an argument that may have been familiar to some of its readers as distinctly Machiavellian. It also links the spiritual reformation — the overthrow of episcopacy — with a political reformation, which was perceived as presently going astray.

The Moderate *Numb*. 51.

26 June – 3 July, 1649 413.2051 {9.10}

HE that overcomes by Conquest and keeps his Trophies of *Victoria* by love, will challenge a high applause of being a good Souldier, and a better Christian; but he that looses all (after Conquest) for want of Affection, deserves the just brand of Infamy, and a weak Politician. Man being deeply afflicted, both in outward and inward condition, will make desperate adventures to bring himself to a long expected ease thereof and his oppressor to a speedy ruine; and though once, or more supprest in the attempt, yet no sooner opportunity smiles upon him, but its embraced again with the dearest affection, and managed with the greatest depth of Judgement, and strength of Reason. Hence it is, that all Tyrants and Oppressors have been alarmed in all ages (especially this) with the desperate On-sets and Carreers of the distressed multitude; who no sooner enter by storm, but they make their enemies (though never so great) drink the dregs of their cup of Fury; and not onely so, but leaves them, and their issue, odious to all posterity. For the Lord will break the Rod of the Oppressor, and make his people free indeed, not onely in Christ, as to a spiritual, but also the world, a temporal condition; so shall they submit to no power on earth, but such as they shall choose for their good and wel being. All creatures being in subjection to them, and they to none, but God, or such as they themselves shall please to appoint, for the end aforesaid.

Laurence Clarkson, or Claxton, was a Ranter. He had been an army chaplain before exploring several of the more interesting heresies of the 1640s.

Mercurius Politicus Numb. 17.

26 September – 3 October, 1650 361.017 {9.11}

Edenburgh Sept. 25. 1650.

Yesterday, upon the confession of one *Laurence Clarkson*, touching the making & publishing of a blasphemous Book, called *The single eye*; and also upon a Report made of the carriage of Major *Rainsborow*, passed severall *Votes:* That the said *Major* be disabled from his Justiceship in *Middlesex*, or any other County: That *Clarkson* be sent to *Bridewell* for a Moneth, and after banished, not to return upon paine of death: That the said Book be burnt by the *Hangman*: Lastly, that whosoever hath any of the Books, shall deliver them up to the next Justice of peace. The severity of which *Votes* may serve to stop the slandrous mouths of those that publish abroad such vile reports of this *Commonwealth*, as if they intended to countenance impious and *licentious practises*, under pretence of *Religion* and *Liberty*.

This account suggests the way the term 'Ranter' could be an undefined category of abuse, as fictional as Chaucer's epic of storytelling. The writer twists the usual radical connotations around and shows how the king's supporters could be equally unconcerned with notions of the heinousness of sin.

Mercurius Politicus Numb. 33.

16–23 January, 1651 361.033 {9.12}

From *Leyden* we had this accute representation of Affaires in *Holland*, of this 17. instant, *stilo novo*. {...}

The Kings Agent here hath his Intelligencers at *London*, which doe him little good, but to tell Stories of exorbitant practices of some men in power among you, and to make his party merry with *Canterbury* tales of *Ranters*. I had thought all the Ranters had been Kings men, and spued out of your Land: for, I have seen good store of them here, among whom *Ned Broughton* the Captain of Hachsters and Dammees of your Nation, as one of his Comrades told me, is newly gone over in secret to *London* to his wife there, from whose friends he hath a Passport to compound for his lands, or receive money from them. If this shall goe cleverly, then may the Devill be a compounder in *England*. I have heard him glory how many women he hath defiled, and how many Round-heads he hath kild with his own hand. But enough of him. {...}

The following heresies, described as Ranter, combine prophecy and aspirations to divinity with ingenuity and exegetical confidence.

A Perfect Account *Num*. 21.

28 May – 4 June, 1651 496.021 {9.13}

Munday, June 2.

Several persons called Ranters, were very lately apprehended in the Suburbs of London, and being carried before Justice *Hubbert*, their examinations were taken, a true copie of those that are more remarkable here follow.

The examination of *Elizabeth Haygood*, taken the 24 of *May* 1651. before *Thomas Hubbert* Esquire, one of the Justices of the Peace for the County of Middlesex, who being taken in the company of a blasphemous sort of people, commonly called Ranters, and examined, she confesseth and saith, That *Iohn Robbins* is her God Almighty, & that he is the eternal God & Father of our Lord Jesus Christ, and that Jesus Christ is now in the womb of *Ioan Robbins*, one of her society, and that he shall be born of her about five weeks hence, and she looks to be saved by none other God but her God *Iohn Robbins*. And further she saith, That the said *Iohn Robbins* is the Mediator between God and her, and that Christ is the Mediator between *Iohn Robbins* and her. And further, she refuseth to set her name to this her examination, for she saith, She will not take the Divels pen into her hand, or acknowledg the Divels power.

Ioan Robins confesseth and saith, That she lived with *Ioshua Garment* (by the word of the Lord) as his wife 3 years; and that she hath lived with the above said *Iohn Robins* these three quarters of a year, as her Flesh and Bone; and that the said *Iohn Robins* is her Deliverer; and that the Lord told her about four years since, that she should conceive of a child that should be great in the work of the Lord, of which child she is now big, and that the said *Iohn Robins* begat it, and that about 5 weeks hence she expects to be delivered of it.

Ioshua Garment being examined confesseth and saith, That in the year 1631, as he was lying in his bed, the glory of the Lord did shine about him, & the Angels of the Lord appeared unto him saying, fear not thou servant of the most high God, I am sent unto thee to declare unto thee things that shall be suddenly done in the world; which is the gathering and deliverance of the twelve scattered Tribes, but the religious men of the times must and shall oppose it; be thou silent untill thou art commanded to declare it to thy God. In the year 1647. the word of the Lord came to me to the ear, by the voice saying. Thou art within my new Covenant I will teach thee. The day following the Lord told him, I the Lord have appointed thee to salvation from eternity, thou shalt eat of the bread of life, and shalt live; and brought him some bread and he did eat. A voice came to him within few days following, saying *Iosherbah, Iosherbah*, the time draws near that the Jews must be gathered and delivered. Then he saw the man *John Robins* riding upon the wings of the wind in great glory and Majesty; the word of the Lord came unto him in great power saying: This is thy Lord, Israels King, Judge, & Law-giver: he it is that must deliver the scattered Hebrews; proclaim his day; but he shall be opposed by all men, but they shal be brought in subjection to him by the word of his mouth, he being so set by his Creator.

This Examinant confesseth and saith, That the said *Iohn Robins* is his Almighty God, so set by his Creator. And further saith, That *Ioan Robins* is the mother of the Church, both of Jews and Gentiles, to bring forth that seed which was promised to *Adam in the Garden*; and the said *Iohn Robins* is the same *Adam* that was in the Garden. His several names written with his own hand.

Josherbah, Tangan, Tangarden, Pesautaviah, Phstanvah, Acher, Ahsha, Ba, Ha, Jah.

Moses, the servant of the Lord.
Joshua Garment.

This account of a female heretic brought before Cromwell is evidence of the importance of the army to the spreading of Ranterism.

Mercurius Politicus *Numb. 52.*

29 May – 5 June, 1651 361.052 {9.14}

TEUSDAY, *June* 3.

Take another of the 27 *of* May *from* Edenburgh.

{...} A woman ranter being brought before my Lord, when he had examined her before some of us, he told her she was so vile a creature, as he thought her unworthy to live, and committed her to the Marshal, she being wife to a Lieutenant, till further order could be taken with her, according to her desert.

Mercurius Politicus *Numb*: 211.

22–29 June, 1654 361.211 {9.15}

From Notingham Iune 9.

In Major *Groves* Troop, at his first coming to it, were many persons of subtle Ranting Principles, divers of which have been cast out through the Majors diligent endevors; only there remained 2, or 3, one of whom about 9 weeks since, in a most distracted howling condition, being touched for his folly, continually cryed out he was damned, there was no mercy for him, confessing he had bin a desperate *Ranter* for 3 years, denying God, jeering at Christ, and Scriptures, and all Religion, and working all wickedness in secret but whoredom. Many sad hours we had with him for 3 weeks together. At first he had many fits for divers dayes, like Convulsion fits, and those he called the conflicts of the Devill within him, and when those began to abate, he had some temptations to destroy himself; for which, together with some rude Passages, he was shut up in prison. By means of good company that came to him, there seemed to be divers symptomes of a good change in him, many good Christians having put up prayers in his behalf.

After divers sober dayes, he was permitted to goe out of prison. He walked 3 weeks or more abroad among us, and nothing worthy of blame appeared in him, save only some Fits of passion, which he was naturally addicted to; he Rode and went with us to divers

Meetings in the Country. Hence we conceived him to be so well, that we suffred him to goe out upon a party, and he returned so well home, that the less care was taken of him: But on the 13 instant, while we and some of the Troop were out at a Lecture, one brought him news that his Hors was put in the Pound, wherupon he presently snatching up a Rapier, ran to the Pound, and kild the man that kept it, before he so much as looked upon the horse, and when the deed was done, the hors appeared to be none of his. Immediatly then, he threw away the weapon, lay down & wept, saying, *Now the Devil had what he would have, and done his worst*. He went quietly to prison, and weeps and complains bitterly against himself for shedding innocent blood. There seems to bee hope of grace in him; but if the Lord do shew him loving kindness this is a sad way to it, that he should commit murther, ere the Lord humble him to purpose.

This hath opened the peoples mouths sadly, but you have the Truth in substance. It is (Sir) a black Relation, that one should live a Professor some years, as he did, converse with Gods people, and pray among them and then to despise Ordinances, and from thence go to the *Adamites*; then to fly out against God himself, and say there was none, no heaven, no hell, fall into all wickedness, and lay therin 3 years together, then to be afflicted in conscience, have many symptoms of Gods love returning to him, and afterwards that he should let Satan make this advantage by him. Oh, that this might be a warning to some, and an awaking to others, that have embraced the same Ranting opinions!

The Quakers, here apparently confused with the Shakers, were initially particularly strong in the north; here they are characterised by their egalitarian language and gestures and by their emphasis on the inner light over scripture.

Severall Proceedings of State Affaires
Num. 258

31 August – 7 Sept, 1654 599.258 {9.16}

Berwick 28 August. The Members from *Scotland* are some on their way, others following. And so those for *Northumberland*, who I hope will cause something to bee done about the Shakers, as they call themselves, that swarm about *Northumberland*, many hundreds of them meet together in the fields, and there pretend an Assembly of Devotion. They are a people that say they fare hard, eat little, and pretend that they give up themselves to a devout life, but they in practice appear to bee such as shew respect neither to God nor men; not to God, for they dispise his Word written in the Holy Scriptures, and make their own notions to be exalted above Gods Word; and they are above and trample upon Gods Ministers and Ordinances, and esteem their own phancies to bee as infallible as God himself; and for their carriage towards men, the best man they speak to they *Thou* him, and will put off their hats to no body, nor own any Authority as Magistrates over them; and say the Spirit within them teacheth them in all things, a people they are every way fitted to plant Atheism.

Theareaujohn was the inspired name of Thomas Tany, who has been described as a Ranter as well as a Quaker. He may well have been something entirely different.

Mercurius Politicus *Numb*: 238

28 December – January 4, 1654{5} 361.238 {9.17}

Saturday, 30. A hair-brained fellow or Quaker, who calls himself *Theareau John*, and useth now and then to live in Tents, which he erects sometimes at *Lambeth*, and sometimes at *Greenwich*, saying, *He is to gather the dispersed Jews, and carry them to the Holy-Land*. This man came in an antique habit, with a long rusty Sword by his side to the Room at the Parlament House door, where a Toy taking him, in the head, he suddenly fell a slashing of the By-standers, cutting the Cloaths of some; and in that fury, he ran with his sword drawn and bounced with his foot at the house door, to have forced and entred it; but being laid hold on, he was sent for in, and coming to the Bar, he stood covered; but the Serjeant was commanded to take off his Hat. He was there asked divers questions, and afterwards committed to the Gatehouse. He was formerly committed to Newgate for Blasphemy; and last week, at *Lambeth*, he openly, with great solemnity burnt a sword, a great Saddle, a Pair of Pistols, and the Bible together, declaring them the three grand Idols of *England*. This is the fruit of that Phrensie, called *Quakerism*.

Fox, along with Naylor, was a prominent Quaker leader. This report is dated 26 February.

Mercurius Politicus *Numb:* 246

22 February – 1 March, 1654{5} 361.246 {9.18}

Feb 26. {...}

Divers *Quakers* having been apprehended as they were roving about the Country in *Leicestershire*, and among them one *Fox*, a principal leader of that phrentick party, they are brought up hither, and detained in custody. It hath been observed, that in the said County, there have been of late many meetings of those people, called *Quakers, Ranters*, and others, which are dispersed by some of our horse. This *Fox* being brought to *Whitehal*, had divers followers, poor silly melancholly people, and among the rest, a woman in mean habit, who pretended she had fasted ten days together, and resolved not to eat, till she had uttered a Message, which she said she had from Heaven to deliver to some body, but whom she would not name.

In this period newsbooks were competing over who could make the most damaging accusations against the Quakers: Fox is here accused of witchcraft. The association between Quakerism and popery was a recurring one. *The Weekly Post* ran an identical story five months later.

Perfect Proceedings of State-Affaires *Num.* 283

22 February – 1 March, 1654{5} 599.283 {9.19}

Munday 26 *February*. {...}

This afternoon *Fox* the great Quaker, who is said to be one of the chief, old ringleaders of them, was at White-hall, he came out of *Leicestershire*, some say hee was sent up from thence, and divers Quakers were at White-hall following him. It is said that he (two years since) seduced Collonell *Fells* Wife, who following him up and down the Country, and still is of that gang, and divers others. And I heard a Gentlewoman say this day at White-hall when he was there, that shee heard him boast of his favours, shewing bunches of ribbon in the Country (about *Lancashire*) that hee had from Collonell *Fells* Wife and others. And divers strange stories were told of him and others. As that a Gentlewoman comming where they met, had a Ribbon tyed about her hand, and when shee came home talked much of *Holy Fox* as shee called him, and that shee rose in the morning, and caused her horse to be sadled, and would not be perswaded by her husband, but go shee must; But her husband going with her, in the way spyed the Ribbon, and pulling it off from her hand, shee then desired to go no further, but was ashamed and rid back again home with him, where hee tyed it about a maids hand, who also desired then to go to *Fox* untill it was pulled off, and last of all the Gentlewoman herself, (to try conclusions) would have it tyed about his wrist, charging them if hee did so strive to go, not to let him, but take it off again; who having it on, was as mad to go as either the Maid or the Wife, untill it was pulled off, and then he took the Ribbon and threw it into the fire; which is said did stink very noysomely, and there appeared a flash of lightening. Some think this *Fox* is a Popish Priest, because of his Popish tenents of *Salvation by works*; *universallity of the True light to all that are born into the world*; and the like, but others think he hath not wit enough to undertake that designe for the Papists, but some are confident, that there are Witches among them, and that many are bewitched that come to them.

After *Fox* and divers other Quakers had been at *White-hall* some hours; A Gentleman came to *Fox*, and asked him touching his hair, (which was unreasonable long) whether that did become one that pretended to live in God? It being so clearly contrary to an expresse Text of Scripture, as also his fine Buttons on his coat, (which seemed to bee Silver) if hee pretended to have nothing to do with the world, why did he so follow the fashions of the world? to which hee gave a very surley scornfull answer, and abused divers before, calling a Minister a Lyer, and judging almost every body that spake to him; And at last both *Fox* and the rest of them was bidden to go about their business, and thrust down the staires and dismist.

This story is an example of stereotypical Puritan despair and obsession with Providence. Calvinist theology required the scrutinisation of one's own thoughts and actions in order to determine whether you were numbered among the elect. The consequences could be difficult to live with.

Mercurius Politicus *Numb*. 301.

13–20 March, 1655{6} 361.301 {9.20}

An Advertisement.

About a fortnight agoe, we printed that Sir *Thomas Alcock* made away himself with stabbing; but since it appears, hee cut his own Throat with a kinde of a Skeyne which used to lye over his Bed's-head. What the occasion might be, is not certainly known, but it is collected since by divers circumstances, that he laboured under a troubled Conscience. Upon perusall of his Papers by certain persons appointed for that purpose, there was found among them this following Memoriall under his own Hand-writing, of the many notable Deliverances he had received, by the good hand of God, from his Childhood. And therefore it is the more remarkable, that he should after all, be so farr forsaken by God, as to commit that act of violence upon himself.

To the Eternall praise and glory of my good God, I will set down the many and most apparent Dangers he hath preserved me from, for which his great mercy I will ever praise his holy name.

1. IN the time of my Childhood, I was by a Drunken man cut with a Sword in the hinder part of the Head, to the very Skull.

2. And being at School, I was by a Boy stabbed in the Forehead between the Eye-brows. It was a most mercifull deliverance.

3. Being alone sliding on the Ice, I fell with half my Body into the water, dangerously so hanging, untill it pleased God to send one to my rescue.

4. I fell from the Top of a Bridg over the River *Thames*, there being a Boat not farr from the place; and although I could not then swim, it pleased God that I got to it, and thereby escaped drowning.

5. Being on the Moat at the *Grave* in the *Low-Countreys* in Frosty weather, I fell up to the Chinn; the place was so dangerous

and brittle, that my Company feared to assist mee, yet by the hand of a stranger, who did hazard himself to help me, I was delivered.

6 I stepped in to part two Souldiers that were fighting at *Numigen*; one of the Souldiers made a Thrust which cut the loop of my Girdle, passed through it, and but for the stiffning, had gone into the mortall place of my Belly.

7 At the Isle of *Rhè* I was shot through and through the Crown of my Hat, in the middle part of my Hat, it being pulled fast on my head; the Bullet making a noise with the resistance it found; and yet it pleased my good God, that onely some small part of my hair was taken off, without any other harm; to the wonder of my Company, who were then present.

8 Before divers at *Portsmouth*, I was on a sudden run at by a Drunken man with a broad Sword, my Face being from him; he ran at me so violently, the Sword bended to the very Hilt, which the standers by judged to have been through my Body: but it pleased God so to order it, that the point of the sword met with a Hook of my Breeches, and so most miraculously I escaped.

9 At the siege of the *Busse*, there came a Cannon-shot through the Breast of a Work in which I was; it hit me on the Arm, making it onely discoloured.

These particulars of mercy, besides many and sundry other Preservations from visible dangers (as before besieged places in severall Storms, and many infected Places when Souldiers perished on all sides) have I received, and through the great goodness of God have been still preserved.

Much about the same time that this Knight committed that lamentable Fact, another of the same nature was done by a Book sellers Apprentice at the sign of the Talbot in Fleetstreet; whose Master finding his Maid with the said Boy in Bed at Midnight, turned her out into the hands of the Constable, but leaving his man to himself, he hanged himself in the shop before morning. {...}

We had news likewise, That on the Lords day Mr. *Tison*, Minister of *Botolph Billingsgate*, destroyed himself by cutting his own Throat. He had attempted it about a fortnight before, having cut himself about the Throat, but was prevented from doing it effectually; and being under cure of the Chirurgeon, he was in a fair way of cure; but last Lords day, having privily gotten a Knife into his Bed, he ripped open the wound again, and most sadly made an end of this mortal life. He had been some time in the condition of a distracted man, which (it is thought) was caused by some distress of Conscience. *A wounded spirit, who can bear?*

or who can think of these and other lamentable cases lately faln out among us, without a serious reflection and compassion?

The following accounts document in detail the examination, heresies and punishment for blasphemy of James Naylor, the spectacular Quaker leader. Parliament wasted two weeks preparing his sentence, though it rejected a proposal that he should be stoned to death. Cromwell, generally an advocate of toleration, would not oppose their vicious judgement because of his serious political and economic concerns. Naylor's cruel punishment wounded his spirit and his behaviour thereafter was tragically subdued.

Mercurius Politicus *Numb*. 340.

11–18 December, 1656 361.340 {9.21}

A briefe Account concerning James Naylor the Quaker.

Having been released out of Excester Gaole, hee began immediatly to play his Pranks at divers Places in the West; among the rest, he passed by Wells and Glastenbury, through which Towns hee rod on horsback, a man going bare before him, and others walking a foot on each side of his Stirrup, and others strewing their garments in the way; from thence he took his way toward Bristol, and coming to a little Village called Bedminster about a mile from Bristol, he rode through that place likewise, a young man bare-headed leading his horse by the Bridle, and another man before with his Hat on. There accompanied him two men, with each a woman behind him on horseback; which women alighted when they came to the Suburbs of Bristol, and footed it along on each side of Nailors horse, the man still bare-headed leading the horse; and as they advanced along, they sung, and entred Bristol singing, *Holy, Holy, Holy Lord God of Israel*, and then the Women led the horse with the Reins in their hands, up to the high Cross of Bristol, and from thence to the White-Hart-Inn in Broad-street. Then the Magistrates sending for Nailor and his Companions, they came singing all the way Hosanna, and *Holy, Holy, Holy, &c.* His name that went bare before him is Timothie Wedlock, a Devonshire man. The one woman is named Martha Simonds wife of Thomas Simonds Stationer of London; the other Hannah Stranger wife of Iohn Stranger of London Comb maker.

The Magistrates having convented Nailor and the rest, divers strange blasphemous Letters and other Papers were found about them, wherein it appeared, that this deceiver had so farr gained upon his Followers by his Impostures, that they ascribed to him divine Honors, and gave him in Scripture-Phrase the same Titles which are applicable to none but Christ himself.

In a Letter of one *Richard Fairman* from Dorcester-gaole to *Nailor*, are these horrid Expressions [*I am fild with joy & rejoycing when I behold thee in the eternal unity. O my Soul is melting within me, when I behold thy beauty and innocency, dear and precious son of Zion, whose Mother is a Virgin, and whose birth is immortal.*]

Another writes of him thus [*All the Wisemen shall seek for him, and when they have found him, they shall open their ears, and shall give unto him of their Gold, Frankincense and Myrrh*]

Hannah Stranger writing from London to *Nailor* in September last, begins her Letter most blasphemously thus: [*In the pure fear and power of God, my Soul salutes thee, thou everlasting son of Righteousness, and Prince of Peace. O how my Soul travelleth to see thy day, which Abraham did, and was glad*. Then towards the latter end she useth these expressions, [*O let Innocency be thy beloved, and Righteousness thy Spouse, that thy Fathers Lambs may rejoice in thy pure and clear unspoted Image of Holiness and Purity*] And a line or two after it follows thus [*The Lord shall not suffer his Holy one to see corruption, nor his soul to lie in Hell, but will cause the mountains to melt at his presence, and the little Hils to bring him peace.*

The same woman, in another Letter to him, proceeds thus, [*O thou fairest of Ten Thousand, Thou only begotten Son of God, how my heart panteth after thee. O stay me with Flagons, and comfort me with wine. My well beloved thou art like a Roe, or young Hart, upon the Mountaines of Spices*. Then, by way of Post-Script her husband Thomas Stranger adds this. *Thy name is no more to be called* Iames *but* Iesus.]

Also, *Martha Simonds*, begins a Letter of hers to him in these words, [*O, let me for evermore be tried by the hands of* Iesus. *But should it enter into the heart of my Lord, concerning his Servant, of being guilty in this matter?*]

And her husband, *Thomas Simonds*, In a Letter to the said *Naylor*, hath these expressions of high Blasphemy [*Thou King of Israel, and Son of the most high; arise, arise in thy might power: show thy selfe a Lyon to thine Enemies, a lamb to the Innocent; make haste, and come away in the beauty of Holiness; because of the Sweet Odour of thy oyntment poured forth, therefore do*

the virgins love thee. They wait to see thy day, and the innocent doth crie, come away.

Thus much of the Letters which were found about them.

Then being examined before the Magistrates of Bristol, Martha Simonds professed she ought to fall down and worship Nailor; also, that he is her Lord, Lord of righteousnes & Prince of Peace, and anointed King of Israel by a Prophet; but who that Prophet was, she would not tell.

Likewise, Hannah Stranger upon examination declared him to be the Prince of Peace, and his Name Jesus.

Also, a Maid names Dorcas Erbury, being examined, declared James Nailor to be the Holy one of Israel, the only begotten son of God, and that she pulled off his Stockins, and put her Clothes under his Feet, because he is the Holy Lord of Israel, and that she knew no other Saviour but him; affirming more over; That the Spirit of the Lord within her commanded her to call him Lord and Master, and to serve him; That in Excester-Gaole, he had raised her from the dead, after she had been dead two daies; And that James Nailor shall sit at the right hand of the Father, and judge the world.

Thus you see, how this wretched Impostor hath prevailed upon his Followers, to bewitch them to the committing of strange Absurdities, and the uttering of many horrible Blasphemies, the like for all Circumstances, never heard of in any Age before. An Account whereof I had hitherto forborne; but have now given it in briefe, that the honor and Justice of the Parlaments Sentence passed upon him may be made evident to the People. {…}

Wednesday, 17 Decemb. {…}

This day *James Naylor* was according to the order made yesterday, brought to the Bar of the house, where being come, Mr. *Speaker* pronounced on him the Judgement of the House, for those high Crimes whereof he had been found guilty; which Judgment was as followeth.

THat *James Nailor* be set on the Pillory, with his head in the Pillory, in the new Pallace, *Westminster,* during the space of two hours on Thursday next, and shall be whipped by the Hangman through the streets from *Westminster*, to the *Old Exchange, London*; and there likewise be set upon the Pillory with his head in the Pillory, for the space of two hours, between the hours of eleven and one, on Saturday next; in each of the said places, wearing a Paper containing an Inscription of his Crimes: And that at the *Old Exchange* his Tongue shall be bored through with a hot Iron; and that he be there also stigmatised in the Forehead with the Letter *B*. And that he be afterwards sent to *Bristol*, and conveyed into, and through the said City on a Horse bare ridged, with his face backward; and there also publickly whipped the next Market day after he comes thither.

That from thence he be committed to prison in *Bridewel, London,* and there restrained from the Society of all people and kept to hard labor, till he shall be released by Parliament; and during that time, be debarred from the use of Pen, Ink, and Paper, and shall have no relief but what he earns by his daily labor.

This letter from New England conveniently arrived during the controversy over Naylor. While the account suggests how magistrates could find heretics if they wanted to, its compendious detail eventually permits the Quakers to speak for themselves.

Mercurius Politicus *Numb.* 341.

18–24 December, 1656 361.341 {9.22}

As touching the Extraordinary Diligence used by the Quakers to spred their sottish humors and opinions, it appears now, that (like the Pharisees of old) they compasse Sea and land to make Proselyts. This weeks Letters from Hamburgh speake of two men that came thither, but are now by order there shipped back again for England.

And this week also came to hand this following account concerning some that have rambled as farr as New-England, and arived there at a Town called Boston. What passed there betwixt Mr. John Endecott *the Governer of New-England and the Court there, you may read as followeth in Terminis, as it came from that Country.*

At a Court of Assistants held at Boston, Sep. 8. 1656.

THe Court taking into serious consideration the dangerous effect; and evill consequences that accursed sort of those vpstart hereticks commonly called Quakers might by their damnable Doctrins, and Blasphemous opinions produce here amongst us, to the subverting of the truth of the Gospel, and poysoning the souls of simple and ignorant people to their vtter destruction, And having seen and read divers of their hellish Printed Pamphlets sent hither into these parts before any of the cursed generation arived in this jurisdiction, (that wee know of) and perceiving thereby the inveterate, and malicious spirit of that abominable brood, bent against the servants of God, especially against Magistrates, and Ministers and all order, and ordinances, that Christ hath established in Churches and Commonwealths; and generally against all persons professing the feare of God; which are not of their abominable and soul-murthering way, thought it necessarie for the preventing of such a mischiefe as might likely ensue upon any of their comings over unto us, and spreading of their detestable books and opinions amongst us, to take such a course as (according to God and the Laws of this jurisdiction) might be for the safety of the Churches, and peace of the people of God here with us, and to preserve them by Gods assistance from being bewitched and infected with the spreading Leprosie; their poysonfull and deadly doctrines, which use to run over a whole Country where it is suffered, to the confusion and destruction of thousands of souls. The ship being arived that some weeks before we had intelligence of namely, the Speedwell of London, *Robert Lock* Commander, the Court then in being sent some Officers according to our usuall custom and Laws made in that behalf, to see what passengers came in her; when they landed they found besides other passengers, 9. of those Quakers, 5 men and 4 women, whose names are (as they say) after the flesh *William Brend, Thomas Thurston, Christopher Holder, John Copeland, Richard Smith, Mary Prince, Dorothy Waugh, Sary Gibons, and Mary Whitehead*, who were all brought before the Court then sitting. And being examined and demanded wherefore they came into this Country; and what their busines was here, they answered, to do the work of God; being asked who sent them, they answered God, being demanded every one of them how they would make it appear that God sent them, they made a great pause and answered nothing, but that they had the same call *Abraham* had to come out of his Country: being asked divers other questions and they not returning any satisfactory answers to them, but carrying themselves very unreverently and contemptuously in the face of the whole Country and many hundreds of the Country, and having brought with them many hereticall books full of Blasphemie, with intent to spread and skatter them through the plantations, they were all committed to prison and their books siesed on, which are reserved for the fire. After these things the Governor going from the publick Assembly on the Lords day towards his owne house, and more gentlemen with him, *Mary Prince* one of the said Quakers called out unto him from a Window of the Prison, and reviled him, saying, Woe unto thee that art an

Oppressor, denouncing divers Judgments of God upon him in a most impudent and bold maner, contrary to the Word of God, and the Laws of the Country. And she not being content therewith, sent to the Governor a Letter stuft with opprobrious revilings both against Magistrates and Ministers; and some other of them did the like. After all this, the Governour sent for this Mary Prince from the Prison to his house twice, laboring to turn her from her abominable ways, and to that end desired two reverend and godly Elders to be at his house when they came; where being met, she not being able to answer to such questions as were put unto her in moderation of spirit and soberness; All that she returned these reverend men for their pains and love was reviling and bitter Speeches such as these, *Thou art the seed of the Serpent, of the brood of Ishmael, Baals Priest, deceiver of the people, hireling*, with other such like language which comes from the bottomless pit, and not from the Spirit of Jesus Christ; what the blasphemous and Heretical opinions the Sect of the Quakers do maintain in their Books, is known to those that have read them, what these persons hold that are with us, many are ear witnesses of. Amongst many others these are some, 1. *That they have an infallible spirit.* 2. *That they sin not.* 3. *That the light in every mans conscience that comes into the world is Christ, and that that light would save him, if obeyed.* 4. *That the Baptism with water is not an Ordinance of God.* 5. *That if they had not the Scriptures to direct them, yet they have that within them which was before the Scriptures, and that would guide them.* All which, and many other such erronious opinions and bitter speeches spoken by, and held by the said *Mary Prince*; and other damnable opinions held by the rest of them. And notwithstanding means of Conviction, they maintain and persist in, declaring also, The end of their coming was to publish their Light (which in truth we call darkness) unto the people; which evidently tends to destroy Truth and Peace amongst us.

This Court doth sentence them to banishment; and in order thereunto, Do require they be carried back to prison, and there continued without Bail or Mainprise; and to be kept, men and women apart, and no person, but the Gaoler, permitted discourse with them. And it is ordered by the Council, That at such time as the Ship *Speedwel, Robert Lock* Commander, is ready to depart the Countrey, or the first ship, then the Marshal to deliver them aboard the said ship, to the Master, who is hereby required to export them to the place from whence they came. And for that end, The said *Robert Lock* is hereby required to give in sufficient security to the value of 500. *l*. to the Secretary, That it be performed according to the Act of Council. Dated 11 *July*. 1656

Vera Copia. Edward Rowson, Secretary.

An Examination of the Quakers *before the Court of* Assistants, 8 *Sept,* 1656.

1 *Quest.* Whether you own not your selves to be such as are commonly called and known by the name of Quakers.

Answ. We are all so called; we are of one minde.

2 *Quest.* Whether you brought not hither several Books, wherein are contained the several Opinions of that Sect or people.

Answ. *Mary Prince*, and another; yea, those that were taken from us.

3 *Quest.* Wherefore came you into these parts.

Answ. By all; To do the Will of God, what ever he should make known to be his Will.

4 *Quest.* How do you make it appear, that God called you hither.

Dor. Waugh He that believes hath the Testimony in himself.

Brend. By the power of the Spirit of the Lord; it was a cross to my will, I would not have come, but the Lord hath brought me down to obey him in his call.

5 *Quest.* Do you acknowledge the Light that comes into every mans Conscience; that comes into the world is Christ, and that Light would save him, if obeyed.

Books under all their names.

The Answer to this in their Books, is this, The Light is but one, which is Christ, who inlightens every one; and all are inlightened with one Light, as in the third page of that Book: And in the close of the Book adde, That this is called the Light of your Consciences, the true Teacher; and said to be the first step to peace.

6 *Quest. Mary Prince*, Do you own that Letter you sent me, which was shewed her.

Answ Yes, and said it was the eternal Word of the Lord, which must stand for ever, and should stand; and said further, She wrote this as a Prophetess of the Lord, and was guided by the Infallible Spirit of the Lord.

7 *Quest.* Whether you own the Scriptures, are the rule of knowing God, and living to him.

Answ. This Eternal Word is the rule of their lives, and not the written Word: And in answer to this question, propounded from thence, That if you had not the Scriptures to direct you, yet you have that within you, which was before Scripture, that would guide you aright. To which *Mary Prince* answered: Yea, and it was a sufficient guide.

8 *Quest.* Do you acknowledge, that Christ is God and Man in one person.

Answ. This they will not acknowledge.

9 *Quest.* Do you acknowledge one God, subsisting in three persons, Father, Son, and Holy Ghost.

Answ. They acknowledge no Trinity of Persons.

10 *Quest.* Whether you acknowledge, that God and man in one person, remains for ever a distinct person from God the Father, and God the Holy Ghost, and from the Saints, notwithstanding their Union and Communion with him.

Answ. This they will not acknowledge.

11 *Quest.* Do you acknowledge your self a sinner.

Answ. This they will not acknowledge.

12 *Quest.* Do you acknowledge Baptism with Water to be an Ordinance of God.

Answ. This they will not acknowledge.

Mary Prince *her Letter to the Governor*.

John Indicot.

Thus saith the Lord, I am against thee, and against them that sit in Council with thee, and against those that Divine unto you, that do uphold you, that oppress my servants whom I have sent. Verily I will utterly and suddenly destroy you together; for the Beast that upholdeth the false Prophet, and the false Prophet, shall down into the Pit together: For you have joyned together, Magistrates and Priests, and took Council against me, and seek to make my determination void; and you have dealt treacherously, and have imprisoned my Messengers, and evily intreated my servants, whom I have sent to gather my sheep, out of the mouths of the devourers. But wo, wo unto the then oppresser, and to them that conspire with thee, against me and my little ones, whom I love as the Apple of mine eye. I, even I am risen as a mighty Man of War in great fury, and in an hour, when you are not aware, will I come upon you, and sweep you away, and lay you low.

The B, written on the body to represent the crime, stood for Blasphemer.

Publick Intelligencer *Numb*. 63.

22–29 December, 1656 575.063 {9.23}

Wednesday, 24 Decemb.

Mr. *Caryl*, Mr. *Manton*, Mr. *Nye*, and Mr. *Griffith*, were ordered to repair to Newgate to *James Nailor*, to try if they could bring him to a Recantation of his Errors; but after divers Questions and

Answers betwixt them, during the space of half an hour, or thereabouts, the said Ministers returned, not effecting any thing.

Saturday, 17 Dec.

This day according to Order of Parliament, the said *James Naylor* was conveyed from Newgate to the Old Exchange, where he stood in the Pillory from twelve till two of the Clock: After which, he was bored through the Tongue with an hot Iron, and stigmatized on the Forehead with the Letter *B*. Which Execution being done, he was conveyed back to Newgate.

This is observable, That Mr. *Rich*, formerly a Merchant, was on the Pillory most part of the time that *Naylor* suffered, and held him by the hand while his Tongue was bored, and his Forehead stigmatized.

Mercurius Politicus *Numb*. 345.

15–22 January, 1657 361.345 {9.24}

From *Bristol, Saturday* 17 *January*.

This day the order of Parliament was executed here upon *James Nailor*, in a manner as is described by the following order.

Mr. *Roach*,

C*Ause* James Nailor *to ride in at Lawfords-gate upon a horse bare ridged, with his face backward, from thence along Winestreet to the Tolzey, thence down High street over the Bridge, and out of Rackly-gate; there let him alight, and bring him into St. Thomas-street, and cause him to be stript and made fast to the Cart-horse; and there in the Market first whipped, from thence to the foot of the Bridge there whipt, thence to the end of the Bridge there whipt, thence to the middle of High-street there whipt, thence to the Tolzey their whipt, thence to the middle of Broadstreet there whipt, and then turn into Tailors-hall, thence release him from the Cart-horse, and let him put on his cloaths, and carry him from thence to Newgate by Tower-lane the back way.*

There did ride before him bearheaded, *Michael Stamper*, singing most part of the way, and several other friends, men and women; the men went bare headed by him, and *Robert Rich* (late Merchant of *London*) rode by him bare headed and singing, till he came to Redcliff gate, and there the Magistrates sent their officers, and brought him back on horse-back to the Tolzey, all which way he rode, singing very loud, where the Magistrates were met.

Quakers were famous for their aggressive challenges to ungodly ministers, particularly during sermons. This asserted the priority of the inspired individual over formal worship and church hierarchies. What follows was not the only instance of an attempt to resurrect the dead.

Mercurius Politicus *Numb.* 351

26 February – 5 March, 1656 361.351 {9.25}

From Worcester, February 28. 1656.

Sir, having certain knowledge of the truth of what followes, I thought it my Duty to impart it to your selfe, that the World (especially all good people of this Common-wealth) may by your means receive some further hint of the Palpable seduction and delusion, the apparent Arrogancie, frantick Conceits and Attempts of the Popes English Younglings, the Brood, Sect, and Sort of people called Quakers; the Narrative is of known truth, and will ere long be printed at large, to the open Unmasking of these notorious deceivers, and eminently deceived people, here and elsewhere, too too abundantly spread and increased throughout this Land.

One Susan Peirson, having formerly been a pretended Lover of, and a Zealous contender for Christ, Scriptures, Ordinances, Ministers, Members, &c. But all being but (as the end concludes it) meerly pretended, she hath since proved an Appostate from, and been (as I may say) halfe madd against each of the former, and at length she imbarqued among that idle Sect called the Quakers.

Her wonted practice for these late months (Morality, Modesty, and Civilty, together with her fomer pretence of piety, being now laid aside) was this, to wag from one Assembly to another, requiring the Ministers then, and there Preaching, to prove their Call by Miracles, as the Apostles did, and to shew what grounds they had to Preach, by the Book, viz. the Bible; and for their non-performance of the one, and practise of the other, she alledged ordinarily, she was sent by God, and did witness against them, and would often bid them come downe, and forbid them to come and delude the people in such a manner any more; but whether it were to prove her reall call to this practise, or what other end else, I know not; but let the reader judge, and say when all is heard how well she did it.

There was in this City one William Pool an Apprentise to George Knight, (and *qualis est herus talis fuit servus*) both quakers; the young man was aged about 23 years, and on Friday the 20 of February, he went forth of his Masters house about evening into the Garden, and (as tis reported) being asked where he had been, he said he had bin with Christ, Christ had him by the hand, and he had appointed and must be gone again to him.

But being gone, he came not again, nor was heard of till Sunday following, *February* 22. and then it was found he had stripped himself, laid his cloaths by the water side, and drowned himself, and accordingly by the Coroner and his quest was judged guilty of self-murther, and was buried in the Parish of *Clains*, by four of the clock on Monday morning, his Mother, an honest and (by report of some judicious people that know her) a godly woman, being much troubled hereat, the aforesaid Mistress *Peirson* endeavored to comfort her with this perswasion, That she would fetch her son to her alive again; and about six or seven hours after he was buried, the said Mistress *Peirson* and other Quakers went to the grave, digged up the yong man, opened the shroud and laid the Corps upon the ground, rubbed his face and brest with her hand (and some say, laid her face upon his face, and her hands upon his hands) and commanded him to arise. But he not moving, she kneeled down and prayed over him, and so commanded him in the name of the living God, to arise and walk. This being done, and he not obeying, she caused him to be put into the Grave again, and thence departed, having onely this excuse left her, *That he had not yet been dead four days*. Since this we have enjoyed one Lecture days Sermon without her disturbance; she like the Snail, pulling in her Horns. And I hope, that by these and such like eminent detections, it will be known, by what spirit it is, that they are guided, and how they deceive and are deceived.

This will be attested by many witnesses of known credit

Mercurius Politicus *Numb*. 364

28 May – 4 June, 1657 361.364 {9.26}

From *Foy* in *Cornwal*, May 25.

I must needs acquaint you with a Mercy-passage, lately happened at St *Minver*: On a Lords day a Quaker (of which cattle we have here great store) in an audacious manner interrupted Mr *Weals*, the Minister in his Sermon, charging him with false Doctrine, and deceiving of the people; a yongman hearing it, strook him down, he instantly was revenged on him, and a third coming in to assist his friend; one blow begetting another, the whole Parish was suddenly together by the ears at fisty-cuffs: The Wednesday after, there was a meeting to decide the quarrel by dispute, but they at length grew to such a height, that one of them told the Quaker, he had yet a very strong argument left to convince him, and withal reached him such a lusty box, as made him reel; hereupon they all fell again by the ears, worse then before; but in both combats, the end proved very prejudicial to the Noses and sides of the Quakers. This calleth into my memory a handsom passage between *Luther* and *Carolstadius*, the latter having met *Luther* at his own house to dispute, and contemning all Reasons, Divine and Humane; *Luther* at last in lieu of Logical Arguments, made use of a good cudgel to beat *Carolstadius* out of his Error; and I think this is the best way to be rid of them: I am sure they would use worse means to arrive at their purposes: But they might spare us that labor, if they would follow the example of that Soldier of the Castle, a man of their own humor, who last Thursday after he had stabbed himself on both sides of his throat, running through the streets all bloody, the people flocking towards him to apprehend him, he very valiantly cut his own throat in sight of them all.

Mercurius Politicus *Numb.* 415.

6–13 May, 1657 361.415 {9.27}

In the Strand May 2.

This day in the French Church at Somerset-house, was a Turk baptized, by the Reverend *Iohn Despagne*; the ceremonies followed in this manner. After the Sermon was ended, wherein the several kinds of Religions that have been and are owned in the World were handled and learnedly treated of, there were chairs placed in order over against the Pulpit to keep off the press of people. Monsieur *Despagne* descended, and seated himself in one of them, the Turk standing at his right hand, who was about 30 years of age. And then the Sexton was sent to a noble man that sate in the Gallery, to desire him to be a Witness to the Sacrament that was there to be administred; he came down having a Gentlewoman with him; and being come to the place where they were expected, the Minister acquainted them in brief to what end he desired their assistance at that time, and the Turk having saluted them, the Church called upon God for a blessing upon the ordinance that was then to be dispenced; but the Turk was before interrogated by the Minister in the face of the congregation of Christ, why he would change his religion? why he beleeved not and embraced the Roman rather than the Reformed? & lastly what he beleeved of the Trinity and that Sacrament whereof he was about to partake, to each which he made satisfactory, though not ample replication by reason of his unskilfulness in the French tongue. At length he was baptized in the name of the Father Son and holy Ghost, being named *Arman Adrian* after the names of his God-father and God-mother, he kneeling all the time the Sacrament was in administration. And so the Minister invocated God for a blessing upon what was done, and dismissed the Assembly.

There were many stories of sacrilegious behaviour in the provinces in the summer of 1659, when the future of central government was so unstable.

The Weekly Intelligencer of the Common-Wealth *Numb.* 12.

19–26 July, 1659 689.12 {9.28}

Monday *July* 25. {...}

We had yesterday, two strange stories, of two more strange Christians, the one did go up into the Pulpit, a little before the Sermon did begin, and sitting crosse legged on the Cushion, did pull forth his bottome of thread, and his work out of his pocket, and fell a soeing very busily; belike he had a design, to disgrace that Cushion, with his crosse leggs, on which he thought the Crosse had been too much praised, and honored: But he was pulled down from thence, and carried away by force. The other was at *Norwich*, and it is also very certain, where a bold bad man did pull down his breeches on the Communion Table, and laid there his most odious; and nasty burden, but observe and tremble at the divine vengeance, he was suddainly tormented with the griping in his guts, and lamentable roaring out, he was never able to go to the stool afterwards. And will any man now say that this is a generation of men indued with new lights, surely these lights are from the Prince of Darkness.

CHAPTER TEN

To Amuse and Abuse the People: The Restoration

Less than ten years after Charles I was executed outside his own Banqueting House in the name of the free people of England, Oliver Cromwell developed a political illness. There had been a constitutional crisis through 1657–8, when the Second Protectorate Parliament had laid claims to political supremacy and tried to divide the army, which had jeopardised Cromwell's own relationship with some of the officers. He dissolved the parliament on 4 February 1658, and thereby prevented any chance of paying the army's arrears.[1]

Through the summer Cromwell followed through the logic of the metaphor of the body politic, and faced with the stubborn refusal of Britain to mould itself into a permanent and stable state, an insoluble financial crisis, and deaths in his own family, he internalised this political disease and, with a fine sense of timing, died. He held on until 3 September, his birthday, the anniversary of his great military triumphs at Dunbar and Worcester {2.32}, and the day that everyone expected him to die {10.01}. There had been rumours after his great victory at Worcester that on the eve of the battle he had sold his soul to the Devil in return for a military triumph and seven years rule. According to a myth started by Edmund Waller's poem 'Upon the Late Storm', his soul was carried away in a great storm, and some saw this as a verification of the diabolic pact. The storm actually took place a few days earlier.

1 This skeletal reconstruction of events should be sufficient to assist the reader in understanding the passages from newsbooks which follow. Because the story is so complicated, I have devoted this introductory section to outlining a narrative.

According to John Evelyn, at Cromwell's funeral {10.03} 'there were none that cried but dogs'.[2]

Richard Cromwell inherited the Protectorate in an impossible situation. His father had increasingly controlled the polity through a dynasty, the personal relations of which only he had the ability to juggle. Needing finances, Richard elected to call a parliament, and immediately, like his father, he found himself negotiating between the commonwealthsmen and the republicans in the army. Being a civilian made him initially popular; but it also left him with no basis for power in the army. Consequently he was unable to command the allegiance of officers as Oliver Cromwell had, and when parliament and the army came into conflict in late April 1659, his response was to order the dissolution of the Council of Officers. The army resisted and Richard summoned those faithful to him to his side. Fleetwood, Desborough and other officers did the same, and mustered a force of thousands at St. James in opposition to Richard's hundreds. They dissolved parliament and a general council took over, under pressure to restore the purged parliament. This consisted of the surviving members of the Long Parliament, minus those who had been excluded by Pride's Purge on 6 December 1648: it was the parliament which Cromwell had angrily dissolved on 19 April 1653. Richard retired {10.04–5}.

The restored parliament met on 7 May. It had an unstable basis in the counties, as demonstrated by the insurrections of the summer {10.07–8}, and was faced with an explosion of pamphlets in London, debating the merits of an election and a free parliament. The parliament soon acquired the name 'The Rump', a derogatory term which has endured {10.22–3}. In October some officers led by John Lambert complained of the House's dilatoriness in following through the brief which it had been granted. Particularly they petitioned for autonomy in the army's command structure and speedier national religious reform. In return the Commons threatened to remove all funding for the army and to change its commissioned officers. Lambert responded

2 Ronald Hutton, *The Restoration: A Political and Religious History of England and Wales 1659–1667* (Oxford: Clarendon press, 1985), p.25. Much of the following narrative is based on Hutton's excellent book. See also Austin Woolrych's introduction to *Complete Prose Works of John Milton*, vol. VII, revised edition (New Haven and London: Yale University Press, 1980). For more on the crisis prior to the death of the Protector, see Hutton, *The British Republic 1649–1660* (Basingstoke: Macmillan, 1990); also the last three chapters of David Underdown, *Royalist Conspiracy in England 1649–1660* (New Haven: Yale University Press, 1960).

by closing the House of Commons and locking the building. Under his influence, the Council of Officers decided to establish a Committee of Safety as an interim government.

Until this point the conflict remained basically between the parliament and the army. Then Colonel Monck, a ex-royalist who had changed sides and become the triumphant commander of the army in Scotland on Cromwell's behalf, wrote from there to express his condemnation of the closing of parliament {10.13}. The army was thus divided.

On 26 October the Committee of Safety met to raise an army under Lambert to deal with the threat of Monck. As Monck advanced, there were disturbances, mainly caused by apprentices in London, which was suffering from severe economic problems. This applied considerable pressure for a free parliament {10.15}. On 13 December the General Council succumbed to this pressure. On the same day John Lawson, in command of the only active fleet, declared his support for the purged parliament, and on 16 December sailed down the Thames {10.16}. Some infantry units around London began to move for the same. Lambert's supporters in the capital, facing defeat, submitted to Speaker Lenthal, and Fleetwood in disgust handed the keys back to parliament. It reconvened on 26 December {10.18}. Lambert, stationed at the Scottish border, decided to turn around and intervene in London; suddenly what had seemed a highly trained force disintegrated, not least because of Monck's close pursuit {10.19}.

Hindered by snow, it took Monck some time to reach London. Meanwhile the apprentices in London rioted for a free parliament, and continued to be suppressed by an army which appeared to be largely republican in sympathy. Monck arrived on 2 February 1660, apparently in favour of the restored parliament {10.21}. A week later Praise-God Barebone, a colourful republican who had lent his name to what was technically the nominated assembly of 1653, petitioned the parliament that they retain their sympathies to the 'Good Old Cause'. Monck, it appears, had other ideas, and reached an agreement with his officers to order that the Commons be dissolved as soon as they had sent out the writs for a new, 'free' parliament.

By 20 February Monck had firmly changed his mind. He ordered the readmission of the secluded members; that is, those who been purged in December 1648. This, like the original exclusion, caused some discontent and required the display of military force. The House of Lords at this point remained closed, as it had been since its abolition in 1649. Some army units and religious radicals were unsettled by this move, though the citizens responded with great celebrations in London, not for the first time breaking the windows of Praise-God Barebone. Monck then shrewdly engineered the weeding of dissenting officers from the army, thereby ensuring that he remained firmly in command; in March the Commons began to swing in favour of a monarchy, which would previously have precipitated a mutiny. After providing for a new election the House dissolved on 16 March after nineteen years and four months of much interrupted existence {10.22}.

Having secured the co-operation of the army Monck began to treat with the Royalists. To these he declared, probably disingenuously, that all his actions over the preceding four months, had been solely oriented towards a restoration of Charles II as King of Britain. After some careful restraint on behalf of exultant royalists in England, the future king agreed to some fairly soft terms on 4 April, which produced the Declaration of Breda. The Council of State had already repeated the action of the restored parliament almost a year earlier, and removed Nedham from the editorship of his newsbook.

John Lambert, the republican army general, managed to escape from the Tower of London to stage an abortive uprising at Edgehill, the famous civil war site, on 22 April {10.25}. There continued to be some active opposition to the prospect of a restored king by both soldiers and civilians, and there were widespread fears of a Quaker uprising: but the process of Restoration was almost complete. On 25 April the Convention Parliament met, including a House of Lords. The election results were broadly disastrous for republicans. The hope of the opposition, known as the 'Presbyterian Knot', now lay in working within parliament to impose some constitutional limitations as the precondition for a monarchy. Monck, by effectively controlling the army and subsuming their interests to those of the parliament, something Richard Cromwell had so signally failed in, had deprived the republicans of support in the army, and made such restrictions unlikely. On 26 April Monck permitted, against the wish of the Presbyterian Knot, the younger Lords to enter the Upper House, thereby ensuring a comfortable royalist majority. On 29 April the Declaration of Breda was formally presented to the parliament, which on 1 May declared itself in favour of government by king, Lords and Commons {10.26}. The British Republic was over.

On 8 May Charles II was formally proclaimed king of England: on 29 May he entered the capital of his largest kingdom {10.27}.

In the city and in the provinces there were bells rung and bonfires lit, a mass of disorderly and extended celebrations which involved revels, excessive drinking, setting up of maypoles, flag burning, the mobbing of radicals in general and attacks upon Quakers in particular, an increase in witchcraft prosecutions and widespread hysteria.[3]

In 1647 Colonel Rainsborough, the Leveller leader who was later to be brutally murdered, had said that 'every man born in England cannot, ought not, neither by the Law of God nor the Law of Nature, to be exempted from the choice of those who are to make laws for him to live under, and for him, for aught I know, to die under.'[4] The Regicide John Cook later said that the people would have been enfranchised, 'if the Nation had not been more delighted in servitude'.[5] This wedge driven between quasi-democratic principles and the interests of 'the people' was the basis for every attempt at a political solution after the execution of the king. There is evidence that in 1660 there was much popular support for a restored monarchy, and the Good Old Cause soon became little more than rhetoric without much effective protest. Nine months before the Restoration, James Harrington blamed 'the Governours' for the errors and the sufferings of the people, and argued that widespread dissatisfaction with the Commonwealth meant that there was no Commonwealth. He also wrote 'A King governing now in *England* by an Army, would for the same causes finde the same effects with the late Protector'.[6] When 'the people' chose to support the return of the king he was proven right: in the offices of power there began the process of following through the exemptions from the king's general pardon. The regicides were, inevitably, permitted rather less dignity than Charles I had been {10.32ff}. Public displays of humiliation had the last word.

3 See David Underdown, *Revel, Riot and Rebellion: Popular Politics and Culture in England 1603–1660* (Oxford: Oxford University Press, 1985), ch.10.

4 *Puritanism and Liberty*, ed. A.S.P. Woodhouse (London: J.M. Dent and Sons, 1986, orig. 1938), p.56.

5 Quoted in Christopher Hill, 'The Poor and the People in Seventeenth-Century England' in ed. Frederick Krantz, *History From Below: Studies in Popular Protest and Popular Ideology* (Oxford: Basil Blackwell, 1988), p.47.

6 James Harrington, *Aphorisms Political* (London, August 25, 1659), aphorisms 1, 12, 54. Wing H804.

Mercurius Politicus *Numb*. 432.

2–9 September, 1658 361.432 {10.01}

Whitehal, Sept. 3.

His most Serene and Renowned Highness *Oliver* Lord Protector, being after a sickness of about fourteen days (which appeared an Ague in the beginning) reduced to a very low condition of Body, began early this morning to draw near the gate of death; and it pleased God about three a clock afternoon, to put a period to his life. I would willingly express upon this sad occasion, the deep sorrow which hath possessed the mindes of his most Noble Son and Successor, and other dearest Relations, had I language sufficient: But all that I can use, will fall short of the merits of that most excellent Prince. His first undertakings for the Publick Interest, his working things all along, as it were out of the Rock, his founding a Military Discipline in these Nations, such as is not to be found in any example of preceding times; and whereby the Noble Soldiery of these Nations may (without flattery) be commended for Piety, Moderation, and Obedience, as a pattern to be imitated, but hardly to be equalled by succeeding generations: His Wisdom and Piety in things divine, his Prudence in management of the Civil Affairs, and conduct of the Military, and admirable Successes in all, made him a Prince indeed among the people of God; by whose prayers being lifted up to the supreme Dignity, he became more highly seated in their hearts, because in all his actings it was evident, that the main design was to make his own interest one and the same with theirs, that it might be subserving to the great interest of Jesus Christ.

And in the promoting of this, his spirit knew no bounds, his affection could not be confined at home, but brake forth into forein parts, where he was by good men universally admired as an extraordinary person raised up of God, and by them owned as the great Protector and Patron of the Evangelical Profession. This being said, and the World it self witness of it, I can onely adde, That God gave him Blessings proportionate to all these vertues, and made him a Blessing to us, by his wisdom and valor to secure our Peace and Liberty, and to revive the antient renown and reputation of our Native Country.

After all this, it is remarkable, how it pleased the Lord, on this day to take him to rest, it having formerly been a day of labors to him; for which both himself and the day (*Sept.* 3.) will be most renowned to posterity, it having been to him a day of Triumphs and Thanksgiving for the memorable Victories of *Dunbar* and *Worcester*; a day, which after so many strange Revolutions of Providence, high Contradictions, and wicked Conspiracies of unreasonable men, he lived once again to see, and then to die with great assurances and serenity of minde, peaceably in his Bed.

Thus it hath proved to him to be a day of Triumph indeed, there being much of Providence in it, that after so glorious Crowns of Victory placed on his head by God on this day, having neglected an Earthly Crown, he should now go to receive the Crown of Everlasting Life.

Being gone, to the unspeakable grief of all good men, the Privy Council immediately assembled, and being satisfied that the Lord Protector was dead; and upon sure and certain knowledge, that his late Highness did in his life-time, according to the *Humble Petition and Advice*, declare and appoint the most Noble and Illustrious Lord the Lord *Richard*, Eldest Son of his said Highness, to succeed him, it was resolved at the Council, *Nemine Contradicente*, That his late Highness hath declared and appointed the said most noble and illustrious Lord to succeed him in the Government, *Lord Protector, &c.* Which being made known to the Officers of the Army, it was pleasant to behold, with how much content and satisfaction they received the notice of it, and unanimously concurred thereunto, being resolved to their utmost to maintain the Succession, according to Law: Which worthy resolution of theirs, as it speaks them men of Honor, Prudence, and Fidelity, mindful of the merits of their late great Leader, and common Father, and of the grand interest of *Establishment*, after all our shakings; so it is but answerable to the worth and nobleness of his Son, who in all respects appears the lively image of his Father, the true Inheritor of his Christian Vertues; a person, who by his Piety, Humanity, and other Noble Inclinations, hath obliged the hearts of all, and thereby filled this people with hopes of much ſelicity, though Gods blessing upon his Government.

Hereupon the Council passed a Proclamation in order to the proclaiming of his Highness; which was signed by the Lord Major of the City of *London*, the Lord President, and Lords of the Privy Council, the most Noble Lord the Lord *Fauconberge*, and the rest of the Officers of the Army; and it was resolved, That Proclamation should be made tomorrow morning at nine of the Clock; in order whereunto the Heralds, Serjeants at Arms, and other Officers were ordered to attend. Also, that Letters be sent to the Judges to repair forthwith to *London*.

The first time Cromwell's body was displayed: as an icon of an individual who united the commonwealth. The second time was quite different.

Mercurius Politicus *Numb.* 438.

14–21 October, 1658 361.438 {10.02}

Octob 15. {...}

On Monday the 18 instant, the Representation of the person of his late Highness in Effigie, will be exposed to publick view at Somerset-house upon a Bed of State vested with his Robe of Estate, a Scepter placed in one hand, a Globe in the other, and a Crown laid on a Velvet Cushion a little above the head, after the antient and most becoming Ceremony of the preceding Princes of this Nation upon the like occasion; which point of Honor is the more due to his memory, by how much he advanced the honor of our Country by his incomparable Actions, beyond the example of any that swayed the Scepter of this Land before him. {...}

A particular and exact Relation how Sommerset-House *is prepared for the Effigies, or representation of his late Highness, by particular Order of the Lords of the Council, which was first shewed publiquely on Monday last.*

THe first Room the people enter, was formerly the Presence Chamber, which is hung compleatly with black, and at the upper end a Cloth of Estate, with a Chair of Estate standing upon the Haut-place under the State.

From thence you passe to a second large Room, which was the Privie Chamber, all compleatly hung with black, and a Cloth of Estate at the upper end, having also a Chair of Estate upon the Haut-place, under the Cloth of Estate.

The third Room is a large withdrawing Chamber, compleatly hung as the other with black Cloth, and a Cloth of Estate at the upper end, with a chair of Estate, as in the other Rooms.

All these three large Rooms are compleatly furnished with Escucheons of his Highness Armes, crowned with the Imperial Crown, and upon the head of each cloth of Estate is fixed a large Majesty-Escucheon fairly painted, and gilt upon Taffity.

The fourth Room, where both the Body and the Effigies do lie, compleatly hung with black Velvet, the roof of the said Room Cieled also with Velvet, and a large Canopie or cloth of Estate of black Velvet fringed over the Effigies; the Effigies it self apparrelled in a rich Suit of uncut Velvet, being robed first in a Kirtle Robe of Purple Velvet, laced with a rich gold lace, and furr'd with Ermins; upon the Kirtle is the Royal large Robe of the like Purple Velvet laced, and fur'd with Ermins, with rich strings, and tassels of gold; his Kirtle is girt with a rich Embroidered Belt, in which is a fair Sword richly gilt, and hatcht with gold hanging by the side of the Effigies; in the right hand is the golden Scepter representing Government; in his left hand is held the Globe, representing Principality; upon his head, the Cap of Regality of Purple Velvet, furr'd with Ermins. Behind the head is a rich chair of Estate of cloth of gold tissued; upon the Cushion of the Chair stands the Imperial Crown set with stones.

The whole Effigies lies upon a bed covered with a large Pall of Black Velvet, under which is a fine Holland sheet upon six stools of cloth of gold tissued; by the sides of the Bed of State lies a rich Suit of compleat Armor, representing his command as General, at the feet of the Effigies stands his Crest, as is usuall in all ancient Monuments.

This Bed of State upon which the Effigies so lies is ascended unto by two Ascents, covered with the aforesaid Pall of Velvet; and the whole work is incompassed about with Railes covered with Velvet; at each corner is a square Pillar or upright, covered with Velvet; upon the tops of them are four beasts, supporters of the Imperial Armes, bearing Banners, or *S*treamers crowned; the Pillars are decorated with Trophyes of Military honor, carved and gilt; The Pedestalls of the Pillars have Shields and Crowns gilt, which makes the whole work Noble and compleat; within the Railes stand Eight great Standerts or Candlesticks of Silver, being almost 5 foot in height, with great Tapers in them of Virgins wax, 3 foot in length.

Next to the Candlesticks are set upright in Sockets, the four great Standerts of his Highness Armes, the Guidons, the great Banners, and Banrolls, all of Taffity, richly gilt and painted; the cloth of Estate hath a Majesty-Scucheon fixed at the head, and upon the Velvet Hangings on each side of the Effigies, is a Majesty-Scucheon. *A*nd the whole room fully and compleatly furnished with Taffity-Scucheons. Much more might be inlarged of the Magnificence of this solemn setting up, and shewing the Effigies at present in *Somerset*-house, where it is to remaine in State untill the Funeral day, which is appointed to be on the Ninth of November next.

Mercurius Politicus *Numb*. 443.

18–25 November, 1658 361.443 {10.03}

Somerset-house Novemb, 23.

THis being the day appointed for the solemn Funerals of the most Serene and Renowned *Oliver* Lord Protector, and all things being ready prepared, the Effigies of his Highness, standing under a rich Cloth of state, having been beheld by those persons of honor and quality which came to attend it, was afterwards removed, and placed on a Herse, richly adorned and set forth with Escutcheons and other Ornaments, the Effigies it self being vested with royal Robes, a Scepter in one hand, a Globe in the other, and a Crown on the head. After it had been a while thus placed in the middle of the Room, when the time came that it was to be removed into the Carriage, it was carried on the Herse by ten of the Gentlemen of his Highness forth into the Court, where a Canopy of state very rich, was born over it, by six other Gentlemen of his Highness, till it was brought and placed on the Carriage, at each end whereof was a Seat, wherein sate two of the Gentlemen of his Highness Bed chamber, the one at the head the other at the feet of the Effigies. The Pall being made of Velvet and fine linen, was very large, extending on each side of the Carriage, to be born by persons of honor, appointed for that purpose; the Carriage it self was adorned with Plumes and Escutcheons, and was drawn by six horses, covered with black Velvet, each of them likewise adorned with Plumes of Feathers. {...}

The whole Ceremnony was managed with very great State to Westminster; many thousands of people being Spectators. At the West-gate of the Abby-Church, the Herse with the Effigies thereon, was taken off the Carriage by those ten Gentlemen who removed it before, who passing on to enter the Church, the Canopy of State was by the same persons borne over it again; and in this magnificent manner they carried it up to the East-end of the Abbey; and placed it in that Noble Structure which was raised there on purpose to receive it; where it is to remain for some time, exposed to publick view.

This is the last ceremony of honor, and less could not be performed to the Memory of him, to whom posterity will pay (when envy is laid asleep by time) more honor then we are able to express.

The Rump was forcibly restored, from which the Army expected an enduring religious and political settlement, a conclusive revolution in government, and Richard Cromwell resigned:

Mercurius Politicus *Numb.* 566.

5–12 May, 1652 361.566 {10.04}

Westminster, May 6.

It was ordered by the Lord *Fleetwood*, and the general Council of the Officers of the Army, that their Declaration should be printed and published, Entituled, *A Declaration of the Officers of the Army, inviting the Members of the long Parliament, who continued sitting till the* 20 *of* April 1653. *to return to the exercise and discharge of their Trust.*

The Conclusion of the Declaration runs thus,

[*And amongst other things, calling to minde, that the long Parliament consisting of the Members which continued there sitting until the* 20 *of April* 1653 *were eminent Assertors of that Cause, and had a special presence of God with them, and were signally blessed in that work (the desires of many good people concurring with ours therein) we judge it our duty to invite the aforesaid Members to return to the Exercise and discharge of their Trust, as before the said* 20 *of* April 1653.

And therefore we do hereby most earnestly desire the Parliament consisting of those Members who continued to sit since the Year 1648 *until the* 20 *of* April 1653. *to return to the exercise and discharge of their Trust, and we shall be ready in our places, to yield them, as becomes us, our utmost assistance to sit in safety; for the improving present opportunity for setling and securing the Peace and Freedom of this Commonwealth; praying for the presence and blessing of God upon their endeavors*.

The Declaration it self at large is printed by *Henry Hills*, and sold at the several Booksellers shops in *London*.

Mercurius Politicus *Numb.* 568.

19–26 May, 1659 361.568 {10.05}

A Letter from the Militia Troop of the County of Durham.
Honored Friends,

IT is deadful to consider the wonderfull workings of the Lord amongst the people of the Nations of this Commonwealth; how hath he set up and thrown down, and overturned first one party and then another, sifted and tried all men, and all sorts of men, as if he had some glorious work to accomplish, if fit Instuments could be found for it? but who can say they have kept their Integrity, and been faithful to the Lord and their own principles, and have not fallen in the Night of our late Apostacy; and amongst all the revolutions that we have had the last is most to be admired; how sudaine, how seasonable was it, as if it were the Lords one time for some great work to be brought forth, and if the Lord shall please to strengthen your hands to go on in uprightness and sincerety of heart, happy days are near us; This is the third opportunity put into your hands, do not neglect it; the hearts, the hands, the prayers of all good men are with you, and their hopes are much upon the issue of this undertaking, and we know your Enemies hang their heads, and their hearts faile them. {...}

May 25 1659,

The Committee that were appointed to attend the Eldest Sonne of the late Lord General, touching his aquiescing in the present Government, among other things according to a former Vote, did this day present a paper to the House, Signed with his own hand *Richard Cromwel*, in these words following.

I Have perused the Resolve and Declaration which you were pleased to deliver to me the other night; and for your Information touching what is mentioned in the said Resolve, I have caused a true state of my debts to be transcribed and annexed to this Paper, which will shew what they are, and how they were contracted.

As to that part of the Resolve whereby the Committee are to inform themselves how far I do acquiesse in the Government of this Commonwealth, as it is declared by this Parliament.

I trust my past carriage hitherto, hath manifested my aquiessence in the will and disposition of God, and that I love and value the peace of this Commonwealth much above my own concernments; and I desire that by this a measure of my future deportment may be taken, which through the assistance of God, shall be such as shall bear the same witness, having I hope in some degree learned rather to reverence and submit to the hand of God, then to be unquiet under it: And (as to the late providences that have faln out among us) however in respect of the particular engagements that lay upon me, I could not be active in making a change in the Government of these Nations; yet through the goodness of God I can freely aquiesse in it being made, and do hold my self obliged, as (with other men) I expect protection from the present Government, so to demean my self with all peaceableness under it, and to procure to the uttermost of my power, that all in whom I have any interest do the same,

Richard Cromwel.

Mercurius Politicus *Numb*. 571.

9–16 June, 1659 361.571 {10.06}

Whitehall, June 15. {...}

From *Scotland* also its written that General *Monck* and the Army there, are confirmed in their Resolutions to adhere to the Parliament. Also, that *Charls Stuart* hath lately had an Agent at work in the *Highlands*, in design to create new Troubles by stirring up the old Enemy, some few of the forward Malcontents of that party got together, in hope to have inflamed the rest to an Insurrection, but they were quickly prevented, and forced to hide themselves, by a party of our owne sent from the next garrison to suppress them.

Mercurius Politicus *Numb*. 278. {i.e. 578}

7–14 July, 1659 361.578 {10.07}

Whitehal, July 9.

Yesterday Col. *Henry Cromwel* retired into *Cambridgeshire*, having (as was ordered by the Parliament) given his account concerning *Ireland* to the Council of State.

Affairs being managed here with diligence and prudence by the Parliament and Council of State; a strict eye being kept upon the common Enemie in their plottings; and the Soldiery being vigilant and active on their Guards and in their Rounds, to prevent them in the present designes, its a main ground of hope (through Gods goodness) that this cheerful concurrence of Parliament and Army in the common work, will effect a speedy settlement of the Commonwealth, in despight of the idle Rumors which run up and down to Proclaime division, and are raised on purpose by the Adversaries to create it if they could, but however to amuse and abuse the People. {...}

The saying is, *The burnt child dreads the fire:* But too many in this Nation mind not the proverb: And hence it is that they have been often *burnt*; some twice, others thrice, and some many times more. Now it is well known to such as know the dark ways of the Common Enemy, howsoever he hath many destructive designs on foot against the publick peace and welfare of the Commonwealth, yet nothing that he doth more daily practise then devising lyes: And among the several kinds of his falsehoods and lyes, (for he hath lyes of all sorts and sizes) this is one (and a special one at this time) namely, to possess the people of huge discontents and divisions between the Parliament and the Army, and what Risings there are in several parts of the Nation: A plot meerly devised to ensnare ignorant and simple people. And whereas such a wicked plot was lately hatched here in *London*, and probably by this time it is spread abroad through the Nation; It cannot be amiss thus much to declare to all people in all places, That whatsoever is reported abroad about raising the Parliament, or any discontent in the Army tending that way, it was only a *Malignant lye*, without any ground at all for it. And therefore out of compassion to the poor people of the three Nations, this *Caveat* is given them, To beware of *Malignant Lyes*. If they will not take warning, but rather take encouragement to be seditious from such false Reports and lying Incendiaries, they will be the more inexcusable when Justice shall lay hold of them, having had before so fair a warning given them. For doubtless they shall not prosper (poor nor rich) who are for the corrupt Interest of the *Charls Stuart* or any Single person, against a Free Commonwealth setled upon a good foundation of Truth and Righteousness, as it is hoped *England* ere long will be. {...}

Whereas divers Reports pass up and down, touching a late Tumult in Enfield-Chase, *The Reader is to take notice, that (as to matter of Fact) the true account of that business is as followeth.*

M*onday July* 11. Enfield-Chase being newly inclosed and Houses built thereupon, some pretending right of Commonage, threatned to pull down the said Houses, and to lay open the Inclosure, whereupon four Files of foot Soldiers, were sent by order of the Commander in Chief to quarter in the said Houses, to the end they might preserve them; notwithstanding, about Two Hundred and Fifty men, Inhabitants in and about the Town of *Enfield* came armed with Pitchforks, Sythes, Axes, and Long-Staves, drew nigh the Quarters of the Soldiers, making great shouts, upon which the Serjeant who commanded the said Soldiers, sent two of them to demand of this Company what they intended; who instead of an answer, beat down both the Soldiers, one of which recovering himself, brought word to the Serjeant of their usage; whereupon the Serjeant marched up with about fourteen Soldiers to them, to demand his Soldier, and to reason the Case with them; but the Multitude immediately fell upon the Soldiers, in which diverse Conflict divers were wounded on both sides, and one of the Country-men killed upon the place. The Serjeant very much wounded, and run through the Thigh. In the end the Multitude over-powring the Soldiers, they took nine of them Prisoners, violently carrying of them before the next Justice of the Peace, who committed the Soldiers to *Newgate*, where at present they remaine, Notwithstanding the Multitude proceeded in their disorders, seting on fire some stacks of wood and hedges cutting down a Barn, and forcing all the workmen out of the Ground.

As the polity was thrown into confusion and uncertainty once again, the common people took out their fears on the enduring symbols of subversion: religious radicals.

Mercurius Politicus *Numb*. 580.

21–28 July, 1659 361.580 {10.08}

Tiverton in Devon, July 21. 1659.

Upon the Fourteenth day of this month, about midnight the whole Town of *Tiverton* as also several Families in the Parish were raised up out of their Beds by a false Rumor and Alarm; That the Ministers of the Town, and others fearing God, should be all massacred that night; whereupon the Magistrates, Ministers and several others, gathered themselves together (many of them being in Arms) consulting in whose hands to put Arms, it being so dangerous a Time. Neighbors rouzed up each other out of their Beds, crying pittifully one to another, *Take Arms, take Arms, else they would have their Throates cut in their Beds*. And when they came forth of their Houses, and asked the reason of this Hurliburlie and feare, the common Replie and general Crie was, that, *the Anabaptists and Quakers were joyned together, and intended that night to cut the Throats of the Ministers, and all the Godly people*, Whereupon some (being wiser then the rest) returned to their Beds, as judging there was no Cause of Feare. But others (being thereto invited) took Arms, and walked through the Town. The Crie for a while increased and grew higher and higher, to wit, That, *the Fifth Monarchie men, Anabaptists and Quakers were joyned together, not only to cut the Throats of the Godly in that Town, but the Throats of all the Godly in the Nation that Night.* They had an intent to have beaten their Drums, and rung the Bells at Midnight, but some perswaded to the contrary, which was a great mercie to a few Anabaptists (so called) living in that Town: for it is probable, had such a thing been done, the rude multitude in their rage, by reason of the false Report, would have pluckt their houses down upon them. But they did only set a Guard about their Houses (which were 10 or 12 Families) as their Neighbors told them the next day.

The occasions of this Commotion, as it appears by inquiry, was from a Letter which a Parish Minister wrote to several of his Bretheren, That there was a designe on foot by the *FifthMonarchie Men, Anabaptists and Quakers to CUT THROATS THAT NIGHT:* Whereupon for fear they left their Houses.

It is necessary that a word be added: 1. To undeceive many simple ones in the Nation, that is, to warn all men in their places to take heed of the secret Plotters, and cunning designs now every where on foot, to ensnare poor people. It is well known the Cavaliers in City and Country are waiting for an opportunity to rise for *Charls Stuart* against the Commonwealth neither care they what the way be, so they may reach their malicious end, against the Government by a Commonwealth; and what way more likelie then this of *Tiverton*?

But Secondly, It is very strange that men professing to fear God, should not make more conscience of Lying, especially to devise such a thing as every one that shall hear of (if he be sober and discreet) will cry out against it as a most absurd and groundless thing. Truly this way will not do it, to bring in Monarchie; God hath hitherto cursed it, and therefore let men know they do but *kick against the pricks* in seeking to set up *a King and House of Lords*, it will not be, because the Lord himself is against it.

This providential story is thinly veiled propaganda pressing for the Restoration. Black letter, conspicuously emphasising the child's prophetic words, was sometimes used in newsbooks to indicate official documents.

The Loyall Scout *Numb.* 17.

19–26 August, 1659 151.017 {10.09}

In the Suburbs of London, in the lower end of East-Smithfield, at a place called Knockfergus, a young woman was brought to bed with a Child that was born with two Tongues, the one in some measure covering the other, but the lower Tongue appearing to be the more firm and longer then the other. The Father of it is a poor man, and of a poor Trade, but such a one that the best Lady in the Land, when she is troubled with Corns, would be glad of his Assistance. Having a sharp Knife, and a good dexterity in his Art, doth get an easie subsistence in a hard world by cutting of Corns. His name is John Clark, living next door to the Sign of the Soldier and Trumpet at Knockfergus. His Wife is an honest woman, and well beloved amongst her Neighbours, who were many of them with her, at the time of her delivery, and did assist her in her Childing Throws. Three days after she was brought to bed many of her neighbours came to give her a visit; and it was baptized *John*. After which, Mrs. *Silk* the Midwife, handing it to the Godmother, it began to wayl, and cry out, A King, A King, A King. In a silence full of amazement, they did look on one another; the speaking Child having made the women dumb. And thus it continued for some time; putting out its hand, and crying to any spectators that it does not like, Away, Away. The Child is 3 quarters old.

The Weekly Intelligencer of the Common-Wealth *Numb.* 20.

13–20 September, 1659 689.20 {10.10}

On *Thursday Septemb.* 7. in the afternoon there was seen at *Markfield* in *Leicestershire* extraordinary flashes of lightning, which breaking from the angry clouds made way for the ensuing thunder, the claps whereof were terrible and continued chiding and roaring in the Air for the space of an hour: At every silence and respite of the thunder, the lightning during this dreadful storm did break forth with great force: And the next voyce of the thunder was louder, and more affrighting then that which was before; There were no showres of raine, but at the last there was a most black, and dreadful storn of Haile, and in stead of Hail-stones there fell ratling down from the Air, Halberts, Swords, and Daggers, which being taken up were found to be of the same nature, and to be begotten of the same extremity of Cold as were the Hail-stones, and after a little time, both the sight and the fright which the sight brought with it, did melt away at once. Many of the Town of *Markfield*, and places adjacent were much amazed at this prodigious spectacle, which to increase their wonder, was seconded by another terrible noise in the Air, as if two great Armies had been on their march, and advancing one against the other; The Canons were heard to play with importunate fury, and the muskets on both sides in repeated volleys did discharge their cholerick errands: During this incounter there were beheld many prodigious erruptions of fire, which with great violence did fly in the Air, and running lower, did tear in pieces many strong Houses, and laid great Trees on their backs, which in an instance were plucked up by the roots. There was not far off a Lime-kiln, on which some part of the tempest did fall with so great violence that all the Lime was blown up in the Air, just as in a high storm the waters of the Sea are blown, when the winds and the waves do wrastle for supremacy. This being done, this part of the fiery tempest which came so low, was seen by all to take its course up the hill, where it vanished away, and there was heard no more noyse of it.

It is certified by several letters, that this Tempest at the first did appear like a thick and rowling Smoak, and sometimes it would cast it self into a great Circumference, like to a great wheel, or an Orbe, not easie to be compassed.

There is no man ignorant of the late great Indevours to ingage this Nation again in a new War, which by the Almighty goodnesse is now quieted, and since we enjoy peace on Earth, let us pray for the Continuance of it, that so these Daggers and these Halberts, may fall in vain from the Armory of Heaven.

The Publick Intelligencer *Numb*. 195.

19–26 September, 1659 575.195 {10.11}

From Calais, Sept. 24. *S.N*.

MEn are amazed in these parts to hear, that the Insurrections in England have been so strangely suppressed; the Scotish King and his Friends made reckoning of great matters like to be done for them, and meant to have transported themselves with some Forces, which were prepared for that purpose; for this end they came from Brussels, and he and his brother, the Duke of York, were seen about Boloigne, but incognito, and they had a good sail of small Vessels ready upon the coast, to waft them over and their men, if their party could have made way sufficient for them, and had not been suppressed so quickly; upon the news whereof, his men were immediately dispersed, and he returned again (as is supposed) to Brussels with his Company.

The October coup, when the army led by Lambert locked the members out of Parliament:

The Weekly Intelligencer of the Common-Wealth *Numb*. 24.

11–18 October, 1659 689.24 {10.12}

Thursday *Octob*. 13.

Some disturbance being this day expected in the Parliament House, the Parliament in the afternoon, having as strong guards to defend them, as in so short a time could be provided five of the Commissioners, who were appointed for the Government of the Army, sate all night in the Parliament House, in that room which was called the *Speakers* Chamber: On *Thursday* morning, those Regiments which stood for the Parliament, which were Colonel *Mosseys* heretofore. Colonel *Prides* Regiment of Foot, and Col. *Morleys* Regiment drew early down to *Westminster*, and possessed themselves of the Hall, and Palace yard, and the Court of Wards, and parts adjacent: There were also some Troops of Horse under the Command of Colonel *Okey*. All *King-street*, and the further parts were possessed by the discontented party of the Army. The Lord *Lamberts* Regiment of Foot were placed next to

King-street, and the Abbey of *Westminster*, and Colonel *Hewson's* Regiment maintained the Out-places.

A strong Barricado was made at the *Mill-bank*, to hinder all Accesse from those places: And some Boates were well manned with Souldiers, did row up and down the *Thames* about *Westminster*, and permitted none to land thereabouts.

The greatest part of Colonel *Lamberts* Horse were drawn up behind the *Mewes*, in those Fields commonly called *Leicester-House* Fields. Major *Evelin*, who commanded the Parliaments Life-guard was dismounted, and Major *Creed* was immediately mounted on the same Steed: The Life-guard perceiving this, with a flourish made with their hats in their hands, did express a willingness to adhere to Colonel *Lamberts* party. And to speak the truth, the whole Army for the Generality of them, did seem to be much discontented, that a Gentleman, who had done such remarkable Service for his Country, as Col. *Lambert* had performed, not onely in suppressing the late Insurrection, but who had shewed himself very active, and fortunately couragious all along, as well, in *Scotland*, as in *England*, and who had received many honourable wounds in his Countries Service, should now be dis-authorited by them whom so faithfully he had served, and be bereaved of those many laurels, which were so justly due unto his valour, and his Conduct.

About ten of the Clock, the Drums did beat, commanding the City bands to appear presently, at the place of Randezvous upon pain of Imprisonment, but upon better considerations there came immediately a Countermand, and none appeared.

The forces of the discontented party of the Army, and the two Regiments who adhered to the Parliament stood all the while at *Westminster*, and many of them within a pikes length one of another, their Muskets charged, and their Matches lighted and in a churlish silence staring on one another, and far from those friendly Incouragements which in all former dangers they were accustomed to give to one another.

Nevertheless, in *Southwark* the *Militia* and Trained bands were raised, and eight Companies or there abouts appeared in Armes in St. *Georges-fields*, where they continued till evening, and brought with them the good news of a hopeful reconcilement betwixt both parties.

The Souldiery also in *Westminster*, keeping their stations, on both parts, the whole day continued in the same posture until the Evening, at which time came an Order from the Council of State requiring all of them to draw off, and to return to their respective quarters, whereupon both sides marched off from their weary stations, and gave many volleys of shot to testyfie their joy at their drawing off.

This was about four of the Clock in the afternoon, at which time Coll. *Mosse* his Regiment (which as I have already said, was heretofore Col. *Prides*) being drawn off from *Westminster*, Col. *Lambert* did ride through their Ranks and Files, and took a perfect view of them, and many of them (although that day opposite to him) yet in the acknowlegment of so brave a Souldier did salute him with several volleys of shot. {...}

Monday *October* 17. {...}

It is observeable that not long before there was one, a person of Honour, who meeting my Lord *Lambert*, told him that his Sword was too long, to whom my Lord suddenly and gallantly replyed, that if it were a foot shorter, it were too long for him.

The blow from Scotland, which divided the army and threatened a fourth civil war.

The Weekly Post *Numb* 26.

25 October – 1 November, 1659 704.26 {10.13}

Westminster, Octob. 29. {...}

Yesterday came a Letter hither to the Officers of the Army, from Gen. *Monck*, importing somwhat of dissatisfaction in himself, and some Officers of the Army in *Scotland*, touching the interruption & force put upon the Parl. in *England*. Insomuch, that he secured most of the strong Holds in that Nation, and several Officers of his own in *Tyntallon* Castle, who could not concur with him. He hath possessed himself of the strong Town of *Berwick*, in which Col. *Cobbet* was a while detained by Lieu. Col. *Mayr* the Governour; but afterwards coming to know, that he was going with Letters to Gen. *Monck* from the Officers of the Army in *England*, he permitted him to proceed in his journey. In the *interim*, for the security of the Northern parts, Orders are sent to dispose of what Northern Forces they can, and to command other Regiments out of the more Southerly parts to joyn with them, so that a considerable Army will (ere long) be rendezvouzed in the North.

The Weekly Intelligencer of the Common-wealth *Numb*. 27.

1–8 November, 1659 689.27 {10.14}

THE business which first began the unhappy war was the *Militia*, and the business which now ends the war is the *Militia*; the Parliament would have it from the King, and claimed it as due unto them, and now the Army would have it from the Parliament, for by whom should the Army (they say) be better Commanded then by the Commanders of it: And from hence we are threatned with new Alarms, and the effusions of more blood. *How just are the Councels of God, and his wayes past finding out*!

The Weekly Intelligencer, covering the following incident, claimed that the apprentices had gathered to play foot ball.

The Weekly Post *Numb*. 31

29 November – 6 December, 1659 704.31 {10.15}

London, Decemb. 5.

The Apprentices of the City of *London*, having presented a Petition to the Lord Mayor, Aldermen, and Common-Council; wherein they remonstrate, the manifold Troubles and Distractions the Nations are involved in, and the great Decay of Trade: Humbly imploring a speedy and timely Redress of these sad and heavy grievances; and withall praying, the establishing & preserving of a faithful, pious and Orthodox Ministry, the maintaining of the two Universities of *Oxford* and *Cambridge* as Schools of Learning, Nurceries, and Piety; and to endeavour the Restauration of Trade, both to City and Countrey. Upon the presenting of this Petition, divers Apprentices gathered together in *Cheapside, Cornwall*, and other places; which occasioned the drawing together of several Regiments of Horse and Foot, to prevent Commotions & Insurrections, in these times of imminent danger, which otherwise might inevitably threaten a new involving into intestine Troubles, and indanger the publike peace and safety of the Nations: Yet notwithstanding the great care and prudence both of the City Magistrates and Officers, some coales of Dissention were kindled and brake forth between the Apprentices and

Souldiers; for as the horse and foot were marching through Cornhill, several stones were cast at them from the tops of houses, and elsewhere, and great shoutings, and pressing upon the Rear: insomuch, that some of the Musquetiers faced about, and fired, killing 6 or 7, and wounding 19 or 20. some of which were carryed to the Hospital for cure. During this disturbance, the shops were shut up in several parts of the City; and the Lord Mayor was very diligent in preserving of the publike peace, desiring the Apprentices and others, to depart home, and to return to their respective habitations; for that they had received their Petition, and the things therein contained should be speedily taken into consideration. Whereupon they departed, and appointed 6 young men to wait his Lordships pleasure for an Answer, which is expected this present Tuesday.

The army was divided in the provinces, and as Lambert rode north, some rose to protest for a free or restored parliament.

The Publick Intelligencer *Numb*. 207.

12–19 December, 1659 575.207 {10.16}

December 18.

This day came the following Letter, giving a Relation of an endeavor to make a Rising in *Essex* at *Colchester*, to promote the Cavalier-designe, under the stale pretence of a Free Parliament.

From Colchester, Decemb. 17.

Last Thursday in the afternoon, Captain *John Rayner* came to the market place of this Town, and there declared who ever would adhere to him, and appear for a Free Parliament he would see them paid, which if he failed to do, then let them come to his House first and plunder. Hereupon the rude multitude began much to resort to him: When he had got a considerable number (as he thought) to answer his end, he bade them *Fall on*, now was the time to play their game; but the Soldiers in this place quickly secured him, and dispersed the multitude; and so all being quiet, we are providing to secure the peace of the Town for the future, and shall leave Captain *Bourchier* of Colonel *Salmons* Regiment, to command the forces here.

This day also by Letter from *Graves-End*, it is certified, that Vice-Admiral *Lawson* was come hither with several of his Captains, where upon conference with those persons before

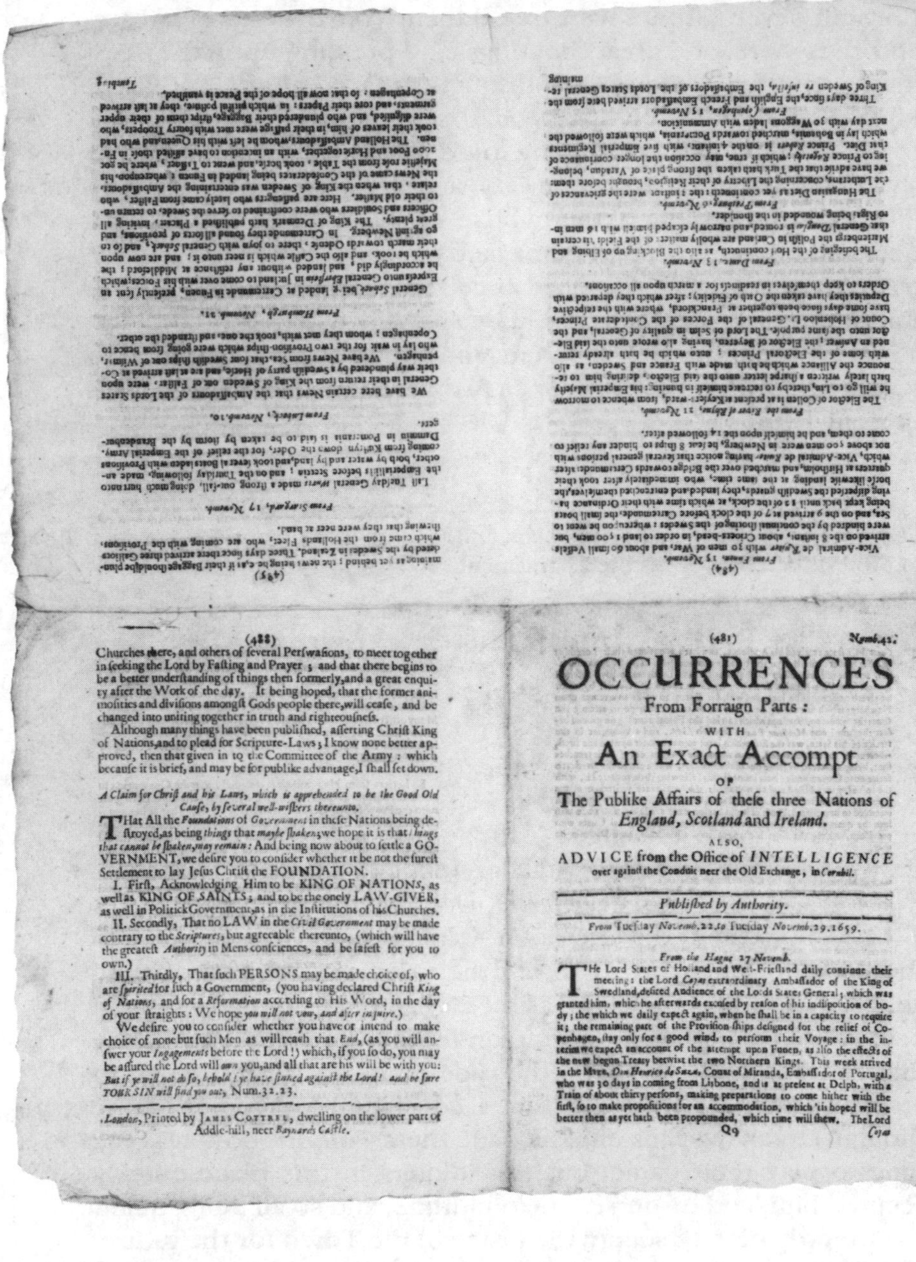

(481) *Numb.42.*

OCCURRENCES

From Forraign Parts:

WITH

An Exact Accompt

OF

The Publike Affairs of these three Nations of *England, Scotland* and *Ireland*.

ALSO,

ADVICE from the Office of *INTELLIGENCE* over against the Conduit neer the Old Exchange, in *Cornhil*.

Published by Authority.

From Tuesday *Novemb.* 22. *to* Tuesday *Novemb.* 29. 1659.

From the Hague 27 Novemb.

THe Lord States of Holland and West-Friesland daily continue their meeting: the Lord *Coyat* extraordinary Ambassador of the King of Swedland, desired Audience of the Lords States General; which was granted him, which he afterwards excused by reason of his indisposition of body; the which we daily expect again, when he shall be in a capacity to require it; the remaining part of the Provision ships designed for the relief of Copenhagen, stay only for a good wind, to perform their Voyage: in the interim we expect an account of the attempt upon Funen, as also the effects of the new begun Treaty betwixt the two Northern Kings. This week arrived in the Maes, *Don Henrico de Suza*, Count of Miranda, Embassador of Portugal, who was 30 days in coming from Lisbone, and is at present at Delph, with a Train of about thirty persons, making preparations to come hither with the first, so to make propositions for an accommodation, which 'tis hoped will be better then as yet hath been propounded, which time will shew. The Lord

Q9 *Coyat*

(488)

Churches there, and others of several Perswasions, to meet together in seeking the Lord by Fasting and Prayer; and that there begins to be a better understanding of things then formerly, and a great enquiry after the Work of the day. It being hoped, that the former animosities and divisions amongst Gods people there, will cease, and be changed into uniting together in truth and righteousness.

Although many things have been published, asserting Christ King of Nations, and to plead for Scripture-Laws; I know none better approved, then that given in to the Committee of the Army: which because it is brief, and may be for publike advantage, I shall set down.

A Claim for Christ and his Laws, which is apprehended to be the Good Old Cause, by several well-wishers thereunto.

THat All the *Foundations* of *Government* in these Nations being destroyed, as being *things* that *maybe shaken*; we hope it is that *things that cannot be shaken, may remain*: And being now about to settle a GOVERNMENT, we desire you to consider whether it be not the surest Settlement to lay Jesus Christ the FOUNDATION.

I. First, Acknowledging Him to be KING OF NATIONS, as well as KING OF SAINTS; and to be the onely LAW-GIVER, as well in Politick Government, as in the Institutions of his Churches.

II. Secondly, That no LAW in the *Civil Government* may be made contrary to the *Scriptures*, but agreeable thereunto, (which will have the greatest *Authority* in Mens consciences, and be safest for you to own.)

III. Thirdly, That such PERSONS may be made choice of, who are *spirited* for such a Government, (you having declared Christ *King of Nations*, and for a *Reformation* according to His Word, in the day of your straights: We hope *you will not vow, and after inquire*.)

We desire you to consider whether you have or intend to make choice of none but such Men as will reach that *End*, (as you will answer your *Ingagements* before the Lord!) which, if you so do, you may be assured the Lord will *own* you, and all that are his will be with you: *But if ye will not do so, behold! ye have sinned against the Lord! and be sure YOUR SIN will find you out*, Num. 32. 23.

London, Printed by JAMES COTTREL, dwelling on the lower part of Addle-hill, neer *Baynards Castle*.

13. An uncut copy of *Occurrences From Forraign Parts*, recto

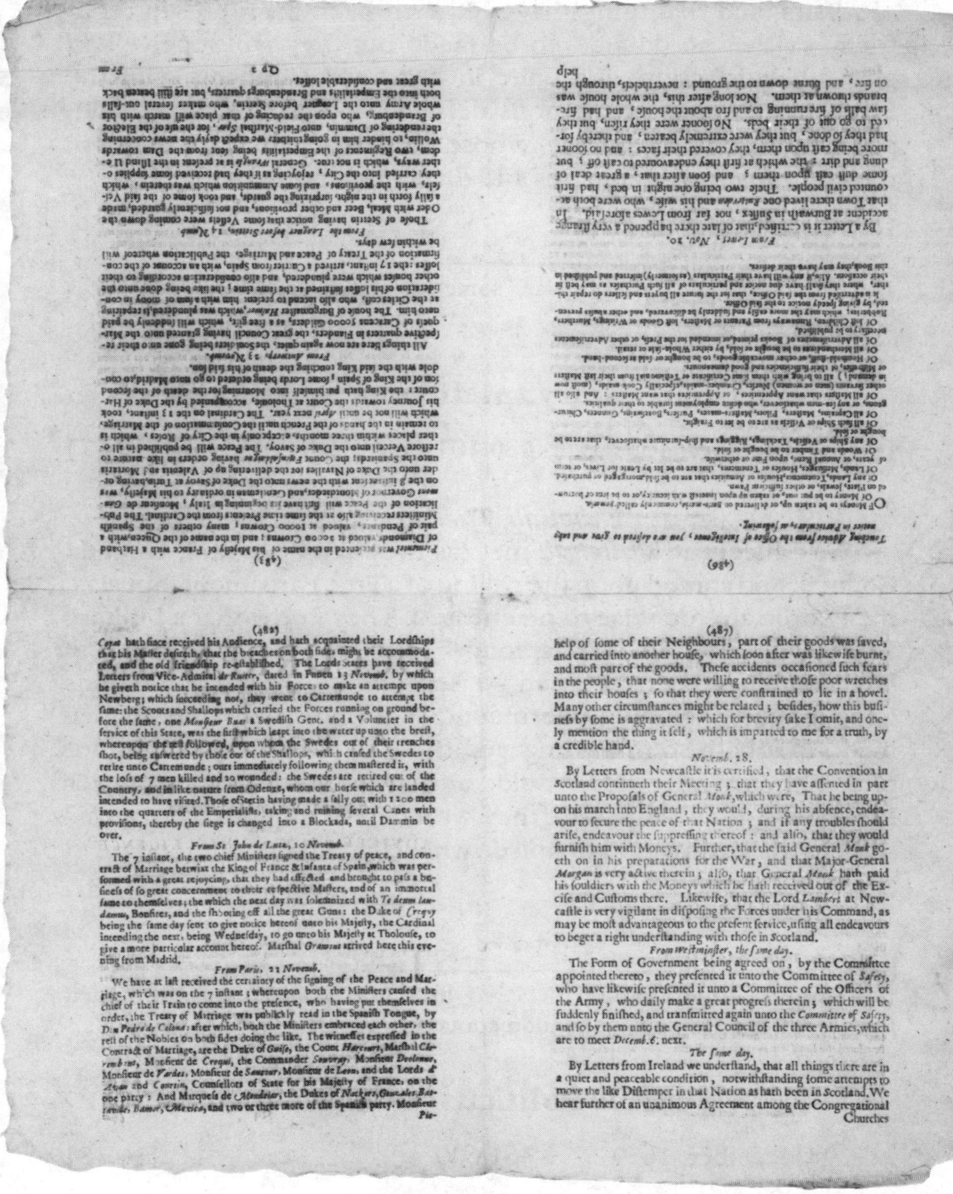

(482)

Coyet hath since received his Audience, and hath acquainted their Lordships that his Master desireth, that the breaches on both sides might be accommodated, and the old friendship re-established. The Lords States have received Letters from Vice-Admiral *de Ruiter*, dated in Funen 13 *Novemb.* by which he giveth notice that he intended with his Forces to make an attempt upon Newberg; which succeeding not, they went to Cattemunde to attempt the same: the Scouts and Shallops which carried the Forces running on ground before the same, one *Monsieur Buat* a Swedish Gent. and a Voluntier in the service of this State, was the first which leapt into the water up unto the brest, whereupon the rest followed, upon whom the Swedes out of their trenches shot, being answered by those out of the Shallops, which caused the Swedes to retire unto Cattemunde; ours immediately following them mastered it, with the loss of 7 men killed and 20 wounded: the Swedes are retired out of the Country, and in like nature from Odenze, whom our horse which are landed intended to have visited. Those of Stetin having made a sally out with 1200 men into the quarters of the Emperialists, taking and ruining several Canes with provisions, thereby the siege is changed into a Blockada, until Dammin be over.

From St. John de Luza, 10 Novemb.

The 7 instant, the two chief Ministers signed the Treaty of peace, and contract of Marriage betwixt the King of France & Infanta of Spain, which was performed with a great rejoycing, that they had effected and brought to pass a business of so great concernment to their respective Masters, and of an immortal fame to themselves; the which the next day was solemnized with *Te deum laudamus*, Bonfires, and the shooting off all the great Guns: the Duke of *Crequy* being the same day sent to give notice hereof unto his Majesty, the Cardinal intending the next, being Wednesday, to go unto his Majesty at Tholouse, to give a more particular account hereof. Marshal *Gramont* arrived here this evening from Madrid.

From Paris, 21 Novemb.

We have at last received the certainty of the signing of the Peace and Marriage, which was on the 7 instant; whereupon both the Ministers caused the chief of their Train to come into the presence, who having put themselves in order, the Treaty of Marriage was publickly read in the Spanish Tongue, by *Don Pedro de Colona*: after which, both the Ministers embraced each other, the rest of the Nobles on both sides doing the like. The witnesses expressed in the Contract of Marriage, are the Duke of *Guise*, the Count *Harcourt*, Marshal *Clerembaut*, Monsieur de *Crequi*, the Commander *Souvray*, Monsieur *Deolmue*, Monsieur de *Vardes*, Monsieur de *Saucour*, Monsieur de *Leon*, and the Lords *d'Avau* and *Contin*, Counsellors of State for his Majesty of France, on the one party: And Marquess de *Mondeiar*, the Dukes of *Nockers*, *Gonzales Barrande*, *Bamer*, *Mexico*, and two or three more of the Spanish party. Monsieur *Pie-*

(487)

help of some of their Neighbours, part of their goods was saved, and carried into another house, which soon after was likewise burnt, and most part of the goods. These accidents occasioned such fears in the people, that none were willing to receive those poor wretches into their houses; so that they were constrained to lie in a hovel. Many other circumstances might be related; besides, how this business by some is aggravated: which for brevity sake I omit, and onely mention the thing it self, which is imparted to me for a truth, by a credible hand.

Novemb. 28.

By Letters from Newcastle it is certified, that the Convention in Scotland continueth their Meeting; that they have assented in part unto the Proposals of General *Monk*, which were, That he being upon his march into England, they would, during his absence, endeavour to secure the peace of that Nation; and if any troubles should arise, endeavour the suppressing thereof: and also, that they would furnish him with Moneys. Further, that the said General *Monk* goeth on in his preparations for the War, and that Major-General *Morgan* is very active therein; also, that General *Monk* hath paid his souldiers with the Moneys which he hath received out of the Excise and Customs there. Likewise, that the Lord *Lambert* at Newcastle is very vigilant in disposing the Forces under his Command, as may be most advantageous to the present service, using all endeavours to beget a right understanding with those in Scotland.

From Westminster, the same day.

The Form of Government being agreed on, by the Committee appointed thereto, they presented it unto the Committee of *Safety*, who have likewise presented it unto a Committee of the Officers of the Army, who daily make a great progress therein; which will be suddenly finished, and transmitted again unto the *Committee of Safety*, and so by them unto the General Council of the three Armies, which are to meet *Decemb. 6.* next.

The same day.

By Letters from Ireland we understand, that all things there are in a quiet and peaceable condition, notwithstanding some attempts to move the like Distemper in that Nation as hath been in Scotland. We hear further of an unanimous Agreement among the Congregational Churches

14. An uncut copy of *Occurrences From Forraign Parts*, verso

mentioned, they begin to have a right understanding of the nature of Affairs, and that things have hitherto been misrepresented to them; so that no doubt is to be made but they will receive and give full satisfaction, and unite in heart and Councels with the Land-forces, for an unanimous defence of this Commonwealth against the common Enemy, whose long expected Harvest lies in the continuation of Enmities and divisions among our selves.

The army conceded to popular, sometimes disorderly pressure, for a parliament.

The Parliamentary Intelligencer *Numb*. 1.

19–26 December, 1659 486.101 {10.17}

Whitehall, Tuesday, 20

The Officers at *Whitehall* met (as they call it) in their General Council, and agreed upon the calling of a Free Parliament: but alas, the People are too wise to be cheated. They know that a Military Parliament may do well among *Mammalucks*, but not true Englishmen, who have been so sensible of these Gentlemens impatience under any Government, that if this renowned Parliament, that hath so much engaged them by their favours, cannot please them, no other would; and we know, that whatever Parliament, they had set up, they would have thought themselves sufficiently impowered to pull down again, if they had not danc'd after their pipe.

The garrison at Portsmouth declared itself for Monck and the purged parliament, and the army at London conceded.

Mercurius Politicus *Numb*. 600.

22–29 December, 1659 361.600 {10.18}

Whitehal, Decemb. 22.

This day came a full Information, that the forces which had laine for some-time near *Portsmouth*, and in the Country about, for the blocking up of that Garrison, upon consideration of the manifold dangers and Inconveniencies already seen, and of more ready to break forth, through the practises of the Common Enemy, in the late time of Division, had been sufficiently instructed concerning their own and the publick hazzard through a long *Interregnum*; and therefore chose rather to return to the obedience of the Parliament, the old Assertors of the *Good Cause* which hath been contended for, then stand out any longer, and so they submitted to the Authority of Parliament, exercised there by Sir *Arthur Hesilrigg*, Colonel *Walton*, and Colonel *Morley*, as Commissioners appointed by Act of Parliament for the Government and Conduct of the Army; by whose prudent improvement of the opportunity of an unsetled state of Affairs, this leading example was given to the rest of the Soldiery at *London*, to remember their duty, and from whom they had received their Commissions.

Accordingly, this day most of the Soldiery about Town began to declare themselves of opinion, that there was no visible meanes so conducing to the preservation of the Commonwealth, as the Parliament re-sitting, and a resolution to adhere unto them, that they may sit with honor, freedom and safety, to repair the Breaches made by this unhappy interruption, and conquer the difficulties thereby encreased upon them. {...}

December, 24.

According to the Orders given yesterday, this afternoon the Horse and Foot (except those on the Guards) which are about Town, were Rendevouzd in *Lincolns-Inn* Fields, and there with one consent resolved to live and die with the Parliament, using many high expressions in declaring their resolution. After this, they marched in good order down *Chancery-lane*; at the *Speakers* dore they made a stand, and several of the principal Commanders sending in word, that they there attended to know his pleasure, His Lordship came down to them in his gown to the gate in the street, where standing, the Officers as they passed with the Forces, made Speeches to him, signifying in the name of themselves and the whole soldiery, their hearty sorrow for the great defection in this late Interruption, with their absolute purpose of a firm adherence for the future; the like was done by the soldiers in their countenances and acclamations to the *Speaker*, as they passed, owning him in words also, in the behalf of the Parliament, as their General and the Father of their Country. Hereupon his Lordship issued forth Orders for disposing of them for the preservation of the Peace till the Parliament can Assemble, and he also for this night gave them the *Word*, and they gave him many volleys of shot.

From *Brussels*, Decemb. 27. S.N. {...}

The *Scotish* King is here, expecting somewhat will be done for him, upon the present divisions in *England*; he hath gained this by his Journey, that the King of *Spain* hath given order for a good summ of money to pay his debts in this Country, which are not small, and some supply he gained from his Mother in his return; which hath enabled him for the present to appear in more splendor than formerly, and his Retinue encreaseth by the return of such as formerly belong'd to him, but have been for a good while forced to shift elsewhere for a subsistance. {...}

Westminster, Munday Decemb. 26.

The Parliament having asserted their own Authority, and by their diligence, prudence, and courage, reduced all the Forces both here and abroad in the South, to the obedience of Parliament; the House began this evening to sit again, in order to the commanding of the remaining forces in the North to their duty, the providing of present Pay for the Souldiery, the remedy of Grievances, and the settling of the Great Work of the Commonwealth upon the wheel again, toward a sure and happy Settlement. The *Speaker* (who for his prudence and fidelity, upon this great occasion, will be for ever renowned) together with the Members of Parliament that were in Town (which were a Member {i.e. number} much exceeding the *Quorum*) met at *Whitehall* in the Council Chamber, and from thence came on foot through *Chanon*-row (the Mace being being carried before the *Speaker*) to *Westminster* Hall, where, as they passed, the Souldiers upon their Guard standing in rank, welcomed them with hearty expressions of joy, and loud Acclamations. And when the House arose, the Souldiers, as they departed, shouted for joy again, remembring they never have had so good days for constant Pay, as under the Government and care of this Parliament.

Mercurius Politicus *Numb*. 601.

29 December – 5 January, 1660 361.601 {10.19}

Whitehall, Jan. 4.

This night came a Messenger with Letters from General *Monck*, who was at *Kelsal* in *Scotland*, wherein is signified the continued resolution and good condition of his Army for the Parliament, intending to march on, in case the Forces in the North should not conform to the commands of Parliament.

But the same Messenger giveth an account of this great News; That as he came on the road by *North-Allerton* in *York-shire*, he found Major-General *Lambert* was there with only about fifty horse, the rest of the Forces having upon such notice of what hath passed here in the South, submitted to the Authority of Parliament, and declared for the Parliament, as himself also hath done, and the Forces are all dispersed into several Quarters, expecting what Orders will be sent from hence for the disposing of them for the service of the Commonwealth. The same Messenger comming also by *York*, saith, that the Lord *Fairfax* being there with about 2 or 300 horse, and Col. *Lilburn* likewise with some Troops, had both of them declared for this present Parliament, together with the City of *York* it self: So that, by the good hand of God, the Affairs of the Commonwealth in all the three Nations are in a miraculous manner reduced to a quiet state (as it were in an instant) under the obedience of the Parliament. This is certain: For late this night also Letters are come from the Lord *Fairfax* himself, and from some of the Gentry in Yorkshire, to the *Speaker*, signifying the same; which Letters are this Thursday to be communicated to the Parliament, together with another Letter from the Lord *Lambert*.

An Exact Accompt Of the daily Proceedings in Parliament *Numb*. 55.

6–13 January, 1659{60} 491.055 {10.20}

Courteous Reader,

T*Hou art desired to take notice of a Passage in a* Scandalous Pamphlet *called* MERCURIUS POLITICUS, *who after the Resolve of the House concerning Sir* Henry Vane, *pretends it was rendered in an abusive manner by another hand: certainly he had no eyes, or wanted a Pair of Spectacles to read daily Notes of Parliament where these Words are Verbatim*, Viz. Several Members of the House accused Sir *Henry Vane*, and charged him with several Crimes, Miscarriages and Misdemeaners against the Parliament and Commonwealth, since the late interruption of the Parliament, *&c. But our POL. covertly strikes the Parliament, and not the publisher, for charging one of their Members with just Crimes, wherein he himself hath been so lately involved, as to render the Letters of*

Generall **Monck** ***unto the City a-Fiction, and scandalizing many eminent persons,*** **&c.** ***For which 'tis hoped the Parliament in convenient time will send him unto his due place.***

General Monck entered London on 3 February.

The Publick Intelligencer *Numb.* 214.

30 January – 6 February, 1660 575.214 {10.21}

On Friday the Soldiers being marched, tumults quieted, and all both within and without the City in a great calm, General *Monck* with the Parliaments Army under his conduct, drew near the Town, and after noon, his Lordship and his Army entred by the way of Greys Inn-lane into *Holborne,* and from thence down Chancerylane, and so through Temple Bar, along the Strand, to *Whitehal.*

The Horse marched first, and himself on Horsback in the head of them, gallantly mounted; before him rode his Trompeters richly habited; so also were his Footmen, and there were several Led horses in compleat equipage.

After him followed many of his Officers, and other persons of honor and quality, and then the Horse in their order. After them marched the Foot, which are reputed as good as any in the world, trained up under an excellent Discipline, and they discovered it both in their countenances and their order.

The Speaker of the Parliament having notice of his approach, with the leave of the House set forward in his Coach from *Westminster* to meet his Lordship. In the Strand, over against Somerset-house they met, and as the Speaker was descending from his Coach, the General alighted off his Horse, and imbracing each other with all demonstrations of respect and honor, after mutual expressions of civility, they parted; the Speaker home, and General *Monck* advanced as before towards *Whitehal*, where his Lordship is setled in the Lodgings prepared for him, and hath received particular visits from all the Members of Parliament, and hath the like daily from many other persons of the highest rank and quality.

The restored purged parliament was dissolved, to the sound of catcalls and scatological eschatology, on March 16.

Mercurius Phanaticus. Or Mercury Temporizing *Numb*. 2.

14–21 March, 1660 354.2 {10.22}

The Long Parliament have at last shooke hands with the House and parted Friends, they went in one day but could not find the way out in twenty years; and although they became excellent Masters at Resolving, they could never find out the knack of Dissolving till now. The restoring of this Parliament was the distroying of that so famous *Rump*, who with a Squirt Blew down King, Lords and Commons: the Rumpling of whose Guts made not onely *England*, but Neighbouring Nations to Tremble; their fall was like *Lucifers*, Legions fell with both, there is but this difference; these are reserved in Chains, those left at Liberty.

Mercurius Honestus. Or, Tom Tell-truth Num. 1.

14–21 March, 1660 332.1 {10.23}

Tuesday March 13.

Resolved that the Rumps Engagement against a single person and House of Lords be discharged, and taken off the File, *as 'tis fit it should*, and that all Orders concerning the taking thereof should be vacated and expunged out of the Journal Books, Mr. *Prin*, Serjeant *Maynard* and Col. *Harley* being to see it done. {...}

March 16. {...}

A Bill engrossed for dissolving the Parliament begun and holden at *Westminster Nov*. 3. 1640. And for the calling and holding of a Parliament at *Westminster, April* 25. 1660. was this day read the third time, with a proviso to the said Bill upon the Question agreed unto, *viz*. Provided alwayes, and be it declared, that the single Actings of this House enforced by the pressing necessities of the present times are not intended in the least to infringe, much less take away that ancient native right which the House of Peers had, and have to be a part of the Parliament of *England. Good Boyes, make the body compleat, and you shall not long want a Head.*

Mercurius Politicus *Numb*. 615.

5–12 April, 1660. 361.615 {10.24}

From *Brussels April* 7. *S.N.*

HEre is no other talk now, but of the affairs of England, the King of Scots, and his followers being in great hopes that they shall shortly returne for England, upon which score, the people here are very forward to supply them with money and credit. His Retinue increaseth, and his Country men in those parts begin to flock about him, in expectation of some great matter for themselves.

Lambert's last stand ended with the ignominy of his fine Arab steed being unable to deal with a ploughed field. This was read as more a matter of providence than of style. *Mercurius Publicus* was the Thursday paper of Henry Muddiman, who already edited *The Parliamentary Intelligencer*. In 1660 Muddiman supplanted Nedham as the dominant journalist in Britain.

Mercurius Publicus *Numb*. 17.

19–26 April, 1660 378.117 {10.25}

From St. James, April 23.

On Sonday, April 22. Colonel Ingoldsby having notice of Col. Lamberts being with a party near Daventry, marched with his own Regiment, Captain Linleys Troop of Col. Rossiters Regiment, and two Companies of Col. Streaters Regiment, commanded by the Colonel himself to the place where Lambert was, about two miles distant from Daventry, with four Troops of Horse, viz. Col. Alureds and Major Nelthrops, (which two Gentlemen were then in London about the affairs of the Regiment, not in the least acquainted nor consenting, but declaring against the defection of their Troops,) Captain Hesilriggs Troop and Cap. Clares Troop, besides several Anabaptists, Quakers, and other Fanaticks. Col. Ingoldsby's Forlorn commanded by Cap. Elsemore, met with Cap. Hesilrigg, whom he took prisoner; but upon giving his Parol, and a promise to send his Troop to them, he was dismissed. Cap. Hesilriggs Troop not long after came in to Colonel Ingoldsby according to his engagement, led by the Cornet and Quarter Master, and was placed in the left Wing.

The Enemy thinking himself well gifted as to the perswasive faculty desired to parley, thinking by that means to gain some of our party. Our Officers were not unwilling to admit it, knowing such treacherous actions could not be upheld by the subtlest insinuations, and that all their arguments could never shake a truly resolved courage. The business they did drive at was under pretence of security to all Interests, to perswade a readmission of the Lord Richard to his Protectorship, which was well answered by a stout Officer, telling them their only end in that was to set up one again, who they themselves had already learnt to pull down, that they are under command, and knew it their duty not to dispute, but to submit to what orders they received from their superiors, which they wished them likewise to do. Thus the first dispute ended, and our party prepared to make use of sharper arguments to convince those whom reason and duty could not prevaile with. When the Enemy saw our men fully resolved to fall on them, and that Captain Barkers Troop was joyned with us, they were much disheartened, and upon our march horse and foot to force upon them, after a wheel about, and a little pause, colonel Alureds Troop came into us. Then did Lambert find himself forsaken by his brethren, Clare's Troop, which were his greatest Confidents growing rather an hinderance to his flight then a defence for his person, their guilt had unmann'd them, and he who before had gaind the name of stout and valiant in many battels, when he saw Colonel Ingoldsby rid up to him, and demanded him as his Prisoner, was presently taken without drawing his Sword, and driven to that pityfull shift to cry out PRAY MY LORD LET ME ESCAPE, PRAY MY LORD LET ME ESCAPE. Yet one of his desperate Villains after he was taken, discharged a Pistol at colonel *Ingoldsby*, whose courage and mercy are in this most justly to be commended, which could command his passions at that time not to revenge himself on such miscreants. One thing is very remarkable, that though Colonel Lambert was mounted on a Barb which might have hastened him in his flight, providence had so ordering it, that he was on ploughd land, where his horse could prove of little advantage to him. Colonel Lambert was taken by Colonel Ingoldsbys own hands. The rest of his party took Col. Cobbet, Major Creed. Lieut: col: Young, captain Timothy Clare, captain Gregory and captain Spinage and some other private Soldiers. Colonel Okey, col. Axtel, and capt. Cleer, Okeys Son-in-law escaped, though pursued four miles. {...}

On Tuesday April 24 {...} *Col. Lambert* and some of his confederates were brought up Prisoners to the Council, who after examination committed him, Colonel *Cobbet* and Major *Creed,* to the Tower to be kept close Prisoners. An happy Omen of our future settlement, that the day before the sitting of the Parlament; there should not onely appear so gallant a body of honest Citizens to defend them, but the chief of that Faction that endeavored the disturbance of the Nation should be delivered into their hands, and the rest of his Accomplices timely discovered and dispersed.

The Treaty of Breda, which formed the basis for the Restoration, became public in late April.

Mercurius Publicus *Numb*. 18.

26 April – 3 May, 1660 378.118 {10.26}

May 1.

OUr Chronicles make mention of an *Ill May-day*; Let this of 1660. henceforward by called the *Good one* for ever, as having produced the most desired, the most universally satisfactory, and the most welcom News that ever came to these Three Nations since that of 29. of *May* which was the Birthday of our Soveraign *Charls* the Second, whom God preserve; viz. *His Majesties gracious Letter and Declaration sent to the House of Lords by Sir* John Greenvil *Knight, one of His Majesties Bedchamber, from* Breda. *His gracious Message, with the Declaration to the House of Commons; and His gracious Letter, with the Declaration inclosed, to his Excellency the Lord General* Monck, *to be communicated to the Officers of the Armies under his Command*. In all which I refer you to the printed Copies at large, giving you only the heads of the Declaration, wherein His Majesty grants a free general Pardon to all his Subjects whatever that shall within forty days after the publishing thereof lay hold upon that grace and favor, and by any publick act declare their doing so, excepting onely such persons as shall hereafter be excepted by Parliament; such onely excepted, His Majesty promiseth upon the word of a King, that no Crime committed either against Him, or His Royal Father, shall (as far as lies in His Majesties power) endamage the least either in Lives, Liberties, Estates, or Reputation; it being His Majesties desire that all Notes of Discord should be laid aside among all His Subjects. His Royal Majesty doth further declare a Liberty to Tender Consciences, and that no man shall be called in question for differences of Opinion in matter of Religion, which do not disturb the Peace of the Kingdom: And that all differences, and all things relating to Grants, Sales and Purchases, shall be determined in Parliament, which can best provide for the just satisfaction of all men who are concerned. His Majesty doth farther declare, that He will be ready to consent to any Act or Acts of Parliament to the purposes aforesaid, and for the full satisfaction of all Arrears due to the Officers and Soldiers of the Army under the Command of General *Monck*, and that they shall be received in His Majesties service upon as good pay and conditions as they now enjoy.

The gracious Message, with the Letter to His Excellency, and the Declaration, were read in the House of Commons with the accustomed ceremony and reverence due to Majesty, and entertained with so general a consent, that the House never appeared so truly the Peoples full Representative. The first that spake to it was Mr. *Luke Robinson*, a person whose former actings evidenced his Judgement Antimonarchical; but now as ingenuously acknowledged his conviction, and cordially professed his loyal submission. If a Message from His Majesty hath such influence as to beget so eminent a Concert, why may we not hope that His glorious Appearance will be an universal healing to the Nations? Men will recover their Senses again, as well as their Liberties; all Clouds of Discontent will vanish, all Fanatick Vapors, all Fantastick Mists will be dispelled and dispersed into nothing.

The Letter to his Excellency being communicated to the House of Commons and read there, the Speaker desired it might be put to the Question, Whether it should be return'd to him, or kept there as a perpetual monument of his Honor? But his Excellency desired that he might have the favor to communicate it to his Officers; after which he humbly referred it to their discretion to do with it as they thought fit.

The proclamation was a long and ritualistic procedure, followed by great celebrations.

The Parliamentary Intelligencer *Numb*. 20.

7–14 May, 1660 486.120 {10.27}

May 8. 1660.

Let this day in its order as well as the first never want a distinguishing mark in the Calender for signal Joy and Festivity, in which his Sacred Majesty with an universal Testification of Loyalty from all degrees was solemnly proclaimed by the Lords and

Commons, the Lord Mayor &c. in the Cities of *London* and *Westminster*. The manner whereof followeth.

The Lords House being risen between One and Two of the clock, they went all forth into the Painted Chamber, where they continued till they were placed in order, The Earl of Manchester Speaker first, then the Duke of Buckingham, the Earl of Oxford &c. Thus they walked all along with the Heralds before them through the Court of Requests and Westminster-Hall to the Palace, where they staid before the Hall-gate. A little while after the House of Commons came down to them in the Palace-yard, where all stood bare both Lords and Commons near the Hall-gate, whilst Mr. *Bish*, dictated, and Mr. *Ryley King* at Arms with a loud voice proclaimed *Charls* the Second, in these words.

ALthough it can no way be doubted, but that his Majesties Right and Title to his Crowns and Kingdoms, is and was every way compleated by the death of his most Royall Father of glorious memory, without the ceremony or solemnity of a Proclamation: Yet since Proclamations in such cases have been always used, to the end that all good Subjects might upon this occasion testifie their duty and respect; And since the armed violence, and other the calamities of many years last past, have hitherto deprived us of any such oportunity, wherein we might express our loyalty and allegeance to his Majesty: We therefore the Lords and Commons now assembled in Parliament, together with the Lord Major, Aldermen, and Commons of the City of London, and other Freemen of this Kingdom now present, do according to our duty and allegeance, heartily, joyfully, and unanimously acknowledge and proclaim, That immediately upon the decease of our late Soveraign Lord King *Charls*, the Imperial crown of the Realm of *England*, and of all the Kingdoms, Dominions, and Rights belonging to the same, did by inherent Birthright, and lawful and undoubted succession, descend and come to his most excellent Maiesty, *Charls* 2. as being lineally, justly, and lawfully next heir of the Blood-Royal of this Realm; and that by the goodness and providence of Almighty God, He is of *England, Scotland, France* and *Ireland*, the most Potent, Mighty, and undoubted King: And thereunto we most humbly and faithfully do submit and oblige our selves, our heirs, and posterities for ever.

The Proclamation being ended, the Lords and Commons took their coaches and proceeded in this order. First, the Head-Bayliff of Westminster, and his Servants did ride along with white staffs, to prepare the way. Then followed a gallant troop of Officers of the Army and other Gentlemen with trumpets before them, then the Life-guard very stately mounted, and richly clothed, after them a class of six Trumpets and three Heralds, then a Herald between the Serjeant to the Commons, and the Mace of the Council, next Mr. *Ryley* King at Arms in his rich coate of the Kings Arms, between Serjeant *Norfolk* and Serjeant *Middleton*, after whom came the Usher of the Black-Rod and Mr. *Bish* together. These thus ushering the way, came, the Right Honorable the Earl of *Manchester* in his coach and six horses, the Speaker of the House of Commons in his, then his Excellencie the Lord General Monck in his, after which followed both Houses of Lords and Commons, some in coaches of six horses, some four, some two, and then a Troop of Horse. In this manner they came to *Whitehal*, where they proclaimed His Majesty a second time, and then in like order proceeded. Being come to *Arundel* house, they made a stand, where Mr *Ryley*, King at Arms, taking one of the Heralds and six Trumpets with him, advanced forward toward Temple Bar; perceiving at a distance the Gates open, he paused a while Col. Alderman *Bateman*, and some other Gentlemen came to him to acquaint him, that the Lord Major, Aldermen, Colonels, and other Officers of the City, were there ready to receive him. Whereupon the King at Arms having some discourse with the Colonel, the Colonel went back to Temple Bar, and caused the Gates to be shut; Upon this the King at Arms with Trumpets before him went to the Gate, knocked and demanded entrance. The Lord Major appointed some to ask who it was that knock'd; the King at Arms replied, that if they would open the Wicket, and desire the Lord Major to come to the Gate, he would deliver to him his Message: The Lord Major came on Hors-back attended with several Officers to the Gate, and Col. *Bateman* told the King at Arms, he might now deliver his Message to the Lord Major, who was come to receive it. The Trumpets immediately sounded, after which, silence being made, it was demandeed of the King of Arms, *Who he was, and what was his Message*; to which he answered on Hors-back with his Hat on, *We are the Heralds at Arms appointed and commanded by the Lord and Commons in Parliament assembled, to demand entrance into the famous City of* London, *to proclaim* Charls *the Second, King of* England, Scotland, *and* Ireland, *and we expect your speedy answer to this demand*. To this they returned, *If it please you, Sir, to have a little patience, we shall speedily give you an answer to your message*, shutting the Wicket again. After some conference between the Lord Major, and Aldermen, the Colonel returned, and opening the Wicket, told the King at Arms, That his Message was accepted, and the Gates should be immediately opened, which was done accordingly. The King at Arms entred trumpets sounding before him, and was joyfully received by the Lord Major in his crimson velvet Gown and Hood, the Aldermen and Sheriffs in Scarlet, and the Officers of the Militia gallantly accoutred on horse-back.

Both sides of the streets were guarded by the Militia forces of London from Temple-bar to the Old-Exchange, and stood all with their swords drawn; as also the Officers and several spectators in windows. The City Horse fell in next the life-guard, then the Lord Major and Aldermen, after whom the Heralds and the rest as formerly. When they came to Chancery lane end they proclaimed his Majesty a third time, where the word CHARLS the second in the Proclamation, the King at Arms lifting himself up with more then ordinary cheerfulness, and expressing it with a very audible voice, the people presently took it, and on a sudden carried it to the Old Exchange, which was pursued with such shouts, that near a quarter of an hour was spent before silence could be made to read the rest of the Proclamation. After this they went to Cheapside, where His Majesty was proclaimed a fourth time, where the shouts of the people were so great, that though all the Bells in the City rung, Bow bells could not be heard there. Thence to the old Exchange where his Majesty was again proclaimed.

The shouts and acclamations of the people to this gallant and well ordered Procession, are not easy to be exprest. But then the doubling and redoubling of them when the ceremony of Proclaiming was performed, none but he that was an eye and ear witness, can conceive. Sometimes they looked upward and presently cast their eyes toward the General, as if they had intended at once to pay a tribute of thanks to Heaven, and his Excellency, who had been so signally instrumental in this happy change; and then again with one voice cryed out, *God save King Charles the Second*, as if they had acknowledged this days joy a recompence for all their former pressures and grievances; so excellent a Tutor is the want of that, which long fruition makes us not rightly understand.

When the solemnity was thus ended, then did the people severally begin to express their joys with ringing of Bells, Bonfires and Shooting, Major *Nichols* of his Excellencies Regiment, who then commanded in the Tower, ordered three severall times 35 great Guns to be shot off at each time, which were ushered in by three several peals of small shot, to testifie how freely he will pay that duty which he ows His Majesty. The Forein Ambassadors were not wanting in declaring their satisfaction with the work of this great day, amongst whom the Swedish Ministers were eminently forward, throwing out money at their Bonfires, to raise the hearts of those whom want might otherwise have dejected.

A shortened version of the account of the Proclamation of the King at Sherborne in Dorsetshire on Monday 14 May: one of many proclamations which made the official newsbooks tedious, as they had been in September 1658. This is an extreme example, and the degenerate pleasure the royalists take in their mock trial (their refusal to acknowledge the authority of the court is a parody of a more famous incident) was soon to be realised in the grim punishments inflicted on Cromwell's disinterred corpse.

Mercurius Publicus *Numb*. 21.

17–24 May, 1660 378.121 {10.28}

{...} The very earth did seem to quake, and the air to tremble at the mighty rending shouts that were that day iterated. On the top of the Tower of the antient Cathedral, were four large white Flags with red Crosses in them, displayed on high Poles; the Conduit that day and the next ran with Clarret, besides many Hogsheads of March Bear, and large Baskets of White Loaves set out in the street for the poor. In the close of the day, some of the witty Wags of the Town, did very formally represent an High Court of Justice at the Sessions Bench, whither, by a formidable Guard was brought a grim Judge or Lord President in a Blood-red Roab, and a tire for his head of the same hue; who being gravely set down in the Chair of Judicature, together with sundry Assessors, the Cryer in the name of the supream Keeper of the Liberties of *England* did command silence. After the appointing of an Attorney General, a Solicitor General, and other Officers for the due constituting of so high a Court, and the empanelling of a Jury, *John Bradshaw* and *Olivers Cromwels*, whose effigies were artificially prepared and brought thither by a guard of Soldiers, were endited of High Treason and murdering of the King, commanded to hold up their bloody hands, which for the purpose were besmeared with blood. They were asked whether they did own the Authority of the Court, at which, being silent the whole multitude present cryed out, Justice! Justice! my Lord, Justice for these bloody Traitors and murderers. They were asked again, whether they owned the Authority of the Court, and upon refusal, sentence was passed upon them to be dragged to the place of Execution, to be there hanged upon two Gibbets of forty foot high, on both sides the States Arms, which had lately been erected by Captain *Chasie*, one of *Lamberts* Champions; which sentence was accordingly executed. The honest Officers that dragged them to execution, from the lower part of the Town to the upper, had many a blow with fists, swords, halberts, and pikes, which were aimed at the execrable malefactors: As they hung upon the Gibbets, they were so hacked and hewed, so gored and shot throw, that in a short time but little remained, besides *Cromwels* Buff Coat and Bloody Scarff, that was worth the burning. Yet would not the people be satisfied till they had made a fire between the Gibbets and burnt all they could get of their Garbage or Garments, and at last tore down the States Arms to help make up their funeral pile. At night besides the multitude of Bonfires in the streets (which no doubt made the inhabitants of the World in the Moon, if there be any there) think there was an apparition of some Blazing-star: there were three huges piles of Faggots fired on the broughes of three of the highest Hills, about a mile distant from the Town, which were visible over all the Marshes of Somersetshire, in part of Wales, and the greatest part of Blackmore, which the Lunarians might take for three locks or beards of the aforesaid Comets.

This extraordinary joy of the people of this Town might perhaps proceed from the Native *Genius* of the place, which having enjoyed formerly the residence of many a King and Bishop, and the felicities that attend those Governments in Church and State, did cause them to be even transported with joy at the restitution of the one, and the fair hopes of restauration of the other, to these long harassed Kingdoms and Churches. {...}

Charles embraced Monck at Dover on 25 May.

An Exact Accompt *Numb.* 95.

25 May – 1 June, 1660 491.095 {10.29}

From the *Downes* we have this accompt, that the Fleet came in there on Friday at three of the clock in the afternoon, that the Guns in the Castles did speak his Majesties welcome into *England*; that the Commissioners of the Parliament Landed at *Deale*, and went away immediately to *Canterbury* to make provisions for his Majesty against he came thither; that his Majesty came unto *Dover*, where the Dukes of *York* and *Glocester* landed first, and afterward his Majestie at the *Peer-Head*, who immediatly as soon as he came on *English* Ground was observed to take of his Hat lifting up his eyes and hands to the great Creator of Heaven and Earth in so wonderfully bringing him in Peace into his Hereditary Dominions.

His Excellency the Lord General *Monck* with the Lords and Gentlemen attended the coming of his Majesty, that the Gentry made a guard for his Majesty from the landing place unto the House, where he refreshed himself: that at his comming a shore, the Generall presented himself unto his Majesty upon his knee, desiring to kisse his Majesties hand, who kindly took him up and would not suffer him to doe it. That after his Majesty had taken notice of the Lords and Gentlemen with the Generall, who having performed their duties unto his Majesty with the Dukes of *York* and *Glocester*, his Majesty took the Generall by the hand, and walkt with Him unto the House appointed for Him, where having refreshed Himself some short time, he took Coach and came unto *Canterbury* being met by the Mayor Aldermen, &c. unto whom the Recorder after he had made a speech presented his Majesty with a Gold Tankard, after which he was conducted unto the Pallace, where he will remaine untill Munday.

The arrival of the restored king in London on 29 May was described in extensive detail.

Mercurius Publicus Numb. 22.

24–31 May, 1660 378.122 {10.30}

At Black-heath the Army was drawn up, where his Majesty received them, giving out many expressions of his gracious favour to the Army, which were received by loud shoutings and rejoycings. Several bonfires were made as his Majesty came along; and one more remarkable then the rest for its bigness, where the States Arms were burned.

Thence the Army being placed according to his Excellencies Order, his Majesty marched towards London. And now because God himself, when he would set a mark of observance upon his own *Magnalia*, hath taken notice of the circumstance of time, it is very considerable here, that it was his Majesties Birth-day: He was Heir apparent when first born, but had *Jus in re* now, when entring the Metropolis of his Kingdome he took possession. All letts and hinderances which have intervened since his Majesties just Right, are now so many Arguments of his future fixed and peaceable enjoyment. This the Ancients intimate, when they tell us *Jupiter* himself was not quiet in Heaven, till after a long War with the Giants. May that God by whom Kings reign, long preserve Him and the Nation a mutual blessing to each other.

When his Majesty came to St. Georges Field, the Lord Major and the Aldermen were in a Tent ready to receive him. There the Lord Mayor delivered unto his Majesty a sword upon his knees, which his Maiesty gave back to him; after a repast taken there, his Majesty came to White-Hall in this manner, All the streets being richly hang'd with Tapistry, and a lane made by the Militia forces to London-Bridg, from London-Bridg to Temple-bar by the Trained Band on one side, and the several Companies in their Liveryes, and the streamers of each Companie on the other side by the Railes; from Temple-barr to Westminster by the Militia forces, Regiments of the Army, and several Gentlemen formerly Officers of the Kings Army, led by Sir John Stawel. First marched a Troop of Gentlemen led by Major General Brown, all brandishing their Swords in cloathes of silver doublet in all about three hundred, besides their servants. Then another Troop of about 200 in Velvet coats, the footmen and Liveries in purple. Then another Troop led by Alderman Robinson, with Buff coats, silver sleeves and green scarves. After this a Troop with blew liveries and silver lace, colours red, fringed with silver, about 130. After that a Troop 6 Trumpets 7 footmen in sea green and silver, their colours pinck, fringed with silver. Then a Troop with their liveries gray and blew, with silk and silver laces thirty Footmen, four Trumpets, consisting of about 220. their Colours skie fringed with silver. Another of gray liveries, six Trumpets, Colours skie and silver, of about 105 Gentlemen. Another Troop of 70 Gentlemen, five Trumpets, Colours sky and silver. Another Troop led by the Lord Cleveland, of about 300 Noblemen and Gentlemen, Colours blew fringed with gold. Another Troop of about 100, black Colours fringed with gold. Another Troop of about 300.

After these came two Trumpets with His Majesties Arms; The Sheriffs men in red Cloaks and silver Lace, with Half-pikes, 79 in number. Then followed the several Companies of London, with their several Streamers, all in black Velvet Coats, with Gold

Chains, every Company having their Footmen of their several Liveries, some red and white, some pink and white, some blew and yellow, &c. Three Trumpets in Liveries, richly laced, and cloth of Silver sleeves, went before the Company of the Mercers. After all these came a Kettle-drum, five Trumpets, and three Streamers, and very rich red Liveries with silver Lace: The number of the Citizens were about 600. After these twelve Ministers, another Kettle-drum, four Trumpets. Then his Majesties Life-guard, led by the Lord Gerard, another party led by Sir Gilbert Gerard and Major Rosecarron, and the third Division by Colonel Pragues. Then three Trumpets in rich Coats and Sattin Doublets; the City Marshal with eight Footmen in French green, trimmed with crimson and white; the City Waits, the City Officers in order, Dr. *Warmstry*, the two Sheriffs, and all the Aldermen of London in their Scarlet Gowns and rich Trappings, with Footmen in Liveries, red coats laced with Silver, and cloth of Gold and Silver; the Heralds and Maces in their rich Coats: The Lord Mayor bare, carrying the Sword, his Excellency and the Duke of Buckingham bare, and then the Glory of all, his Sacred Majesty, rode between the Dukes of York and Glocester. Afterwards followed a Troop bare with white colours, then the Generals Life-guard: after which another company of Gentry, sky coloures fringed of gold: after which five Regiments of the Army horse, led by Col. Knight, viz. his Excellencies Regiment, Colonel Knights, Colonel Cloberries, Lord Faulkenbergs, Lord Howards; after whom came two Troops of Nobility and Gentlemen, red colours fringed with gold. There was never such a sight of Noblemen and Gentlemen that marched then brandishing their swords all along. Soon after his Majesty was passed all the Musketiers that lined the street gave many Vollies of shot. {...}

The Solemnity of this day was concluded with an infinite number of bonfires, it being observable, that as if all the houses had turned out their Chimneys into the streets, the weather being very warm, there were almost as many bonfires in the streets, as houses throughout London and Westminster. And among the rest in Westminster a very costly one was made, where the effigies of the old Oliver Cromwel was set up on a high post with the Arms of the Commonwealth, which having been exposed there a while to the publick view, with torches lighted, that every one might take better notice of them, were burnt together.

Mercurius Publicus *Numb*. 27.

28 June – 5 July, 1660 378.127 {10.31}

☞ ***We must call upon you again for a Black Dog, between a Grey-hound and a Spaniel, no white about him, only a streak on his Brest, and his Tayl a little bobbed. It is His Majesties own Dog, and doubtless was stoln, for the Dog was not born nor bred in*** England, ***and would never forsake his Master. Whosoever findes him may acquaint any at White-hal, for the Dog was better known at Court, than those who stole him. Will they never leave robbing His Majesty? must He not keep a Dog? This Dogs place (though better then some imagine) is the only place which no body offers to beg.***

Hugh Peters, a Regicide and a favourite preacher of Cromwell, was punished not least because of his powerful preaching. He was singled out for particularly cruel treatment in print.

Mercurius Publicus *Numb*. 36

30 August – 6 September, 1660 378.136 {10.32}

Westminster.

And now we can tell News which all the good subjects of three Kingdoms will rejoice at; how that great Instrument of sedition and Firebrand, *Hugh Peters*, is close prisoner in the *Tower* of *London*. The particulars take impartially thus. On Friday last intelligence was given that *Peters* privily lurked about *Southwark*; whereupon Sir *Edward Nicholas* his Majesties principal Secretary of State, sent two Messengers of his Majesties Chamber in ordinary to apprehend him: That night they entred the house where he lay, which was one *Broad's* a Quaker in S. *Thomas* parish, whose daughter Mrs. *Peach* then lay in. The Messengers search'd, but miss'd *Hugh Peters*, who *according to his custom* had crept into bed to the young woman, where the Messengers modesty forbad their search; she having been delivered but two days before. There lay *Hugh*; and the Messengers finding a private passage out of that into the house of another Quaker call'd *John Day* the Cobler, (thus *Quaking* runs from house to house;) they search'd there also: In the interim *Peters* escap'd from childbed, leaving behind him his Cane with a Rapier in it, a small pocket-Bible, and a gray Cloak, (for possibly now he was in his Frock.) But on Sunday last about six at night, in a place call'd the *Maze*, in the same parish near *Hors-way Down*, at *Nathanael Mun* a Tape-weavers house, *Hugh Peters* again lay in. The Messenger Mr. *Wickham* coming to the door, found it not lock'd nor latch'd, but kept fast by the Tape-weavers wife, (how faithful that sex are to *Peters!*) who thrust her back to the door, till the Messengers strength prov'd Mrs. *Mun* was the weaker vessel, and suddenly running up stairs, found that door also kept fast like the other; 'twas *Hugh* himself, whose shoulder at the door put the Messanger hard to it, for *Peters* now thought he thrust for his life. But the Messenger encourag'd, in hopes 'twas *Peters*, whose strength fail'd, as his fear increased, at last the door flew open, where *Hugh Peters* was found (a true Quaker) trembling after an incredible manner: Yet now (in his wonted way of confidence) he stifly denied himself to be *Peters*, but said his name was *Thompson* (perhaps *Hugh* the son of *Thomas*) threatning the Messengers with an Action at Law for offering to affirm he was *Hugh Peters*; and therefore refused to go down with the Messenger, till Mr. *Arnold* (servant to Mr. *Blagge* of his Majesties Bedchamber) Mr. *Hopkins* a good neighbour, and Mr. *Harris* the honest Constable came us stairs, who all expressed much diligence and heartiness in assisting the Messenger. And yet after all, he refused to come down (still wondring they would think him *Peters*,) so as they began to force him down, and then he promised to go along, *but first*, said he, *give me leave to gather up my spirits*; whereupon he call'd for Drink, and drank two quarts (two full quarts) of small Beer, for the House had no strong. The *Hugh* desired he might speak privately with Mris. *Mun*, which they denied, unless hee would speak in their hearing; after which hee said, *I will go, but I beg for the Lords sake that you call mee not Mr.* Peters, *for*, said hee, *if it be known that I am* Hugh Peters, *the people in the street will stone mee*. At last out hee came, but suddenly stept in again, saying, *I must speak privately with the woman of the House*, (a woman was his chief Confident) and now they had some tugging to fetch him back, in which struggle, feeling his skirts hard, they unript them, and found five peeces of Gold and some Silver Medals, and out of his pocket they took his Almanack, for which hee struggled more than for his Bible. Thence they forced him to the Constables House, where they sent for his Landlord *Broad* (an old Accuser of honest men) who being absent, his Son-in-law *Peach*, (whose happiness it was that his Wife had been but 2. daies delivered) came in his stead, who being asked if hee knew that Cloak, Cane, and Gloves, answered, *that they belonged to that*

Gentleman; pointing to *Peters*. But *Hugh* still with his wonted modesty denied it, name and all; though soon (forgetting himself) hee unawares put on the Gloves, and said, *they were his own*; and then without more trifling they brought him to the *Tower*, and delivered him into the custody of the worthy Lieutenant Sir *Iohn Robinson* (in the blood of whose Uncle, that ever-renowned *William* late Archbishop of *Canterbury*, *Hugh Peters* was elbow deep, and got the Archbishops Library of most choise Books, as well as his Majesties Library at St. *James's)* which he hath now turn'd to a pocket Bible and an Almanack. All this while, and at the *Tower* also, *Hugh* averred his name was *Thomson*, and denied himself to be *Peters* though there his Cosin Mr. *Birch* the Wardour knew him and called the man by his name; til at last in privat to Sir *Iohn Robinson* he confessed who hee was, and then (with most ingenious modesty) accused the Messenger and the rest *for taking him and bringing him to the* Tower *by the name of* Thomson. So that he who before threatned an *Action* against those who offered to call him *Hugh Peters*, doth now accuse them for calling him *Thomson*. This is St. *Hugh*, who when our Glorious Soveraign was led to Matyrdom, fel so heavy upon his righteous soul, blaspheming him upon his then Text (*Psal*. 149. *To bind their King in Chains, &c.*) {...}

These represent just part of the extensive reports of the trials and executions of the regicides and others exempted from the king's mercy. The 'Lady from the Gallery' may have been Lady Fairfax.

Mercurius Publicus *Numb*. 42.

11–18 October, 1660 378.142 {10.33}

Monday, Octob. 15.

To day Mr. *John Carew* was executed within the Rails where *Charing-Cross* stood. Before his execution he spake much like what he did at his Arraignment, and that was after the rate and manner of *Thomas Harrison*. He quoted several places out of the *Apocalyps*; neither gave nor asked forgiveness of any friend or enemy: After he was hanged and cut down, he was quartered, and his quarters conveighed back on the same Hurdle that brought him from *Newgate*.

While Mr. *John Carew* was executed, *Daniel Axtel* (heretofore called Col. *Axtel*) was arraigned at *Justice-Hall* before His

Majesty's Commissioners of *Oyer* and *Terminer*; where by divers witnesses it was proved, That he guarded that abominable *High Court of Justice*, at the *Kings* Tryal; that when *Bradshaw* said His late *Majesty* was charged *by and in the name of the people of England*, and a Lady from the Gallery crying out, *It was a lye, and not half the people. Axtel* then gave command to his soldiers, that if one word more were spoken they should shoot her: Whereupon the soldiers mounted the Muzzles of their Muskets toward that place; that he stroke his soldiers for not crying out *Justice* against the *King*; and on the day when His *Majesty* was sentenced, he incited his soldiers to cry out *Execution, Execution!* That he commanded *Lashaw Axtel* to fetch the *Executioner*, and was very active about the *Kings* death. That he carried 16 or 17 soldiers who had formerly served the King, to be examined by *Cook* as witnesses against His *Majesty*, compelling them to examination, being strangely eager to finde out witnesses against the King: That he was one of the five who managed the Kings Execution.

To which Charge upon Oath, he answered, That he was a Commissioned Officer under the Lord *Fairfax* (as he had been before under the Earl of *Essex*) and by Commission was to obey his Superior Officer (who commanded him that day to *Westminster-Hall*) according to the customs of War, so that if he had disobeyed his Superior Officer, then he had died, and now must die for obeying him.

But the Court told him he might have refus'd without any danger as well as Colonel *Hunckss*, and that *Passive* as well as *Active* obedience was required from every man; and that neither *His* nor his *Imperial Officers* Commission bid him kill his Father, much less the Father of his Countrey. As for the Muskets mounted toward the Lady, he said, That if a Lady grew uncivil to disturb the Court, he could do no less then check her (so he called shooting her dead;) that his *striking the soldiers for not crying Justice* was a mistake; for he said he strook them, because they did it, saying, *I'll give you Justice*. That his inciting them (at the Sentence) to cry *Execution*, was the *Execution of Justice*, and that could do no hurt; with such little evasions as these (repeated over and over) he took up three hours, but received so full and satisfactory answers from the Court, that the Jury (observing how fully that high Charge was proved) stirred not from the Bar, where they brought him *Guilty*.

Then Mr. *Francis Hacker* (usually called Col. *Hacker*) was tryed, who (without calling witnesses) confessed he signed a

Warrant for Execution of His late *Majesty*; but pretended he was no Lawyer, no contriver, but drawn in by the art of *Cromwel*; and said, he liked not the fact so well, to go about to excuse it. So as the Jury (from his own mouth) gave in their verdict that he was *Guilty*.

After *Hacker*, came *William Howlet alias Hewlet*, who was charged by His *Majesties* Counsel, as one of those disguised persons in a Frock on the Scaffold, which was proved by several witnesses who had heard it confessed out of his own mouth; he having several times gloried, That he was the man who had done that monstrous fact; which though he (with very much boldness) denyed, the Jury after some little consultation gave him in *Guilty*.

Tuesday, Octob. 16.

This day *John Cook*, (of whose Tryal you heard at large in our last) was executed at *Charing-Cross*. He carried himself at his execution (as well as at his Tryal) much better then could be expected from one that acted such a part in that horrid Arraignment of our late Soveraign; for, (not to wrong him) he expressed exceeding much Penitence; and (which best became him) heartily prayed for His *MAJESTY* that now is; and taking notice of *Hugh Peters* (that was executed next after him) wished he might be reprieved, because at present (as he conceived) *Peters was not prepared to die*.

And in earnest, Mr. *Cook* in this was not mistaken, for when *Hugh Peters* came to die, he was as far to seek, as to *Answer* at his *Tryal*. And (without any reflexion on the wickedness of the man) there never was person suffered death so unpitied, and (which is more) whose Execution was the delight of the people; which they expressed by several shouts and acclamations, not onely when they saw him go up the Ladder, and when the Halter was putting about his Neck; but also when his head was cut off, and held up aloft upon the end of a Speir, there was such a shout, as if the people of *England* had acquired a Victory.

And here we cannot forget, how some years since, he preached so often, so vehemently, and indeed so fondly for the necessary pulling down of Old *Charing-Cross*, crying out, *It was as old as Popery it self, and that it had caus'd more superstition, and done more mischief, than any Pulpit in England had done good*; (though amongst sober men, the Superstition was begotten only by pulling it down) and that now this Trumpet of Sedition should be hang'd upon a Gibbet in the same place where the Old Cross stood, with his Face towards the place where the Scaffold was erected, and where *Peters* gave order for knocking down Staples to tye our Martyr'd Soveraign fast to the Block.

At the self same time these two were executed, these one and twenty persons were again brought to the Bar at the *Old Baily, viz.* Sir *Hardress Waller, William Heveningham, Isaac Penington, Henry Marten, Gilbert Millington, Robert Tichborne, Owen Rowe, Robert Lilbourne, Henry Smith, Edmund Harvey, John Downs, Vincent Potter, Augustine Garland, George Fleetwood, Simon Meyne, James Temple, Peter Temple, Thomas Wayte, Francis Hacker, Daniel Axtel*, and *William Hewlet*.

All which persons (except Mr. *Heveningham*) were condemned to be hanged, drawn, and quartered, seventeen whereof have their Execution suspended until His *Majesty* by the advice and assent of the Lords and Commons in Parliament, shall order the Excecution by Act of Parliament to be passed for that purpose.

Wednesday, October 17

And this morning *Thomas Scot, Gregory Clement, Adrian Scroop*, and *John Jones*, (who were excepted by Parliament, and last week were Arraign'd and Condemn'd) were executed at the aforesaid place at *Charing-Cross*.

Thomas Scot dy'd as he liv'd, (there's few in *England*, but know how that was) who last year publickly boasted, that he was one of those that adjudg'd his late *MAJESTY* to death, and desired *he might have That written upon his Tomb*, in some sort now hath his desire, only he hath no Tomb; for after (according to Law) he was half-hang'd, cut down, his Members cut off, and burnt in his sight, his Quarters were convey'd back upon the Hurdle that brought him; to be dispos'd so far asunder, that they will scarce ever meet together in one Tomb.

Gregory Clement, at his death, express'd a great deal of sorrow and penitence, confessing, That he most justly suffer'd both from God and Man, and that his Judges had done nothing but according to Law, begging the Prayers of all Spectators.

Adrian Scroop, of a noble antient Family (and of whose name there have been and are Gentlemen most eminent for their Loyalty to his Majesty and his Glorious Father) behav'd himself at his Tryal, as well as any Guilty of so foul a Fact; for he confess'd, and saved the Witnesses a Labour, only he deny'd those words witnessed against him formerly in the House of Commons, and again at his

Tryal. He dyed somewhat pityed, as well in regard he was a comely person, as because he beg'd the Prayers of all good People.

John Jones (the last of the four) all along as he was drawn upon the Hurdle, as well as at the place of Execution, lifted up his hands and turned his head to all that beheld him, to gain their prayers; expressing very much sense of the horror of his fact; nor did he offer to justifie it his Tryal: He formerly in *Ireland* declared against that Monster *Oliver Cromwel*, whereby he saw his own destruction designed, so as for an Atonement he chose to marry *Oliver's* own Sister, which (were she like her Brother, as 'tis said she is not) none were fit for, but he that had his hand in the murther of a King.

Mercurius Publicus *Numb*. 48

22–29 November, 1660 378.148 {10.34}

On Sunday last {25 November} *Tench*, the Carpenter (employ'd to build the Scaffold wherein His late *Majesty* of ever glorious memory was martyr'd) was apprehended and sent close prisoner to the Gate-house, *Westminster*.

The day of this vote, like the week in which Cromwell died, witnessed tempestuous winds ...

Mercurius Publicus *Numb*. 50

6–13 December, 1660 378.150 {10.35}

On Saturday (*Decemb*. 8,) the most Honourable House of *Peers* concurr'd with the Commons in the Order for the digging up the carkasses of *Oliver Cromwel, Henry Ireton, John Bradshaw*, and *Thomas Pride*, and carrying them on an Hurdle to *Tyburn*, where they are to be first hang'd up in their Coffins, and then buried under the Gallows.

And we must not conceal that while the Noble Peers and Commons of *England* are taking up the Carrion of the English Regicides; the Loyal *Scots* are taking down the Martyr'd Corps of that most Renowned *James* Lord Marquess of *Montrose*, to give it just and honourable Burial as a Tribute too long due from that Nation.

The posthumous executioner gets the very last word. Here we see the moral ambiguities of history being erased, and its lifeless protagonists turned into a spectacle for a grim public.

Mercurius Publicus *Numb.* 4.

24–31 January, 1661 378.204 {10.36}

London.

This day *Jan.*30 (we need say no more but name the day of the Moneth) was doubly observed, not only by a solemn Fast, Sermons, & Prayers at every Parish Church, for the precious blood of our late pious Soverain King *Charles* the First, of ever glorious memory; but also by publick dragging of those odious Carcasses of *Oliver Cromwell*, *Henry Ireton*, and *John Bradshaw* to Tiburn. On Munday night *Cromwell* and *Ireton* in two several Carts were drawn to *Holborn* from *Westminster*, after they were digged up on Saturday last, and the next morning *Bradshaw*; To day they were drawn upon Sledges to Tiburn, all the way (as before from *Westminster*) the universal outcry of the people went along with them. When these their Carcasses were at *Tyburn*, they were pull'd out of their Coffines and hang'd at the several angles of that Triple Tree, where they hung till the Sun was set; after which they were taken down, their heads cut off, and their loathsome Trunks thrown into a deep hole under the Gallows. And now we cannot forget how at *Cambridge* when *Cromwell* first set up for a Rebell, he rode under the Gallowes, where his horse corvetting threw his cursed Highness out of the Saddle just under the Gallowes (as if he had been turned off the Ladder) the spectators then observing the place, and rather presaging the present work of this day, than the monstrous Villanies of this day twelve years. But he is now again thrown under the Gallows (never more to be digg'd up) and there we leave him.

Mercurius Publicus *Numb.* 5.

31 January – 7 February, 1661 378.205 {10.37}

The Heads of those three notorious Regicides, *Oliver Cromwell, John Bradshaw*, and *Henry Ireton*, are set upon Poles on the top of *Westminster-hall* by the common Hangman: *Bradshaw* is placed in the middle, (over that part where that monstrous Court of High Justice sate,) *Cromwell* and his Son in Law *Ireton* on both sides of *Bradshaw*.

Numb. 44

A
PERFECT
DIVRNALL
OF THE
PASSAGES
In Parliament:

From the 10. of Aprill to the 17. of Aprill.

Collected by the ſame hand that formerly drew up the Copy for William Cook *of Furnifulls Inne, and now printed by* J. Okes, Fr. Leach, *and are to be ſold by* Fr. Coles *in the Old Baily.* 1643.

Munday the 10. of Aprill.

THe Houſe of Commons received information that divers perſons through the neglect of the Courts of Guard come daily to London from Oxford, and other parts of the Kings Army, notwithſtanding their former order againſt it; and they thereupon drew up another order to this effect. That whatſoever perſon ſhall come from Oxford, or any part of the Kings Army to London, or any parts adjacent, or to any other part of the Army under the Command of the Earle of Eſſex, or to any Fort, or Court of Guard, kept by the authority of both Houſes of Parliament, or of the Lord Generall the Earle of Eſſex, ſhall apprehend as Spies and Intelligencers, and be proceeded againſt according to the Rules and grounds of War; and it is

Two meſſages from his Majeſty, and the Parliaments anſwer, the L. Generals his advance, Sir Will. Wallers happy ſucceſſe & other matters of note this weeke.

X a further

15. *A Perfect Diurnall of the Passages of Parliament*, 10 April 1643

Chronology of Events 1640–1660

1640	Jan	Thomas Wentworth made Earl of Strafford and appointed Lord Lieutenant of Ireland.
	April	Short Parliament sits — until May
	Aug	Second Bishops' War begins.
	Oct	The English are defeated by the Scots. Charles calls a Parliament.
	Nov	Long Parliament meets and begins its process of reform. The Arminian canons of 1640 are condemned; Laud and Strafford are impeached.
1641	July	High Commission and Star Chamber are abolished.
	Nov	News of the Irish Rebellion causes increasing divide among members of the Long Parliament, which begins to break down into Royalist and Parliamentarian parties. The Grand Remonstrance is passed. The first newsbook appears.
	Dec	Protests on the streets of London.
1642	Jan	The king attempts to arrest the Five Members: then leaves London.
	April	Sir John Hotham denies the king entry to Hull.
	June	19 Propositions. The king takes Newcastle and begins to form an army.
	July	Parliament send troops to Leicester. Essex is appointed to command the parliamentary army. Warwick takes command of the Navy. First bloodshed of the Civil War at Manchester, soon followed by encounters at Hull.
	Aug	The king raises his Standard.

	Sept	Battle of Edgehill. The theatres are closed by order of parliament.
	Dec	Peace protests in London.
1643	Jan	*Mercurius Aulicus* appears.
	June	Parliament establishes Westminster Assembly to discuss a religious settlement.
	Aug	*Mercurius Britanicus* appears as parliament's answer to *Aulicus*.
	Dec	John Pym dies.
1644	Jan	Royalist Parliament summoned at Oxford.
	July	Parliament wins important victory at Marston Moor.
	Dec	Self-denying Ordinance first suggested in response to parliamentary defeats and divisions within the army leadership. Rejected by Lords.
1645	Jan	Laud and the Hothams are executed. Peace negotiations at Uxbridge — they fail in February. New Directory of Worship, devised by Westminster Assembly, is approved by parliament.
	April	Self-denying Ordinance passed. New Model Army created.
	June	Parliament wins battle of Naseby.
1646	Mar	Presbyterian church formally established.
	May	Charles I surrenders to Scots.
	June	Oxford surrenders to parliament's forces: the First Civil War ends.
	Oct	Episcopacy abolished.
1647	Jan	Scots deliver Charles to parliament.
	June	Cornet Joyce seizes king on behalf of New Model Army.
	Aug	Heads of Proposals presented by army to king.
	Oct	Levellers' *Agreement of the People*. Debates of Army Council begin at Putney.
	Nov	King flees to Isle of Wight, then signs Engagement with Scots.
1648	April	Second Civil War breaks out. Many short-lived newsbooks appear due to laxity of press controls.
	July	Scots invade England.
	Aug	Scots defeated at Preston: Second Civil War ends.
	Sept	Treaty of Newport.
	Oct	Treaty of Westphalia ends Thirty Years War.
	Dec	Pride's Purge: creating of what becomes known as the 'Rump'.

1649	Jan	King tried and executed by Supreme Court of Justice. Proclamation of a successor declared treasonable.
	Feb	Charles II proclaimed King in Scotland.
	April	Diggers establish agrarian commune in Surrey.
	May	England declared a commonwealth, Leveller mutiny in the Army.
	Aug	Cromwell arrives in Ireland.
1650	May	Cromwell returns from Ireland.
	June	Cromwell succeeds Fairfax as commanded-in-chief of the commonwealth forces. Charles II lands in Scotland. Marchmont Nedham's *Mercurius Politicus* established.
	July	Cromwell invades Scotland.
	Aug	Blasphemy Act passed by purged parliament, chiefly directed at Ranters.
	Sep	Cromwell defeats Scots at Dunbar.
1651	Jan	Charles II crowned at Scone.
	Aug	Scots army invades England.
	Sept	Scots defeated at Worcester by Cromwell. Charles escapes to France.
1652	May	War breaks out with United Provinces as a consequence of trade disputes.
	Aug	Irish Settlement Act begins land confiscations in Ireland.
1653	April	Cromwell expels the purged parliament
	July	Nominated Assembly (known as 'Barebone's Parliament) meets. Dutch defeated at Battle of Texel, leading to end of Anglo-Dutch war.
	Dec	Instrument of Government, a written constitution, nominating Cromwell as Lord Protector of England and Wales, Scotland and Ireland.
1654	April	Union of Scotland and England. Treaty of Westminster with United Provinces.
	Sept	First Protectorate Parliament meets.
	Dec	Launch of Hispaniola expedition to West Indies.
1655	Jan	Cromwell dismisses his parliament.
	May	Jamaica captured by Hispaniola expedition.
	Oct	Suppression of unofficial newsbooks. Major-Generals introduced to rule provinces and military.
	Dec	Effective readmission of Jews into Britain.
1656	Sept	Second Protectorate Parliament meets. Economic depression begins.

	Oct	The Quaker James Nayler enters Bristol in imitation of Christ.
1657	May	*Humble Petition and Advice*: Cromwell declines offer of crown. Major-Generals abolished.
	June	Second, more ceremonial inauguration of Cromwell.
1658	Jan	Second Protectorate Parliament reconvenes, increasing political division and economic problems.
	Sept	Cromwell dies and is succeeded by his son Richard.
1659	Jan	Richard Cromwell calls a parliament, which lasts until April.
	April	Unofficial newsbooks begin to reappear.
	May	Richard Cromwell resigns and Concludes the Protectorate. The Army restores the purged parliament.
	Oct	Army expells purged parliament. General George Monck, in Scotland, condemns the action, and begins to march south.
	Dec	General Council of Army succumbs to pressure to recall the purged parliament for a second time.
1660	Feb	General George Monck arrives in London. He readmits the secluded members of the Long Parliament.
	Mar	Long Parliament dissolves itself.
	April	Declaration of Breda, establishing the terms for the Restoration. General Lambert's uprising at Edgehill fails. Convention Parliament meets. Nedham flees country and *Politicus* ceases publication.
	May	Charles II proclaimed king, and he enters London.
	July	Charles II's dog is stolen.

Index of Newsbooks (by entry number)

(titles preceded by N&S serial numbers)

36] Certaine informations, 3.04, 4.03, 6.01
Wing C5194] Collection of speciall passages and certaine informations, 1.48
52] Compleate intelligencer and resolver, 4.02
61] Continvation of certain speciall and remarkable passages, 6.03
68] Continuation of the true diurnall of all the passages in Parliament, 1.17
97] Diurnall occurrences in Parliament, 1.05, 1.07
100] Diurnall occurrences in Parliament, 1.20
106] Diurnall occvrrances, touching the dayly proceedings, 1.06
109] Diurnall: or, the heads of all the proceedings, 1.03, 1.04
110] Diurnall out of the North/ Diurnall and particula [sic], 1.25
150] Faithfull scout/ Armies scout, 3.35, 4.12, 4.13, 4.18, 4.19, 4.20, 4.21, 4.23
151] Faithfull scout/ National scout/ Loyall scout, 10.09
181] Heads of severall proceedings/ Divrnall occvrences/ Continuation of the divrnall, 1.01, 1.02, 1.08, 1.10, 1.12
198] Informator rusticus, 2.18
210] Kingdomes faithfull scout/ Kingdomes faithfull and impartial scout, 4.06, 6.08, 9.07
214] Kingdomes vveekly intelligencer, 3.29, 3.32
248] Man in the moon, 3.11, 3.19, 3.20, 4.08, 5.18

275] Mercvrivs avlicvs, communicating the intelligence, 2.09, 2.10, 2.11, 2.12, 2.13, 2.14, 2.19, 2.21, 2.23, 2.24, 3.06, 3.08, 3.09

279] Mercurius bellicus, 2.30

286] Mercurius britanicus: communicating the affaires of great Britaine, 2.15, 2.20, 2.22, 8.01, 8.02, 8.03, 8.04

298] Mercurius civicus, Londons intelligencer, 3.07, 6.02, 9.03

312] Mercurius elencticus. Communicating the unparallell'd proceedings, 2.29, 3.12, 3.27, 5.05

322] Mercurius fumigosus, or the smoking nocturnall, 3.30, 3.31

332] Mercurius honestus. Or, Tom Tell-truth, 10.23

336] Mercurius jocosus, 3.28

344] Mercurius melancholicus: or, newes from Westminster, 4.04

346] Mercurius militaris: communicating from all parts/ Mercurius militaris of the armies scout, 2.31, 4.05

354] Mercurius phanticus, 10.22

361] Mercurius politicus. Comprising the summ, 2.32, 3.14, 3.15, 3.17, 3.22, 3.25, 3.33, 3.38, 4.09, 4.10, 4.11, 4.14, 4.22, 4.24, 4.25, 4.26, 4.27, 4.28, 4.29, 4.30, 4.31, 4.32, 4.33, 4.34, 6.12, 6.14, 6.15, 6.17, 6.18, 6.19, 6.20, 6.22, 6.23, 6.24, 6.25, 6.26, 7.03, 7.04, 7.05, 7.06, 7.07, 7.10, 8.12, 8.13, 8.14, 8.15, 8.16, 8.17, 8.18, 8.19, 8.20, 8.21, 9.11, 9.12, 9.14, 9.15, 9.17, 9.18, 9.20, 9.21, 9.22, 9.24, 9.25, 9.26, 9.27, 10.01, 10.02, 10.03, 10.04, 10.05, 10.06, 10.07, 10.08, 10.18, 10.19, 10.24

369] Mercurius pragmaticvs. Communicating intelligence from all parts, 5.14, 5.16, 8.05, 8.06, 8.07, 8.08, 8.09, 8.10, 8.11, 9.04

370] Mercurius pragmaticus, (for King Charles II.), 9.08, 9.09

378] Mercurius publicus: comprising the summ, 10.25, 10.26, 10.28, 10.30, 10.31, 10.32, 10.33, 10.34, 10.35, 10.36, 10.37

Wing W3171] Mercurius rusticus: or, a countrey messenger, 2.16

384] Mercvrivs rusticus, or the covntries complaint, 3.10, 9.01

413] Moderate: impartially communicating, 5.01, 5.02, 5.10, 5.13, 6.10, 9.10

419] Moderate intelligencer: impartially communicating, 3.05, 3.16, 3.26, 6.05, 6.06, 6.07, 6.09

465] Occurrences of certaine speciall and remarkable passages/ Perfect occurrences of Parliament/ Perfect occurrences of

both Houses/ Perfect occurrences of every dayes journall, 5.03, 5.06, 5.07, 5.08, 5.12, 5.17
485] Parliament scout, 3.34
486] Parliamentary intelligencer/ Kingdomes intelligencer, 8.22, 10.17, 10.27
487] Parliaments post, 2.28, 3.23
no entry] Perfect diurnall of all the proceedings of the English and Scotch armies in Ireland, 2.01
491] Particular advice from the office/ Occurrences, from forraigne parts/ Exact accompt, 10.20, 10.29
492] Particular relation of the severall removes/ Continuation of true intelligence/ Particular relation of the most remarkable occurrences, 2.25
496] Perfect account of the daily intelligence, 3.01, 3.21, 9.13
498] Perfect declaration/ True informer, 6.04, 9.02
503] Perfect diurnall of some passages and proceedings of, and in relation to the armies, 4.16
504] Perfect diurnall of some passages in Parliament, 5.04, 5.09, 5.11, 5.15, 7.01, 7.02, 9.06
507] Perfect diurnall of the passages in Parliament, 1.09, 1.13, 1.16, 1.18
509] Perfect diurnall of the passages in Parliament, 1.21, 1.26, 1.32
510] Perfect diurnall of the passages in Parliament, 1.29, 1.30
511] Perfect diurnall of the passages in Parliament, 1.34, 1.39, 1.44, 2.05
512] Perfect diurnall of the passages in Parliament, 1.36, 2.04
515] Paerfect [sic] diurnall of the proceedigns [sic] in Parliament, 1.42
517] Perfect diurnall or the proceedings in Parliament, 1.27
533] Perfect weekly account containing/ Perfect weekly account concerning, 9.05
544] Politique post/ Grand politique post/ Weekly post, 2.33, 3.36, 4.17, 6.16
575] Publick intelligencer, 7.11, 9.23, 10.11, 10.16, 10.21
579] Quotidian occurrences in and about London/ England's memorable accidents, 1.41, 1.43, 2.06
594] Scotish dove. Sent out, and returning/ Scotish dove sent out the last time, 2.26, 3.02
599] Severall proceedings in Paarliament/ Severall proceeding sof state affaires/ Perfect proceedings of state affaires, 3.13, 3.24, 3.37, 4.07, 6.11, 6.13, 6.21, 7.08, 7.09, 9.16, 9.19

605] Some speciall and considerable passages/ Speciall passages from divers parts/ Speciall passages and certaine informations, 1.33, 1.37, 1.49, 2.03, 2.07, 2.08, 3.03, 4.01

606] Some speciall passages from London [Westminster] [Hull], 1.19, 1.22, 1.23, 1.24, 1.28, 1.31

621] True diurnal occvrrances: or, the heads, 1.11

625] True diurnall of the passages in Parliament, 1.14

626] True diurnall of the passages in Parliament, 1.15

638] Trve relation of certaine speciall and remarkable passages/ Certaine speciall and remarkable passages/ Continvation of certaine speciall and remarkable passages, 1.35, 1.38, 1.40, 1.45, 1.47, 1.50, 2.02

671] Weekly account/ Perfect weekly account, 2.27

686] Weekly intelligence from severall parts of this kingdome, 1.46

688] Weekly intelligencer of the common-wealth, 3.18, 3.39, 4.15

689] Weekly intelligencer of the common-wealth/ Kingdomes intelligencer, 9.28, 10.10, 10.12, 10.14

704] Weekly post: truly communicating/ Faithfull post, 10.13, 10.15

708] Welch mercury/ Mercurius Cambro-Brittanus, 2.17

Index

Adams, Mary, 185
Advertisements, 20, 142, 160, 193, 195, 200–1, 201, 237, 268–70, 408–10
Africa & Africans, 102, 130, 155
Agnew, Alexander, 317–20
Alborne, 101
Alcock, Sir Thomas, 408–10
Allen, Oliver, 331–6
America, 253–6; *see also* New England, Virginia, Maryland
Amerindians, 115 (chapter six, *passim*)
Amsterdam, 197
Anabaptists, 262, 438, 454; *see also* Sectarianism
Antichrist, 35, 161, 258, 357
Antinomianism, 390, 262; *see also* Sectarianism
Archer, Thomas, 4
Ashe, Simeon, 109
Ashton, Colonel, 321–3
Atheists, 71–4, 98; *see also* Sectarianism
Audley, Captain Thomas, 21, 84, 333
Axtel, Colonel Daniel, 455, 468–9, 471

Banbury, 172
Baptists, 125, 388–90; *see also* Sectarianism
Barbados, 281–2, 287–9
Barclay, Sir William, 259
Barebone, Praise-God, 425–6
Barril, Chester County, 196
Barton, Elizabeth, 166
Bastwick, John, 294
Berkenhead, John, 84
Berwick, 443
Betteley, John, 324–6
Bible, printing of, 46–7
Bills of Mortality, 180
Bohemia, Queen of, 73–4
Book of Common Prayer, 28, 211, 251, 386
Border, Daniel, 254–5
Bourne, Nicholas, 3, 4, 21
Bradshaw, John, 224–42, 461, 469, 472–3
Brainford, 79–80, 227

Brathwait, Richard (author of *Whimzies*), 12
Breda, Treaty/Declaration of, 426, 456–7
Bridewell, 126, 133, 400, 413
Bristol, 418
Bristol, John Digby, Earl of, 76
Brockeford, Sussex, 184
Brookes, Lord, 78, 95, 104
Browne, James, 388–90
Buckingham, George Villiers, 2nd Duke of, 458, 465
Buchanan, George, 349
Buggery, 106, 107, 151, 317, 318
Burford, 92–5
Burton, Henry, 294
Butter, Nathaniel, 3, 4, 12, 21, 338
Byron, Sir John, 92–5

Caesar, Julius, 176, 368, 372
Cambridge, University of, 56, 444; Sidney-Sussex College, 161; Trinity College, 179
Cardigan, 142
Carew, John, 468
Carolina, 268–70
Censorship, 3, 7, 11, 333, 335–6, 358, 375
Charles I, 1, 5, 8, (chapter one, *passim*) 84, 91, 92, 96, 101, 112, 113, 162–3, 178–9, 203–252, 259, 296, 297, 299, 321, 333, 339–53, 356–7, 359–64, 386, 473
Charles II, 1, 179, 216, 249–50, 277, 321, 336–7, 342–3, 364, 367 (chapter ten, *passim*)
Chartier, Roger, 172
Cheapside, 97, 324, 446, 460, 470–1
Chipping Norton, 137
Church-Lawton, Chester, 186
Circumcision, 159, 257, 270–2
Clarkson, Laurence, 400
Clement, Gregory, 471
Cobbet, Colonel Ralph, 119, 229, 443, 455
Cobham, Kent, 127
Colchester, Essex, 445
Commissions of Array, 30, 31, 53
Cook, John, Solicitor General, 228, 231, 234, 427, 470
Corantos, 2–4
Corbet, Miles, 115, 124, 155–6, 252, 361
Cornwall, 128, 152, 166
Cotton, Sir Robert (his house), 225, 226, 227, 234, 237
Coventry, 66
Cromwell, Oliver, 25, 115–6, 124, 126, 161, 162–3, 190, 191, 244, 252, 256, 294, 298, 310, 321, 336, 356–7, 363, 371 (as Prince Archon), 383, 391, 396–9, 403, 410, 423–4, 428–32, 461, 465, 472–3
Cromwell, Richard, 116, 335, 433–4, 455
Crouch, John, 20, 24, 124, 126, 149, 158
Culpepper, Sir John, 68
Cyrencester, 93, 96

Davis (Douglas), Eleanor, Lady, 125
Davis, J.C., 384
Denmark, 89, 148
Defoe, Daniel, 23–4
Derbyshire, 90
Desborough, Colonel John, 426
D'Ewes, Sir Simonds, 361
Digby, George, Lord, 49, 76, 82, 349
Digby, Sir Kenelm, 290–1
Diggers, 125, 381, 384, 392–5
Dillingham, John, 161, 263
Donne, John, 19
Dorset, Thomas Sackville, Earl of, 68, 107
Dover, Henry Carey, Earl of, 37
Dunbar, 117, 163, 423, 429
Dundee, 187
Duppa, Brian, Bishop of Salisbury, 207
Durham, 434

East Indies, (chapter six, *passim*)
Edge-Hill, 78, 174, 227, 426
Edward II, 352
Edwards, Thomas (author of *Gangraena*), 385
Edinburgh, 151, 309–11, 340
Eliot, John, 272–77
Elizabeth I, 297
Endecott, John, 413
Enfield Chase, 436–7
Essex, Robert Devereux, Earl of, 32, 56–7, 59, 60, 63, 65–9, 79, 96, 98, 129
Evans, Arise, 162–3
Evelyn, John, 424
Evelyn, Sir John, 77–80, 442
Everard, John, 392–3
Executions, 106, 140–1, 142, 154–5, 170, 172, 180, 182, 245–9, 272, 286, (chapter seven, *passim*), 396, 461–2, 468–72

Fairfax, Lady, 131, 339, 468–9
Fairfax, Thomas, Lord, 118, 130–1, 210–11, 214, 217, 220, 223, 225, 244, 252, 339, 360–3, 392, 396–8, 451
Featley, Daniel (author of *The Gentle Lash*), 7
Fiennes, Nathaniel, 362
Fifth Monarchists, 126, 162–3, 438
Filmer, Robert (author of *Patriarcha*), 123–4
Five Members, 38–41, 104, 223
Fleetwood, Charles, Lieutenant-General, 118, 424–5, 433
Florio, John, 254
Fox, George, 383, 406–7
Fox, Somerset, 312–3
France & French, 33, 99, 121, 178, 185, 201, 225, 244, 253, 263–5, 268, 289–90, 321, 331, 340–7, 368, *see also* Paris
Fuller, Thomas, 14
Fynes, Nathaniel, 105

Gauden, Dr. John, 208
Genoa, 307
Gerard, John, 312–3, 315–6
Germany, 89–90, 174, 179, 368

Gloucester, 97–8
Gloucester, Henry Stuart, Duke of, 463, 465
Glyn, John, 45
Goring, George, Lord, 150
Grand Remonstrance, 9, 24, 28–9, 382
Grant, James, 15
Green, Anne, 170–2, 182–4
Griffin, Lewis, 85
Grimston, Harbottle, 361

Haberdashers Hall, London, 91
Hacker, Colonel Francis, 118, 226, 228, 246, 248, 469–70
Hackluyt, John, 176
Hackney, 163
Hakluyt, Richard, 256
Hall, John, 19, 20–1, 349, 371
Hampden, John, 78, 104, 212
Harley, Brilliana, Lady and Sir Robert, 6, 362
Harrington, James, 336, 427
Harris, John, 116
Hartford, William Seymour, Marquis of, 93, 238, 251
Haruney, Luke, *see* Henry Walker
Henrietta Maria, Queen, 29, 32, 43, 101, 131, 210, 329–48
Henry VIII, 251
Hewlet, William, 470–1
Heylin, Peter, 84
Hobbes, Thomas, 31, 277, 336, 371
Holborn, 138, 66–7
Holland, 54, 73–4, 89, 130, 198, 292
Holland, Henry Rich, Earl of, 58, 59, 63
Holles, Denzil, 60, 78
Hopkins, Mathew, 310–11
Hotham, Sir John, 32, 53, 54, 55, 57, 61–2, 105, 299–303
Hull, 32, 51, 52, 54–5, 57, 58, 60, 61–2, 101, 188, 299–304
Huntingdon, 131
Hyde, Edward, First Earl of Clarendon, 24, 297
Hyde Park, 116

Ireland & Irish, 7, 8, 28, 33, 36, 37, 42, 43, 48–9, 50, 76, 86, 87, 90, 108–9, 113–4, 133, 137, 149, 181, 211, 225, 243
Indians, *see* Amerindians
Ingoldsby, Colonel Richard, 118, 454–6
Ireton, Henry, 124, 204–5, 221, 244, 472–3
Infanticide, 127, 141, 170–2, 318
Isle of Wight, 181, 228, 229
Ipswich, 184

Jamaica, 287–9
Jefferson, Thomas, 32–3
Jermyn, Henry, 49, 76
Jews, 155, 391, 393, 402
Jones, Inigo, 101
Jones, John, 471–2
Jonson, Ben, 11, 26
Julian of Norwich, 126
Juxton, William, Bishop of London, 245, 247, 248–51

Kineton, *see* Edge-Hill
Kempe, Margery, 126
Kingston, Surrey, 140–1

Lambert, John, 424–6, 441–3, 451, 454–6
Laud, William, Archbishop of Canterbury, 5, 8, 28, 103, 161, 304–8, 468
Lawson, Admiral John, 425, 445
Leicester, 37, 112–4, 128–9, 406
Leicester, Robert Sidney, Earl of, 206
Lenox, Duke of, *see* Richmond/Lenox
Lenthal, William, 115, 214, 340, 425, 449–52
Lesbury, Northumberland, 195
L'Estrange, Roger, 299, 302, 337
Letters, interception of, 54–6, 60–1, 98–9, 339
Levellers, 24, 204, 206, 208, 253–5, 268, 362, 373, 384–5, 394–9, 427
Lilburne, John, 222, 244, 352, 395, 451
Lilly, William, 126, 139–40
Lincolnshire, 101
Lindsay, Montague Bertie, 2nd Earl of, 251
Lisbon, Portugal, 194, 257–8
Lock, Tom, 156
Lorraine, Charles III, Duke of, 340–1
Lothian, William Kerr, Earl of, 160
Louis XIV, 253–4
Lucan, 121
Lunsford, Thomas, 37, 96
Lupton, Donald, 12
Luther, 421
Lynn, Norfolk, 190

Maastricht, 311
Mabbot, Gilbert, 206, 208
Macaulay, T.B., 294
Machiavelli (-anism), 116, 256, 336, 359, 365, 367, 399
Manchester, Edward Montague, Earl of, 115, 458–9
Markfield, Leicestershire, 439–40
Marten, Henry, 115, 124, 150, 151, 222, 363, 471
Maryland, 259
Marvell, Andrew, 85, 190, 208
Maynard, John, 45, 453
Mazarin, Cardinal, 340
McKenzie, D.F., 1
Micham, Surrey, 175
Mildmay, Sir Henry, 115, 137, 155, 361
Milford Haven, 108
Milton, John, 7, 117, 161, 208, 277, 282
Moll Cutpurse, 75
Monck, General George, 425–7, 435, 443, 448, 450, 452, 457, 459, 463
Monsters & monstrous births, 102, 106–7, 115, 130, 156, 173, 176, 180–1, 185, 197, 198–200, 439
Montaigne, Michel de, 254–5
More, Sir Thomas, 336, 369–70
Muddiman, J.G., 337, 379, 454

Naples, 272
Naseby, 127–8, 339
Nashe, Thomas, 19, 338

Naylor, James, 294, 383, 406, 410–18
Nedham, Marchamont, 8, 13, 18, 19, 21, 22, 84, 117, 126, 172, 178, 195, 206, 243, 249, 277, 280, 332–79, 395, 396, 426, 454
New England, 261–3, 270, 272, 280, 413
Newcastle, William Cavendish, Earl of, 130–1
Newbury, 101, 227
Newport, Isle of Wight, 178, 203
Newport, Mountjoy Blount, Earl of, 57
Nicholas, Sir Edward, 466
Nineteen Propositions, 52, 53
Northampton, 87
Northampton, James Compton, 3rd Earl of, 96
Northumberland, Algernon Percy, Earl of, 55, 63, 78
Norton, Lady, 136
Norwich, 132, 175, 422
Nottingham, 67–8
Nye, Philip, 417

Okey, Colonel John, 441, 456
Old Bailey, 141
O'Neal, Philem, 90
Ormond, James Butler, Marquis of, 215, 349
Oxford, 56, 69, 71, 80, 96, 182–4, 340, 352–3, 444; All Souls College, 396; Christ Church College, 89, 183; Corpus Christi College, 89; Magdalen College, 71, 89, 183; New College, 89; Queens College, 89; St Johns College, 89
Oxford, Aubrey de Vere, 20th Earl of, 458

Palatine, Charles Louis, Prince Elector of, 73–4, 245, 265
Paris, 49, 268, 277, 289–90
Parliament of 1628, 10; Short Parliament, 26–7; Long Parliament, *see* chapters one, five and ten, *passim*
Partridge, John, 24
Pebmarsh, Essex, 386
Pecke, Samuel, 299, 304
Pembroke, Philip Herbert, Earl of, 30, 63, 115, 352–3
Pennington, Sir John, 55
Peters, Hugh, 230, 303, 362–3, 466–8, 470
Petitions—by men, 7, 36–7, 45; by women, 43–4, 122–3, 132–3, 136
Petty, Dr. William, 182–3
Physicians, 170–1, 173, 181–4, 199–200, 334, 370–1
Piedmont, massacre at, 282–6
Poland, 89, 179
Pool, Elizabeth, 125–6
Pope, 75–6, 103, 155, 258, 278–80
Portugal & Portuguese, 148, 266–7
Presse full of Pamphlets, A, 13
Pride, Colonel Thomas, 150, 362, 441, 472

Prideaux, Edmund, 361, 398
Pride's Purge, 204, 359–64, 424
Prostitution, 149–50, 156
Prynne, William, 5, 46–7, 115, 453
Putney Debates, 350–2
Pym, John, 28–9, 38–41, 47, 57, 105–6

Quakers, 125, 281, 382–3, 385, 404–7, 410–21, 426–7, 438, 454, 466–7

Ranters, 124, 125, 158–9, 159, 382, 384–6, 390, 400–4, 406
Rape, 52, 62, 91, 127–31
Rainsborough, Colonel Thomas, 427
Reading, 129–30
Regicides, trials & executions of, 461–2, 465, 468–73
Renaudot, Theophraste, 4–5
Rennes, 170, 172
Richelieu, Cardinal, 5
Richmond/Lenox, James Stuart, Duke of, 41–4, 245, 251
Robinson, Henry (author of *Liberty of Conscience*), 7
Robinson, Luke, 457
Rochel, 225
Rochester, John Wilmot, Earl of, 158
Rome, 49, 75, 154, 176, 278–80
Rudyerd, Sir Benjamin, 361–2
Rumbold, Richard, 23
Rupert, Prince, 83, 87–88, 94, 96, 103
Rushworth, John, 6, 72, 213–20
Rutland, John Manner, Earl of, 63
Rutlinguen, 192
Ryves, Bruno, 84, 338, 386

Sa, Dom Pantaleon, 312, 314–6
St. George's Hill, 392–4
St. Pauls, London, 95
Salmasius, Claudius, 277
Say and Sele, William Fiennes, Viscount, 71, 115
Scott, Thomas, 471
Scotland & Scottish, 8, 27, 64, 70, 86, 87, 102, 117–21, 154, 160, 181, 187, 188–9, 195, 207, 211–3, 220, 225, 231, 309–10, 317–20, 340, 349–50, 356–7, 404, 435, 443, 472
Scroop, Adrian, 471–2
Sectarianism, 71–4, 112, 125, 161–2, 262, 373, 381–422, 438
Shrewsbury, Shropshire, 90–1
Sidney, Lady, 52, 62
Smith, George, 110
Southam, Warwickshire, 69
Southampton, Thomas Wriothesley, Earl of, 68, 251
Spain & Spanish, 33, 257–8, 263–5, 272, 288–9, 290, 291–2, 368
Sprigge, Joshua, 230
Stacy, Edmund, 297–8, 326–31
Staffordshire, 95
Star Chamber, 5, 50

Stationers, Company of, 5, 46
Stowe, 93–4
Strafford, Thomas Wentworth, Earl of, 10, 28, 103, 211, 238, 246, 250
Stratford-upon-Avon, 157
Stuart, Elizabeth, 181
Suicide, 180, 408–10
Sumner, John, 326–31
Swanley, Captain, 108
Suffolk, 175
Surrey, 175
Sweden, 89, 179
Sweden, Queen Christina of, 143–9
Swift, Jonathan, 254

Tany, Thomas ('Theareau-john'), 405
Tetbury, Gloucestershire, 93
Thirty Years War, 3, 257, 263
Theatres, 1, 69
Thomas, John, 8, 15
Thomason, George, 6, 17
Thompson, Hunter S., 21–4
Tillingham, Essex, 185
Tiverton, Devon, 437–8
Tomlinson, Colonel, 245–6
Trapnel, Anna, 126, 162–3, 163–6
Tripoli, 291
Truro, Cornwall, 166
Turkey & Turks, 130, 257, 265–6, 270–2, 421–2

Underdown, David, 23–4, 123–4
Uxbridge, Treaty of, 340–1

Valentines Day, 387
Vane, Sir Henry, 361, 451
Venice, 49, 107, 266
Virginia, 149, 256, 258, 260, 268–70
Vowel, Peter, 312–3, 315

Wales & Welsh, 84, 102–3, 115, 162–3, 348, 353, 371, 462
Walker, Henry, 14, 103, 163, 176–7
Waller, Edmund, 423
Waller, Lady, 136
Waller, Sir William, 96, 130, 362
Wallington, Nehemiah, 5, 6, 10, 83
Walwyn, William, 255
Warmestry, Dr., 321–3, 326–30, 465
Warwick, 157
Warwick, Philip, 340
Warwick, Robert Rich, Earl of, 52, 55, 60–1, 66–7, 78, 115
Wenman, Elizabeth, 163
West Indies, 258, 260–1 *see also* Barbados and Jamaica
Wharton, George, 115, 139–40, 221
Whately, William, 123
White, Dorset, 79
White, Major Francis, 205
Whitelocke, Bulstrode, 334, 398
Wight, Sarah, 126
Willoughby of Parham, Lord, 55
Wilmot, Henry, Lord, 82
Winstanley, Gerard, 381, 392–3
Witches & witchcraft, 124–5, 152, 153–4, 163–6, 309–11, 384–5, 406–7

Wither, George, 101
Women, 43-4, 52, 88, 91, 98-9, 106-7, 113, 122-67, 182-4, 185, 284-6, 289, 343-8, 468-9
Worcester, Battle of, 117-21, 423, 429
Wylde, Sergeant, 36

York, Archbishop of, 57-8
York, James Stuart, Duke of, 67, 216, 463, 465
Yorkshire, 130-1